APPLIED POLITICAL THEORY AND CANADIAN POLITICS

Bringing together political theorists and specialists in Canadian politics, *Applied Political Theory and Canadian Politics* combines conceptual frameworks from political theory and empirical evidence to offer fresh perspectives on political events in contemporary Canada. Examining complex and timely subjects such as equality, social justice, democracy, citizenship, and ethnic diversity, contributors present current and archival research supplemented with insights drawn from political theory to give readers a deep and nuanced understanding of increasingly pressing issues in Canadian society.

For scholars and students seeking a work of political theory that is tangible, focused, and connected to the real world of everyday politics, *Applied Political Theory and Canadian Politics* will be an important resource, combining philosophical insights and empirical evidence to enhance our understanding of contemporary Canadian politics.

DAVID McGRANE is associate professor in the Department of Political Studies at St Thomas More College and the University of Saskatchewan.

NEIL HIBBERT is associate professor in the Department of Political Studies at the University of Saskatchewan.

Applied Political Theory and Canadian Politics

EDITED BY DAVID McGRANE
AND NEIL HIBBERT

UNIVERSITY OF TORONTO PRESS
Toronto Buffalo London

Toronto Buffalo London
utorontopress.com

ISBN 978-1-4426-5047-3 (cloth) ISBN 978-1-4426-2843-4 (paper)

Publication cataloguing information is available from Library and Archives Canada.

This book has been published with the help of a grant from the Federation for the Humanities and Social Sciences, through the Awards to Scholarly Publications Program, using funds provided by the Social Sciences and Humanities Research Council of Canada.

University of Toronto Press acknowledges the financial assistance to its publishing program of the Canada Council for the Arts and the Ontario Arts Council, an agency of the Government of Ontario.

Canada Council for the Arts
Conseil des Arts du Canada

Funded by the Government of Canada
Financé par le gouvernement du Canada
Canada

Contents

Acknowledgments

The genesis of this project was a series of panels at the Prairie Political Science Association (PPSA) annual meeting in Banff in 2014; the editors would like to thank the PPSA for accepting to host these panels and providing such a wonderful environment in which to deliberate. The PPSA, held yearly at the Banff Centre, is truly an excellent venue for these types of book projects.

The editors would like to thank the anonymous reviewers for their insightful comments and criticisms, which greatly strengthened the quality of the manuscript. Peter Bruce and Helana Obuobisah, graduate students at the University of Saskatchewan, are also to be thanked for their excellent research assistance in editing and organizing various versions of the manuscript. The editors are also grateful to all of the staff at University of Toronto Press, especially Daniel Quinlan, who offered valuable advice and encouragement from the earliest stages of the project to its completion. We would also like to thank freelancer Barry Norris, who did an excellent job of copy editing the manuscript before it went to publication. The editors are very appreciative of the Social Sciences and Humanities Research Council of Canada for its grant to aid in defraying the costs of publication.

A special thank you is extended from the editors to the contributors of the volume. The contributors were exceedingly patient as the manuscript travelled through the various stages of the publication process. They met their deadlines on time and responded graciously to requests for modification of their chapters by the editors and the reviewers. It was a genuine delight to work with such a hard-working, dedicated, and generous group of scholars!

Finally, the editors would like to thank our department and our families. It is a pleasure and a joy to work with our colleagues at the political studies departments at the University of Saskatchewan and St Thomas More College. It difficult to imagine a better intellectual home to have. And a special thanks to our families – Lisa, Caroline, Anne, and Gabriel – for supporting us throughout this endeavour. We could not have completed this project without your support.

David McGrane
Neil Hibbert
Saskatoon, September 2018

APPLIED POLITICAL THEORY AND CANADIAN POLITICS

Introduction

DAVID McGRANE AND NEIL HIBBERT

How can bringing together the study of political theory and Canadian politics deepen our understanding of the policy, ideological, and legal issues that define Canada today? It is this intriguing question that motivates our edited collection. The authors' interest in exploring this question is based on their shared view that the relationship between political theory and political practice is symbiotic. That is to say, we believe that the conceptual tools of political theory can be used to make our political practices more comprehensible, salient, and meaningful. At the same time, using political theory to understand political experience can beneficially reflect back, making our theorizing more concrete and hedging against tendencies towards excessive abstraction.

Although this two-way relationship between political theory and practice holds in general, Canadian politics traditionally has been fertile ground for the application of political theorizing to concrete practice. Indeed, an enduring feature of Canadian politics is how it has been marked by an ongoing discussion of the nature of the basic building blocks of citizenship and identity. Due perhaps to the ongoing contestation of the core elements of a political community as a seemingly permanent feature of political life in Canada, Canadian political theorists have made important contributions to the issues of nationality, diversity, Indigeneity, and a variety of different rights claims. Although pluralist in its normative commitments and methodological approaches, the collective work of Canadian political theorists over the course of the past few decades is on the whole characterized by an orientation towards applying their theoretical insights to pressing problems that animate the Canadian political context.

Using an approach that we call "applied political theory," this collection brings together a diverse group of scholars who use concepts derived from political theory to explore a range of debates and problems within Canadian politics. As opposed to political theory that exclusively focuses on detailing abstract moral arguments, or comparing canonical thinkers, the chapters in this book apply principles and conceptual frameworks from political theory to problems and situations in the Canadian political community. Whether it is the platforms of political parties, methods of public consultation on public policy, the design of social assistance programs, or dress codes for government employees, the authors illustrate how an applied political theory approach enhances our understanding of the politics that play out on a daily basis in Canada.

The overall argument of the collection is that, through using an applied political theory approach, we can understand Canadian politics much better than if we bracket off the study of Canadian politics from the resources available from both current and historical political theory. Moreover, the use of practices from the real world of Canadian politics to set the grounds of theorizing has the effect of making research in political theory more tangible, focused, and reflective of political reality.

As a work of applied political theory, the chapters in this collection are situated at the crossroads of the study of Canadian politics and the study of political theory. The criterion for inclusion in the book was not that the scholar hail from Canada or work in Canada, but simply that the researcher wanted to bring together political theory with Canadian political practice and experience. We intentionally looked for contributors from the fields of both "political theory" and "Canadian politics." Thus, the attentive reader will note that some of the authors are political theorists first and Canadianists second, while others are primarily scholars of Canadian politics with a background in political theory.

The marriage of political theory and the study of Canadian politics inherent in applied political theory is particularly effective when examining subjects that are vast, historical, and hard to draw boundaries around. It is these types of subjects that this book tackles: ideology, equality, social justice, democracy, citizenship, ethnic diversity, minority rights, nationalism, and Canada's place in the world. As such, when exploring such foundational topics in Canadian politics, future scholars should consider using an applied political theory approach.

Applied political theory provides tools to illuminate and critique Canadian political practices. Political scientists can use the applied political theory approach to understand the ideational foundations of what happens in Canadian politics and how Canadian politics fails or succeeds in meeting normative standards and goals. In this way, applied political theory deepens our understanding of what we observe in Canadian politics, and helps us make value judgments about what we observe. We hope that the explorations in this collection demonstrate that applied political theory is a fruitful approach for political scientists who are looking to combine empirical observation and normative evaluation in their study of Canadian political practice.

Defining Applied Political Theory

Before introducing the contributions found in this volume, we would like to outline briefly our definition of applied political theory and to explore previous work in this area produced by Canadian scholars. We define "applied political theory" as the study of concrete political practices that combines empirical evidence with the concepts and normative arguments that emanate from a recognizable tradition of political theory. As such, research would have to meet two criteria to be considered a work of applied political theory.

First, the object of research is not abstract, like Plato's cave or Rawls's veil of ignorance. Rather, the research must deal with political practices and events that have taken place, are ongoing, or might take place. Applied political theory can be used to examine the past, analyse the present, or speculate about the future. It must explore real-world political examples such as speeches by political leaders in the heat of an election campaign, a specific public policy that is currently being implemented, or the possibility of a referendum to decide an important political issue. Applied political theory shies away from hypothetical situations and thought experiments in favour of examining actual political phenomena.

Applied political theory thus involves an empirical analysis of the political practices or events it is exploring. When it comes to the gathering of empirical evidence, applied political theory allows for methodological pluralism. Often, the empirical evidence offered to the reader consists of qualitative description of a real-world political practice, such as outlining the implementation of a public policy using government documents or the description of historical events using political documents from the past. There is no reason, however, that applied political theory must limit itself to generalized qualitative description. Case studies using different forms of data collection such as semi-structured interviews, content analysis, or participant observation could also yield empirical evidence to be used in applied political theory research. It is also possible to use more positivist methodologies such as opinion surveys to conduct applied political theory research. For instance, David Miller (1992) compares survey data on public opinion concerning different principles of justice derived from political theorists such as Rawls and Walzer. The important point is that applied political theory research relates concepts derived from a tradition of political theory to empirical evidence based on the observation of concrete political practices. How exactly the applied political theorist wishes to gather that evidence is left up to his or her discretion.

The second criteria is that applied political theory research must relate the political practice or event it is exploring to concepts that originated within the western canon or another recognizable tradition of political theory. An applied political theorist will include explicit statements of the use of concepts of political theory and how they correspond to the empirical evidence presented. Similar to the methodological pluralism exhibited in the gathering of evidence, the concepts and principles used by applied political theory can come from diverse sources. As such, a scholar could engage directly with passages from canonical texts within traditional western political theory. It would also be acceptable for applied political theory research to use concepts elaborated by contemporary political theorists working off of canonical works and western political schools of thought. Further, researchers may draw upon non-western political philosophy such as Indigenous oral tradition or eastern philosophy to study political practices. The important consideration is that the concepts the researcher uses to explore a political practice or event have a traceable lineage within the western canon of political theory or another tradition of political theory.

Even though they have not always explicitly used the term "applied political theory," Canadian scholars have often used the approach described above in developing their work. Indeed, Canadian theorists have an ongoing tendency to bring political theory to bear on some of the most existential questions facing our politics, such as continentalism, multiculturalism, Indigenous/non-Indigenous reconciliation, and Quebec-Canada relations. What Joseph Carens (2000, 2) has called the "back and forth" application of principles drawn from political theory to corresponding empirical understanding of cases grounded in the Canadian political experience has resulted in a significant body of scholarly work that yields important insights into the normative dimensions of politics in Canada and beyond. Although an exhaustive treatment of all the research that could be considered "applied political theory" that has emanated from Canada is outside the scope of this introduction, we can note several examples to situate the aims of this book.

In English Canada, one of the first examples of scholarly work that could be considered applied political theory is George Grant's *Lament for a Nation* (1965). It compares a qualitative description of John Diefenbaker's prime ministership (particularly, Canadian-US relations) to a diverse set of canonical sources ranging from Locke to Rousseau to Marx. In the 1990s, three Canadian scholars engaged in applied political theory – Will Kymlicka, Charles Taylor, and James Tully – garnered a considerable amount of attention in Canada and well beyond its borders for their work on ethnocultural and national diversity in liberal democratic states. In *Multicultural Citizenship* (1996), Kymlicka relates concepts of liberal theorists such as Mill and Rawls to qualitative analysis of the kinds of claims for group-differentiated rights made by Canadian minorities such as Hutterites, immigrant groups, Indigenous peoples, and the *Québécois*. In *Reconciling the Solitudes* (1993), Taylor provides detailed descriptions of specific events and policy developments within the Quebec-Canada relationship, and analyses those moments using the thought of western canonical political philosophers. James Tully's *Strange Multiplicity* (1995) provides empirical descriptions of the history of various Canadian Indigenous bands that are juxtaposed with the work of British social contract theorists such as Locke and Hobbes. As the 1990s closed, all three of these scholars wrote chapters in a collection edited by Ronald Beiner and Wayne Norman entitled *Canadian Political Philosophy: Contemporary Reflections* (2001). Affirming the tendency of Canadian political theorists to engage in applied political theory, many of the chapters in that important collection used concepts from the western political theory canon to explore concrete aspects of Canadian political life.

The early twenty-first century saw the publication of several works of applied political theory using Canadian practices as their object of research. Carens's *Culture, Citizenship, and Community* (2000) develops what he calls "contextual political theory," bringing together his analysis of case studies of Indigenous Canadians, Muslim Canadians, and *Québécois* and critical engagement with the work of Kymlicka and Walzer. Joseph Heath's *The Efficient Society* (2001) uses the writings of western canonical theorists ranging from Aristotle to Rawls, and empirical evidence such as quantitative economic statistics and the qualitative description of federal government policies, to argue that "efficiency is the central value in Canadian society" (xviii). Another good example of how qualitative and quantitative methodology can be mixed within applied political theory is the collection edited by Keith Banting and Will Kymlicka entitled *Multiculturalism and the Welfare State* (2006). This collection brings together empirical evidence from a variety sources (such as public opinion polls and government documents) and compares those empirical findings to theoretical work on how multicultural policies might affect the condition of solidarity in pluralistic societies. The work of Melissa Williams and Daniel Weinstock is also notable on this front. For instance, Williams's "Toleration Canadian-Style: Reflections of a Yankee Canadian" (2001) qualitatively describes Canadian policies on asylum seekers, deportation, and the wearing of the *hijab* in public institutions in the light of the concept of toleration found in US and British liberal political theory. In "Towards a Proceduralist Theory of Secession" (2000), Weinstock evaluates specific claims of Quebec sovereignists using the theoretical reflections of David Miller.

One of the best recent examples of applied political theory coming from a Canadian scholar is the work of Genevieve Fuji Johnson – in particular, her two books *Deliberative Democracy for the Future: The Case of Nuclear Waste Management in Canada* (2008) and *Democratic Illusion: Deliberative Democracy in Canadian Public Policy* (2015). These books provide empirical evidence in the form of four case studies of exercises in deliberative democratic decision-making by the Toronto Community Housing Corporation, Nova Scotia Power Incorporated, the Nuclear Waste Management Organization, and the government of Nunavut. The data for these case studies came out of semi-structured interviews with organizers and participants, as well as the examination of policy documents and public submissions pertaining to these decision-making processes. Fuji Johnson develops a novel framework that interprets her data using criteria for deliberative democracy arising from the writings of a diverse range of contemporary and western political theorists from John Stuart Mill to Iris Marion Young.

Although the above examples have focused on English-Canadian scholars, it should be noted that Indigenous and *Québécois* scholars have also actively engaged in applied political theory. In a critique of European-American theories of nationalism, Gerald Alfred's *Heeding the Voices of Our Ancestors* (1995) compares detailed quantitative and qualitative descriptions of Kahnawake Mohawk politics with Iroquois political philosophy that can be traced back to an oral law called the *Kaienerekowa* that was created in the fourteenth century. James (Sákéj) Youngblood Henderson (2002) uses British liberals such as Blackstone to examine cases concerning Indigenous rights that have come before the Supreme Court of Canada. Glen Coulthard's *Red Skin, White Masks: Rejecting the Colonial Politics of Recognition* (2014) relates conceptual frameworks from the theories of Marx and Fanon to the history of the Dene nation and the recent Idle No More protests.

The application of political theory to understanding the situation of the *Québécois* within Canada has been common in French literature on the subject, which reaches back to Louis-Joseph Papineau and the *Patriotes* who drew inspiration from British and US liberal philosophers in the middle of the nineteenth century (Lamonde 2000, 85–237). More contemporary examples include Fernand Dumont's *Genèse de la société québécoise* (1993) and Gérard Bouchard's *La pensée impuissante: échecs et mythes nationaux canadiens-français, 1850–1960* (2004). These two authors provide very thorough descriptions of the formative historical events of the *Québécois* nation using a variety of archival resources that they compare with concepts within the writings of French and British canonical political theorists, as well as the writings of seminal *Québécois* political theorists of the twentieth century such as Lionel Groulx and Henri Bourassa.

The Value of Applied Political Theory

The chapters in this collection demonstrate the different ways applied political theory can provide value to the study of Canadian politics. These principally include contributions that take the form of *illumination* or *critique* of Canadian political practice.

The first group of chapters uses applied political theory to illuminate Canadian political practices. In this case, applying political theory to political practice in Canada can provide us with interpretations of those practices insofar as they are in alignment with a set of normative underpinnings. Such interpretive modes of inquiry can reveal degrees of conceptual consistency in Canadian politics by showing how policies and programs embody particular justificatory ideas. As such, these chapters aim to illuminate how certain Canadian political practices align with broader conceptual frameworks within traditions of political theory. The result of these contributions is to provide a more thorough understanding of the underlying ideational structures of Canadian political phenomena and how diverse practices can be understood through classification within established theoretical frameworks.

In the case of the relationship between the platforms, messaging, and policy development by Canada's major political parties, the chapters by Brooke Jeffrey and David McGrane advance the type of illumination to which we refer. Jeffrey compares key principles from liberal political theory with a detailed qualitative analysis of the policies of Liberal federal governments and the ideas of Liberal prime ministers, including Justin Trudeau, to argue that there is a distinctive Canadian liberal ideology that has guided Liberal Party politics across generations. McGrane begins his chapter by explaining how T.H. Green, John Dewey, and John Rawls exemplify the ideology of twentieth-century reform liberalism, while the writings of the Fabians, Anthony Crosland, and contemporary European political theorists such as Thomas Meyer and Brian Barry embody the ideology of twentieth-century social democracy. McGrane's applied political theory approach compares the prototypical ideas of reform liberalism and social democracy to the platforms of the Liberal Party and the New Democratic Party in the 2015 federal election. He contends that there are important ideational differences between Canadian social democrats and Canadian liberals. What both chapters have in common is that they illuminate how the practices and ideas of Canadian political parties align with broad ideological traditions within political theory.

Shifting to problems of state formation and legitimacy, the chapters by Catherine Frost and Marc Chevrier connect concepts found in canonical political thought to produce interpretive analysis of key moments in Canadian political history. Frost applies Hannah Arendt's work on the founding of both ancient and modern states to a qualitative description of the historical events surrounding Canadian Confederation and the 1982 patriation of the Canadian Constitution. She uses applied political theory to argue that these were incomplete attempts at political founding and, as such, Canada lacks the main features of a founding moment according to Arendt's criteria. Chevrier compares a detailed historic-legal sketch of the British conquest of Canada to how political theorists – specifically Hobbes, Hume, Locke, and Montesquieu – treat the possibility of a legitimate founding of a state through conquest. His applied political theory approach illustrates that, even if the Canadian state has been democratized, it maintains several characteristics of an "empire-state, where conquest continues to be a basis of its legitimacy." Both Frost and Chevrier show that political theory can be used to illuminate the deeper structures of Canadian political history, and help us understand what happened, how it happened, and what are the effects of those historical events today.

The chapters by Raffaele Iacovino, Stephen Winter, and Mark Blythe and Jay Mararenko seek to use political theory to illuminate the contours of contemporary Canadian political debates in the areas of public policy and jurisprudence. Iacovino applies the thought of contemporary theorists of liberal pluralism to the case studies of the Bouchard-Taylor Commission and the Charter of Quebec Values. He reveals a dialectic between the view of the *Québécois* nation as a single "political subject" for the purpose of legitimating claims to self-determination and a widespread acceptance of a universal view of political justice within the province, part of which involves a civic commitment to respecting cultural diversity. Winter uses applied political theory to compare the work of Mark Tushnet and others to a thorough legal description of the Canadian Charter of Rights and Freedoms as well as human rights bills from other Commonwealth countries that have emulated the Canadian innovation of "weak-form review" of legislative decisions by the judiciary. He clarifies how weak-form judicial review secures legitimacy for a legislature's decisions by establishing more effective and diverse accountability channels for legislative authority. Blythe and Mararenko apply Rawls's deliberations about constitutional essentials as matters of basic justice to the empirical description of two case studies: the Supreme Court of Canada judgment in *Andrews v. Law Society of Canada* and the federal Conservative Party's framing of the *niqab* debate in the 2015 election campaign. They illuminate how disparate elements of Canadian multiculturalism can be brought together when seen as part of public reason in Canadian legal debates and during election campaigns.

Other chapters operating in this manner take steps beyond the use of political theory to illuminate and interpret by discussing the conditions under which ideas guide policy and programmatic change. Applied political theory allows us to see how ideas appear to push or guide political actors towards certain paths and away from others. As some ideas emerge and gain popularity and others fade away, political change happens. Paying attention to ideas can help us tell descriptive stories of Canadian politics and understand why players in those stories act the way they do.

The chapters by Jim Farney, Neil Hibbert, and Darin Nesbitt are good examples of using applied political theory in an elucidatory manner.

Hibbert's chapter engages with the work of Joseph Heath to develop the concept of a "normative model of the Canadian welfare state." He argues that the guiding ideas behind the development of the Canadian welfare state changed in the 1990s from an egalitarian model to a public economic model of the welfare state, where efficiency is the overriding principle. These ideational changes surrounding the concept of social citizenship are shown to have connections to programmatic changes by governments of different ideological stripes. Farney's study of contemporary conservatism in Canada compares the policy and ideas of the Conservative Party of Canada under Stephen Harper to concepts developed in the work of George Grant and F.A. Hayek. He details the change in the core commitment of Canadian conservatism away from nationalism, statist Keynesianism, and *noblesse oblige* towards the supremacy of individual choice within the free market. Nesbitt uses an applied political theory approach to relate Mill's idea of autonomy to the historical development of the moral and legal status of euthanasia in Canada, leading up to the Supreme Court's 2015 ruling in *Carter v. Canada*. He contends that the "*Millian proviso*," in which the state can override individual autonomy only when someone's decisions and actions violate the rights of others, slowly emerged as the basis for Canadian policy concerning physician-assisted death. His chapter helps us understand how the Supreme Court is pushing Canadian society towards a distinctively individualist conception of personal autonomy.

Similarly, the chapters by Michael Murphy and Paul Saurette and Kathryn Trevenen analyse how political theory can provide clues to the emergence of certain political phenomena in Canada. Murphy combines self-determination theory, which is founded on an Aristotelian conception of well-being, with empirical evidence of unequal physical and mental health outcomes between Indigenous and non-Indigenous Canadians. In this sense, applied political theory helps us understand the political imperative for Indigenous self-determination, given the connections between autonomy and mental health. Similarly, Saurette and Trevenen aim at a greater appreciation of the role and force of emotions in politics than is provided by traditional "intellectualist" approaches to ideology such as those of Marx and the French *Idéologues*. They apply "evolutionary functionalist" theory (exemplified by Drew Westen) and "critical affect theory" (represented by William Connolly, Lawrence Grossberg, and others) to the study of ideology in Canada. They conclude that these two alternative approaches offer a more sophisticated analysis of how emotions have become central drivers of ideological commitment and can better account for right-wing populist backlashes and Justin Trudeau's surprising electoral victory in 2015.

Taken together, this first group of chapters show how applied political theory can be used to advance our understanding of core Canadian political practices by illuminating how they align with, and are structured by, theoretical ideas and frameworks emanating from diverse strands of political theorizing. In doing so, the ideational foundations that underlay these practices are brought into relief, and by identifying instances of ideational and institutional alignment with political theory we are much better positioned to understand and to classify the origins and evolution of these practices.

A second group of chapters use political theory as a tool to *critique* Canadian political practices. Instead of pointing out cases in which political theory and political practice in Canada are in alignment, these chapters illustrate instances of disconnect between normative claims and concepts within political theory and practices on the ground in Canadian political life. There is a misalignment between what theory holds could be possible and what is actually happening. Using political theory to indicate where areas of practice are misaligned with appropriate justificatory ideas can motivate and guide programmatic reform. In this sense, the examination of empirical evidence using political theory can lead to suggestions for improvement of concrete political practices.

Several chapters lay out a quite robust critique of existing public policies in Canada. Using qualitative analysis of the K-12 education policies of several provincial governments, Stephen Lecce explores the extent to which private schools can be justified using the principles of egalitarian liberalism established by philosophers such as Rawls and Mill. He reaches the provocative conclusion that private schools are inconsistent with the principle of equal opportunity that is central to the Canadian ethos of social justice and, as a result, they are unjust and should be abolished. Mireille Paquet's chapter relates the work of liberal theorist Joseph Carens on immigration and border control to Canada's Express Entry Program, a new set of procedures for admitting immigrants that was implemented by the federal government in 2015. Using a conceptual framework inspired by Carens, she criticizes the program for departing from Canada's commitment to equal membership within the Canadian polity. Kirsten Fisher and Cristina Stefan relate ideas emanating out of liberal cosmopolitanism (rooted in Kant's writings) to a detailed description of recent developments regarding the Responsibility to Protect (R2P) and the International Criminal Court (ICC). They conclude that the current practices of R2P and the ICC lack legitimacy and are misaligned with liberal cosmopolitanism, setting up a duty for Canada to lead efforts to reform them.

Other chapters use applied political theory to critique current practices of Canadian democracy and public dialogue. Marlene Sokolon's applied political theory approach relates concepts arising from the work of several contemporary theorists of the deliberative democracy to recent Canadian attempts to establish "deliberative forums" on electoral reform, health policy, and environmental policy. She illustrates that, although citizens in such forums demonstrated the capacity to understand and contribute to debates in complex policy areas, the forums did not go far enough in addressing the deeper problem of enhancing the voice of marginalized or disadvantaged groups against elite-led politics. Lee Ward is also concerned with the failure of Canadian political institutions to fulfil their democratic promise. He evaluates the amending formula of the Canadian Constitution using Lockean concepts of popular sovereignty and writings on community and rights by Charles Taylor and James Tully. Using insights gained from his applied political theory approach, he argues that the Constitution's amending formula is unnecessarily complex and prohibitive, and he makes a provocative proposal for "renegotiating, formalizing, and codifying our provincial constitutions" through convening constitutional conventions in each province and territory.

Other chapters use applied political theory to critique broader and overarching political phenomena as opposed to focusing on specific public policies, institutions, or political events. Ann Ward draws on the work of George Grant, Aristotle, and Michael Byers to assemble a conceptual framework that critiques the present state of English-Canadian nationalism as flagging and in need of renewal. Her applied political theory approach then relates this framework to the concrete examples of Canada's unique role in peacekeeping around the world and combatting climate change to show that, as opposed to being insular, English-Canadian nationalism can "comprehend a cosmopolitanism that looks to the good of the planet." Marc Woons critiques liberal multiculturalism, found in the work of theorists such as Kymlicka, for imposing an "illegitimate political framework" onto Indigenous peoples by virtue of squeezing out Indigenous normativity from the scope of "reasonable" political debate. Using a qualitative description of contemporary treaty negotiations in Canada, Woons endorses a "realist" view of political disagreement where conflict could strengthen Indigenous peoples' political footing and open up new forms of political action. Jill Vickers develops a feminist critique of traditional theories of federalism, notably the idea of "legal pluralism." Applying this theoretical framework to a "small n" comparative analysis of family law reforms across federations, including Canada, she argues that legal pluralism can "fragment" women's citizenship in ways detrimental to the ideal of individual equality.

The common thread of this group of chapters is that they use concepts derived from political theory to critique specific policies enacted by Canadian governments and broader political practices within Canada. As such, they use applied political theory to point out problems within Canadian politics and to provide a basis for thinking about potential reforms that might solve those problems. Political theory is used here both to provide a critical lens on practices and to enlighten the road towards changing those practices.

As can be seen in the description of the two groups of chapters above, an applied political theory approach allows the authors in our collection to understand various elements of Canadian political practice in innovative and novel ways. Indeed, the collection highlights the benefit of engaging in applied political theory in the Canadian context both for political theorists and for Canadian specialists.

The benefit for political theorists is that engaging in applied political theory using Canadian practices brings empirical evidence to bear on their theorizing. As is illustrated throughout this book, the types of empirical evidence used in applied political theory are quite varied, and include quantitative statistics, court cases, election platforms, and government documents. The application of theoretical approaches to an empirical understanding of real-world propositions, puzzles, and cases yields useful normative and critical insights for political theorists. As applied political theory moves "back and forth" between theory and practice, political theorists can come to a greater understanding of the concept they are developing and of how their theories reflect (or do not reflect) political realities.

The benefit for Canadianists in engaging in applied political theory is that it gives them a tool with which to analyse broad topics in the Canadian political experience. A commonality of all the chapters in this book is that they deal with relatively broad objects of research that often stretch over long periods of time. Further, their objects of research are difficult to define and delineate precisely. As the reader will see, applied political theory is a particularly effective approach for Canadianists studying aspects of Canadian politics that defy simple definition and that have elements spanning decades or even centuries. As opposed to shying away from the examination of difficult subjects, the study of Canadian politics is undoubtedly enhanced when Canadianists take up the challenge to tackle a broad and potentially unwieldy topic.

Overall, this volume demonstrates the value of using an applied political theory approach in the Canadian context, and encourages future researchers to use this approach when studying Canadian politics. In bringing together scholars working in both political theory and Canadian politics, our collection offers empirically based theoretical reflections on a wide range of social, policy, and legal questions that constitute the main threads of Canada's political tapestry. In this way, it provides an opportunity for the theorists in our collection to make their research more concrete and less abstract, while giving the Canadianists an opportunity to ground their empirical research in a more salient normative and conceptual terrain. It offers effective conceptual tools with which to illuminate and critique Canadian political practices. We hope that other scholars will want to embark on a similar journey.

REFERENCES

Alfred, Gerald. 1995. *Heeding the Voices of Our Ancestors: Kahnawake Mohawk Politics and the Rise of Native Nationalism*. New York: Oxford University Press.

Banting, Keith, and Will Kymlicka. 2006. *Multiculturalism and the Welfare State: Recognition and Redistribution in Contemporary Democracies*. New York: Oxford University Press. https://doi.org/10.1093/acprof:oso/9780199289172.001.0001

Beiner, Ronald, and Wayne Norman. 2001. *Canadian Political Philosophy: Contemporary Reflections*. New York: Oxford University Press.

Bouchard, Gérard. 2004. *La pensée impuissante: échecs et mythes nationaux canadiens-français, 1850–1960*. Montreal: Boréal.

Carens, Joseph. 2000. *Culture, Citizenship, and Community: A Contextual Exploration of Justice as Evenhandedness*. New York: Oxford University Press. https://doi.org/10.1093/0198297688.001.0001

Coulthard, Glen. 2014. *Red Skin, White Masks: Rejecting the Colonial Politics of Recognition*. Minneapolis: University of Minnesota Press. https://doi.org/10.5749/minnesota/9780816679645.001.0001

Dumont, Fernand. 1993. *Genèse de la société québécoise*. Montreal: Boréal.
Fuji Johnson, Genevieve. 2008. *Deliberative Democracy for the Future: The Case of Nuclear Waste Management in Canada*. Toronto: University of Toronto Press. https://doi.org/10.3138/9781442687837
Fuji Johnson, Genevieve. 2015. *Democratic Illusion: Deliberative Democracy in Canadian Public Policy*. Toronto: University of Toronto Press.
Grant, George. 1965. *Lament for a Nation: The Defeat of Canadian Nationalism*. Toronto: McClelland & Stewart.
Heath, Joseph. 2001. *The Efficient Society: Why Canada Is as Close to Utopia as It Gets*. Toronto: Viking.
Henderson, James (Sákéj) Youngblood. 2002. "Sui Generis and Treaty Citizenship." *Citizenship Studies* 6 (4): 415–40. https://doi.org/10.1080/1362102022000041259
Kymlicka, Will. 1996. *Multicultural Citizenship: A Theory of Minority Rights*. Oxford: Oxford University Press. https://doi.org/10.1093/0198290918.001.0001
Lamonde, Yvan. 2000. *Histoire sociale des idées au Québec, 1760–1896*. Anjou, QC: Éditions Fides.
Miller, David. 1992. "Distributive Justice: What the People Think." *Ethics* 102 (3): 555–93. https://doi.org/10.1086/293425
Taylor, Charles. 1993. *Reconciling the Solitudes: Essays on Canadian Federalism and Nationalism*. Montreal; Kingston, ON: McGill-Queen's University Press.
Tully, James. 1995. *Strange Multiplicity: Constitutionalism in an Age of Diversity*. New York: Cambridge University Press. https://doi.org/10.1017/CBO9781139170888
Weinstock, Daniel. 2000. "Towards a Proceduralist Theory of Secession." *Canadian Journal of Law and Jurisprudence* 13 (2): 251–64. https://doi.org/10.1017/S0841820900000424
Williams, Melissa. 2001. "Toleration Canadian-Style: Reflections of a Yankee Canadian." In *Canadian Political Philosophy: Contemporary Reflections*, ed. Ronald Beiner and Wayne Norman, 216–31. New York: Oxford University Press.

PART I

Ideology

1 From Grant to Hayek: The Shifting Nature of Canadian Conservatism

JAMES FARNEY

This chapter seeks to define Canadian conservatism using an applied political theory approach. The political theories of George Grant, the quintessential Canadian Tory, and F.A. Hayek, the Austrian economist and social theorist, can be applied in understanding the evolution of conservatism in Canada from the 1960s until today. In particular, the writings of Grant and Hayek can be compared with empirical evidence of the rhetoric and ideas of the Conservative Party of Canada under Stephen Harper's leadership with reference to Harper's ideological predecessors in the Reform Party/Canadian Alliance and the Progressive Conservative Party. An applied political theory approach reveals the main argument of this chapter: that the core of contemporary Canadian conservatism over a wide range of policy areas is a commitment to individual choice, understood in a way heavily influenced by free market economists. Around this core commitment are arrayed other, secondary, commitments: to smaller government generally and to a smaller federal government in particular, a particular vision of nationalism, and a view of Canada's role in the world that emphasizes *realpolitik* more than the liberal internationalism of other Canadian parties and political movements.

This articulation of Canadian conservatism, at first glance, seems relatively straightforward and uncontentious. It does not take long, however, for two problems to emerge: the first, one of continuity; the second, one of differentiation. Continuity is a problem because the foundational examinations (Horowitz 1966) or articulations (Grant [1965] 1995) of Canadian conservatism identify as its most important feature a Tory sensibility critical of the market logic of liberal society. How, then, did Canadian conservative thinking transform itself into one in which the central commitment is to the free market? To identify and resolve this problem, I begin by contrasting Grant with Hayek. Although other thinkers have been influential for Canadian conservatives – Leo Strauss, Milton Friedman, and a variety of religious thinkers all have their followers – and although Canadian commentators and politicians have written at length about what it means to be conservative,[1] Grant and Hayek stand out as political thinkers who allow us to understand the contours of the contemporary Canadian right.

The contrast between Grant and Hayek highlights the nature of the core commitment of contemporary Canadian conservatives: a vision of the good society in which market mechanisms of exchange are the preferred way to ensure economic growth and protect individual rights. These were principles promoted by Hayek and opposed by Grant.[2] Although Grant's British-inspired Toryism, or the more pragmatic, Keynesian Toryism articulated by Robert Stanfield as leader of the Progressive Conservatives, is often remembered as defining Canadian conservatism in the 1960s and 1970s, it is important to remember that there was significant internal debate about the ideology. Grant's famous *Lament for a Nation* ([1965] 1995), after all, contains as much criticism of the pro-American capitalism promoted by the Ontario provincial Progressive Conservatives as praise of John Diefenbaker. Similarly, the Alberta government of Ernest Manning and a variety of provincial and national pro-business groups all articulated *laissez-faire* principles. What is missing is a Canadian embodiment of this free market–centric position of the intellectual heft and influence of George Grant. Given his later influence on the Canadian right, it seems fair to turn to Hayek as a theorist whose

---

1 Commentary by William Gairdner (1992, 2010), David Frum (1994), Janet Azjenstat and Peter Smith (1995), as well as Ted Byfield's journalism have all been influential for Canadian conservatives. From practising politicians, the reflections of Preston Manning (2002) and Hugh Segal (1997, 2006) on the nature of Canadian conservatism are very helpful.

2 Neoliberalism, as Patten (2013, 60) defines it, is "a political ideology, a set of individualistic and market-orientated values, assumptions, and beliefs that shape how adherents approach government and the challenges of policy and governance. It informs policy frameworks that aim to achieve economic competitiveness by rolling back the state and reining in expenditures … monetarism, supply-side economics, public choice theory, and the return to neo-liberal economic analysis all contributed to the consolidation of neoliberalism."

ideas can be applied to the empirics of Canadian politics. In the 1960s, either Hayek's or Grant's principles would have had equal claim to be at the core of Canadian conservatism. By the 2000s, this was no longer the case, for Canadian conservatism had redefined its core to be much closer to Hayek's vision than to Grant's.

My applied political theory approach acknowledges the fundamentally contested nature of ideology using what Freeden (1996) called the "morphology" of ideological commitments. For my purposes, what is important is differentiating among the core, secondary, and peripheral concepts that make up the shifting definition of an ideology. At the core of conservatism, Freeden argues, is a fundamental concern with change, a "belief in the extra-human origin of the social order," and a reactive or mirror image response to progressive ideology (1996, 330–6). These core commitments are positional, not definitional, meaning that conservative ideology is fundamentally flexible and might often appear defined by radically different principles, depending upon which ideological opponent conservatives are facing at any given time and in which particular political context they find themselves. That the core of Canadian conservatism has changed does not mean that we should read Grant as the "real" or "true" Canadian conservative and later articulations as somehow imposters or fallings away. Instead we should understand that different substantive commitments can be inserted into larger, morphological, structures, and it is the structural component of the ideology that identifies someone as conservative.[3] Recognizing this structural reality is especially important to understanding conservatism, as its contemporary form is built on a core set of concepts usually seen, even by Hayek, as part of classical liberalism. This requires a notable flexibility and attention to self-definition as we seek to apply the concepts of ideology, as defined by political theory, to the empirical development of Canadian conservatism.

3 This structural component is also an explanation for the absence of Quebec and of French-language conservatism from this account. Before the Quiet Revolution, there was a sustained intellectual tradition that articulated analogous positions to what I am describing here. Since then, while significant parts of Quebec society hold some of the secondary commitments I have identified and have voted for the Conservative Party at one time or another, there is no sustained intellectual attempt to construct an overarching conservative framework.

George Grant: A Canadian Tory

A quick glance at George Grant's biography or a superficial reading of his most famous book, *Lament for a Nation*, would seem to make finding his place in Canadian conservatism a relatively straightforward process.[4] Born into one of the country's most prominent families and educated at Upper Canada College (where his father was principal), Queen's (where his grandfather had been principal), and Oxford (on a Rhodes Scholarship), Grant (1918–88) was undoubtedly a scion of Canada's upper class. A resolute Canadian nationalist and defender of the British connection, Grant was also deeply religious and, later in life, vocally pro-life on abortion. To the modern audience, all of these positions seem perfectly, if sometimes perhaps quaintly, conservative. More difficult to typologize are his arguments for a strong state capable of resisting Americanization and the forces of international capital. To the historically minded reader, this should call to mind politically active contemporaries of Grant – especially Robert Stanfield – who saw as one implication of their own financial well-being and elite status the need to build a welfare state capable of aiding the less fortunate members of their community. These "Red Tories" held a position made possible by a combination of *noblesse oblige* and Keynesian economics.

But if this is the characterization of Grant, why ought we read mediations on half-century-old political contestations by a rather unsystematic member of a now-extinct colonial ruling class? I argue that Grant is still worth reading because, among other things, he articulates a credible vision of conservatism that stands in stark contrast to that most often in present-day use and, through this contrast, helps us understand the later.[5] Articulated most clearly in *Lament for a Nation* (1965) and *English-Speaking Justice* (1976), this is a political vision that sought to defend a notion of public virtue as the core of conservatism. Grounded in a philosophical vision that preferred the Ancient Greek vision of justice to that of modern liberal theorists, Grant's notion of virtue was undoubtedly both conservative and religious, but presented in a way that opened up ground for discussion with Canada's socialist left.

---

4 For Grant's biography, see Christian (1993). For the most up-to-date introduction to his life and thought and a very useful bibliographic essay, see Forbes (2007).

5 The other reasons to read Grant centre on the questions he raises with regards to technology, philosophy, and faith. For a guide to these issues, see Forbes (2007).

In *Lament for a Nation*, the hook that ties all of this together is the defeat of the Progressive Conservative government of John Diefenbaker in 1963. Although aware of Diefenbaker's failings, Grant argued that his electoral defeat by Lester Pearson's Liberals marked the final impossibility of the Canadian effort to "build, along with the French, a more ordered and stable society than the liberal experiment in the United States" (Grant [1965] 1995, 25). Pearson, with his internationalism and closeness to big multinational business, embodied what we would now call globalizing forces. Diefenbaker, especially in his attempt to retain an independent Canadian defence policy, represented what Grant (citing Eric Voegelin) saw as nationalism: "the process through which human beings form and reform themselves into a society to act historically" (31). Diefenbaker's great failure, for Grant, was that his rural commitments to populism and small- town free enterprise blinded him to the Canadian reality that, "after 1940, nationalism had to go hand in hand with some measure of socialism" (34) and a very strong civil service (37).

The first half of *Lament for a Nation* is clearly nationalistic and deeply, perhaps unfairly, partisan. His emphasis on an independent foreign policy (especially his resistance to Canada's acquiring nuclear weapons), his criticism of capitalism and industrialization, and his defence of a strong state all made him popular with the social democratic left of the day – thus, his title of Red Tory.[6] What makes this position conservative at the level of political theory, and not simply partisanship, is articulated in the book's second half. For Grant, foreign policy considerations and economics are only the proximate causes of Canada's eventual disappearance. At its core, it is the "aspirations of progress that have made Canada redundant. The universal and homogeneous state is the pinnacle of human striving ... achieved by means of modern science – a science that leads to the conquest of nature [and] ... makes all local cultures anachronistic" ([1965] 1995, 69). Progressive aspirations are fundamentally liberal, and liberals, to Grant, "recognize that no appeal to human good, now or in the future, must be allowed to limit

6 Grant did see a philosophical similarity as well, for he believed that Marx's commitment to a teleological view of history produced stronger commonalities between Marx and the Ancients to whom Grant was committed than existed between the Ancients and a modern liberal such as John Rawls, who lacked such a teleological commitment.

their freedom to make the world as they choose. Social order is a man-made convenience, and its only purpose is to increase freedom" (70). But Grant established to his satisfaction that no alternative to this progressive or liberal vision is possible, bearing with it the reason for his lament that "the impossibility of conservatism in our era is the impossibility of Canada" ([1965] 1995, 67).

It is telling that it is the context of discussing its impossibility that Grant defined conservatism as a "conception of society requiring a high degree of law and respect for a public conception of virtue" ([1965] 1995, 81). (It is a belief in public virtue that made Grant see socialism as an ally of his definition of conservatism). Explicitly, he argued that American conservatives of his time (typified by Barry Goldwater) were not genuine conservatives but only "old-fashioned liberals. They stand for the freedom of the individual to use his property as he wishes, and for a limited government that must keep out of the marketplace ... [T]his has more to do with 19th century liberalism than traditional conservatism, which asserts the right of the community to restrain freedom in the name of the common good" (76). For a genuine alternative to modern liberalism, Grant suggested, we must turn either to the Christian Gospels, to Greek philosophy, or, the approach he himself took, to some combination of the two.[7]

Why such an alternative is necessary Grant articulated in 1974's *English-Speaking Justice*. Beginning with a history of modern political thought that identified the practical success of the English-speaking world with its ability to fuse technological advancement with liberal politics, Grant then turned to John Rawls's recently published *Theory of Justice* ([1971] 1999) for the best articulation of modern liberal theory. Although Grant found deeply problematic Rawls's identification of reason with self-interest absent a concept of some higher good ([1974] 1998, 13), the fundamental problem Grant found in Rawls was ontological: there was no conception of human nature or an answer to why we ought to pursue justice (32, 43–4). While acknowledging this was a significant analytic advantage in some ways, as it overcame other philosophic or religious conceptions of the good and provided support to some public policies Grant found praiseworthy (42), the absence of a

7 Grant never fully articulated what such a combination would look like, but it is clear that it was through an engagement with Leo Strauss, Martin Heidegger, and Simone Weil that he believed it could be found (Forbes 2007).

robust conception of human nature was fundamentally dangerous. For Grant, the danger was practically embodied in the *Roe v. Wade* decision on abortion. It "raised a cup of poison to the lips of liberalism"(70) by enshrining a vision of justice that "will exclude liberal justice from those who are too weak to enforce contracts – the imprisoned, the mentally unstable, the unborn, the aged, the defeated and sometimes even the morally unconforming" (83–4). Countering this danger would require what was practically impossible: the reassertion of a traditional definition of justice as an "overriding order which we do not measure and define, but in terms of which we are measured and defined" (74).

Although Grant's political thought was deeply rooted in the English-Canadian experience, he drew heavily on international intellectual figures, of whom the most important near-contemporary influences on his mature political thought were Simone Weil, Leo Strauss, Martin Heidegger, and Eric Voegelin. His defence of an ordered and virtue-seeking society could find parallels in more politically oriented contemporaries such as Viscount Hailsham in the United Kingdom and Russell Kirk in the United States. There are strong parallels between Grant's thinking and later proponents of virtue ethics, perhaps most notably Alistair MacIntyre, as well as attempts by Christian thinkers, such as Oliver and Joan O'Donovan or John Milbank, to find a philosophically robust way of engaging modern politics from the standpoint of the Christian theological tradition.[8]

Finding a legacy for Grant in Canadian politics is more difficult, which poses problems for the simple application of his theoretical arguments to contemporary politics. Today, Red Tories are rare animals indeed, and the polarity of the term has been reversed. Grant was a Red Tory because he tilted left on economics and right on social issues such as abortion. At the federal level, contemporary exemplars of the breed – Hugh Segal and Joe Clark being prominent examples – are described as Red Tories because they tilt right on economics and left on social issues: they are *Progressive* Conservatives. Provincially, Alison Redford and Jim Prentice in Alberta were often described as Red Tories, but, again, they reversed Grant's social and economic policies. Perhaps the closest one might find to a contemporary Red Tory by Grant's definition is former Saskatchewan premier Brad Wall – who has deep religious roots and

8 In all these cases except that of the O'Donovans (Joan O'Donovan 1984), these are family resemblances, rather than direct intellectual connections to Grant.

sometimes seemed more moderate than his party on many economic and social issues. That Wall himself actively rejected the use of the term (Taube 2015), then, suggests that "Red Tory" has become nothing more than a synonym for "moderate conservative." Perhaps it is best to say that Grant's conservatism represents a road left untravelled for the Canadian right. In its nationalism, its turn towards classical philosophical sources, its nuanced engagement with religious traditions, and its critique of a market economy pursuing economic growth, Grant's thought is undoubtedly conservative. However, if we are to understand the arguments that have driven Canadian conservatives in a different direction, it is best to turn to a contemporary of Grant's who had very little direct connection to Canada.

F.A. Hayek: Cosmopolitan Classical Liberal

F.A. Hayek (1899–1992) is a more unusual figure to appear in histories of Canadian conservatism than Grant. And, to be fair, there are good reasons for this. The Austrian-born economist spent much of his career in the United States and England, and never himself intervened in Canadian political debates. Trained as a psychologist and economist, much of Hayek's early work revolved around business cycle theory and was conducted at the London School of Economics. There, he lost a famous debate with John Maynard Keynes over technical aspects of understanding business cycles. After the Second World War, Hayek moved to the University of Chicago and shifted his intellectual focus to a remarkably wide-ranging variety of political theory. A self-described "Burkean Whig," Hayek embraced modernity, internationalism, and individualism, and rejected the label "conservative" for his own work.[9] Hayek was also a successful institution builder and, in founding the Mont Perelin Society in 1947, started a network that would diffuse free market ideas throughout the developed world.

It is the diffusion of these ideas, rather than any personal interest that Hayek took in Canada, that makes him important for this study. As one of the formative influences on what became known as neoliberal

9 Both Hayek's own writing and the secondary literature on it are very extensive. A good starting point is the by Bruce Caldwell (2004), who is also general editor of Hayek's collected works. Jones (2012) provides a very good introduction to Hayek's intellectual context and contribution.

economic thinking, Hayek's arguments underpin our contemporary "common sense" about the relationship between state and market. Paying more attention to politics than did contemporaries such as Milton Friedman, Hayek added authority to an intellectual movement that sought direct political influence (as detailed in the next section). A more systematic thinker and more prolific writer than Grant, Hayek drew on nineteenth-century liberal theorists, classical economists, and a wide swathe of mid-twentieth-century social science filtered through his academic training as an economic theorist and methodologist.

There are two contextual intellectual difficulties in understanding Hayek's influence on conservative ideology. The first is that, although conservatives have embraced neoliberal views on economics more warmly than have other parts of the political spectrum, such views have been influential across the ideological spectrum and, at the level of practical governance, are determinative of parties of almost all political stripes. The warmth and shape of the embrace help us determine whether someone is conservative, but the mere fact that someone embraces neoliberalism does not.

Second, in his own terms, Hayek was explicitly not a conservative, but stood in opposition to the sort of principles that Grant defined as truly conservative. In both his first popular book, *The Road to Serfdom* ([1944] 2007), and in the postscript to his central *The Constitution of Liberty* (1960), Hayek went out of his way to articulate "Why I am not a Conservative." For Hayek the fundamental political threat was totalitarianism, of which fascism/Nazism and socialism/communism were but variants. In its "fear of change" (1960, 400), conservatism could not articulate an alternative to the totalitarian/planned society direction in which these ideologies were trying to drive western countries. Indeed, in its "fondness for authority and lack of understanding of economic forces" (401), conservatism was often complicit in the growth of the state and of economic planning, trends which Hayek argued were necessarily connected to the development of totalitarian regimes. Moreover, the "characteristic concern that this authority not be weakened rather than that its power be kept within bounds" (401) too often meant that the conservative desired only that the right person be in charge, not that there was any fear of the nature of authority itself. Conservatives, in their attachment to traditional authority, lacked "political principles which enable him to work with people whose moral values differ from his own for a political order in which both can obey their convictions" (401). For Hayek, "neither moral nor religious ideas are proper grounds for coercion" (402) and "conservatives deceive themselves when they blame the evils of our time on democracy. The chief evil is unlimited government, and nobody is qualified to wield unlimited power" (403). Conservatives fail to see that human knowledge is advancing, and are far too attached to nationalism (404). Not only are conservatives wrong in many key aspects of their thinking, but there is real danger present in confusing the type of liberalism that Hayek was arguing for and conservatism. For Hayek, "[c]onservatism, though a necessary element in any stable society, is not a social program; in its paternalistic, nationalistic, and power adoring tendencies it is often closer to socialism than true liberalism; and with its traditionalistic, anti-intellectual, and often mystical propensities, it will never, except in short periods of disillusionment, appeal to the young and all those others who believe some changes are desirable" ([1944] 2007, 45).

Very clearly, Hayek differentiated himself from the sort of virtue-concerned, religiously inspired, nationalist traditionalism that Grant articulated. While not as dangerous as socialism or fascism – conservatism is a "necessary element," after all – the worldview Grant articulated is clearly deeply mistaken from Hayek's point of view. What, then, was Hayek's own position and how are we to understand it as conservative by the framework with which we began this essay?

The second question is easier to answer. Hayek saw himself as an Old Whig or, perhaps, as a libertarian, updating and defending the fundamentals of nineteenth-century British liberalism. His concern with our moving away from these positions meant that he was concerned with the topic of change and, at least initially, reacting to the positions taken by others. In Freeden's terms, this meant that, from Hayek, one can take concern with the extra-human origins of social order (originating in the market rather than in divine law for the agnostic Hayek), which is in opposition to progressive or left-wing changes. Whether this is an entirely fair reading of Hayek is a difficult matter – Freeden (1996) categorized him as a libertarian with conservative tendencies – but there is sufficient overlap for Hayek to have become a very influential figure for conservatives.

Within that positioning, Hayek can be described as arguing that freedom and progress are the most desirable political goals. These goals are best achieved by allowing individuals (who best know their own situation) to make decisions while bound only by general and stable laws and by minimizing the coercion to which they are exposed. These decisions, aggregated (usually) through market mechanisms will lead to the most satisfactory spontaneous order possible in a given situation. Differentiating liberalism from democracy, Hayek argued that the former is more important than the latter. Although fond of arguments that acknowledged differences in national culture, Hayek was profoundly against nationalism, as one might expect of an Austrian, naturalized in the United Kingdom, who spent his most productive years in the United States and ended his career in Germany.

This position rested, throughout Hayek's life, on a significant degree of pessimism about our ability to know enough about the complex social and political environments we find ourselves in to make plans to control them. Although the price system is a powerful mechanism for exchanging information, and "money one of the greatest instruments of freedom ever invented by man" (Hayek [1944] 2007, 133) the working of a free market system depends upon individuals acting within the narrow sphere they know best. Following this argument, private property is an important guarantor not only of economic but also of personal freedom, since without it the state will end up making important decisions for individuals. And this cannot be, since "morals are of necessity a phenomenon of individual conduct [which] exist only in a sphere in which individuals are free to decide for himself" (211).

What changed was the threats he saw this vision facing as the welfare state grew. In *The Constitution of Liberty* (1960), he articulated what he saw as the traditional nineteenth-century vision of a free society, focusing on the central topics of "The Value of Freedom," "Freedom and the Law," and "Freedom and Welfare State." Freedom, for Hayek, was not itself a value, but "that which is the source and condition of most moral values" (1960, 6). Defining liberty primarily as being free from coercion by other people, not material conditions (12–13), it is protected, fundamentally, by equality before the law. It is threatened by the modern belief that the state can pursue equality of outcome, for that necessarily means the state will treat people unequally to offset the inequality that is the natural result of liberty. Although Hayek was clear that his liberalism was not utilitarian (175), he also argued that "the ultimate end of freedom is the enlargement of those capacities in which man surpasses his ancestors and to which every generation must endeavor to add its share" (394).

This goal required a limited state. Importantly, such a state should not necessarily be limited in the extent to which it intervened in the economy: Hayek at various points expressed support for the United Kingdom's National Health Service, public funding of education, regulation of workplace safety, and collective goods such as national defence and transportation. Rather, the limit should be in *how* the state intervened. The state ought to set the general conditions for economic life – he argued, for example, for flat taxes (1960, 295) and a fixed monetary framework (324–40) – and then change them as little as possible. What the state should not do is pursue changeable policies designed to alter the places of specific individuals or groups.

By the end of the 1960s, Hayek had come to believe that it was not enough simply to rearticulate this set of ideological arguments; it was also necessary to find a new mechanism for defending it. This was necessary because the combination of constitutionalism and democracy was a failure: it made genuine liberalism impossible by creating a situation in which society lost "belief in a justice system independent of personal interest; a consequent use of legislation to authorize coercion, not merely to prevent unjust action but to achieve particular results for specific persons or groups; and the fusion in the same representative assemblies of the task of articulating the rules of just conduct with that of directing government" (1973, 2). In the three-volume *Law, Legislation, and Liberty* project (1973, 1976, 1979), Hayek articulated what he believed to be a manageable return to these principles, which meant reaffirming three core positions. The first was a recognition of "the fundamental principles [of liberalism] that in the ordering of our affairs we should make as much use as possible of the spontaneous forces of society" ([1944] 2007, 71), and that these spontaneous forces are fundamentally distinct from planned organizations such as governments (1973, 2). This principle, which he believed conservatives did recognize in the growth of social institutions such as language, was only roughly embodied in *laissez-faire* economics. Competition would encourage the efficient evolution of such an order, and the role of the state was to provide a stable framework of unchanging general laws within which the forces of organic change and market competition could work. This position, he acknowledged, meant accepting considerable economic inequality, but this was defensible so long as it was not the product of laws or policies that deliberately targeted specific groups, but the operation of forces operating within the framework of general laws.

Hayek's second core position was that social or distributive justice only has meaning within specific, bounded organizations (1973, 2). Developing his critique in *The Mirage of Social Justice* (1976), Hayek argued that both the market order and the liberal society he defended were fundamentally incompatible with the type of planned reordering proposed by advocates of social justice.

Finally, Hayek believed that the design of liberal democratic institutions "in which the same representative body lays down the rules of just conduct and directs government, necessarily leads to the gradual transformation of the spontaneous order of a free society into a totalitarian system conducted in the service of some coalition of organized interests" (1973, 2). To avoid this danger, in the final volume of the project, entitled *The Political Order of a Free People* (Hayek 1979), he developed an elaborate – and frankly somewhat odd – scheme for separating the creation of public policy from the writing of overarching legislation.

Although Hayek was careful to specify that he was not promoting a vision of the state that would leave collective decisions solely in the hands of the market, his vision did push in that direction at a time when mainstream economists and political scientists were pursuing a Keynesian vision that left a great deal of room for state intervention. Together with the economically focused work of his colleague Milton Friedman and the technical work of public choice economists, Hayek helped create the blueprint for neoliberalism, the dominant framework by which we understand the interaction between state and market today. A conclusion that comes into relief using applied political theory is that much of the history of English-speaking conservatism since 1980 has been – to put it very simply – the result of the successful application of Hayek's theories by practical politicians in ways that have supplanted other traditions of conservatism. Canadian conservatism, as we will see, is no exception.

Ideas in Practice: Rebuilding around a Hayekian Core

Grant and Hayek offered very different social and political visions drawing on different intellectual resources. Both fit within Freeden's broad definition of a conservatism as defined, at its core, by fundamental concern with change, a "belief in the extra-human origin of the social order," and a reactive or mirror-image response to progressive ideology (Freeden 1996, 330–6), even as both men stood in an uneasy relationship with both conservative ideology and conservative politics. The challenge of this final section is to apply the political theory outlined above to Canadian political history in order to sketch how Canadian conservatism shifted from a diverse and contested understanding of its core – which included followers of both Grant and Hayek – to one defined in overwhelmingly Hayekian terms, and how that new understanding moved out to secondary or peripheral locations.

The shift towards Hayekian dominance occurred during the 1980s and 1990s, when Canadian conservatives – in common with political actors across the ideological spectrum – sought solutions for the apparent failure of the post-war Keynesian economic models (Lewis 2003). Much of the debate about Keynesianism was found in technical discussions about monetary policy, but Hayek's ideas about the impossibility of state planning and the power of market choice were influential at the broader political and social levels across most of the English-speaking world and, to a lesser degree, in continental Europe. The connection between Hayek and political action was clearest in Britain, where Margaret Thatcher had long-standing connections to free market think tanks indebted to Hayek and where Hayek's influence on the Thatcher government was evident (Jones 2012). But thanks in part to the Mont Perelin Society, Hayek's free market ideas had already travelled through a developed institutional network across the English-speaking world. By the 1970s this network included the Fraser Institute in Canada, joined later by think tanks such as the Atlantic Institute for Market Studies, the Frontier Institute, and the Macdonald-Laurier Institute, and lobby organizations such as the Canadian Taxpayers Federation, which worked hard to promote free market ideas (Gutstein 2014). In the 1980s and 1990s these ideas were forcefully articulated by conservative politicians such as Preston Manning, Mike Harris, and Ralph Klein, and distributed widely through the economics profession and public policy communities (Lewis 2003), coming to define the policy options available to most governments, including the Chrétien Liberals and even New Democratic Party governments such as that of Romanow in Saskatchewan and Rae in Ontario.

In a more lasting and important way than in other developed countries, conservatism in Canada was pushed towards Hayek by the emergence of a powerful set of right-wing populist movements in the 1980s. Populism is not necessarily right wing – indeed, most previous Canadian populist movements had been progressive (Laycock 1990) – but 1980s populism saw the state and its associated elites as the problem. The solution was the common wisdom of the person on the street, direct democracy, limited government, and an end to the accommodation of special interests. This argument found its most visible articulation in the federal Reform Party, but it was also influential in provincial conservative parties. No logical necessity linked conservative economics with populism, but Hayek's argument that only individuals know enough to make informed economic decisions for themselves did provide a politically powerful linkage between free market economics and populist democratic principles (Manning 2002; Patten 1996, 2013).[10] Both institutionally (by undercutting the Progressive Conservative Party) and ideologically (by undercutting trust in elites of all sorts), this right-wing populism pushed Grant-style Tories to the margins while opening up room for *laissez-faire* conservatives at the centre of the ideology. Organizationally this consensus was reinforced by the way in which federal conservatives reunited as the Conservative Party of Canada in 2003 – a unification that clearly identified the dominance of the populist/free market wing, with its roots in the Reform Party. In this regard Canadian conservatives shared some fundamental similarities with their American cousins, who had found that a similar combination held the key to electoral success.

But as Freeden's core/secondary/peripheral distinction identifies, there is more to any ideology than just the set of principles at its core. And if we are to understand Canadian conservatism with reference to articulations of the ideology in other settings, it is important to examine how it is that secondary or peripheral commitments can be made to fit with a free market core. In Canada, questions of group identity – especially national and religious identity – have been very important in determining the character of these secondary commitments. And at least as defined by the Harper government, secondary characteristics have been held in a way that makes them more compatible with Hayek's principles in Canada than is the situation in other countries.

For a combination of pragmatic and principled reasons, contemporary Canadian conservatism has seen the abatement of the thick nationalism that was so important to Grant and that continues to be visibly important to both American and European conservatives. The Harper Conservatives changed the citizenship test to emphasize Canadian history, yet until the 2015 election they were unique among conservative parties in both the effort they put into reaching out to immigrant and ethnic communities and the success they met with in garnering support from those communities (Marwah, Tiadafilopoulos, and White 2013). Some of this outreach must have been due to the electoral importance of minority and immigrant voters in swing ridings; some was also likely

10 Important voices argued, however, that this combination was fundamentally unstable and that the Reform Party should recognize that, to govern, it would have to be conservative (Flanagan 1995).

due to the economic benefits and lower labour costs that Canadian business saw significant immigration, both permanent and temporary, as underpinning. But important matters of principle were at play, too, and it seems that some of Hayek's internationalism and commitment to individualism found a home on the Canadian right.

The 2015 election campaign and the Conservative leadership race that followed made it unclear whether this comparative openness would continue. The Conservatives' handling of the refugee crisis in the dying days of the Harper government and their embrace of the *niqab* issue in the last days of the campaign suggested the very real possibility that Canadian conservatives – like their counterparts in western Europe and the United States – would make the questioning of multiculturalism and immigration a more central part of their identity. Although Kellie Leitch did not do well when the leadership votes were counted, her courting of nativist sentiment met with surprising success in setting the tone of the campaign debate. Time will tell if this holds and whether it plays out in a particularly Canadian way. Given the deep ties the Conservatives developed with immigrant communities, perhaps what they were exploiting was not simply a divide between old and new Canadians, but also between, say, Hindus or Sikhs and Muslims, which made the electoral costs of painting Muslims as the "other" quite low, even within immigrant communities.

It might be that the deeper embrace of a relatively open notion of citizenship and nationality by the Canadian right has been made possible by the difficulty Canadian conservative politicians have encountered in dealing with Quebec, one they resolved simply by taking the issue off the table. Stephen Harper's generation of conservative leaders cut their political teeth in the Reform Party, which made opposition to distinct status for Quebec a key part of its platform. That this status was being promoted by a Progressive Conservative prime minister, Brian Mulroney, only added to the betrayal many English Canadians felt in the 1980s, triggering a set of constitutional debates that came close to tearing the country apart. The Harper government did give symbolic recognition to Quebec as a "distinct nation within a United Canada," but most of that government's actions on constitutional matters were driven by its pursuit of an "open federalism" that, by devolving power to the provinces, allowed for regional differentiation across the country and limited the federal government's ability to intervene in the economy (Behiels and Talbot 2011; Harmes 2007; Jeffrey 2010). As the Harper government pursued policies that limited its taxing capacity – through cuts to the goods and services tax, the introduction of tax-free savings accounts, and an aggressive program of tax credits – it also limited its capacity to intervene in provincial jurisdictions by using the federal spending power. As tax cuts are politically difficult to reverse, there is a strong argument that this was a deliberate strategy by the Harper Conservatives to entrench a Hayekian small state.

That Canadian conservatives grounded their accommodation of minority rights claims in a fundamentally Hayekian individualism is clear if one compares their (relative) openness to immigration and immigrants to their strong resistance to claims by First Nations. Although there were many other, more proximate political reasons for the adversarial relationship between the Harper government and First Nations groups, there was an important challenge of principle as well. Any serious engagement with contemporary First Nations' claims for self-government would have meant accommodating collective claims to self-governance, not the recognition of the cultural practices of individuals and the acceptance of important orders of government that reject the notion of private property rights. Such claims are fundamentally incompatible with the Hayekian core of contemporary Canadian conservatism – an incompatibility that has produced some important similarities between how Canadian conservatives view First Nations groups and how American and European conservatives view immigrants.

So, on questions of identify, nationalism, and federalism, it seems clear that Canadian conservatives have evolved a secondary set of commitments that is more consistently classically liberal than its counterparts in other countries: they have pushed thick descriptions of national identity out to the periphery of the ideology, and in so doing they necessarily have rejected Grant.

One area where this was more complicated concerned religious freedom and social conservatism. Here the Harper Conservatives shifted positions a number of times, though each shift seemed to bring them closer to Hayek. Initially opposed to the idea of gay marriage, the party dropped its open opposition after 2006. Harper worked hard to keep the abortion issue off the table in ways that very clearly differentiated Canadian conservatives from their American counterparts (Farney 2012). But the Harper Conservatives did go some way to capturing both the rhetorical and policy ground of defending traditional family values and religious identity by opposing a national childcare program, refusing to fund international maternal health initiatives that included abortion access, and creating an office of religious freedom. That this constituency in the party was less influential at the end of the Harper government than at the beginning was probably due primarily to social changes and secularization, but some part of the change must also have been the result of the deliberate marginalization of these concerns by the party leadership. If permanent, this shift should be seen as away from some idea that government exists to enforce common societal conceptions of virtue and towards a classically liberal emphasis on individual autonomy.

One final issue where Canadian conservatives' move from Grant-style Toryism to Hayekian *laissez-faire* conservatism can be seen to have played out was in the area of foreign policy. This issue was central to Grant's identity as a conservative, although his pacifism and opposition to American hegemony probably mark the points at which he stood furthest from practical Canadian conservatives in his own day. Foreign policy was much less central to Hayek's thinking, but he clearly opposed nationalism, and hoped that free trade and the free exchange of ideas would have the same effects internationally as he believed they did domestically. Certainly, the Harper government made the signing of free trade agreements a central part of its foreign policy, which could be seen as a shift in Hayek's direction. It also made military support of American interventions and, in general, a narrower view of which countries Canada was partnered with on security matters important aspects of Canadian foreign policy. This cannot be seen as a shift towards Hayek, but it certainly was a shift away from Grant.

The comparative ease with which each of these secondary commitments was grafted in an intellectually coherent and practically expedient manner onto the free market core of contemporary Canadian conservatism speaks to the flexibility of that core. It also offers an example of the usefulness of applied political theory for understanding the changes such a flexible position can undergo. Understanding the nature of this flexibility is important because the geographic and organizational forums within which Canadian conservatives have worked out their differences of principle have often changed dramatically over the past generation: whether as members of the Progressive Conservatives, the Reform Party, the Canadian Alliance, or the Conservative Party of Canada, or one of a constellation of provincial parties, Canadian conservatives have worked out different aspects of conservatism. But underpinning each of these parties has been a gradual move towards a Hayekian commitment to classical liberalism, the free market, and a small state as the defining ideology. In the broad outlines of this movement, Canadian conservatives are similar to their counterparts in other countries, but they have pushed the implications of this approach further, especially regarding national identity – although whether the change will prove durable at a time of so much political contestation over identity and diversity is impossible to forecast.

REFERENCES

Azjenstat, Janet, and Peter Smith. 1995. *Canada's Origins: Liberal, Tory, or Republican?* Ottawa: Carleton University Press.

Behiels, Michael, and Robert Talbot. 2011. "Stephen Harper and Canadian Federalism: Theory and Practice 1987–2011." In *The State in Transition: Challenges for Canadian Federalism*, ed. Michael Behiels and François Rocher, 15–86. Ottawa. Invenire Books.

Caldwell, Bruce. 2004. *Hayek's Challenge: An Intellectual Biography of F.A. Hayek.* Chicago: University of Chicago Press.

Christian, William. 1993. *George Grant: A Biography*. Toronto: University of Toronto Press.

Farney, James. 2012. *Social Conservatism and Party Politics in Canada and the United States*. Toronto: University of Toronto Press. https://doi.org/10.3138/9781442699618

Flanagan, Tom. 1995. *Waiting for the Wave: The Reform Party and Preston Manning*. Toronto: Stoddart.

Forbes, Hugh Donald. 2007. *George Grant: A Guide to his Thought*. Toronto: University of Toronto Press. https://doi.org/10.3138/9781442684379

Freeden, Michael. 1996. *Ideologies and Political Theory: A Conceptual Approach.* Oxford, UK: Clarendon.

Frum, David. 1994. *Dead Right*. New York: Basic Books.

Gairdner, William D. 1992. *The War Against the Family: A Parent Speaks Out*. Toronto: Stoddart.

Gairdner, William D. 2010. *The Trouble with Canada...Still! A Citizen Speaks Out*. Toronto: Key Porter.

Grant, George. [1965] 1995. *Lament for a Nation: The Defeat of Canadian Nationalism*. Ottawa: Carleton University Press.

Grant, George. [1974] 1998. *English-Speaking Justice*. Toronto: Anansi.

Gutstein, Donald. 2014. "The War on Ideas: From Hayek to Harper." In *Publicity and the Canadian State: Critical Communications Perspectives*, ed. Kirsten Kozolanka, 93–111. Toronto: University of Toronto Press.

Harmes, Adam. 2007. "The Political Economy of Open Federalism." *Canadian Journal of Political Science* 40 (2): 417–37. https://doi.org/10.1017/S0008423907070114

Hayek, F.A. [1944] 2007. *The Road to Serfdom*. Ed. Bruce Caldwell. Chicago: University of Chicago Press. https://doi.org/10.7208/chicago/9780226320533.001.0001

Hayek, F.A. 1960. *The Constitution of Liberty*. Chicago: University of Chicago Press.

Hayek, F.A. 1973. *Law, Legislation, and Liberty*. Vol. 1, *Rules and Order*. Chicago: University of Chicago Press.

Hayek, F.A. 1976. *Law, Legislation, and Liberty*. Vol. 2, *The Mirage of Social Justice*. Chicago: University of Chicago Press.

Hayek, F.A. 1979. *Law, Legislation, and Liberty*. Vol. 3, *The Political Order of a Free People*. Chicago: University of Chicago Press.

Horowitz, Gad. 1966. "Conservatism, Liberalism and Socialism in Canada: An Interpretation." *Canadian Journal of Political Science* 32 (1): 143–71.

Jeffrey, Brooke. 2010. "Prime Minister Harper's Open Federalism: Promoting a Neo-Liberal Agenda?" In *The Case for Centralized Federalism*, ed. Gordon DiGiacomo and Maryantonnett Flumian, 108–36. Ottawa: University of Ottawa Press.

Jones, Daniel Stedman. 2012. *Masters of the Universe: Hayek, Friedman, and the Birth of Neoliberal Politics*. Princeton, NJ: Princeton University Press.

Laycock, David. 1990. *Populism and Democratic Thought on the Canadian Prairies*. Toronto: University of Toronto Press.

Lewis, Timothy. 2003. *In the Long Run We're All Dead: The Canadian Turn to Fiscal Restraint*. Toronto: University of Toronto Press.

Manning, Preston. 2002. *Think Big: My Adventures in Life and Democracy*. Toronto: McClelland & Stewart.

Marwah, Inder, Phil Tiadafilopoulos, and Stephen White. 2013. "Immigration, Citizenship, and Canada's New Conservative Party." In *Conservatism in Canada*, ed. James Farney and David Rayside, 95–119. Toronto: University of Toronto Press.

O'Donovan, Joan. 1984. *George Grant and the Twilight of Justice*. Toronto: University of Toronto Press.

Patten, Steve. 1996. "Preston Manning's Populism: Constructing the Common Sense of the Common People." *Studies in Political Economy* 50 (1): 95–132. https://doi.org/10.1080/19187033.1996.11675338

Patten, Steve. 2013. "The Triumph of Neoliberalism within Partisan Conservatism." In *Conservatism in Canada*, ed. James Farney and David Rayside, 59–76. Toronto: University of Toronto Press.

Rawls, John. [1971] 1999. *A Theory of Justice: Revised Edition*. Cambridge: Belknap Press.
Segal, Hugh. 1997. *Beyond Greed: A Traditional Conservative Confronts Neoconservative Excess*. Toronto: Stoddart.
Segal, Hugh. 2006. *The Long Road Back: The Conservative Journey in Canada, 1993–2006*. Toronto: HarperCollins.
Taube, Michael. 2015. "Brad Wall for Conservative leader." *Toronto Sun*, 29 October.

2 Canadian Liberalism as a Distinctive Tradition

BROOKE JEFFREY

I am a liberal. I am one of those who think that everywhere in human beings, there are abuses to be reformed, new horizons to be opened up, and new forces to be developed.

– Sir Wilfrid Laurier (1877)

Liberalism is a philosophy for our time, because it does not try to conserve every tradition of the past, because it does not apply to new problems old doctrinaire solutions, because it is prepared to experiment and innovate, and because it knows that the past is less important than the future.

– Pierre Trudeau (1984)

Liberalism, Berlin taught us ... is a fighting creed for those devoted to the fate of their particular communities. The Canada I grew up in, the Canada that shaped me, is a liberal Canada.

– Michael Ignatieff (2009)

In Canada, better is always possible.

– Justin Trudeau (2015)

Liberalism has often been described as the dominant political philosophy in Canada, but it has also been criticized as a pseudo-philosophy based more on opportunism and brokerage politics than on values or beliefs. Part of the problem in conceptualizing liberalism in Canada is that it has become so closely identified with the Liberal Party and the actions of Liberal governments when that party is in power. This linkage is particularly significant since the party is recognized as the most successful in the western democratic world. It dominated the political landscape in Canada throughout the twentieth century – indeed, its dominance was so overwhelming that noted scholar John Meisel (1972) once declared, "the line between the government and the Liberal Party has become tenuous."

This reality was acknowledged by Tom Flanagan, a former adviser to Stephen Harper, when he cautioned that the new Conservative Party should move slowly and incrementally to implement change because "Canada is not yet a conservative or Conservative country" (2007, 274). It was also recognized by Harper himself, who once declared he wanted to create "a country built on solid conservative values ... a country the Liberals wouldn't even recognize" (2003).

The applied political theory approach can be particularly useful for understanding this close relationship between the Liberal Party and the ideology of liberalism in Canada. I begin by outlining the evolution of liberal principles emanating from a range of thinkers from John Locke to Isaiah Berlin, and the additional liberal values and beliefs developed in the Canadian context over time. I then compare these ideas with the policies of Liberal federal governments and prime ministers since the turn of the twentieth century. Combining the empirical analysis of Liberal federal government policies with liberal political theory, I show that the Liberal Party of Canada has stood consistently for a clear set of values and beliefs, some of which are distinctively Canadian.

Seen in this context, the Liberal Party's rapid fall from grace – losing two elections to the Harper Conservatives in 2006 and 2008 and then losing even its status as the Official Opposition after the 2011 federal election – becomes all the more significant. The party's unprecedented reversal of fortunes immediately led Prime Minister Stephen Harper to declare that liberalism itself was on the wane: "I believe the long Liberal era has truly ended. As with disco-balls and bell-bottoms, Canadians have moved on ... We are moving Canada in a conservative direction, and Canadians are moving in that direction with us" (2011).

Nor was Harper alone in his belief that both the party *and* its underlying philosophy were a spent force. As leader of the Official Opposition, New Democratic Party (NDP) leader Tom Mulcair claimed that the philosophical landscape in Canada was rapidly polarizing between conservatism and socialism. A number of academics agreed. Political scientist Nelson Wiseman, for example, predicted the demise of the Liberal Party, and offered his view of the dilemma facing a moderate centrist philosophy bracketed by two more hardline alternatives: "Today," Wiseman declared, "the Liberals are a dilapidated annex of the Canadian party system. Their prospects are bleak. In this respect Stephen Harper and the NDP pursue a common strategic objective, the further marginalization of their common foe" (2011).

Wiseman's views were widely shared. Author Peter Newman's analysis of the 2011 election was titled *When the Gods Changed: The Death of Liberal Canada* (Newman 2011), a theme repeated by *Globe and Mail* columnist Jeffrey Simpson as late as 27 June 2015 – on the eve of the next federal election – in an article entitled "Are we witnessing the strange death of Liberal Canada?" (Simpson 2015). Similarly pollster Darrell Bricker and *Globe and Mail* Ottawa bureau chief John Ibbitson's widely cited work, *The Big Shift*, declared that "the centre isn't there anymore" and the "odds are good" the Liberal Party would die. More important, they not only concurred with Wiseman that liberalism was no longer a viable philosophy; they also predicted Harper's new right-wing conservatism would triumph over socialism as represented by the NDP: "The Conservative Party will be to the twenty-first century what the Liberal Party was to the 20th, the perpetually dominant party, the natural governing party" (Bricker and Ibbitson 2013, 126).

The 2011 election undoubtedly represented the Liberal Party's worst setback, but it was hardly the first time its demise was predicted. In 1984 the party was reduced to an all-time low of forty-four seats in the House of Commons under leader John Turner. Its imminent collapse became conventional wisdom, even though it retained its status as the Official Opposition. NDP leader Ed Broadbent declared that Canadian liberalism was an outdated and essentially artificial concept, based on what he saw as a hazy set of "centrist" values he termed the "mushy middle" – values he believed were easily sacrificed to opportunism and political expediency by liberalism's proponents. These centrist values, he argued, were now causing its demise, squeezed out by more "legitimate" philosophies on the right and left.

The widespread perception that the Liberal Party was on its last legs vanished in 1988, when the party doubled its representation in the House. But concerns about Canadian liberalism – and its allegedly opportunistic centrism – lingered even after the Chrétien Liberals' return to power in 1993 and their subsequent decade of ascendancy. Moreover, the source of the criticism changed, and its tone and tenor was far more strident. The new, more aggressive criticism came from the far right, rather than from the left. And instead of merely accusing Liberals of practising brokerage politics to maintain their position in the "mushy middle," it charged liberalism with having no values or principles at all.

A primary reason for this harsh new critique of liberalism was the advent of so-called neoconservative regimes in much of the western world in the late twentieth century. Epitomized by the governments of Margaret Thatcher and Ronald Reagan, the far right's political discourse was significantly different from that of more traditional conservatives. Liberalism was directly in their sights, accused of being both dangerous and unacceptable, rather than simply an alternative philosophy. Thatcher herself once declared that modern liberals were "abandoning all values, beliefs and principles" (Katwala 2013, 7).

Under the Harper Conservatives, whose admiration for Thatcher and Reagan was well-known, this critical discourse took root in Canada as well. In his June 2003 speech to the Civitas Society, Stephen Harper spelled this out quite explicitly. Liberalism, he declared, was really another word for "moral nihilism." As such it should no longer be viewed as a legitimate competing philosophy, but as a dangerous "system of moral relativism, moral neutrality and moral equivalency."

Many political theorists disagreed, however, arguing that the advent of the new Conservative Party's right-wing philosophy did not represent a clash between morality and nihilism, but, rather, between two diametrically opposed value systems (McCullough 2010; Nadeau 2011). This argument gained credence when prominent Canadian "progressive" conservatives categorically rejected the new conservatism (for example, former PC prime minister Joe Clark, in remarks on CTV's *Question Period*, 26 April 2014; Stevens 2008). Indeed Clark actually had declared he would vote for the Liberal Party in the 2011 federal election rather than for Stephen Harper's new Conservative Party.

As the following discussion will outline, the values and beliefs underpinning Canadian liberalism have been clearly identified and upheld by its proponents. As Pierre Trudeau warned in his speech at the June 1984 Liberal leadership convention held to choose his successor, the real challenge for each generation of Canadian liberals has been to determine how to apply these values and beliefs to the issues of the day and to articulate them in a meaningful framework of policy initiatives for each generation of Canadians.

For much of the twentieth century, Canadian liberals met this challenge. But more recent developments, such as globalization and the technological revolution – and the new right's strident rhetoric in response to them – have proven far more difficult for liberals, in Canada and elsewhere, to address, a fact Robert Reich (1989) made clear in the case of the United States, where Democrats were actually afraid to use the word "liberal" for decades.

Although recognizing the problems liberalism has faced in recent times, I reject this negative assessment. Refuting both the NDP's "mushy middle" and the Conservatives' "moral nihilism" critiques of Canadian liberalism, I argue instead that its proponents have outlined a cohesive and distinctive set of values and beliefs. As a corollary, I also argue that the difficulties the Liberal Party of Canada faced during the Harper era were the result, not of declining public support for liberalism, but of the failure of the party leadership to articulate those values clearly and cogently, and to offer a convincing alternative narrative to neoconservative rhetoric.

I begin with an overview of the distinctive evolution of modern liberalism in Canada, identifying key values that have become closely identified with it. The following sections demonstrate the commitment of leading Liberal Party politicians to those values in theory and their practical application of those values when in power. In a final section, I identify the difficulties recent Liberal leaders have faced in light of the new conservative rhetoric, and I conclude with the return to power of the federal Liberal Party in 2015, a victory that arguably represented a successful response by liberals to that rhetoric.

The Distinctive Evolution of Reform Liberalism in Canada

The classic liberalism of philosophers such as John Locke, which evolved in Europe in the seventeenth and eighteenth centuries, emphasized individual liberty as the pre-eminent liberal value. The rights of the individual over the power of the state engendered the values of life, liberty, and the pursuit of happiness, while the arguments put forward by Adam Smith promoted the mercantilist view of the economy and the right to individual ownership of property. The institutional results of classic liberalism included the adoption by states of written constitutions and limited constitutional monarchies and, ultimately, of citizenship and democracy, albeit in a majoritarian sense.

By the early nineteenth century, however, the failure of classic liberalism to deal with major social and economic upheavals in society led to the evolution of a reform liberalism in which the role of the state as a force for good was increasingly seen as desirable. It rejected Adam Smith's concept of the invisible hand of the marketplace in favour of limited state intervention to reduce inevitable and serious inequalities, and similarly sought to protect the rights of minorities within society. Thus tolerance of diversity became an essential element of reform liberalism. As Roberts has explained, "[t]olerance was seen as a positive good to be embraced enthusiastically and championed both because it reflected the diverse reality of mankind, but also because diversity constitutes the driving force behind human imagination and intellectual competition that (are) the source of human advancement" (2003, 9). In this regard it is important to note that human advancement – the belief in the possibility of constantly improving the human condition, and a focus on progress and the future, rather than an emphasis on tradition and the past – were important components of that vision. At the same time, reform liberalism emphasized a pragmatic, rather than a rigid ideological, approach to government in which balance and moderation were key attributes. "Pragmatism rather than righteousness should govern the public agenda. Moral rectitude is not the purpose of government, but practical action to enhance the opportunity for individuals to be self-enhancing" (79).

Over time, further evolution of reform liberalism led to the concept of the state's taking positive, rather than simply negative, actions vis-à-vis individuals. From John Stuart Mill to Isaiah Berlin and John Rawls, the increasing emphasis on the legitimate role of the state in providing all citizens the tools to achieve self-improvement led to the creation of the programs of the welfare state and to increasing government intervention in the marketplace. In the vision of reform liberalism, individual liberty could not be considered meaningful if there was no equality of opportunity. Similarly the economic chaos of the early twentieth century led John Maynard Keynes to argue for the obligation of the state, in order to protect its citizens, to mitigate against the inevitable upheavals of the marketplace by intervening more intensively with formal checks and balances domestically and internationally.

In Canada the country's geographic and demographic circumstances – including its British and French origins and the arrival of waves of immigrants from eastern Europe – played an important role in the evolution of Canadian reform liberalism, leading to some distinctive characteristics. As Horowitz (1966) argued, the presence of Tory and socialist "fragments" in Canadian society ultimately produced a liberalism that acknowledged the importance of certain collectivist principles, and accepted a greater "protective" role of the state. At the same time, liberalism's emphasis on pragmatism led it to reject both the equality of condition and massive state intervention promoted by socialism as hopelessly utopian goals.

Meanwhile the situation of Canada as a geographically large but underpopulated country located next door to the United States also produced a fragment related to American ideals of independence. Nation building in the face of American cultural dominance, and the construction of a Canadian identity, therefore became another important and distinctive element of Canadian liberalism.

There are a number of practical implications of this unique approach to liberalism in Canada. First and foremost, tolerance of diversity played a significant role in the framing of the Canadian Constitution (the Constitution Act, 1867) and in the choice of a federal system of government. Subsequently it led to the adoption of official bilingualism, multiculturalism, and the Charter of Rights and Freedoms. Similarly the dominant themes in federal-provincial relations as well as in government decision making have been compromise and consensus. The practical application of this approach can be seen in the development of "cooperative federalism" to achieve the programs of the welfare state, and in the concept of horizontal equity among regions, through programs such as equalization and regional development. Moreover, the extension of such values to foreign policy has resulted in Canadian liberalism's preference for a multilateral approach to international issues and a commitment to international organizations designed to promote such values.

In the end, Canadian liberalism has come to be situated to the left of the European liberalism from whence it came and, to an even greater extent, to the left of American liberalism, which retains closer ties with classic rather than with reform liberalism. As a result, the centrism of Canadian liberalism, while reflecting a middle position between the extremes of conservatism and socialism, has also traditionally been one that has articulated progressive concepts such as equality of opportunity, economic nationalism, and multilateral foreign policy, even while reinforcing the values of pragmatism and balance through its emphasis on consultation and compromise.

As the following sections demonstrate, for much of Canada's history a succession of Liberal Party leaders has actively articulated these liberal values and, in power, have operationalized those values in their public policy initiatives.

Liberal Values and the Liberal Party

Virtually every leader of the Liberal Party has outlined his vision of liberalism. Each successive leader has repeated a number of basic values, but there is also evidence of the evolution of liberal thinking over time, which has added new dimensions to its basic tenets.

To begin with, Liberal leaders from the time of Laurier have viewed liberalism as favouring reform but eschewing radical options, a crucial distinction in a country with both conservative and socialist strands. An early advocate of a distinctive Canadian liberalism, Laurier is particularly well known for his emphasis on conciliation and compromise, which he clearly saw as virtues, rather than an absence of values and beliefs. In a speech to the House of Commons, Laurier declared, "[n]o great reform can be achieved except at the sacrifice of some opinion, even by those who are the most ardently in favour of it. The true reformer is not he who always adheres stubbornly to his own ideas, but the true reformer is he who, after having earnestly combatted for his opinions then yields in order to attain some greater end, and to facilitate the change from the old to the new order of things" (Hansard, 25 March 1907). For Laurier the need for compromise was particularly self-evident between Canada's two founding linguistic groups and in his pursuit of national unity and a pan-Canadian identity. In one of his most famous addresses, he declared, "I have had before me, as a pillar of fire, a policy of true Canadianism, of moderation, of reconciliation."

Laurier's vision of Canadian liberalism also emphasized individual liberty: "Canada is free and freedom is its nationality ... Nothing will prevent me from continuing my task of preserving at all cost our civil liberty." At the same time, Laurier emphasized the legitimate limitations society (through government) could impose on individual liberty – and, by extension, on the rights of the majority – noting in his landmark 26 June 1877 speech in Quebec City on liberalism that "[w]e have no absolute rights among us. The rights of each man, in our state of society, end precisely at the point where they encroach upon the rights of others" (quoted in Bélanger 2007, 42).

By contrast, in the post-war era, with the advent of the United Nations and the development of international declarations and conventions on human rights, Liberal leaders increasingly addressed their concerns about individual liberty in the context of the protection of human rights and the promotion of equality of opportunity. In his seminal speech, "On Liberalism," Liberal leader Lester Pearson spoke of liberalism's "belief in man, and that is the first purpose of government, to legislate for the benefit and liberation of the human personality ... liberalism must also ensure that all citizens, without any discrimination, will be in a position to take advantage of new opportunities and of freedoms that have been won" (1962).

In the same vein, Pierre Trudeau stressed the importance of individual liberty vis-à-vis the power of the state, arguing that the Charter of Rights did not transfer powers from the provinces to the federal government, as some premiers claimed, but actually constrained the power of *both* levels of government from interfering with the basic human rights of citizens.

This blend of consistency and evolution can also be seen in Liberal politicians' pragmatic support for government intervention in the economy. In his 1918 treatise on labour relations, Liberal leader Mackenzie King argued for limited government intervention in the economy for specific ends such as the protection of workers and consumers. Forty years later, Lester Pearson declared government should play a more significant role in the post-war era: "Government must keep pace with the changing needs of the times and accept greater responsibilities than would have been acceptable to a Liberal a hundred years ago." But any such intervention could be justified only by determining that it "will truly benefit the individual, [and] will enlarge (not restrict) his opportunity for self-expression and development" (Pearson 1962).

Years later, Pierre Trudeau promoted new forms of government intervention, but his memoirs still referred to the classic "inevitable inequities" produced by an unfettered marketplace and his belief that, "[a]gainst the invisible hand of Adam Smith, there has to be a visible hand of a society that is caring and humane" (Axworthy and Trudeau 1990, 190). Likewise, Trudeau's successor, Jean Chrétien, stated: "The basic principles of liberalism are timeless and immutable. Liberalism is founded on freedom of the individual, equality of opportunity, compassion for the underprivileged and protection of the weak, and tolerance of diversity. Liberalism certainly relies on free markets, but it recognizes, at the same time, the necessary role of government in facilitating change, and in delivering necessary public goods and services" (Chrétien 1992, 12).

The evolution of liberalism's emphasis on equality of opportunity, tolerance of diversity, and minority rights was epitomized in Pierre Trudeau's 1974 campaign slogan, "Towards a Just Society" and in his speech unveiling his party's platform:

> The Just Society will be one in which all of our people will have the means and the motivation to participate. The Just Society will be one in which personal and political freedom will be more securely ensured than it has ever been in the past. The Just Society will be one in which the rights

> of minorities will be safe from the whims of intolerant majorities. The Just Society will be one in which those regions and groups which have not fully shared in the country's affluence will be given a better opportunity. (Trudeau 1998, 16–20)

In much the same way, liberal values of balance, compromise, and consensus have been increasingly articulated in terms of the pursuit of national unity. In the post-war era, with the advent of the welfare state and especially with the selection of Pierre Trudeau as Liberal leader, strong central federalism emerged as a key tenet of Canadian liberalism. Given the significance of federalism in the evolution of Canada, this is perhaps hardly surprising. All three mainstream ideologies, and the political parties that represent them, have identified their position on the federal centralist-decentralist axis as defined by Livingston (1963). The Conservatives and NDP historically have taken a decentralist approach to federalism, while only the Liberal Party has favoured a strong central government. More important still, the Liberal Party's commitment to centralized federalism has become a crucial element of its underlying philosophical framework, rooted in its deeply held views about the positive role of federalism in promoting tolerance and respect for diversity in a plural society, in protecting individual rights, and in facilitating a pan-Canadian vision. As former Trudeau adviser Senator Michael Kirby noted during an intense debate over the 1985 Meech Lake Accord – proposed by the Mulroney Progressive Conservative government and vigorously opposed by former prime minister Trudeau and the vast majority of Liberals: "The Conservatives' accord reinforces the concept of Canadian federalism as some type of 'provincial compact' in which the rights or powers of provincial governments are more important than the rights of individuals." This vision, Kirby argued, "is precisely the opposite" of the liberal vision in which the rights of individual Canadian citizens are paramount" (1988, 57).

The Accord was also the opposite of the Trudeauvian vision of a pluralist, pan-Canadian society, since it promoted the nationalist concept of Quebec as a "distinct society" that he had consistently rejected. "It is Canada," Trudeau declared, "that is the distinct society" because of its pluralism. The importance of the pan-Canadian vision and strong central federalism was underlined by Prime Minister Jean Chrétien in a speech at a Forum of the Federations meeting at Mont-Tremblant, Quebec, shortly after the 1995 referendum on Quebec sovereignty: "Over time, our federal experience has helped shape the Canadian personality.

It has imbued us with important values – our instinctive tolerance, our search for understanding and accommodation, our appreciation of diversity, our sense of solidarity, our commitment to dialogue. Minority rights are an essential part of Canadian federalism." More than twenty years later, Liberal leader Michael Ignatieff, in delivering the 2009 Isaiah Berlin lecture, reminded his British audience that "Canadian rights culture strikes a distinctive balance between the individual and the collective ... The enduring character of our linguistic and cultural differences has also shaped our philosophy of government ... From the beginning we had to compromise, to reach out across divides that have broken other countries apart. Government is central to Canadian survival, but at the same time our federation distributes powers so that no single order of government can dominate. Because our unity cannot be taken for granted, we understand that pragmatic leadership and moderate government are conditions for our survival" (Ignatieff 2009).

Liberalism's focus on the future and desire for positive change has also been recognized by a succession of Liberal politicians. In a speech marking the adoption of the new Canadian flag in 1965, Lester Pearson declared: "This ceremony today is not a break with history but a new stage in Canada's forward march. This is inevitable in the succession of new beginnings that mark a nation's progress." His views were echoed by Pierre Trudeau in a speech delivered at the Liberal Party's 1968 leadership convention: "Liberalism is a philosophy for our time, because it does not try to conserve every tradition of the past, because it does not apply to new problems old doctrinaire solutions, because it is prepared to experiment and innovate, and because it knows that the past is less important than the future."

Trudeau's reference to experimentation and innovation was also reflective of liberalism's ability to adapt to changing realities, the characteristic seen by proponents as a strength, but by critics as opportunism or lack of commitment. The importance of adaptation was underlined by future Liberal leader Jean Chrétien in the preface to *Finding Common Ground*. "The basic principles of liberalism are timeless," Chrétien wrote, "but while its basic values are unchanging, changing times always require new policies and fresh approaches" (1992, 12).

Finally, the accusation that liberalism represents only a "mushy middle," bereft of meaningful values and principles, has been repeatedly and categorically rejected by Liberal thinkers. In "On Liberalism," for example, Pearson specifically asserted the legitimacy of liberalism as a centrist philosophy: "Liberalism stands for the middle way, the way of progress. It stands for moderation, tolerance and the rejection of extreme courses, whether they express themselves in demands that the state should do everything for the individual … or in demands that the state should do nothing except hold the ring so that the fittest survive under the law of the jungle. In other words, liberalism accepts social security but rejects socialism; it accepts free enterprise but rejects economic anarchy; it accepts humanitarianism but rejects paternalism" (Pearson 1962).

A similar defence of centrism can be found in a treatise by former Trudeau adviser Senator Jack Austin. Austin compared liberalism with its philosophical counterparts on the right and left, the appeal of which, he argued, stems from their appearing to offer more certainty and clarity. But simplistic guarantees, he maintained, are dangerous. For Austin, another great virtue of liberalism is its ability to recognize the complexity of policy issues and avoid extremes at all costs. In this sense, moderation is a value in and of itself, epitomized by liberalism's commitment to equality of opportunity, rather than equality of *condition*, as promoted by socialism: "The polarities of public opinion are always so clear, so coherent, so well-organized, so outwardly sure of themselves, that they cannot tolerate public dissent for fear of a loss of their momentum. The centre (liberalism) is committed to accommodating a spectrum of opinion, a balancing of views, a trade-off of demands, and the most progress for the greatest number." Austin also wrote presciently that, "[w]e live today in a world filled with fear and anxiety … We are frightened of changes taking place around us that we barely understand. At such times, there is a great temptation to go where strength seems to be – whatever the substance that may be offered." Against this tendency, he argued that "holding the centre" is the "public trust" of liberals and of the Liberal Party as its standard-bearer (Austin 1981).

The role of Canadian liberalism as the guardian of the centre was reinforced after the Liberal Party's disastrous 1984 election campaign, which reduced it to a mere forty seats and delivered a massive majority to the right-wing Mulroney government. As one of the young opposition MPs who formed the highly partisan "Rat Pack" in Question Period, Brian Tobin was an unlikely spokesperson for the philosophical merits of liberalism. But in an interview years later, when asked about his role in the party's rebuilding process, he stressed that he and his colleagues had been "crystal clear" that their first task was to defend liberalism: "We knew there was more at stake than the survival of the party … We were really in a battle to preserve our world view – to keep alive a moderate, progressive voice in Canadian politics" (quoted in Jeffrey 2010, 142).

The Liberal Party in Power: Operationalizing Liberal Values

An important part of an applied political theory approach is the presentation of empirical evidence, and it is to this that I now turn. A brief examination of some major policy initiatives undertaken in the post-war era by four Liberal governments – those of Mackenzie King, Pearson, Pierre Trudeau, and Chrétien – suggests their policies were closely aligned with liberal values. More important, statements by these Liberal prime ministers reveal *their policy choices were motivated by their commitment to liberalism*. Indeed, the strength of their convictions is evident in their championing of certain policies despite the lack of popular support.

Beginning with the lengthy tenure of Mackenzie King, which spanned the Great Depression and the Second World War, Liberal governments pursued domestic policy initiatives that emphasized a positive role for government in the economy and society. Under King these included fair wage legislation, the Old Age Pension, unemployment insurance, which involved a lengthy tussle with the provinces over jurisdiction, and the Family Allowance. At the same time, King's actions epitomized balance and moderation, compromise and consensus. Frequently criticized for slow, incremental decisions, King was unapologetic, and his government often proposed compromises to ensure opposition support during difficult times. This approach is exemplified by his handling of the Great Depression. As King's principal biographer has noted:

> King's response reflected his fundamental commitment to finding a consensus among "liberally-minded" Canadians. He did not expect to convert the Tories, whom he believed were wedded to big business, or the socialists, who wanted a monopoly of power for the workers … The most controversial issue for his party would be inflation ... King's compromise was a government-controlled "central bank" that could modify the money supply on the basis of "public need." The significance of this compromise should not be minimized. It recognized that the state should play a positive role in determining fiscal policy. It placed the party in the centre of the political spectrum, more open than the Conservatives to regulating business without resorting to the socialist panacea of government ownership. (Neatby 2003, 248)

Meanwhile, in his handling of the war effort, King was a staunch follower of Laurier, stressing above all the need to ensure a united Canada. This balancing act was crucial in accommodating French-speaking Canadians in Quebec, particularly during the conscription crisis. Given King's lack of bilingualism and his recognition of the important cultural differences involved, he had already ensured a linguistic and regionally representative cabinet and appointed Quebec lieutenants Ernest Lapointe and Louis St-Laurent. King's focus on national unity also drove him to stress Canada's independence from Britain, playing key roles in the Imperial Conference of 1926, the adoption of the Statute of Westminster, and the creation of the United Nations.

During Lester Pearson's relatively brief time in office, and despite its minority status, his government passed a wide range of national social programs – including the Canada Pension Plan (CPP), medicare, and the Canada Assistance Plan – that expanded on King's efforts and became the backbone of the Canadian welfare state. Pearson also established the Royal Commission on the Status of Women, which ultimately led to the implementation of affirmative action and employment equity programs in the public service, and the Royal Commission on Bilingualism and Biculturalism. Pearson's economic initiatives were deliberately designed to enhance both equality of opportunity and economic nationalism. These included the introduction of student loans and the Canada Labour Code, the signing of the historic Canadian-US auto pact, and the creation of the Economic Council of Canada and the Science Council of Canada. In 1967 Pearson's government adopted the first non-discriminatory set of immigration regulations (the points system), which promoted immigration as an important aspect of Canadian economic independence.

Another building block of Canadian identity was laid with the Liberals' establishment of the Canadian Radio and Television Commission (CRTC, later the Canadian Radio-television and Telecommunications Commission) and the introduction of Canadian-content regulations. Pearson summed up his liberal vision of national identity when speaking about the new Canadian flag his government inaugurated in 1965 after a lengthy parliamentary debate: "As the symbol of a new chapter in our national story, our Maple Leaf Flag will become a symbol of that unity in our country without which one cannot grow in strength and purpose, the unity that encourages equal partnership of two peoples on which this confederation was founded; the unity also that recognizes the contributions and the cultures of many other races ... May the land over which this new Flag flies remain united in freedom and justice … tolerant and compassionate towards all men – and just in the giving of security and opportunity equally to all its cultures" (Hansard, 15 June 1964, 4325).

Building on King's progress in achieving an independent Canadian presence on the world stage, Pearson charted a course for Canada as a "middle power," concerned primarily with peacekeeping and development aid and the adoption of a multilateral approach to foreign policy. Nowhere was the balanced approach of liberalism more evident than in the growing international recognition that Canada's chosen role was one of "honest broker."

The influence of liberalism on Pearson's successor, Pierre Trudeau, was evident early on. As minister of justice in the Pearson government, Trudeau stressed the importance of individual liberty and the need to restrain the powers of the state. When introducing major (and controversial) revisions to the Criminal Code concerning abortion, divorce, and homosexuality, he famously declared that the state "has no place in the bedrooms of the nation." Later, justice reforms under his own government included the creation of a correctional investigator, adoption of the United Nations Convention on Standard Minimum Rules for the Treatment of Prisoners, introduction of Aboriginal support programs, and abolition of the death penalty.

Trudeau's government undertook a wide variety of economic and social measures that built on the existing liberal-inspired framework, including the expansion of unemployment insurance to include training and enhanced income support, the amendment of the National Housing Act to promote assisted and cooperative housing, the introduction of the Child Tax Credit, and the indexing of the Family Allowance, Old Age Security, and income tax brackets. Meanwhile his appointments to the Senate and the Supreme Court and as speakers of the House and governors general reflected an ongoing concern with gender equality and cultural diversity, as did his promotion of participatory democracy and numerous reforms to the Liberal Party's constitution and the Elections Act.

Trudeau also continued Pearson's emphasis on development assistance, creating the Canadian International Development Agency and establishing the North-South Institute as a think tank on development policy. Despite considerable opposition from neoconservative leaders such as Thatcher and Reagan, Trudeau continued to push for an independent Canadian foreign policy based on multilateralism. He promoted east-west détente, championed Canada's early recognition of regimes in China and Cuba, promoted North-South dialogue, and argued for greater power sharing with Third World countries in international institutions.

Following Pearson's lead with respect to the promotion of a pan-Canadian identity, Trudeau introduced legislation establishing official bilingualism, another controversial measure that flew in the face of accusations about liberalism's mushy middle. In his 17 October 1968 speech in the House of Commons on tabling the Official Languages Act, Trudeau stressed the importance of government's giving formal recognition and support to cultural diversity in order to promote both equality of opportunity and national unity. He stated the bill "is a reflection of the nature of the country as a whole," and declared that Liberals "believe in two official languages in a pluralist society, not merely as a political necessity but as an enrichment." Similarly, in 1971, responding to concerns about rising discrimination resulting from increased non-European immigration, his government introduced a multiculturalism policy and established a program to promote human rights and intergroup understanding.

These initiatives culminated in the entrenchment of the Charter of Rights and Freedoms in the Constitution Act, 1982. In addition to the guarantee of classic liberal values such as freedom of speech and religion, the Charter contained sections reflecting the distinctive aspects of Canadian liberalism, such as official bilingualism, multiculturalism, and equalization, as well as Aboriginal rights. Similarly, section 1 of the Charter demonstrated the liberal commitment to balance, declaring that the rights it enshrined were "subject to such reasonable limits prescribed by law as can be demonstrably justified in a free and democratic society."

The mix of private sector regulation and public enterprise begun by earlier Liberal leaders also continued under Trudeau. For example, "regional equity" was the driving force behind the creation of the Department of Regional Economic Expansion and the (highly controversial) introduction of a National Energy Policy, including the creation of Petro-Canada. Trudeau's principal adviser, Tom Axworthy, wrote in his memoirs that, "economists have often emphasized that we promoted regional equity as much as economic efficiency. To those charges we happily plead guilty" (Axworthy and Trudeau 1990, 206). Similarly the introduction of measures such as the Foreign Investment Review Agency were specifically justified as fostering Canadian independence.

Both Pearson and later Trudeau for much of his time in office were fortunate that their tenure coincided with periods of strong economic growth. Jean Chrétien, however, faced an economic crisis upon taking office. Consequently he presided over a variety of controversial funding cuts in the early years of his mandate in order to eliminate the substantial deficit left by the Mulroney government. Such actions were notable exceptions for a Liberal government, and were criticized widely as "illiberal." Chretien, however, said such temporary austerity measures were necessary to allow the government to pursue social policy initiatives and enhance the opportunities of individual Canadians in the longer term. Chrétien's explanation demonstrated the philosophical dilemma he believed he faced, one reflected in his earlier statement that "the Liberal Party has always been at the forefront of social change in Canada," but, *unlike socialism*, "liberalism has always recognized that a strong economy with growing personal incomes is an essential requirement for progressive and generous system of social security" (Chrétien 1992, 12). Once the deficit was eliminated, Chrétien's actions reflected this thinking, as he moved to restore social program funding to the provinces, particularly for health care. He also introduced new social policy initiatives such as the National Child Benefit, the Early Learning and Child Care Program, improvements to social housing through Canada Mortgage and Housing Corporation, Millennium Scholarships, and Canada Research Chairs.

In the area of foreign policy, Chrétien's commitment to the United Nations and his refusal to participate in the US-led invasion of Iraq mirrored Pearson's earlier peacekeeping and "middle power" policies, while his New Partners for Africa's Development initiative and his support of development aid as chair of the G7 in 2002 followed closely on Pierre Trudeau's commitment to focus development assistance on "the poorest of the poor." Meanwhile initiatives such as the International Criminal Court, the international convention on landmines, and the "Responsibility to Protect" principle reflected liberalism's flexibility and willingness to adopt new methods. Chrétien closely followed Trudeau's thinking on the importance of promoting national unity and the role of the Charter, having served as Trudeau's justice minister during the 1981 constitutional negotiations. Chrétien's response to the second Quebec referendum on sovereignty, in 1995, involved a series of initiatives designed to bolster Canadian unity, such as the addition of more Quebec ministers to cabinet, the distribution of Canadian flags across the country, and the adoption of a federal-provincial Social Union

Framework Agreement – as well as the expansion of a federal advertising program in Quebec that led to the so-called Sponsorship Scandal. Perhaps most important, the Canadian unity initiatives included the Clarity Act, a measure designed to ensure certainty in any future referendum process and reinforce the role of the federal government.

Chrétien also created the Forum of the Federations, an international think tank promoting the adoption of federal systems in plural societies and best practices in existing federations. As he stated when launching the Forum's first international conference at Mont-Tremblant in 1999, "[t]he essence of federalism is balance. A balance between different identities. A balance between local interests and larger interests. Federalism helps democracy flourish in complex societies. It does not just recognize and accommodate diversity; it sees diversity as something to celebrate and cherish. Federal countries often find unity in their very diversity."

Canadian Liberalism and the Challenge of Neoconservative Rhetoric

Virtually all of the long-standing values of reform liberalism were categorically rejected by the new conservatism of Thatcher, Reagan, and, in Canada, Stephen Harper and his new Conservative Party. They drew their inspiration not from Locke, Rawls, or Keynes, but from Hobbes, Hayek, and Friedman (Nadeau 2011). Moreover, as Jonathan Haidt (2012) has demonstrated, the new conservatives' opposing set of values are not only radical, but deeply held, resulting in greater political conflict due to their rigid belief in the "rightness" of those values and their unwillingness to compromise.

Despite what scholars consider to be significant differences, however, the distinction between liberalism and its philosophical counterparts on the right and left appeared to be increasingly unclear to many Canadians after 2006. As I have argued elsewhere (2010), this situation was primarily due to the failure of liberals themselves to underline those differences, a failure that actually began much earlier. Following his unsuccessful run for the Liberal leadership in 1984 and the subsequent defeat of the Liberals by the Mulroney Conservatives, former Trudeau cabinet minister John Roberts outlined what he saw as the crucial problem facing Canadian liberalism. In *Agenda for Canada*, Roberts noted:

> Canada has entered a period of rapid and extraordinary change … one that is especially challenging to our traditional liberalism … But if

> Canadians are questioning their traditional liberalism, it is not, I believe, because of any inevitable rejection of an active role for government. Rather it is because the methods of government have grown increasingly cumbersome and inept ... The challenge now for liberals is to show that we do have a vision of how Canada can grow in response to the different times ahead, and how Canada can use government to achieve that growth ... This calls for a new balance. The liberal agenda must now not only concern itself with social justice – with the politics of distribution – but must focus equally on how to establish the conditions for the generation of sustainable, environmentally sound growth. (1985, 30–1)

Although the Chrétien government did stress balance in its policies, and responded to some of Roberts's concerns with concrete policy measures, it failed to appreciate the semantic and philosophical threat posed by the rhetoric of its new right-wing opposition. Simply put, the lack of credibility of the messengers – the fringe Reform Party and its equally ineffective successor, the Canadian Alliance – masked the potential effect of their far-right message on public opinion in turbulent times. This failure to recognize the very real danger of a simplistic but persuasive alternative ideology had devastating consequences for the Liberal Party. Speaking at the University of Toronto in 1998, Canadian academic Michael Ignatieff decried the neoconservative attack on liberal values and, equally, the failure of liberals to respond, declaring, "nothing has done the electoral and moral credibility of liberalism more harm than the failure to take this attack seriously" (Ignatieff 1998).

Ignatieff's views echoed those of well-known American liberal Robert Reich (1989), who argued that the now-dominant neoconservative "parable" about the incompetence and ineffectiveness of "big government" to protect citizens in times of major upheaval could be overcome only if liberals presented an alternative and more compelling narrative. The continued failure of American liberals to do so – and the consequent rise in conservative Republican fortunes – was underlined by economist John Kenneth Galbraith (1992) and historian Christopher Lasch (1995) in graphic detail. The Democrats eventually were able to offer successful alternative narratives under Bill Clinton and Barack Obama.

In Canada, meanwhile, a succession of Liberal leaders struggled to find their own relevant discourse. For example, when Chrétien's former environment minister Stéphane Dion was elected leader of the Liberal Party in December 2006, it was with the support of a large community of dedicated environmentalists, many of whom had joined the party for the sole purpose of supporting him, and on the clear understanding that the party would move to reposition Canadian liberalism in the twenty-first century by adding to its fundamental values and beliefs and incorporating in its policies the preservation of the environment and the concept of sustainable development. Dion stated the case succinctly in his victory speech: "Underlying our Liberal philosophy is a conciliation of two great human ideals: individual freedom and equal opportunity. I propose we add another: a healthy environment." His remarks introducing the Green Shift, the party's key platform plank in 2008, repeated this stance: "I want Canada to be the country that is the best in the world at combining economic growth, social justice and environmental sustainability" (Liberal Party of Canada 2008). Unfortunately, during the election campaign, Dion almost never again mentioned this underlying rationale, and the Green Shift was soon seen as an isolated initiative or, worse, as representing the whole Liberal platform, rather than as part of a comprehensive and compelling liberal vision. Moreover, the Green Shift was presented without adequate repudiation of the neoconservative rhetoric lauding small government, balanced budgets, and lower taxes. Consequently the Harper Conservatives successfully discounted it as a "tax grab" and an economically unsustainable assault on the private sector and on federal finances. Despite the inaccuracy of these claims, the initial popularity of the Green Shift quickly turned to public scepticism and rejection (Jeffrey 2008).

Dion resigned soon after the Liberals' poor showing in the 2008 federal election. The party turned next to Michael Ignatieff, who had finished second to Dion in the last leadership race. Ignatieff was leery of pursuing environmental sustainability to reposition liberalism. He chose instead to focus on the concept of "intergenerational fairness." In his speech unveiling his party's platform in 2011, he justified this theme as a new expression of equality of opportunity, an approach suggested by party icon Tom Kent (2010). In practical terms, the concept was represented in the platform by the "Family Pack" measures designed to finance early childhood care and learning, provide tuition for low-income students and lifelong learning measures for adults, support those (predominantly middle-aged) caring for sick or elderly relatives, and enhance the CPP and Guaranteed Income Supplement for low-income seniors.

But, like Dion, Ignatieff failed to emphasize his overarching theme of intergenerational fairness in his speeches or to underline its relationship to equality of opportunity. As individual planks were released during the campaign, they too appeared to be unrelated initiatives with no comprehensive *raison d'être*. Moreover, rather than denouncing the new conservative economic mantra, as he himself had urged in 1998, Ignatieff's platform actually appeared to *accept* many of the underlying premises of the neoconservative parable. Months before the writ was dropped, Ignatieff ruled out income tax increases or an increase in the goods and services tax, while also promising that the party would not run a deficit to finance its programs. Not surprisingly the Liberal platform was once again judged to lack credibility (Jeffrey 2011). In the end, Ignatieff failed to communicate an alternative, liberal parable in a manner that resonated with Canadians or to convince them that the Liberal Party would be a solid economic manager, as he himself admitted in his memoirs (Ignatieff 2015). This fatal combination produced the party's worst showing ever, and caused Ignatieff to resign immediately. The Harper Conservatives had a significant majority in Parliament, while the Liberals were reduced to third place behind the Official Opposition NDP. Once again, predictions of the Liberals' imminent demise, or eventual merger with the NDP, began to surface.

Liberalism and the Resurgent Liberal Party

The selection in April 2013 of Justin Trudeau to head the Liberal Party initially was seen by some as a desperate (and opportunistic) move by the party to rely on a charismatic leader for its salvation. This view began to change, however, as Trudeau framed many of his early policy announcements in terms of a liberal narrative of "fairness." Whether the issue was child benefits, pension provisions, income tax reductions for the middle class, or support for veterans, the term fairness was used throughout as the underlying rationale for Liberal policies. By implication this liberal narrative was one that rejected conservatism as leading to unfair policies both for individuals and for regions of the country. Throughout 2014 and early 2015, this approach appeared to be having an effect: the Liberal Party consistently placed first in the polls, while the Conservatives trailed and the NDP was far behind.

By spring 2015, however, the Liberals began a precipitous slide to third place as they repeatedly took ambiguous positions on a number of government initiatives, thereby diluting their message. Nowhere was this more obvious than in their convoluted stance on Bill C-51, the Conservatives' legislation on national security, introduced in the aftermath of terrorist attacks. Critics denounced the bill as draconian – of providing the government too much unfettered authority and lacking sufficient civilian oversight to protect civil liberties. Harper's government defended the bill without compromise; the NDP rejected it categorically. The Trudeau Liberals, however, attempted to chart a self-described "middle course," saying they would support the admittedly flawed bill because it improved security for Canadians, but would introduce amendments once elected in order to better protect individual rights. Many Canadians – including Liberal supporters – disapproved of this position and even questioned Trudeau's commitment to the Charter. Numerous public opinion polls confirmed that Canadians saw his stance as opportunistic, not principled, and was a prime reason Liberal fortunes had plummeted.

Experts had long predicted the upcoming federal election would be a contest between the NDP and the Liberals for the nearly 65 per cent of voters who were determined to replace the Harper Conservatives. At the start of the campaign, the NDP appeared to have won that contest, but their lead dissipated, for two fundamental reasons. Although polls demonstrated that the Liberals had made up lost ground in the early part of the campaign on the basis of their overall positive performance – Trudeau's charismatic appeal on the hustings, an attractive liberal platform, and a positive advertising campaign – this was still not sufficient to distinguish them from the NDP and break out of the three-way race that had developed. Indeed, many observers began to predict a split progressive vote and a Conservative minority.

This situation changed dramatically when Trudeau announced he would run "modest" deficits for the first three years of his mandate in order to kick-start the stagnating economy and invest in national infrastructure projects. The polls, Liberal insiders, and expert observers agreed this was the turning point in the campaign: the Liberals had finally and forcefully rejected the conservative parable of lower taxes and smaller government, arguing that government had a positive role to play in the economy and taxes were necessary to provide services to citizens. And, in so doing, they had provided a credible basis for their own platform costing.

This decision proved crucial to the Liberal campaign, and saw the party begin to break out of the three-way tie. But it was hardly the whole story. As the campaign progressed, a second factor became crucial. Perhaps having learned from Bill C-51, Trudeau began aggressively promoting liberal values while criticizing various Conservative policies, and – equally important – as the underlying justification for his own platform. Whether he was rejecting Harper's position on the *niqab* and Syrian refugees or the NDP's positions on the Clarity Act and balanced budgets, Trudeau stressed the need for tolerance of diversity, the importance of individual rights, compassion, fairness, and equality of opportunity. His impassioned defence of Liberal icons such as the Charter, official bilingualism and multiculturalism, the Clarity Act, and the programs of the welfare state resulted in positive reviews of his performance in opinion polls and in media coverage. Similarly his campaign speeches ("In Canada, better is always possible") and the party's campaign slogan ("Real Change, now!") provided symbolic reinforcement of liberalism's belief in progress and vision for the future. Regardless of the election outcome, it was increasingly clear that Trudeau had successfully distinguished the Liberal Party's philosophical approach from those of his opponents.

Conclusion

On 19 October 2015 the resurgent Liberals obtained a comfortable majority of 184 seats in the House of Commons, and Justin Trudeau became the twenty-third prime minister of Canada. Barely a month later, a major EKOS/2020 poll concluded that the primary reason for the Liberals' remarkable come-from-behind victory was that "the election shifted from being about the economy to a historic election about values." This shift, in turn, resulted from Trudeau's rejection of the conservative mantra on the economy, which removed the Harper Conservatives' advantage. According to EKOS president Frank Graves, "[i]t was pretty clear that the values vision that Trudeau and the Liberals were offering up, backed up by an accounting framework that says we are actually going to find the money to do this, is what won the election for them" (quoted in Kennedy 2015).

The EKOS findings were reinforced by a comprehensive Ensight study, "The Back to the Future Election," which found that "[v]oters made a deliberate decision to restore the values they view as traditionally defining Canada and Canadian society … They embraced Justin Trudeau's agenda of hope and optimism at the core of what they perceive as the values traditionally defining Canada." Moreover, the Harper Conservatives were specifically rejected for what voters described as their "Reform or Tea Party style and substance." Similarly the study found that "Canadians reported a lack of trust in the commitments of [Tom] Mulcair, raising a nagging concern the NDP were, in fact, socialists.'" The NDP's return to third-party status was seen as an appropriate outcome (Ensight 2015, 7–8).

The applied political theory approach once again proves useful. The empirical evidence of the Trudeau Liberals' first two years in office demonstrates that liberal values have been backed by concrete actions. From gender balance in cabinet to an emphasis on diversity in appointments, the decriminalization of marijuana, initiatives in support of the LGBT community and Indigenous Canadians, increased acceptance of refugees, a renewed commitment to international development assistance, active participation in the United Nations, and support for international efforts on sustainable development, the liberal philosophical approach driving the Trudeau government's actions is readily apparent. As did his predecessors, Trudeau has taken controversial positions based on liberal values, notably in providing an apology and redress for former child soldier Omar Khadr, a position originally opposed by nearly 70 per cent of Canadians. In defending this action, Trudeau specifically stated: "The measure of a society – a just society – is not whether we stand up for people's rights when it is easy or popular to do so, but whether we recognize rights when it is difficult and unpopular."

Perhaps equally significant are polling data demonstrating that, when the Liberals have found themselves at odds with popular opinion, it has been due more often to their perceived failure to implement platform commitments based on liberal values, such as electoral reform, or to move quickly on others, such as assistance for Indigenous communities. Nevertheless – and despite declining popular support for Trudeau personally – a compilation of polls released in mid-2017, at the half-way point in its mandate – showed that the Liberal government had retained strong public support nationally, with a nearly twenty-point lead over the Conservatives and in some regions exceeding the levels the party obtained in the October 2015 election (Grenier 2017).

More recent polls in the spring of 2018 suggest that the situation for the Liberals is deteriorating, due partly to their perceived failure to implement many of their campaign commitments and also to their increased reliance on extended deficit projections. At the same time these polls reveal that support for the party's leader, Prime Minister Justin Trudeau, has decreased substantially as questions arise concerning his competence and political judgment, exemplified by unanticipated events such as a disastrous trip to India and an apparent inability to mediate a successful conclusion to the pipeline dispute between Alberta and British Columbia. Although these numbers might reflect a normal mid-mandate slump, they should not be taken lightly. As the 2011 election demonstrated so dramatically, if the Liberal Party is perceived as incapable of implementing a liberal agenda, it might be replaced by another centre-left party. As Pierre Trudeau warned in 1984, the party must not take Canadians' faith in liberalism for granted. With its distinctive emphasis on compromise and consensus, Canadian liberalism must adapt both the philosophical narrative *and* the practical application of liberal values to changing circumstances, and to the specific Canadian context, if it is to continue to be relevant.

REFERENCES

Austin, Jack. 1981. *Themes in Canadian Liberalism*. Ottawa: Liberal Party of Canada.

Axworthy, Tom, and Pierre Trudeau. 1990. *Towards a Just Society: The Trudeau Years*. Toronto: Viking.

Bélanger, Réal. 2007. *Wilfrid Laurier: Quand la politique devient passion*. Quebec City: Presses de l'Université Laval.

Bricker, Darrell, and John Ibbitson. 2013. *The Big Shift: The Seismic Change in Canadian Politics, Business, and Culture and What It Means for Our Future*. Toronto: HarperCollins.

Chrétien, Jean. 1992. *Finding Common Ground*. Hull, QC: Voyageur Publishing.

Ensight. 2015. *The Back to the Future Election*. Ottawa: Ensight.

Flanagan,Tom. 2007. *Harper's Team: Behind the Scenes in the Conservative Rise to Power*. Montreal; Kingston, ON: McGill-Queen's University Press.

Galbraith, John Kenneth. 1992. *The Culture of Contentment*. Boston: Houghton Mifflin.

Grenier, Éric. 2017. "Poll tracker." *CBC News*, 14 June.

Haidt, Jonathan. 2012. *The Righteous Mind*. New York: Pantheon Books.

Harper, Stephen. 2003 Speech to the Civitas Society, Toronto, June.

Harper, Stephen. 2011. Speech to the Calgary Southwest Riding Association, 8 July.

Horowitz, G. 1966. "Conservatism, Liberalism and Socialism in Canada: An Interpretation." *Canadian Journal of Political Science* 32 (2): 143–71. https://doi.org/10.2307/139794

Ignatieff, Michael. 1998. "Does the Liberal Imagination Have a Future." Keith Davey Lecture, Victoria University, Toronto, 8 January.

Ignatieff, Michael. 2009. "Liberal Values in Tough Times." Isaiah Berlin Lecture, delivered to the Canadian Club, London. Reproduced in *Maclean's* as "Liberalism Is Not a Bloodless Breviary for Rootless Cosmopolitans." 9 July.

Ignatieff, Michael. 2015. *Fire and Ashes: Success and Failure in Politics*. Toronto: Random House.

Jeffrey, Brooke. 2008. "Missed Opportunity: The Invisible Liberals." In *The Canadian Federal Election of 2008*, ed. Jon Pammett and Bruce Dornan, 63–97. Toronto: Dundurn.

Jeffrey, Brooke. 2010. *Divided Loyalties: The Liberal Party of Canada, 1984–2008*. Toronto: University of Toronto Press.

Jeffrey, Brooke. 2011. "Caught in the Crossfire: The Disappearing Liberals." In *The Canadian General Election of 2011*, ed. Pammett and Dornan. Toronto: Dundurn.

Jeffrey, Brooke. 2015. *Dismantling Canada: Stephen Harper's New Conservative Agenda*. Montreal: McGill-Queens University Press.

Katwala, Sunder. 2013. "Ideology in Politics: Reflections on Lady Thatcher's Legacy." *Juncture*, 8 April. Available online at https://www.ippr.org/juncture/ideology-in-politics-reflections-on-lady-thatchers-legacy

Kennedy, Mark. 2015. "Liberal values won the election, says poll." *Ottawa Citizen*, 19 November.

Kent, Tom. 2010. "A few questions for Ignatieff and the Liberals." *Globe and Mail*, 3 July.

Kirby, Michael. 1988. "Meech Lake pact reflects traditional Tory views." *Toronto Star*, 4 June.

Lasch, Christopher. 1995. *The Revolt of the Elites*. New York: Norton.

Liberal Party of Canada. 2008. "The Green Shift: Building a Canadian Economy for the 21st Century." Available online at https://www.poltext.org/sites/poltext.org/files/plateformes/ca2008lib_plt_eng._05012009_111617.pdf

Livingston, William. 1963. *Federalism and Constitutional Change*. Oxford: Oxford University Press.

McCullough, H.B. 2010. *Political Ideologies*. Don Mills, ON: Oxford University Press.

Meisel, John. 1972. *Working Papers on Canadian Politics*. Montreal; Kingston, ON: McGill-Queen's University Press.

Nadeau, Christian. 2010. *Rogue in Power: Why Stephen Harper Is Remaking Canada by Stealth*. Toronto: Lorimer.

Neatby, Blair. 2003. *William Lyon Mackenzie King: A Political Biography*. Toronto: University of Toronto Press.

Newman, Peter C. 2011. *When the Gods Changed: The Death of Liberal Canada*. Toronto: Random House.

Pearson, Lester. 1962. "On Liberalism." Available online at http://www.canadahistory.com/sections/documents/Primeministers/pearson/docs-onliberalism.htm

Reich, Robert. 1989. *The Resurgent Liberal*. New York: Random House.

Roberts, John. 1985. *Agenda for Canada: Towards a New Liberalism*. Toronto: Lester & Orpen Dennys.

Roberts, John. 2003. "Liberalism: The Return of the Perennial Philosophy." In *Searching for the New Liberalism: Perspectives, Policies, Prospects*, ed. Thomas S. Axworthy and Howard Aster. Toronto: Mosaic Press.

Simpson, Jeffrey Simpson. 2015. "Are we witnessing the strange death of Liberal Canada?" *Globe and Mail*, 27 June.

Stevens, Sinclair 2008. "One Canada or ten Canadas?" *Toronto Star*, 25 April.

Trudeau, Pierre. 1998. *The Essential Trudeau*. Ed. Ron Graham. Toronto: McClelland & Stewart.

Wiseman, Nelson. 2011. "The Withering of the Liberal Party?" *Hill Times*, 4 November.

3 What Does "Progressive" Mean? The Political Theory of Social Democracy and Reform Liberalism in Canada

DAVID McGRANE

With the 2015 Canadian federal election only days away, a Liberal news release claimed that "the most progressive platform is the Liberal platform" and that the Liberals' plan will "deliver strong progressive change for all Canadians ... to bring an end to the Harper decade" (Liberal Party of Canada 2015a). Similarly, when presenting his platform ten days before the election was held, New Democratic Party leader Thomas Mulcair stated, "[o]nly the NDP is in a position to defeat Stephen Harper and form a more progressive government in Ottawa" (New Democratic Party of Canada 2015). Clearly, both parties were marketing themselves as the "progressive" alternative to the Harper Conservatives. But were both parties equally "progressive"? What does it even mean to be "progressive" in the Canadian context?

Applied political theory can help us cut through the marketing and actually understand the ideological differences between the federal NDP and federal Liberals. Using an applied political theory approach, this chapter illustrates that the term "progressive" is analytically unhelpful. To achieve a more nuanced and exact understanding Canadian politics, it is more appropriate to talk about reform liberals and social democrats.

In constructing this argument, I begin by defining the ideologies of social democracy and reform liberalism using the writings of certain political theorists associated with these intellectual traditions. I use T.H. Green, John Dewey, and John Rawls to exemplify reform liberalism, while the Fabians, Anthony Crosland, and contemporary European political theorists such as Thomas Meyer and Brian Barry represent social democracy. I argue that, although both ideologies are concerned with a lack of egalitarianism in society – hence, the common moniker of "progressive" – differences between social democrats and reform liberals emerge in their definitions of society's main problems, their vision of a good society, and their policy prescriptions on how to attain the ideal society they envision. I then shift to an examination of empirical evidence in the form of two primary documents, the platforms of the Liberal Party of Canada and the NDP in the 2015 federal election, which I compare to the writings of the political theorists examined earlier in the chapter. The comparison reveals genuine differences between the two parties that were reflective of their social democratic and reform liberal ideologies. I conclude by arguing that use of the term "progressive" in contemporary Canadian politics, which has little grounding in political theory, masks distinctions between the federal NDP and the federal Liberals and creates more confusion than illumination.

Social Democratic and Reform Liberal Approaches to the Economy and the Environment

In the conventional view of a political spectrum going from left to right, reform liberalism and social democracy would be placed side by side. Their proximity on the political spectrum is predicated, I would argue, on a shared sense that society's primary problem is a generalized lack of egalitarianism. Hence, if a definition of "progressive" in the Canadian context is possible, it would be as follows: progressives hold that the main problems of society are, first, the economic inequality and ecological damage created by *laissez-faire* capitalism and, second, social inequalities stemming from the persistence of discrimination based on one's identity, society's overreliance on tradition, and the lack of secularization of the state apparatus. It is this commitment to basic egalitarianism that entitles New Democrats, social democrats, Liberals, and reform liberals to declare themselves "progressive." The ideological traditions of reform liberalism and social democracy diverge quickly, however, from this similar starting point. Thus, an appreciation of these two ideological traditions gained through an applied political theory approach allows one to construct a more precise understanding of Canadian politics than a term such as "progressive" could ever entail.

The differences in how social democrats and reform liberals approach economic equality and environmental protection originate in their deeply held values concerning human nature. Social democrats maintain that humans are naturally altruistic, and have the capacity (and possibly even the desire) to limit their appetites. Humans work together because it is in their nature to care for one another, and they limit their appetites both so that everyone can share in society's material wealth and to protect our natural environment. Humans also tend towards solidarity with one another, and seek the convergence of societal values around commonly held goals and aspirations. Society does not need to be fiercely pluralistic; it can coalesce around universal ideals and agreements about what the good society entails.

Although social democrats evidently understand the economic differences in the interests of the classes that make up society, they believe that class collaboration is possible. For example, in Britain the Fabians saw the state as a neutral site where classes could cooperate, and argued that the Labour Party should compromise with other political parties in order to advance social democratic reforms. Indeed, the Fabians believed that there were social democrats in all classes and that the working classes should welcome the middle classes and business owners into their political party (Fabian Society [1889] 1967, 247–68). For social democrats, the free market is the main barrier to a more caring, altruistic, and cooperative society. The operation of the unfettered free market forces people to pursue their own selfish interests instead of caring for others and seeking solidarity with others through empathy and collaboration. As such, the free market does not work with human nature; rather, it deforms it by making people antisocial.

In contrast, reform liberals generally see humans as being fundamentally self-interested and as having a limitless appetite for the acquisition of material goods. Individuals have a natural desire for autonomy that makes society inherently pluralistic, and notions of solidarity and submission to the collective will can be dangerous impediments to the exercise of freedom and lead to illiberal dictatorial forms of government (Rawls 2001, 34). Reform liberals are clear that humans do find fulfilment in cooperation. Dewey stated that it is in humans' nature to live in association and to realize that their community needs to use its collective resources to promote the good of each of its members through "organized social action" (Dewey 1935, 5). But that cooperation is founded upon the realization that, working together, humans can achieve goals that are in everyone's mutual self-interest. Rawls follows up on Dewey's idea that cooperation is founded on mutual self-interest. He describes people in the state of nature prior to entering the social contract as free, rational, "not taking an interest in one another's interests" (1971, 12), and preferring a "larger to a lesser share" of what society produces (4). At the same time, society is a "fair system of social cooperation over time from one generation to the next" that is based upon its members rationally seeking to advance "their own good." People cooperate because they realize that it "makes possible a better life for all than any would have if each were to live solely by their own efforts" (Rawls 2001, 5). The free market takes advantage of the tendency inherent in human nature to strive for mutual self-advantage by rewarding humans who work well together (Dewey 1935, 67–9), and by creating a situation of reciprocity where cooperating with others means the accumulation of more goods for ourselves (Rawls 2001, 6, 96–7).

The differences in how social democrats and reform liberals see human nature affect how they conceptualize economic inequality and humans' relationship with their natural environment. Social democrats argue that property rights and wealth accumulation have potentially negative consequences for the entire society. In the writings of the Fabians, it is the institution of private property that creates economic inequality within capitalism. The Fabians' understanding of economic inequality started from the premise that the operation of monopolies and the concentration of wealth, property, and surplus production create a class of idle rich who, unlike the first capitalists, perform no meaningful task for society (Fabian Society [1889] 1967, 46–84). According to the Fabians, this system of unrestrained private property is responsible for the poverty of the labouring and middle classes, forces individuals into greedy antisocial behaviour, and denies citizens the material base on which to develop their own unique capacities and seek moral goodness (165–73). The right to private property, as well as the rate of wealth accumulation, needs to be limited to ensure that the gap between rich and poor decreases and that the development of individuals and society towards more altruistic behaviour is not stunted.

Writing shortly after the defeat of the Atlee Labour government, Crosland argued that capitalism had been transformed to ensure that the poverty that produces "physical squalor" would soon disappear and Britain's post-war mixed economy would produce high levels of employment, productivity, and stability (Crosland 1956, 77–9). Nonetheless, he argued, post-war capitalism, and the system of private property and unlimited wealth accumulation on which it was based, still did not generate a widespread societal concern for the welfare of the needy, a belief in equality, or the rejection of "competitive antagonism" in favour of the ideals of fraternity and cooperation (77).

Contemporary European social democratic theorists are less optimistic than Crosland was, and echo the Fabians' concerns about society's main problems. Meyer argues that contemporary capitalist societies based on underregulated free markets, conspicuous consumption, overly robust property rights, and insufficient universal social entitlements do not provide for basic rights such as a clean environment for all citizens, an adequate standard of living, fair wages, just working conditions, stimulating cultural opportunities, and quality health care and education (Meyer 2007, 23). Barry holds that liberal capitalist societies place too much emphasis on how wealth accumulation of individuals benefits the entire society, because it conceives of equality of opportunity in the narrow sense of giving everyone an equal chance to achieve things based on their own choices and efforts (Barry 2005, 39). He is adamant that children in liberal capitalist societies start their lives and grow up with vastly different resources. Over time these initial disadvantages accumulate, and the unequal distribution of resources and, subsequently, opportunities creates profound social injustices that are embedded in the institutions of society (16–17). The standard of living of citizens becomes intimately connected with the socio-economic status of their parents, rather than with their natural ability or intrinsic merit (48). Accumulation of wealth does not correct this situation but perpetuates it.

For reform liberals, in contrast, the free market, property rights, and wealth accumulation are fundamentally good things. Economic inequality is perceived to be the obvious result of the unwillingness of the state to impose regulation upon the free market. Such regulation should not include unduly limiting property rights or undermining the societal benefits associated with the accumulation of wealth. Both Green and Dewey were adamant that the relatively unhindered acquisition of property is required for the free market to increase production, thereby creating new sources of income for the working class, business owners, and society as a whole (Dewey 1935, 48, 76; Green 1882, 244–6). Theirs was, in fact, a sophisticated formulation of the argument later made by US president John F. Kennedy, a reform liberal himself, that a "rising tide lifts all boats" – that the ability to accumulate wealth has benefits for the whole society.

Rawls is also protective of property rights, and sees wealth accumulation as having positive societal benefits. Individuals' right to exclusive use of their personal property is part of his first principle of justice, and must not be overridden in the name of reducing social and economic inequalities or any other considerations about the overall well-being of the collectivity (Rawls 2001, 114–15). Under certain circumstances, however, it might be permissible to regulate private property that relates to the ownership of natural resources, or means of production as a way to attain greater economic equality. Rawls prefers to avoid "prejudging" the cases where property rights concerning the means of production are not sacrosanct, suggesting that legislatures should determine such circumstances by taking "historical and social conditions" into consideration (114–15). Nonetheless he does seem to subscribe to the "rising tide lifts all boats" logic when he argues that inequalities generated by the free market can be justified as long as they increase the income of those less well off in society (42–3). Indeed the better endowed are encouraged to use their endowments to seek benefits for themselves because through doing so they create wealth that contributes to the good of all, particularly those who are less endowed (122–4).

When it comes to realizing their ideal society through policy prescriptions, reform liberalism believes that the state should ensure equal opportunity for all to develop their own unique capacities in such a way as not to restrict unduly the right of individuals to acquire property or undermine the societal benefits of wealth accumulation. After all, it is the relatively unlimited right of property acquisition and humans' nature as inexhaustible acquirers in a relatively free market that is responsible for producing wealth. Due to the free market's constant generation of new wealth, Green argued, the working class can accumulate savings if they have "education and self-discipline" and can even become capitalist themselves "to the extent of owning their houses and a good deal of furniture, of having an interest in stores, and of belonging to benefit-societies through which they make provision for the future" (Green 1882, 225–6). Thus, for Green, the free market, wealth accumulation, and property rights provide a good society in which the working class may attain at least some of the trappings of capitalists and thereby pursue their own self-development if they have the merit and ability to do so. He believed that such a society could be reached through legislation that encouraged the self-improvement of the working class, such as the expansion of the franchise, public education, and temperance (Green [1881] 1964, 43–74). Further, minimal interference by the state in the economy should be tolerated in the form of basic labour standards, building codes, and rules to ensure non-exploitative contracts in order to protect the health of the working class and allow it to build up property (ibid.).

In Dewey's ideal society, government would introduce "social legislation" to ensure that all individuals have the equal opportunity both to act freely and to realize their purposes or desires (1935, 88). Such social legislation would leave property rights untouched, and put in place very minimal regulation of the free market. It would include a basic welfare state to increase material security and the "basis of life" for all members of society (57). Like Green, Dewey placed special emphasis on public education, because it would "permit the average individual to have access to the rich store of the accumulated wealth of mankind in knowledge, ideas, and purpose" (52). Educated, the average individual could then contribute "in his own way" to the enrichment of his society (57). The basic welfare state should be undergirded by restrictions on the most pernicious elements of free market capitalism, such the growth of powerful monopolies, the lack of citizens' protection from unlawful foreclosures, and an underregulated stock market.

Rawls's good society is one ordered in accordance with his famous two principles of justice: every citizen should be assured an equal set of basic liberties, and social and economic inequalities should be attached to offices and positions that all have an equal opportunity to obtain and be of the greatest benefit to the least advantaged (Rawls 2001, 42–3, 198–9). The good society should not be conceived as a cohesive community with "shared values and ends," since individuals always differ about what the good life entails (20). There will be some overarching agreements about the benefits of cooperating, but also frequent disagreements about how benefits and burdens should be allocated. The best that can be hoped is for individuals to come to a consensus about the basic institutions of society (193–5).

Although Rawls slyly asserts that an undefined "liberal socialism," in which the state owns part of the economy, might satisfy his two principles of justice (2001, 138), he has a clear bias towards market-based solutions that do not involve public ownership or infringe on property rights. Rawls's preference for the free market is based on his belief in its efficiency, its ability to ensure that citizens have a free choice of career, and the importance that the distribution of goods and services is the result of impersonal forces, rather than of the preferences of government bureaucrats (1971, 239–42). His set of policy prescriptions is encompassed in his concept of a "property-owning democracy" (2001, 135–79), which bears a number of similarities to the policy programs of Green and Dewey. Following those two theorists, Rawls places high importance on the provision of public education for all citizens in order create equality of opportunity. As citizens become more educated and trained, ownership of productive assets becomes more widespread and wealth less concentrated in the hands of a few rich owners who possess large parts of the means of production (139–40). He even toys with the idea of public subsidies to worker-owned firms as way to accelerate this process (178). As property owning becomes democratized (that is, more widespread), the underclass in society might become very small or even cease to exist (140). Rawls endorses government-provided health care for all citizens and social assistance to the poor as ways to underwrite fair equality of opportunity and to ensure that all may enjoy their basic rights and freedoms (129–32, 171–4). He is critical, however, of the unbridled growth of the welfare state. He argues that the welfare state merely redistributes wealth after it has been accumulated, while a property-owning democracy would equalize the manner in which wealth is created within the free market (139–40). Indeed, he argues for progressive taxation and inheritance taxes, not on the grounds that they would fund social programs, but to prevent the unequal distribution of income (161).

On the environment, Rawls argues that basic protections are needed because a cooperative society of free and equal citizens requires a healthy environment to sustain human life, find medicines to cure human illnesses, and provide recreational opportunities (Rawls 1993, 245). As with public ownership of natural resources, he is content to leave it to legislatures to determine the level of basic environmental protection needed to meet these goals (2001, 152). Andrew Dobson convincingly argues, however, that several aspects of Rawls's philosophy – such as its support for wealth accumulation, the view of the market as the most efficient distributor of resources, and opposition to the state's supporting a single definitive version of the good society – would lead away from stringent regulation of the free market in the name of environmentalism (Dobson 2001, viii–ix).

As we can see, for reform liberals, a basic welfare state, moderately graduated taxation, and limited intervention by the state in the economy are sufficient to ensure equality of economic opportunity, which would permit all citizens to attain the material security needed to fulfil their potential if they have desire to take advantage of the opportunities afforded them. Basic health care and good public education allow everyone to participate to their fullest in the capitalist economy. Nationalization is generally unnecessary, and state intervention in the economy should be limited to restricting monopolies and ensuring that everyone has a similar starting point in terms of skills training and education and a healthy environment in which to live.

In contrast, proponents of social democracy believe that the good society should ensure a basic equality of condition for all citizens regardless of merit, and that the regulation of property and wealth accumulation in the interests of the common good is necessary to achieve this goal. This deeper notion of equality is based on the value that humans can overcome their acquisitive impulses, at least partially, to become social beings who realize themselves in the tempering of their appetite and the advancement of their community *if their basic material needs are filled*.

As opposed to a classless society of absolute equality, the Fabians argued that the end result of social democracy would be a "new birth of happiness in the households of the five men out of six in England who live by the weekly wage," who could escape the "dreary squalor of their homes" and the "constant apprehension of undeserved misfortune, which is a peculiar result of capitalist production" (Fabian Society [1889] 1967, 185). For capitalists the achievement of social democracy would mean they would have to live more modestly to ensure the "equal rights of their fellows," but they would also embark on a "new and nobler life," feeling relieved that they no longer lived off the misery of others (186). To obtain such an idealized society, the Fabians prescribed a whole menu of state intervention in the economy, such as the regulation of monopolies, adequate labour standards, the encouragement of cooperatives and trade unions, investment in public works to employ those without a job, a rudimentary welfare state, and the nationalization of industries that were monopolistic, key to the country's industrial structure, or that provided essential services to the public (1889, 213–46). Private property would continue to exist, but it would be regulated in the interests of the common good through progressive taxation and the creation of a mixed economy comprising public, cooperative, and private ownership.

For Crosland, the continued expansion of the welfare state and public ownership will lead to a society in which people work as much for the common good as for personal gain; private businesses learn to cooperate with one another, unions, and government for the betterment of society; and the more egalitarian distribution of status and privilege produces less resentment between classes (Crosland 1956, 79–90). He expressed the optimistic view that, as standards of living rise for all citizens, both the rich and the less well off will become satisfied and conspicuous consumption will be seen as "positively unfashionable, and may even give way to conspicuous under-consumption" (244). Crosland advised social democrats, in addition to continuing to improve the welfare state already in place, to encourage economic growth through implementing economic planning mechanisms, providing private industry with risk capital, and following Keynesian policies of demand stimulation and deficit financing (325–41). In many ways, these suggestions represent a less radical reform of capitalism than envisioned by the Fabians, who believed in wide-ranging nationalization. Indeed, Crosland called for a more flexible approach to nationalization that would focus less on the expropriation of existing private companies and the creation of state monopolies and more on competitive public companies, joint ventures, and new public enterprises (355–87).

Following Crosland and the Fabians, the focus of a good society for contemporary European social democratic theorists is the filling of material needs regardless of one's merit and as an entitlement of citizenship. Meyer talks about a "material understanding of freedom," where the basis of genuine citizenship is a minimum equality of condition (Meyer 2007, 23). Only when a minimum equality of condition for all citizens flows from the basic structures of society can humans be liberated from fear and want. In this way, government entitlements aim not to equalize economic resources or social status, but to ensure that all individuals have the same set of basic resources to equalize their chances to reach their full potential (Rothstein 2012, 97). Further, political institutions and state entitlements can do more than just give a basic set of resources to all citizens: they can promote good decisions and discourage bad ones, and they can incentivize mutual trust, altruism, solidarity, and reciprocity among citizens (Barry 2005, 157; Rothstein 2012, 101). In a good society, political institutions encourage citizens to make healthy lifestyle choices, increase their level of educational attainment, and engage in responsible consumption that respects the environment and workers' rights. Contemporary European social democratic theorists explicitly recognize the nefarious effect of overconsumption on the environment, and see curbing wealth accumulation, as opposed to increasing it, as having the greater societal benefit.

On policy prescriptions to reduce economic inequality, contemporary European social democrats and modern reform liberals such as Rawls do appear to veer quite close to each other, but there are important differences. First, social democrats envision a more comprehensive and generous welfare state based on universal entitlements than do reform liberals. Interestingly, Rawls is idiosyncratic among the latter in that he does not insist that citizens' entitlements generally should not be based on merit. Other reform liberals, such as Will Kymlicka, critique

Rawls on this score, and argue that considerations of merit are acceptable when allotting entitlements (Kymlicka 2002, 53–101). Within contemporary social democratic thought, the purpose of the welfare state remains to secure the material well-being of all citizens, as opposed merely to providing equality of opportunity. This requires an enduring commitment to universal entitlements that are not targeted at a particular income group or merit based. Barry and Meyer advocate policy options such as free tuition for post-secondary education, extending the public school system to cover children under age five, expanding parental leave to include fathers, and a guaranteed income for all citizens as opposed to means-tested social assistance (Barry 2005, 208–28; Meyer 2007, 140–58). What these policy prescriptions have in common is a preference for aggrandizing the welfare state through universal entitlements, as opposed to the narrower expansion of the welfare state through targeted programs based on need or merit.

A second difference between contemporary social democrats and reform liberals is that the former have a more expansive view of public ownership. For social democrats, private property should be regulated through publicly owned corporations that channel their profits towards funding the welfare state and securing a better material basis of life for lower-income citizens by providing essential services at an affordable price. Another fundamental aim of public ownership is the decommodification of certain essential goods and services, which should lead to greater economic equality (Meyer 2007, 140–7). Decommodification does not necessarily mean the provision of services "free of charge" to all citizens; rather, it is the disallowing of wealth accumulation, profit making, and property acquisition through certain activities in the name of the common good. A good example is child care, which social democrats believe should not be for-profit, but provided publicly to ensure high-quality care, low fees, and strong democratic oversight of the system.

Third, although reform liberalism does advocate progressive taxation, social democrats would push for an even stronger redistributive bent to narrow the gap more aggressively between rich and poor. In general terms, this would mean making "ability to pay" the guiding principle of taxation (Barry 2005, 188–92). Such a move would entail reducing or eliminating taxes on low-income earners, while simultaneously increasing taxes on high-income earners and corporations.

Finally, social democrats want a higher level of coordination of the free market than do reform liberals. In the German and Swedish cases,

Pontusson (2011) notes how this coordination entails robust labour legislation, leading to strong unions that can engage in corporatist arrangements along with business and government. The result is a high-wage economy in which government intervenes to ensure high productivity and promotes responsible consumption that respects the natural environment.

It would not be unfair to characterize the two ideologies' policy disagreements about how to reduce economic inequality and protect the environment as differences of degree, rather than of kind. Nonetheless, compared to current versions of reform liberalism, contemporary social democracy still prescribes a *larger* scope for the welfare state, *higher* levels of public ownership, a *more* redistributive tax system, and *greater* coordination of free markets. These are real-world policy differences, undergirded by differences in values concerning human nature, the individual's place in society, and the responsibilities of government. Social democracy sees human nature as inherently altruistic, cooperative, and able to moderate appetites, whereas reform liberalism holds that humans are naturally acquisitive, self-interested, and autonomous. For social democrats, the individual's place in society is as part of a greater whole, and the interests of the collectivity come before those of the individual. It is the responsibility of government to create and strengthen forms of solidarity, such as the welfare state, public ownership, unions, and cooperatives, that restrict the operation of the unfettered free market and achieve equality of condition. For reform liberals, individuals should strive to exercise their liberty to develop their own unique capacities in a pluralistic society in which cooperation is based on mutual self-interest. For them the responsibility of government is to promote wealth creation through the protection of property rights in a relatively free market, while ensuring basic equality of opportunity through a well-structured welfare state.

Social Democracy, Reform Liberalism, and Economic Equality in Canada

As prescribed by the applied political theory approach, I now relate the writings of reform liberal and social democratic theorists discussed above to empirical evidence in the form of the 2015 election platforms of the federal NDP and Liberals. Those platforms presented an interesting mix of commonalities and dissimilarities when it came to questions of economic inequality and environmental protection. Below I show that the ensemble of these commonalities and dissimilarities reflects how important differences in the policy prescriptions of the NDP and the Liberals arose from their social democratic and reform liberal ideologies.

In terms of enlarging the scope of the welfare state, the two parties' platforms agreed on enhancing the Canada Pension Plan, increasing investment in affordable housing, expanding parental leave, and boosting income support of low-income seniors and students. The NDP, however, promised two key universal expansions: a $15-a-day national child care program and a publicly owned insurance scheme for all Canadians that promised to lower prescription drug costs by 30 per cent. For their part, the Liberals pledged a means-tested monthly allowance that would decrease as income rose for parents of children under age eighteen. Reflecting a preference for individual choice and autonomy in social policy, this allowance could be spent on child care costs or anything else parents chose. As for prescription drugs, rather than pursue universal coverage, the Liberals promised to work with the provinces on bulk purchasing, in the hope of lowering prices for Canadians.

On expanding the publicly owned portion of the Canadian economy or decreasing the privatization of public services, the Liberal and the NDP platforms agreed that CBC funding should be increased and door-to-door mail service by Canada Post restored. The NDP was more committed to public ownership, however, in its calls to expand the number of destinations served by VIA Rail and to reverse the privatization of the Canadian Wheat Board. The NDP also pledged to prevent all new municipal projects built with federal funding from being public-private partnerships, whereby the private sector owns, operates, and maintains infrastructure such as bridges. Interestingly, although the Liberals voted against the Conservatives' bill privatizing the Canadian Wheat Board in 2011, after the Justin Trudeau Liberals won the 2015 election, the NDP criticized the new government for refusing to reverse the privatization. The NDP also criticized Liberals for their creation of the Canada Infrastructure Bank in the 2017 federal budget, charging that the bank's promotion of public-private partnerships would lead to the "privatization of public infrastructure … that will only make private investors wealthy, to the detriment of the public interest" (New Democratic Party of Canada 2017). As Rawls would council, the Trudeau government appears to approach public ownership on a case-by-case basis, referring to existing social and historical conditions to determine if public ownership is appropriate.

Both the 2015 Liberal and NDP platforms promised to undo two moves by the Harper Conservatives – income splitting and the doubling of tax-free saving accounts – that reduced the redistributive nature of the Canadian tax system. From this common starting point, there was an interesting divergence in their taxation plans. The Liberals promised to raise personal income taxes on the wealthiest 1 per cent in order to allow the reduction of income taxes on "middle-class Canadians" – those making between $45,000 and $200,000 annually – by reducing the middle income bracket from 22 per cent to 20.5 per cent (Liberal Party of Canada 2015b, 5). As Andrew Jackson (2015) pointed out, the Liberals' plan was not as redistributive as it appeared at first glance. The plan did not provide any benefit to the one-third of tax filers who are working poor and have taxable incomes under $45,000. Further, the benefits of reducing the middle income tax bracket would have gone disproportionately to the upper middle class – that is, "individuals with incomes between $89,200 and $200,000, roughly the top 10%, minus the top 1% who will pay higher taxes to pay for the tax cut for those below them on the income ladder" (Jackson 2015). The NDP, in contrast, chose a different tack, promising to increase the corporate tax rate from 15 per cent to 17 per cent, as well as the tax rate chief executives pay on their stock options, and to use the revenue generated by these measures to increase income supplements to low-income individuals and families and funding for universal social programs such as a national child care program and drug insurance.

The logic behind the Liberal plan to redistribute wealth from the top 1 per cent to middle-income earners – particularly the upper middle class – through shifting income tax brackets reflected reform liberalism's belief that the accumulation of wealth has social benefits. Indeed, the platform justified the plan by stating, "[w]hen middle class Canadians have more money in their pockets to save, invest, and grow the economy, we all benefit" (Liberal Party of Canada 2015b, 5). On the other hand, the NDP's plan to redistribute wealth from corporations and CEOs to the working poor through income supplements and to the entire society through universal benefits was based upon solidarity and altruism. In justifying its choice to use revenue from increased corporate taxes for programs to combat poverty, the NDP platform stated: "[W]e shouldn't be leaving anybody behind ... The NDP knows that one of the most important ways to judge the conscience of our country is how we treat our most vulnerable citizens" (New Democratic Party of Canada 2015, 28). As opposed to speaking about how wealth accumulation has societal benefits, the NDP appealed to voters' morality and their innate desire to help others in need.

Both the NDP and the Liberals agreed that the federal government must take the lead on coordinating free markets through lowering taxes on small businesses to encourage them to create jobs, increasing funding for skills training, investing in transportation and green infrastructure, and subsidizing research and development. In some areas, however, the NDP illustrated a penchant for greater coordination of the free market than did the Liberals. While the Liberal platform pledged to further reduce barriers to trade, the NDP platform committed to ensuring that trade agreements improved social, environmental, and labour standards in partner countries. Unlike the Liberals, the NDP also came out strongly against the Trans-Pacific Partnership during the final two weeks of the 2015 election campaign because it feared the loss of jobs in the dairy and auto sectors. The NDP platform, like that of the Liberals, pledged to repeal several pieces of labour legislation passed by the Harper government, but the NDP went further than the Liberals by promising to introduce anti-scab legislation and a $15 per hour federal minimum wage. While the Liberals vaguely promised to allow provinces to set their own frameworks on greenhouse gas emissions, the NDP promised to enforce a pan-Canadian cap-and-trade system that would put a price on carbon emissions and reduce missions by 34 per cent of 1990s levels by 2025.

Finally, while some media outlets seized on the fact that the Liberals promised to go into deficit to finance their infrastructure spending to claim that they were more "left wing" than the New Democrats (Kohut 2015), my analysis of the ideologies of reform liberalism and social democracy finds no support for such an argument. Both social democrats and reform liberals have endorsed Keynesian notions of demand stimulation and deficit financing over the years. Deficit financing is compatible with both ideologies as an occasionally necessary measure to raise funds to coordinate markets or build up the welfare state. At the same time, strict fiscal responsibility could also be compatible with both ideologies. For instance, the Fabians argued that because graduated taxation would provide revenue for new government programs, government debt loads would be "easily and sternly restricted" (Fabian Society [1889] 1967, 179). Green was also sceptical of the need to acquire large amounts of government debt (1889, 242–3). In short, deficit financing is not a critical fault line between social democrats and reform liberals.

Social Democratic and Reform Liberal Approaches to Social Equality

Throughout most of the twentieth century, social democrats offered the same package of rights and a similar view on social inequality as did reform liberals. In the United Kingdom, Crosland, because he believed that the advent of the British welfare state and the rising abundance of the post-war period were reducing the importance of problems of wealth redistribution, encouraged the Labour Party to focus more on issues that increased citizens' freedoms – such as abortion, divorce, censorship, civil rights, and protection from discrimination for minorities (Crosland 1956, 402–9). He conceived of rights for women and ethnic minorities in a manner that mirrored reform liberalism and liberalism in general.

For both ideologies, social inequalities were unjust because they were created by an overreliance on traditional thinking about gender or sexual orientation, the lack of secularization of the state apparatus, or racism. A regime of liberal rights to ensure legal equality, pursue affirmative action programs, and introduce penalties for discrimination was the appropriate policy prescription. It is important to realize, however, that social democracy's initial defence of liberal rights has always come from a different value set than that of liberal reformism. Social inequality is a problem for social democrats because it tears at the bonds of solidarity in society as certain members, such as women or ethnic minorities, feel excluded from the collectivity. Reform liberals, in contrast, feel that liberal rights are necessary to ensure the protection of individual freedom and autonomy.

Recently, more substantive differences have emerged between reform liberal and social democratic approaches to social inequality that boil down to the question of accommodation versus integration, particularly with respect to multiculturalism. Rawls holds that political institutions cannot countenance inequalities based on arbitrary traits, but must be fair to all members of society regardless of race or gender (2001, 64–6). Civil rights, such as freedom from discrimination for women and ethnic minorities, are required to allow these citizens the same equality of opportunity as other citizens (64–6). According to Phil Ryan, an application of Rawlsian reform liberalism to multiculturalism would place "reasonable pluralism" in the foreground, where the most important principle is respect for the freedom of others to be themselves, including respect for freedom of conscience and religious freedom (Ryan 2014, 92). This respect for the freedom of others is based on the firm belief that there is no overriding vision of a good society or comprehensive doctrine to which we should refer when constructing political institutions. As such, when it comes to multiculturalism, reform liberalism becomes quite interested in accommodating diversity, individuality, and autonomy, even if it means tolerating non-liberal views of the good society.

In reform liberalism's view of the good society, individuals' right to preserve their homeland culture and follow their religion within the host society is the overriding concern. In difficult situations, described in the work of Janice Gross Stein (2007), where homeland religious traditions contradict the dominant view of the host society concerning feminism or gay rights, reform liberalism generally councils tolerance and accommodation of religious freedom. Will Kymlicka (a reform liberal himself), in his response to Stein, admits that the beliefs both of newcomers to Canada and those of established religions such as Catholicism create practices of inequality, but he is adamant that "we have to stop somewhere. Pushing equality norms all the way down would effectively abolish any meaningful right of religious freedom, or indeed freedom of association more generally" (Kymlicka 2007, 143). He looks to for the courts to apply the Criminal Code to limit extreme behaviour, such as child abuse and other forms of violence, based on religious belief. He expresses optimism that liberal activists in these religious or ethnic communities eventually will push them to disregard practices that create inequalities.

Contemporary European social democratic theorists are critical of the liberal multiculturalism espoused by thinkers such as Kymlicka. The first element of their critique is that group-differentiated rights have the potential to jeopardize the egalitarianism that is the basis of social democracy's view of a good society if they are used to defend practices that systemically discriminate against women, ethnic minorities, gays, or other groups. Meyer states quite clearly that "[s]ocial democracy assumes the primacy of civil and human rights. Violations of such fundamental rights in the name of cultural difference cannot be tolerated" (Meyer 2007, 200). To use a real-world example, social democrats would argue that it should be illegal for First Nations to discriminate against women by excluding them from membership in their band if they marry a non–First Nations man while allowing men to maintain their membership in the band if they marry a non–First Nations woman. Similarly, Catholic hospitals should not be able to use arguments of religious freedom to refuse to perform abortions or assisted dying procedures.

The second element of the social democratic critique of liberal multiculturalism is that group-differentiated rights can undermine the universalism that underlies social democratic policies. The starting point for this criticism is the realization that a common identity and common sense of belonging are essential bases for universal social policies or collective projects such as publicly owned utilities. A strong collective identity creates feelings of reciprocity, leading to growing support for a "social" view of citizenship based on universal entitlements and publicly owned corporations benefiting the common good (Barry 2001). If ethnocultural communities become isolated from their host society, the collective identity and bonds of solidarity on which social democratic projects depends weakens (Cuperus and Elchardus 2012, 139–41). To guard against this danger, multiculturalism policies must avoid widening the perceived gap between immigrant groups and their host society, and should not leave the impression that immigrants are under no obligation to adapt to the norms and practices of the society that has taken them in or entail one-sided support for sectional group identities at the expense of an inclusive national identity. As such, multiculturalism policies should be visibly combined with national citizenship policies whose aim is to integrate immigrant groups culturally and encourage them to become involved in democratic politics.

When it comes to policy prescriptions, social democrats are more comfortable with the civic republican approach to multiculturalism or the interculturalism approach to embracing ethnic diversity. Elsewhere I have argued that NDP governments in Manitoba turned away from liberal multiculturalism during the early 2000s (McGrane 2011). Instead, when it comes to the rights of ethnic minorities, Manitoban social democrats are more comfortable within a civic republicanism tradition (Honohan 2002) that stresses how citizens can retain their cultural distinctiveness while also integrating and participating in the broader society. Similarly the Quebec government's version of interculturalism stresses that new immigrants to the province must participate within the polity and culture of the civic *Québécois* nation, whose unique language and history is the defining feature of Quebec society (Bouchard 2015). Both the culture of newcomers and that of the *Québécois* nation are transformed and enriched through interaction, leading to greater mutual understanding. The commonality of both approaches is that individuals are encouraged to retain their homeland culture, but only to the extent that it does not interfere with their participation in the broader society.

In summary, social democrats approve of group-differentiated rights designed to improve the prospects of marginalized groups or to seek historical redress in most instances. The expansion of such rights, however, must not harm the solidarity of the society on which social democracy is based or run counter to the social democratic vision of a good society that is free from systemic discrimination based on race, gender, and sexual orientation. A similar test could be applied to the expansion of individual rights to increase liberty. As long as a practice such as, for example, the recreational use of marijuana does not lead to the isolation of a certain group from society, undermine the accomplishment of collective projects, or is discriminatory, social democrats should favour it.

Canadian Social Democracy, Reform Liberalism, Social Inequality

Once again, as prescribed by the applied political theory approach, I now relate the thought of the social democratic and reform liberal political theorists analysed above to empirical evidence in the form of primary documents – in this case, the 2015 NDP and Liberal election platforms. When it came to their promises to reduce social inequality, there were almost no differences between the NDP and Liberal 2015 election platforms. Both parties wanted to increase funding for shelters for abused women, hold a national inquiry into missing Indigenous women, create a nation-to-nation relationship between the federal government and Indigenous peoples, improve legislation on the rights of the transgendered, and boost investments in infrastructure and education on First Nations reserves. The NDP went slightly farther down the road of promoting group-differentiated rights than the Liberals did by promising pay equity in the public sector. Once in government, however, the Liberals did vote in favour of a NDP motion to implement the recommendations of a 2004 task force on pay equity in the public service, and appointed a special committee that would propose a pay equity regime for Canada. When it came to the expansion of individual rights, the Liberals were in favour of legalizing marijuana for recreational use, whereas the NDP favoured only decriminalizing the possession of personal amounts of marijuana. On the other hand, the NDP wanted to repeal Bill C-51, which it said allowed federal security agencies to invade the privacy of Canadians unduly, while the Liberals stated they would merely remove the bill's most problematic elements.

Undoubtedly the highest-profile social equality issue during to the 2015 election campaign was a court decision, handed down in the middle of the campaign, allowing Muslim women to wear the *niqab* at citizenship ceremonies. Both NDP leader Mulcair and Liberal leader Trudeau came out in favour of the decision, while the Conservatives and the Bloc Québécois opposed it. Allowing Muslim women to wear the garment in that context clearly was the establishment of a group-differentiated right based upon respect for religious freedom. Although the Liberal Party united behind Trudeau's position, the issue caused internal friction in the NDP, with its English-Canadian wing being quite supportive and several members of the Quebec wing expressing their opposition to Mulcair on this point.

One might observe here that a social democratic case could be made for both the prohibition and the allowing of the *niqab* at citizenship ceremonies. If one sees the *niqab* as a symbol of the oppression of women in the name of organized religion, it could be argued that permitting the wearing of that garment at a public ceremony to become a Canadian citizen runs counter to the social democratic vision of a good society that firmly believes in gender equality. Further, allowing the *niqab* to be worn at a citizenship ceremony sustains this religious group's isolation from the rest of society, and is counterproductive to Muslim women's full integration into their host society and their participation in the polity of the host society. This appeared to be the position of many Quebec members of the NDP. On the other hand, one could argue that the state's telling women what they can and cannot wear in the public sphere is contrary to the social democratic vision of a good society that respects women's right to control their own bodies and appearance. Further, the very low incidence of women taking the citizenship oath veiled in a *niqab* means that the broader inclusion and participation of Muslims within Canadian society is not unduly jeopardized: the practice simply is not widespread enough to constitute an actual threat to the solidarity of Canadian society, and denying Muslim women the right to wear the *niqab* at a citizenship ceremony would only have supported the Conservatives' attempt to whip up Islamophobia for electoral gain. This appeared to be the position of most of the English-Canadian members of the NDP.

Conclusion

From a marketing standpoint, it might have made perfect sense for either the federal NDP or the federal Liberals to label themselves "progressive" during the heat of the 2015 electoral battle. Certainly "progressive" rolls off the tongue much more easily and sounds much more inclusive than "social democrat" or "reform liberal." The applied political theory approach illustrates, however, that "progressive" is too broad and imprecise a term, and its use by both parties led to confusion about their respective ideologies. Most likely to the detriment of the NDP, there was a lack of clarity about what it meant to be "progressive" and which party was more "progressive." The use of the term might have led to a masking of the real differences between the platforms of the two parties. Indeed one media narrative running through the entire campaign questioned whether the NDP or the Liberals were the more "progressive" party (Macfarlane 2015).

It is here that applied political theory helps us more than does political marketing. The term "progressive" as it has been used in the Canadian context has a very weak grounding in the writings of either contemporary or canonical political theorists. Although Canadian progressives can be said to share a concern about the growth of economic and social inequality, the term "progressive" does not get us much farther than that. In contrast, the 2015 NDP and Liberal election platforms illustrate that these parties are representative of two quite different ideological traditions – social democracy and reform liberalism – that have different values and, consequently, different views on the primary problems of society, the good society, and what needs to done to achieve the good society. Despite areas of agreement, these differences are embedded in the history of Canadian politics and in the philosophical traditions underpinning the two parties.

This precise illumination of the differences and similarities between the NDP and the Liberals can help citizens and political scientists understand the intellectual foundations of the agreements and disagreements between the two parties, both in the House of Commons and in future election campaigns. Further, the applied political theory approach allows for a more nuanced evaluation of calls from, for example, former journalist Paul Adams and former prime minister Jean Chrétien for the Liberals and the NDP to merge (Adams 2012; Curry 2011). Finally, sketching the philosophical differences between the two "progressive" parties might help the NDP in its deliberations on how to revitalize the party after its disappointing electoral defeat, and aid the now-governing Liberals in defining their direction. All of these cases illustrate the practical utility of applied political theory for the field of Canadian politics.

REFERENCES

Adams, Paul. 2012. *Power Trap: How Fear and Loathing between New Democrats and Liberals Keep Stephen Harper in Power – and What Can be Done About It*. Toronto: Lorimer.

Barry, Brian. 2001. *Culture and Equality: An Egalitarian Critique of Multiculturalism*. Cambridge, MA: Harvard University Press.

Barry, Brian. 2005. *Why Social Justice Matters*. London: Polity Press.

Bouchard, Gérard. 2015. *Interculturalism: A View from Quebec*. Toronto: University of Toronto Press.

Crosland, Anthony. 1956. *The Future of Socialism*. London: Cape.

Cuperus, Rene, and Mark Elchardus. 2012. "Social Cohesion, Culture Politics, and the Impact of Migration." In *After the Third Way: The Future of Social Democracy in Europe*, ed. Olaf Cramme and Patrick Diamond, 125–42. London: I.B. Tauris.

Curry, Bill. 2011 "Liberal-NDP merger could 'come very quickly,' Chrétien predicts." *Globe and Mail*, 6 September.

Dewey, John. 1935. *Liberalism and Social Action*. New York: G.B. Putnam's Sons.

Dobson, Andrew. 2001. "Foreword." In *Sustaining Liberal Democracy: Ecological Challenges and Opportunities*, ed. John Barry and Marcel Wissenburg, vii–ix. New York: Palgrave.

Fabian Society. [1889] 1967. *Fabian Essays in Socialism*. Garden City, NY: Dolphin Books.

Green, T.H. [1881] 1964. "Liberal Legislation and the Freedom of Contract." In *The Political Theory of T.H. Green*. Ed. John R. Rodman. New York: Appleton-Century-Crofts.

Green, T.H. 1882. *Lectures on the Principles of Political Obligation*. London: Spottiswoode, Ballantyne.

Honohan, Iseult. 2002. *Civic Republicanism*. London: Routledge. https://doi.org/10.4324/9780203460894

Jackson, Andrew. 2015. "So-called 'Middle Class' Tax Cut Leaves Out Most Canadians." *Broadbent Institute Blog*, 14 November. Available online at http://www.broadbentinstitute.ca/andrew_ajackson/so_called_middle_class_tax_cut_leaves_out_most_canadians

Kohut, Tania. 2015. "Trudeau skirts suggestion Liberals leaning further left than NDP." *Global News*, 27 August. Available online at https://globalnews.ca/news/2189566/trudeau-skirts-suggestion-liberals-leaning-further-left-than-ndp/

Kymlicka, Will. 2002. *Contemporary Political Philosophy: An Introduction*. 2nd ed. Oxford: Oxford University Press.

Kymlicka, Will. 2007. "Disentangling the Debate." In *Uneasy Partners: Multiculturalism and Rights in Canada*, ed. Janice Gross Stein, 137–56. Waterloo, ON: Wilfrid Laurier University Press.

Liberal Party of Canada. 2015a. "Liberal plan will deliver strong, progressive change for all Canadians." News release, 17 October.

Liberal Party of Canada. 2015b. *Real Change: A New Plan for a Strong Middle Class*. [N.p.].

Macfarlane, Emmett. 2015. "Who's more progressive, the Liberals or the NDP?" *Ottawa Citizen*, 13 August.

McGrane, David. 2011. "From Liberal Multiculturalism to Civic Republicanism: An Historical Perspective on Multiculturalism Policy in Manitoba and Saskatchewan." *Canadian Ethnic Studies* 43 (1–2): 81–107. https://doi.org/10.1353/ces.2011.0019

Meyer. Thomas. 2007. *The Theory of Social Democracy*. London: Polity Press.

New Democratic Party of Canada. 2015. *Building the Country of Our Dreams*. [N.p.].

New Democratic Party of Canada. 2017. "NDP to force vote on Liberal privatization bank." News release, 10 May.

Pontusson, Jonas. 2011. "Once Again a Model: Nordic Social Democracy in a Globalized World." In *What's Left of the Left: Democrats and Social Democrats in Challenging Times*, ed. James E. Cronin, George W. Ross, and James Shoch, 89–115. Durham, NC: Duke University Press. https://doi.org/10.1215/9780822394518-004

Rawls, John. 1971. *A Theory of Justice*. Cambridge, MA: Havard University Press.

Rawls, John. 1993. *Political Liberalism*. New York: Columbia University Press.

Rawls, John. 2001. *Justice as Fairness: A Restatement*. Cambridge, MA: Havard University Press.

Ryan, Phil. 2014. "Our Multiculturalism: Reflections in the Key of Rawls." In *The Multiculturalism Question: Debating Identity in 21st Century Canada*, ed. Jack Jedwab, 89–106. Montreal; Kingston, ON: McGill-Queen's University Press.

Rothstein, Bo. 2012. "Equality, Social Trust, and the Politics of Institutional Design." In *After the Third Way: The Future of Social Democracy in Europe*, ed. Olaf Cramme and Patrick Diamond, 95–110. London: I.B. Tauris.

Stein, Janice Gross. 2007. "Searching for Equality." In *Uneasy Partners: Multiculturalism and Rights in Canada*, ed. Janice Gross Stein, 1–22. Waterloo, ON: Wilfrid Laurier University Press.

4 It Don't Mean a Thing if It Ain't Got that Swing: Ideology in the Age of Emotion

PAUL SAURETTE AND KATHRYN TREVENEN

There are few currents in political thought that embody the idea of applied political theory more than the tradition of ideological analysis.[1] For although tales of the death of ideology were greatly exaggerated in the 1990s, the term "ideology" remains pervasive in the public sphere, employed to explain everything from voting behaviour to language politics to the resurgence of populism/nationalism to social movements such as Black Lives Matter to contemporary popular culture to the Arab Spring.

But what, exactly, is ideology in the twenty-first century? Is it a set of ideas? Principles? Beliefs? Assumptions? Values? Concepts? Policy prescriptions? A pattern of discourse? A jumble of symbolic markers? Must an ideology be logically coherent? Or can it be a contingent assemblage of signifiers? Is it a rational system whose meaning and impact are derived from the validity of its argumentation? Or are its core meaning and motivational power profoundly linked to emotional and affective dimensions?

Although some might dismiss these questions as overly abstract for those interested in applied political theory, we would argue the opposite. For the applied value of any analysis (theoretical or empirical) rests squarely on the robustness and utility of its foundational assumptions and concepts – elements that not only have been the subject of intense contestation since the term ideology was itself coined, but that are also particularly in need of reconsideration in the image-saturated, communications-obsessed, twenty-four-hour news/social media cycle context that envelopes modern politics.

1 An early version of some of this material appeared first in French; see Saurette and Trevenen (2013).

In this chapter we focus on one particular dimension of this general problem: the ways that the relationship between ideology and emotion is theorized. On one hand, popular analyses of contemporary North American and European electoral politics talk about the importance of emotion and ideological rhetoric as if it explains everything. On the other hand, there has been surprisingly little conceptual work on exactly what this might mean. So those of us who believe that theoretical reflection and clarity is an important precursor to practical analysis are left with many questions. Do the dominant methods of studying political ideas and ideology in Canada allow us to understand properly the ways that emotion and ideology are connected? If they do not, are there contending approaches that better help us explore these dimensions? What difference would understanding the emotional dimension make to our analysis of contemporary ideology in Canada and the United States? These are the key questions of this chapter.

We believe that exploring these conceptual complexities helps demonstrate not only that the tradition of ideological analysis is a classic example of applied political theory, but also that rigorous, critical, and theoretical self-reflection is inextricable to any applied political theory. We therefore set the stage, in the first two sections of the chapter, by showing that the foundational assumptions of the main traditions of ideological analysis are deeply intellectualist and, to their detriment, have largely ignored and/or dismissed the affective and emotional dimensions of ideology. In the third and fourth sections, we demonstrate that there are other traditions of ideological analysis that conceptualize and explore the emotional dimension of ideology in much more convincing ways. We conclude by demonstrating that a practical application of these approaches to ideology allows us to account for and understand the emotion-laden appeals of the Harper Conservatives and Trudeau Liberals in ways that traditional ideological analyses cannot. In doing so, we argue not only that ideological analysis remains an important example of applied political theory, but also that theoretical self-reflection is key to ensuring that applied political theory reaches its full potential.

All Head, No Heart: The Origins of the Intellectualist Tradition

Even if we limit ourselves to the "western" tradition of theorizing over the past several centuries, there is a dizzying array of competing conceptualizations of, and methods for studying, ideology (Eagleton 1991;

Saurette, Gunster, and Trevenen 2009). Beneath this diversity, however, also lies a set of (often unstated) foundational assumptions and characteristics that are shared by the vast majority of the dominant approaches to ideological analysis.

Given our focus in this chapter, one of the most notable shared characteristics is the "intellectualist" orientation of the dominant traditions – that is to say, the tendency to study ideology as if its core nature and persuasive force can be understood on purely rationalist grounds without any consideration of the affective and/or emotional content and dynamics of a given ideological assemblage. This, of course, is not coincidental, for as political theorists well know, a deep ontological rationalism has characterized western political theory at least since Plato and his insistence that truth is to be found in the world of forms and concepts, and that empirical reality is but flickering shadows dancing on cave walls. Although some political theorists have challenged the intellectualist tradition throughout the history of political thought, the dominant tradition of theorization, particularly since the Enlightenment, has consistently denigrated the importance and value of emotions.

It is unsurprising, then, that this intellectualist sensibility defined the very core of the first modern attempt to study ideology. Coined by Comte Destutt de Tracy, a late-eighteenth-century French Enlightenment *philosophe*, the study of "ideology" was championed by a classical liberal republican group named the *Idéologues*, who shared a profound optimism about rationality and believed that a study of the systems of human thought and ideas would uncover the fundamental laws of reason, which would then allow humanity to reform and correct the irrationalities of human thought (Carver 2006; Head 1985; Lichtheim 1965). The origin of the modern concept of ideology, then, was marked not only by empirical assumptions about the rationalist nature of ideas, but also by a profoundly normative faith in rationality.

Although the *Idéologues*' vision – and their normative faith in the potential offered by the study of ideology – was quickly challenged by other perspectives (Kennedy 1979), even the most critical voices tended to retain their analytic intellectualist assumptions. Consider Marx's seminal rewriting of the study of ideology. On one hand, Marx unstintingly attacked the *Idéologue* tradition, referring to their analysis as "*fischblütige Bourgeoisdoktrinär*": a cold-blooded bourgeois doctrine that used ideas to naturalize and legitimize the material class interests of the bourgeois. In one sense, Marx's approach fundamentally challenged certain aspects of the philosophical and intellectualist orientation by rejecting the conceptualization of ideas as pure laws of reason or autonomous and free-floating principles. By insisting, as he put it most bluntly in the *German Ideology*, that "the ideas of the ruling class are in every epoch the ruling ideas, i.e. the class which is the ruling material force of society is at the same time its ruling intellectual force" and that therefore "the ruling ideas are nothing more than the ideal expression of the dominant material relationships, the dominant material relationships grasped as ideas," Marx rejected the belief that ideas are simply intellectual constructs and instead insisted that political ideas are heavily influenced (if not completely determined) by material conditions and very specific class interests (Marx 1978, 172). For Marx, political ideas are not simply the result of pure "thought" or "mind" or "spirit." Rather, they are the result of our ontological nature as material, productive beings; they largely reflect current power relations; they ultimately serve to rationalize the power of the dominant class; and they cannot alone change the course of history, but can do so only to the extent that the entire social context of the material relations of production are characterized by sufficient contradictions. The aim of studying ideology, then, was not to identify and clarify a series of rational and intellectual laws of reason, but rather to critique the dominant ideas of society and to expose their role in naturalizing alienating social practices and in justifying inequalities of power. In this sense, Marx's perspective deeply challenged the rationalist utopianism dimension of the *Idéologues'* intellectualist orientation.

In another sense, however, Marx's approach nonetheless reproduced important elements of the intellectualist orientation insofar as he retained the view of ideology as a system of *thought* that is essentially defined by *rational interest* – that is, one's material class position. Moreover, although Marx did recognize that people could hold political ideas and values that contradicted their true "rational" class interest, he tended to suggest that the phenomenon of false consciousness could largely be explained by mistaken intellectual beliefs – for example, by accepting and reifying ruling class concepts such as private property or the commodity. As such, in various ways, the intellectualist tradition not only deeply characterized the *Idéologues'* conception of ideology; it remained heavily present in the Marxist rewriting of ideological analysis that would influence so many of the "critical" approaches to ideological analysis of the twentieth and twenty-first centuries.

All Head, No Heart, Part II: The Contemporary Intellectualist Tradition

Intellectualist orientations continue to define the bulk of contemporary ideological analysis, particularly in the Anglo-American world. A quick scan of virtually any mainstream Anglo-American introductory political science textbook demonstrates that the vast majority of students are taught that ideology is something like "a fairly coherent and comprehensive set of ideas that explains and evaluates social conditions" (Ball 2002, 5); a "socially constructed and transmitted system of political beliefs with some significant measure of formal articulation, scope, internal consistency and durability" (Gibbins and Youngman 1996, 6); or "sets of ideas, perceptions, values and beliefs through which we interpret social, political and economic events" (Patten 2006). Although these definitions differ slightly, they share the assumption that ideologies can best be understood as a systematic, largely coherent framework and sets of political beliefs that act as the rational basis for explanation and evaluation. On these definitions, understanding what a particular ideology *is* – for example, how it functions as a political factor – does not require us to examine any questions of emotion and affect. Rather, we can understand its essence simply by intellectually reconstructing the beliefs, principles, and supporting intellectual assumptions that make it a coherent, consistent, explanatory, and evaluative framework. Similar assumptions are at the base of some of the most sophisticated contemporary methods of analysing political texts and the history of political ideas as well. Although Quentin Skinner, for example, argues that we must reconstruct historical patterns of political discourse and ideas – he often calls them "ideologies" or "conventions" – to discover the illocutionary force of specific texts and the overall political discourse of a given era (Skinner 1988), his method disallows any exploration of the ways that conventional affective and emotional investments and triggers might be crucial factors in determining what certain discourses and texts "meant" to their audiences and why their arguments and appeals were or were not persuasive.

The intellectualist orientation has also characterized many, if not most, of the influential contemporary Marxist and post-Marxist approaches to ideological analysis. Most of the dominant debates in twentieth-century Marxist thinking on ideology largely focused on questions about how far the economic base determines the ideological superstructure (questions that operate on assumptions about how rational "class interests" determine the nature and force of ideology) and how false consciousness operates and can be challenged (a framework of analysis that also takes for granted a variety of intellectualist assumptions). In the Anglo-American world, the intellectualist and rational choice traditions were so strong that they came to define explicitly some of the most influential contemporary Marxist perspectives – culminating in the emergence of "Analytic Marxism," an approach that sought to reinterpret Marxism according to the intensely intellectualist axioms of rational choice theory (see, for example, Cohen 1988; Elster 1985). Similar tendencies were also evident in the continental post-Marxist tradition – perhaps most famously with Jürgen Habermas's rearticulation of the Frankfurt School tradition in a way that posited that beneath the oppression of contemporary society lay the universal and rationalist moral and communicative foundations whose rearticulation would dissolve the historically ideological and instrumental formations that currently blocked emancipation (see Habermas 1984).

Even many twentieth-century Marxists and post-Marxists whose perspectives seem to have been most open to questions of emotion did not pursue them. Althusser's late-modern Marxist conceptions of "interpellation" as the subjective ground zero of ideology and Ideological State Apparatuses as the key training grounds of ideological formations failed to carve out much room to explore the role of affect and emotion in these processes (Althusser 1972). And although Gramsci's analysis of ideology and common sense offers many openings for a consideration of emotion and affect, some of the best-known applications and development of his concept of hegemony continued to ignore this possibility entirely: Laclau and Mouffe's *Hegemony and Socialist Strategy* (1985), for example, does not use the word "emotion" once. Even some of the most trenchant cultural studies observers of contemporary American politics, such as Thomas Frank, fail to escape from the intellectualist tradition even as they underscore its profound limitations. For although Frank explicitly argues that emotion is critical to understanding the popularity and functioning of American right-wing populism, he still reproduces certain rationalist assumptions by often implicitly suggesting that the emotion driving this is irrational and stems from a misunderstanding of the more important issues – for example, rational class interest (see Frank 2004).

The intellectualist orientation has also deeply characterized the main currents of theoretical analysis of ideology in Canadian political science. Essentially all mainstream textbook introductions to ideology in Canadian political science reproduce the intellectualist perspective outlined at the beginning of this section (see, for example, Gibbins and Youngman 1996; McCullough 1995). Despite disagreeing on a variety of substantive issues, all sides of the debate over "fragment theory" and its applicability to understanding the origins and nature of Canadian political ideologies share the intellectualist presumption that political ideology should be viewed as a set of rational and explicit political beliefs, values, and principles that have been passed down historically and institutionally; see Ajzenstat and Smith (1995); Hartz (1964); Horowitz (1966, 1977, 1978); Lipset (1991); Wiseman (1988).

Even the critical tradition in Canadian political thought has been heavily intellectualist in its approach, for although the ideological analyses of Marxists such as C.B. Macpherson (2010) and Ellen Wood (1992, 1997; Wood and Wood 1978) have produced innovative and thoughtful intellectual histories that take seriously Marx's injunction to treat ideas as deeply implicated in material struggles, they have also treated ideological texts largely as principled puzzles to solve. For example, Macpherson has sought to identify the rationally consistent assumptions that resolved the apparent contradictions in the texts of a variety of seventeenth-century English political theorists, while Wood has sought to demonstrate that the classic political texts rationally reflected the material relations of production and class interests of each historical era. Similarly, critical Gramscians such as Robert Cox (1981) and Stephen Gill (2010) have consistently offered analyses of global politics in ways that treat hegemonic formations more or less as coherent sets of class-defined ideas, with little or no use of the tools of cultural theory or analyses of the "cultural" and affective/emotive bases of hegemony. And most critical analyses of ideology from the perspective of Canadian political economy tend to focus on the clash of ideas, as if it was exclusively a battle over economic principles or relatively straightforward class interests (see Albo 2002; Banting 1992; Clarkson 2002).

The intellectualist orientation has also defined most empirical studies of ideology in Canadian politics, the bulk of which treat ideology as a set of principles, values, beliefs (see, for example, Farney 2012, 2013; Harrison 1995; Jeffrey 1999; Langford 1991; Laxer 1996; Laycock 2002; Patten 2001; Piotte 2003).[2] Even Canadian studies of "political culture"

2 Harrison's *Of Passionate Intensity* (1995) gestures towards some fascinating potential avenues of exploration regarding the role of emotion as a factor in the rise of the populist Reform Party, but these ultimately are not systematically pursued.

have tended to focus similarly on articulating the intellectual principles and values presumed to be at the "core" of Canadian belief systems as revealed by interpretations of historical events, broad value-surveys, the implicit and explicit nature of constitutions and institutions, and so on (Wiseman 2007). Even recent and otherwise highly innovative studies of political culture and ideology continue to embody this tradition. Jared Wesley's *Code Politics* (2011), for example, offers a fascinating examination of the ways that implicit and subterranean messaging – "codes," in his nomenclature – have determined the meaning and persuasive force of Prairie political discourse or ideology. But even Wesley's (2011, 11) definition, and subsequent analysis, of these "codes" continues to treat them as primarily intellectual values and systems of ideas in ways that avoid analysis of their emotional dimension.

"We're all just a bit emotional right now": Evolutionary Functionalist Perspectives

Over the past decade, however, more and more theorists have begun to challenge the intellectualist bias and argue that understanding the emotional register of politics is crucial for our understanding of ideology and political ideas. Although these approaches embody significant methodological and theoretical pluralism, for the purposes of this chapter we discuss two broad traditions that represent influential, but very different, approaches to these questions. The first tradition encompasses approaches that embody "evolutionary functionalist" perspectives on the role of emotion in politics – and have come primarily from the field of political psychology. One of the best-known examples is Drew Westen's *The Political Brain: The Role of Emotion in Deciding the Fate of the Nation* (2007), in which he argues that emotional factors are central to processes of human judgment and thus central to understanding the creation, adoption, and power of political ideologies.

Although space does not allow a detailed analysis of Westen's book, several points about his work are worth underscoring. First, he argues that the dominant enlightenment and academic belief that the average human is a "dispassionate calculating machine, objectively searching for the right facts, figures and policies to make a reasoned decision" (Westen 2007, xv) is profoundly misleading. According to Westen, "the political brain is an emotional brain" and even though we may consider rational arguments and interests – and we certainly justify our emotional decisions post-facto using rational arguments – we are beings that primarily "think with our guts" even when we are engaged in rational evaluation (xv).

Second, Westen argues that we should not be surprised by this because this is precisely how our brains evolved to function. On Westen's telling, the brain is a complex organ with a long and very particular evolutionary history and role, which means that it has a deeply emotional component that cannot be wished away by the intellectualist/rationalist theories of the past several hundred years: "The human central nervous system (which consists of the brain and the spinal cord) is essentially a living fossil record of its own history. The further down you go (almost literally, from the upper layers of the brain to the spinal cord), the more you see ancient structures that evolved hundreds of millions of years ago and continue to be shared by our vertebrate cousins. Most of us would be truly embarrassed if we realized the extent to which the more primitive structures of our brains, particularly the structures that regulate basic motives such as sex and hunger, resemble those of a sheep" (Westen 2007, 51). As Westen puts it, "primitive feeling and thinking (sensation and perception) were always linked. Smell and taste not only convey *information* about what is in front of our noses or in our mouths but inherently arouse *feelings*" (53). Feelings such as anxiety evolved to help organisms avoid danger by motivating them either to approach or to avoid. This is why some of our most basic sense perceptions and even certain thought processes seem to have built-in emotional triggers. If something smells rotten, we feel repulsion. If something smells delectable, we feel the desire to approach. In humans these processes of emotional judgment are performed not only in some of the oldest and most rudimentary layers of our brainstem functions, but also in some of the fastest processors of the cerebrum – in particular, the amygdala.

In humans, the amygdala is responsible for processing complex emotional judgments: "from identifying and responding to emotional expressions in others, to attaching emotional significance to events, to creating the intensity of emotional experience, to generating and linking feelings of fear to experience"(Westen 2007, 57). But what is particularly important about the amygdala is that it responds to stimuli – and thus helps frame/make "decisions" about how to react – infinitely more quickly than conscious thought does. The amygdala, for example, can "respond to stimuli even when the person has no awareness of having seen them. Presenting a threatening stimulus subliminally (i.e. so quickly that the person cannot report seeing it) can lead to activation of the amygdala, suggesting an emotion system that is constantly processing emotionally relevant information faster than we can consciously register it" (58). As the body's oldest processor of "last instance," the messages sent by the amygdala are not just faster, they are also more powerful (57). In comparison, the processes of the cerebral cortex – the home of what we would mostly identify as our capacities of rational analysis and decision making – are both much slower and a much more recent (and thus weaker) evolutionary addition to our brain. According to Westen, then, the human brain is, at the very least, a thinking brain *and* an emotional brain. And he would argue that many political phenomena – including political rhetoric and ideology – can be best understood if we analyse them as the result of the emotional brain.

Although functionalist evolutionary approaches help highlight the insufficiency of the intellectualist tradition and its assumptions, they also suffer from some serious limitations. For example, at their core these perspectives tend to assume that all emotions (like other senses and skills) have evolved (and continue to evolve) to serve life-preserving "adaptive" functions such as communication, motivation, self-preservation, reciprocal care, and so on (Westen 2007, 70–3). These are crucial assumptions, since they then function as the key explanations for why individuals and groups of people today become emotionally engaged about a given issue. On these tellings, then, everything from jingoism and nationalism to the tendency to ignore disconfirming evidence to support for welfare programs to Arendt's conception of the banality of evil can be explained simply by reference to basic and emotional fight/flight/freeze emotional drives in the brain's oldest and most basic sensory and decision-making processes. In the context of this chapter, the problem with this is that, since these assumptions potentially can explain anything, they are unable to explain the specificities of any concrete situation. Three issues in particular stand out with this in reference to applying Westen's theory to ideological analysis.

First, Westen's evolutionary and functionalist approach means that he never asks whether the meaning, intensity, and/or relevance of the specific emotions that play a central role in contemporary political judgment have some degree of cultural and/or historical specificity. Rather, Westen's story tends to assume that we can identify and explain the appeal of successful contemporary political themes – "survival, reproduction, connection to kin" – as the direct result of a functional evolutionary process of "natural selection" that favoured those animals whose emotions helped them "survive, reproduce, take care of their children and relatives" (Westen 2007, 73). But this does not help us understand why abortion, for example, has been an intensely emotional, gut-level issue in the United States since the 1970s, whereas it was not a particularly emotional issue before that and it certainly is not in many other countries (Saurette and Gordon 2015).

Second, Westen's evolutionary and functionalist framework encourages him to offer a largely one-way explanatory model of the link between emotion and discourse/ideology. The issue is not that Westen ignores the role that discourse and ideology can play in the emotional landscape of politics. He does not. Rather, the issue is that, because Westen's perspective on emotion tends to naturalize emotions and present them as profoundly shaped by millions of years of evolution, he never explores the possibility that patterns of discourse, political ideas, and/or broader cultural elements might be capable of impacting and altering the content, relevance, direction and force of those emotions. Instead, Westen tends to represent the issue as largely unidirectional: ideologies and political discourse are important, but only to the degree that they can speak to, and thus resonate and activate, the pre-existing and largely unalterable emotions that exist within us.

This, in turn, leads to a third issue. Given his functionalist framework, Westen's practical applied "takeaways" are limited to helping partisan rhetoric and ideology become more efficient at tapping into and resonating with the pre-existing emotional structure of the voting public (Westen 2007, 165). But this eliminates any possibility of working on those emotional structures and of cultivating different ways to interpret and productively respond to the emotional dynamic in politics – despite the very clear evidence that both individuals and societies can react very differently, emotionally speaking, to potential "threat" stimuli across time and space.

Culture and Emotion: Critical Affect Theory

Evolutionary functionalism is not the only theoretical tradition that takes seriously the question of emotions, however. Another contending theoretical tradition – one we might call critical affect theory – builds on the insights of continental political and social theory, as well as on contemporary neuroscience, in order to take political emotion seriously while avoiding some of the weaknesses of the evolutionary functionalist perspective. Perhaps the best-known Anglo-American exemplar of this tradition is William Connolly. For the past three decades and longer, he has mined social and political theory, philosophy, and neuroscience to explore the political relevance of what he calls the "visceral register" by tracing the effect of diverse psychological and emotional drives – such as the need to secure one's identity, feelings of insecurity, the drive to revenge a perceived wrong, or the sense of generalized "ressentiment" – on political behaviour and ideational phenomena (Connolly 1991, 1995, 1999, 2002).

Like Westen, Connolly believes that we cannot understand why certain ideologies defend certain positions, or why these positions appeal so strongly to some constituents, without exploring the emotional and psychological reactions they stimulate. Take the example of ideologies that espouse "tough-on-crime" policies and moral positions. An intellectualist analysis of the ideological discourse of North American "tough-on-crime" policies invariably would construct a philosophical map that centred on a set of "deep principles" such as "justice," "deterrence," "just deserts," "merit," "security," and so on as both the motivation and the justification of those policies. As Connolly and others have shown, however, the problem with this type of picture is that it cannot explain why these so-called deep principles are not consistently applied, even within the issue area of crime policy, nor help us understand why "tough-on-crime" agendas are espoused even though the data clearly show that these policies not only fail to lower crime rates; they also contribute to a broader loss of confidence in the justice system by creating deeply unequal outcomes for different demographic populations.

So what explains the intensity and longevity of "tough-on-crime" approaches? According to Connolly, it is the ways these policies both activate and answer certain pre-existing subterranean emotional undercurrents (Connolly 1995, 1999). According to Connolly's analysis, "tough-on-crime" ideology has four main attributes. First, it derives its meaning primarily by speaking to a wide and deep set of fears, insecurities, and resentments ranging from existential resentment of the instability of our identities to philosophical resentment of the profound imperfections that racialized inequality reveals to economic resentment of a globalized system that radically reduces our employment security to personal fears about physical security. Second, it uses coded language to activate, enflame, and then often redirect/refocus these fears, insecurities, and resentments towards concrete, but often unrelated, phenomena such as crime, racialized populations, foreigners, scapegoats, rival sports teams, and gendered/sexual/religious minorities. Third, "tough-on-crime" ideology addresses these fears, insecurities, and resentments by promising small (and often only symbolic) moments of revenge. Fourth, it completes the circle by employing principles and values such as justice, fairness, merit, just deserts, and so on to rationally justify these emotional responses – a process that, as Westen shows, ironically provides the brain with further emotional pleasure. In Connolly's view, this also has implications for how we imagine contesting emotionally fused ideology: when the driving motivation is lodged deeply in the visceral level, it is not enough to provide data, rational counterarguments, or even court judgments. Until the emotional dimension is addressed and altered, the energy that drives those ideological positions will continue to fuel it.

It is clear, therefore, that one important difference between the two approaches is that, although they agree that emotions are critical to politics, critical affect theory highlights a far more wide-ranging and philosophically tinged set of politically relevant emotional needs and drives than does the evolutionary functionalist approach. A second, and equally important, distinction, however, is how the two approaches address *why* and *how* feelings of disgust, fear, anger, or resentment are linked to specific issues. Where Westen explains everything by reference to universal and unchanging flight/fight/freeze responses, Connolly insists that the meaning, relevance, focus, and intensity of politically relevant emotions vary enormously over time and across cultures. Building on theorists and scientists as diverse as Nietzsche, Foucault, Deleuze and Guattari, and Joseph LeDoux, Connolly argues that emotional "instinct is more than a brutish, biologically fixed force"; that even the deepest of our contemporary emotions are more accurately described as culturally and historically cultivated "second nature"; and thus that these "instincts [which] are culturally formed can sometimes be modified by cultural strategies applied by groups to themselves and by individuals arts of the self" (Connolly 1999, 27). Like Westen, Connolly believes that the processes of amygdala-infused judgment are crucial to understanding politics and ideology. But unlike Westen, Connolly insists that we must also remember that even neuroscience is showing that "cultural learning is inscribed to some degree in memory traces of the amygdala" (Connolly 2002, 8).

One way of clarifying and sharpening this key difference between Connolly and Westen is to distinguish between emotion and affect in the way cultural theorist Lawrence Grossberg does. Grossberg is also convinced that the real meaning, and the core appeal, of American conservative ideology over the past several decades has "been built on an affective politics, on sentimentality and passion, in which meaning and political positions have become secondary" (1992, 269). Grossberg insists, however, that the success of conservative ideology lies not in its ability to identify and exploit pre-existing "gut-level issues." Rather, Grossberg suggests, it is "more accurate to say that the conservative strategy *transforms political struggles into 'gut' issues*. After all, no issue is intrinsically a gut issue; it is produced as such only by reducing the complexity of the debates, the various interpretations and contradictions that surround it, to a matter of affective investment" (269, emphasis added).

Grossberg and others therefore split what we call "feelings" into two distinct components. These scholars use the term "affect" to describe the physiological processes, hormonal responses, and physical experiences that exist in all humans (to a lesser or greater extent, of course). Brian Massumi (1996), for example, has suggested that we separate "affective energies" from "emotions." According to this perspective, affective energies are the physiological "intensities" that virtually all of us experience due to the way human bodies and minds have evolved to function over millions of years. In contrast, emotion should be understood as the *culturally and historically shaped articulation* of an affective intensity. "An emotion is a subjective content, the socio-linguistic fixing of the quality of an experience which is from that point onward defined as personal. Emotion is qualified intensity, the conventional, consensual point of insertion of intensity into semantically and semiotically formed progressions, into narrativizable action-reaction circuits, into function and meaning. It is intensity owned and recognized" (Massumi 1996, 221).

Critical affect theorists, then, would argue that Westen basically treats political emotions as if they are synonymous with physiological affect, and, in doing so, fails to explore the questions that really matter from a political point of view: those of how and why diffuse and redirectable affective intensities actually have been captured by a given, socially shared and defined emotion that is then aimed and focused towards a particular ideological principle or policy issue. Without this second level of analysis, Westen can make the broad point that politics is infused by affective intensities as much as rational debate, but he cannot explain or understand any particular phenomenon in any detail. To do this, we must not only understand the importance of affective intensities in general; we must also trace out the ways they become concretized into shared emotions and attached to specific issues and discourses at historically specific conjunctures.

Critical affect theory allow us not only to better understand why certain ideological principles and issues are able to call forth certain emotions, but also to explore how ideological discourses, narratives, principles, and so on evoke and *transform* the intensity and target of shared emotions over the long term. To paraphrase the song, for Connolly, Massumi, and Grossberg, feelings are always so much more than feelings. Where Westen would find "disgust" to be a natural emotion that is relatively fixed, these thinkers see it as a much more complicated phenomenon: "Disgust is a *thought-imbued feeling* … it is thought-imbued in that it responds acutely to some events and activities while remaining quiescent before others, and these thoughts are bathed in an intense feeling that can unsettle or overwhelm those sunk in it" (Connolly 1999, 163, emphasis added). Central to Connolly's project is highlighting the degree to which complicated and multiple processes in the body, brain, culture, and ideological discourse interact to create the thought-imbued feelings, and feeling-imbued thoughts, that influence our political judgment. To study what Connolly calls "neuropolitics," then, is to study "the politics through which cultural life mixes into the composition of body/brain processes. And vice versa" (Connolly 2002, xiii).

This is also why Connolly has long argued that, in addition to studying politics and ideology from a "macro" point of view, we also need to study how ideological phenomena interact with the "micro-political" level. According to Connolly, once we acknowledge the importance of affect to politics and the ways affect is trained into politically relevant shared emotions, we need to study the vast array of micro-techniques through which these emotions – and thus the broader political "sensibility" – are cultivated. In Connolly's view, this means studying elements as varied as "techniques organized and deployed collectively by professional associations, mass-media talk shows, TV and film dramas, military training, work processes, neighborhood gangs, church meetings, school assemblies, sporting events, charitable organizations, commercial advertising, child rearing, judicial practice and police routines … the micro-political dimension of each is potent because of the critical functions the institution performs in organizing attachments, consumption possibilities, work routines, faith practices, child rearing, education, investment, security and punishment" (Connolly 2002, 20–1). Where the intellectualist tradition encourages us to ignore the "emotional" dimension, and Westen's functionalist political psychology reduces and naturalizes politics and ideology as unchanging affect, critical affect theory offers a third model that both acknowledges the importance of understanding the emotional resonance of given ideologies and discourses and insists that doing so requires us to trace the historical and emotional specificity of the particular context surrounding the precise phenomena and events in question.

The Emotional Dimension of Contemporary North American Ideology

So, what difference does all this make for the practice of ideological analysis in Canadian political science? Throughout this chapter we have suggested that we can no longer assume that it is only (or even primarily) the persuasiveness of the "rational content," the ubiquity of the messaging, the credibility of its spokespeople, or the self-interested benefits it offers that explain the meaning and persuasive force of a given ideology. Rather, we have argued that, in many cases, we must also analyse the emotional dynamics and resonance of an ideology if we are to fully understand its core meaning and persuasive force.

But what does this approach mean in practice? Although a full exploration of this is obviously beyond the scope of this chapter, in this concluding section we want to examine several examples to give an idea of what this might mean. Given that most attempts to understand Canadian political ideology do so in a comparative light, often with a view to our neighbours to the south, let us begin by looking at the ways that observers have tried to explain the nature of contemporary ideology (and in particular American conservatism) before posing the same question to Canada.

We might say that there are two mainstream ways of understanding the ideological roots of the explosion of right-wing populism in the United States. One approach is exemplified by Thomas Frank (2004) who explains the appeal of the ideology of what he calls "backlash populism" as having its root in baiting working-class voters using what Stuart Hall et al. (1978) would call moral panics – priming, activating, and intensifying social wedge issues that allow voters to channel and express the insecurity and anger that have been caused largely by conservative economic policies. In contrast, the other explanation rejects the "bait-and-switch" argument, and suggests that conservative ideology has been successful because its economic policies align more closely with voters' beliefs/desires (Bartels 2006; Smith 2007).

None of these authors, however, explores the emotional dynamics too deeply. Smith and Bartels ignore this dimension completely, and while Frank plays up the importance of emotion, he tends to reduces it to anger about economic opportunity. The lost opportunity here is that these authors fail to examine the possibility that the appeal of American conservative economic ideology is understandable only in light of its emotional content. An analysis of the emotional triggers embedded in conservative economic discourse, in fact, would reveal a rich rhetorical system designed to capture and define affective energy in a variety of ways. On the positive, aspirational side, for example, the constant use of the language of "free choice" to justify and characterize conservative economic policy taps into the deeply positive emotional associations that many voters have with regard to the question of choice – positive associations that have been cultivated by many other ostensibly apolitical discourses, practices, and roles that highlight the value of choice – for example, as consumers, as "moral" agents, as members of various voluntary communities and associations, as individuals proud of their own life choices, and so on. In this sense, even the very bedrock concepts of conservative economic ideological discourse are neither technical nor intellectualist, but instead are already highly moralized and emotional (Gunster and Saurette 2014; Saurette 2006; Saurette and Gunster 2011, 2013).

On the other side of the emotional ledger, we would argue that the Trump phenomenon is a textbook case study of the power and relevance of the darker emotions in contemporary American ideology today. In many ways, the nature of Donald Trump's electoral victory and his presidency has made it impossible to deny the centrality of the emotional dimension of US politics. As has become commonplace to acknowledge now, Trump's appeal and victory cannot be explained by analysing any of the normal elements political scientists examine: the "principles" of his ideology, his policy pronouncements, the support of the Republican Party establishment, the amount of money spent, his personal "character," or any other "rational" factor. Instead his success can be explained only in reference to the ways his ideological discourse resonates in the deeply volatile and angry emotional landscape that underlies contemporary US politics. Trump has been successful because he has discursively triggered and amplified a set of "moral panics" (Hall et al. 1978), which have become "affective magnets" (Grossberg 1992) that allow voters to channel and collectively express deep and widely shared pre-existing emotions such as fear, xenophobia, insecurity, and resentment, which, in turn, have fused together to form a popular emotional wave that Trump has been able to surf to success simply by associating himself with it.

This strategy, of course, is not particularly new. Activating fears of racialized, stereotyped and other scapegoats by dog-whistling and using coded discourse and then capitalizing on the resulting moral and political hysteria has long been a key technique of the US conservative movement. What makes Trump distinctive, however, is that his technique is almost entirely explicit. He does not dog-whistle moral panic or code his appeals to underlying emotions; rather, he speaks to those issues and emotions explicitly and sensationally. Rather than deny it, he affirms it. And when questioned and criticized, rather than apologize he doubles down and responds with even more outrage and anger.

Although to many pundits with an "intellectualist" sensibility this seemed like an absurd vaudeville spectacle destined to crash and burn, Trump understands that his refusal to apologize, while alienating some and outraging many, actually emotionally binds his core supporters to him all the more closely, for, in refusing to apologize, he mirrors, amplifies, and defends the legitimacy of the emotions and alienation that many conservative voters themselves feel. And this might be the most important way in which he literally embodies politics as reality TV: both reveal just how deep, intense, volatile, and powerful drivers are the emotional landscapes underpinning US society today.

In comparison, it is tempting to view the emotional register of Canadian politics as paper-thin, and argue that an analysis of the emotional dimension is unnecessary for understanding it. An applied analysis of the Canadian ideological context from a critical affect theory perspective, however, suggests that the story is much more interesting.

On one hand, although much of contemporary Canadian conservatism is very different than the backlash populism that dominates American conservatism (Saurette and Gunster 2013), important swathes of the Canadian ideological spectrum have mobilized somewhat comparable emotional dynamics. Historically, for example, the previous century saw many populist movements – many of which led directly to our contemporary mainstream political parties – whose core ideological and political appeal lay in the ways they passionately articulated, and promised to resolve, a variety of grievances and emotionally perceived threats (see Harrison 1995; Laycock 2002). Moreover, as Rob Ford's 2010 Toronto mayoral campaign proved, backlash populist discourse, under the right circumstances, sometimes can be a successful strategy in Canada. In some ways, as the pre-eminent example of recent mainstream backlash populism in Canada, Ford's campaign showed just how far apart the Canadian and American variants are – for example, his campaign did not mimic the highly racialized (and racializing) scapegoating tendencies so characteristic of American backlash populism.[3] On the other hand, central to Ford's discourse was another classic emotional scapegoating strategy of portraying bureaucrats and political "elites" as lazy, self-satisfied, and entitled know-it-alls whose appetite for waste makes them the enemy of all hardworking people. In this sense Ford's political discourse clearly functioned to prime and capture a variety of negative affective energies, and use them to attract voters to his candidacy in ways very similar to American backlash populism. Beyond proving that this mode can achieve electoral success in Canada, it also it proved that the emotional pull of backlash populism also can be used to build an extremely strong, loyal, and vocal community of supporters. Indeed, the moniker "Ford Nation" was particularly appropriate, since it underlined the fact that Ford's strategies embodied dynamics that were similar to the emotive inside/outside identity appeals that are at the core of many patriotic and nationalistic ideologies.

Even though they often fly under the radar, there are many other examples of emotion-laden backlash populist ideological appeals in other parts of the Canadian conservative movement. We have, for example, analysed the ideological and emotional content of Canadian conservative political talk radio, a phenomenon that is a surprisingly widespread vehicle for ideological discourse in Canada (Saurette and Gunster 2011). We found that Canadian conservative political talk radio employs many deeply emotive rhetorical patterns characteristic of the ideological discourse of American backlash populism. In particular, both share a deep hostility to expert knowledge and structural analysis, and instead embody what we call "epistemological populism": a championing of everyday, individual "common sense" experience where the legitimacy of that experience is based on a combination of the subjective characteristics of the speaker and the emotional intensity of the speech. And both practise a form of what we call "argutainment": a

3 This is not to suggest that there weren't racializing dynamics at work in Ford's campaign or in his mayorship. Rather, it is to suggest that these dynamics did not play the prime discursive and emotional roles they do in most American variants.

mode of discourse that favours highly emotional (usually outraged), polemical, fast-paced, attack-and-move-on-and-never-apologize political commentary that justifies itself as filtering out the "political BS" and allowing people access to the plain and simple truths of common sense. In the same way that the Tea Party and Donald Trump essentially have invoked and justified an authoritarian sensibility in response to a variety of emotional anxieties in the name of democracy – for example, "saving/rebuilding/making America great again" – clearly there are strains within the Canadian conservative movement that seek to apply similar, emotionally resonant ideological strategies in Canada.

The emotional dimension of contemporary ideological discourse, however, is not confined to the more marginal phenomena of Canadian politics. Over the past decade, for example, the Conservative Party of Canada clearly has focused on the emotional dimension of Canadian politics. One of the architects of the rebuilt party, Tom Flanagan, has made it very clear that its conservative electoral, fundraising, legislative, and ideological strategy has focused heavily on the emotional dimension – in particular, on cultivating and using fear to attract and mobilize supporters (Flanagan 2007, 2014). In fact, in many circles it has become something of a truism that Harper's essential strategy for the second half of his mandate rested heavily on intensifying Canadians' fears of terrorism and crime, and then framing the Conservatives as the only party "tough enough" to protect citizens from these dangers (see, for example, Hepburn 2015).

In our view the story is more complex than that. We would argue that a close analysis of their legislative and electoral strategy suggests that the federal Conservatives were not so much playing off of fears of terrorism per se as priming and responding to a much wider and more nuanced set of anxieties and discomforts. During the 2015 election campaign, for example, the main strategy the Conservative Party used to blunt the NDP's momentum was to create a moral panic around *identity issues* – banning the *niqab* in citizenship ceremonies, the "barbaric practices" hotline, and so on – in order to activate and enflame emotional anxieties about supposed threats to Canadian values and identities, which, while obviously fused with terrorism in conservative discourse, remains a distinct issue. The fact that the Conservatives were able to use these panics successfully to erode NDP support – even though there was no evidence suggesting that specific threats existed – demonstrates the ways the actual meaning and effect of ideological discourse and policies are intrinsically related to emotional dynamics. On the other hand, the fact that a large majority of Canadian voters ended up rejecting these emotional strategies also demonstrates that appeals to "fear" – even if we understand that in an expansive way – do not always trump other emotional investments.

Which brings us to our last point: the emotional lessons of Justin Trudeau. It is notable that many pundits first dismissed Trudeau's chances, and then explained his victory, by reference to his style: a great head of hair, a few policy ideas that appealed to "the youth," his "sunny ways," and the fact that he was not Harper. But this perspective – itself a combination of an intellectualist orientation, with its implied judgment that politics should be about rational principles and policy, and the journalistic habit of treating all of politics as if it were a cynical game of emotional manipulation (he's just a pretty face wooing the voters) – deeply misrepresents the nature of politics. For once we acknowledge the importance of the emotional dimension of politics, we should not be surprised that voters reacted "emotionally" to the different leadership styles – and the values/ethos they implicitly communicated – portrayed in the parties' ideological discourse, campaign promises, advertisements, policy pronouncements, and debate comments.

Moreover, one might argue that these emotional markers conveyed highly valuable information to voters, for the vast bulk of decisions a government makes during its mandate go far beyond the dozen or so explicit policy pronouncements of an election campaign. In our contemporary Westminster system, with its high degree of policy- and decision-making centralization, voters essentially are asked to pick someone they can trust to make decisions that reflect their preferences (broadly speaking) on a wide set of questions that are not explicitly discussed in the campaign. In this context, using emotional intelligence to try to evaluate a leader's character, leadership style, and broad values set might be a more relevant and reliable guide to voting than a close and tightly "rational" analysis of party platforms and statements. The catch, of course, is that everything in politics is subject to potential marketing spin – including the emotional presentation of leaders and parties, their styles and values. But this is true of all political judgments in our age, not just those that rely on emotional evaluation.

Regardless of normative judgments, however, it seems hard to argue that one can understand the outcome of Canada's 2015 federal election without taking emotion into account. The emotional dimension of politics might not always be the deciding factor in elections. But in 2015 – with polling reporting widespread and intense negatives characterizing voters' (other than core conservative supporters) feelings about Harper's style, a Conservative ideological discourse and policy platform that were largely viewed as highly divisive, polemical, and angry, and the ideological and marketing representations of Trudeau and the Liberals as optimistic, open, young, innovative, and communicative – there is little question that the emotional dimension lay at the heart of both the campaign and the outcome. In fact, it might even be the case that emotions explain not only why Harper lost, but also why the anti-Harper "change" mandate coalesced under Trudeau, rather than under Mulcair. If Trudeau's style clearly conveyed emotionally that he was the essential anti-Harper, Mulcair's style – a lawyer by trade and an extremely skilled and pugnacious debater in Parliament – marked him less as anti-Harper and more as the Harper of the left. It was not coincidental, for example, that, in the debates, viewers and commentators tended to overlook Trudeau's inexperience and instead focus on his perceived openness, while largely ignoring Mulcair's content expertise and focusing on how deeply uncomfortable Mulcair looked when he tried to smile and remain light. Contrary to what many might suggest, this was a sign not of voters' ignorance or irrationality, but that they were using their emotional intelligence to evaluate the ideological and political messages of the election campaign in a context filled with far too much smoke and too many mirrors.

Conclusion

In our view, applied political theory is a fair descriptor of any use of theoretical methods that seek to understand/explain/describe how political phenomena function and/or offer us practical and normative guidance about how they should function. In this chapter, we have focused on demonstrating how the theoretical tradition of ideological analysis attempts to do this, concentrating primarily on the former task. In particular, we have argued that, although a valuable tradition, its utility would be improved if it paid more attention to the emotional dimension.

We would never argue that the emotional dimension is the only relevant factor in politics. Nor would we suggest that ideological discourse appeals only to our emotions. Intellectualist methods offer important perspectives, and help us understand various aspects of the meaning and impact of ideology as well. We have tried to show, however, that exclusively adopting the intellectualist perspective has significant costs – including eliminating our ability to understand the emotional meaning at the core of certain ideological discourses and to explain why and how these discourses actually move people. This is why developing new and better ways to study the emotive dimension of contemporary ideology is worth the effort – not because it promises to replace all other methods and perspectives, but because the failure to consider the emotional and affective components of ideology leaves us unable to comprehend fully the messy, emotive, and fascinating nature and force of a variety of ideological phenomena in our world today. That is something that no approach to ideology that aspires to call itself applied political theory should accept.

REFERENCES

Albo, Gregory. 2002. "Neoliberalism, the State, and the Left: A Canadian Perspective." *Monthly Review*. May. https://doi.org/10.14452/MR-054-01-2002-05_4

Althusser, Louis. 1972. "Ideological State Apparatuses (Notes Towards an Investigation)." In *Lenin and Philosophy and Other Essays*. New York: Monthly Review Press.

Ajzenstat, Janet, and Peter J. Smith. 1995. *Canada's Origins: Liberal, Tory or Republican?* Ottawa: Carleton University Press.

Ball, Terrence. 2002. "Ideology and Ideologies." In *Political Ideologies and the Democratic Ideal*. 4th ed., ed. Terrence Ball and Richard Dagger, 3–18. New York: Longman.

Banting, K.G. 1992. "Neoconservatism in an Open Economy: The Social Role of the Canadian State." *International Political Science Review* 13 (2): 149–70. https://doi.org/10.1177/019251219201300202

Bartels, Larry. 2006. "What's the Matter with 'What's the Matter with Kansas?'" *Quarterly Journal of Political Science* 1 (2): 201–26. https://doi.org/10.1561/100.00000010

Carver, Terrell. 2004. "The Career of a Concept." In *Ideals and Ideologies: A Reader*. 4th ed., ed. Terrance Ball and Richard Dagger, 1–10. New York: Longman.

Clarkson, Stephen. 2002. *Uncle Sam and Us: Globalizaton, Neoconservatism, and the Canadian State*. Toronto: University of Toronto Press. https://doi.org/10.3138/9781442689541

Cohen, G.A. 1988. *History, Labour, and Freedom: Themes from Marx*. Oxford: Oxford University Press.

Connolly, William E. 1991. *Identity\Difference*. Ithaca, NY: Cornell University Press.
Connolly, William E. 1995. *The Ethos of Pluralism*. Minneapolis: Minnesota University Press.
Connolly, William E. 1999. *Why I Am Not a Secularist*. Minneapolis: University of Minnesota Press.
Connolly, William E. 2002. *Neuropolitics*. Minneapolis: University of Minnesota Press.
Cox, Robert W. 1981. "Social Forces, States and World Orders: Beyond International Relations Theory." *Millennium – Journal of International Studies* 10 (2): 126–55. https://doi.org/10.1177/03058298810100020501
Eagleton, Terry. 1991. *An Introduction to Ideology*. London: Verso.
Elster, Jon. 1985. *Making Sense of Marx*. Cambridge: Cambridge University Press.
Farney, James. 2012. *Social Conservatives and Party Politics in Canada and the United States*. Toronto: University of Toronto Press. https://doi.org/10.3138/9781442699618
Farney, James. 2013. *Conservatism in Canada*. Toronto: University of Toronto Press.
Flanagan, Thomas. 2007. *Harper's Team*. Montreal; Kingston, ON: McGill-Queen's University Press.
Flanagan, Thomas. 2014. *Winning Power: Canadian Campaigning in the Twenty-First Century*. Montreal; Kingston, ON: McGill-Queen's University Press.
Frank, Thomas. 2004. *What's the Matter with Kansas?* New York: Owl Books.
Gibbins, Roger, and Loleen Youngman. 1996. *Mindscapes: Political Ideologies towards the 21st Century*. Toronto: McGraw-Hill Ryerson.
Gill, Stephen. 2010. *Gramsci, Historical Materialism and International Relations*. Cambridge: Cambridge University Press.
Grossberg, Lawrence. 1992. *We Gotta Get Out of This Place: Popular Conservatism and Postmodern Culture*. New York: Routledge.
Gunster, Shane, and Paul Saurette. 2014. "Storylines in the Sands: News, Narrative and Ideology in the Calgary Herald." *Canadian Journal of Communication* 39 (3): 333–59. https://doi.org/10.22230/cjc.2014v39n3a2830
Habermas, Jürgen. 1984. *The Theory of Communicative Action*, vol. 1. Boston: Beacon Press.
Hall, Stuart, Chas Critcher, Tony Jefferson, John Clarke, and Brian Roberts. 1978. *Policing the Crisis: Mugging, the State and Law & Order*. London: Palgrave Macmillan.
Harrison, Trevor. 1995. *Of Passionate Intensity: Right-Wing Populism and the Reform Party of Canada*. Toronto: University of Toronto Press.

Hartz, Louis. 1964. *The Founding of New Societies: Studies in the History of the United States, Latin America, South Africa, Canada, and Australia*. New York: Harcourt Brace Jovanovich.

Head, Brian. 1985. *Ideology and Social Science: Destutt de Tracy and French Liberalism*. Boston: Lower Academic. https://doi.org/10.1007/978-94-009-5159-4

Hepburn, Bob. 2015. "How Stephen Harper came to love politics of fear." *Toronto Star*, 21 March. Available online at https://www.thestar.com/opinion/commentary/2015/03/21/how-stephen-harper-came-to-love-politics-of-fear-hepburn.html

Horowitz, Gad. 1966. "Conservatism, Liberalism and Socialism in Canada: An Interpretation." *Canadian Journal of Economics and Political Science* 32 (2): 143–71. https://doi.org/10.2307/139794

Horowitz, Gad. 1977. "'The Myth' of the Red Tory." *Canadian Journal of Political Science* 1: 87–8.

Horowitz, Gad. 1978. "Notes on 'Conservatism, Liberalism and Socialism in Canada.'" *Canadian Journal of Political Science* 11 (2): 383–99. https://doi.org/10.1017/S0008423900041135

Jeffrey, Brooke. 1999. *Hard Right Turn: The New Face of Neo-conservatism in Canada*. Toronto: HarperCollins.

Kennedy, Emmet. 1979. "'Ideology' from Destutt De Tracy to Marx." *Journal of the History of Ideas* 40 (3): 353–68. https://doi.org/10.2307/2709242

Langford, T. 1991. "Left/Right Orientation and Political Attitudes: A Reappraisal and Class Comparison." *Canadian Journal of Political Science* 24 (3): 475–98. https://doi.org/10.1017/S0008423900022654

Laclau, Ernesto, and Chantal Mouffe. 1985. *Hegemony and Socialist Strategy: Towards a Radical Democratic Politics*. London: Verso.

Laxer, James. 1996. *In Search of a New Left: Canadian Politics after the Neoconservative Assault*. Toronto: Viking.

Laycock, David. 2002. *The New Right and Democracy in Canada: Understanding Reform and the Canadian Alliance*. Toronto: Oxford University Press.

Lichtheim, George. 1965. "The Concept of Ideology." *History and Theory* 4 (2): 164–95. https://doi.org/10.2307/2504150

Lipset, Seymour Martin. 1991. *Continental Divide: The Values and Institutions of the United States and Canada*. New York: Routledge.

Macpherson, C.B. 2010. *The Political Theory of Possessive Individualism*. Oxford: Oxford University Press.

Marx, Karl. 1978. *Marx-Engels Reader*, ed. R. Tucker. New York: W.W. Norton.

Massumi, Brian. 1996. "The Autonomy of Affect." In *Deleuze: A Critical Reader*, ed. Paul Patton, 217–39. Oxford: Blackwell.

McCullough, H.B. 1995. *Political Ideologies and Political Philosophers*. Toronto: Thompson Educational Publishing.

Patten, Steve. 2001. "'Toryism' and the Conservative Party in a Neo-Liberal Era." In *Party Politics in Canada*. 8th ed., ed. Hugh G. Thorburn and Alan Whitehorn, 135–47. Toronto: Prentice Hall.

Patten, Steve. 2006. "New Right Politics." In *Canadian Politics: Democracy and Dissent*, ed. Joan Grace and Byron Sheldrick, 273–99. Toronto: Pearson Education Canada.

Piotte, Jean-Marc. 2003. *ADQ, à droite toute! le programme de l'ADQ expliqué*. Montreal: Hurtubise.

Saurette, Paul. 2006. "Conservatives for Choice." Paper presented at the *American Political Science Association*, Philadelphia, September 2006.

Saurette, Paul, and Kelly Gordon. 2015. *The Changing Voice of the Anti-Abortion Movement*. Toronto: University of Toronto Press.

Saurette, Paul, and Shane Gunster. 2011. "Ears Wide Shut: Epistemological Populism, Argutainment and Canadian Conservative Talk Radio." *Canadian Journal of Political Science* 44 (1): 195–218. https://doi.org/10.1017/S0008423910001095

Saurette, Paul, and Shane Gunster. 2013. "Canada's Conservative Ideological Infrastructure: Brewing a Cup of Cappuccino Conservatism." In *Tax Is Not a Four-Letter Word: A Different Take on Taxes in Canada*, ed. Alex Himelfarb and Jordan Himelfarb, 227–66. Waterloo, ON: Wilfrid Laurier University Press.

Saurette, Paul, Shane Gunster, and Kathryn Trevenen. 2009. "Un conservatisme renouvelé? l'étude des idéologies au Canada." In *Les politiques publiques au Canada: pouvoir, conflits et idéologies*, ed. Dimitrios Karmis and Linda Cardinal, 11–34. Quebec City: Presses de l'Université Laval.

Saurette, Paul, and Kathryn Trevenen. 2013. "Feelings, Nothing More than Feelings: affects, émotions et étude des idées politiques populaires." In *Ceci n'est pas une idée politique: réflexions sur les approches à l'étude des idées politiques*, ed. Dalie Giroux et Dimitrios Karmis, 381–404. Quebec City: Presses de l'Université Laval.

Skinner, Quentin. 1988. "Some Problems in the Analysis of Political Thought and Action." In *Meaning and Context: Quentin Skinner and His Critics*, ed. James Tully, 97–118. Princeton, NJ: Princeton University Press.

Smith, Mark. 2007. *The Right Talk*. Princeton, NJ: Princeton University Press.

Wesley, Jared. 2011. *Code Politics*. Vancouver: UBC Press.

Westen, Drew. 2007. *The Political Brain*. New York: Public Affairs.

Wiseman, Nelson. 1988. "A Note on 'Hartz-Horowitz at Twenty: The Case of French Canada.'" *Canadian Journal of Political Science* 21 (4): 795–806. https://doi.org/10.1017/S0008423900057450

Wiseman, Nelson. 2007. *In Search of Canadian Political Culture*. Vancouver: UBC Press.
Wood, Ellen. 1992. *The Pristine Culture of Capitalism*. London: Verso.
Wood, Ellen. 1997. *Peasant-Citizen and Slave: The Foundations of Athenian Democracy*. London: Verso.
Wood, Ellen, and Neal Wood. 1978. *Class Ideology and Ancient Political Theory*. Oxford: Oxford University Press.

PART II

Equality and Social Justice

5 The Changing Normativity of the Canadian Welfare State

NEIL HIBBERT

A generally accepted view is that democratic welfare states, including Canada's, have undergone significant transformations in recent decades. They now exist in societies quite different than those from which they emerged, address new kinds of social risks, rest on new configurations of interests, and are oriented towards different kinds of justificatory ideas. And, although the evolution of welfare states has been complex, a broad consensus exists on the further point that they interfere less with market processes and produce fewer redistributive effects than during their developmental peak in the middle of the twentieth century. These changes are of particular note to political theorists given the welfare state's historical status as a primary mechanism of social justice.

An applied political theory approach is particularly useful for addressing the changing politics of the Canadian welfare state as it can identify the underpinning normative changes that connect a wide range of institutional and discoursive developments. Using political theory, one can generate the idea of a "normative model" of welfare states, and then show how the contemporary Canadian welfare state is guided by a set of standards for intervention in the economy and society that differs from that of previous eras in its development. In particular, I argue that the new normative logic of the Canadian welfare state represents a shift from an "egalitarian" to a "public economic" normative model. This change is characterized by the less redistributive politics of increasingly individuated approaches to protection against risk and uncertainty, as opposed to the redistributive effects produced by the egalitarian model's linkage of the welfare state to the idea of universal rights of social citizenship.

The chapter is organized as follows. I begin by presenting the idea of a normative model of the welfare state in general and egalitarian and public economic models in particular. I then advance the claim that the post-war development of the Canadian welfare state was guided by an egalitarian normative logic by virtue of connecting welfare state entitlement to the idea of equal social citizenship. Drawing on four major areas of programmatic and discoursive change beginning during the 1990s, I demonstrate that the still-ongoing period of welfare state reform can be understood as a shift towards the new normative logic of a public economic model, in which the welfare state is increasingly disconnected from an ideal of equal social citizenship.

Normative Models of the Welfare State

The idea of a normative model of the welfare state combines moral and sociological aspects of norms. That is, it presumes that welfare states can serve some moral purposes, even if their foundations are not necessarily moral, and that these norms inform, to some degree, their ongoing development and functioning. If so, we can get a firmer grip on changes to welfare state practices by developing a "reconstructive account" of the "norms and ideals that are implicit and play a structuring role in our practices" (Heath 2011, 28). Developing a normative model involves a "reflection on practice," and proceeds through institutional interpretation of current practices to ascertain what normative purposes welfare states plausibly can be seen serve (Weale 1983, 9). A normative model will identify the "norms and values that are embedded in welfare policies, how they are justified and which consequences they may have" (Kidal and Kuhnle 2005, 3). As a work in applied political theory, this chapter draws on qualitative and quantitative literature on the history and current politics of the Canadian welfare state. Building on this work, I apply concepts from the normative literature on welfare states to the major institutional developments in welfare state formation in Canada to ground a general idea of its basic normative structure. I presume the norms that are couched in welfare state practices guide the actions for state intervention in society and the economy, and so, if the normative underpinnings of the welfare state change over time and we accept some degree of normative efficacy, we can expect that change to give rise to, and consolidate, subsequent institutional change. I therefore treat the relationship between norms and institutions as dynamic, in the sense that institutional change affects the normative structure of welfare states, which can be expected to feed back into subsequent institutional development.

A survey of the literature on the different "worlds" of welfare state practices reveals significant plurality in the normative purposes the welfare state is thought to serve. As an example of a reconstructive theory, Goodin et al. classify welfare states using "six moral values which [they] have traditionally been supposed to serve" – namely, economic efficiency, poverty reduction, social equality, social integration, social stability, and autonomy (1999, 22). Esping-Andersen's (1990) influential typology reduces the normative grounds of welfare states somewhat to three distinct normative types: the social democratic, liberal, and conservative varieties. Prescriptive political theory exhibits an even greater diversity of normative purposes the welfare state could be justified in pursuing, even if current practices are not based on such norms. These include, but are not limited to, meeting basic needs (Goodin 1988), decommodification (Walzer 1983), mitigating bad luck (Dworkin 2002), preserving democratic community (Wolff 1998), and ensuring persons' capabilities (Sen 2009).

To narrow the matter for the purpose of assessing the normative development of the Canadian welfare state, I draw on Joseph Heath's (2006, 2011) work on the normativity of welfare states, and use a two-part typology: a public economic model and an egalitarian model. In the public economic model, the primary normative aim of the welfare state is to promote efficiency, understood as "Pareto-improving" mutually beneficial outcomes. In the egalitarian model, the primary normative aim of the welfare state is to promote greater equality in the distribution of income and in-kind goods and services that are central to persons' welfare. Unlike the public economic model, this might require inefficient change to a distributive status quo that makes some advantaged people worse off.

The egalitarian model of the welfare state is probably the one with greatest currency in contemporary political theory. By distributing core primary goods and services either as entitlements of citizenship or as means-tested entitlements, the welfare state limits market-generated inequalities, and is thus treated as the core mechanism of social justice in liberal democratic societies. This view is applied in practice through Esping-Andersen's link between the "decommodification" of core elements of the provision of welfare and social equality in welfare states. Decommodified forms of welfare distribution "crowd out" the market and distribute according to right, rather than capacity to pay (Esping-Andersen 1990, 20). Short of decommodifying labour (and therefore income) itself, the egalitarian strategy of pursuing equality through the decommodifying effects of unconditional social policy has been the main route to greater social equality in democratic welfare states (47).

This approach is mirrored in egalitarian political theory in, for example, Rawls's claim that the distribution of primary social goods is grounded in entitlements of justice, rather than in capacity to pay (1999, 78–81). The welfare state works towards greater equality by limiting the scope of market incomes in determining entitlements to the various goods and services that constitute persons' welfare (65). Equal social rights to primary goods diminish the role of market-generated "money incomes" in the distribution of the goods and services that constitute what Marshall (1964) calls the "real income" of citizens.

The public economic model of the welfare state, as mentioned, holds that its primary normative function is to promote mutually advantageous – that is, efficient – outcomes. This conception of the welfare state has received remarkably little by way of attention from political theorists. What might be termed the conventional view in political theory distinguishes between the normative grounds of any social cooperation whatsoever and the regulatory principles that subsequently apply within it for the distribution of cooperative gains. Rawls's view is perhaps most emblematic of this distinction. For him, social cooperation is justified as a system of mutual advantage – that is, as an efficient move from a non-cooperative baseline whereby everyone is made better off (Rawls 1999, 4). In addition to personal security, the primary benefits secured through social cooperation, according to Rawls, are those produced by the market mechanism, particularly gains from trade and economies of scale (see also Heath 2006, 319). A basic gain of cooperation, then, is the presence of the material resources that allow for better lives than those that would be obtainable through individual efforts. However, although cooperative schemes are justified by the principle of efficiency, market-created inequalities can call into question their moral legitimacy and even basic stability. It is here, on the conventional view, that the welfare state enters the picture as a residual mechanism, based on the idea of equality, to redistribute the cooperative gains produced by the market in accordance with some conception of justice.

According to Heath, the view of the welfare state as a residual egalitarian mechanism suffers from "catallactic bias" by obscuring non-exchange forms of efficiency promotion (2006, 315). The public economic model of the welfare state, in contrast to the conventional view, treats it, like the market, as a "sui generis source of collective benefit" (323). The primary cooperative benefit produced by the welfare state is risk pooling. This, Heath argues, is evidenced by the fundamental insurance structures of the welfare state. Because of uncertainty, pooling risks is mutually advantageous, suggesting that the logic of the major elements of the welfare state – such as pensions (the risk of outliving one's savings), health (the risk of illness), and unemployment insurance (the risk of losing paid employment) – best correspond with the norm of efficiency, not equality. In the public economic model, both the market and the welfare state represent the same normative logic of efficiency, in contrast to the normative dualism of the conventional view. The welfare state, rather than overriding market-generated inequalities, is justified in cases of market failure in providing insurance in crucial areas of social risk and uncertainty (Barr 2012; Heath 2011, 23). As such, both the welfare state and the market are based on common interests in optimizing the production of mutually beneficial gains from cooperation (Heath 2011, 17). Unlike the principle of equality, which entails redistribution and therefore "winners and losers," the principle of efficiency, by ruling out making some worse off to improve the condition of others, is a "win-win" norm (24).

Further critical consideration of the public economic model of the welfare state would be a welcome addition to political theory. One significant reason is that it would bring the theory of the welfare state closer to the actual interests of persons with respect to the risks and uncertainties presented by liberal market societies that welfare states historically have mitigated. This would bring the theory of the welfare state closer in line with actual welfare state forms that, in the main, are modelled along the logic of insurance. Relatedly, it also would go a significant distance in addressing motivational concerns that the conventional view confronts in attempting to explain why self-interested persons motivated to cooperate in systems of mutual advantage subsequently would accept equality-delivering social policies that might cut against their interests.

There are problems, however, with Heath's further claim that the main features of the welfare state that are usually thought of as egalitarian in nature – particularly decommodification and universalism – can be accounted for by the norm of efficiency. Many nascent welfare state institutions reflect the idea of efficient risk pooling among roughly equally situated persons, generally delineated by occupational differences

(Esping-Andersen 1990, 39–41; see also the discussion of early forms of decommodification in Polanyi [1944] 2001). Frequently, however, they were exclusive schemes of common protection limited to sectoral interests, and did not cover persons with different risk profiles. Indeed, much of the progressive politics associated with welfare state formation involved making existing program structures more inclusive, extending common protections to differently situated persons (Weale 1990). Thus, although the public economic model is successful in explaining the presence of some form of welfare state institutions, it has difficulty explaining variations in their form – such as, programmatic differences involving levels of benefit generosity, stringency of eligibility conditions, duration of benefit eligibility, extent of earnings relatedness, and so forth – and why some forms that are more egalitarian than others emerge in some instances and not in others. The public economic model of the welfare state has difficulty accounting for the emergence of what we might see as more egalitarian forms of social policy because, as Sen puts it, the principle of efficiency is inherently "silent" on the question of the fairness of any particular distribution that might constitute the baseline from which assessments of the efficiency of any given change are made (Sen 1970, 99; see also Rawls 1999, 61).

If the identified baseline is as stratified as societies such as Canada's were during the formative years of the welfare state, the principle of efficiency, by virtue of giving all persons a "veto" over potential changes, precludes equal protection against unequally shared risks and uncertainties. As Baldwin argues, this inequality exists on two primary levels. The first is inequality of exposure and uncertainty with respect to any particular risk. This is more salient in certain areas of socio-economic life than others – persons can be more secure in facing the risk of becoming unemployed or outliving their savings than, say, of becoming ill or disabled. The second level is capacity to deal effectively, drawing on one's own resources, with actualized foreseeable or unforeseeable types of risk (Baldwin 1990, 12–17). In both cases, if the inequality is of a sufficient degree, common protections will not be supported by shared interests; advantaged persons will lack interest in joining with disadvantaged persons in risk-pooling arrangements, and can be expected to cooperate exclusively with like-situated persons.

Despite different interests tied to immediate susceptibility to socio-economic risks, Barr argues, advantaged persons might be motivated to include the disadvantaged in risk-pooling arrangements from a range of indirect interests tied to the externalities involved in cases of those unable to insure themselves against potential risks. Using the case of unemployment insurance, he argues that, when a vulnerable, uninsured, person becomes unemployed, society has the choice of either paying out a "non-contributory benefit" or offering no help and allowing the person to "starve." The latter option, too, involves externalized costs, including those of the care of dependents, increased crime, and disposing of the body, as well as "psychic externalities" in the sense that we do not want to live in a society in which people starve (Barr 2012, 138). This kind of interest, one hopes, might ground a certain kind of cross-class solidarity and motivate some degree of support for protections against core socio-economic risks. However, state insurance against insecurities based on interests tied to externalities involved in non-protection is likely to be either minimal or differentiated across social class and status (Weale 1990, 477). The move to common forms of protection is very difficult politically, following the public economic model, due to interests rooted in existing market-position differentials (478).

The challenge of this dynamic can be seen in the nature of the first, pre-war, phases of welfare state formation in Canada and other industrial capitalist societies. During this phase social policy makers confronted a disunity of interests rooted in a range of socio-economic cultural positions that presented barriers to broad-based entitlement programs. Such barriers included, in addition to basic economic inequality, the "exclusionary corporatism of narrow status-solidarity that … permeated early trade unionism and friendly societies" (Esping-Andersen 1990, 65). Canada, in particular, faced significant regional and cultural barriers to broad-based solidarity rooted in a shared nationality that might support encompassing institutions (Banting 2005; Brodie 2002, 381). The existence of societal fractures and conflicting interests in social protections led to the two initial trajectories of either status-differentiated entitlements or targeted minimal protections. In the case of Canada, the development of the nascent welfare state followed the targeted minimalist track. As Myles puts it, Canadian welfare state development began "in the 'poor law' tradition, providing means-tested mother's allowances to indigent women with children … (and) a means-tested old age pensions in 1927" (1998, 350). To the extent this can be explained by the principle of efficiency, early Canadian social policy reflected concern with the negative externalities associated with extreme poverty. Subsequently, however, the post-war period of welfare state expansion in Canada increasingly involved the creation of common protections extended to all persons as a social right of citizenship. If it is the case that early social policy makers faced significant conflict of interests rooted in differential socio-economic positions, as well as other cultural and societal dynamics, such that common protections against shared risks and uncertainties are unlikely to represent an efficient change from some pre–social policy status quo, how might the normative shift of the Canadian welfare state go beyond the "poor law" tradition of minimal, and often stigmatizing, protections?

For some political theorists, the explanation must extend beyond interests and appeal to an altruistic sense of justice. David Miller, for example, argues that, for advantaged persons to support social policies that are explicitly redistributive and not rooted in shared interests in common protections against risk or uncertainty, "they must see this as a matter of social justice" (2006, 328). Titmuss similarly argues that the nature of social policy beyond that rooted in shared interests depends on the "morality of society" and on its members' willingness to "give to strangers" (1971, 11). Although this kind of moral-motivation explanation of the welfare state has significant currency in contemporary political theory, adding altruism to shared interests in protections against common risks and uncertainties muddies the motivational picture in accounting for the growth of the welfare state by holding that, although persons have an interest in cooperating and pooling certain kinds of risk, and so are motivated by mutual advantage, they are also, in other areas of social life, willing to act against their interests from impartial motives. It is also difficult to ascertain how the level of altruism might grow or diminish and how it might correlate to phases of welfare state growth or retrenchment. As Jon Elster puts it, the "the justice motive in social behaviour" is extremely elusive (1987, 715). Although some egalitarian norms are more robust than others – particularly negative norms of justice on the exercise of power over individuals – most are "extremely context-dependent in the way they are interpreted and applied" and can be used to "both criticize and justify ... [a policy]... by suitable choice of reference group and dimension" (715). Furthermore, altruism has difficulty accounting for the important normative developments of the welfare state – in particular, the move away from the poverty-relief (and modestly redistributive) orientation of the poor law paradigm to the encompassing insurance model of "income maintenance" and horizontal redistribution (Barry 1990, 501). A targeted, or "prioritarian," form of social policy is more consistent with the justice motive than are common protections. What is needed in light of these explanatory and motivational issues, then, is an account, using the applied political theory approach, of the reorganization and articulation of interests that underpinned the move to common protections against the risks and uncertainties experienced by persons in different socio-economic situations. How, in other words, were advantaged persons brought into the same risk pools as the disadvantaged, when such inclusion sat at odds with an efficiency model of the welfare state?

Following the applied political theory approach, the next section presents an empirical analysis of the transition of the Canadian welfare state in the post-war phase of its development away from the poor-law model to encompassing and common protections. It suggests that egalitarian norms were built into the welfare state without extending beyond a predominantly interest-based account of political motivation, and argues that the construction of social citizenship in Canada created a new egalitarian status quo.

The Egalitarianism of the Post-war Development of the Canadian Welfare State

The Canadian welfare state developed significantly over the middle decades of the twentieth century. After the adoption of the means-tested Old Age Pension in 1927, the welfare state shifted from the poor law tradition, and the "Canadian trajectory of programme design closely resembled the Scandinavian" approach of universal and flat-rate benefits (Myles 1998, 350–1). Major program additions during this time included unemployment insurance (1940), the Family Allowance (1944), Old Age Security (OAS, 1951), hospitalization insurance (1961), the Canada Pension Plan (CPP, 1965), the Canada Assistance Plan (1966), sickness insurance (1971), health insurance (1972), and the Canada Health Act (1984) (see Olsen 1994, 5–13). The post-war expansion of the welfare state resulted in a hybrid model that combined "traditional means-tested benefits, a Beveridge core of universal benefits based on citizenship, supplemented by social insurance for retirement, unemployment and sickness" (Myles 1998, 351–2). The institutional result of this expansion was what Banting calls a system of "embedded liberalism" that entrenched a liberalized economy in an "impressive set of social programs ... [including a] rapidly growing education system [that] would expand equality of opportunity, a comprehensive health insurance [system] ... [a]nd a full range of income transfer programs" (Banting 2006, 419–20). The main orientation of these programs was economic security. Unlike in the poor law tradition, however, economic risks were reconceptualized to "confront virtually the entire population," not just the poor, and so "social security programs [were] designed to provide economic security for the population as a whole" (417, 420).

As discussed, the principle of efficiency faces limits in accounting for the development of common protections and universal risk-pooling structures, as well as reasonably generous targeted programs, in situations characterized by diverse and conflicting interests rooted in different socio-economic positions. Instead, significant equality of exposure to risk, and capacity to deal privately with actualized risk, is needed to make universal protections and risk-pooling arrangements efficient. In situations of radical uncertainty, there is convergence between the partial and impartial perspectives such that the imperatives of equality and efficiency overlap – effectively the realization of Rawls's veil of ignorance in the real world (Dryzek and Goodin 1986). Canada, during the expansion of its welfare state, however, was defined by significant class, cultural, and regional barriers to shared interests in inclusive schemes of social protection (Banting 2005; Brodie 2002). There existed, in other words, a lack of solidaristic interests rooted in homogeneous socio-economic experiences and expectations that would make common protections an efficient change from the pre-war status quo. How, then, can the encompassing normative structure of the post-war Canadian welfare state be explained? I suggested above that "altruistic" explanations face significant problems in accounting for the nature of the growth of social policy in Canada. What is needed, then, is an account that sits between self-interested risk pooling and altruism.

In both of those approaches, the welfare state is treated as largely reflective – reflective of either a pre-political confluence of interests or levels of altruistic sentiments. Both pictures, however, sit at odds with the historical conditions of welfare state growth. Rather than reflecting prior unity, the welfare state itself historically has been instrumental in creating a distinctly political sort of solidarity. As Esping-Andersen argues, the welfare state is a unique mechanism of social stratification and can order social relations in different ways that are more or less conducive for grounding support for common protections: "[t]he welfare state is not just a mechanism that intervenes in, and possibly corrects the structure of inequality; it is, in its own right, a system of stratification. It is an active force in ordering social relations" (1990, 23). The key in this process was connecting the welfare state to the idea and character of citizenship. Whereas targeted programs "prevented the generation of social solidarity" (Brodie 2002, 384), and in fact reinforced class-based interests, universal programs, accompanied by the idea of "social rights," have had the effect of diminishing the salience of class-based interests, replacing them with a new shared set of politically defined experiences and expectations attached to equal citizenship.

What social citizenship in effect has accomplished is the creation of a new, distinctly political status quo, or baseline, from which mutual interests in common protections flow from increasingly homogenized risk pools delineated by shared expectations and experiences of economic life. As Brodie puts it, "[s]ocial citizenship rights ... promised a new foundation for building social solidarity in advanced capitalist societies by engaging all citizens in a collective project grounded in state-based assurances of citizens equality" (2002, 378). Social citizenship can be seen to represent a state-led, inefficient alteration of a status quo marked by a conflict of interests to a new political baseline from which the equality of citizenship generates mutual interests that can support common protections. In this sense, the welfare state itself "can be viewed as [an] intervening variable ... on one hand reflecting causal factors such as actions by coalitions of interests groups, and on the other hand potentially having feedback effects on distributive processes via [its] effects on the formation of interests, preferences and coalitions among citizens" (Korpi and Palme 1998, 664). In so doing, social citizenship effectively brings the interests of the advantaged into alignment with the welfare state by crowding out class perspectives and experiences across a range of socio-economic areas by, as T.H. Marshall puts it, "the invasion of the contract by status [and] ... the replacement of the free bargain by the declaration of rights" (1964, 122). This process of linking the welfare state to the shared status of citizenship represents the egalitarian normative logic of the post-war development of the Canadian welfare state.

The development of social citizenship through the expansion of welfare state programs and entitlements has created a new, distinctly political egalitarian baseline by levelling out exposure or vulnerability to risk and uncertainty and the capacity to manage actual occurrences. Over time, this has diminished the salience of interests rooted in class inequality. With a robust conception of social citizenship in place, Marshall argues, the public perceives subsequent equalization measures as "not so much between classes as between individuals within a population which is now treated for this purpose as though it were one class" (1964, 102–3). New interests rooted in the shared experiences and expectations of citizenship lend solidaristic support to the subsequent deepening of common protections. This is a distinct, egalitarian political logic that the state has created in "framing policy in such a way" as to instigate a "two-way process" between institutions and interests where the welfare state can function as a "perpetual motion-machine," organizing the grounds for its own stability (Rothstein 1998, 150–6). Like the public economic model, this approach appeals, in the main, to mutual advantage, but it is egalitarian in the sense that it places justice "prior to efficiency and requires some changes that are not efficient" (Rawls 1999, 69). Once such changes are made, and a more or less egalitarian baseline is consolidated through social citizenship, shared interests rooted in efficiency can offer ongoing support to the relevant institutions and entitlements.

This conception of the egalitarian normativity of the development of Canada's welfare state can be questioned, however, on a number of grounds. One straightforwardly rejects the idea that social citizenship in Canada has made the extensive inroads into reducing market inequalities and other sources of differentiated interests that mark it off from the public economic model. According to this objection, rather than replace the market, the Canadian welfare state has largely functioned to re-enforce it as a source of interests and welfare. This view aligns with Esping-Andersen's categorization of Canada's welfare state under the "liberal" regime type (1990, 41–4). This type, he argues, does not aim to diminish the role of the market in providing welfare and ordering social relations; rather, "the state encourages the market" as the main source of welfare (26). It does so through strict and stigmatizing conditions for "typically modest" benefits, with the result of minimizing the "decommodification effects" of social policy and containing "the realm of social rights, and erect[ing] an order of stratification that is a blend of relative equality of poverty among state-welfare recipients, market-differentiated welfare among the majorities, and a class-political dualism between the two" (26–7).

It is certainly the case that Canadian public social expenditures as a percentage of gross domestic product historically have lagged significantly behind the levels found in the Scandinavian and other western European countries – generally 10–15 percentage points behind at any time since 1960. It is important to note, however, that overall spending levels do not necessarily determine the normative standing of a welfare state, as evidenced most clearly in the case of the high spending levels in continental European countries that, in the main, have had the effect of stabilizing "traditional status relations" (Esping-Andersen 1990, 58). Despite its relatively modest overall spending levels, the Canadian welfare state has been effective in generating "re-distributive impacts" (Banting and Myles 2013, 1). According to a recent study on inequality and social policy by the Organisation for Economic Co-operation and Development, at its peak prior to the beginning of the retrenchment era in the mid-1990s, the "Canadian welfare state was as effective as those in the Nordic countries in stabilizing inequality, offsetting more than 70 percent of the rise in market income inequality" (OECD 2011, 2; see also Banting and Myles 2013). Today that rate is down to about 40 per cent, placing Canada near the bottom in producing a redistributive impact through the welfare state.

A further kind of objection accepts the general thrust of the development of the Canadian welfare state as described above, but objects to characterizing its normative underpinnings as egalitarian in nature. In particular, this line of objection holds that universal insurance and earnings-related forms of the welfare state, by virtue of not directing the bulk of resources towards the poor, are insufficiently redistributive to represent an egalitarian logic. As Brian Barry argues with respect to these constitutive features of the welfare state, the "case for compressing the distribution of income between strata defined by lifetime market-derived incomes is entirely independent of the case for a [universal] welfare state" (1990, 505).

On the face of it, universal social programs appear to have core egalitarian, or redistributive, dimensions by virtue of entitlement to the relevant good or service being based on the right of citizenship, rather than on capacity to pay. This would seem to work against market-based income inequalities in structuring people's life chances and to produce more equitable outcomes than do market distributions. Heath, however, argues that the main form of universal welfare programs is nevertheless insurance, and that using egalitarian norms to explain social insurance is "quite misleading" (2011, 33). Insurance is, in a certain sense, redistributive by virtue of transferring resources from the "lucky to the unlucky." However, because these categories do not necessarily overlap with the better- and worse-off classes, the redistributive logic of insurance programs is "assurentiel," rather than egalitarian (33). Insurance, he argues, is "Pareto-improving ex ante," and subsequent "back-end" transfers are not necessarily progressive or regressive "with respect to income" (33–4). From a redistributive perspective – which holds that the primary function of welfare states is to promote greater equality – this kind of program design, and its "back-end" redistribution, lacks "target efficiency" compared to programs that directly redistribute resources from the better to the worse off.

There are, however, grounds for the view that universal social insurance programs represent an egalitarian normative logic. First, it is important to note the significant degree of "front-end" redistribution in the funding of social programs themselves, to the extent that the relevant tax system is progressive in nature. The egalitarian logic, in this case, takes the form of unequal contributions to a system of equal entitlements. Heath, however, argues that this does not affect the normative logic of social programs themselves: "[t]he way that public health care systems are paid for is redistributive, and progressive with respect to income, but this is a property of the tax system, not the health care system (and the tax system is not a social program, it is the mechanism used to pay for social programs)" (2011, 35). This kind of division between front- and back-end distributive dimensions of social programs is an unnecessarily narrow way of rendering the issue, and prevents consideration of how the different sources of welfare – social programs, the tax system, markets, families – work together. To capture the broader normative thrust of a welfare state, we should think more holistically, using the idea of a "welfare regime" that not only includes those welfare state institutions that are "often associated narrowly with public transfers, in cash or in kind," but that also treats these as "embedded in larger socio-economic orders which promote people's welfare" (Goodin et al. 1999, 5). Taking these institutions as part of a coherent welfare regime allows for theorizing the normative logic of social policy as part of the interworkings of the "larger constellation of socio-economic institutions, policies and programmes all oriented towards promoting people's welfare quite generally. It certainly includes the transfer-oriented welfare state sector … [b]ut it also includes the tax as much as the transfer sector of the public economy" (5).

In addition to the front-end redistribution produced by the progressive funding of universal social programs, a right to social insurance itself can be seen as entitlement to an important resource, or primary good, independent of whether any particular risk is actualized that requires the use of insurance. Access to insurance is of value in itself because of the way it reduces uncertainty and "stabilizes expectations." As Goodin argues, a primary function of the welfare state is to "provide a certain measure of stability to people's economic affairs" (1995, 192).

Stable expectations are of free-standing value to persons by allowing them "to enter into long-term commitments" (201). To the extent that this is so, the universal distribution of insurance as a right of citizenship represents a front-end egalitarian logic, regardless of the extent of progressivity of after-the-event transfers.

A further concern with the "target efficiency" critique of the egalitarian standing of universal programs is that it presumes the level of available resources for social programs is static. The egalitarian recommendation, as such, is to redirect resources away from society as a whole towards the worse off, thereby enhancing target efficiency. The problem with this idea is that program design informs the level of resources available for social spending. As Korpi and Palme argue, the "size of budget available for redistribution is not fixed and … the institutional structures of welfare states are likely to affect the definitions of identify and interests among citizens" (1998, 663). Different forms of social policy, they argue, "can be expected to … encourage or discourage the formation of risk pools with varying degrees of homogeneity in terms of socioeconomically structured distribution of risks and resources" (670). Universal forms of social insurance can lead to the "creation of risk pools within which risks and resources are shared … [and] to delineated risk pools that are more or less homogeneous in terms of risks and resources" (671). In contrast, "the targeted model creates a zero-sum conflict of interests between the poor and the better-off … who must pay for the benefits of the poor without receiving any" (672). The "paradox of redistribution," then, is that, by "providing high-income earners with earnings-related benefits, encompassing social insurance institutions can reduce inequality and poverty more efficiently than can flat-rate or targeted benefits" (681).

Finally, in addition to organizing interests into cross-class solidarity groups in support of common protections, the universal welfare state also contains a moral logic that is egalitarian in nature. Beyond stabilizing existing entitlements, the connection of the welfare state to social citizenship also generates an iterative dynamic that conditions subsequent institutional development. This is a central idea in Marshall's theory of the normative connection between egalitarianism and social citizenship. Citizenship, he argues, is a "principle of equality" that functions as an ideal status "set against structural inequalities" (1964, 112–13). In this respect, the idea of social rights constitutes a normative "target [that] is perpetually moving forward and the state may never be able to get quite within range of it" (115). Nevertheless, consolidated citizenship rights and status can be reiterated in novel areas of social governance, with the effect, as Benhabib puts it, of raising "the threshold of justification to which formerly exclusionary practices are now submitted" (2006, 60).

To summarize, the development of universal social citizenship through the formation of welfare states in the middle decades of the twentieth century reflected a transition from a public economic model to an egalitarian model of state intervention in the economy. Canada's welfare state underwent this process in the development of social policy in the post-war period. In the next section, however, I apply normative ideas of the welfare state derived from political theory to show that the significant changes to the Canadian welfare state during the 1990s were characterized by the disconnection of the welfare state from ideas of social citizenship. As a result, the Canadian welfare state now increasingly reflects the normative logic of the idea of efficiency that characterizes the public economic model.

Disconnecting Citizenship and the Welfare State: The New Normative Logic of the Canadian Welfare State

It is generally accepted that, beginning in the 1990s, the Canadian welfare state began to reverse the trajectory of previous decades and instigate a process often described as "retrenchment." By the end of that decade, the proportion of federal expenditures on social policy was back to the levels of the pre–welfare state era of the 1950s (Brodie 2002, 388). Although certainly important, retrenchment consisted of more than overall spending reductions; it also involved a major rethinking of the role of the state in providing for the welfare of its population and in securing the traditional concept of social citizenship. During this still-ongoing shift in direction, the institutions and justification of the welfare state have become increasingly disconnected from the practices and language of citizenship. As a result, the nature of the experiences and expectations surrounding social risk and uncertainty has become increasingly individuated. This development has led, in turn, to new kinds of increasingly differentiated interests in the kinds and extent of institutional protections against social risk. Taken together these developments have generated a shift away from an egalitarian normative logic of the Canadian welfare state to one that is increasingly modelled along the lines of the public economic model.

The changing nature of the politics of the Canadian welfare state began in the early 1990s with a series of policy changes, which in a short time were accompanied by new kinds of justificatory ideas and norms. These programmatic changes included "virtually every program with … direct implications for labour market performance [that were] restructured in important ways reducing the level of economic security" (Banting 2006, 424). Notably, the unemployment insurance program underwent significant changes that lowered the replacement rate (from 66 per cent in 1971 to 50 per cent by 1996) and duration of eligibility while raising eligibility conditions and increasing clawbacks of benefits through taxation (425). For many observers, however, the change that was most emblematic of the new politics of the Canadian welfare state concerned the core piece of social citizenship in Canada: the health care system. In 1995 the federal government introduced the Canada Health and Social Transfer (CHST). As Brodie puts it, the CHST "effectively reduced the federal government's participation in social policy to the transfer of block funds to the provinces' consolidated revenue funds" (2002, 388) with essentially no strings attached, often ending in tax cuts rather than reinvestment in social policy institutions.

To get a handle on the cumulative effect of the range of changes made to the welfare state over the past three decades on its underpinning normative structure, I look at four major areas of programmatic and discoursive social policy developments – universal programs, income-support programs, the new direction of Canadian social policy, and the changing social policy discourse – which, taken with decreasing progressivity in the tax system, reflect a general shift away from an egalitarian normative model that links the welfare state to social citizenship to one more consistent with the public economic model of increasingly salient inequality of exposure to socio-economic risk and uncertainty.

Changes to universal programs

A widely supported claim in the literature on welfare state reform is that universal programs are less prone to retrenchment than are targeted programs (Pierson 1994). This is broadly consistent with the argument above concerning the role of social citizenship in generating new kinds of experiences and expectations rooted in shared-risk pools. However, although the respective cores of universal health and pension programs have remained stable, the margins of these programs have undergone notable policy "drift." Both of these trends are consistent with an emerging public economic normative logic. The preserved core attends to the nature of the relevant risks and the significant levels of uncertainty – such as incurring catastrophic illness or outliving one's savings – that makes basic insurance structures in these areas efficient. Drift at the margins reflects differing levels of uncertainty regarding non-catastrophic risks based on market differentiation and the capacity privately to manage such risks and needs.

In the case of health care, while stable, the relative scope of the core of the single-payer system has shrunk significantly: from covering 60 per cent of the health care system in 1975, it had fallen to below 40 per cent by 2012 (Tuohy 2013, 293). Technological and demographic changes mean that drug and long-term care take up increasing amounts of health care spending. Public interventions in these areas of health policy have not extended the universal approach, however, but have been uneven and non-redistributive. This is consistent with a move towards the public economic model, and reflects the significant labour-market-position-based differentiation of persons with respect to these risks – particularly between those with and without employer-based drug plans – and the barriers this presents to developing common protections.

The core of the universal pension programs – the CPP, OAS, and Guaranteed Income Supplement – similarly has remained stable, although with some recent moves towards retrenchment in raising the OAS eligibility age from sixty-five to sixty-seven. This, too, is consistent with expectations under the public economic model, given the radical unpredictability of people's lifespan, which makes basic levels of common protections efficient. As with health care, there has been drift around the margins of the pension system away from an egalitarian logic. Of note is that the decline in workplace pensions has not been met by an expansion of the universal public pension. Rather, public funds increasingly go to supporting private individualized retirement programs, re-enforcing, rather than crowding out, the market as a source of welfare and interest formation (Banting and Myles 2013).

Changes to income-support programs

Income-support programs have also been transformed in ways consistent with the transition to a public economic model. These programs never became encompassing institutions by which the middle and upper classes were brought into citizenship-based risk pools with the disadvantaged. As a result, programs targeted towards the unemployed and otherwise marginalized members of society have undergone significant retrenchment. In the case of employment insurance (EI), benefit levels have been substantially reduced, while eligibility conditions have been tightened. In the decade from the late 1980s to the late 1990s, the share of unemployed Canadians receiving EI fell from 80 per cent to 40 per cent (Banting and Myles 2013, 22), while, over roughly the same period, the replacement rate dropped from 66 per cent to 50 per cent (Banting 2006, 425). These changes are consistent with the public economic model, given the increasingly differentiated labour market positions and degrees of uncertainty about future employment prospects in post-industrial economies (Vosko 2000), and reflect the interest of advantaged persons in not pooling the risk of unemployment with those in precarious sectors of the labour market. This is evidenced in part by policy inaction in response to the changing nature of employment in Canada, defined by part-time and contract-limited forms of work that remain outside the EI program.

If the heightened salience of risk differentiation in the case of temporary unemployment has led to the retrenchment of EI, the case is even more pronounced in non-contributory forms of social assistance. In 1995 the Canada Assistance Plan was abolished and replaced by diminished block grant transfers to the provinces. This led to retrenchment politics across the country, characterized by intensified conditionality (such as workfare policies), heightened eligibility conditions, and benefit reductions. The ease with which governments pursued these changes is consistent with what would be expected under the public economic model, assuming a highly differentiated baseline relative to the relevant risks, with the advantaged lacking any strong interest in generous, non-stigmatizing social assistance programs, and perceiving them as redistributive, not mutually advantageous.

The nature of new social policy

The nature of new social policy making during the retrenchment era of the Canadian welfare state is consistent with the public economic model, and exhibits little interest in connecting social policy to the rights of citizenship, as per the egalitarian conception. Two predominant trends indicate this new normative direction in Canadian social policy. The first is the nature of new social policy itself, which reflects, and re-enforces, an unequal baseline rooted in differentiated market positions, rather than attempting to replace it with the shared interests of citizenship. The result is policies that reflect individuated mitigation of risk. One example is the new policies in the area of retirement income that encourage private savings, rather than strengthening universal risk pools. The development and expansion of Tax-Free Savings Accounts is a strong indication of the new social policies' rootedness in market-determined interests in a stratified society.

The other trend indicative of the rise of public economic norms in the Canadian welfare state is the absence of new social policies designed to pool and mitigate new kinds of socio-economic risks and inequalities. In a very real sense, the federal government in recent decades essentially has abandoned the field of social citizenship, and increasingly linked welfare provision to the private sphere (individuals and families) (Brodie 2002, 388). Two policy areas demonstrate that social policy has failed to keep up with the changing nature of socio-economic risk and needs in Canadian society. One is child care policy, where the decline of the so-called male breadwinner model, or the family wage, and the rise of two- or single-parent working households have not been addressed with the creation of a universal public child care system. This reflects the lack of an interest on the part of those who can provide child care through either family or privately funded arrangements in pooling child care–related costs with those who lack this capacity and have an interest in public provision. A second social policy failure concerns the challenges to health care posed by changing technologies and demographics. Although the single-payer system has remained more or less stable in its current form (universal insurance for hospital and physician services), it has not kept pace with growing areas of health care costs, such as pharmaceuticals or long-term care. As a result, the single-payer system covers a third less of total health care expenditures today than it did in the 1970s (Tuohy 2013, 286). The rise of private and mixed-financed approaches to health care coverage is consistent with the shift away from a citizenship model to the public economic model in conditions of market-differentiated individual capacities to deal with health risks and uncertainties.

Changing social policy discourse

In addition to programmatic changes, the new politics of the Canadian welfare state has also been characterized by changes to the discourse surrounding social policy that are similarly consistent with the public economic model. Because of the increasing salience of exposure and the capacity to mitigate risk privately, to be seen as efficient, and to garner the support of advantaged persons, social policy must be justified on grounds other than mutually advantageous risk pooling. In other words, advantageously situated persons in market relations must be seen to have an interest in social policy from which they have little or no expectation of ever directly benefiting.

Most notable in this regard is the rise of rhetoric surrounding the idea of the "social investment" or the "enabling" state. Rather than providing welfare directly to persons, the social investment state contributes to persons' "human capital" and capacity to provide for their welfare through market participation. The rise of the human capital discourse has attended the decline of the "social security" discourse that characterized the post-war expansion of the Canadian welfare state (Marsh [1943] 1975). It reflects an attempt to insert the idea of mutual advantage into social policy discourse in an era in which social security programs are not seen as mutually advantageous but as redistributive. All persons have a presumptive interest in the social investment state, in contrast to the redistributive welfare state. The advantaged benefit from social policy that invests in the human capital of the disadvantaged by virtue of the enhanced contribution of human capital to the overall productivity and global competitiveness of the economy. They also benefit from its enabling of persons to (re)join the labour force and provide for their own welfare, rather than being dependent on public support. As Banting puts it, the new discourse surrounding social policy reconceptualizes social security from "security as protection from change to security as capacity to change" (2006, 422). As such the human capital discourse has been accompanied by other norms related to labour market activation as the prime source of welfare, such as the supposed moral hazard of unconditional support, and imposed conditionality on benefit entitlement, such as workfare policies.

Conclusion

Through using an applied political theory approach, this chapter has illustrated that the Canadian welfare state has become unmoored from the status of citizenship. This has been the result of policy change, policy neglect, and changing justificatory ideas for new social policy. As a result, the welfare state is playing a new role in structuring social relations, in which risks have been depooled and interests have been reorganized to reflect market-differentiated positions. The connection of the welfare state to citizenship effectively produced cross-class solidaristic interests in support of common protections. The now-ongoing disconnection is undoing these political sources of solidarity, and creating new barriers to the wide support of common protections. The politics of welfare state reform in Canada offer the lesson that the condition of citizenship is crucial to the prospects for social justice.

REFERENCES

Baldwin, Peter. 1990. *The Politics of Solidarity*. Cambridge: Cambridge University Press. https://doi.org/10.1017/CBO9780511586378

Banting, Keith. 2005. "Canada: Nation-Building in a Federal Welfare State." In *Federalism and the Welfare State: New World and European Experiences*, ed. Herbert Obinger, Stephan Leibfried, and Francis G. Castles, 89–137. Cambridge: Cambridge University Press.

Banting, Keith. 2006. "Disembedding Liberalism? The New Social Policy Paradigm in Canada." In *Dimensions of Inequality in Canada*, ed. David A. Green and Jonathan R. Kesselman, 417–52. Vancouver: UBC Press.

Banting, Keith, and John Myles. 2013. "Introduction." In *Inequality and the Fading of Redistributive Politics*, ed. Keith Banting and John Myles. Vancouver: UBC Press.

Barr, Nicholas. 2012. *The Economics of the Welfare State*. 5th ed. Oxford: Oxford University Press.

Barry, Brian. 1990. "The Welfare State Versus the Relief of Poverty." *Ethics* 100 (3): 503–29. https://doi.org/10.1086/293208

Benhabib, Seyla. 2006. *Another Cosmopolitanism*. Oxford: Oxford University Press. https://doi.org/10.1093/acprof:oso/9780195183221.001.0001

Brodie, Janine. 2002. "Citizenship and Solidarity." *Citizenship Studies* 6 (4): 377–94. https://doi.org/10.1080/1362102022000041231

Dryzek, John, and Robert E. Goodin. 1986. "Risk Sharing and Social Justice: The Motivational Foundations of the Post-War Welfare State." *British Journal of Political Science* 16 (1): 1–34. https://doi.org/10.1017/S0007123400003781

Dworkin, Ronald. 2002. *Sovereign Virtue*. Cambridge, MA: Harvard University Press.

Elster, Jon. 1987. "Comment on Van der Veen and Van Parijs." *Theory and Society* 15 (4): 709–21.

Esping-Andersen, Gosta. 1990. *The Three Worlds of Welfare Capitalism*. Princeton, NJ: Princeton University Press.

Goodin, Robert. 1988. *Reasons for Welfare*. Princeton, NJ: Princeton University Press.

Goodin, Robert. 1995. *Utilitarianism as a Public Philosophy*. Cambridge: Cambridge University Press. https://doi.org/10.1017/CBO9780511625053

Goodin, Robert, Bruce Headey, Ruud Muffels, and Henk-Jan Dirven. 1999. *The Real Worlds of Welfare Capitalism*. Oxford: Oxford Univeristy Press. https://doi.org/10.1017/CBO9780511490927

Heath, Joseph. 2006. "The Benefits of Cooperation." *Philosophy & Public Affairs* 34 (4): 313–51. https://doi.org/10.1111/j.1088-4963.2006.00073.x

Heath, Joseph. 2011. "Three Normative Models of the Welfare State." *Public Reason* 3 (2): 13–43.

Kidal, Nanna, and Stein Kuhnle. 2005. "Introduction." In *Normative Foundations of the Welfare State: The Nordic Experience*, ed. Nanna Kidal and Stein Kuhnle, 1–10. London: Routledge.

Korpi, Walter, and Joakim Palme. 1998. "The Paradox of Redistribution and Strategies of Equality: Welfare State Institutions, Inequality, and Poverty in the Western Countries." *American Sociological Review* 63 (5): 661–87. https://doi.org/10.2307/2657333

Marsh, Leonard. [1943] 1975. *Report on Social Security in Canada*. Toronto: University of Toronto Press.

Marshall, T.H. 1964. *Class, Citizenship and Social Development*. New York: Doubleday.

Miller, David. 2006. "Multiculturalism and the Welfare State: Theoretical Reflections." In *Multiculturalism and the Welfare State: Recognition and Redistribution in Contemporary Democracies*, ed. Will Kymlicka and Keith Banting, 323–38. Oxford: Oxford University Press. https://doi.org/10.1093/acprof:oso/9780199289172.003.0012

Myles, John. 1998. "How to Design a 'Liberal' Welfare State: A Comparison of Canada and the United States." *Social Policy and Administration* 32 (4): 341–64. https://doi.org/10.1111/1467-9515.00120

Olsen, Gregg. 1994. "Locating the Canadian Welfare State: Family Policy and Health Care in Canada, Sweden, and the United States." *Canadian Journal of Sociology* 19 (1): 1–20. https://doi.org/10.2307/3341235

OECD (Organisation for Economic Co-operation and Development). 2011. "Divided We Stand: Why Inequality Keeps Rising." *Country Note*. Paris: OECD Publishing.

Pierson, Paul. 1994. *Dismantling the Welfare State?* Cambridge, MA: Harvard University Press.

Polanyi, Karl. [1944] 2001. *The Great Transformation*. Boston: Beacon Press.

Rawls, John. 1999. *A Theory of Justice*. Rev. ed. Cambridge, MA: Harvard University Press.

Rothstein, Bo. 1998. *Just Institutions Matter: The Moral and Political Logic of the Universal Welfare State*. Cambridge: Cambridge University Press. https://doi.org/10.1017/CBO9780511598449

Sen, Amartya. 1970. *Collective Choice and Social Welfare*. New York: Holden Day.

Sen, Amartya. 2009. *The Idea of Justice*. Cambridge, MA: Harvard University Press.

Titmuss, Richard. 1971. *The Gift Relationship: From Human Blood to Social Policy*. New York: George Allen and Unwin.

Tuohy, Caroline Hughes. 2013. "Health Care Policy after Universality." In *Inequality and the Fading of Redistributive Politics*, ed. Keith Banting and John Myles, 285–311. Vancouver: UBC Press.

Vosko, Leah. 2000. *Temporary Work: The Gendered Rise of Precarious Labour*. Toronto: University of Toronto Press. https://doi.org/10.3138/9781442680432

Walzer, Michael. 1983. *Spheres of Justice: A Defense of Pluralism and Equality*. Princeton, NJ: Princeton University Press.

Weale, Albert. 1983. *Political Theory and Social Policy*. New York: St Martin's Press.

Weale, Albert. 1990. "Equality, Social Solidarity and the Welfare State." *Ethics* 100 (3): 473–88. https://doi.org/10.1086/293206

Wolff, Jo. 1998. "Fairness, Respect and the Egalitarian Ethos." *Philosophy & Public Affairs* 27 (2): 97–122. https://doi.org/10.1111/j.1088-4963.1998.tb00063.x

6 "How We Treat Our Women Is Our Business!": Legal Pluralism's Impact on Women's Citizenship in Federations

JILL VICKERS

This chapter explores the concept of *legal pluralism* and its impact on women's citizenship in federations, including Canada's. In its 2011 report, UN Women maintained that discriminatory family law is the greatest barrier to equality women face worldwide and is highly correlated with legal pluralism: the presence of two or more legal codes in a country (UN Women 2011). Legal pluralism is a basic design feature of, and constitutionally sanctioned in, federations. Moreover, proponents of federalism think it promotes equity by giving minority nations some measure of self-rule, and enhances democracy by letting "local" communities govern "moral issues," which is how most of them categorize family law. But gender scholars point to the fragmentation of women's citizenship that results from legal pluralism, a danger for both majority- and minority-culture women if it denies the universality and human rights status of women's rights. For feminists the main issue involves the ethics of women's rights and the allocation of benefits according to where they live. Where family law reform is part of a minority nation's claim to self-rule, central governments might deny women security when community leaders claim that "how we treat our women is our business." But in other cases, women's rights have become part of minority communities' or nations' progressive agendas for gaining greater autonomy. Some central governments are willing to oversee how legal pluralism affects women, but they lack the capacity; as well, a major barrier is the degree of diversity and resulting conflict in the federation.

This chapter takes a methodological approach that combines applied political theory and normative analysis to focus on theories of federalism and the effects of legal pluralism on women's citizenship. I draw ideas from contemporary political theorists of federalism, gender/federalism scholarship, and feminist theorists' critiques of federalism. I then combine theoretical and normative reflections with statistical evidence drawn from WomanStats, a database that rates family law equitability across many countries (see Watts 1996). Starting with analyses of the Canadian federation is useful because the case includes close comparisons of majority- and minority-nation women's perspectives on various aspects of federations. Scrutiny of feminists' loyalties to Quebec nationalism, for example, shows that minority women are more likely to view legal pluralism favourably, while majority – that is, English-Canadian – feminists consider it a negative feature. But federations take different forms mainly depending on the extent of their diversity and the resulting conflict they must manage. Comparing such differences within a single federation raises interesting theoretical, normative, and empirical puzzles, but comparisons across federations of different types, and between federations and unitary states, are necessary to generate new theories.

As the prism through which to explore these puzzles, I chose family law: the rules and legal doctrines that shape *gender regimes*, the rules governing sex/gender relations in both the public and private spheres. Indeed, the UN Women report asserts that "inequality in the family is the most damaging of forces in women's lives, underlying all other aspects of discrimination and disadvantage" (UN Women 2011, 3). This makes the reform of family law necessary for women to be full citizens. In their seventy-country study, Htun and Weldon (2012) find that discriminatory family law is strongly correlated with legal pluralism, as well as with high levels of violence against women (Hudson, Bowen, and Nielsen 2011). Family law thus can help focus attention on the divide between the public and private spheres: the metaphor that underlies all western political theory and marks the "proper" limits of state power according to liberal theory, and continues to deny women full citizenship long after they have gained the right to vote. Within an applied political theory framework, we find that legal pluralism helps preserve the public/private divide – indeed family law reforms often require redrawing or eliminating the metaphoric divide, as in the slogan "the personal is political," which grounds feminist theories.

In federations, legal pluralism may be territorial or non-territorial: territorial when a national minority community (such as Quebec francophones) govern a regional unit in which it (currently) is the majority; non-territorial when communities or nations that are not territorially organized have more limited forms of self-rule. In India and Malaysia, non-territorial pluralism involves personal status codes legislated by central governments to regulate the family affairs of larger, minority cultural/ religious communities wherever their members live. There is some self-rule because the content of the legislated rules is provided by minority religious/ traditional authorities. These categories do not always fit concrete cases, however – for example, Canada's First Nations make both territorial and non-territorial claims to govern both on- and off-reserve members. Difficult questions arise, such as if Canada's Charter of Rights and Freedoms applies on First Nation territories, while to non-Indigenous Canadians the concept of "Aboriginal multilevel governance" is a recent addition to the discourse.

Since leaders of cultural minority communities or nations often consider family relations central to how they reproduce their populations and identities, they also consider control of family law important to the preservation of self-rule. To preserve traditional practices, community leaders often claim the right to control women's behaviour, assuming a passivity that no longer accords with many women's lives as they assert their agency in both private and public affairs. Using applied political theory, we can see that this claim reveals some of the normative questions raised by legal pluralism, and illustrates the difficulty of balancing minorities' rights to *self-rule* with the need for *shared rule* and the state's capacity to manage diversity-promoted conflicts effectively. The issues also highlight conflicts between collective and individual rights, especially in very diverse federations. UN Women maintains that legal pluralism obstructs the reform of family law needed for women's full citizenship. The effects of legal pluralism depend on the types used, how power is divided, and central governments' capacity and willingness to reform discriminatory family laws. The extent to which legal pluralism produces negative outcomes for women depends on how diverse a federation is (Vickers 2013a, 2013b, 2014), how much conflict it has, and how effectively the conflict is managed. Consequently legal pluralism produces more negative outcomes for women in very diverse federations than in their mono-national counterparts – that is, in federations with just one national identity – making the reform of family law harder. So, where diversity and conflict are extensive, central governments will be under more pressure to federalize their institutions – for example, by creating new regional (or local) governments and/or institutions and devolving more powers to them. This makes the central government's regulation of legal pluralism more politically "costly" and likely making them less willing to act.

In the United States, the first modern federation, family law was assigned to state governments, supported by an ideology of "localism" that valorized the importance of local communities controlling so-called "moral" relations within and between families that, until the 1860s, included slaves. In Canada, in contrast, the central government was assigned responsibility for regulating marriage and divorce, although the provinces have authority for the administrative arrangements, ceremonies, and courts involved. Nonetheless legal pluralism exists in Canada regarding other aspects of family law, notably Quebec's civil law and the federal *Indian Act*. More recently formed federations usually are more diverse and conflictual, and their central governments retain concurrent legislative control over most aspects of family law; moreover, in most civil law federations, family law is centrally or concurrently controlled.

This chapter conceptualizes three types of federation from the least to the most diverse – namely, *(mono) national*, *multinational*, and *very diverse*. Although the extent of diversity and conflict might change over time, "conflict management" remains a key goal of federal governments. For example, after partition, India's central government reorganized its states around language, while also adopting non-territorial form of legal pluralism to manage "personal status" codes for larger religious minorities. Similarly, after the civil war that resulted from Biafra's attempt to secede, the Nigerian central government created many new regional states, and devolved responsibility for aspects for family law to them and to some local governments. All types of federations have territorial legal pluralism resulting from the division of powers; however, very diverse federations also have non-territorial forms.

Federations are both societal and institutional phenomena – which one might call "federal arrangements" – as well as an ideology of governance. A major question feminists and gender scholars ask is if "federalism" is "good" or "bad" for women. Empirical evidence from many federations suggests that the answer depends on conditions such as the diversity and conflict the federation faces. In federations with a single national identity and no strong territorial minorities pressing for federalization, autonomous women's movements can take advantage of multiple levels by moving from "unfriendly" to "women-friendly" governments. In multinational federations such as Canada, however, territorial minorities (for example, in Quebec and Nunavut) make "national" claims and demand more powers for their regional government. Feminist movements might align with regional nationalists and "piggyback" their claims for gender reforms onto collective claims for self-rule or even independence. For example, francophone feminists supported Quebec's (unsuccessful) demand that all aspects of family law be devolved to it so that a unified family policy could be created around Quebec's civil code. They also supported the (successful) devolution of social programs to Quebec to promote nation building – notably, programs aimed at women, such as better parental leave and inexpensive child care – which created a greater social citizenship than women in other provinces enjoyed.

Therefore, feminists' views about legal pluralism tend to vary according to their location, since being part of a majority or minority nation reflects different relationships to central and regional governments. The francophone feminist movement became aligned with Quebec nationalism, judging that a modern nationalist government would be more progressive on gender issues and more open to their influence. In the 1970s and early 1980s, in contrast, English-Canadian feminists considered the central government more progressive and open to their influence, a relationship then disrupted by the Mulroney government. Nonetheless, the treatment of Quebec women before 1960 shows that decisions about such alliances are specific to the time and to the gender ideology dominant in the period. The nationalism that present-day Quebec promotes is inclusive, leading feminists to support greater self-rule for "their" regional government – even independence, despite women's usual aversion to risky political ventures. But many gender scholars consider central governments more progressive on gender issues because they are more open to international or transnational agencies, whereas regional governments are seen as less progressive and more easily captured by those who oppose reforms.

Legal pluralism, therefore, tends to create higher risks for women because regional governments are often insulated from progressive international organizations. The effectiveness of international regimes also depends, however, on rules governing the mechanisms to implement rights accords. In Nigeria, for example, family law reform was blocked because, although the central government signed on to the *Convention for the Elimination of All Kinds Discrimination Against Women* (CEDAW), its rules and norms were not "domesticated" through the passage of laws. In 2006, efforts to "domesticate" CEDAW failed to pass Nigeria's state-dominated Senate. In Australia, by contrast, the central government may occupy fields the constitution assigns to state governments simply by signing treaties in those fields.

The chapter has five sections. The first draws insights from feminist theory to examine how family law affects women's citizenship in federations. I then explore the role of legal pluralism both in "federalism" as an ideology of governance and in relation to "federal arrangements" – that is, institutions, practices, and discourses. In the third section I examine different types of legal pluralism, and in section four I consider UN Women's claims about the effects of discriminatory family law. Consistent with an applied political theory approach, in the final section I test the chapter's proposition about the theorized effects of legal pluralism using data regarding family law reform from the Womanstat Project.

Why Family Law?

Although the problems women encounter when attempting to reform family law should be part of normative political theory, political theorists rarely consider them in relation to citizenship because they assume the same rules apply to everyone in a nation-state. Although many feminist theorists think women relate to the state differently as a status group, this does not account for the different experiences of, for example, women in majority and minority cultures and nations, which result from the conflict produced by diversity, including conflicts over family law reform. For example, Boko Haram's kidnapping of hundreds of Nigerian schoolgirls and the Taliban's attacks on Pakistani schoolgirls are part of campaigns to stop the spread of girls' education. Indeed many cases involve resistance to new gender regimes (Vickers 2011a, 2011b, 2013b) and efforts to block the development of more effective citizenship for women. Family law may apply to everyone within geographic boundaries (territorial) or to members of cultural communities (non-territorial) anywhere they live. Very diverse federations (India, Nigeria) have multiple codes: territorial for the dominant cultural/religious group, and personal status codes for large minorities.

Family law regulates relations between the sexes, sexualities, and generations; specifies gender roles, rights, and responsibilities; governs the transmission of family property; and specifies "appropriate" relations within the family. It also governs children's legitimacy and permitted marriage partners. Glendon (1989) theorizes that family law originated in the rules religious, clan, and tribal leaders used to maintain their communities' boundaries by controlling women's sexual and reproductive partners, targeting women's conduct because it was easier to control than men's.[1] Joseph (2000, 16) notes that, where citizenship is based on kinship and blood ties, especially if conferred by regional communities, "family law [is] crucial to citizenship law and practices" and "a critical site in the struggle between feminists, nationalists and state builders." Htun and Weldon (2012, 2–3) theorize that "family law provisions … reflect the history of state formation, particularly … bargains over the … extent of public power" in conflict between "traditionalists" and "modernists," competing nationalists or both.

A federation's family law often predates the federation in origins – for example, the English common law that governs former British colonies is over a thousand years old. The common law doctrine of *coverture* legitimized practices that denied married women economic, political, and most civil rights until governments passed laws to nullify many of its effects, but some persist. Federations in Europe and South America are governed by civil law codes and doctrines derived from Roman law, which generally assign family law to the central government. Quebec and Louisiana both have versions of civil law, exercised under federal supervision. In both common and civil law, the legal concept of "privacy" insulates family relations, including male dominance, from state intervention and public justice. But it also insulates governments from kinship demands. Many gender scholars (such as Motiejunaite 2005) think the public/private divide that "privatizes" family relations denies women full access to the public sphere – the site of citizenship. In the nineteenth century, legal pluralism was effective in imposing regional moral codes because populations were not very mobile. But in the twentieth century, increasing mobility created major problems. For example, in the United States, marriage and divorce were under state control for almost two centuries, supported by the ideology of *localism* as a way of governing gender regimes and moral codes. Legal pluralism caused problems when people divorced and remarried in one state, moved, and were even jailed for "bigamous cohabitation" by another state that refused to honour the first state's more progressive divorce laws. Publicity about such cases in the United States led Canadian and Australian founders to make divorce the responsibility of their central governments.

1 Mark Tilse (2011, 94–134) explains how the Prussian state's "Germanization" policies of 1871–1914 aimed to restrict sex and marriage between Germans and Poles.

Women eventually gained political and civil rights, but the public/ private divide remains a part of constitutional divisions of power that let (some) communities retain "traditional" family law while the central government facilitates a modern economy with secular rules. Hueglin and Fenna (2007, 166–7) theorize that federations resulted from "a compromise between modernizers [wanting] … common economic space and 'social traditionalists' who would accept a modern economy only if "there was no attempt to impose … cultural uniformity." This often denied married women a direct relationship with and protection from central governments – a consequence that persists in some cases. Family law reform remains the focus of conflict between those who want a society based on individual rights and those who support customary or religious law, or nationalism based on collective rights. The international rights revolution that began in the 1950s and intensified when the Cold War ended has promoted both individual gender and communal rights. This often put advocates of the two on a collision course over family law reform as feminist activism surged. Politicized religion and the release of small, long-encapsulated nations within larger states also made family law reform central to many conflicts.

Reform of family law is an important part of the process of achieving gender equality. As noted, "inequality in the family … [is] the most damaging of all forces in women's lives, underlying all other aspects of discrimination and disadvantage" (UN Women 2011, 3), and legal pluralism is a major barrier to its reform in most federations. But the negative outcomes of legal pluralism are reduced when central governments regulate regional laws (Vickers 2012, 2013b). One approach is to "domesticate" provisions of international gender equality regimes such as CEDAW by incorporating them into the federation's constitution so that they "trump" ordinary laws. Legal pluralism's effect on family law reform depends on its type in specific federations and on the central government's *ability* and *willingness* to regulate the actions of regional governments. That willingness, in turn, will be inflected by government ideology, its support for or resistance to localism, and how it conceptualizes rights. The more diverse the federation the more conflict there is in reforming family law. Moreover, multiple codes make reform pragmatically harder to achieve – for example, it was easier to reform laws to permit same-sex marriage in Canada than in the United States because in Canada the federal government is responsible for laws governing marriage (Smith 2008). Central governments are more likely to have the capacity to overrule regional governments in older federations, while great diversity and multiple forms of legal pluralism might undercut this capacity. Moreover, claims by regional governments that they are entitled to regulate moral affairs as part of self-rule might lessen central governments' willingness to overrule them.

For women, effective citizenship depends on freedom and equal authority in the private sphere, supported by non-discriminatory family law (UN Women 2011). Marshall (1950, 28) defined citizenship as "a status bestowed on those who are full members of a community," but clearly women were not full members of any federation despite having gained the right to vote. Lister (2003) theorizes citizenship as a combination of rights and participation, animated by agency; but for this, women require self-determination in the private sphere and social adulthood in the public sphere.

Support for women's privatization has diminished with changes in political culture, the rise of human rights doctrines, and reduced tolerance for legal pluralism when rights are involved. Fenna (2011, 15) argues that "feminism's focus on universal rights … [puts it] at odds with … federalism's premise that local communities should … constitute and reproduce their own identities through control … of the social and cultural rules that determine how these rights will be defined and exercised." Many federalists consider that family law involves matters of morality and the collective rights of minority communities/nations, not matters of individual rights. But governments' efforts to regulate the sexual and reproductive behaviour of individual citizens' have declined, and to many, especially feminists, no longer seem justified. To federalists, however, this sanctions legal pluralism and privatization.

Feminists' views on legal pluralism differ: majority-culture women often oppose it along with other federal principles and practices (Gray 2010), and favour strong central governments willing and able to defend women's rights, provide uniform social benefits, and enact a reformed family law code as part of shared rule. Such *autonomous* women's movements act independently of governments, parties and other movements to represent the identities and interests of women of the dominant culture, although they claim to represent "women" as a status group. Especially in multinational federations, however, *aligned* women's movements often work with nationalist governments or movements to represent minority-culture women. Those with enough clout to have their own regional government usually also want their own family laws and social programs consistent their nation's or community's values. Moreover, minority women generally support federal arrangements that deliver self-rule. This allows gender equality to be enacted in ways consistent with women's national or communal identity and way of life, so long as they consider "their" regional government more women-friendly than the central government. Multinational federations usually have both autonomous and aligned women's movements; in very diverse federations, however, women's organizing usually is less coherent, with some co-opted organizations, such as women's wings of ruling parties, while others align with opposition groups. In Malaysia, for example, competition between Malay and minority nationalist parties has made participation by the Women's Wing of the United Malays National Organization necessary for Malay political dominance to be maintained. Although this promoted Malay women's formal citizenship, for a long period they lacked the autonomy and political agency needed for full citizenship. Where there are multiple women's movements, they must cooperate to achieve family law reforms. But where there are multiple forms of legal pluralism, as in Nigeria, the diversity and conflict they produce are especially hard to manage.

"Federalism" and Legal Pluralism

Most historical models of federalism are static and can't explain interactions between their institutional and discursive aspects over time. The applied political theory framework used in this chapter combines insights from feminist institutionalism (Krook and Mackay 2010) with an original typology based on the extent of diversity in federations, the conflict it produces, how this changes over time, and how such conflict is managed. It also focuses on the federalization of institutions and discourses in the non-democratic periods many federations go through as they develop into democratic federations.[2] Elazar (1987) theorizes that federalism must combine shared- and self-rule. Kincaid (2010b, 218) considers the essential purpose of dividing power as protecting "the right of constituent communities ... to govern themselves in all matters of local relevance and to maintain their ways of life." Consequently, federalism combines *self-rule* for regional and minority-nation interests and *shared rule* for general/common purposes. So, for federalists, legal

2 As in most comparative federalism scholarship, I do not consider failed federations in this chapter.

pluralism is an essential mechanism for self-rule and more important than women's individual rights.

Federations have four essential design features. First, sovereignty is divided between central and regional governments, manifested through varying divisions of power. Second, each level governs citizens directly. Third, each government must control at least one major jurisdiction, and no regional government nor its (formal) powers can be eliminated or changed without its consent. In some cases (India, Mexico, Nigeria), the powers of local governments are also constitutionally protected. In practice, however, most policy fields are concurrently exercised in ways citizens find confusing. In some mono-national federations (Argentina, Austria, Germany), central governments legislate a policy framework that regional governments administer. In others (Australia, the United States) and in multinational federations (Belgium, Canada), both central and regional government legislate and administer their own laws, although central governments' superior resources let them shape regional policies. In very diverse federations, the central government often alternates between dictatorships and weak democracies, with power highly centralized in the former and more decentralized in the latter. Fourth, all federations require a written constitution that specifies how powers will be divided, how central government institutions will be organized, how the constitution can be amended, and which institution will serve as referee in disputes between governments or interpret the meaning of constitutional provisions. Intergovernmental relations (IGRs) modify formal arrangements through negotiations or informal institutions. The less conflict there is in a federation the more it is possible to institutionalize such relations, making IGRs more accessible and open.

Watts (2005, 324) theorizes that "processes by which federations are established affect the formal distribution of powers." In federations combining previous states or colonies (Australia, the United States), the powers associated with social functioning, including family law, usually stay under regional control as they are still considered part of the private sphere. Feminist constitutional theorist Helen Irving (2008, 65) maintains that, "as a constitutional model … [federalism] has a major impact on women's lives." In earlier studies Vickers (2010, 2011a, 2011b) maintains that the impact is two-way, because some organized women's efforts to *regender* federal arrangements have succeeded. Based on observations about the achievement of gender equality reforms before and after the Charter of Rights and Freedoms was incorporated in the

Canadian Constitution, she suggests that opportunities exist most often when constitutions are being restructured. Baines and Rubio-Marin (2005, 12) think that the effect of conditions surrounding a federation's formation is evident in its division of powers, notably in the "allocat[ion of] 'private matters' to the regional entities." Irving (2008, 65, 68) also believes that the law of central governments "commonly … trumps state law" because "the scope of 'the national' has enlarged." But for central governments to trump regional governments, they must intervene in matters many consider "private." In very diverse federations (Brazil, Nigeria), inchoate party systems and weak central governments often make such interventions virtually impossible. But as party systems and IGRs become more institutionalized and central power increases, this might change. Even in a mono-national federation such as Argentina, family law reform associated with abortion and contraception has been blocked by powerful religious authorities.

Some federalists believe that imposing a uniform, federation-wide law on *moral* issues – matters of right and wrong argued on first principles, not on expertise or evidence – would "greatly reduce aggregate social welfare" (Baker 2001, 441). For Baker it is just to allow local communities to enact diverse laws in "areas of … moral disagreement" because it conforms with the right of self-rule on "moral issues" – which many federalists consider a basic principle of federalism. Kincaid (2010a, 38) suggests that federal democracies use legal pluralism "to balance individual and communitarian identities and liberties," and to permit appropriate responses to regions' diverse needs. But over half the issues he considers legitimate for "moral disagreement," self-rule, and legal pluralism relate to reproductive and sexual freedom, gender equality, and women's rights. Federalists claim that legal pluralism promotes "democracy" because it lets local communities dissent from centrally-enacted gender-equality provisions when "morality" is involved – even provisions sanctioned by countrywide majorities. Mooney (2001) argues that it is "democratic" to allow local communities to determine how to reproduce their families, perpetuate their identities, and preserve their traditions.[3] But Kincaid (2010a) insists that regional policies cannot

3 Federalist scholarship largely ignores issues of gender, including legal pluralism and family law, and conceptualizes them as "moral issues." But there is extensive scholarship on education controlled by regional governments, making comparison useful.

violate federal constitutional provisions; however, when gender issues are involved, purported "morality policies" impinge on human rights. Indeed, most feminists believe legal pluralism should not be tolerated. Mooney (2001) maintains that morality policy is based on concepts of privacy and the private sphere that historically insulated communities and powerful men from outside supervision or interference – and from public justice – just as Westphalian principles insulated nation-states. In liberal state theory, "the demarcation between public and private has marked the limits of state power, with most 'morality issues' located in the classic divide and insulated from central government scrutiny" (Carbone 1996, 267). Mucciaroni (2011) challenges the idea that any policies are intrinsically about morality and so the proper subjects for self-rule, as federalists claim. He considers "designating things morality" a strategy to minimize the complexity of core issues, undervalue evidence and expertise, and minimize possibilities of compromise. By framing an issue as technically simple and subject only to first principles drawn from religion or nationalism – that is, ideology – it becomes something on which anyone can have a view and can be politically mobilized around. The strategy fosters high participation, and frames issues as not amenable to compromise, which increases the potential for conflict and violence if central governments try to impose a resolution. It also empowers religious and traditional authorities.

Some theorists conceptualize "federalism" as a type of society. Erk (2010, x), for example, thinks that federal political institutions "adapt to achieve congruence with the underlying social structure." But studies of federal societies focus mainly on ethnolinguistic diversity, ignoring other types of territorial diversity that also could promote federalization. How gender relations are organized also affects the federalization of institutions; for example, in most federations, the public/private divide is mapped onto constitutional power divisions, and "blood" and kinship are often used to determine citizenship. Many gender scholars (Bashevkin 1998; Chappell and Curtin 2013; Franceschet and Piscopo 2013) consider unitary democracies more responsive to gender issues than are their federal counterparts. Empirically, moreover, less diverse, conflictual national federations are more responsive to gender issues than more diverse, conflictual types. Indeed one might theorize that the central government's capacity to facilitate family law reform is inversely related to the extent of diversity and conflict in a federation. Women's movements are fragmented by diversity and the conflict it fosters, weakening women's citizenship and political agency, but the fragmentation that legal pluralism creates can be overcome if women organize successfully and insert their demands for gender reform into contests between regional and central governments. In the least diverse (mono) national federations, organized women also can promote the establishment of women's policy agencies at government access points, and foster cooperation across levels of government to increase their responsiveness to reform demands, as occurred in Australia (Chappell 2002), Austria, and Germany (Lang and Sauer 2013). In multinational federations, fragmented party systems often make gender equality reforms harder to achieve, while very diverse federations (India, Pakistan, Nigeria) have many minorities seeking self-rule and multiple forms of legal pluralism.

Federalists' Claims and Feminist Critiques

Federalists make many claims about the benefits of federalism. One is that it fosters liberty by limiting government – that is, by dividing sovereignty, each government becomes a counterweight to other governments' power, protecting citizens from governments seeking greater power. But few feminists see many advantages in divided government. Gray (2010) maintains that, although limited government might work for "insiders" who already have rights, it disadvantages "outsiders" seeking rights by weakening the capacity of willing governments to promote change. Moreover, making one government respond to reform demands is easier than making many governments respond. Haussman (2005) and Gray (2010) show how federal arrangements fragment the advocacy and resources of women's movements. Although federalists think divided government enhances citizenship by providing many access points through which citizens can engage governments, feminists stress the many veto points divided government offers anti-reform opponents and the difficulty they face in accessing multiple sites.

Baines (2006) shows how federalism has fragmented women's citizenship in Canada. In the United States, Mettler (1998) finds that New Deal policies relegated both women and African Americans to second-class, regional citizenship, inferior benefits, and little protection from state governments, while white men gained first-class citizenship, rights and benefits. The US Supreme Court reinforced women's inferior status when it struck down provisions Congress had legislated to combat violence against women, ruling that anything associated with the family is essentially local because women as a group are defined by their roles in their families. The Supreme Court of Canada ruled that, under the doctrine of federalism, women are federal citizens for maternity leave, despite the request of women's organizations in Quebec that women be considered provincial citizens, eligible for Quebec's superior benefits. Ironically, all (non-First Nations) women are deemed provincial citizens when it comes to child care and reproductive health care, unless they work for a federal agency. This fragmentation of women's citizenship is problematic because it often results in varied benefits from place to place. Moreover, women cannot "vote with their feet," which federalists consider a benefit of federalism, because their family responsibilities limit their geographic mobility more than for men's.

Many gender scholars have identified disadvantages associated with federal arrangements, but some have also identified certain "federalism advantages" (Vickers 2010, 2011a). Moreover, when asked if federal arrangements "good" or "bad" for women, most gender scholars now answer with a conditional, "it depends." Many federalists believe divided government promotes democracy, since regional representatives govern fewer people over fewer issues and give citizens more opportunities for political expression, as well as giving (territorial) minorities some self-rule. But this idealized model rarely corresponds with reality – especially for women. Often the boundaries of the territory that minority communities claim are not congruent with those of any constituent state because of social engineering. For example, the US Congress refused to grant statehood until white English speakers were a majority in a territory, which sometimes resulted in citizenship for white English-speaking women. But in multinational federations in which some larger territorial minorities have regional governments, smaller territorial, and especially non-territorial, minorities have been denied both a regional state and legal pluralism. So the lauded self-rule is a privilege of only some groups.

Federalists consider divided government more efficient than a unitary state because it lets taxpayers determine the services they want, and "vote with their feet" accordingly. But this claim is *gender biased*: since women are unpaid caregivers in all societies, and access state services for the children, sick, elderly, and others they care for, as well as for themselves, they are considered consumers of state services, not contributors. This weakens their claim to full citizenship. Federalists also consider divided government more market friendly because it restricts citizens' ability to pressure the state to intervene in markets. But most feminists oppose federalism because they believe that gender reforms require governments to intervene in the market. Another claim, that federalizing government institutions and discourses facilitates conflict management, is hotly contested by those who believe it promotes secession by giving (territorial) nations a regional, institutional base on which a new state can be formed. Women have a particular interest in having a "capable state" that can manage conflict, since their bodies and behaviour often are the focus of such conflict. But the increased emphasis on "national security" might make federal states less "capable" of managing conflict as the focus of providing security to citizens shifts from internal to external security threats.

Federalists also think divided government creates opportunities for experimenting with policies without risking countrywide implementation, with successful experiments later being diffused to other jurisdictions. When it comes to gender equality policies, however, diffusion is uncommon. For example, Canada's anglophone provinces did not imitate Quebec's $5 a day child care program and Mexico City's progressive abortion policies resulted in a backlash, with many other Mexican states making their policies more repressive. Minority communities and nations consider family relations and gender regimes part of the identity they want to preserve, hence the lack of diffusion. The ideologies of different regional governments, the values of regional nations or communities, and the strength and strategies of women's movements in diverse regional polities combine to promote or block the diffusion of gender reforms.

Types of Legal Pluralism

There are three main types of legal pluralism. *Territorial* legal pluralism involves the constitutional division of government powers vertically. Regional governments, although they often have little power in practice, especially under dictatorships (Argentina, Brazil), or one-party rule (Mexico, Malaysia, Russia), often remain in charge of family law. Htun and Weldon (2012), for example, find a significant correlation between former communist states and egalitarian family law (Bosnia-Herzegovina) – a legacy of communist ideology. In Russia, however, Vladimir Putin demanded the elimination of all differences between central and regional laws, so that the 1995 family law code, though much amended since, may trump any laws the regional republics pass. At the same time, concern about population decline has fostered tolerance for underage marriages, especially in the non-Russian republics central to Putin's power base; for example, the central government did not react when Chechen authorities allowed violent attacks on women by traditionalists who considered them immodestly dressed (Human Rights Watch 2011).

A second, non-territorial form of legal pluralism involves *personal status codes*, as enacted by central governments in India and Malaysia. Nigerian legal pluralism combines positive, common, and customary law, as well as minority religious codes. The British classified Sharia law as customary, but it now is territorially legislated in Nigeria's Muslim-majority states. Constitutional divisions between family and criminal law left by the British have become problematic in some Muslim-majority states that have criminalized adultery despite the Nigerian constitution's assignment of criminal law to the jurisdiction of the central government, as in Canada. Territorializing Sharia law – that is, moving from non-territorial to territorial legal pluralism by applying Sharia to everyone, including non-Muslims living within a state's territory – has caused much conflict. Cases of women who bore a child after being raped and were condemned to death for adultery have raised global protests.

A third type of legal pluralism *delegates control over family law* to non-state religious or customary authorities. This may involve the formal or informal delegation of responsibility for determining the content of the rules to religious authorities. But the administration of family law usually remains with governments, as in India. In very diverse federations,[4] all three types occur and often conflict, as is increasingly the case in Nigeria.

Using an applied political theory approach to examine legal pluralism provides valuable insights. Although the western canon of political theory contains discussions of family relations, family law reform is rarely considered. This is likely because reform would involve exposing gender regimes to women's demands for more equal gender relations, greater autonomy, and the deconstruction of the public/private divide. In practice, however, many states apply public standards of justice to behaviour within families by criminalizing violence against women, marital rape, and child abuse, disrupting long-standing theoretical

4 Obiora and Toomey (2010) outline the many negative effects resulting from the Nigerian government's incapacity to regulate legal pluralism, manage conflict, or provide security for its citizens.

assumptions about privacy. Despite the expansion of central government activity, in common law federations, family law usually remains the responsibility of regional governments, and many federalist advocates of "localism" still consider the family private and local. Frustration with the effects of legal pluralism and localism makes organized, majority-culture women keen to "nationalize" gender reform by getting it onto the agendas of central governments.

Federal arrangements have a greater impact on gender equality reforms in multinational federations with diverse societies. The extent of federalization also matters – for example, institutionalized IGR in Australia allow women's movements to gain access to and advocate for women, whereas in Canada IGRs remain elite interactions that are largely closed to women's movements (Chappell, Brennan, and Rubenstein 2012; Vickers 2014). Moreover, the effects of federalization change over time – for example, until the 1970s, Swiss women were denied the national vote, and the reforms they proposed were blocked by the Swiss system of elite accommodation, super majorities, and direct democracy; after winning the vote, Swiss women used the same practices that previously excluded them to their advantage. Some women's movements combat or circumvent the effects of federalization by using federal features effectively, especially in national and multinational federations, where they can engage in "forum shopping" under some circumstances (Sawer and Vickers 2010; Vickers 2010).

Family Law Reform and Types of Federations

On the family law scale developed by Rose McDermott (2007)[5] – see Table 6.1 – all *national* federations are rated "equitable" or "generally equitable," while in *multinational* federations family law has been reformed to these standards in five of nine cases. Only one *very diverse* federation has "generally equitable" family law, while family law remains "somewhat inequitable" or "inequitable" in the other five. On this scale, then, reform is most advanced in older federations with the least conflict and the fewest forms of legal pluralism. The McDermott

5 See Vickers (2013b) for a discussion of the effects of different scales in measuring family law equity. I use the McDermott scale because it is the only one that includes majority and minority family law or personal status codes in each country, which approximates reality in many federations.

Table 6.1. Family Law Reform Ratings by Type of Federation

Family Law Rating (McDermott Scale 2011)	Type of Federation		
	National	Multinational	Very Diverse
Equitable	Australia	Belgium	
	Austria	Canada	
	Germany	Spain	
Mostly equitable	Argentina		
	Brazil	Malaysia[a]	Bosnia-Herzegovina
	Russian Federation	Switzerland	
	United States		
Somewhat inequitable		Ethiopia	Iraq
		Mexico	South Africa
		Nepal[b]	
Inequitable		United Arab Emirates	India
			Nigeria
			Pakistan

Source: WomanStats database, available online at http://www.womanstats.org/, accessed 3 October 2014.

a On other scales, Malaysia is "somewhat inequitable" because of (state-regulated) polygamy.

b Nepal's conflict might be ideological, not cultural.

scale, however, does not include laws regarding access to contraception and safe abortion. So, for example, Germany's ranking is "equitable," despite its repudiation of the former East Germany's progressive laws and programs on reunification and the imposition of the former West Germany's restrictive Basic Law on all women in the country. In this case, legal pluralism, which would have advantaged some East German women, was not adopted. In other federations (Australia, Mexico, the United States), legal pluralism also applies to laws governing contraception and abortion, with mixed outcomes for women.

Unequal family law undermines women's citizenship, as do extensive diversity, conflict, physical insecurity, and the lack of reproductive freedom. Before the invasion of Iraq, women of the then-dominant Sunni community had achieved some family law reform by promoting progressive interpretations of Sharia. But post-war conflict and insecurity made cooperation among Sunni, Shia, and Kurdish women difficult, and the project was suspended (Vickers 2012). As well, although the United States promoted electoral quotas for Iraqi women, it did not empower them to participate in constitutional negotiations. Instead the Iraqi negotiators adopted the "Lebanese model," which devolves family law to communal/religious authorities, most of whom apply more restrictive interpretations of Sharia law.

Bosnia-Herzegovina is a highly diverse federation in which a unitary and federal entity were brought together in a framework imposed by the 1995 Dayton Accords to solve a military stalemate by freezing relations between the ethnic entities. It established a complex form of legal pluralism that prevented development of a strong central state, and permitted the exclusion of Jews and Roma from citizenship in the ethnic entities. External pressure from the United States and the European Union strengthened the central state by joining the entities' armies and integrating their tax systems. Although external actors want a citizen-based federation, with individual rights trumping collective rights, internal actors want ethnic citizenship. Women in Bosnia-Herzegovina benefit from a "fairly equitable' family law code they inherited from socialist Yugoslavia that the Dayton Accords froze in place. Women also benefit from (externally imposed) electoral quotas for both regional and central elections – in 2012 women were 21 per cent of the central government's lower house. But there is little civil society activism among women, especially across ethnic boundaries.

Conclusion

Asking if "federalism" is "good" or "bad" for women, and applying feminist and federalist political theories to different types of federation, shows the value of applied political theory. When applied to a range of federations, UN Women's claim that legal pluralism invariably has negative outcomes for women must be modified to take into account federations of different types, the extent of the diversity and conflict in each , the type of legal pluralism, and the strength of the women's movements involved. Undoubtedly, unreformed family law is a major barrier to women's struggles for gender equality and full citizenship, but legal pluralism also could have positive outcomes for women, as the German case shows. Legal pluralism is a basic design feature of all forms of multilevel governance, and so is not something that could be eliminated. Moreover, feminists who align with a regional government often consider legal pluralism part of their nation's identity and self-rule and so the basis for more equitable citizenship. Indeed, my personal understanding of the value of legal pluralism in some contexts comes from discussions with feminist nationalists in Quebec. Legal pluralism is central to power sharing in divided governments, and hence a key approach to conflict management. In very diverse federations it requires multiple forms, as central governments rarely have the capacity to manage the conflict that diversity produces, especially if all types of legal pluralism are involved. Indeed, just one very diverse federation, Bosnia-Herzegovina, has "somewhat equitable" family law, inherited from socialist Yugoslavia.

In using applied political theory, some cases – such as Canada, because of its long experience with legal pluralism – are especially germane, although the gender dimension of that experience is only now being explored. In federations with relatively little conflict resulting from national diversity, legal pluralism has not blocked family law reform much. Nonetheless, women's struggles for access to effective contraception and safe abortion persist. Analyses of relations among Canada's various feminist movements and multicultural minorities also reveal much about legal pluralism, morality issues, and justice in federations. In the end, however, how federations develop and how they are able to manage conflict will determine if it is possible for women to achieve all aspects of family law reform without violence and the importance of allies in that task.

REFERENCES

Baker, Lynn A. 2001. "Should Liberals Fear Federalism?" *University of Chicago Law Review* 70: 433–54.

Bashevkin, Sylvia. 1998. *Women on the Defensive: Living in Conservative Times*. Toronto: University of Toronto Press.

Baines, Beverley. 2006. "Federalism and Pregnancy Benefits." *Queen's Law Journal* 32 (1): 190–232.

Baines, Beverley, and Ruth Rubio-Marin, eds. 2005. *The Gender of Constitutional Jurisprudence. Cambridge*: Cambridge University Press.

Carbone, June. 1996. "Morality, Public Policy and the Family: The Role of Marriage and the Public/Private Divide." *Santa Clara Law Review* 36: 267–86.

Chappell, Louise A. 2002. *Gendering Government: Feminist Engagement with the State in Australia and Canada*. Vancouver: UBC Press.

Chappell, Louise, Deborah Brennan, and Kim Rubenstein. 2012. "A Gender and Change Perspective on Intergovernment Relations." In *Tomorrow's*

Federation: Reforming Australia's Government, ed. Paul Kildea, Andrew Lynch, and George Williams, 228–45. Sydney: Federation Press.

Chappell, Louise, and Jennifer Curtin. 2013. "Does Federalism Matter? Evaluating State Architecture and Family and Domestic Violence Policy in Australia and New Zealand." *Publius* 43 (1): 24–43. https://doi.org/10.1093/publius/pjs030

Elazar, Daniel J. 1987. *Exploring Federalism*. Tuscaloosa: University of Alabama Press.

Erk, Jan. 2010. *Explaining Federalism: State, Society and Congruence in Austria, Belgium, Canada, Germany, and Switzerland*. New York: Routledge.

Fenna, Alan. 2011. "Federalism, Feminism and the Comparative Method." Paper presented at Feminism and State Architecture Workshop, European Consortium for Political Research Joint Sessions, St Gallen, Switzerland, 12–16 April.

Franceschet, Susan, and Jennifer M. Piscopo. 2013. "Federalism, Decentralization and Reproductive Rights in Argentina and Chile." *Publius* 43 (1): 129–50. https://doi.org/10.1093/publius/pjs021

Glendon, Mary Ann. 1989. *The Transformation of Family Law*. Chicago: University of Chicago Press.

Gray, Gwendolyn. 2010. "*Federalism, Feminism and Multilevel Governance*: The Elusive Search for Theory?" In *Federalism, Feminism and Multilevel Governance*, ed. Melissa Haussman, Marian Sawer, and Jill Vickers, 19–35. Farnham, UK: Ashgate.

Haussman, Melissa. 2005. *Abortion Politics in North America*. Boulder, CO: Lynne Reiner.

Htun, Malta, and S. Laurel Weldon. 2012. *Sex Equality in Family Law, World Development Report*. West Lafayette, IN: Purdue University, Global Institute for Gender Research.

Hueglin, Thomas, and Alan Fenna. 2006. *Comparative Federalism: A Systematic Inquiry*. Toronto: Broadview Press.

Hudson, Valerie M., Donna Lee Bowen, and Perpetua Lynne Nielsen. 2011. "What Is the Relationship between Inequality in Family Law and Violence against Women? Approaching the Issue of Legal Enclaves." *Politics & Gender* 7 (4): 453–92. https://doi.org/10.1017/S1743923X11000328

Human Rights Watch. 2011. *Country Reports*. New York: Human Rights Watch. Accessed 20–25 May 2012.

Irving, Helen. 2008. *Gender and the Constitution: Equity and Agency in Comparative Constitutional Design*. New York: Cambridge University Press. https://doi.org/10.1017/CBO9780511619687

Joseph, Suad, ed. 2000. *Gender and Citizenship in the Middle East*. Syracuse, NY: Syracuse University Press.

Kincaid, John. 2010a. "Democracy versus Federalism in the United States of America." In *Federal Democracies*, ed. Alain-G. Gagnon and Michael Burgess, 119–41. Abington, UK: Routledge.

Kincaid, John. 2010b. "Federalism and Democracy: Comparative Empirical and Theoretical Perspectives." In *Federal Democracies*, ed. Alain Gagnon and Michael Burgess, 299–324. Abington, UK: Routledge.

Krook, Mona Lena, and Fiona Mackay, eds. 2010. *Gender, Politics and Institutions: Towards a Feminist Institutionalism*. Basingstoke, UK: Palgrave Macmillan.

Lang, Sabine, and Birgit Sauer. 2013. "Does Federalism Impact Gender Architectures? The Case of Women's Policy Agencies in Germany and Austria." *Publius* 43 (1): 68–89. https://doi.org/10.1093/publius/pjs048

Lister, Ruth. 2003. *Citizenship: Feminist Perspectives*. New York: New York University. https://doi.org/10.1007/978-0-230-80253-7

Marshall, T.H. 1950. *Citizenship and Social Class*. Cambridge: Cambridge University Press.

McDermott, Rose. 2007. "Inequity in Family Law." (MULTIVARSCALE-3). Accessed 10–14 June 2012.

Mettler, Suzanne. 1998. *Dividing Citizens: Gender and Federalism in the New Deal*. Ithaca, NY: Cornell University Press.

Mooney, Christopher. 2001. *The Public Clash of Private Values: The Politics of Morality Policy*. Washington, DC: Georgetown University Press.

Motiejunaite, Jurate. 2005. *Women's Rights: The Private/Public Dichotomy*. New York: IDEA.

Mucciaroni, Gary. 2011. "Are Debates about 'Morality Policy' Really About Morality? Framing Opposition to Gay and Lesbian Rights." *Policy Studies* 39 (2): 187–216. https://doi.org/10.1111/j.1541-0072.2011.00404.x

Obiora, L. Amede, and Sarah Toomey. 2010. "Federalism and Gender Politics in Nigeria." In *Federalism, Feminism and Multilevel Governance*, ed. Melissa Haussman, Marian Sawer, and Jill Vickers, 211–26. Farnham, UK: Ashgate.

Sawer, Marian, and Jill Vickers. 2010. "Introduction: Political Architecture and Its Gender Impact." In *Federalism, Feminism, and Multilevel Governance*, ed. Melissa Haussman, Marian Sawer, and Jill Vickers, 3–18. Farnham: Ashgate. https://doi.org/10.1057/9780230248588_1

Smith, Miriam. 2008. *Political Institutions and Lesbian and Gay Rights in the United States and Canada*. New York: Routledge.

Tilse, Mark. 2011. *Transnationalism in the Prussian East: From National Conflict to Synthesis, 1871–1914*. Basingstoke, UK: Palgrave Macmillan.

UN Women. 2011. In Pursuit of Justice: Progress of the World's Women. N.p.: UN Women. Available online at http://asiapacific.unwomen.org/en/

digital-library/publications/2011/1/progress-of-the-worlds-women-in-pursuit-of-justice. Accessed 15 May 2012.

Vickers, Jill. 2010. "A Two-Way Street: Federalism and Women's Politics in Canada and the United States." *Publius* 40 (3): 412–35. https://doi.org/10.1093/publius/pjq006

Vickers, Jill. 2011a. "Gender and State architectures." *Politics & Gender* 7 (2): 254–62. https://doi.org/10.1017/S1743923X11000092

Vickers, Jill. 2011b. "Gendering Federalism: Institutions of Decentralization and Power-Sharing." In *Gender, Politics and Institutions*, ed. Mona Krook and Fiona Mackay, 129–46. Basingstoke, UK: Palgrave Macmillan.

Vickers, Jill. 2012. "Gender Implications of Federalism in Post-Conflict Zones." Working paper for UN Women, Research Gate.

Vickers, Jill. 2013a. "Is Federalism Gendered?" *Publius* 43 (1): 1–23.

Vickers, Jill. 2013b. "Territorial Pluralism and Family Law Reform: Conflicts between Gender and Culture Rights in Federations North and South." *Politikon: South African Journal of Political Studies* 40 (1): 57–82. https://doi.org/10.1080/02589346.2013.765675

Vickers, Jill. 2014. "Gendering Inter-Governmental Relations." Paper prepared for Symposium on Comparing Intergovernmental Relations, Sydney, Australia, April.

Watts, Ronald L. 1996. *Comparing Federal Systems*. 2nd ed. Kingston, ON: Queen's University. WomanStats database, available online at http://www.womanstats.org, accessed 25–28 May 2012; Codebook, available online at http://www.womanstats.org/CodebookCurrent.htm, accessed 2–5 June 2012.

Watts, Ronald L. 2005. "Comparative Conclusions." In *Distribution of Powers and Responsibilities in Federal Countries*, ed. Akhtar Majeed, Ronald L. Watts, and Douglas M. Brown, 322–50. Montreal; Kingston, ON: McGill-Queen's University Press.

7 Autonomy, Rights, and Euthanasia Policy: Lessons from John Stuart Mill

DARIN NESBITT

End-of-life decisions are by their nature highly controversial and deeply contested. The ethics and morality of assisted death have long been a subject of intense inquiry and debate by philosophers, theologians, and jurists (Mitchell 2007, 5). Euthanasia involves a range of issues including policy, law, social change, public opinion, professional medical standards, and religious, moral, and ethical considerations (Otlowski 1997, 4). The political and legal debate over physician-assisted death and voluntary euthanasia may be understood as a clash of two widely held beliefs: the values of personal autonomy and dignity versus the view that the state as a matter of policy ought to protect all human life no matter its quality. Yet a rules-based (that is, non-arbitrary) legislative method to balance these objectives remains elusive.

Euthanasia encompasses numerous conceptual and practical dimensions from active to passive euthanasia (ranging from introducing something to cause death to withholding treatment or other supporting measures), voluntary to non-voluntary to involuntary euthanasia (ranging from obtaining individual consent or consent from a guardian or other authorized person to euthanasia without explicit consent to forced or coerced euthanasia), to physician- and other-assisted death (where physicians prescribe and administer medicines or authorized third-parties administer medicines to cause death). Supporters of voluntary euthanasia typically invoke the right to self-determination, individual autonomy, and dying with dignity as their principal justifications. Opponents reject the practice variously on ethical and religious grounds, the physician's role to preserve life, the potential for social distrust in the medical community, and the risks of misuse with respect to involuntary euthanasia.

Using an applied political theory approach, this chapter presents an interpretive reconstruction of how Canadian courts have dealt with these concerns, leading to the current jurisprudential landscape that confronts policy makers as they craft and refine legislation on medical aid-in-dying. I relate the political philosophy of John Stuart Mill to an empirical analysis of the standards that have resulted from Canadian court decisions. Mill's philosophy, both its insights and its weaknesses, proves highly useful for navigating the balance between legislative and judicial decision making that surrounds assisted death.

Canadian courts and federal governments historically have been deeply resistant to support medical aid-in-dying. In the first constitutional challenge to Canada's criminal prohibition of assisted death in 1993, *Rodriguez v. Canada (Attorney General)*, the Supreme Court of Canada upheld the prohibition on the grounds that the courts have a general duty to protect human life. In 1995 a special Senate committee affirmed its opposition to assisted death on the basis, it was stated, that government's basic role is to uphold respect for life (Canada 1995). Yet a number of recent landmark political, legislative, and legal developments mean Canada has joined jurisdictions such as Belgium, the Netherlands, Luxembourg, Switzerland, Colombia, India, Germany, South Korea, Japan, and the US states of Oregon, Washington, Colorado, Hawaii, Montana, California, and Vermont that now support limited forms of voluntary euthanasia and medical aid-in-dying.

The first such development came about when the Quebec provincial government passed Bill 52, "An Act respecting end-of-life care," in June 2014 by a vote of ninety-four to twenty-two. In doing so, the province became the first jurisdiction in Canada to enact right-to-die legislation. The legislation provides Quebec residents medical assistance to die so long as they have an "incurable serious illness" and an advanced, irreversible decline in their abilities. Adult patients must be in constant, unbearable physical or psychological pain that cannot be treated, and be capable of providing consent. The legislation was expected to come into effect in December 2015, but its implementation was delayed due to some unsuccessful legal challenges.

The second occurred on 6 February 2015 when the Supreme Court of Canada, in *Carter v. Canada (Attorney General)* ([2015] S.C.C. 5) invalidated sections 241(b) and 14 of the Criminal Code on the basis that both provisions unjustifiably infringed upon section 7 of the Charter of Rights and Freedoms to the extent they prohibited physician-assisted death for a competent adult person who clearly consents to the termination of life and who has a grievous and irremediable medical condition – including an illness, disease, or disability – that causes enduring suffering that is intolerable to the person. The Supreme Court suspended enforcement of the decision initially for one year, then for another four months, to allow the federal government to craft a legislative response.

The third development transpired on 17 June 2017, when federal legislation entitled "An Act to amend the Criminal Code and to make related amendments to other Acts (medical assistance in dying)" came into effect, creating a national regulatory framework for medical assistance-in-dying. The procedure is legal under section 241.2 of the Criminal Code if the patient is a Canadian citizen, is at least eighteen years of age, capable of providing informed consent, and has a grievous and irremediable medical condition. The legislation, unlike the Supreme Court's *Carter* ruling, defines what constitutes a "grievous and irremediable medical condition": a person with a serious and incurable illness, disease, or disability in an advanced state of irreversible decline in capability that is causing enduring physical or psychological suffering where natural death is reasonably foreseeable.

The Supreme Court in *Carter* did not impose any specific or particular policy requirements on the federal or provincial governments. Although the courts have developed decisional methodologies to navigate constitutional disputes and complexities, there does not appear to be anything analogous in the political and policy realms to guide federal and provincial governments in their efforts to support or limit individual rights and freedoms in the interest of public order or public good. The absence of such criteria to guide medical aid-in-dying policy and legislation is problematic to the extent that how to weigh and balance the harms in either prohibiting or supporting physician-assisted death is unclear or, worse, arbitrary. This wide legislative discretion is now the source of a profound challenge: how can governments rebalance and reconfigure the right to die with protecting human life in light of the Supreme Court's ruling?

Considering the judicial and legislative dynamics regarding medical assistance-in-dying in Canada, applied political theory is uniquely able to provide direction to government policy making and how it might arrange, rank, preserve, and balance basic goods such as security, order, liberty, equality, and community. In the context of voluntary euthanasia, governments and courts have attempted to balance the rights of individuals to exercise their autonomy in end-of-life decisions with the interest to protect and preserve all human life. Whether in terms of policy making, law, or jurisprudence, the effort to balance such competing interests is fraught with theoretical and practical difficulties. The decision as to which values and goods are to be balanced and how specifically to decide which will receive priority are two such examples.

The challenge of balancing the right of individuals to exercise autonomy and self-determination against broader societal interests is, of course, not unique to the topic of euthanasia, but finding that balance has particular relevance because of the unmapped legislative terrain federal and provincial governments face as a result of the Supreme Court's *Carter* decision. Building on interpretation of Canadian jurisprudence on the issue of assisted death, I suggest there are, for Canadian courts, two constitutional standards to balance individual rights and societal interests when they conflict. The first involves whether government laws or policies that restrict rights can be upheld as reasonable limitations on those rights. The second, and more recent, standard is found in the Supreme Court's application of a three-pronged test involving fundamental justice.

Based on this interpretive understanding of the current legal and legislative landscape of assisted death in Canada, in this chapter I aim to apply principles formulated in the liberal tradition on balancing individual liberty with societal interests to help set potential parameters for subsequent policy making. One classic formulation to weigh individual autonomy or self-determination against the authority of the state to limit freedoms originated in John Stuart Mill's classic treatise *On Liberty* ([1859] 1991). As he observed, there is "no recognized principle by which the propriety or impropriety of government interference is customarily tested" (13). Mill attempted to derive a rules-based principle to balance individual rights against social and political needs. The core of *On Liberty* is widely taken to revolve around the claim that the only legitimate exercise of political power over individuals is to prevent harm to others. This "one very simple principle," as Mill put it, continues to be a source of intense debate, with such disputes usually focusing on the difficult question of what constitutes harmful behaviour. Differences over the meaning and application of Mill's harm principle have arisen partly because he failed to supply a clear answer to that basic question. He did suggest a principle, which will be called the *Millian rights proviso*, to determine when it is legitimate to override individual autonomy: when someone's decisions and actions violate the rights of others. I hope to show that applying Mill's proposed solution to when it is legitimate for governments to limit citizens' rights and freedoms to the current legal and legislative landscape concerning assisted death offers a compelling basis for developing future aid-in-dying policy.

The Legal Background: Assisted Death and Voluntary Euthanasia

Although suicide is legal in Canada, until the *Carter* decision both voluntary euthanasia and assisted death violated the Criminal Code. Section 14 of the code stated that no person was entitled to give his or her consent to die and that criminal liability for causing the death of a person was not affected by that person's giving consent to die. This section was intended to prevent a person charged with murder from claiming as a defence that the other person consented to die. Someone who committed voluntary euthanasia could be convicted of first- or second-degree murder, the former carrying with it a mandatory minimum life sentence with no possibility of parole for twenty-five, while the latter means a mandatory minimum life sentence with no possibility of parole for ten years. Such charges were laid in at least seventeen cases: in one case, the accused fled the country, another was not taken past a preliminary hearing, three were acquitted, seven were convicted with suspended sentences, four were convicted on the lesser charges of manslaughter or administration of a noxious substance, and two were convicted of murder and received life sentences (Schüklenk et al. 2011, 28). In addition, section 241(b) of the Criminal Code stated: "Every one who (a) counsels a person to commit suicide, or (b) aids or abets a person to commit suicide, whether suicide ensues or not, is guilty of an indictable offence and liable to imprisonment for a term not exceeding fourteen years." In comparison, the Dutch criminal code prior to 2002, when the Netherlands became the first country to allow a physician to terminate a patient's life on request, had a legal penalty of no more than three years for assisting another's death (Weyers 2012, 35). Up to 2011 at least eighteen cases were known to have come to the attention of Crown prosecutors in which a charge under section 241(b) was either not laid, stayed, or dropped, the defendants were found not guilty, or, if convicted, were given a suspended or conditional sentence. It is unknown how many other cases of assisted death have come to the attention of Crown prosecutors or simply happened without the knowledge of the police (Schüklenk et al. 2011, 27)

Although Canada had some of the most restrictive and punitive laws concerning euthanasia of any of the democracies – in theory, in Canada euthanasia constituted first- or second-degree murder – it was generally dealt with as administering a noxious thing or manslaughter. Euthanasia in Canada was, as Jocelyn Downie concluded, "*de jure* murder but *de facto* a considerably less serious crime" (2004, 38). The severe legal penalties formerly outlined in the Criminal Code contrasted sharply with sentences in criminal cases where individuals found guilty – typically physicians and other health care workers – served little or no jail time. This contrast was problematic for a number of reasons, not the least of which is that laws should reflect the commonly held values of the community (Scherer and Simon 1999, 115). If the severity of Canada's laws that prohibited assisted death genuinely reflected Canadians' views, then the real concern should have been the Crown's inability to prosecute consistently those accused of aiding or abetting someone to end his or her life. At a minimum there was a notable disjunction between the putative intention of the laws and their application.

Rodriguez v. British Columbia (Attorney General), *1993*

The constitutionality of the prohibition against assisted death in Canada was initially tested in *Rodriguez v. British Columbia* (1993). Sue Rodriguez, a forty-two-year-old mother, was diagnosed with amyotrophic lateral sclerosis (ALS) – oftentimes referred to as Lou Gehrig's disease. ALS is an incurable and progressive disease that ultimately results in the full loss of all muscle function, including the ability to swallow and breathe. The prognosis for her type of ALS was a steady loss of physical abilities such as walking, speaking, swallowing, and breathing, followed by death in two to fourteen months. ALS patients near the end of their lives are conscious of their surroundings, but bedridden and completely dependent upon the care of others and the support of artificial respiration, hydration, and nutrition. Ms Rodriguez wished to live as long as she had the capacity to enjoy life, but realized at some point she would no longer be able to end her life without assistance.

In 1992 Ms Rodriguez commenced a court action, asking that the Criminal Code provisions prohibiting assisted death be declared unconstitutional. She applied to the Supreme Court of British Columbia for an order declaring then-section 241(b) invalid under the Charter, and requested the Court to allow a qualified physician to set up the technological means by which she could end her life at the time of her choosing. The BC Supreme Court dismissed her application, and a majority of the British Columbia Court of Appeal affirmed the trial judge's decision. Ms Rodriguez then argued at the Supreme Court of Canada that denying her access to assisted death under section 241(b) violated her constitutional rights as stated in the Charter in sections 7 (the right not to be deprived of the rights to life, liberty, and security except in accordance with the principles of fundamental justice), 12 (the right not to be subjected to cruel and unusual punishment), and 15 (the right to equal treatment under the law).

In a five-to-four decision, the Supreme Court dismissed the appeal, holding that, although section 241(b) infringed Ms Rodriguez's Charter rights to liberty and security of the person, it did not do so in a manner contrary to the principles of fundamental justice. The majority wrote that the prohibition against assisted death was grounded on a societal consensus against the practice. It was also argued on Ms Rodriguez's behalf that a handicapped person wishing to end her life but physically unable to do so had a right to assisted death under the equality provisions of the Charter, since the act of suicide is not criminalized for those capable of ending their own lives. Mr Justice Sopinka assumed Ms Rodriguez's equality rights under section 15 of the Charter had been infringed, but the central question for him was whether the infringement could be saved by section 1 of the Charter, which "guarantees the rights and freedoms set out in it subject only to such reasonable limits prescribed by law as can be demonstrably justified in a free and democratic society." He concluded that the infringement under section 15 was justified under section 1: the purpose of section 241(b), he stated, is to protect individuals from others who may wish to end their lives. To create an exception to the prohibition against assisted death for certain groups of persons would occasion a "slippery slope" towards full recognition of euthanasia. He dismissed claims that legal and policy safeguards would prevent such abuse.

There were three dissenting opinions. Chief Justice Lamer held that the prohibition against assisted death limited the right to equality guaranteed under the Charter, a limitation not justifiable under section 1. He concluded that the vulnerable could be legislatively protected in a manner that would not violate the equality rights of the disabled. Madam Justice McLachlin (Madam Justice L'Heureux-Dubé concurred) held that the prohibition infringed the right not to be deprived of life, liberty, and security of the person except in accordance with the principles of fundamental justice, and is not demonstrably justified in a free and democratic society. She further held that the vulnerable could be protected in a manner that did not arbitrarily limit Canadians' right to liberty. Mr Justice Cory agreed with the section 7 analyses of Justices McLachlin and L'Heureux-Dubé, but he also claimed the prohibition violated Ms Rodriguez's right to equality.

The *Rodriguez* ruling revealed the justices were deeply divided over the constitutionality of assisted death. They were sharply at odds in particular over the meaning and requirements of fundamental justice. Some of the justices evoked the same ethical concepts in support of their opposing positions: Justice Sopinka stated that sanctioning assisted death undermined human dignity, whereas Justice McLachlin argued prohibiting the practice did so. All agreed the prohibition limited a person's autonomy, but they disagreed whether allowing assisted death would threaten vulnerable persons. Another relevant dividing line was over the constitutional limits of individual autonomy and self-determination, with the majority holding that the interest in protecting human life was sufficiently compelling to dismiss the appeal (*R. v. Big M Drug Mart Ltd.*, [1985] 1 S.C.R. 211). The majority's belief of a "societal consensus" against assisted death was also noteworthy given that determining levels of public support concerning euthanasia – let alone making definitive judgments about it – is fraught with interpretive difficulties (Glick 1992, 9).

Courts have legitimate authority as a result of their role as arbiters of constitutional disputes. They can present two faces – unanimous or divided – to the public concerning contentious moral and constitutional issues such as physician-assisted death. In five-to-four votes, such as the Supreme Court's first assisted-death decision, courts might resolve an issue momentarily from a constitutional perspective, but are unable to establish clear direction for public and policy purposes. Non-unanimous rulings such as *Rodriguez* present both governments and the public with conflicting rationales that might lead to a greater polarization of issues among governments, the courts, and the public over the merits of physician-assisted death. Although differences of opinion among the justices provide some assurance that the constitutionality of euthanasia, whether of law or of fact, was carefully scrutinized, it is difficult not to conclude that *Rodriguez* was a form of unprincipled jurisprudence (Beširević 2006, 295).

Carter v. Canada (Attorney General), *2015*

The period between the Supreme Court's *Rodriguez* decision and its landmark *Carter* ruling witnessed increasing elite and public support for assisted death in Canada. Private members' bills proposing physician-assisted death became a staple of post-*Rodriguez* parliaments. In 2005 former Bloc Québécois Member of Parliament Justine Lalonde introduced Bill C-407, which endorsed legalized assisted death. The most recent private member's bill on the issue was Bill C-581, "An Act to amend the Criminal Code (physician-assisted suicide)," sponsored by former Conservative MP Steven Fletcher. On 4 December 2009 the Quebec National Assembly unanimously adopted a motion to establish a select committee to study the issue of dying with dignity, which subsequently recommended aid-in-dying. In 2011 a report on end-of-life decision making issued by the Royal Society of Canada, the country's main national scholarly academy, proposed that the Criminal Code be amended to allow physician-assisted death. By 2014 the Canadian Medical Association changed its long-standing policy of opposition to euthanasia, and proposed that its members follow their conscience in deciding whether to oppose or support medical aid-in-dying. In June 2014 Quebec became the first jurisdiction in Canada to enact right-to-die legislation. The *Carter* ruling needs to be placed in this wider public context.

Carter v. Canada had its origins in 2009, when Gloria Taylor was diagnosed with ALS, the very illness that had afflicted Sue Rodriguez. Ms Taylor brought a claim before the British Columbia Supreme Court challenging the constitutionality of the Criminal Code provisions that prohibited assisted death – specifically, sections 14, 21, 22, 222, and 241. Ms Taylor was joined by Lee Carter and Hollis Johnson, who had assisted Ms Carter's mother, Kathleen ("Kay") Carter, to travel to Switzerland to use the services of DIGNITAS, an assisted-death clinic. By 2010 Ms Taylor's physical condition had deteriorated to the point that she required a wheelchair for short distances, and was suffering severe pain from muscle degeneration. As she explained to the Court, Ms Taylor wanted neither to live in a bedridden state stripped of dignity and independence nor an "ugly death." Unable to afford to travel to Switzerland, where assisted death is legal and available to non-residents, Ms Taylor described the "cruel choice" she faced between ending her life while she was still physically capable of doing so or abandoning control over the manner and timing of her death (*Carter v. Canada*, 11–13).

In a unanimous ruling, the Supreme Court justices held the laws prohibiting physician-assisted death infringed Ms Taylor's section 7 rights. The justices also concluded the infringement was not justified under section 1. Their remedy was to hold that sections 241(b) and 14 of the Criminal Code were void insofar as they prohibited physician-assisted death for a competent adult who clearly consents to the termination of life, and has a grievous and irremediable medical condition (including an illness, disease, or disability) that causes enduring and intolerable suffering to the individual (*Carter v. Canada*, 127).

The case revolved around section 7 of the Charter: "Everyone has the right to life, liberty and security of the person and the right not to be deprived thereof except in accordance with the principles of fundamental justice." As the justices explained, those who claim a government decision or action violates this section must demonstrate that the law or policy interferes with, or deprives them of, their life, liberty, or security of the person, and does so in a matter inconsistent with the principles of fundamental justice. A central issue for the Court to resolve was whether the unconditional prohibition against physician-assisted death did so.

The Court determined that the prohibition did, in fact, infringe the right to life. The justices accepted the evidence provided at the trial level that the prohibition forced some individuals to take their own lives prematurely for fear they would be incapable of doing so if their physical mobility were impaired at some future and foreseeable point. The prohibition thus deprived some individuals of life. The justices rejected the claims that the right to life requires either an absolute prohibition of assisted death and that persons in certain circumstances cannot waive their right to life. They recognized that an absolutist position requiring that all human life be preserved no matter the circumstance is inconsistent with the established and recognized legal rights of individuals to withdraw or to refuse life-saving or life-sustaining medical treatment (*Carter v. Canada*, 57–63; Schafer 2013, 526).

The Court also held that the prohibition against assisted dying infringed the rights to liberty and security of the person. The justices again adopted the trial judge's reasoning that the prohibition interfered with the ability to make fundamentally important and personal medical decision making, and thus the subsequent stress imposed by the absence of physician-assisted death violated security of the person. The justices wrote that "an individual's response to a grievous and irremediable medical condition is a matter critical to their dignity and autonomy. The law allows people in this situation to request palliative sedation, refuse artificial nutrition and hydration, or request the removal of life-sustaining medical equipment, but denies them the right to request a physician's assistance in dying. This interferes with their ability to make decisions concerning their bodily integrity and medical care and thus trenches on liberty. And, by leaving people like Ms. Taylor to ensure intolerable suffering, impinges on their security of the person" (*Carter v. Canada*, 66).

The additional section 7 question the Court addressed was whether constitutional recognition of physician-assisted death is consistent with the principles of fundamental justice. As the justices explained, section 7 provisions are not guarantees that the state will never interfere with a person's life, liberty, or security of the person; rather, the issue is whether a law or policy violates the principles of fundamental justice. Although a number of basic principles of fundamental justice have emerged, three are considered central to section 7 jurisprudence: laws that encroach upon life, liberty, or security of the person must not be (1) arbitrary, (2) overbroad, or (3) have consequences that are grossly disproportionate to their objective. Careful consideration of the fundamental justice criterion reveals that the Supreme Court justices conceived and applied it more consistently in *Carter* than they did in *Rodriguez*.

The federal government's prohibition of physician-assisted suicide was not arbitrary to the extent its objective was to protect vulnerable persons from being induced to commit suicide at a time of weakness (*Carter v. Canada*, 78). The justices, however, held that the laws prohibiting physician-assisted death were overbroad insofar as there were individuals who were competent, fully informed, and free from coercion or duress – in other words, individuals who were not vulnerable – who wished assistance to end their own lives (86). While the justices believed the injunction against assisted death was grossly disproportionate to the objective of the law – "it imposes unnecessary suffering on affected individuals, deprives them of the ability to determine what to do with their bodies and how those bodies will be treated, and may cause those affected to take their own lives sooner than they would were they able to obtain a physician's assistance in dying" – the Court did not claim the laws violated the principle of gross disproportionality since the determination had already been made that they were overbroad (90). Similarly the Court did not address whether the prohibition violated section 15, since the justices had already determined it violated section 7.

The section 1 analysis revolved around (1) whether the government had demonstrated that the absolute prohibition of physician-assisted dying was rationally connected to the goal of protecting the vulnerable from being induced to take their own lives in times of weakness; (2) whether the limitation on section 7 rights was reasonably tailored to the objective; and (3) whether there was proportionality between the deleterious and salutary effects of the law. The justices believed there was a rational connection between the prohibition of assisted death and its objective. The issue whether the prohibition was reasonably tailored to the objective depended on whether the laws as enacted were the least drastic means of achieving the legislative objective. The justices concluded that this question "lies at the heart of this case" (*Carter v. Canada*, 104). They accepted the trial judge's conclusion that a more permissive assisted-death regime with administrative safeguards could protect vulnerable people from abuse and error. The judgment whether there was proportionality between the deleterious and salutary effects of the law – that is, "an assessment that weighs the impact of the law on protected rights against the beneficial effect of the law in terms of the greater public good" – was unnecessary since the Court concluded that laws prohibiting assisted death were not minimally impairing (122). The justices decided that sections 241(b) and 14 of the Criminal Code could not be saved by section 1 of the Charter.

The Court explained its reasoning for overturning *Rodriguez*. First, vigorous public debate continued despite the *Rodriguez* decision. Second, more recent policy reports, such as the Royal Society of Canada's on end-of-life decision making and the Quebec National Assembly's Select Committee on Dying with Dignity – which established a policy framework for provincial legislation sanctioning medical aid-in-dying in Quebec – constituted clear evidence of increasing societal support for physician-assisted death. Third, in 1993, no jurisdiction lawfully permitted assistance in dying, but by 2010 an increasing number did. Examination of the varied regimes had led to an extensive body of literature concerning the legal and policy dimensions of physician-assisted death, including current end-of-life practices, the risks and benefits associated with assisted death, and the efficacy of procedural safeguards (*Carter v. Canada*, 5–8).

The Supreme Court's decision to provide constitutional protection for the practice of physician-assisted death will have profound effects on the evolution of Canadian law and health care policy concerning end-of-life issues. Canada was firmly implanted in an "emerging policy development stage" (Ogden 1994, 7) until the Court sent a clear and decisive message to federal and provincial governments that assisted death must be permitted for those who wish to have that end-of-life option. The Court also gave the federal government substantial berth to craft a policy response – evidenced by the fact the justices chose not to specify what constitutes a "grievous and irremediable medical condition" – but it noted that neither the federal nor provincial governments would be able to act alone or impose a set of unilateral constraints. The Court's unwillingness to provide specific policy requirements might have the unintended effect of complicating the development and implementation of uniform provincial health care policies concerning assisted death, given that delivery and administration of health care is ultimately a provincial constitutional responsibility. In the end, though, *Carter* is a more principled and definitive judicial determination than was *Rodriguez*.

Autonomy, Rights, and the Millian Rights Proviso

A recurring theme in the discussion and assessment of euthanasia is the need to balance competing political and ethical goals and objectives. Governments and courts have tried to balance the harm that might result if even one person is wrongfully euthanized against that of compelling a person who is suffering to live despite his or her wish to request aid-in-dying. The courts have provided decisional criteria to assess the constitutional claims of the right to assisted death. Comparable criteria by Canadian governments are more difficult to locate, to the extent they even exist. The Special Senate Committee on Euthanasia and Assisted Suicide's report *Of Life and Death* (Canada 1995), which was the last comprehensive parliamentary policy recommendation on assisted death in the past two decades (Schüklenk et al. 2011, 3), urged the federal government to maintain its strict prohibition. The report's authors wrote: "the Committee was consistently confronted with the question of how to balance two different interests: individual rights and the interests of society. To what extent can the individual rights of autonomy and self-determination be protected without compromising society's interest in upholding the principle of respect for human life?" (Canada 1995). Yet the report provided no assessment of the social risks of governments either allowing or prohibiting assisted death, no analysis of the social and legal consequences of doing or not doing so, and no data concerning the costs to the health care system of a policy that restricts or permits medical aid-in-dying. Most important, it did not explain how testimony and evidence that formed the basis for its recommendation to support the prohibition of physician-assisted death were weighed and assessed.

As Mill pointed out in *On Liberty*, governments typically rely on religious faith, traditions, or simply "the likings and dislikings of society" to justify legislation. Yet in the absence of a clear principle to distinguish between the legitimate interests of individuals and those of society, either customs and traditions or the most "powerful portion" of society – that is, majority rule – will be the justification for laws (Mill [1859] 1991, 11). The outcome, Mill ominously suggested, is that the reasons to restrict individual freedoms will be either ad hoc in nature or ultimately arbitrary. In *On Liberty* Mill sought to explain how to distinguish instances where political authority is legitimate from cases where it threatens individual autonomy, and to address which activities ought to be exempt from legal regulation and which may be legitimately limited. In essence Mill defended a "liberty principle" limited by a "harm condition" (Archard 1990, 453): rational adults should be free from legal or societal constraints provided their actions do not adversely affect, injure, or harm others' interests or rights. Governments are justified through the use of laws to prevent people from harming others, but not on the basis of what might be harmful to a person alone. *On Liberty* is therefore anti-paternalist to the extent it consistently denies that a person's own good is sufficient justification for limiting liberty.

Although Mill did not specifically pronounce upon the euthanasia issue, his contributions to our understanding of autonomy and choice have greatly shaped subsequent debate over it. He especially made a case for privileging forms of life under conditions of rational autonomy in that individuals should actively endorse their opinions and decisions. Individuality, as Mill explained, is a person's ability to make significant decisions in life, and thus the area where individuals should not just have, but require, the freedom to do so. The ability to make one's own decisions was so important to Mill that it should be recognized and protected under the rubric of the right to freedom (Nys 2006, 317). For Mill, people are autonomous when they possess rational competence, such as the ability to observe, to reason and judge, and to gather resources to implement decisions, and the self-discipline to pursue what deliberate decision making counsels. Mill's defence of individuality helps us understand how the final stages of degenerative and terminal diseases can erode autonomy; it also deepens our understanding of why those who support medical-aid-in-dying do so. As Michael Gill explains, just as progressive bodily deterioration can limit and ultimately eliminate one's ability to undertake physical action, so mental deterioration does the same to the ability to make any decision at all. It is this "lingering half-life" that assisted death is intended to prevent – the decision to end one's life reveals that what the person values about herself is not simple existence, but the ability to decide what happens to her (Gill 2005, 56).

Despite its rhetorical, moral, and legal force, autonomy cannot in and of itself be a sufficient justifying principle for voluntary euthanasia, since it is the involvement of other agents and institutions – for example, the doctor and other medical practitioners in assisted death – that requires justification. Autonomy underlies the patient's right to end her life, but beneficence or some other moral principle is required to justify the involvement of a physician or other party (Weyers 2012, 49–50). In the context of euthanasia, aid-in-dying involves not just the health care teams; friends, family members, and other caregivers too are part of this complex relational web. Many interests must be recognized in deciding whether and under what circumstances assisted death should take place.

Mill's main objective in *On Liberty* was to examine the nature and limits of "the power which can legitimately be exercised by society over the individual" ([1859] 1991, 5). Initially his answer was that the only legitimate basis for restricting individual freedom is to prevent someone from doing harm to others. He famously proclaimed that "the sole end for which mankind are warranted, individually or collectively, in interfering with the liberty of action of any of their number is self-protection. That the only purpose for which power can be rightfully exercised over any member of a civilized community, against his will, is to prevent harm to others" (14). It is important to note that the liberty principle is neither unqualified nor absolute. Governments are justified in restraining conduct and actions harmful to non-consenting persons – that is, a definite, palpable injury to the life, health, freedom, or material goods of identifiable, not hypothetical, persons. Mill presumed social or public utility is maximized by a weighing and balancing of conflicting ideas, values, and interests to determine whether promoting individual freedom or restraining it is more likely to achieve the greatest happiness of the greatest number.

Mill's harm principle is a continuing source of debate over *On Liberty*. His struggle to provide clear and consistent meaning to it informs us there are deep problems with concepts and notions such as "harm" and "social harm." Even cursory reflection upon the meaning of harm exposes its inherent ambiguity and excessive elasticity. What is regarded as harmful is not infrequently the fashionable and fleeting, and often those claiming an activity is harmful confuse what is affecting their private interests with the public good. Mill's original formulation of the harm principle underwent several iterations. Later in *On Liberty* he claimed it is legitimate for governments to limit freedoms if people harm the interests of others, and he then attempted to distinguish between individual and state interests as a basis for determining when it is legitimate for states to limit freedoms.

While Mill struggled to provide content and coherence to the harm principle, he was more resolute that, "in things that do not primarily concern others, individuality should assert itself" ([1859] 1991, 63). Mill provided first an interest-based and then a rights-based liberty-limiting principle. Governments may place limits on individuals' freedoms when their conduct "affects prejudicially the interests of others" (83). However, the success of this criterion depends, as Mill recognized, on being able to distinguish between decisions and acts that affect only the interests of the individual and those that affect others. Mill was compelled to concede that any decision or action, no matter how personal, innocuous, or remote, could undermine the interests of others. My decision, for example, to purchase coffee at a small, family-owned café can plausibly be said, as Mill variously put it, to "harm," injure," or "damage" the interests of Tim Hortons insofar as the latter loses sales when I do so.

Mill explained, however, that "certain interests" are so important they "ought to be considered as rights" ([1859] 1991, 83). Adult citizens have a moral claim to autonomy – a right to make important decisions defining their own lives for themselves – which is a part of the general right to freedom. For Mill, to possess and exercise a right meant there is an established and recognized rule or principle that a person is entitled to do or not do something, or is entitled to have or forsake something or some object. These rules and principles that form the basis of rights are, for Mill, justified by reference to social or public utility. Rights are claims to be treated a certain way – particularly to protect people by freeing them from undesirable and exploitative dependence on others. They are also moral claims that no one may prevent you from doing what you have a right to do or pursue, or in other cases that someone must provide you what you have a right to receive. Mill claimed that governments may place restrictions on individual freedoms or rights if their exercise by some violates the rights of others. One can call this the Millian rights proviso: the main justification for restricting or limiting, either through policy or law, the freedom of individuals is when their actions violate others' rights.

Does voluntary euthanasia or physician-assisted death violate anyone's rights? If a moral agent freely and rationally consents to have his or her life ended, it is difficult to see any substantive second- or third-party rights violations from a Millian perspective. Mere hypothetical violations of rights are not, Mill insisted, sufficient justification for governments to limit activities. Laws may legitimately limit freedoms only when there is certainty that decisions and actions will violate others' rights. By legalizing voluntary euthanasia and assisted death, options would exist for those who choose to exercise their rights in accordance with their personal beliefs and conscience. The needs of those who do not hold those same beliefs would also be met by continuing to provide medical treatment and pain control until death occurs naturally (Scherer and Simon 1999, 16). The Millian rights proviso offers the kind of principled balance between conflicting claims that Mill believed is necessary to prevent laws and policies from being merely arbitrary in nature.

The Millian condition in its incarnation above specifies that governments may not place restrictions on individuals unless it is to remedy a rights infraction or there are deeply compelling reasons that particular activities could compromise the system of rights itself. One thing is clear: there is no right – whether as individuals, groups, or communities – to compel individuals to die as others wish. The value of life and meaning of death ultimately are what we as individuals assign to them (Dworkin 1993, 216). The right to aid-in-dying is a moral (and now constitutional) claim to pursue assistance to exercise that right without the fear or threat of legal reprisals. The *Carter* ruling is unambiguous that publicly funded health institutions must provide at least the option of assisted death to those Canadians eligible to request it.

Mill's theory of rights prioritizes the interests of individuals where there might be a conflict between their needs and those of the community, and attempts to balance conflicting moral and social claims on the basis of principle. His non-deontological rights theory recognizes that governments have a legitimate claim to limit rights and freedoms: individuals may not end their lives in any manner they choose; the state has the authority to prevent people from exercising the freedom to end their lives in a way that threatens the physical safety of others. The state also may limit how a person *exercises* the right to die, but it cannot deny that person's *possession* of the right itself. Euthanasia and physician-assisted death are not matters that affect only the individual; assisted death goes beyond the individual insofar as the participation of another party, by either the actual commission of the act or by providing the means to complete the act, turns the death into a social consideration (Scherer and Simon 1999, 108). The community has an interest in upholding safety, public order, and health that justifies regulation of the manner in which one exercises the right to end one's life (Paust 1995, 475).

Reconceptualizing Assisted Death Policy

Using an applied political theory approach, it is possible to use the Millian rights proviso to tackle the significant challenges governments face when crafting legislation and policy on assisted death. As the Supreme Court of Canada justices observed, "Parliament faces a difficult task in addressing this issue; it must weigh in balance the perspective of those who might be at risk in a permissive regime against that of those who seek assistance in dying" (*Carter v. Canada*, 98). The Court also deferred to Parliament with respect to the content and substance of future policy by noting that "complex regulatory regimes are better created by Parliament than by the courts" (125).

Canadian courts have developed decisional criteria to adjudicate constitutional disputes and to assess when it is legitimate to restrict constitutional rights and freedoms. Governments are obligated to assess proposed legislation and policy with respect to their consistency with the Constitution, but how they do so frequently is unclear. In developing legislation, governments cannot adopt the decisional methods used by the courts, since they must take into consideration much wider social and political concerns than those the courts require in their role as interpreters of the Constitution. Past injunctions against assisted death were largely based on near-absolutist grounds of protecting human life. Yet policy should not be based on abstractions such as the "sanctity of life" (Schramme 2013, 478–9), since it places the emphasis in the wrong place: the issue is each individual's way of living and manner of death. As Ronald Dworkin notes, "the question posed by euthanasia is not whether the sanctity of life should yield to some other value, like humanity or compassion, but how life's sanctity should be understood and respected" (1993, 217). Dialogue and discussion about assisted death should take place within a discursive context where citizens and public officials alike share basic self-understandings, the most important of which is that citizens in liberal democracies are rights-bearing moral agents. Indeed, as Penney Lewis states, in jurisdictions "with constitutionally entrenched human rights, the debate over the legalization of assisted suicide is likely to continue in the form of rights discourse" (2001, 99).

It is often claimed, however, that rights-based approaches to resolving policy problems are fraught with insurmountable difficulties. Gunter Lewy asserts that deontological arguments are "unlikely to lead to the kind of compromise that often is necessary in the development of public policy" (2011, 16). Definitional vagueness and conceptual confusion, for example, can reveal the limitations of rights-based approaches. Conceptually there are different kinds of rights: personal rights, civil and political rights, moral rights, legal rights, and constitutional rights. There is also deep disagreement over the specific meaning of the rights to life, freedom, and equality, let alone when conflict arises among them. However, the argument that rights-based discourse is ill-suited to guiding discussion and policy is quite mistaken. The problem, as Douglas Amy reminds us, is that "questions of right and wrong, justice and injustice, are rarely amenable to compromise" (1984, 584). It is not rights claims as such that create intractability, but rather the intensity of core commitments over autonomy and compassion versus sanctity of life and protection of the vulnerable that makes compromise difficult.

Indeed it is difficult to understand how rights claims will not govern the terms of debate over future assisted death policy, given their primary basis in liberal democratic political and legal cultures, practices, and institutions. The steady evolution and primacy of rights in political and legal discourse reveal a crucial change in the burden of justification for laws. From a rights-based perspective, the evidence should be incontrovertible that restricting autonomy and choice is absolutely necessary before legislation and policy is enacted that does so. As Margaret Battin soberly counsels, in the absence of overwhelming evidence that others will be harmed, "we ought not compromise the choices of some individuals in order to protect others" (1994, 180). Since assisted-death policy involves both private and public morality, any change to laws must attempt to bridge the gap between the private and the public – in the former to ensure legitimacy and in the latter to protect and preserve human life. All the considerations – the need to respect the principles of autonomy and the sanctity of life, for example – are important in the development of policy, but the basic consideration must be the right of individuals to live and die on their own terms.

One cannot develop a comprehensive, rights-based policy framework in the context of this chapter – such a project would be a considerable and complex undertaking – but it is possible to sketch an outline. Safe, clear, and consistent guidelines need to be established to ensure decisions to end life are based on genuine voluntariness and consent – the hallmarks of a constitutionalized system of rights. At the same time, it is crucial that assisted-death laws and policies not require unrealistically high and policy-thwarting standards of proof of individual choice or general wishes (Paust 1995, 482). Patients might lack specific knowledge of treatment options and the advantages and disadvantages of treatment protocols, but they do have the most comprehensive knowledge to evaluate their own life circumstances and financial and social support networks, and, most important, the capacity to decide on their own terms what constitutes a flourishing human life and a dignified and meaningful death (Hall 2010, 65).

Policy makers will need to tread carefully around the competence issue, however, especially as it revolves around mental infirmities. It is a requirement in all jurisdictions currently offering physician-assisted death that individuals be competent to make medical decisions at the time of assistance, to ensure that assisted death is limited to those who genuinely wish to die and have the cognitive ability to make such a choice. One way to satisfy the voluntariness criterion is through the use of advance euthanasia directives such as used in the Netherlands (Menzel and Steinbock 2013, 484). Clear evidence of one's wishes is a carefully considered and crafted directive, written while still competent, that speaks to one's current situation and that one has reiterated over time. There is a strong *prima facie* case for following such an advance directive, whether for withdrawal of life-sustaining treatment or for aid-in-dying (496). Indeed, governments should encourage the careful and considered drafting of such directives as a part of will and estate planning, while minimally compelling hospitals and health care workers to follow their established terms. Because young children lack the mental capacity to weigh different and often conflicting factors and make their own decisions, the rights they possess to exercise such choices should be considerably narrowed, with their best interests becoming the relevant and appropriate decisional procedure.

It is crucial that federal and provincial ministries of health provide detailed and current information and data on the implementation and administration of medical-assistance-in-dying. In fact, it might be preferable to establish a national agency to monitor and report on provincial euthanasia practices to encourage consistent nationwide best-practice standards. There must also be every good faith effort to prevent the bureaucratization of medical-assistance-in-dying, such as the proliferation of situational rules and overly cautious protocols that, in effect, become institutional disincentives for patients to choose assisted death.

Relatedly, end-of-life decisions should not be made by remote government officials, health administrators, or courts unless there is clear evidence of force, fraud, or mental infirmity (Hall 2010, 65). Greater resources also should be directed towards palliative care – providing patients relief from the symptoms, pain, and physical and mental stress of chronic, degenerative, and terminal illnesses – so that there are no policy and institutional biases with respect to any specific end-of-life option. Neither assisted death nor palliative care ought to be privileged from a policy vantage point.

Conclusion

The development of medical-assistance-in-dying policy will necessarily incorporate a strongly normative dimension. As such the analysis of this policy area lends itself to an applied political theory approach. When it comes to assisted suicide, powerful principles often examined in political theory, such as autonomy, conscience, compassion, and duty, are values that necessarily clash. In a democracy, differences over value and principle are resolved by a political process where the decisional priority of such values is established largely by policy makers. It is expected that legislators and policy makers will bargain and compromise to accommodate competing and conflicting interests. Broadly speaking, policy is shaped by reference to pragmatic, ethical, and logical considerations (Keown 2002, xiv). As Mill pointed out, however, it is vastly preferable that government officials develop policy and law on the basis of principle rather than political prudence or raw majoritarianism. As medical costs continue to outpace inflation and provincial governments struggle to control health care spending, the implications of ad hoc policy decision making concerning assisted death become clearer. Physicians, hospitals, and insurers are increasingly under pressure to contain costs, and it is already the case that age is a criterion for who does or does not receive certain health care treatment. In this context it would be alarming if future medical-assistance-in-dying policy were driven by economic necessity, rather than based on principles such as the recognition and preservation of rights.

Mill's struggle to derive a clear and decisive way to balance autonomy against other public values that might conflict with it is of particular relevance for contemporary political, moral, and legal debate over medical aid-in-dying. Where there are deep divisions, democratic deliberation requires a common basis for reasonable people to accept public decisions. A rights-based dialogue and framework such as Mill suggested is most consistent with Canada's constitutional and democratic system. His theory of rights is based on utility, not on deontological or absolutist grounds. Thus Mill's approach is not vulnerable to the charge that rights-based discourse is unduly inflexible for developing practical policy. If one voluntarily consents to having one's life ended in the event of grievous suffering, the decision, from a rights perspective, does not infringe upon or violate others' rights. We might conclude that the Millian rights proviso establishes a theoretical framework concerning euthanasia policy, but it is not itself entirely free of ambiguity in providing grounds for a clear solution to the problem of balancing conflicting values. A rights-based approach, however, minimally would compel governments to provide more persuasive reasoning why citizens may not exercise their own judgment and decide on their own terms how to live and die.

REFERENCES

Amy, Douglas J. 1984. "Why Policy Analysis and Ethics are Incompatible." *Journal of Policy Analysis and Management* 3 (4): 573–91. https://doi.org/10.2307/3324545

Archard, David. 1990. "Freedom Not to Be Free: The Case of the Slavery Contract in J. S. Mill's *On Liberty*." *Philosophical Quarterly* 40 (161): 453–65. https://doi.org/10.2307/2220110

Battin, Margaret Pabst. 1994. *The Least Worst Death*. Oxford: Oxford University Press.

Beširevi , Violeta. 2006. *Euthanasia: Legal Principles and Policy Choices*. Florence: European Press Academic Publishing.

Canada. 1995. Parliament. Senate. Special Committee on Euthanasia and Assisted Suicide. *Of Life and Death: Final Report*. Ottawa. Available online at https://sencanada.ca/content/sen/committee/351/euth/rep/lad-e.htm

Dworkin, Ronald. 1993. *Life's Dominion: An Argument about Abortion, Euthanasia, and Individual Freedom*. New York: Alfred A. Knopf.

Downie, Jocelyn. 2004. *Dying Justice: A Case for Decriminalizing Euthanasia & Assisted Suicide in Canada*. Toronto: University of Toronto Press.

Gill, Michael B. 2005. "A Moral Defense of Oregon's Physician-Assisted Suicide Law." *Morality* 10 (1): 53–67. https://doi.org/10.1080/13576270500031055

Glick, Henry R. 1992. *The Right to Die: Policy Innovation and Its Consequences*. New York: Columbia University Press.

Hall, Lauren K. 2010. "A Classical-Liberal Response to the Crisis of Bioethics." *Independent Review* 15 (1): 53–70. Available online at http://www.jstor.org/stable/24562265

Keown, John. 2002. *Euthanasia, Ethics and Public Policy: An Argument against Legalisation*. Cambridge: Cambridge University Press. https://doi.org/10.1017/CBO9780511495335

Lewis, Penney. 2001. "Rights Discourse and Assisted Suicide." *American Journal of Law & Medicine* 27: 45–99.

Lewy, Gunter. 2011. *Assisted Death in Europe and America: Four Regimes and their Lessons*. Oxford: Oxford University Press.

Menzel, Paul T., and Bonnie Steinbock. 2013. "Advance Directives, Dementia, and Physician-Assisted Death." *Journal of Law, Medicine & Ethics* 41 (2): 484–500. https://doi.org/10.1111/jlme.12057

Mill, John Stuart. [1859] 1991. *On Liberty*. Ed. John Gray. Oxford: Oxford University Press.

Mitchell, John B. 2007. *Understanding Assisted Suicide: Nine Issues to Consider*. Ann Arbor: University of Michigan Press. https://doi.org/10.3998/mpub.171846

Nys, Thomas. 2006. "The Tacit Concept of Competence in J. S. Mill's *On Liberty*." *South African Journal of Philosophy* 25 (4): 305–28. http://dx.doi.org/10.4314/sajpem.v25i4.31453

Ogden, Russel. 1994. "The Right to Die: A Policy Proposal for Euthanasia and Aid in Dying." *Canadian Public Policy* 20 (1): 1–25. https://doi.org/10.2307/3551832

Otlowski, Margaret. 1997. *Voluntary Euthanasia and the Common Law*. Oxford: Clarendon Press.

Paust, Jordan J. 1995. "The Human Right to Die with Dignity: A Policy-Oriented Essay." *Human Rights Quarterly* 17 (3): 463–87. https://doi.org/10.1353/hrq.1995.0030

Schafer, Arthur. 2013. "Physician Assisted Suicide: The Great Canadian Euthanasia Debate." *International Journal of Law and Psychiatry* 36 (5–6): 522–31.

Scherer, Jennifer M., and Rita J. Simon. 1999. *Euthanasia and the Right to Die: A Comparative View*. Lanham, MD: Rowman & Littlefield.

Schramme, Thomas. 2013. "Rational Suicide, Assisted Suicide, And Indirect Legal Paternalism." *International Journal of Law and Psychiatry* 36 (5–6): 477–84. https://doi.org/10.1016/j.ijlp.2013.06.008

Schüklenk, Udo, Johannes J.M. Van Delden, Jocelyn Downie, Sheila A.M. McLean, Ross Upshur, and Daniel Weinstock. 2011. "End-of-Life Decision-Making in Canada: The Report by the Royal Society of Canada Expert Panel on End-of-Life Decision-Making." *Bioethics* 25: 1–73. https://doi.org/10.1111/j.1467-8519.2011.01939.x

Weyers, Heleen. 2012. "The Legalization of Euthanasia in the Netherlands: *Revolutionary Normality*." In *Physician-Assisted Death in Perspective: Assessing the Dutch Experience*, eds. Stuart J. Younger and Gerrit K. Kimsma, 34–68. Cambridge: Cambridge University Press. https://doi.org/10.1017/CBO9780511843976.007

8 What's Wrong with Private Schools?

STEVEN LECCE

By some accounts approximately 6 per cent of grade 10 students in Canada attend private schools, and there is compelling evidence that they routinely outperform their public school counterparts: "at age 15, private high school students scored significantly higher than did public high school students on reading, mathematics, and science assessments, and by age 23, had higher levels of educational attainment" (Frenette and Chan 2015, 23). To the extent that educational success in these areas is typically correlated with greater subsequent earning potential, status, and interesting work, private schools appear to put those who do *not* attend them at a competitive and comprehensive disadvantage (Frenette 2014).

Self-selection effects are at work that make establishing the causal connections between private schooling and academic achievement very difficult: rich parents can more easily afford to send their kids to private schools in the first place; private schools often have more stringent admission criteria, which stream some of the brightest students out of the public school system; private school students are more likely to live in stable two-parent families, with more books and computers around; private school students tend to have better-educated parents; and so on (Van Pelt, Allison, and Allison 2007). Perhaps private schools are not better than public ones, then, because they have superior resources and teachers, but because they have better *students* for some/all of the previous reasons (Frenette and Chan 2015, 14). Notice, however, that the latter explanation, even if sound, reinforces, rather than undermines, the putative unfairness of private schooling: even if it is not the case that private schooling creates inequality where none would otherwise exist, it certainly magnifies broader socio-economic inequalities that do violence to fundamental liberal democratic values.

Liberal democratic justice requires that we all have the same basic civil and political liberties and equal, or at least fair, access to whatever resources we need to exercise our rights and responsibilities as citizens and to lead decent and meaningful lives on our own terms. Education is one of the most pre-eminent, potentially architectonic, of such resources: it is valuable for its own sake, but it also conditions and structures how (and whether) we make use of all the other resources that matter – health, political influence, and economic security, to mention but a few. Given that education is central to democratic citizenship and human flourishing in this way, should we be worried about the existence of private schools?

Perhaps. But sometimes parental motivations are likely to be less thoroughly mercenary, and therefore potentially objectionable. For example, imagine that, instead of sending their child to a private school to improve her chances of being admitted to, say, Harvard Law, parents go private so that she might be raised and educated as they were: as devout and observant Jews. In this context, we should not think of private schooling primarily as a tool for competitive advantage, but as a vehicle for the intergenerational transmission of culture: in extending a shared history, language, religion, and culture beyond the home, private schools act as institutional trustees for parental fiduciary responsibilities that are mediated by the religious/cultural values and practices in question (Reshef 2013).

Given (for many of us) the centrality of religious convictions to personal identity and intergenerational continuity, and also how threatening an increasingly secular and consumerist popular culture can be to religious practices and beliefs, it is readily apparent why faith-based schools might be attractive to parents, and why the alleged moral right to have one's children attend one ought to be legally recognized, perhaps even at some public expense. K–12 children typically spend *more* time in school than they do with their families, so it is easy to understand why, given a focus on the intergenerational transmission of culture and religion, parents want schooling to reflect rather than subvert their fundamental ethical commitments.

Religious private schools, though, also seem problematic from the perspective of liberal democratic justice. Their pedagogy, their rules and structures of authority, and significant parts of their formal curricula are intentionally designed to encourage children's belief in a particular religion. Also, religious schools are typically more or less closed to those outside the community of faith. This has the predictable result that both the student body and faculty are drawn heavily from that community, with little effort to encourage interaction with kids who attend other schools that are either secular or organized around other religious traditions.

The religious mandate of such private schools invites the charge that they are necessarily indoctrinatory, and in a way that violates the liberal commitment to personal autonomy. There are many accounts of autonomy in the contemporary literature, but a common reading of the idea is to link the capacity for a self-directed life to reason: we live an autonomous, rather than a manipulated or coerced, life when our fundamental choices reflect our own best and informed assessment of what matters in life and why, given the evidence at our disposal, and ample opportunity and encouragement to question things from time to time. Some people think autonomy is so important that it is a necessary (but not sufficient) condition of any valuable or worthwhile life. If their suggestion is correct, we have a fundamental moral right to an autonomy-supportive educational environment. At bottom, schools must teach critical thinking skills, rather than impart specific substantive ideals; if they cannot help imparting such ideals, they should do so through, rather than by circumventing, critical thinking skills. The central worry about religious private schools is that, to the extent they succeed in imparting religious beliefs, they do so at the expense of autonomy, because faith cannot be evidence based, and non-evidence-based teaching is indoctrinatory.

In sum, although parents opt for private schools for many reasons, two stand out: first, such schools bestow competitive advantages in the race for money, status, and power; second, they reinforce parental influence by institutionalizing the intergenerational transmission of religious/cultural beliefs and practices. At least at first glance, private schools seem unfair because they violate equality of opportunity, and religious ones also seem unjust because they violate children's right to an autonomous education and upbringing. Are appearances deceptive?

In this chapter I use an applied political theory approach to address the question of liberal democratic justice and the current practice of private schools in Canada. Based on a qualitative assessment of the role of private schools in Canada's educational system, I consider how the two main forms of private schooling, and their attendant parental motivations and educational outcomes, sit in accordance with the broader set of liberal democratic principles that constitute Canada's political morality. The applied political theory approach reveals significant tensions between current private schooling practices in Canada and principles of liberal democratic justice, and points to potential policy reforms to address these concerns.

The chapter proceeds in the following way. I first set the stage for the analysis by briefly introducing some of the instrumental and intrinsic benefits of schooling, suggesting that schooling is both a useful tool and an aspect of human flourishing itself. I then focus on equality of opportunity. Upon establishing the empirical dimensions of how certain types of private schools provide quantifiable socio-economic advantages to their graduates compared to public schools, and given that private schools confer on their students significant educational, social, and material advantages, I ask if some parents should be allowed to send their kids to these schools when others cannot do so. Is conferring educational advantage in this way protected by equality of opportunity, or would the abolition of private schools be a radical consequence of finally taking that idea as seriously as we should? Finally, I shift the focus to applying liberal democratic principles of justice to an interpretation of the aims and outcomes associated with religious private schools, and ask, given the importance of personal autonomy, if such schools are objectionably indoctrinatory. If they are, should they be banned or simply reformed?

Instrumental and Intrinsic Benefits of Schooling

It is commonly thought that parents have the right, and possibly also the duty, to do *everything* they can to benefit their children in ways that will both give them a decent childhood now and prepare them for responsible adulthood when they grow up. The thought might be a widely held one, but it cannot be sound. My daughter's chances of being admitted to a prestigious medical school would be improved by my secretly killing all the other applicants, but this particular parental strategy is impermissible because it would violate other people's rights. So although it is true that parents have rights (and duties) to advance their children's interests, somewhere there is a line that helps us distinguish between just and unjust ways of doing so. Reading to your kids at night is clearly on one side of that line; murdering strangers is on the other. Along that continuum, where should we place parents' decisions to send their children to elite private schools?

The question itself can take one of two forms. On the one hand, there is a moral question about the boundaries of legitimate parental partiality under the unequal circumstances of the real world: to the extent that there are private schools now in operation against a background of highly unequal resources, is sending your child to such a school consistent with an otherwise attractive principle such that, morally speaking, no one's life is more important than anyone else's (Brighouse and Swift 2009; Swift 2003)? In short, is going private morally permissible? On the other hand, there is a question of political philosophy and, ultimately, of law: in a liberal democracy such as Canada, should there be private schools at all? It is the latter question with which I am concerned, and answering it presupposes that, in the first place, we have some idea about what education is and why it matters. Only then can we articulate the appropriate educational distributive principles to see whether those principles, in fact, condone or condemn private schooling.

In the broadest of terms, education is the process of learning and practising a variety of different interpretive, analytical, and communicative skills, and acquiring knowledge about myriad natural and social subject matters. Clearly schools are only one locus of education so understood: much education happens informally in the family home, in the neighbourhood, in religious organizations, and in civil (and uncivil) society more generally. But there *are* reasons to focus more narrowly on schooling. To begin with, many recent public debates about education do so. For example, in 2007 Ontario Progressive Conservative leader John Tory announced that if he were to form the next provincial government, he would appoint former premier Bill Davis to examine how religious schools could be brought into the public school system. The goal was for Ontario's schools to reflect twenty-first-century diversity and to treat all religions fairly. Critics argued that extending public funding beyond the Catholic school system to all faith-based schools would compound unfairness by further depressing state funding to the public system, as well as segregate children from diverse backgrounds who should grow up together (Gillespie 2007). As it happened, on Election Day, the critics won out (McCluskey 2007).

At its core, the Ontario schooling controversy implicated three sets of interests: those of students/children, those of parents/religious communities, and those of third parties/the general citizenry. Political theory can clarify these interests and formulate proposals to advance public debate on an issue – schooling – that remains intensely controversial everywhere: "Politicians, parents, employers, even children, are constantly proclaiming on what schools should be doing" (Brighouse 2006, 1).

Another reason for focusing on schooling, even though education is a much broader category, is that unless the state limits its focus in this way, whatever balancing of educational interests justice requires will be nearly impossible to oversee and implement absent monstrous invasions of familial autonomy. In order to provide people their distinctive benefits, healthy families require a modicum of immunity from public scrutiny. Justice requires that we contribute to the common good, but we also have lives of our own to lead, and there are limits to what we can be expected to sacrifice in the name of social ideals. For example, one way of securing equality of educational opportunity would be to abolish families. Plato once proposed something of this sort, but no one else has recently advocated this. As it stands, then, the issue is not whether to defer to families, but how, and schools are precisely where this delicate balancing act gets played out. Evidence suggests that schools can strongly influence people's identities, abilities, and overall life prospects, and anyone interested in social and political justice would do well, then, to pay attention to what is happening (or not) in schools.

Schooling is supposed to deliver two different kinds of benefit. First, social, numeracy, and literacy skills, among others, provide competitive advantages in market economies where the benefits and burdens of social cooperation are very unevenly distributed. In western industrialized societies such as Canada, education is in large part a competitive positional good: "As an instrumental means to jobs and the money that goes with them, what matters is not how much education one has, or how good it is, but how much one has, or how good it is, relative to the others with whom one is competing for jobs. This gives education something of a zero-sum aspect: the better educated you are, the worse for me (and vice-versa)" (Swift 2004, 11). Schooling, and education more generally, is a tool that enables one to succeed in the competition for desirable things such as job security, income, status, and political influence.

Schooling is also indirectly linked to the possibility of a good or flourishing human life. While reasonable people might disagree about precisely what a good life must include, obvious candidates are: a basic understanding of social and natural phenomena; the ability to understand and experience art; the capacity for intimate and loving relationships; the capacity to participate in the political affairs of one's community; and so on. Such activities and relationships are valuable in and of themselves, and not only because of whatever material rewards they also happen to generate, if any. To the extent that schooling prepares us for such valuable things, it also "provides non-competitive opportunities for fulfilling life experiences: not only the reward of executing excellently those tasks which demand the skills one has learned ... but also the rewards which come from entertaining, executing, and reflecting on those tasks in a social context" (Brighouse 2008, 117).

If schooling delivers instrumental and intrinsic benefits such as these, what might motivate parents to select private schools for their children? The short answer is simple: on average, private schools deliver such benefits better than do public schools, notwithstanding important differences across English-speaking western democracies. In the United Kingdom, for example, private schools are predominantly elite institutions seen by both proponents and critics as "important mechanisms in the reproduction of the British class system" (Swift 2004, 8). By contrast, in the United States, private schools are primarily faith based and populated by children from across a much broader socio-economic spectrum than in the United Kingdom (8). Canada appears to follow the United States in this regard: 81 per cent of Canadian private (secondary) schools are faith based or "sectarian" (Frenette and Chan 2015, 15).

States can intervene in schooling on at least three levels: provision (they can supply buildings and employ teachers); funding (they can subsidize school places); and regulation (they can mandate attendance, set national curricula, and devise assessment systems) (Tooley 2003, 427–8). Now imagine a continuum between two ideal types: at one end of the spectrum is the Fully Private System in which there is *no* state involvement at any of the three levels; at the other end is the Fully Public System in which the state provides, funds, and regulates everything. To be sure, virtually any imaginable school system will be a kind of hybrid, but it is worth asking about the attraction of the pure types in order to establish what, if anything, justice might single out, even if only in rough approximation, along that continuum.

How should a liberal democratic state respond to parents who want a Fully Private School for their kids? This way of framing the question is apt because private schools have interests that generally coincide with those of (some) parents – namely, that their students/kids outperform outsiders (Merry 2007, 260–1). As Lynch and Baker (2005, 136) note:

> In a market system, what schools want are parents who will invest time and resources in their children thereby boosting performance, and

> correlatively the status of the school. Middle class and upper class parents fit this profile more fully than those from working class households. Working class students are more likely to be perceived as a liability, a risk to the status of the school in a market-driven system ... professional parents in particular are more likely to operate as active consumers in an education market; they have the knowledge, contacts, confidence, time and money to exercise choice and promote high educational performance.

Wealthy parents typically wish to send their kids to private schools, then, in order to secure them competitive advantages in the pursuit of lucrative and rewarding careers. In Canada, taxpayers are actually partly complicit in conferring these competitive benefits. We do not have a Fully Private System. Instead private schools often receive *public* subsidies that routinely trigger accusations of unfairness. Are private schools ultimately unfair? If so, does that putative unfairness wane (or is it actually compounded) when the underlying parental motivation for going private, as it were, is religious/cultural rather than economic?

Equality of Opportunity

Equality of opportunity is *the* master distributive principle of liberal democracy in theory and in practice; it implies that justice is fundamentally about fairly "rationing opportunities to become unequal" (Fishkin 1983, 8), rather than securing equal outcomes, no matter what. On the one hand, then, liberalism offers an interpretation of the basic equal moral standing of individuals; on the other, it also assumes that, because such individuals are rational and therefore, in some morally relevant sense, free, they must take personal responsibility for their own choices. On this view, justice is undermined rather than served when other people either unfairly benefit from, or are penalized by, our own prudent or reckless choices, as the case may be.

The connection between equality and freedom is therefore a constitutive one: the liberal state does not endorse any particular comprehensive ethical doctrine, and democratic citizens are free to pursue the good life on their own terms. Instead the state's business, as it were, is to identify various resources and goods that are valuable for pursuing whatever (justice-respecting) goals and relationships people wish to pursue, and then to ensure that each citizen has an equal chance to access those resources and goods. None of this implies that, for liberals, social life is necessarily and inherently competitive. Instead the claim is a *pro tanto* one: to the extent that social life is predictably competitive, the competition should be fair, and the fairness-versus-unfairness distinction piggybacks upon prior intuitions and arguments about personal and collective responsibility (Brighouse 2008, 89).

In a nutshell, equality of opportunity tells us that unequal life prospects are morally (and therefore politically) permissible only if, and to the extent that, they result from informed and voluntary choices, but not if they arise from unequal circumstances over which people have little or no personal control: "This idea, sometimes dismissed as weakly reformist or even conservative is, in fact, startlingly radical in its implications. If taken seriously, it would require systematic intrusions into the family and a vast reform in the way of life we commonly take for granted" (Fishkin 1983, 1).

At bottom, opportunity is an agency concept. To make use of their opportunities, people have to *do* something. But how should we construe the link between agency and the various outcomes that people pursue? One suggestion is that there is a necessary correlation between the two such that "one has an opportunity to do something or have something provided one can do it or have it if one chooses" (Lloyd Thomas 1977, 388). This cannot be right, though, for the simple reason that it implies that genuine opportunities are (provisional) guarantees. If equality of opportunity is meant to yield a principled mechanism for rationing *scarce* but valuable goods (jobs, educational positions, status), it does not make sense to tie the concept to outcomes that everyone can have, if only they would try (Barry 1995, 37–8). This solves distributive problems, but only by defining them away.

A more promising analysis postulates a triadic formula according to which (a) an agent has an opportunity when she or he has a chance to realize or attain (b) a goal without the hindrance of (c) some obstacle (Westen 1985). This formulation avoids the problem just mentioned by loosening the connection between choice and outcome, but it is also quite formal and therefore vacuous without further elaboration. In order to see whether or not equality of opportunity condemns private schooling, we need to move beyond the abstract concept and focus upon the leading substantive conceptions – those that fill in the relevant agents, goals, and obstacles in light of broader normative commitments.

Suppose that the agents in question are democratic citizens and that their goals are familiar things such as education, interesting careers, good health, economic security, and meaningful relationships. The general concept of equality of opportunity only tells us that, for justice to prevail, people should be free from certain irrelevant obstacles to the successful pursuit of such goals. Even if we accept that, in principle, there is nothing wrong with people having different levels of, say, wealth and health, provided those differences are traceable to different choices against the backdrop of a fair or level playing field, precisely *which* obstacles are irrelevant? When is that playing field level? In the literature, there are several possibilities.

Formal equality of opportunity only requires that law and public policy not discriminate between citizens based upon supposedly arbitrary and irrelevant characteristics such as gender, race, religion, socio-economic class, and so on. At the birth of the liberal era, this view was a radical one: equality before the law for all citizens was certainly an improvement over arbitrary submission to the whimsical preferences of kings. As critics have rightly pointed out, however, this conception of equality of opportunity is not particularly demanding: its focus on the formal and public aspect of rules is "compatible with private discrimination, implicit bias, and unequal distributions of resources" (Stanford University n.d., 2).

Especially when they are pursuing goods such as education, economic security, and health, people should be equally free from more than just state-sanctioned discrimination. Perhaps we can strengthen equality of opportunity, then, by basing the distinction between relevant and irrelevant obstacles to successful pursuit upon some notion of moral deservingness or individual merit? This is the strategy of meritocracy. In the competition for scarce and valuable societal goods, success should be determined solely by reference to merit. The idea finds its most natural expression in connection with jobs: a job should be given to whoever would do it best, given the demands of the role, and irrespective of other factors such as gender and race that are not obviously related to those demands. Meritocracy generalizes this intuition more broadly to cover a range of competitions for societal goods and resources. We are not unfairly disadvantaged simply because other people manage to get what we also happen to want. In order for competitive harm of this kind to be not just disappointing, but also unjust, we must be, in some relevant sense, less meritorious than other people.

Meritocracy assumes that equally talented people willing to exert the same amount of effort should be equally likely to succeed in a competition for a scarce resource. Thus, talent + effort = merit. As John Rawls noticed, though, "even the willingness to make an effort, to try, and so to be deserving in the ordinary sense is itself dependent upon happy family and social circumstances" (1971, 74). If this is right, then not everyone will be (equally) well placed or motivated to develop the particular talents, traits, and dispositions valued by any given specification of the meritocratic ideal. Unless meritocracy somehow controls for the unfair influence of, say, bad or absent parenting and poverty, equality of opportunity will be an engine of injustice rather than its opposite.

Fair equality of opportunity builds upon these insights. If each citizen must have the same chance to develop merit in the first place, then just institutional arrangements will somehow neutralize and/or compensate for the effects of differential family and socio-economic circumstances. Only then will otherwise equally talented and similarly willing individuals from every socio-economic background have genuinely equal opportunities to secure valued resources and opportunities.

But if the problem with meritocracy is that it allows morally arbitrary factors such as family background and socio-economic status to influence one's life chances, why care only about social disadvantages as obstacles to equal opportunity? That is, why stop at fair equality of opportunity, as Rawls does? Perhaps it makes sense to hold people partially responsible for the extent to which they develop their talents, but it is implausible to suppose that people are responsible for having – and therefore deserve – those natural talents in the first place. Does Sidney Crosby deserve his stick-handling abilities with a puck? Did Stephen Hawking deserve his scientific genius?

The most demanding conception of equality of opportunity is equality of opportunity for welfare or, as it has also been called, "luck egalitarianism." The view takes to its logical conclusion the foundational opportunity egalitarian insight that people should not be held responsible for disadvantages that are not of their own doing or making, and such disadvantages are equally likely to be generated by both social and natural circumstances. Having poor and uneducated working-class parents is one kind of competitive disadvantage that a child can suffer in the pursuit of status-conferring and well-paid work later in life. Equally damaging, however, is being born not particularly bright, or with a debilitating disease. For luck egalitarians, the state must do what it can to underwrite equal life chances for everyone, not just between equally talented and motivated children, but also between children born with varying levels of talent and motivation. Typically this underwriting takes the form of state compensation for things such as disadvantaged social background, and bad luck in the form of natural disasters, disease, and disability. By contrast, people who take informed and voluntary risks against the backdrop of a level playing field have no legitimate claim to compensation from others.

Now that we have a clearer picture of the motivation behind the opportunity egalitarian ideal, what are we to make of its application to the case of K–12 private schools? There are two decisive problems with equality of opportunity in this context; however, defenders of such schools should probably wait to celebrate. Although these problems undermine one type of argument (equality of opportunity) for the abolition of elite private schools, they also lead to an even stronger principle of educational equality (equality of condition) that clearly supports such abolition.

To begin with, there is something fundamentally misplaced about the meritocratic underpinnings of all conceptions of equality of opportunity as they apply to schooling. As Elizabeth Anderson has noticed: "Equality of opportunity is a valid ideal for deciding who, among those with *already developed talents* and motivation, should have access to the best jobs in an *exogenously* given occupational hierarchy. It cannot guide us in the allocation of K–12 educational opportunities, where both the talent and motivation of those seeking education, and the structure of educational opportunities, are *endogenous* to the decision being made" (Anderson 2004, 102). On the one hand, then, the kind of merit at the core of meritocracy is developed talent and demonstrated motivation, not something called "potential"; on the other, from the indisputable fact alone that children are born with different levels of potential, nothing necessarily follows about how we should structure opportunities to *develop* such potential (102).

The greatest difficulty, however, is that the norm of personal responsibility that recommends the ideal of equality of opportunity in connection with adults simultaneously weakens its appeal in connection with children. What do people find most attractive about equality of opportunity? That it is a distributive ideal that balances equal political concern with freedom: democratic citizens should be free to make their own choices, and they, not others, should bear primary responsibility for the costs of those choices. But K–12 children are not the informed, rational, independent, autonomous individuals presupposed by liberal theory. Although things typically improve over time, at least when they are very young, children suffer from all sorts of physical, cognitive, informational, emotional, social, economic, and political limitations. They are bad at both predicting and understanding the consequences of their choices; their options are limited and controlled by others;

and their preferences are unstable. For example, many children would rather play video games than study math: should their choice to do so be respected, and should they fully bear the subsequent costs of their juvenile preferences? Part of the reason for denying children many of the rights of democratic citizens (such as voting) is that they cannot effectively discharge the associated responsibilities. The criminal law is another obvious place where this differentiated capacity between adults and children is routinely (and rightly) taken into account.

All of this means that children have diminished responsibility in two interrelated ways: first, their "choices" are not always properly attributable to them; second, it is often inappropriate to saddle them with the costs of such choices. So whatever one might think about liberalism's notion of freedom and personal responsibility for adults, the view will have to be modified significantly for children. Even if people should be responsible for their choices, clearly, children do not choose their parents.

Although adults might be justly entitled to vastly unequal bundles of resources, then, there is no reason to think that their discretionary control over such resources also extends to spending on expensive private schooling, irrespective of the competitive disadvantage thereby generated for the children of other adults who either cannot afford it or who choose to spend their money on other self-indulgent or otherwise frivolous things. Nothing in equality of opportunity recommends having children's overall life chances dramatically influenced by their parents' bank account, intelligence, or preferences.

If children's entitlement to resources (including educational resources) cannot be choice differentiated, then equality of opportunity is inappropriate. But the paradoxical effect of this is that we are led to an even stronger principle: equality of condition. In broad outline, equality of educational condition for children seems to require (at least) three things in connection with K–12 schooling: first, children's access to educational resources should *not* correlate positively with inequalities of parental wealth; second, children's access to such resources should *not* correlate positively with differences in parental educational attainment and/or decision-making ability; and third, all else being equal, children with special needs and developmental disabilities should receive more educational resources than those without such disadvantages. Admittedly, these requirements might be realized in a variety of different institutional settings, so there is no logical or conceptual connection between equality of educational condition and the abolition of private schools. However, to the extent that, in practice, K–12 private schools subvert all three requirements of justice, they should be abolished.

Does this mean that we must abandon equality of opportunity for adults altogether? Not necessarily. Colin Macleod has suggested an ingenious response to the intergenerational problem that is meant to harmonize a norm of personal responsibility for adults with equality of condition for children:

> First, we identify the class of children-focused resources that: a) can be publicly provided to children and b) have the most direct and significant impact on the current and prospective well-being and opportunities of children. The most obvious candidates for inclusion in this class are quite familiar – quality education, health care, nutritious food, and adequate shelter. Second, these resources are made available to all children on a fair and equal basis. Third, for this class of special resources only constraints on the discretionary control over privately held resources should be established that prevent adults from using private resources in ways that violate the standard of equal public provision. (Macleod 2002, 227)

There is much to be said for this institutional division of labour, as it were, because it permits choice-based inequalities between adults, but constrains how economically successful adults can use their prosperity to confer competitive advantages on their children.

Liberal Democratic Principles of Justice and Religious Private Schools

Using an applied political theory approach, one can compare the liberal democratic principles described above to the current situation of private schools in Canada. Provincial governments tolerate, but for the most part do not directly fund, religious private schools. The glaring exception is Ontario, which fully funds the Catholic school system. In 1999 a United Nations human rights committee concluded that this system was clearly discriminatory and that Ontario should either withdraw such funding or else extend it to all faith schools (*CBC News* 1999). Since then, it has done neither.

Another way of balancing religious freedom with other political values such as fairness or neutrality would be for the state to tolerate but *not* fund any religious private schools, as is the case in the United

States. There are, however, two decisive problems with this approach. First, it generates unequal access to religious schooling on arbitrary and irrelevant grounds: rich parents who want their children to receive religious schooling can secure this; poor parents cannot. If people do have fundamental interests in religious schooling, why should the size of one's wallet determine whether or not such interests are advanced? Second, at least in Canada, all religious schools must teach the same mandated curriculum that is found in the public system. What distinguishes religious schools, then, is precisely their additional faith-based mission: to explain, teach, and inculcate particular religious practices, beliefs, values, and principles. As we are about to see, it is precisely this mission that invites the charge that such schools are indoctrinatory, and if they *are*, then the case for *both* tolerating and funding them seems to collapse. Now, a supporter might object that, even if religious schools are indoctrinatory, at best this generates only a *prima facie* case for reforming, not abolishing, them. However, to the extent that the indoctrination charge is thought to be linked to a necessary feature of religious schools – namely, the inculcation of belief – the reform in question amounts to their abolition: without that feature, they are indistinguishable from public schools. So the key question looms: does the indoctrination charge stick?

The argument against religious schooling is premised upon the importance of individual autonomy. That idea, however, needs some refinement, because some of its more ambitious formulations invoke unnecessarily controversial ethical claims – ones that are at least as contentious as the positions they are invoked to sustain.

In *On Liberty*, John Stuart Mill famously argued that, "it is the privilege and proper condition of a human being, arrived at the maturity of his faculties, to use and interpret experience in his own way ... He who lets the world, or his own portion of it, choose his plan of life for him, has no need of any other faculty than the ape-like one of imitation. He who chooses his plan for himself, employs all his faculties" (Mill [1859] 1991, 64–5). Mill's essential point was that, for people to flourish and thereby live worthwhile or ethically valuable lives, they must be self-governing, or autonomous. That is, they must actively shape their lives in accordance with their own considered assessments of which relationships, projects, and goals ultimately matter, and these commitments must also be open to periodic reexamination and, if necessary, either revision or abandonment. Any other kind of life, Mill thought, was "ape-like" to the extent that, in all likelihood, it only mirrored or parroted conventional expectations, traditional values, or common practices. Mill further supposed that people's characters differed in basic and important ways, which also meant that, to flourish, they needed a wide range of options to choose from, because the same lifestyle that is, say, the pinnacle of flourishing for one person is often simultaneously a crushing burden for another.

Now recall that a religious school – its pedagogy, its rules and structures of authority, and significant parts of its formal curriculum – is intentionally *designed* to encourage and stabilize children's faith in a particular set of religious ideas and practices (MacMullen 2007, 31). That is, the mission of a religious school seems particularly hostile to a character ideal that has Millian individuality and autonomy as it core. Religious schooling is supposed to create firm believers, not free thinkers. It was no accident that Mill thought Christianity a religion for the meek and the unoriginal. It is difficult to see how schooling that tries to fix one's convictions and render them more or less impervious to the countervailing influences of the broader society advances, rather than hinders, well-being – if well-being is understood as a life of detached scepticism and reversible commitment.

However, a democratic society committed to treating all its citizens with equal concern and respect cannot base law and public policy, including educational policy, on controversial character ideals such as personal autonomy. To do so would be to invoke perfectionist values that would be reasonably rejectable by free and equal citizens. In a pluralistic society, the state must remain, as far as possible, neutral between the competing ethical ideals that divide us. So even if religious schooling is hostile to personal autonomy in Mill's sense, the latter cannot be invoked to condemn it without violating an otherwise attractive principle of political legitimacy. Telling parents that they cannot send their kids to religious schools because, in light of the value of personal autonomy, those kids have a fundamental interest in freedom from religion would be using the state to advance a sectarian conception of the good life. If this is the rationale for banning religious schools, parents should feel justifiably insulted.

But there is another notion of autonomy that does *not* similarly run afoul of the neutrality constraint. Rather than invoking a comprehensive ethical claim about human flourishing, some defenders of autonomy have advanced an epistemological thesis about the connection between critical thinking and well-being, irrespective of the substantive content of people's chosen projects and relationships:

> [W]e might usefully compare mandatory education for autonomy with mandatory instruction in what used to be called the "three Rs": reading, writing, and arithmetic. Most, if not quite all, liberals accept that the state can impose these latter basic curricular requirements despite the objections of cultural or religious groups who say, for example, that it is contrary to their way of life for women to learn such skills ... When schools teach children how to read, write and perform mathematical calculations, they should not claim to be agnostic about the wisdom of using these skills throughout their lives. Similarly, I suggest, there is nothing illiberal about the idea that schools should urge their students to adopt the method of autonomous reflection as a lifelong approach to ethical issues. (MacMullen 2007, 105)

Understood in this way, autonomy is not a particular way of life, but an indispensable instrument with which we must equip children if they are to identify for themselves what kind of life is a good one for them, including a possibly religious one. This conception of autonomy as all-purpose life skill does not obviously run afoul of liberal neutrality, so if it can be shown that religious schooling undermines it, then parents cannot justifiably demand such schooling for their kids, in the same way that they cannot justifiably demand, say, that their children remain illiterate and innumerate.

Of course, what distinguishes faith schools from public ones is precisely the mission of inculcating religious beliefs: "When parents choose a faith school for their child (assuming that they are choosing it *qua* faith school and not simply because it is local or performs well in academic league tables), they do so because they want their child to receive an education that includes religious nurture" (Hand 2003, 91). Given that mission, however, there appears to be something necessarily objectionable about the means that are deployed to conduct it. As Michael Hand has argued, "[w]e are normally prepared to count a person's beliefs as knowledge only when they are justified in a fairly strong sense, when the reason for them is decisive and recognized as such by all reasonable people. We count a person's beliefs as a matter of faith when they go beyond the evidence available, or are based on a reading of the evidence with which others may reasonably disagree. In this straightforward sense, there is currently no such thing as religious knowledge: to hold religious beliefs at all is to hold them by faith" (2003, 93). For Hand this distinction between knowledge and faith is exhaustive, which implies that faith-based schools are in trouble because they try to impart in students controversial beliefs by bypassing, rather than appealing to, their reason. That is, religious schools teach "not known to be true" propositions as though there was sufficient evidentiary support for them. Teaching students to believe in such propositions in this way is therefore the essence of indoctrination: faith schooling subverts, rather than develops, the very interpretive and analytical skills that lie at the basis of the instrumental argument for autonomy. On this view, religious schools teach their students to believe unthinkingly, rather than to think critically, and to their obvious detriment.

This conclusion might be unnecessarily hasty, though, for two reasons. To begin with, there will often be a kind of slippage between what religious students are taught to believe and what they actually believe. Claiming that faith schools are necessarily indoctrinatory, then, falsely assumes that they always actually succeed in their avowed mission. Second, virtually all of our beliefs about the social and physical world are typically mediated by various kinds of intellectual authorities. For example, I am not an economist, which means that my so-called knowledge about the links between progressive taxation and economic productivity is entirely dependent upon the expertise of trained social scientists. I am also sure that climate change deniers are delusional, but I can only point to the overwhelming consensus among natural scientists as evidence for my certainty. In both cases, then, my "knowledge" of the social and scientific facts derives not from my own expertise – I have none – but rather from evidence vouchsafed for by appropriately qualified others. To the extent that my economic and climactic beliefs *are* rational at all, then, I must have some reason in the first place to trust others as competent authorities. But if this is the case, why cannot religious beliefs also be susceptible to an analogous justification? Perhaps students in faith schools are similarly justified in trusting the intellectual authority of religious teachers. If so, they are not indoctrinated, because, as we just saw, sometimes deferring to such authority is itself an exercise of reason.

Neither point actually defuses the objection, however, which can be easily reformulated to take each one into consideration. The slippage issue can be dealt with by incorporating a success condition to the effect that, when successful, religious schooling is indoctrinatory. Admittedly this is a weaker conclusion. However, to the extent that religious schooling is precisely aimed at inculcating religious belief, even with this proviso, such schooling is caught on the horns of a dilemma: if teachers do not manage to inculcate the relevant beliefs, then faith schools are not indoctrinatory, but they are also pointless; if and when teachers do inculcate those beliefs, this very success is objectionable because it debases students' reasoning capacities.

What about K–12 teachers as possible intellectual authorities on religion? This suggestion also collapses once we distinguish between perceived intellectual authority and the exercise of psychological power, and we also notice an important difference between parents and teachers. Practical reason tells us what we have reason to do; theoretical reason tells us what we have sufficient epistemic warrant to believe. In each case an authority is someone whose utterances or commands are, themselves, pre-emptive reasons for doing or thinking as they direct. Now consider the case of young children. They instinctively regard their parents as intellectual authorities on practically everything, including religion (Hand 2003, 97). This implies that, as long as parents are so regarded by their children, they can transmit their religious beliefs and practices to their kids without indoctrinating them.

Elsewhere (Lecce 2008), I have argued that liberal neutrality does not directly constrain parental behaviour, so parents are not under an obligation to avoid enrolling their children in controversial religious and ethical beliefs and practices. But it is a mistake to think that this permission also extends to teachers. Without having any very determinate view about precisely where we should draw the line, there comes a point – variously located for different children – when older children stop regarding adults, especially teachers/strangers, as reliable guides of what to do and believe in connection with ethical or religious questions: "Children learn very quickly that there are no legitimate religious authorities, that equally rational and well-informed people hold widely differing opinions on religious matters" (Hand 2003, 98). The implication is that, although K–12 children might be justified in treating their teachers as authorities on the history or sociology of religion, there is no reason to treat them also as authorities on questions of religious truth. Given that reasonable people can and do disagree about such questions, the only way for teachers (rather than parents) to inculcate faith is to exercise psychological power so that, in believing, children are, in fact, responding either to the force of their teachers' personalities or to the fear of threatened consequences for non-compliance. In either case, they are being indoctrinated, because there is insufficient evidentiary warrant for the underlying religious "truths." If we accept the instrumental argument for autonomy, then, such that children's well-being is dependent upon their acquiring and then deploying critical reasoning skills, then religious schooling harms students' capacities for human flourishing: it trains them to believe in people and things for wrong or inadequate reasons. This seems like a decisive reason to abolish religious schools.

Now someone might retort that the case against religious schools rests upon a division between knowledge and faith that is far too crude to support its weight. If "knowledge" only counts as such when the evidence in question is so decisive that there cannot be reasonable disagreement, and if faith is a residual category for everything else, then it seems as though virtually nothing we believe can ever be rationally justified. On this view, it sounds as though almost all of the central findings of contemporary social and natural science are also articles of "faith"; if so, teachers should be forbidden from teaching, say, both climate change and the biblical story of Genesis. Call this the slippery-slope problem. Any proposed amendment to our theory of reason that includes climate change will, on pain of inconsistency, also draw in the biblical account of creation and a host of other things. Call this the can-of-worms problem. Can we distinguish between knowledge and faith without falling victim to either of these traps?

Yes. Both misunderstand the indoctrination charge. If we insist that teachers can avoid indoctrinating their students only when the taught beliefs in question are beyond all reasonable dispute (because the evidence is decisive), then we *do* expose the case against religious schools to slippery slopes and cans of worms. The solution, however, is simply to sharpen the focus so that the central harm of indoctrination is not linked to the actual truth or falsity of whatever is being taught, but, rather, to the non-evidentiary way that indoctrinated beliefs are transmitted and then subsequently held. As Siegel has observed: "Difficult to shift beliefs are problematic when that difficulty is a result, not of the strength of their supporting evidence, but rather of the non-evidential way in which they are held. Holding beliefs in that way is problematic because the autonomy of the believer is compromised. The believer who believes non-evidentially is the prisoner of her convictions – her beliefs are deeply held, but she cannot subject them to critical scrutiny, even when they would benefit from such scrutiny and it is in her own interest to so subject them" (Siegel 2004, 80).

The claim, then, is that the religious mission of K–12 schools cannot be undertaken without teaching children to believe in epistemically unjustified propositions, and seeking to inculcate beliefs in such a non-evidentiary way is the essence of indoctrination. Because indoctrination is a violation of the autonomy to which children have a right, faith schools are morally objectionable and therefore should be abolished. This kind of argument is not similarly vulnerable to the slippery-slope or can-of-worms problems because it does *not* assert that teachers indoctrinate children whenever contested topics (such as climate change) are taught.

Conclusion

An applied political theory approach is a fruitful way to analyse the thorny issues of private schools in Canada. When we fuse a qualitative analysis framework with the right sort of empirical evidence in connection with elite private and religious schools – that is, when we do what I have done in this chapter – we are led to conclude that such schools are eminently unjust and should be abolished. If we care about equality of opportunity, then it is intolerable that some children who are already socio-economically advantaged in so many ways *also* have access to a quantity and quality of K–12 education that is a distant fantasy to less fortunate others. And if our individual and collective flourishing as Canadians depends upon both our willingness and our capacity to rethink and, at times, even revise our beliefs and practices in light of an open confrontation with the best available evidence at our disposal, then we should seriously question the existence of schools whose very purposes subvert those things.

A shift in this direction any time soon is exceedingly unlikely, however, as several things conspire against it. First, in Canada as in the other advanced liberal democracies, the wealthy have disproportionate influence on the agenda of politics, and it is unreasonable to expect that they will voluntarily relinquish one of the primary mechanisms for the intergenerational transmission of their own advantage. Second, Canada's policy of official multiculturalism is deeply embedded in both our institutions and our broader public political culture. Questioning not only the funding, but also the very existence of faith-based schools likely would strike many people as deeply un-Canadian. If the injustice of private schooling is to be recognized for what it is, then political theorists must do a far better job of convincing a wider audience that two-tiered schooling is as un-Canadian as the bogeyman of two-tiered health care and also that religious schools violate, rather than bolster, the best understanding of multiculturalism as a social ideal.

REFERENCES

Anderson, Elizabeth. 2004. "Rethinking Equality of Opportunity: Comment on Adam Swift's How Not to Be a Hypocrite." *Theory and Research in Education* 2 (2): 99–110.

Barry, Brian. 1995. *Justice as Impartiality*. Oxford: Clarendon Press.

Brighouse, Harry. 2006. *On Education*. New York: Routledge.

Brighouse, Harry. 2008. *School Choice and Social Justice*. Oxford: Oxford University Press.

Brighouse, Harry, and Adam Swift. 2009. "Legitimate Parental Partiality." *Philosophy & Public Affairs* 37 (1): 43–80. https://doi.org/10.1111/j.1088-4963.2008.01145.x

CBC News. 1999. "UN says funding of Catholic schools discriminatory." 5 November.

Fishkin, James. 1983. *Justice, Equal Opportunity, and the Family*. New Haven, CT: Yale University Press.

Frenette, Mark. 2014. "An Investment of a Lifetime? The Long-term Labour Market Premiums Associated with a Postsecondary Education." Analytical Studies Branch Research Paper Series. Cat. no. 11F0019M — No. 359. Ottawa: Statistics Canada.

Frenette, Mark, and Ping Ching Winnie Chan. 2015. "Academic Outcomes of Public and Private High School Students: What Lies Behind the Differences." Analytical Studies Branch Research Paper. Cat. no. 11F0019M — No. 367. Ottawa: Statistics Canada.

Gillespie, Kerry. 2007. "Tory would expand religious school funding." *Toronto Star*, 23 July.

Hand, Michael. 2003. "A Philosophical Objection to Faith Schools." *Theory and Research in Education* 1 (1): 89–99. https://doi.org/10.1177/1477878503001001006

Lecce, Steven. 2008. "How Political Is the Personal? Justice in Upbringing." *Theory and Research in Education* 6 (1): 21–45.

Lloyd Thomas, D.A. 1977. "Competitive Equality of Opportunity." *Mind* 86 (343): 388–404. https://doi.org/10.1093/mind/LXXXVI.343.388

Lynch, Kathleen, and John Baker. 2005. "Equality in Education: An Equality of Condition Perspective." *Theory and Research in Education* 3 (2): 131–64.

Macleod, Colin. 2002. "Liberal Equality and the Affective Family." In *The Moral and Political Status of Children*, ed. David Archard and Colin M. Macleod, 212–30. Oxford: Oxford University Press. https://doi.org/10.1093/0199242682.003.0012

MacMullen, Ian. 2007. *Faith in Schools: Autonomy, Citizenship, and Religious Education in the Liberal State*. Princeton, NJ: Princeton University Press.

McCluskey, Peter. 2007. "How faith-based schools sunk John Tory's dreams." *CBC: Ontario Votes*, 11 October.

Merry, Michael. 2007. "Should the State Fund Religious Schools?" *Journal of Applied Philosophy* 24 (3): 255–70. https://doi.org/10.1111/j.1468-5930.2007.00380.x

Mill, John Stuart. [1859] 1991. *On Liberty*. Ed. John Gray. Oxford: Oxford University Press.

Rawls, John. 1971. *A Theory of Justice*. Cambridge, MA: Harvard University Press.

Reshef, Yonatan. 2013. "Rethinking the Value of Families." *Critical Review of International Social and Political Philosophy* 16 (1): 130–50. https://doi.org/10.1080/13698230.2012.680745

Siegel, Harvey. 2004. "Faith, Knowledge and Indoctrination: A Friendly Response to Hand." *Theory and Research in Education* 2 (1): 75–83.

Stanford University. N.d. "Stanford University's McCoy Family Center for Ethics in Society." Available online at https://edeq.stanford.edu/sections/equality-opportunity-introduction

Swift, Adam. 2003. *How Not to Be a Hypocrite: School Choice for the Morally Perplexed Parent*. London: Routledge.

Swift, Adam. 2004. "The Morality of School Choice." *Theory and Research in Education* 2 (1): 7–21.

Tooley, James. 2003. "Why Harry Brighouse Is Nearly Right about the Privatization of Education." *Journal of Philosophy of Education* 37 (3): 427–47. https://doi.org/10.1111/1467-9752.00337

Van Pelt, D.A., P.A. Allison, and D.J. Allison. 2007. "Ontario's Private Schools: Who Chooses Them and Why." Fraser Institute Occasional Paper. Vancouver: Fraser Institute.

Westen, Peter. 1985. "The Concept of Equal Opportunity." *Ethics* 95 (4): 837–50. https://doi.org/10.1086/292687

PART III

Democracy and Citizenship

9 Deliberative Democracy: The Canadian Experience

MARLENE K. SOKOLON

Even though voter turnout in the October 2015 federal election was the highest in twenty years, with over 68 per cent participation, over a third of eligible voters still did not vote. It remains uncertain whether this reversal represents a new trend of increasing political participation in voting or a mere blip in the general decline in voter turnout found not only in Canada, but across most western democracies. Many prominent political scientists, such as Robert Putnam (2000), have tied this declining voter turnout to other of forms of citizen dissatisfaction with their democracies, such as decreasing confidence in the core institutions of government and civil society. Alarmed by this growing apathy in democratic governance, many scholars (for an overview, see Bohman and Rehg [1997]) have turned to a potential solution inspired by ancient Athenian democracy. Although direct voting and holding office were important, these ancient democrats valued most highly each citizen's equal right to speak and deliberate in their assembly (Woodruff 2005). Modern democratic theorists call their ideas for reviving direct citizen participation "deliberative democracy." By the end of the twentieth century, almost every major political theorist had weighed in concerning the goals and potential of deliberative democracy, including Habermas (1990), Rawls (1997), and Benhabib (1996), to name only a few. Importantly, and almost exceptional in political theory, deliberative democracy moved very quickly from abstract theoretical debate to applied political theory as both empirical scholars across several disciplines and policy makers in many jurisdictions attempted to incorporate the theoretical ideas into the practice of real-world cases of political and policy decision making.

This chapter focuses on the Canadian experience with deliberative democracy. In many ways, the approach to deliberative democracy in Canada is not unique. Canada shares with most other western democracies an increasing citizen dissatisfaction with politics, which is one of the main reasons cited for not voting in elections; research also reveals that Canadians increasingly are not interested in politics and sceptical that their vote makes a difference (Bilodeau, Scotto, and Kanji 2012). As well, major Canadian political theorists, such as Taylor (1994), Kymlicka (2001), and Warren (2001), are among those who have made significant contributions to the more than thirty years of theoretical debate on how deliberative democracy might reverse growing citizen dissatisfaction. Finally, as in other western democracies, the theoretical ideas of deliberative democracy in Canada have been applied to empirical research and incorporated in the policy process by engaging citizens through different mechanisms, especially in highly contentious public policy areas such as resource management, environmental sustainability, and health policy, as well as electoral reform.

Using an applied political theory approach, this chapter explores the unique contribution of these real-world deliberative forums in Canada to the broader theoretical debates concerning the assumptions and goals of deliberative democracy. Deliberative democracy is a good candidate for the use of the applied political theory approach, or the application of theoretical discussions to concrete political practices, as proponents have moved very quickly from abstract theoretical debates to testing its normative and theoretical expectations in empirical research as well as real-world policy and political decision making.

I begin by outlining some of the crucial theoretical expectations and values of deliberative democratic theory. I then apply the concepts, requirements, and goals of the theory to the two most salient types of deliberative forums in Canada: electoral reform, and public policy debates in the environmental and health contexts. Using applied political theory to assess Canadian deliberative democracy reveals a myriad opportunities for citizen engagement. Crucially the Canadian experience provides additional evidence for the oft-cited tension in deliberative democracy between the theoretical goal of genuine citizen deliberation and the reality that such deliberation does not always result in desired outcomes, but can reinforce inequalities, further marginalize disadvantaged groups, and do little to counteract elite-driven politics. Importantly, however, assessing the Canadian experience with an applied political theory approach confirms a key theoretical assumption of deliberative democracy: given the opportunity, the average citizen is capable of understanding, deliberating, and contributing to the policy-making process. Yet the applied political theory approach also reveals that citizen deliberation is more successful in debates concerning specific processes or concrete decisions than on questions of competing principles or contested values. In the final assessment, an applied political theory approach indicates that, in many cases of concrete decision making, rather than relying exclusively on the traditional elites of politicians, bureaucrats, and scientific experts, the time is ripe to think of innovative ways to encourage Canadian citizens to engage in the political decisions that affect their shared democratic lives.

What Is Deliberative Democracy?

As a theory of democracy, deliberative democracy draws from, develops, and challenges the foundational ideas and concepts of the long tradition of liberal democratic theory. In this tradition, it responds most directly to post-war theories of democracy, in which democratic politics were understood from the perspective of elite or interest group competition, and which downplayed or ignored the possibility of citizen participation in political decision making. Elite theory, for example, assumed citizens to be generally uninformed, apathetic, and easily manipulated; thus, from this perspective, policy was best made by elites who faced only a negative control through the mechanism of elections (Schumpter 1942). Other theories of democracy, such as the pluralist model of Dahl (1956) or the economic theory of Downs (1957), were less elitist, as they assumed citizens were rational. Such theorists, however, still viewed citizens as primarily passive consumers of competing political interests, which formed prior to, and aggregated in, acts of political participation such as elections. In contrast, deliberative democratic theory also assumes that citizens are rational, but stresses their capacity to contribute actively and directly in the policy-making process (Cohen 1998). In addition, rather than viewing democracy as an aggregation of already-established preferences, deliberative democratic theory emphasizes the act of public deliberation as crucial to the formation and transformation of citizen preferences.

As a response to growing citizen apathy, the proponents of deliberative democracy argue that it could revive democratic politics in several diverse ways (Gutmann and Thompson 2004; Jacobs, Cook, and Delli Carpini 2009). Citizen deliberation, for example, would enhance policy outcomes, it is suggested, because it would result in more egalitarian policy that goes beyond benefiting elites and powerful interest groups and more likely "accords with principles of justice" (Johnson 2015, 16). In addition, deliberative democracy could result in more thoughtful argumentation concerning the principles and values of the common good (Cohen 1998). In consequence, this increased empowerment of citizens should also reverse the declining trends in other forms of civic and political engagement, such as voting, as well as increase democratic legitimacy, as government officials would become more responsive to their communities.

Thus far the theoretical debate has yielded no consensus on a definition of deliberative democracy, its necessary conditions, or whether certain conditions are goals or outcomes. For example, is equality of participants a condition for deliberation, an outcome of deliberative process, or both? Is the goal of consensus in the deliberations unrealistic? Despite these debates, deliberative democratic theorists (see Bohman and Rehg 1997) tend to agree that deliberative democracy requires more than an increase in political participation in referendums, public opinion polls, or even improved public consultations. Deliberative democracy requires a genuine and open exchange of a diversity of ideas and the willingness to assess one's own views and challenge the views of the elites and status quo (Johnson 2015). Again, although there is no consensus on the specific criteria, at a minimum deliberative democracy requires the following: (1) procedures for genuine deliberation in which participants are autonomous and the discussion is inclusive and equal of all viewpoints; (2) discussions based on rational principles of mutual and reciprocal reason giving; and (3) procedures that offer some assurance that the outcome of discussions will affect policy and empower citizens (see Jacobs, Cook, and Delli Carpini 2009; Ryfe 2005). In other words, deliberative democracy requires a genuine, open, and engaged process in which citizens are involved in deliberation that has the potential to promote citizen understanding and political literacy, create policy that goes beyond elite interests, and encourage government accountability and legitimacy.

Since its inception, this promise of deliberative democracy has faced criticism, especially regarding the theory's underlying assumptions and feasibility. Can ordinary citizens, for example, really understand complex policy problems, especially those related to scientific and technical areas? Are the conditions of democratic deliberation possible and practical, or are they potentially deleterious for democratic legitimacy?

Critics, for example, have noted that the conditions of equality and inclusiveness might promote the opposite result: marginalized groups might self-exclude from the process since entrenched inequalities affect whether a citizen is even willing to engage in deliberation (see Dryzek 2005; Mansbridge 1983; Sanders 1997; Young 2000). Similarly, without equal education and access to the same degree of knowledge and resources, it is doubtful that every position can receive equal attention in the debate. Deliberative democracy is also challenged because the theory does not account for the diversity of how different human beings discuss and engage on political issues. Certain research findings indicate, for example, that, when confronted by a diversity of ideas, some participants do absorb a deeper consideration of issues (Munz 2006; Ryfe 2005), while other research has found that the more homogeneous the group the greater the tendency to avoid paying attention to opposing views (Eliasoph 1998). Research from social network studies (Green, Visser, and Tetlock 2000) confirms this selective exposure bias, in which we engage in political discussion only with those who have similar views, and actively avoid any exposure to challenges to our position. Thus it is not clear whether all citizens are willing to participate or are open to the views of others.

The deliberative conditions of rationality and reciprocity have also been the subject of sustained critique. Several scholars (Jacobs, Cook, and Delli Carpini 2009; Mansbridge 1983; Morrell 2010; Mouffle 1996) have challenged the requirement or assumption that political deliberation is based solely on reasoned arguments; in contrast, public talk often uses simplistic assumptions, argumentation, and the manipulation of stereotypes. Feminist theorists, in particular, have argued that the condition of rationality can be used to dismiss women's opinions, as the higher inflections and tone of women's voices are viewed as "emotional," rather than reflecting "the man of reason" (Forester and Kahane 2010, 224). Sanders (1997) and Young (2000) emphasize that democratic communication is not always rational, and should include alternatives to procedural reasoned argument, such as public protests, testimony, narration, and storytelling. These theoretical claims are often backed by empirical studies (see Mazzocco, Green, and Brock 2007; Ryfe 2005) that reveal the extent to which human beings rely heavily on emotional content and narrative during political discussion and decision making.

Finally, other critiques of deliberative democracy have focused on the practicality and feasibility of genuine citizen deliberation in contemporary large democracies, such as Canada, with millions of people living across large geographical areas. As I explore below, one response to this problem has been to use "mini-publics" or smaller sample groups of citizens, which might or might not be randomly selected, to obtain a cross-section of citizen involvement on specific policy decisions. These mini-publics have been criticized (see Goodin 2008) as tending to over-represent individuals with the luxury of spare time and resources, while underrepresenting marginalized economic and social populations. In addition, even if chosen randomly, mini-publics can be viewed as "undemocratic," since they would give a small group of unelected citizens more input on policy making than legally elected representatives. Relying on increased input from social media might not resolve this dilemma, since such sites might overrepresent the views of citizens with leisure time and access to, and a level of comfort with, such technology. In other words, such experiences with deliberative democracy might undermine democratic legitimacy by embedding more or a new kind of elitism and interest group competition.

In summary, the proponents of deliberative democracy argue that increased opportunity for citizen deliberation could produce well-informed debate, be more inclusive of a diversity of opinions, increase the quality of policy decisions, and enhance government accountability and legitimacy. At their best, such deliberations could have an educative effect on citizens, whose greater participation would improve their own arguments, enhance the quality of public debate, and ultimately contribute to policy that reflected the common good for all Canadians. In contrast, critics of deliberative democracy, while typically agreeing with the importance of increasing participation and the legitimacy of democratic governance, nevertheless argue that the conditions or assumptions of deliberative democracy could undermine these valuable goals. Greater citizen inclusion in the political processes would not necessarily bring societal divisions together, but, as Dryzek (2005, 235) points out, could lead to "deadlock, frustration, and failure." Rather than challenging elite politics, such deliberations might entrench existing inequalities by marginalizing women and other groups whose argumentative style failed to live up to rationalized ideals.

The Canadian Experience

Using an applied political theory approach, what can the Canadian experience with deliberative democracy contribute to these long-standing and overarching theoretical debates? As noted above, many of Canada's most notable political theorists, such as Taylor (1994) and Kymlicka (2001), have contributed to the theoretical understanding of deliberative democracy. As Steiner (2012) suggests, however, it is Charles Taylor's role as co-chair, with Gérard Bouchard, in Quebec's Consultation Commission on Accommodation Practices Related to Cultural Differences (commonly referred to as "Reasonable Accommodation") that potentially represents his most important contribution to the ongoing debates concerning citizen engagement. These kinds of commissions have a long history in Canada, as they developed out of the monarchy's prerogative power to order investigations: the first Canadian Royal Commission in 1886, for example, investigated class relations by interviewing hundreds of Canadians, with the result of creating Labour Day as a national holiday. Although such commissions are not technically deliberative democratic forums, as citizens do not deliberate with one another, they are a kind of citizen participation that focuses attention on issues and fosters broader community discussions. Importantly, as with critiques of deliberative democracy, the result of the public debate fostered by commissions is not always positive, but, as Ajzenstat (1994) argues, can solidify social cleavages in Canadian society.

The Canadian experience with more genuine deliberative democracy includes diverse types of deliberative formats, from citizen assemblies with randomly selected membership and strict rules of debate to open-ended town hall meetings where interested individuals contribute to policy debates. Deliberative democracy has also cross cut a variety of policy arenas, from language policy in Nunavut to environmental and transportation policy (see Johnson 2015). Specifically, this chapter explores two categories of policy that directly applied the theoretical ideas of deliberative democracy. First, starting in the early 2000s, proponents of electoral reform saw deliberative democracy as an opportunity to change Canada's first-past-the-post (FPTP) electoral system, which undermines the voices of smaller parties and interests. It was suggested that citizen deliberation forums could bypass the stalled reform efforts of governments that benefited from the artificially created majorities of FPTP. Second, from the early 1990s, deliberative democracy was incorporated into the policy process of developments in health, science, and the environment, which became salient during the same period as deliberative democracy took hold in academic circles. For such policy areas, deliberative democracy was considered a way to broaden public input as rapidly developing technologies and growing environmental concerns put pressure on policy makers, since they required new and broader ethical assessments of major social and environment risks, often with long-term consequences (Johnson 2008). Using an applied political theory approach, in the remainder of the chapter I assess whether the cases of these concrete practices in Canada confirm or challenge the main assumptions and criteria of deliberative democratic theory. In particular, I examine whether Canadian deliberative democracy represents a real challenge to elite and interest group theories of democracy by providing a forum for autonomous, inclusive, and equal expression of a diverse range of opinions. I also evaluate whether such debate involves mutual and reciprocal reason giving on policy options, and would lead to greater efficacy, more empowered citizens, and more responsive government.

The Politics of Electoral Reform in Canada

Two major attempts in Canada to reform the FPTP electoral system used principles derived from deliberative democratic theory. The better known is the British Columbia Citizens' Assembly on Electoral Reform (for a full analysis, see Warren and Pearse 2008). The use of a citizens' assembly to debate electoral reform is not unique to Canada; the Netherlands, for example, was successful with electoral reforms using a similar type of assembly in 2006 (Leenknegt and van der Schyff 2007). Funded with $5.5 million, the BC Citizens' Assembly was created in 2003 with 160 participants chosen by random selection, with some consideration to ensure there were two members from First Nations communities. Meetings were held from January to November 2004 in distinct phases that included learning about alternative electoral systems, public hearings, and finally direct deliberation, which resulted in a near-consensus vote (146 in favour, 7 against) to change the province's FPTP system to a single transferable vote (STV) electoral system. To reach this near-consensus, the deliberative process revealed that participants did move beyond their initial opinions and consider different viewpoints. The last phase required approval of the proposal by a direct democratic referendum, which needed a supermajority of 60 per cent. This referendum was held in 2005, but failed, gaining the approval of 57.4 per cent of the vote; a second referendum, in 2009, also failed, with just 38.8 per cent support.

The second case, that of Ontario's Citizens' Assembly on Electoral Reform, similarly failed to achieve electoral reform in 2006. This assembly consisted of 103 randomly selected citizens, one from each riding, with controls for equal male/female distribution, one First Nations member, and diversity in demographic makeup and age. The assembly held meetings for eight months, first focusing on learning about different electoral systems, then moving to a series of public consultations, and ending with six weekends of deliberation. As in the BC example, there was a broad consensus for reform (in a final vote of 94–3), but the Ontario assembly chose instead a mixed member proportional (MMP) representation electoral system. This example also ran into difficulty at the direct democratic stage as a referendum on the proposal failed to pass, with only 37 per cent approval (with a historically low turnout of 53 per cent). According to LeDuc (2011), any gains for deliberative democracy were undermined in the referendum phase, which was marked by an inadequate public education campaign and little awareness of the Citizens' Assembly's role in the proposal. Reflecting critiques of mini-publics in deliberative democratic theory (Goodin 2008), the media discourse, especially in mainstream newspapers such as the *Globe and Mail* and *National Post*, was highly critical of the process, which it characterized as undemocratic.

Although neither the BC nor Ontario publics ratified these democratic deliberative attempts at electoral reform, the process revealed both the strengths and weaknesses of applying theoretical ideas and concepts to real-world attempts at electoral reform. The Ontario and BC assemblies confirmed that a group of regular citizens, who were not experts in comparative electoral systems, can understand, evaluate, and deliberate highly complicated institutional reform. The assemblies' large mini-publics also proposed reasoned recommendations that were near unanimous. Throughout the process, the participants acted autonomously in complex debates involving mutual and reciprocal reason giving. There were issues, however, with meeting other conditions of deliberative democracy, such as equality and inclusion. In the BC example, the meetings were run by staff who controlled the agenda and determined which experts were consulted; thus the staff influenced the potential outcome by excluding certain perspectives (Ferejohn 2008). Equally problematic, after the deliberative process, both proposals were "captured" by typical adversarial democratic politics during referendum phase. In the Ontario case, the proposal ran into difficulties when the Liberals, who had initiated the deliberative democratic assembly process, failed to "champion" the proposal, preferring instead to concentrate on their own electoral success (LeDuc 2011).

It is important to note that referendums on electoral reform have not always failed to pass with a supermajority: New Zealand changed its FPTP system via a referendum in 2007 (see Renwick 2011). In this case, however, the reform did not involve deliberative democracy, but only a direct referendum in which 70.5 per cent of voters chose to move to a MMP system.

Deliberation in Science, Health, and Environmental Policy

Using an applied political theory approach also reveals important findings in the empirical evidence of "mini-publics" and other kinds of deliberative democratic forums on science and environmental policy in Canada and across most western democracies. These deliberative forums are now so common in these policy areas that the question of whether to involve the public is "no longer under serious debate as decision makers, faced with increasingly difficult resource allocation decisions, welcome the opportunity to share this task (and the associated blame) with the public" (Abelson 2001, 777). Importantly, public concern with developments in science and technology, especially in environmental and health policy, have coincided with growing interest in deliberative democracy. For instance, "lay panel conferences" in Norway in 1996 and 2000 influenced that country's highly restrictive approach to genetically modified organisms (GMOs) (Wandel 2006). In contrast, in Germany, industry officials, anti-GMO activists, and university researchers came together for two years of deliberation on GMO policy development (Charles 2001). In the German case, the deliberative process was highly contentious, and fell apart when the activist representatives walked out of the deliberations, especially around the deliberative democratic condition that agreement must be based exclusively on rational evidence. In Canada similar mixed results are found. Canada has many examples of successful outcomes where participants contributed to the final adopted policy, but the empirical cases of deliberative democracy also reveal the difficulty of expecting citizen deliberation to resolve policy that involves contentious principles or opposing ideological values.

One crucial study concerning deliberative democracy in environmental policy is Johnson's (2008) in-depth analysis of nuclear waste management policy. The deliberative model, in this case, was not a mini-public, but a three-year iterative deliberative process involving twenty sets of discussions with randomly selected citizens representing the diverse normative values of the Canadian population, experts in nuclear waste management, and representatives from organizations and First Nations with articulated interests in the policy area. The process included an information stage, 120 public sessions, public opinion surveys, and several e-dialogues. Despite this serious engagement, Johnson's analysis highlights many ways the process failed to meet deliberative conditions of inclusion, equality, and rationality. Aboriginal participants, in particular, were critical of several elements of the process; rather than inclusive, these participants found the process exclusionary and unequal, as it provided insufficient time for translation and analysis. Other issues with the process included predetermined constraints on debate, which took certain issues such as banning nuclear power off the table. In the end, as with debates on GMOs in Germany, disagreements on moral principles or between the pro- and antinuclear positions remained entrenched. Most significantly, Johnson concludes that the "ultimate success of deliberative democratic policy processes is determined by the actors themselves, and especially actors in positions of institutional and financial dominance" (2008, 110).

Other studies of various deliberative forums on new technologies and resource policy have arrived at similar conclusions. One such case is the more than twenty years of consensus-based decision making (CBDM) forums used in forest planning in British Columbia to resolve disputes over land management (see Mascarenhas and Scarce 2004). In 1992 the province established an independent advisory Commission on Resources and Environment (CORE), which developed a land-use strategy emphasizing inclusive and cooperative decision making with representatives affected by land-use plans, such as industry representatives, community organizations, local government, and environmental and recreation groups. Again, one the main critiques of the process was that significant issues, such as logging targets, were predetermined by government and left off the table. In addition, although agreement on certain practical issues were found, there was little consensus or compromise on divergent positions on larger environmental concerns or ethical principles; over time, some participants became suspicious that the procedure was a political ploy for government to "unload" a contentious issue and divert blame. Mascarenhas and Scarce's (2004) study also highlights other issues with the CBDM process, such as unequal access to resources for all groups. Various people also questioned the inclusiveness of participation, which was perceived as skewed towards forestry experts and industry insiders, with local voices – especially the perspectives of environmental non-governmental organizations and First Nations – underrepresented or absent from discussions. Also salient was the question of whether those involved, even from local communities, really were "representative" of diverse local interests or simply other elite insiders. Despite such concerns, there were many examples of deliberate forums seen as responsive to community needs, which resulted in positive views of the process. In these cases, the success of the CBDM was often attributed to specific individuals in positions of leadership during the deliberations.

In another empirical and real-world example of deliberative democracy, forest management companies have responded to demands for more inclusive and transparent decision making by establishing stakeholder advisory committees (SACs). There have been over 140 such committees across Canada on issues as diverse as airport development, remediating contaminated sites, and the location of logging sites (Parkins et al. 2004). Designed to enhance participatory democracy by ensuring equitable representation, these committees have consisted of a diversity of actors, long-term dialogue, and collaborative problem solving. McGurk, Sinclair, and Diduck (2006) find that, in Manitoba, many SACs experienced successful deliberation encounters marked by greater information sharing, breadth of participant learning, relationship building, and influence on site-specific operational details. Weaknesses of this deliberative process, however, reflect critiques of other kinds of deliberative democratic forums, including questions of legitimacy due to lack of accountability, inadequate or sometimes overwhelming information in the learning stages, and a lack of broad community involvement, especially by First Nations peoples. In particular, participants cited infrequent meetings as highly problematic, since this led to disadvantaging those in the bottom tier of the learning process as well as to poor attendance and frequent changes in participants. Other critiques focus on how the process was not truly deliberative, as there was an overreliance on passive techniques, including mass opinion surveys, and information provision without deliberation, such as news conferences. The authors conclude that the stakeholder advisory committees "represent increments toward meaningful public participation in forest management," but that genuine participation remains elusive (McGurk, Sinclair, and Diduck 2006, 823). To create truly deliberative conditions would require more equitable representation, especially of marginalized groups, and less control by company officials who set the agenda and acted as "gatekeepers" of information.

Turning to empirical evidence from deliberative forums on health care policy, the applied political theory approach also reflects strengths and weaknesses in the procedures and outcomes of such discussions. In 2009 in Vancouver, O'Doherty, Hawkins, and Burgess (2012) recruited a mini-public to investigate the feasibility of incorporating public deliberation into social, ethical, and policy challenges concerning the development of biobanks, which contain biological samples for use in medical research. Biobanks pose new ethical dilemmas about consent and the privacy of personal information connected to biological samples. This twenty-eight-participant mini-public was drawn from a random, demographically stratified sample intended to overrepresent First Nations and individuals with genetic/chronic disabilities. It followed similar stages found in other deliberative forums, such as learning phases and multiple deliberation sessions. These sessions were guided by a workbook, which constrained potential topics for discussion to increase the possibility that dialogue and recommendations would include specific problems identified by biobank development experts. Importantly, unlike critiques of other mini-publics in nuclear waste management or CBDM, the participants were free to reject biobanks on principle. In the evaluation of this process, the study finds that deliberants were able to come to collective decisions and move beyond their original and personal opinions. Most important, although it constrained deliberation, the predetermined and structured approach (such as the use of a workbook) was deemed crucial to creating consensus, or at least a clear articulation of disagreement about the recommendations. Even with the possibility of rejecting biobanks outright, however, control over the agenda by experts constrained participants' autonomy and the inclusiveness of all opinions.

Another study on the use of deliberative forums in the development of health policy assesses citizens' reasoned opinions in the development of personalized medicine (Bombard et al. 2013). Personalized medicine is the use of genetic information to improve medical treatment by personalizing risks: an example would be the use of a gene expression profile, which can aid in predicting how women with breast cancer might respond to treatment. In 2009 citizens' reference panels were created consisting of fourteen individuals chosen by lot to represent each health authority region in Ontario: the panel was 50 per cent Canadian born, with five women and nine men ages eighteen to seventy-one. The panel met five times over eighteen months, with discussion guided by precirculated material that, like the biobank example, included a workbook, but also newspaper stories, academic articles, and draft policy recommendations. Overall the panel came to a strong consensus that personalized medicine had the potential to improve health care delivery, with caveats concerning cost of delivery and the possibility that such technology would stratify treatment access. The panel stressed, for example, that personalized medicine should not determine access to treatment, which should be made available to all patents whether or not the tests indicated any benefit. Although Bombard et al. (2013) are clear that such mini-publics cannot be used to represent public opinion, they stress that this case provides "evidence of the public's ability to form coherent judgments and expectations about a new or future policy issue using structured, facilitated deliberative discussion" (1200). In this example, the outcome confirmed that small-group public deliberation can result in reasoned agreements, but it requires a means of constraining discussion with expert-chosen, predetermined, evidential material.

In another study, Abelson (2001) focuses on four Ontario public participation communities which were undergoing health services restructuring to assess how contextual factors – such as shared values that shaped overall participation, the politicization of contentious community issues, and the roles government officials and health councils performed as "enablers" of discussion – affected public deliberation, including whether individuals were willing even to participate. One important finding emphasizes that the style of deliberation, such as the public interaction with health care experts, varied depending on the socio-economic status of the community and pre-existing cultural norms, either strong or weak, of community participation. In the Hamilton-Wentworth region, for example, deliberations tended to be low key and polite, possibly due to the community's relatively lower socio-economic status, which might contribute to a culture of deference towards health care professionals; such deference was found even among local elites, such as politicians and media, who rarely challenged medical experts. In contrast, with a generally higher socio-economic status as well as a long-standing tradition of public engagement, the deliberative environment in the Ottawa-Carleton region was described as "highly competitive and divisive" (Abelson 2001, 783). Ottawa-Carleton's media also tended to be more critical, and their coverage emphasized long-standing rivalries and controversies underlying the current debate. Thus, in this concrete example of deliberative democracy, the process and outcomes differed depending on socio-economic status and existing cultural norms that varied across regions.

Abelson (2001) also notes that the institutional organization of the public participation communities played a potentially vital role in fostering debate beyond those communities. In some cases, such as in Ottawa-Carleton, the institutional organizations enabled routine participation by community members; in contrast, in more rural regions such as Nipissing, the same institutions had an insignificant effect on building deliberation beyond specific issue-driven participation. Abelson suggests the difference is due to the failure of the institutional design of the Ontario Health Care Councils to take into account unique characteristics of different communities. Thus, one lesson important from this empirical case is that fostering genuine deliberative democracy, especially equal and inclusive deliberation that goes beyond issue-driven politics, cannot rely on a one-size-fits-all institutional design, but must incorporate "the contextual fabric of local communities" (Abelson 2001, 791). Johnson (2015) echoes this finding in her exploration of contextual factors in additional policy areas, such as transportation policy in Toronto and language policy in Nunavut. In the case of language policy, for example, Johnson finds that the policy-making phase was highly deliberative, but the criteria of inclusiveness became limited at the policy implementation phase when faced with entrenched and complicated bureaucratic procedures.

These empirical cases of deliberative democracy in Canada thus reveal the extent to which other factors, such as institutional design and differing norms and styles of engagement, are significant to the process and outcomes of citizen deliberation.

Conclusion

The examples explored in this chapter provide only a very brief snapshot of the myriad recent attempts at deliberative democracy in Canada. By comparing these empirical findings to theoretical expectations, however, an applied political theory approach can contribute both to theoretical debates and to the development of incorporating citizens' deliberation in policy making.

In particular, these cases reveal, first, the limitations of the theoretical expectations of criteria such as autonomy, inclusiveness, equality of opinions, mutual and reciprocal reason giving, and the potential to empower citizens and foster more responsive government. Most significantly, despite the theoretical expectation that deliberative democracy is an alternative to elite and aggregate theories of democracy, the

Canadian experience with deliberative democracy falls short of this goal. In most cases, elites remained crucial to the success of the deliberative process in several ways, including controlling the agenda, acting as leaders during the deliberative process, and by championing (or failing to champion) the proposals of the mini-publics. In the BC electoral reform example (Warren and Pearse 2008), the process of deliberation and flow of information was controlled and influence by staff; in the Ontario electoral reform case LeDuc (2011), the outcomes of the mini-publics underscored the need for a a political champion to be translated into policy. Similarly Johnson (2008), in her analysis of nuclear waste management, points out the inherent tension in real-world experiences with deliberative democracy. On the one hand, the support of actors with financial and political power is crucial if deliberations are to have an effect on policy; on the other hand, elite control was a main obstacle to genuine deliberation, especially as experienced by marginalized groups such as First Nations (see also McGurk, Sinclair, and Diduck 2006 in forestry management). In other cases, elite dominance over the deliberative process, such as the use of a workbook to guide discussion in biobank mini-publics or control of the agenda in CBDM, was critical to the outcome. This dominance led participants, in many cases, to argue that the deliberations simply mimicked existing elite and interest group rivalries (Mascarenhas and Scarce 2004; O'Doherty, Hawkins, and Burgess 2012). In still other cases, participants saw the process as an extension of politics as usual, in which deliberative democracy was simply a way for elites to "unload the blame" onto the deliberative process (McGurk, Sinclair, and Diduck 2006, 30). In other words, the empirical evidence of the applied political theory approach underscores the extent to which deliberative democracy does not replace or supersede elite or interest group politics, but appears to work alongside such traditional political competition.

Second, the empirical evidence also reveals that the oft-cited criteria of deliberative democracy, such as equality and inclusion, were rarely achieved in concrete experiences of Canadian citizen deliberation. For the most part, especially with targeted mini-publics, great effort was made to include a diversity of backgrounds and interests. Yet even with such diversity, the process remained susceptible to the critiques (see Goodin 2008) that such groups are not representative of all citizens' viewpoints, and do not have the legitimacy of elected representation: in Ontario, for example, media criticism of the mini-public on these grounds contributed to the failure of the recommended electoral reforms (LeDuc 2011). Importantly, the deliberative conditions of equality and inclusion of marginalized groups was highly problematic in several empirical cases, especially in the area of resource management. As critics expected (see Dryzek 2005; Mansbridge 1983; Sanders 1997; Young 2000), the deliberative process privileged those with greater access to resources and information; in the case of forestry planning in British Columbia, many volunteer participants felt illegitimate in their role, especially in comparison to government and industry participants who received specialized training and payment (Mascarenhas and Scarce 2004). In Manitoba the lack of First Nations participation in the stakeholder advisory committees was problematic for the process and legitimacy of its decision-making capacity (McGurk, Sinclair, and Diduck 2006). Although individuals declined to engage in deliberation for many reasons, including lack of resources or the timing of meetings, it is possible that elite agenda setting, such as leaving logging targets off the table, delegitimized the deliberations by excluding the position of many individuals. These empirical findings underscore the theoretical requirement of efficacy or assurance that discussion will affect policy (Jacobs, Cook, and Delli Carpini 2009; Ryfe 2005), as citizens were generally unwilling to engage in difficult deliberations without some assurance that the outcome would have policy consequences that genuinely addressed their concerns (Abelson et al. 2003).

The theoretical criteria of autonomy and rational evidence-based decision making also encountered difficulties in the empirical cases. Abelson (2001) emphasizes the importance of contextual factors in deliberation on health care decision making in Ontario. She finds that citizens do not deliberate as autonomous, rational individuals; instead, they are influenced by a complexity of institutional and community norms that shape whether they are even inclined to participate in the deliberative process. In addition, in several cases, science-based epistemology was privileged as "rational" and thus it constrained normative discussion and influenced meaningful outcomes. As several theoretical critiques have predicted (Forester and Kahane 2010; Sanders 1997; Young 2000), expectations of rationality in deliberation did not always limit non-rational displays and "emotional" outbursts. In the case of nuclear waste management, for example, which had specific workshops on different epistemological perspectives and attempted to encourage reciprocity of understanding, the debate still occasionally broke down as participants launched "boisterous attacks on opposing positions" (Johnson 2008, 102). Thus the empirical evidence in the applied political theory approach supports the critique that expectations of rationality do not represent real-world deliberation, and tend to privilege elite perspectives.

Third, in several empirical cases, the reason-giving exchange broke down expressly in deliberations that encountered strong normative disagreements. Most examples of successful deliberation, which ended with near consensus, were premised by prevailing broad agreement on ethical norms. In the case of the biobank mini-publics, support was found to reinforce existing broad, liberal democratic principles, such as "safety for current and future generations" or "respect for informed consent" (O'Doherty, Hawkins, and Burgess 2012, 1608–9). In the electoral reform cases, the participants agreed with general norms of democratic representation. On more contentious issues, such as the use of nuclear energy per se (Johnson 2008) or whether to protect the forest environment from further logging (Mascarenhas and Scarce 2004), successful deliberation was contrived, since divisive principles were left off the table. In contrast, little progress was seen when serious disagreement existed concerning general principles or values at the heart of the deliberation: Johnson (2008, 107) notes that, throughout the three-year process of the case she examines, there remained "persistent disagreements between anti-nuclear activists and pro-nuclear industry representatives." This tendency towards conflictual deliberation was also found in cases where the policy outcomes were tied to specific interests. Forest management deliberations (Mascarenhas and Scarce 2004), for example, became contentious when debates over actual land usage became captured or merely replicated interest group competition for resources.

Thus an important finding of the applied political theory approach to empirical cases in Canada is that deliberative democracy is no panacea for the limitations of elite or interest group competition. As some theorists argue – see, for example, Johnson (2015) – the conditions of deliberative democracy prove more "ideal" than found in practice. In general, deliberation was less antagonistic when dealing with already broadly agreed-upon norms and values or when highly constrained by leaving contentious principles off the table. Deliberative democracy appeared to flourish more when the agenda referred to specific and well-defined options and issues, but was limited in challenging existing norms or resolving highly contentious conflicts over values and principles. As such the empirical evidence reveals that it is misguided to expect deliberative democracy to result in better and more reasoned argumentation about conflicts over the common good (c.f. Cohen 1998). Yet despite these shortcomings, the Canadian experience with real-world examples of deliberation underscores the degree to which the average Canadian, when given the opportunity, can become informed, seriously deliberate, and agree to reasoned conclusions about complex and technical policy areas and political debate. Citizens did learn and deliberate about highly complex issues in the governance of biomaterial and other health care technologies, the use of land and resource management, and the intricacies of comparative electoral systems. Although there is no evidence that such successes influenced citizens' perceptions of Canadian democracy, Abelson et al. (2003) find that the greater degree of understanding of participants translated generally into more respect for existing political decision makers. Thus, it is possible that, with many more such experiences of citizen deliberation over time, the perception of governments' legitimacy will increase.

One final important and overriding lesson from the applied political theory approach is that the average Canadian citizen should be given more opportunities to participate in political decision making, especially in policy areas with widely agreed-upon norms and values. Since citizens, if given the opportunity, can learn about and discuss complex policy issues, policy makers' current overreliance on "epistemic communities" of scientific experts in many policy areas is unwarranted. The practice of citizen deliberations will never reach the ideals of deliberative democracy nor will it replace other kinds of political behaviour, such as elites and interest group competition, or political protest and voting. Despite the limited success of deliberative forums, however, citizens and their government representatives should feel encouraged to continue developing innovative ways to foster greater citizen participation, especially by marginalized individuals, in the messy and always unfinished business of improving Canadian politics.

REFERENCES

Abelson, Julia. 2001. "Understanding the Role of Contextual Influences on Local Health-Care Decision Making." *Social Science & Medicine* 53 (6): 777–93. https://doi.org/10.1016/S0277-9536(00)00386-5

Abelson, Julia, Pierre-Gerlier Forester, John Eyles, Patricia Smith, Elizabeth Martin, and François-Pierre Gauvin. 2003. "Deliberations about Deliberative Methods: Issues in the Design and Evaluation of Public Participation

Processes." *Social Science & Medicine* 57 (2): 239–51. https://doi.org/10.1016/S0277-9536(02)00343-X

Ajzenstat, Janet. 1994. "Constitution Making and the Myth of the People." In *Constitutional Predicament: Canada after the Referendum of 1992*, ed. Curtis Cook, 112–25. Montreal; Kingston, ON: McGill-Queen's University Press.

Benhabib, Seyla. 1996. "Toward a Deliberative Model of Democratic Legitimacy." In *Democracy and Difference: Contesting the Boundaries of the Political*, ed. Seyla Benhabib, 67–94. Princeton, NJ: Princeton University Press.

Bilodeau, Antoine, Thomas J. Scotto, and Mebs Kanji. 2012. "The Future of the Canadian Election Studies." In *The Canadian Election Studies: Assessing Four Decades of Influence*, ed. Mebs Kanji, Antoine Bilodeau, and Thomas J. Scotto, 209–14. Vancouver: UBC Press.

Bombard, Yvonne, Julia Abelson, Dorina Simeonov, and François-Pierre Gauvin. 2013. "Citizens' Perspectives on Personalized Medicine: A Qualitative Public Deliberation Study." *European Journal of Human Genetics* 21 (11): 1197–201. https://doi.org/10.1038/ejhg.2012.300

Bohman, James, and William Rehg. 1997. "Introduction." In *Deliberative Democracy: Essays on Reason and Politics*, ed. James Bohman and William Rehg, ix–xxx. Cambridge, MA: MIT Press. https://doi.org/10.1007/978-1-4615-6327-3_1

Charles, Daniel. 2001. *Lords of the Harvest: Biotech, Big Money, and the Future of Food*. New York: Basic Books.

Cohen, Joshua. 1998. "Democracy and Liberty." In *Deliberative Democracy*, ed. Jon Elster, 185–231. New York: Cambridge University Press. https://doi.org/10.1017/CBO9781139175005.010

Dahl, Robert. 1956. *Preface to Democratic Theory*. Chicago: University of Chicago Press.

Downs, Anthony. 1957. *An Economic Theory of Democracy*. New York: Harper.

Dryzek, John S. 2005. "Deliberative Democracy in Divided Societies." *Political Theory* 33 (2): 218–42. https://doi.org/10.1177/0090591704268372

Eliasoph, Nina. 1998. *Avoiding Politics: How Americans Produce Apathy in Everyday Life*. Cambridge: Cambridge University Press. https://doi.org/10.1017/CBO9780511583391

Ferejohn, John. 2008. "Conclusion: The Citizens' Assembly Model." In *Designing Deliberative Democracy: The British Columbia Citizens' Assembly*, ed. Mark E. Warren and Hilary Pearse, 192–213. Cambridge: Cambridge University Press. https://doi.org/10.1017/CBO9780511491177.011

Forester, John, and David Kahane. 2010. "The Micropolitics of Deliberation: Beyound Argumentation to Recognition and Justice." In *Deliberative*

Democracy in Practice, ed. David Kahane, Daniel Weinstock, Dominique Leydet, and Melissa Williams, 209–31. Vancouver: UBC Press.

Green, Melanie C., Penny S. Visser, and Philip E. Tetlock. 2000. "Coping with Accountability Cross- Pressures: Low-Effort Evasive Tactics and High-Effort Quests for Complex Compromises." *Personality and Social Psychology Bulletin* 26 (11): 1380–91. https://doi.org/10.1177/0146167200263006

Goodin, Robert E. 2008. *Innovating Democracy: Democratic Theory and Practice After the Deliberative Turn*. Oxford: Oxford University Press. https://doi.org/10.1093/acprof:oso/9780199547944.001.0001

Gutmann, Amy, and Dennis Thompson. 2004. *Why Deliberative Democracy?* Princeton, NJ: Princeton University Press. https://doi.org/10.1515/9781400826339

Habermas, Jurgen. 1990. *Moral Consciousness and Communicative Action*. Cambridge, MA: MIT Press.

Jacobs, Lawrence R., Fay Lomax Cook, and Michael X. Delli Carpini. 2009. *Talking Together: Public Deliberation and Political Participation in America*. Chicago: University of Chicago Press. https://doi.org/10.7208/chicago/9780226389899.001.0001

Johnson, Genevieve Fuji. 2008. *Deliberative Democracy for the Future*. Toronto: University of Toronto Press. https://doi.org/10.3138/9781442687837

Johnson, Genevieve Fuji. 2015. *Democratic Illusion: Deliberative Democracy in Canadian Public Policy*. Toronto: University of Toronto Press.

Kymlicka, William. 2001. *Politics in the Vernacular: Nationalism, Multiculturalism and Citizenship*. Oxford: Oxford University Press. https://doi.org/10.1093/0199240981.001.0001

LeDuc, Lawrence. 2011. "Electoral Reform and Direct Democracy in Canada: When Citizens Become Involved." *West European Politics* 34 (3): 551 67. https://doi.org/10.1080/01402382.2011.555983

Leenknegt, Gert-Jan, and Gerhard van der Schyff. 2007. "Reforming the Electoral System of the Dutch Lower House of Parliament." *German Law Journal* 8 (12): 1133–46.

Mansbridge, Jane. 1983. *Beyond Adversary Democracy*. Chicago: University of Chicago Press.

Mascarenhas, Michael, and Rik Scarce. 2004. "'The Intention Was Good': Legitimacy, Consensus-Based Decision Making, and the Case of Forest Planning in British Columbia, Canada." *Society & Natural Resources* 17 (1): 17–38.

Mazzocco, Philip, Melanie Green, and Timothy C. Brock. 2007. "The Effects of a Prior Story-Bank on the Processing of a Related Narrative." *Media Psychology* 10 (1): 64–90.

McGurk, Brett, A. John Sinclair, and Alan Diduck. 2006. "An Assessment of Stakeholder Advisory Committees in Forest Management." *Society & Natural Resources* 19 (9): 809–26. https://doi.org/10.1080/08941920600835569

Morrell, Michael E. 2010. *Empathy and Democracy: Feeling, Thinking, and Deliberation*. University Park: Pennsylvania State University Press, 2010.

Mouffe, Chantal. 1996. "Democracy, Power, and the Political." In *Democracy and Difference: Contesting the Boundaries of the Political*, ed. Seyla Benhabib, 245–56. Princeton, NJ: Princeton University Press.

Munz, Diana C. 2006. *Hearing the Other Side: Deliberative versus Participatory Democracy*. Cambridge: Cambridge University Press.

O'Doherty, Kieran, Alice K. Hawkins, and Michael M. Burgess. 2012. "Involving Citizens in the Ethics of Biobank Research: Informing Institutional Policy through Structured Public Deliberation." *Social Science & Medicine* 75 (9): 1604–11. https://doi.org/10.1016/j.socscimed.2012.06.026

Parkins, J.R., S. Nadeau, L. Hunt, J. Sinclair, M. Reed, and S. Wallace. 2004. *Public Participation in Forest Management: Results from a National Survey of Advisory Committees*. Edmonton: Canadian Forestry Service.

Putnam, Robert. 2000. *Bowling Alone: The Collapse and Revival of American Community*. New York: Simon & Schuster. https://doi.org/10.1145/358916.361990

Rawls, John. 1997. "The Idea of Public Reason Revised." *University of Chicago Law Review* 64 (3): 765–807. https://doi.org/10.2307/1600311

Renwick, Alan. 2011. *The Politics of Electoral Reform*. Cambridge: Cambridge University Press.

Ryfe, David. 2005. "Does Deliberative Democracy Work?" *Annual Review of Political Science* 8 (1): 49–71. https://doi.org/10.1146/annurev.polisci.8.032904.154633

Sanders, Lynn M. 1997. "Against Deliberation." *Political Theory* 25 (3): 347–76. https://doi.org/10.1177/0090591797025003002

Schumpter, Joseph. 1942. *Capitalism, Socialism, and Democracy*. New York: Harper.

Steiner, Jürg. 2012. *The Foundations of Deliberative Democracy: Empirical Research and Normative Implications*. Cambridge: Cambridge University Press. https://doi.org/10.1017/CBO9781139057486

Taylor, Charles. 1994. "The Politics of Recognition." In *Multiculturalism and the Politics of Recognition*, ed. Amy Gutmann, 25–74. Princeton, NJ: Princeton University Press.

Wandel, Margareta. 2006. "Genetically Modified Foods in Norway." In *Biotechnology Unglued: Science, Society, and Social Cohesion*, ed. Michael D. Mehta, 70–94. Vancouver: UBC Press.

Warren, Mark E., and Hilary Pearse, eds. 2008. *Designing Deliberative Democracy: The British Columbia Citizens' Assembly*. New York: Cambridge University Press. https://doi.org/10.1017/CBO9780511491177

Warren, Mark E. 2001. *Democracy and Association*. Princeton, NJ: Princeton University Press.

Woodruff, Paul. 2005. *First Democracy: The Challenge of an Ancient Idea*. Oxford: Oxford University Press.

Young, Iris Marion. 2000. *Inclusion and Democracy*. Oxford: Oxford University Press.

10 Democracy and the Problem of Constitutional Change in Canada

LEE WARD

The patriation of the Canadian Constitution in 1982 was meant to signal a new era in Canadian democracy with the achievement of complete self-government through cutting the last constitutional tie to the British Parliament and through the introduction of a charter laying out judicially enforceable rights limiting the scope and power of government. The patriation process of 1982 also held out the promise of deepening the idea of democracy in Canada – that is, the notion of the country as a national community of democratic citizens and rights-bearing individuals. As David Smith observes, in Canada since 1982, "the word constitution has assumed a different meaning from what it once had" (2007, 15).

In this chapter, I use an applied political theory approach employing the principles of participatory self-government drawn from the tradition of democratic theory to assess the impacts of Canadian constitutional development and practice in recent decades on Canadian democracy. I argue that the prospect of enhanced democracy has been largely unrealized in Canada since 1982. This is the case not because, as is sometimes asserted, the legalistic principle of individual rights embodied in the Charter of Rights and Freedoms has encouraged unrepresentative judicial activism and undermined the idea of shared citizenship (Choudry 2009; Morton and Knopff 2000); arguably the "rights revolution" since 1982 that has increased democratic participation of highly mobilized interest groups has added much to our civic discourse (Russell 2009). Rather, I examine the dynamics of the amendment process established by both the precedent of the constitutional negotiations of 1981 and in Part V of the Constitution Act of 1982, and suggest that it has played a key role in stymying the development of democratic community in

Canada. Any hope that the Canadian constitutional settlement of 1982 could fulfil the promise of becoming a "people's package" has foundered, in large measure due to the amendment process enshrined by the elite-level compromise that practically excluded any direct popular participation in the constitutional amendment process such as national or province-wide referendums.

Applied political theory proves to be a useful approach, as it suggests that Canada's constitutional dilemma embodied by its problematic amendment process results from the tension between the conflicting values that characterize Canadian democracy post-1982. On the one hand, as the Quebec referendums of 1980 and 1995, the 1992 referendum on the Charlottetown Accord, and the demise of the Meech Lake Accord demonstrate, Canadians' perceptions about the meaning of constitutionalism are now in a crucial sense derived from the principle of popular sovereignty – that is, the emerging convention regarding the use of referendums rests on the idea that the people are the ultimate source of constitutional legitimacy (Ackerman and Charney 1984, 126–33; Russell 2004, 5). On the other hand, the formal structures of the constitutional settlement of 1982 still adhere to the more traditional Canadian idea of parliamentary sovereignty, embodied by a constitutional amendment process that is largely insulated from public participation. Although I am sympathetic to the general argument for participatory democracy, my purpose in this chapter is not to argue for one model of democracy over another, but rather to examine whether Canada's amendment process contradicts the democratic principles emergent in Canadian constitutionalism over the past three decades or more. Does the procedural mechanism for constitutional amendment established in 1982 affect, and even undermine, the prospects for popular sovereignty in Canada? Indeed, is the extreme difficulty of our amendment formula partly responsible for what Peter Russell has famously identified as Canadians' inability to constitute "themselves as a sovereign people" (2004, 5)?

The domestic amendment formula set out in Part V of the 1982 Constitution Act is notoriously *complex* and *prohibitive*. The effect of this complexity and degree of difficulty has been to enmesh the Constitution in what Richard Albert has identified as "constructive unamendability," a characteristic derived from a state of affairs that is not legally required but exists as a structural, social, and political fact (2014, 195). The problems arising from an excessively difficult amendment process are manifold. For instance, important recent studies have linked the demise of constitutions to their difficulty to change (Elkins, Ginsberg, and Melton

2009); others demonstrate the salutary effect of a high degree of public participation in constitutional change for increasing the overall level of democracy in society (Eisenstadt, LeVan, and Maboudi 2015). Moreover, the applied political theory approach exposes the degree to which constitutional change is an abiding concern among Canadian political theorists, as many of the practices, policies, and reforms called for by prominent figures such as Charles Taylor and James Tully require a more fluid, flexible, and democratic amendment process than Part V of the Constitution Act, 1982.

This chapter is divided into five sections. I begin by examining the theoretical foundations of the popular sovereignty doctrine, and express why the values of popular sovereignty are important for Canadian democracy. I then consider the importance of constitutional change in Canada in light of the reflections of arguably two of Canada's most prominent political theorists, Charles Taylor and James Tully. This is followed by empirical analysis of the historical and legal context surrounding the patriation process in the 1980–82 period; here I focus on the debate about the drafting of Part V, especially the decision to exclude from the final text populist measures such as referendums. I then provide a qualitative description of the legacy of Part V and its effect on Canadian democracy since 1982, showing that, although there has been some success at minor bilateral or unilateral amendments, major constitutional change has proven practically impossible. Finally, I examine the future possibilities for greater democratic participation in changing the Constitution by considering how the Supreme Court of Canada decision in its *Reference re: Secession of Quebec* ([1998] 2 S.C.R. 217; hereafter *Secession Reference*) provides guidance for methods to generate public involvement in civic discourse of a constitutional nature. I also offer a brief plan for democratic renewal in Canada that includes a proposal for codifying provincial constitutions designed to be ratified and amendable by the people.

Popular Sovereignty and the Constitution

An important part of the applied political theory approach involves tying current political practices to concepts that originated in the western canon of political theory or another recognizable tradition of political theory. Since the 1960s, Canada has been engaged in a constitutional debate involving competing theoretical principles with a long pedigree in the Anglo-American political tradition. In order to understand this debate, however, it is vital to reconsider the theoretical foundations of modern constitutionalism. The defining characteristic of the modern idea of constitutions is the notion of constituent power first articulated by the English philosopher John Locke in the seventeenth century. Writing in the context of the mammoth struggle between Tories and Whigs in the 1680s over who is sovereign, king or Parliament, Locke argued that the power of the sovereign people to establish the framework of government is distinct from, and superior to, the ordinary power of government ([1689] 1988, 2:134, 141). Locke's idea of constituent power rests upon the theoretical construct of the state of nature, according to which the power of government is deduced from the pre-civil, natural rights (what Locke termed a *natural executive power*) of individuals (Ward 2010, chap. 2). Most English Whigs accepted Locke's constitutional conclusion that Parliament could limit the power of the king, but they rejected the radical theoretical premises of a state of nature and constituent power. The sovereignty of Parliament as the institutional expression of the political will of the nation, rather than of popular sovereignty per se, became the fundamental constitutional principle of representative government in Britain and Canada in the eighteenth and nineteenth centuries.

For Locke, popular sovereignty was in part a theory of political obligation according to which, at least in principle, the unanimous agreement of individuals is required to form society, even as the majority legitimately determines the form of government ([1689] 1988, 2:95–8). As such, the sovereignty of the people is typically dormant, but it is activated in times of revolution or serious constitutional change. The tension between popular sovereignty and parliamentary sovereignty comes into stark relief over the question of whether a written constitution is capable of acting as an organizing legal instrument that transcends ordinary legislation. In the dominant strain of British constitutionalism, of course, the constitution is essentially whatever the supreme legislature says it is. The Lockean view, however, was that a written constitution can assume an ontological priority over normal statute law only if it is the product of a process engaging the direct constituent power of the individuals in the community.[1] It was not until the

1 Although, in *The Fundamental Constitutions of Carolina*, Locke did not elaborate an amendment process distinct from normal legislation, he did establish the principle that any proprietor in the colony could legally challenge any act of Parliament that was contrary to "these fundamental constitutions of the government" ([1669] 1997, sec. 71, 175–6).

American Revolution that the Lockean idea of constituent power would achieve full fruition. In the flurry of constitution making in the newly independent states that immediately followed the rupture with Britain, Massachusetts finally approached the Lockean ideal by establishing a written constitution in 1780 devised by a special drafting convention (rather than by the legislature), and ratified directly by the citizens of the state in a popular referendum.[2] The logical corollary of the Lockean idea of popular sovereignty is, of course, the principle that amendments to the written constitution should at least approximate the degree of public participation in the original act of framing.

As Peter Russell has observed, Canadian constitutional development in recent decades has been defined fundamentally by the conflict between, on the one hand, the Lockean idea of popular sovereignty that has taken hold among Canadians and, on the other, constitutional structures that remain anchored in the principle of parliamentary sovereignty, expressed through both the federal Parliament and the provincial assemblies (Russell 2004, 9, 11). To the extent that the patriation process of 1982 held the promise of transforming Canada into a democratic community built upon the Lockean idea of popular sovereignty and written constitutionalism, the period since then makes clear that somehow Canadian constitutional development went astray. But why are the values of popular sovereignty important for Canadian constitutionalism, and what are the problems for Canada in not achieving it?

Popular sovereignty in the Canadian context is a multidimensional political principle that has constitutional, national, as well as civic implications. In constitutional terms, popular sovereignty is a formative principle of institutional organization. In its original Lockean formulation, popular sovereignty means that political supremacy is difficult, or even impossible, to locate in institutional terms (see, for example, Locke [1689] 1988, 2:151–2). Popular sovereignty, in this view, is demonstrated partially through recourse to the people by elections to the legislature and more directly through referendums and ultimately (extraconstitutionally) in popular revolution. In this respect, ambiguity about institutional sovereignty logically reinforces de facto, if not formal, recognition of a community's democratic foundations. In the

2 See the discussion about the drafting of the first US state constitutions in Ward (2004, chap. 15). The Massachusetts example became the precedent for the drafting and ratification of the US constitution in 1787–8.

context of Canadian federalism, popular sovereignty also has national implications insofar as it points towards a potential source of national unity signifying more than simply a mathematical majority, but also a principle of democratic legitimacy that can transcend regionalism. The question of the democratic basis of the Canadian federal state was very much an issue in the patriation debates and negotiations in 1981, in which the prospect of a national referendum as a means to establish a national consensus was seen by many champions of provincial rights as a repudiation of the view of Canada as a fundamentally federal nation (Russell 2004, 111). To other participants in the negotiations, the notion of a constitutional amendment process with public participation was seen as having the potential to solidify a concept of Canadian citizenship that is not simply reducible to regional or provincial loyalties.

Finally, there is an important civic dimension to the principle of popular sovereignty. Popular sovereignty assumes that representative government is sufficient for ordinary legislation, but major constitutional change requires more direct democratic participation. In contrast to the Canadian tradition of elite accommodation, popular sovereignty rests on the expectation that democratic citizenship requires, on some level, a participatory ethos.[3] Popular sovereignty thus bears a kinship with the classical republican ideal that active participation in the public life of the community is what makes someone a citizen by helping to develop the faculties of reason and judgment through civic discourse (Aristotle 2013, 1253a1–20). For our purposes, the chief claim of participatory democracy is that, given the fundamental character of constitutional change, it demands a greater degree of public participation, for example through referendums, than does the normal course of democratic politics. Arguably open plebiscitary instruments allow citizens greater means to participate in opinion formation than what normally precedes voting for representatives. That is to say, referendums signify a purer expression of public will on discrete issues or questions than do partisan elections.

---

3 There is, of course, a considerable and well-known body of literature supporting the benefits of participatory democracy generally (see, for example, Barber 1984; Hilmer 2010; Macpherson 1977; Pateman 1970) and in the context of specific case studies such as the New England town hall (Bryan 2004), Chicago local government (Fung and Wright 2001), and the budget process in Porto Alegre, Brazil (Aragonès and Sánchez-Pagés 2008).

In what follows, I argue that the constitutional amendment process adopted in 1982 has produced an enervating sense of inflexibility – indeed, futility – surrounding any question of major constitutional change in Canada. That the problems flowing out of Canada's "unamendable" Constitution are not simply hypothetical or abstruse can be seen in the importance that Canada's most influential political theorists have placed on the idea of constitutional change, to which I now turn.

Contemporary Canadian Political Theory

An applied political theory approach can reveal how the work of important Canadian political theorists is characterized by an orientation towards applying their theoretical insights to pressing problems that animate the Canadian political context. Indeed the flowering of distinctively Canadian political theory has coincided with the extended period of constitutional debate and suspended national unity crisis that has existed in Canada since the 1960s. Arguably the main constitutional issues confronting political leaders and the courts since that time have also been the central preoccupation of our most important political theorists. Much of contemporary Canadian political theory exemplified by the case studies of Charles Taylor and James Tully has been essentially reflections upon democracy by thinkers whose formative political experiences were (1) the constitutional debates about the status of Quebec as Canada's sole francophone majority province, and (2) the claims for Indigenous self-government. That is to say, the animating concerns of Taylor and Tully about rights and community, while relevant across the democratic world, are rooted in unresolved constitutional issues relating to how, or whether, Canada can make constitutional changes to accommodate the demands of a diverse and complex democratic society.

Charles Taylor is arguably the doyen of Canadian political philosophers. A native-born Quebecer and life-long resident of the province, Taylor's work has engaged with the philosophical and legal dimensions of the division between Quebec and the rest of Canada for five decades. For Taylor, the Quiet Revolution in Quebec and the rise of the independence movement produced profound social and political change that the Canadian Constitution has proven unable to address. The problem of Canada is a problem of democracy or, to put it differently, the Constitution is a problem with a democratic solution, for even as the "deep diversity" (Taylor 1993, 200) rooted in language, culture, and history makes the formation of a single political community in Canada difficult, the principle of democracy extends the possibility of accommodating various distinct social and political realities.

At its deepest level, the problem Taylor identifies is not simply political, but philosophical or even existential. As a philosopher, Taylor's central goal has long been to counter what he takes to be the extreme individualism in modern (that is, Enlightenment) philosophy by insisting that modernity's self-generating self, an intellectual and moral monad set adrift in an ocean of being and left to rely solely on the limited introspective cognitive resources available to it, is not a true reflection of human nature or experience (Taylor 1985, 1989). According to Taylor, the ontological priority of community over the individual makes my identity depend crucially upon "my dialogical relation with others" (1994, 34). Canada's deep cultural diversity means that it is "a natural locus for the experiment in the dialogue society" (1993, 27). The difficulty in perfecting this social and political balance through dialogue only intensified, in Taylor's view, with the introduction of the Charter of Rights and Freedoms in 1982. Since that time, "two conceptions of rights-liberalism have confronted each other," the one dominant in English Canada stressing individual rights and proceduralism, on one hand, and the other view of group rights and substantive protections prevailing in Quebec, on the other (Taylor 1994, 52, 56). The "tragic" events relating to the failure of the Meech Lake Accord (Taylor 1993, 190), which promised distinct constitutional status for Quebec, derived from the incapacity of Canada's dominant cultural and linguistic groups to recognize the claims of the minority group.

What in Taylor's estimation are the prospects for the development of democratic political community in Canada based upon recognition of cultural difference? Clearly the failure of Meech Lake and the Charlottetown Accords was a profound event in Canadian constitutional history. It reflected a basic lack of recognition. Going forward, Taylor suggests that English Canada needs to recognize that, from the perspective of French Quebec, "it is necessary to create anew ... the country has to be remade from top to toe" (1993, 145). Although English Canadians are unlikely to accept the need for radical reorganization of the constitutional order post-Meech and Charlottetown, Taylor is unequivocal in his assessment that the 1982 Constitution is inadequate for the purpose of national renewal. In fact he dismisses the work of 1982 as part and parcel of the "1867 Constitution" that "died morally in Quebec" with the failure of Meech (145). The amendment process outlined in Part V of the Constitution, ostensibly the mechanism for future change, is, according to Taylor, part of the problem: "We must avoid becoming embroiled in the maze of amendment procedures that currently exist. The problem with these procedures is that they leave us with the status quo by default. They put the burden of proof on those who want change" (154). Thus, Part V exposes, and indeed exacerbates, the profound tension in Canada between an aspirational democratic political community, on one hand, and a constitutionalism that is unable to reflect the diversity of the country that it purports to represent, on the other.

For his part, James Tully (2008) presents a new "public philosophy" for democratic societies confronting the legacy of imperialism and the challenges of globalization. Tully's philosophical reflections are, he insists, inspired by Canadian political experience, especially his knowledge of indigenous peoples acquired through his involvement in the Royal Commission on Aboriginal Peoples from 1991 to 1996. The primary theoretical foundation of Tully's new public philosophy is "democratic communicative action," which he argues has the potential to liberate modern societies from imperial and hegemonic power structures through healthy civic participation (Tully 2008, 2:169). Tully praises some aspects of the 1982 Constitution, especially the Charter, which he associates with Pierre Trudeau's vision of "a toolbox that citizens should use to engage in practices of civic freedom against the unequal distribution of power in Canada and the world" (2:167). Although concerned that the 1982 constitutional agreement failed to resolve the legitimate claims of *Québécois* or to entrench Indigenous self-government, Tully finds some solace in the new more agonistic approach to civic engagement that the agreement introduced into Canada. As with Taylor, Tully challenges the regnant concept of the state, which he believes should be replaced by a more fluid and egalitarian concept conducive to the idea of "diverse citizenship." For Tully citizenship is about the "grass-roots democratic or civic activities of the governed" (2:247). In classic Aristotelian terms, "one becomes a citizen through participation" (2:248).

Tully calls upon Canadians to reconceive of their state in terms of a community built upon democratic principles. This new Canada would require a new constitution or, more precisely, an "Aboriginal-Canadian Charter that should govern relations between aboriginal and non-aboriginal peoples" (Tully 2008, 1:229). This novel form of constitutionalism would encourage "intercultural dialogue" by emphasizing a "new dialogue of equality" among Canada's diverse peoples based on Indigenous practices and viewing negotiation as the basis of an ongoing relationship defined by mutual respect and sharing of land and resources (1:241,

287–8). In a more radical sense, however, Tully's new Canada would reject the western idea of a single confederation, for Tully envisions "two confederations" of which "the 'first' confederation (or federation) is the treaty confederations of the First Nations with the Crown and later the federal and, to some extent, provincial governments. The second confederation (or federation) is the constitutional federation of the provinces and the federal government" (1:236–7). This new, multidimensional Canadian state would require not only diverse kinds of institutions and practices, but also diverse forms of citizenship and a continual process of consultation, discussion, and adjudication among the national and provincial governments, as well as among First Nations. This new order, which Tully terms "Treaty Federalism," would recognize First Nations as a "stateless, self-governing and autonomous people, equal in status, but not in form, to the Canadian state, with a willingness to negotiate shared jurisdiction of land and resources" (1:280).

How do Tully's proposals relate to the existing Canadian Constitution? The great challenge lies in forging a path that allows Indigenous and non-Indigenous peoples to feel a "shared sense of destiny together" without either assimilation or exploitation (Tully 2008, 1:242). For Tully, "the mutual acceptance and affirmation of Aboriginal and non-Aboriginal peoples as equal, co-existing and self-governing" requires "public acknowledgement of this in the Constitution" (1:230–1). Past attempts at constitutional reform have proven inadequate, as Tully dismisses the "delegated, municipal style of self-government" for First Nations proposed in the Charlottetown Accord, as well as Supreme Court of Canada interpretations of section 35 of the Constitution Act, 1982 that have "never questioned the legitimacy of the unilateral exercise of sovereignty over the indigenous peoples and their territories" (1:275). The "just Confederation" to which Tully aspires presupposes a new spirit of negotiation and dialogue inseparable from a new more fluid conception of constitutional law, which he believes might include an Indigenous charter, Indigenous courts, and even an Indigenous parliament (1:225, 250). In this sense the connection between democracy and formal constitutional change is as central to Tully's vision of a future Canada as it is to Taylor's.

Constitution Making, Canadian Style

The applied political theory approach involves empirical analysis of the political practices one is exploring. Accordingly I offer empirical evidence from Canada's constitutional history of the absence of a developed theoretical framework or concrete institutional practices of popular sovereignty. The title of Keith Banting and Richard Simeon's edited collection on patriation, *And No One Cheered* (1983), captures the curious mixture of relief and foreboding that settled upon the Canadian political landscape at the conclusion of the long process of adjudication, negotiation, threats, and ultimatums that led to the Constitution Act, 1982. Why this feeling of disappointment and anticlimax? There was the obvious failure to obtain the support of the government of Quebec for the constitutional settlement, a setback that would fixate Canadian political leaders for decades. There was also deep concern in many quarters about the lack of public involvement in the process of negotiations in 1980–81. Such a lack should have been predictable, as constitutionalism in Canada has not traditionally been fertile ground for democratic participation in constitution making. Indeed, given the elite-driven process that produced Confederation and the non-existence of any meaningful process for popular ratification in 1867, Peter Russell concludes that, "at Canada's founding, its people were not sovereign" and, to make matters worse, "there was not even a sense that a constituent sovereign people would have to be invented" (2004, 33).

The idea of finding a domestic amendment mechanism first acquired genuine urgency only after the Balfour Declaration of 1926 and the Westminster Treaty of 1931 instituted complete legislative independence for Canada apart from constitutional amendment. As far back as 1935, Canadian leaders met in a federal-provincial conference to discuss a proposal for four distinct amendment processes crafted to different kinds of amendments (Ward 1987, 331). In the 1960s, amid the spirit of modernization in Quebec, a complex joint proposal by federal justice minister E. Davie Fulton and his Quebec counterpart Guy Favreau would have required unanimous provincial agreement for some kinds of constitutional change relating to language policy, but only a two-thirds' supermajority for other changes and more limited provincial agreement for changes pertaining solely to specific regions. The Fulton-Favreau proposal, like all previous efforts, failed to secure the agreement of enough provinces to produce change. So anomalous had Canada's constitutional amendment process become by the late 1960s that British prime minister Harold Wilson was apparently astonished to be informed that an act of the British Parliament was still required to change the Canadian Constitution (Stevenson 2007, 682).

The background to the negotiations in Ottawa in November 1981 – from the failed Victoria Accord of 1971 to the Supreme Court opinion on unilateral patriation – is well known and need not be rehashed here. The first ministers agreed, with the exception of the government of Quebec, to a constitutional package the highlights of which were a Charter of Rights and Freedoms (Part I) and a multivariate domestic constitutional amendment process (Part V). The main characteristic of the amendment formula is its complexity, including five distinct kinds of amendments requiring various degrees of provincial support ranging from unanimity (section 41) and at least seven provincial governments with more than 50 per cent of the Canadian population (section 38), to areas of bilateral federal-provincial agreement (section 43), and unilateral federal (section 44) or provincial government action (section 45). It also included an "opt-out" clause that allowed provinces to withdraw from certain kinds of amendments with financial compensation from the federal government (section 40, 38[3]), a three-year time limit for ratification of amendments (section 39) and a constitutional requirement that Part V be reviewed by first ministers within a fifteen-year period (section 49).

The question of democratic legitimacy expressed itself at the time in terms of controversial proposals about the role of referendums in constitutional change. The negotiations in 1981 took place while the embers of the Quebec independence referendum of the previous year were still smoldering in the public's mind. Indeed support for Ackerman and Charney's claim that the 1980 Quebec Referendum signified the "embryonic stage" in the development of popular sovereignty principles in Canadian constitutionalism can be found in the fact that, for arguably the first time in Canadian history, there was serious debate among first ministers as to whether to include referendums, either national or provincial, in the new domestic amendment formula (Ackerman and Charney 1984, 128). There was even some discussion as to whether the constitutional package should be submitted directly to the Canadian people for ratification through a referendum prior to its formal enactment by the British Parliament. Prime Minister Pierre Trudeau argued repeatedly in the November 1981 negotiations that a national referendum or a series of regional referendums would be a "deadlock breaker" if the first ministers could not agree among themselves (Leeson 2011, 54, 56). It would, he reasoned, "put pressure on us [the elected leaders]" to make a deal (53).

Trudeau's proposal was not simply a negotiating tactic;[4] rather, it reflected competing visions of the process of constitutional negotiations. The premiers, with the exception ironically of Quebec premier René Lévesque, opposed any suggestion of referendums because, they argued, Canada's constitutional convention required collegiality among government leaders. This assumption of elite responsibility was often reinterpreted, however, in a strangely democratic way. Each time Trudeau brought back the idea of a ratification referendum, premiers – including Allan Blakeney (Saskatchewan), Brian Peckford (Newfoundland), John Buchanan (Nova Scotia), and Peter Lougheed (Alberta) – would respond that Canadians "want us to agree" and do not, in fact, want to be directly consulted in a referendum (Leeson 2011, 51, 53). In response to Trudeau's proposal that the amendment formula be put "to the people" in a national referendum or votes "by region as defined in the [British North America] Act," Lougheed demurred, claiming that referendums are "very divisive" and should be avoided (47, 50).

Why were the provinces so resistant to the idea of a referendum? In addition to fear of augmenting federal government power through providing a mechanism to reinforce claims of a national majority (represented by the federal government), some premiers of a more progressive bent, including Blakeney, feared that a referendum would facilitate rising conservatism, even as others warned about disputes over the wording of a referendum question (Romanow, Whyte, and Leeson 1984, 272). From the perspective of the federal government, the idea of a referendum was connected to the determination of a "national will," an elusive idea in Canadian history that the provincial premiers instinctively distrusted and resented (Leeson 2011, 24).

In the end, the "Kitchen Accord" fashioned among the first ministers in November 1981 was an agreement devised by an exclusive subset of an already elite group. Canadians were not called upon to ratify the agreement or even provided means for serious consultation on the substance of the Constitution, with the notable exception of Indigenous and feminist groups, who mobilized to exert "direct, spontaneous democratic pressure" during parliamentary hearings on the Charter (Whittaker 1983, 257). For Pierre Trudeau, the failure either to include

---

4 The idea of incorporating referendums in the constitutional amendment process was long-standing in Pierre Trudeau's mind, dating back at least to a position paper he drafted for the Privy Council Office in 1950 (Nemni and Nemni 2011, 198).

a referendum mechanism in Part V or to ratify the package through a referendum undermined the legitimacy of the proposed constitutional order: "The Constitution will only truly belong to the nation when the people have the opportunity to endorse it through constitutional amendment" (Romanow, Whyte, and Leeson 1984, 273). The failure in 1981–82 to incorporate direct citizen participation in the process of constitution making arguably would be the great missed opportunity in Canadian constitutional development.

The Legacy of 1982?

Although the domestic amendment formula that had been perhaps the priority throughout Canadian constitutional history was finally achieved with Part V of the Constitution Act, 1982, it is the least loved aspect of the 1982 settlement, enjoying much less support from Canadians than Part I of the Charter. Does Part V facilitate or hinder democratic participation in decision making about the most fundamental political, legal, and constitutional issues? Is there a more democratic way to undertake constitutional change other than the first ministers' conferences model?

The fundamental tension between democracy (popular rule) and constitutionalism (checks on direct popular rule) is crystallized in the amendment process in any constitutional order. The French constitution of 1793 captures this tension well: "A People have always the right of revising, amending, and changing their Constitution. One generation cannot subject to its laws future generations" (quoted in Elkins, Ginsburg, and Melton 2009, 13). Operationalizing this right is, however, a source of debate and disagreement well beyond the context of Canada's tortuous path to patriation in 1982. A recent empirical study on comparative constitutionalism concludes that "constitutions with lower thresholds for amendment will be more flexible and likely to survive in the face of constitutional crisis" (Elkins, Ginsburg, and Melton 2009, 99–100). Donald Lutz concurs, finding that an overly rigid and excessively onerous amendment process "violates the assumption of human fallibility and prevents the effective utilization of popular sovereignty" (1994, 356).

The applied political theory approach invites us to contrast the inflexibility and lack of popular involvement in the amendment process in Canada with the more flexible and democratic features of the process in other comparable federal states such as Australia, Switzerland, India, and the United States. In Australia, where there have been eight amendments, amendment requires a majority of electors nationwide and a majority in a majority of states. The Indian constitution (ninety-eight amendments) has a flexible process including both an absolute majority in the national parliament and ratification by half of the twenty-nine state legislatures. In Switzerland the constitution affirms the right of the twenty-six cantons to call for popular referendums on federal laws and constitutional amendments. The US constitution (twenty-seven amendments) allows for the calling of constitutional conventions in the states – although this has never been used – even as each of the fifty state constitutions provides for a vast array of popular instruments for constitutional amendment (Sturm 1982, 82).

Since 1982 the Canadian Constitution has suffered from functional or "constructive unamendability," for although certain provisions of a limited nature have been changed, amendments of a general character that require national support have proven to be practically impossible (Albert 2014, 195). The only time the general amendment formula in section 38 has been used to effect change was in 1983, in the immediate afterglow of patriation, when Pierre Trudeau was able to obtain sufficient provincial support to amend parts of section 35 relating to Aboriginal rights. Since that time, Canadians have seen only localized constitutional change set in motion either by the section 43 bilateral process involving such matters as education in Newfoundland and Labrador and Quebec, language policy in New Brunswick, and the bridge connecting Prince Edward Island to the mainland. The federal government has also initiated two unilateral changes with respect to representation in the House of Commons. It is remarkable that the domestic amendment formula so long sought by Canadian political elites has had relatively little positive effect on the country's Constitution.

The assessment of Part V among constitutional scholars has been almost universally critical (an exception is Newman 2007). John Whyte charges Part V with "inflicting paralysis on the nation's capacity for formal acts of self-determination" (2011, 421). Garth Stevenson attacks the "extreme complexity, extreme rigidity and the absence of any provisions for popular (that is to say, non-governmental) involvement in the amendment process" (2007, 683). He adds to this scathing criticism some historical and comparative perspective: "No other amending formula in any constitution, past or present, approaches it in complexity and obscurity" (683). David Smith reflects sadly that the promise that the Constitution Act, 1982 would signify an "act of constitutional completion" did not happen "largely because of the rigid amending formula the Act established" (2010, 152). Richard Albert insists that, in the case of Canada, "[u]namendability has undermined the democratic foundations of formal amendment" (2015, 23). The consensus among the many critics of Part V is that, although it happily ended the embarrassing situation whereby Canadians relied on the British to enact changes to their own Constitution, it also entrenched an amendment formula less flexible than the conventions that prevailed prior to 1982.

It might be objected that Canada has flourished under the 1982 Constitution, and thus the difficulty posed by the current amendment formula is not as important as I, and these other commentators, believe it to be. There is clearly much truth in the claim that the difficulty of constitutional amendment has not had dire consequences economically, socially, or politically for Canada. However, this should not obscure the reality that some of Canada's most pressing long-term political, social, and, by extension, economic problems are of a constitutional nature. It is hard to envision how Canada could achieve meaningful democratic reform of the Senate, or a just and comprehensive settlement with First Nations, or the conditions that would encourage the government of Quebec to embrace the 1982 Constitution in a scenario that did not involve constitutional amendment. Indeed, arguably, any real progress on these important issues presupposes first remedying the defects in the amendment process in Part V.

The most fundamental problem with Part V relates to its inability to generate either democratic legitimacy or public confidence in the process for constitutional change. On one level, the tensions, and even incoherence, in Part V are epiphenomena of the deeper conflict between provincial and federal power that has regularly seen federalism subsume democracy in Canadian constitutional history. One commentator has argued that the 1982 settlement was a compromise between a "federally sponsored Charter and an Amending formula fashioned by, and sympathetic to provincial governments" (Cairns 1992, 89). As Katherine Swinton observes, the demise of the Meech Lake Accord was due in large part to the failure of Canadian political elites to recognize the importance post-1982 of the provincial legislatures in the constitutional amendment process (1992, 141). The problem, from the perspective of enhancing democracy, reduces to the perennial question of how, if at all, popular sovereignty can express itself constitutionally in Canada.

Referendums are one participatory means to create and perpetuate political community by encouraging mass communal participation in a "dramatic political act" (Cairns 1992, 53). Yet it was not until 1992, with the federal Referendum Act, that referendums were incorporated, albeit ambiguously, into the constitutional amendment process as non-binding votes that give Canadians a direct voice in constitutional change that is effectively denied to them in Part V. Three provinces – British Columbia, Alberta, and Quebec – require a referendum to approve constitutional change; another, Manitoba, requires public hearings on any new constitutional proposal (Wiseman 1994, 290). The more than fourteen million Canadians who voted in the 1992 Charlottetown Accord referendum did express a form of popular sovereignty, albeit, as Peter Russell assesses, "negatively" in the sense of telling their political elites what they do not want to see happen to the constitution (2004, 190).

Is there any empirical evidence that the perception of "constructive unamendability" adversely affects the way Canadians relate to the Constitution? I would point to at least one recent issue suggesting that constitutional paralysis has had a negative effect on Canadian democracy. The alteration to the rules of monarchical succession in 2013 involved welcome changes that eliminated male-preference primogeniture and discriminatory rules against an heir who happens to marry a Roman Catholic. The general consensus among constitutional scholars is that the change required a constitutional amendment under section 41 rules pertaining to a change in the "office of the Queen" (Benoit and Toffoli 2013; Lagassé 2013; Ward 2013; Whyte 2013). Although section 41 requires unanimous consent of all the provinces, it is hard to imagine a constitutional amendment that would be less controversial or divisive than what was proposed. Yet the Harper government and all parties across the spectrum agreed that a simple parliamentary resolution concurring with the United Kingdom Act would suffice, and thus constitutional amendment was unnecessary. What explains this disjunction between constitutional scholars and political practitioners? The federal government's policy on succession was bad constitutional law, but it typified what passes for smart constitutional politics nowadays inasmuch as provincial unanimity is such a high bar. The 2014 Supreme Court of Canada decision requiring unanimity for abolition arguably has had the same chilling effect on debate about the Senate. Furthermore, that political elites feared a national referendum on changing the rules of succession would transform into a full-fledged national vote on the future of the monarchy in Canada speaks to how fragile is a constitutional order not well grounded on popular sovereignty. It also demonstrates how Canada's amendment process stifled a good opportunity for democratic debate about the Constitution.

Conclusion: Going Forward

The central aim of the applied political theory approach in this chapter is to provide insight regarding the questions: What does political theory teach us about the Canadian Constitution? and what does Canada's constitutional experience have to teach other democracies? I have tried to suggest that many Canadian political theorists contend compellingly that Canada's diverse political community is not, and historically has not been, adequately represented by the Constitution either prior to or since 1982. Canada thus provides a cautionary lesson about the dangers of instituting inflexible amendment processes that lack real means of democratic participation. The perception of unamendability undermines a democratic people's confidence in the value and effectiveness of constitutional government. A good first step towards encouraging greater democracy in Canada would be to act on the spirit of section 49 of Part V, which calls for a complete review of this section of the Constitution Act, 1982 within a fifteen-year period. This remarkable provision, reflecting deep unease about Part V among many parties in 1981, has never been acted upon in good faith. In 1996 the Chrétien government, still shell-shocked from its near-death experience in the Quebec referendum of the previous year, offered a "perfunctory exercise" of review that Garth Stevenson calls an "insult to the Canadian people" (2007, 684). Although this misuse of section 49 signified a missed opportunity, nothing constitutionally speaking precludes a meaningful review of Part V in the future.

Apart from a serious revamping of Part V, there are several other possibilities going forward for linking participatory democracy and constitutional change. The first relates to the Supreme Court's 1998 *Secession Reference*. The context, of course, was the federal government's challenge to Quebec's claim that it has the right to secede following a successful referendum campaign in the province. The Court's main finding was that secession is not an extralegal act, but, rather, requires "that an amendment be negotiated" (*Secession Reference*, 4, 36 [97]). Central to this process is a duty to negotiate with the other parties in Confederation. The Court affirmed that "each participant in the federation" has a right to initiate constitutional change even as it defined the Canadian constitution in terms of a "continuous process of discussion and evaluation" (4). The duty to negotiate is not simply a product of constitutional crisis; rather, it reflects "threads of a thousand acts of accommodation" that are the "fabric of a nation" (Russell 2004, 244). Strikingly, the Court prescribed processes for amendment that are *not* discovered in the text of Part V, a section of the Constitution not typically seen as bereft of superfluous details. The amendment process that would be triggered by secession is discernible only by "inferring rules that meet the purposes expressed in constitutional principles," rather than an exhaustive list of rules in Part V (Whyte 2013, 56; cf. Choudhry and Howse 2000, 163).

In the *Secession Reference*, the Supreme Court also commented upon the ambiguous status of referendums, which have logical legitimacy as a democratic method to ascertain the public's view on issues, but have "no direct role or legal effect in our constitutional scheme" (33 [87]). This is an accurate reading of the decision made in the patriation negotiations in 1981. Clearly, if the federal and provincial governments were to act in good faith on section 49's duty to review, clarifying and further institutionalizing a greater role for public consultation in the constitutional amendment process, as adumbrated in the 1992 Referendum Act, should be central to the discussions. Does the duty to negotiate identified in the *Secession Reference* apply to referendums on other issues apart from secession? For example, the Saskatchewan legislature in the fall of 2013 unanimously passed a resolution calling for the Senate to be abolished, which the federal government and the other provinces basically ignored. If Saskatchewan had held a referendum on Senate abolition, would a strong affirmative vote have produced a correlative duty on other constitutional actors in Canada to negotiate seriously? At the very least, one would hope that a democratic expression of popular will in a province on an issue such as Senate abolition would produce greater deliberation than a few passing (and dismissive) comments over lunch at a first ministers' conference!

A final proposal for enhancing democratic participation in the Canadian constitutional order involves constitutional conventions in the provinces and territories to consolidate and codify their fundamental laws as far as possible into discrete documents ratified by the people and amendable through popular referendums (as opposed to simple legislative majorities). In the *Secession Reference*, the Supreme Court waxed eloquently about the value of a written constitution: "A written

Constitution promotes legal certainty and predictability, and it provides a foundation and touchstone for the exercise of constitutional judicial review" (22 [53]). Consolidating the provincial constitutions potentially could set off a round of grassroots constitution making arguably the likes of which Canada has never seen. Although this process of consolidation would be consistent with sections 43 and 45 of Part V, the great practical advantage of such a new constitutional project is that it would help dispel the impression that provincial constitutions are merely derivative of the federal Constitution, rather than being meaningful expressions of the right of self-government of the people in the provinces. In addition to laying out participatory mechanisms for the amendment process, the subjects treated in the provincial constitutions could include electoral law, relations and negotiations with First Nations, the nature of the connection to the monarchy, the constitutional bases of municipal governments, bills of rights and human rights codes, and codifying relations of the branches of government, especially with respect to executive prerogative. Some provinces might wish to include more specific policy matters in their provincial constitutions, such as provisions relating to education, health, language, natural resources, Crown corporations, and the creation and administration of a provincial pension plan or heritage fund. These areas would also, of course, be subject to the amendment rules stipulated in the Constitution.

Admittedly the idea of provincial constitutions historically has been an inchoate and nebulous concept that Nelson Wiseman memorably observes "barely dwells in the world of the subconscious" (1994, 270). Indeed, with the exception of Quebec, not a single province has ever shown any interest in reframing its constitution. Renegotiating, formalizing, and codifying provincial constitutions would require Canadians to rethink their idea of constituent power, which would need to become an inclusive concept that incorporates groups such as First Nations and immigrants that typically were not fairly represented in the first establishment of the provincial governments. Popular sovereignty provides a theoretical framework that renders it possible to conceptualize constituent power in terms of distinct concurrent and overlapping majorities among Canadians, who delegate their power to multiple institutions and diverse arrangements. Perhaps once this form of constituent power theory is put into democratic practice, Canadians finally could claim ownership of their own Constitution.

REFERENCES

Ackerman, Bruce, and Robert Charney. 1984. "Canada at the Constitutional Crossroads." *University of Toronto Law Journal* 34 (2): 117–35. https://doi.org/10.2307/825517

Albert, Richard. 2014. "Constructive Unamendability in Canada and the United States." *Supreme Court Review* 67: 181–219.

Albert, Richard. 2015. "The Difficulty of Constitutional Amendment in Canada." *Alberta Law Review* 39: 1–29. Available online at https://works.bepress.com/richardalbert/47

Aragonès, Enriqueta, and Santiago Sánchez-Pagés. 2008. "A Theory of Participatory Democracy based on the Real Case of Porto Alegre." *European Economic Review* 53 (1): 56–72.

Aristotle. 2013. *Politics*, 2nd ed. Trans. Carnes Lord. Chicago: University of Chicago Press.

Banting, Keith, and Richard Simeon. 1983. *And No One Cheered: Federalism, Democracy and the Constitution Act*. Toronto: Methuen.

Barber, Benjamin. 1984. *Strong Democracy: Participatory Politics for a New Age*. Berkeley: University of California Press.

Benoit, Paul, and Garry Toffoli. 2013. "More Is Needed to Change the Rules of Succession for Canada." *Canadian Parliamentary Review* 36 (3): 10–2.

Bryan, Frank M. 2004. *Real Democracy: The New England Town Hall Meeting and How It Works*. Chicago: University of Chicago Press.

Cairns, Alan. 1992. *Charter versus Federalism: The Dilemmas of Constitutional Reform*. Montreal; Kingston, ON: McGill-Queen's University Press.

Choudry, Sujit. 2009. "Bills of Rights as Instruments of Nation Building in Multinational States: The Canadian *Charter* and Quebec Nationalism." In *Contested Constitutionalism: Reflections on the Canadian Charter of Rights and Freedoms*, ed. James B. Kelly and Christopher P. Manfredi, 233–50. Vancouver: UBC Press.

Choudhry, Sujit, and Robert Howse. 2000. "Constitutional Theory and the Quebec Secession Reference." *Canadian Journal of Law and Jurisprudence* 13 (2): 143–69. https://doi.org/10.1017/S0841820900000370

Eisenstadt, Todd A., A. Carl LeVan, and Tofigh Maboudi. 2015. "When Talk Trumps Text: The Democratizing Effects of Deliberation during Constitution-Making, 1974–2011." *American Political Science Review* 109 (3): 592–612. https://doi.org/10.1017/S0003055415000222

Elkins, Zachary, Tom Ginsburg, and James Melton. 2009. *The Endurance of National Constitutions*. Cambridge: Cambridge University Press. https://doi.org/10.1017/CBO9780511817595

Fung, Archon, and Erik Olin Wright. 2001. "Deepening Democracy: Innovations in Empowered Participatory Governance." *Politics & Society* 29 (1): 5–41. https://doi.org/10.1177/0032329201029001002

Hilmer, Jeffrey D. 2010. "The State of Participatory Democratic Theory." *New Political Science* 32 (1): 43–63. https://doi.org/10.1080/07393140903492118

Lagassé, Philippe. 2013. "The Queen of Canada Is Dead; Long Live the British Queen." *Maclean's*, 3 February.

Leeson, Howard. 2011. *The Patriation Minutes*. Edmonton: University of Alberta, Faculty of Law, Centre for Constitutional Studies.

Locke, John. [1669] 1997. "The Fundamental Constitutions of Carolina." In *Locke: Political Essays*, ed. Mark Goldie, 160–81. Cambridge: Cambridge University Press.

Locke, John. [1689] 1988. *The Two Treatises of Government*. Ed. Peter Laslett. Cambridge: Cambridge University Press. https://doi.org/10.1017/CBO9780511810268

Lutz, Donald. 1994. "Toward a Theory of Constitutional Amendment." *American Political Science Review* 88 (2): 355–70. https://doi.org/10.2307/2944709

Macpherson, C.B. 1977. *The Life and Times of Liberal Democracy*. Oxford: Oxford University Press.

Morton, F.L. and Rainer Knopff. 2000. *The Charter Revolution and the Court Party*. Peterborough, ON: Broadview Press.

Nemni, Monique, and Max Nemni. 2011. *Trudeau Transformed: The Shaping of a Statesman, 1944–1965*. Toronto: McClelland & Stewart.

Newman, Warren J. 2007. "Living with the Amendment Procedures: Prospects for Future Constitutional Reform in Canada." In *A Living Tree: The Legacy of 1982 in Canada's Political Evolution*, ed. Graeme Mitchell, Ian Peach, David E. Smith, and John D. Whyte, 747–80. Markham, ON: Lexis Nexis Canada.

Pateman, Carole. 1970. *Participation and Democratic Theory*. Cambridge: Cambridge University Press.

Romanow, Roy, John Whyte, and Howard Lesson. 1984. *Canada ... Notwithstanding: The Making of the Constitution, 1976–1982*. Toronto: Methuen.

Russell, Peter. 2004. *Constitutional Odyssey: Can Canadians Become a Sovereign People?* 3rd ed. Toronto: University of Toronto Press.

Russell, Peter. 2009. "The *Charter* and Canadian Democracy." In *Contested Constitutionalism: Reflections on the Canadian Charter of Rights and Freedoms*, ed. James B. Kelly and Christopher P. Manfredi, 287–306. Vancouver: UBC Press.

Smith, David E. 2007. *The People's House of Commons: Theories of Democracy in Contention*. Toronto: University of Toronto Press.

Smith, David E. 2010. *Federalism and the Constitution of Canada*. Toronto: University of Toronto Press.

Stevenson, Garth. 2007. "Twenty-Five Years of Constitutional Frustration: The Amending Formula and the Continuing Legacy of 1982." In *A Living Tree: The Legacy of 1982 in Canada's Political Evolution*, ed. Graeme Mitchell, Ian Peach, David E. Smith, and John D. Whyte, 681–705. Markham, ON: Lexis Nexis Canada.

Sturm, Albert L. 1982. "The Development of American State Constitutions." *Publius* 12 (1): 57–98. https://doi.org/10.1093/oxfordjournals.pubjof.a037387

Swinton, Katherine. 1992. "Amending the Canadian Constitution: Lessons from Meech Lake." *University of Toronto Law Journal* 42 (2): 139–69. https://doi.org/10.2307/825875

Taylor, Charles. 1985. "Atomism." In *Philosophical Papers*. Vol. 1, *Philosophy and the Human Sciences*, 187–210. Cambridge: Cambridge University Press. https://doi.org/10.1017/CBO9781139173490.008

Taylor, Charles. 1989. *Sources of the Self: The Making of Modern Identity*. Cambridge, MA: Harvard University Press.

Taylor, Charles. 1993. *Reconciling the Solitudes: Essays on Canadian Federalism and Nationalism*. Ed. Guy Laforest. Montreal; Kingston, ON: McGill-Queen's University Press.

Taylor, Charles. 1994. *Multiculturalism*. Ed. Amy Gutmann. Princeton, NJ: Princeton University Press.

Tully, James. 2008. *Public Philosophy in a New Key*. 2 vols. Cambridge: Cambridge University Press.

Ward, Lee. 2004. *The Politics of Liberty in England and Revolutionary America*. Cambridge: Cambridge University Press. https://doi.org/10.1017/CBO9780511527944

Ward, Lee. 2010. *John Locke and Modern Life*. Cambridge: Cambridge University Press. https://doi.org/10.1017/CBO9780511761461

Ward, Lee. 2013. "Succession rules: Complicated path to doing the right thing." *Regina LeaderPost*, 2 April.

Ward, Norman. 1987. *Dawson's The Government of Canada*. 6th ed. Toronto: University of Toronto Press.

Whittaker, Reg. 1983. "Democracy and the Canadian Constitution." In *And No One Cheered: Federalism, Democracy and the Constitution Act*, ed. Keith Banting and Richard Simeon, 240–60. Toronto: Methuen.

Whyte, John D. 2011. "Constitutional Change and Constitutional Durability." *Journal of Parliamentary and Political Law* 5 (3): 419–36.

Whyte, John D. 2013. "The Federal Senate Proposals: A Challenge to Canada's Constitutional Principles." *Revue québécoise de droit constitutionnel* 5: 51–82.

Wiseman, Nelson. 1994. "Clarifying Provincial Constitutions." *National Journal of Constitutional Law* 6: 269–94.

11 Does Canada Have a Founding Moment?

CATHERINE FROST

Historian David Armitage believes the American Declaration of Independence had such global impact that any state born in its wake tends to emulate its methods of legitimacy. But Canada's founding does not fit the mould, and Canada does not appear in Armitage's list of 116 declarations of independence representing over half the countries in the world and most countries born in the modern age (Armitage 2007, 146–55). Surely Canada by now can claim the status of an independent sovereign state and clearly it is a modern creation like the others he cites, so how did it manage to escape the global pattern Armitage detects?

Political foundings are especially challenging phenomena for theoretical analysis. Each takes a distinct form in a distinct setting and results in a unique new entity. But to be effective they must also have some broadly recognizable quality. Foundings therefore require an approach that brings theory down to ground level, allowing higher-level claims to be tested against lived experience. By exploring the individual context in which a founding appears, history becomes the teacher, modifying and refining existing theory and bringing new possibilities to light. Because Canada is a rare exception among modern state foundings, an applied political theory approach promises to be especially rewarding in considering the questions it presents. To that end this chapter explores the Canadian case by comparing Hannah Arendt's thinking on political founding to real-world evidence drawn from Canadian constitutional history.

The date conventionally cited for Canada's founding is Confederation on 1 July 1867. But the event has not fared nearly as well as the American Declaration of Independence when it comes to the aura of "exceptionalism" that generally surrounds founding moments (Armitage

2007, 5). One historian explains this effect by saying Confederation was "not what is usually referred to as a popular movement"; rather, it was "imposed on British North America by ingenuity, luck, courage and sheer force." In place of inspiration, it forms "a bitter comment on the machinations of Canadians and the ruthlessness of Downing Street" because, of course, it did not found a new country so much as reorganize relations between remote Dominions of an Empire, with the result being "just the old government of the provinces writ large" (Waite 2001, 345–6).

This dim view of Canada's origins is not limited to historians. In anticipation of Confederation's sesquicentennial, a national survey found that, although 1867 was the most common overall choice for Canada's founding event – largely because older, English-speaking Canadians outside Quebec thought so – it is declining in the popular imagination. Less than half of Canadians under thirty-five identified 1867 as Canada's founding date, with some preferring 1982's repatriation of the Constitution (Jedwab 2013, 2–3). If the younger you are the less likely you are to see Confederation as Canada's founding moment, the long-term outlook leaves us ever more uncertain about our origins. Even the influential constitutional scholar Peter Russell has doubts about Confederation as a founding moment. He opens his famous work on Canadian constitutionalism by suggesting that Canada is "not yet constituted" and might even be "incapable" of becoming so (Russell 2004, 5) unless we adopt a new form of politics.

Still Confederation has dedicated boosters who insist it is "worthy of our admiration and gratitude" (Vaughan 2003, x). In particular Janet Ajzenstat's enthusiasm for the study of Canadian founding has been trail blazing. She takes a theorist's eye to conventional politics and by doing so has pioneered a methodology that should be more broadly used.[1] But even Ajzenstat's formidable powers cannot lift Confederation clear of its pedestrian origins or elevate its architects into the ranks of political genius. It probably does not help that Confederation's boosters cannot agree on its virtues. For Ajzenstat the founding "Fathers" are inspired by Lockean liberalism and a belief in popular sovereignty through parliamentary government (2007, 3). In contrast Frederick Vaughan insists they "deliberately and defiantly" resisted the forces of

1 Ajzenstat's work on Confederation's ratification debates shows theorists can and should learn from enacted politics (2007, 32–3).

the Enlightenment (2003, 5), while Peter Russell notes: "if they had been asked to name a philosophical patron saint it would surely have been Edmund Burke not John Locke" (2004, 11). So despite the best efforts of scholars – not to mention an extensive campaign on the part of the federal government to promote Confederation in the popular imagination[2] – the history of the period remains mired in the administrative wrangling of elites and an early form of interprovincial disagreement that still characterize this country.

Perhaps this explains why efforts to cast the architects of Confederation as intellectual leading lights with a vision for politics seem forced. The best that commentators can say is that, although we do not hear much by way of innovative argument from these figures, we can still *associate* their ideas with great intellectual movements, which lends their contribution conceptual credibility. Constitutionalists Hail and Lange explain: "Since the Fathers of Confederation frequently do not directly quote or give acknowledgement to the philosophical basis of their ideas, it is necessary to be familiar with the tradition of Western political philosophy as well as with the debates, speeches, and writings of the Fathers to recognize the reliance of the latter upon the former" (2010, 385).

In effect we can *read into* Confederation some great founding principle; this is a slender reed upon which to rest the origins of a country. Although following a principle and expressing it in high philosophic terms might be separate skills, this approach requires us to place a great deal of trust in interpreters to say what these figures had in mind. Given that the results of this exercise vary wildly, it is safe to say the method remains unproven. Yet the urge to find an expansive moral vision in Confederation is understandable, mainly because the alternative is unpalatable. What if, when you go looking for the great moment of Canadian founding, it is not there? What if – notwithstanding the efforts of well-intended historians and theorists – we are in reality a founding-less state?

Should this even matter? Armitage's identification of founding documents as a worldwide phenomenon suggests it does. Because, while founding is a rare and exceptional event, unless we believe political authority is sourced in some natural or transcendent order, we have to

2 The federal government launched one of its most expensive ad campaigns to date in an effort to generate enthusiasm for Confederation's 150th anniversary (Levitz 2015).

explain how it came about, making origins pivotal for legitimacy. This helps explain the rise of social contract theory as theocracy waned at the origins of modernity. Yet the idea that authority can be traced to a specific event or action in the past seems troublingly arbitrary, because it empowers a select few to bind all. Theories based on consent are all very well but it is cold consolation to tell present generations that past ones consented on their behalf. Considering that Hobbes, the father of modern social contract theory, conceded the state of nature that preceded it was a fiction ([1651] 1968, 187), and Rousseau suggested that reaching a contract requires a god-like overseer ([1762] 1968, 84), the whole process looks suspect.

To avoid these problems, some thinkers have turned to concepts such as right or rationality to lend a semi-transcendent quality to political authority. For example Rawls uses the idea of right to reinvent social contract theory as a thought experiment rather than as a historic event (1971); Jurgen Habermas turns to communicative ethics to identify principles that frame the moral order (1985). The difficulty is that, in a world characterized by moral pluralism, can we really know what right or rationality looks like for all people? Falling back on such conditions to frame a higher law of politics cannot resolve the problem posed by origins because we still need to explain why some rules should prevail under conditions of disagreement, when disagreement might concern those rules themselves (Kuo 2009). This leads back to questions of origins, which again returns us to political founding.

Being without an identifiable founding is not the end of the world, of course. A classic account of constitutions holds that, although modern constitutions are written – and therefore should have an identifiable author and point of origin – ancient constitutions were organic and emerged from precisely the kind of wrangling and compromise that Canadian Confederation typifies. Simone Chambers, for instance, uses this distinction to suggest that Canadian constitutionalism is rooted in discursive traditions. Instead of seeking constitutional ratification as a form of closure on the political debate, she recommends we institutionalize the ongoing dialogue (1998, 144–5; see also Tully 1994). The difficulty is that Canada is a modern nation – a definite member of the new world order, not the old one. This makes our credentials tricky either way. As an ancient constitution we lack the necessary antiquity; as a modern one we lack the great moment of authorship.

Which is why it is especially grating that one of the foremost theorists of founding ancient and modern, Hannah Arendt, never turned sustained attention to the Canadian case. Perhaps for the reasons already acknowledged: it is not entirely clear we have one, or perhaps because she saw Canada as an overgrown Dominion, rather than a state with its own unique problem of beginning. Either way Canada does not loom large in her imagination when she compares the great revolutions of the eighteenth century and their impact on political freedom. The only mention she makes of "British North America" is to say we inherited a useful two-party system from the British, which, because it includes a loyal opposition, avoids unhealthy universalism, making it possible to bring a federal project together (Arendt 1963, 226). In this regard she would agree with Ajzenstat's assessment that Westminster-style parliamentarianism was the making of the country. She would, however, disagree that *representative* democracy was anything to celebrate. The great failure of the American founding, she felt, was the narrowed sphere of politics that resulted (227).

Yet Canada poses a political puzzle at least as compelling as the other celebrated cases Arendt considers. Canada clearly arrived at modern statehood, and it clearly did not get there by being an ancient regime. So how did Canada get there at all? Although Arendt never turned sustained attention to the Canadian case, her work might help us understand Canada's peculiar origins. Rather than taking for granted Confederation's claim to founding status, we can start by asking: does Confederation have what it takes to be considered Canada's founding moment? And if not, what does?

In an Arendtian light Confederation looks more like continuation than creation – a product of circumstances and imperatives more than novelty, genius, and raw freedom. But Confederation is not our only effort at high politics. The twentieth century produced other notable occasions, including repatriation in 1982, followed by two major constitutional deals that changed the political landscape, even if they ultimately met with failure. Could these supply the founding we are looking for? Even a cursory review shows these events, too, fall short of Arendt's requirements, which raises the question: what's missing in the Canadian equation? How can we generate so much high politics without reaching the high-water mark she set for political founding? Could it be that the Canadian experience, while distinct from the more celebrated French and American revolutions, carries within it some new element, one that Arendt can help us identify?

Arendt on Founding

As the first step in using an applied political theory approach to examine Canadian constitutional history, I turn to Arendt's conception of founding. When it comes to the Canadian founding – or lack thereof – one thing that would *not* concern Arendt is the lack of a major revolution. One distinction she makes in *On Revolution* is that there is a world of difference between breaking old ties and forging new ones (Arendt 1963, 154). Revolutions serve to liberate people, but they do not make them free; only a true founding can do that, and in some cases, a revolution never reaches that point, but instead becomes mired in its own inevitable violence. What distinguishes a founding is the quality of beginning – it brings something new into the world – and in doing so represents a moment of human freedom at its finest. But it is also unsettling, because any true beginning confronts the actor with an "abyss of freedom" (191). True innovation disrupts the narrative chain of causality leading up to it, and thereby carries with it a disturbing note of arbitrariness (Arendt 1971, 207).

In effect, beginning breaks time. The problem, Arendt explains, is that beginning has "nothing whatsoever to hold on to; it is as if it came out of nowhere in either time or space ... it is as though the beginner had abolished the sequence of temporality itself" (1963, 197–8), which is why true beginning requires "thinking the unthinkable" (Arendt 1971, 208). What she calls "the riddle of foundation" is therefore "how to restart time" (214), because, as actors and as creatures that regenerate through birth, humans are a perennial source of newness in the world. Yet it is difficult to live entirely in this manner (Arendt 1963, 191–205; 1971, 217). We generate stability by reaching for something beyond the disrupted timeline. In the ancient world stability was generated through story telling, which weaves divergent events into a narrative. In the modern world we tend to favour "absolutes" – an authority that sits outside time, such as God, History, metaphysical Truth, or morality. However, these absolutes can threaten freedom if they become too entrenched (Arendt 1963, 177, 174).

Surprisingly, in Arendt's view, beginning can itself be an absolute, although unlike other absolutes, it is an expression of freedom. This is a far cry from either a social contract or transcendent ideals, because by breaking the claim of invented absolutes to be what Arendt calls "necessity," we reacquaint ourselves with the arbitrariness that is freedom, and this awareness makes all the difference (1963, 23, 55). The breaking of time emphasizes this quality, but also drives home discontinuity. For this reason Arendt thinks founding is often associated with an interlude or "hiatus" of some kind between the end of the old and the beginning of the new wherein people become reacquainted with the possibilities and exhilaration of freedom (1963, 197, 214; 1971, 206).

Thus the broken chain of time makes possible the distinction between revolution, or the ending of a previous order, and founding and the beginning of something new. It helps to enter the process prepared. The difference between the American and French revolutions, according to Arendt, is that the French emerged out of absolutism and tended to recreate it their new politics. In contrast the American colonial period put men out of reach of authorities in England, but not yet consolidated under a new authority in America. Because this bred participatory politics, it was easier to reconstruct healthy politics in their founding (Arendt 1963, 156–9). Still she notes the colonial period did not amount to the hiatus involved in founding because the colonists remained British subjects "up to the last moment" (303, n40), which means for Arendt that the hiatus begins with the Declaration of Independence and ends with constitution-making – a short eleven years in the American case.

Since Arendt describes a process that is extended in time, where is the founding moment within it? Arendt identifies founding with the framing of a constitution, but she also downplays conventional constitution-making as the "pastime" of "experts and politicians" removed from the realm of true politics by their legalist focus (1963, 116–17, 226). So constitution-making alone is not special. Instead there seems to be, throughout the founding period, a kind of human energy or potential that terminates in constitution-making, but that can also be extinguished by it. This energy is most alive, but also inarticulate, in the revolutionary or hiatus period, when the capacity for beginning is most in evidence.

If they navigate the tricky waters of the hiatus period successfully, would-be founders face another challenge: they must witness their own hand in beginning. In the few cases Arendt cites with qualified admiration – chiefly the American example in modernity and the Roman in antiquity – the founders deal with this disquieting experience in a similar manner: worship and storytelling. She notes that Americans began an almost instantaneous "blind worship" of their constitution that solved the problem of authority (1963, 190). In the case of the Romans, she is fascinated with Virgil's work during the transition period between republic and empire. In the *Aeneid*, Virgil forges a tale that casts the Roman founding as a *re*founding of the lost city of Troy. The legend is genius, Arendt thinks, because it solves the problem of beginning for contemporary Romans by making all foundings a form of refounding, a continuation that takes the edge off the experience by bending time back to its beginnings (1963, 200). This bending back of time was familiar to Romans whose system of authority, she says, was rooted in a backwards-looking approach "bound back" to origins (Arendt 1963, 193; see also Honig 1991). This is why storytelling and "fables" are among the few resources available to founders, and why political founding generally makes – indeed *needs* to make – a compelling story (Arendt 1971, 203). No one needs this imaginative reset more than the losers in an epic conflict such as the Trojan War who supply the heroes of the *Aeneid*. Indeed the losing side in any conflict faces the same difficulty: their narrative chain has been corrupted; the option of continuing life as usual is forcibly removed, which means conflict, and perhaps especially defeat, mandates a new beginning, and this makes the work of founding imperative.

So when it comes to political founding, Arendt's work tells us what to look for: political founding will "break time." It is also associated with a period outside the normal flow of events, a kind of temporal gap or "hiatus" produced by a change of circumstances, perhaps most potently in the case of revolution or defeat. But it is important to remember that the breaking of time is tied to the founding itself, not to the chain of events that led to defeat and its aftermath, which remain situated within ordinary time. The interlude could involve uprising, as in the case of America's revolutionary adventures, or wandering exile, as in the case of the defeated Trojans, and it terminates in the act of founding. Because it stands outside normal temporality, any beginning is disturbingly arbitrary – it carries authority within itself as an act, but is unchained to what went before.

In a sense, then, the work of founding – the challenge it issues or imperative it establishes – is to find a way to bind the arbitrary act of beginning back into ordinary time. We have two ways to soothe the unsettling experience of seeing our own radical freedom at work. One is the creation of stability through the search for absolutes that transcend the founding and contain it within a moral order. This is the default modern solution that Armitage detects in the global influence of the American Declaration, and it poses particular hazards. The other involves the creation of fables that, by binding the founding into an already familiar narrative, contain it in story. This appears to be a healthier method on Arendt's terms. In looking for Canada's founding, we might then keep alert to the following: events that *break time*, periods of *hiatus* associated with change, perhaps in the form of negotiating a loss, a sense of unease with *arbitrary* human action, and finally a drive to embrace *absolutes* and/or weave a new *story* out of an old one.

Canadian Confederation

Taking Confederation as the default image of Canada's founding, Arendt's account suggests a problem right away. Confederation is a product, and in many ways a continuation, of the politics that went before it (Russell 2004, 16). Multiple imperatives fed into Confederation, including concerns about American annexation accelerated by the US Civil War, moves on the part of the Maritime provinces for larger union, and British colonial authorities seeking a streamlined solution to their Canadian responsibilities. As Robert Vipond explains, Confederation is "simply less amenable to myth-making" because "the Fathers of Confederation were not 'founding' a political state in the way it is often said the American constitution-makers were 'Founders'" (1989, 6, 11). The reason Vipond gives for rejecting the resemblance is telling. "In the Canadian case there was no self-conscious break with the past," he says; instead "the Fathers of Confederation went out of their way to emphasize that Confederation represented continuity" (11). This was in part because, in their minds, the "fundamental political choices had already been made" and federalism was considered a "practical or political necessity" (11).

In a similar vein Peter Russell calls the attempt at founding through Confederation "thin and uncertain." More decisively he maintains that, even under the new order, the "final custodian" of the Canadian Constitution remained the "Imperial Parliament" (2004, 31–3). Insofar as it sat at the intersection of, and proved a continuation of, existing British North American history and constitutional practice, Confederation did not "break time" in Arendt's sense. Some participants might have felt their work was revolutionary, but because it took place under the auspices of the Imperial power, change could go only so far. This denied the Fathers of Confederation one crucial element of the equation: founding requires a transition through deep instability in order to encounter the power to begin anew. Insofar as it was understood as a product of necessity and a measure coherent with the established order,

Confederation did not make our capacity for free action apparent, and as such it cannot mark the kind of raw beginning Arendt has in mind.

There is one part of the Confederation story, however, that might be significant in light of Arendt's account. Confederation was the work of people who had experienced significant loss in some form or another. The Anglo population of Canada was swelled with the ranks of United Empire Loyalists – the losing side in the American Revolutionary War, for whom Upper Canada was originally created, temporarily undone, and then created again in Confederation as the province of Ontario. Quebec is part of Canada because of the "Conquest" – a conflict in which they, too, were on the losing side of history. They were initially granted autonomy in Lower Canada, to make way for the Loyalists, before this was temporarily undone and recreated again in Confederation as the province of Quebec. So, in a sense, these twin losses – first the Conquest, then the American Revolution – drove Canadian history forward to the point of Confederation (Noël 1994, 95). At a minimum, Confederation is evidence that Canadians have a legacy of loss to overcome.

And the story does not end there. The infamous myopia of Confederation's "two-founding peoples" myth led its architects to overlook yet another profound loss. Canada is the product of having imposed a European colonial presence on existing Indigenous peoples who, in effect, lost most of a continent to the new arrivals. Confederation merely continued this trend (Russell 2004, 32). Although Confederation might not have resolved the injuries dealt to Loyalists, *Canadiens*, and Indigenous peoples, it does make something apparent: it shows that the people in this land had something to overcome. They needed a new narrative around which to frame a shared political life, which means there is an analogy here to the great Roman myth Arendt admires. The defeated Trojans of the *Aeneid* very nearly ended their travels as permanent exiles in Carthage, settling for what seemed like the best option at the time. Confederation, too, was safe harbour. But because it kept Canadians sheltered under an existing regime, it did not constitute a beginning powerful enough to overcome the legacy of loss.

Repatriation

The next logical candidate for a founding is repatriation, designed to place the Canadian Constitution in Canadian hands. Sometimes referred to as "patriation," this term is a Canadian neologism derived as a kind of backwards innovation from *re*patriation. Since repatriation means returning something or someone to the country of origin, the truncated term "patriation" is a strange admission that Canadians were not getting back something that started with them. Repatriation remains a popular term, however, suggesting that the event is not a raw beginning – not a breaking of time, but some kind of return or relocation. Arendt is far from hostile to such recycling, and suggests that revolution can begin as restoration (1963, 32–4). Indeed she explains that founders often seek ways to bind their innovations back to the beginning. So is *re*patriation a hint that, in fact, this was an event so novel it needed to be cast as a *re*organization of authority?

Consider the Charter of Rights and Freedoms, Pierre Trudeau's novel addition to the Constitution. It has in its favour the appeal to absolutes. Arendt specifically identifies such charters with the concept of transcendent morality reached for by French revolutionaries, to their detriment, as it led to authoritarianism and extremism in that case (1963, 98–9). Absolutes – such as the universal morality associated with Law and Rights – prove especially powerful after a founding, when they are drawn into politics to stabilize affairs. Although Arendt would be unlikely to congratulate Canadians on their adoption of the Charter, its popularity might suggest the country is addressing some kind of political unease. If we keenly embrace an absolute, does it mean we must have had some moment of newness to ameliorate?

Through repatriation Trudeau was determined to work against the legacy of Canadian politics, which he saw as hamstrung by a tradition of unhealthy accommodation between French and English Canada (Trudeau 1968, 196–200). He cut a heroic figure for many in English Canada (McRoberts 1997, 186; Russell 2004, 111), and his actions in power hold the mark of arbitrariness associated with novelty and innovation. But his innovations were more divisive than might be expected of a founding, considering that it should produce stability, not uncertainty. Peter Russell suggests his success "gave a sharper edge ... to constitutional politics," and might have served to "deepen rather than narrow divisions within the populace" (1993, 34). Others go further and say Trudeau's approach was a "violation" of long-standing federalist practice (McRoberts 1997, 182) that "breached trust" within the country (Tully 1994, 173). This too might be a hallmark of founding. Machiavelli suggests it is a solitary task, the work of one man willing to do extraordinary – including extraordinarily destructive – things ([1531] 1970, 132, 170).

Yet precisely because repatriation was Trudeau's attempt at *solving* the problem of Canadian national or sovereign status (Russell 1993, 33), it is less a raw beginning and more a response to what went before. Kenneth McRoberts suggests that even the Charter was born chiefly as an instrument to address language inequality (1997, 258). With the possible exception of the Charter, then, repatriation remains bound by the imperatives that put it in motion. Trudeau might have had the audacity, even "ruthlessness," of one who begins new things (McRoberts 1997, 170), but repatriation did not break free of the constitutional timeline or resolve the internecine struggles of Canadian constitutionalism, although it might have succeeded in redirecting them.

The problem is that necessity drives out freedom – Arendt is emphatic on this point. She is sceptical of the "constitutions of experts" because of their means of arrival (1963, 137). Without the crucial break in political authority, no hiatus takes place, and that means the jarring experience of freedom is forestalled. Like American colonists, Canadians stay British subjects until the last moment,[3] but unlike them, there is no gap before the new order is established. And that means they never struggle with the great questions of founding – and without them, they do not confront their own power. The crucial question for founders, Arendt explains, is not how to organize, exercise, or even limit authority, "but how to found a new one" (139). Moreover, while performed as public spectacle, a specialist or elite process such as repatriation did not involve the public in its realization: "The difference between a constitution that is the act of government and the constitution by which a people constitute a government," she says, is "obvious enough" (137).

Moreover, repatriation went ahead over the objections of Quebec, meaning that province faced loss twice over: once in its involuntary entry into the Canadian project, and again in the repatriation exercise. And although more attention was paid to Indigenous peoples in 1982 than in 1867, it still fell short in many eyes, leaving a second legacy of loss unresolved. For these reasons repatriation left a "deep cleavage" that made it "more difficult than ever" to complete the work of founding (Russell 2004, 126). These omissions fuelled further constitutional debates into the 1990s, providing a continuance of the constitutional timeline.

So it seems that, as far as founding goes, Canada is rich in false starts. Our two major constitutional moments are coloured and constrained by their historical circumstances. And in each case, there is a legacy

3 Arguably Canadians are still subjects in some capacity, as the Queen is Canada's head of state.

of loss to be reckoned with. If it is to represent a moment of political freedom, founding must escape the grip of the past, which means the challenge for Canada is to create a history no longer driven forward by that imperative.

Megaconstitutionalism

The constitutional story does not end with repatriation, of course. Instead that event put even more wheels in motion, largely because of who had been left out, meaning that, once again, the past served as a "political resource" (Cairns 1994, 25). Two subsequent attempts were made to renew the Constitution, first with Quebec (the Meech Lake Accord of 1987) and then also with Indigenous and public participation (the Charlottetown Accord of 1992). Both went down to defeat.[4]

The Meech Lake Accord, which Russell calls "a classic exercise in elite accommodation, this time more secret than ever" (2004, 135), was followed by three years of national debate. It met demise when Elijah Harper, the only Indigenous member of the Manitoba Legislature, obstructed a procedural measure to bring through last-minute endorsements of the deal. The demise of Meech was greeted "jubilantly" by Indigenous peoples (Cairns 1994, 44), but by then polls showed that 59 per cent of Canadians did not like it much either (Russell 2004, 152). A subsequent attempt followed in which elite accommodation was supplemented with broad national consultations, which Alain Noël calls "a cynical public relations campaign" that compounded the problem by doing "more of the same … in the vain hope of escaping it" (1994, 76, 88). The resulting Charlottetown Accord was a bit of a "dog's breakfast," promising "something for everyone," but "maybe not enough for anyone" (Russell, 2004, 173, 187). That accord was defeated in a national referendum in October 1992, leaving the country bruised and exhausted by constitutional politics. In the wake of the Charlottetown defeat, the constitutional problem was shelved indefinitely in a move that became known as "abeyance" – effectively, the agreement to leave well enough alone.

4 Trudeau issued a letter excoriating the Meech Lake Accord because he felt it pandered to Quebec nationalists, whom he called the "perpetual losers" in Canadian politics (quoted in Russell 2004, 139). He also intervened to criticize the Charlottetown Accord, calling it a "mess" (quoted in McRoberts 1997, 218).

Although they are rife with high politics, these events hardly seem like promising material for political founding. Should we just accept this is how Canadian politics goes, that we do best when avoiding the disruptions and unease of raw beginning? Peter Russell suggests Canadians are now increasingly hard to scare with political catastrophes and unwilling to endorse principles dictated by the necessities of the Canadian constitutional legacy (2004, 223). But Janet Ajzenstat worries that we have traded a tradition of civil compact for unruly populism. She warns we might have to "abandon the dangerous battle" of constitutionalism and "live with the damage," as "[r]eturn is impossible" (1994, 116, 126). Simone Chambers, in contrast, sees little reason to grieve for these developments, and suggests we should celebrate the Canadian incapacity for high politics. She draws on a Habermasian idea of deliberative democracy to suggest that we should instead rely on consultation and public opinion to frame an ever-shifting constitutional order. The problem with founding, she argues, is that it is so often associated with Lockean-style contract and therefore with "a privileged moment" that tries to settle the complex issues of politics "unambiguously" and forever (Chambers 1998, 149). The "unitary vision" this entails creates closure against new or diverse views. Add to that a referendum process that "adversarializes politics," and the pursuit of a founding moment does more harm than good (155). Far better to keep alive the tradition of participatory politics that accompanied the "Canada round" (144).

What Chambers does not mention, however, is that for most of its consultations the "Canada round" that birthed the Charlottetown Accord did not include Quebec – with nearly one-quarter of the Canadian population. Instead Quebec held its own separate consultations on a different set of questions. So it is simply not the case that the pre-Charlottetown consultations were a model of inclusivity. They were the product of a breakdown in mutual understanding – what McRoberts calls a "dialogue of the deaf" (1997, 188). Whether or not Habermasian public discourse is the answer for Canadian politics, one thing is clear: it is not an existing tradition to be continued. Alain Noël shares Chambers's enthusiasm for deliberation, but thinks a constitutional solution is still a long way off, more difficult than ever to achieve, and there is no guarantee about the results. The significance of Charlottetown for Noël is that it marked an end rather than a beginning – because its failure ruled out an approach based on "confusion, deception or superficial tinkering" in the future (1994, 66–7).

Although our constitutional history might have arrived at a point where contract-style, high-stakes politics is increasingly distasteful, even Chambers's Habermasian alternative requires a set of basic rules that frame the conditions of discourse, and these rules cannot be subject to disagreement. As noted earlier, unless we believe these rules originate in some semi-transcendent principle or authority, then they too must be established someplace and sometime and by some people. So, minimal though she insists these conditions are, it is not clear that Chambers has evaded the founding moment so much as recast it. If even Chambers's vision requires some beginning, how do we get there from here?

The problem seems especially tricky in a county where deep diversity is a recognized fact of life and Chambers's concerns with the unitary vision of the social contract seem to put the founding process at odds with the country's political makeup. But Arendt is not describing a contract, and homogeneity is not a requirement in her account, nor is unanimity of opinion (1963, 219–21). Indeed the foundings she favours all include deep cleavages: the Roman world encompassed a multi-ethnic order, with different levels of citizenship and status; the American founding was the work of thirteen colonies operating together; and in Virgil's epic founding unfolds when two peoples – wandering Trojans and indigenous Latins – are required to coexist. Founding under conditions of diversity comes with no guarantees, of course – Rome was inegalitarian, the Americans had a civil war, and key figures in the *Aeneid* come to blows – providing a reminder that, important though they are, foundings carry within them the inevitable imperfections of all politics (Honig 1991).

Chambers thinks we can do better. Inspired by diversity, she recommends the approach to politics adopted by Indigenous peoples, who seek agreement but avoid excessive individualism, keeping the process vital in a way that closure-seeking methods do not (Chambers 1998, 150). But even if it avoids closure, it is hard to see why Indigenous politics rules out beginning. In fact if any population has a stake in finding a new path, it would be those so squarely disadvantaged under the old one. One volume on indigenous rights worldwide, for example, insists that the critical questions for indigenous politics include: "How might the narratives of nationhood be retold" and "the founding moments of a state reconstituted" (Ivison, Patton, and Sanders 2000, 3). So, although discursive politics might represent a tradition within the Canadian state – albeit a marginalized one – that tradition *itself* calls for a new beginning.

The problem with the "just keep talking," solution is that it can eliminate or avoid the breaking of time that beginning represents and requires. It would be regrettable if the presence of discursive traditions among Indigenous peoples were taken as their lacking a taste for transformative change. Indigenous traditions might resemble the Roman solution to beginning – a kind of civil piety that involves binding the new back into one's origins in the name of stability – but Arendt suggests that such behaviour is an inspired solution to the problem of radical, time-breaking innovation, not evidence of its absence. There is no reason to think Indigenous politics is at odds with the kind of actions involved in founding, but it might be the case, as Tully suggests, that we are "just finding our feet" as regards an Indigenous-inspired political practice in Canada (1994, 198).

The Lessons of Loss

Chambers is right about one thing, though. A striking thread that runs through Canadian constitutionalism is the search for accommodation among diversity. "Accommodation" suggests making room for someone or something – in essence, creating somewhere to dwell. It also suggests the possibility of change – remaking or sharing space in a manner that can involve compromise. Canadians seek accommodation, then, because the dwelling place is not secure – the living space must be shared, and we are still not sure how. Virgil's violent and heroic fable captures this pathos by showing that those who dwell in a New World are often the children of loss and exile, trying to come to terms with one another.

Arendt embraces Virgil's great fable in part for these reasons. Its heroes are defeated, displaced, and drift from port to port in search of a home, and some accommodation from the locals. Is there something that those who know loss intimately understand about founding that other peoples do not? And is this where we should be looking for the potency of the Canadian founding? Barry Cooper suggests that part of the problem for Canada is that Canadians have been content to stay "sheltered within a stable political world" (1996, 89). Such politics lends itself to obsessions with security and propagates a "garrison" mentality "formed in the strenuous conditions of exile." He explains: "Canadians have been taught, particularly through the myths of the garrison and *la survivance*, that they associated initially (and also thereafter) solely for reasons of life and its necessities" (98, 108). A garrison is "a closely knit society" not because it has created something new or solved the problems of solidarity, but "because it is a beleaguered society." This mentality served for a while, but is now "dreamed out." In its wake we must decide whether Canadians "associate for safety or for some higher purpose" (95, 105, 108).

The *Aeneid*, too, begins with exile. This is emphasized in the opening books, when the destruction of Troy must be retold before a rapt audience. The Trojans encountered the Greek rout with disbelief, but their wandering on the high seas gave them time to come to terms with their situation. Whatever sense of complacency we draw from the normal unfolding of life, the reliable course of events that holds society together in predictable ways, this is shattered for the defeated. The lesson we take from loss, in other words, is that time itself can break, and we find ourselves thrown back on our own resources.

Other than providing a great setting for tragedy, why does this matter? It matters because time *must* break in order to make way for the new. Moreover, the break must be *faced*, dealt with, and lived within before the new can successfully emerge. Time, as the chain of causality, can take the guise of necessity – the opposite of human freedom. This is why all founding, all beginning, breaks time in Arendt's account. What the Trojans knew, as all who lose and face exile understand, is the *difference* between necessity and freedom. They were, in a sense, set free by their defeat, but still must move from a world of loss and necessity to one of creation and freedom in the period of hiatus between exile and founding.[5] For to nurse the wounds of loss is to remain bound to a temporal order that can no longer support the demands placed upon it. Thus the displaced develop a profound understanding of the fragility of continuity under the onslaught of human action. Difficult though it is, this understanding is a rich place for politics to begin. We know Canada arose from a legacy of loss; we have even had our constitutional wanderings. The question is, does Canada ever arrive at the point of beginning?

5 Michèle Lowrie points out that time is undone in the narrative structure of the *Aeneid*. Divine violence – that in the *Iliad* leads to the fall of Troy – is in the *Aeneid* unwound to arrive at a point of freedom where the identity of the loser is shed in favour of something new (Lowrie 2005; see also Arendt 1971, 204).

Breaking, Wandering, Beginning

As pointed out, Canadians bring a diverse legacy of loss to the constitutional table – it is what makes our high politics so loaded. The effort to overcome this legacy has driven repeated efforts to find a formula that can once and for all rectify past grievances. If this has been our *modus operandi,* then a new beginning would require us to abandon that pursuit. Yet what, if anything, has come closest to breaking this constitutional obsession? Unlike Confederation, which affirmed our constitutional preoccupations, or the high politics of repatriation and megaconstitutionalism, which perpetuated them, the most extraordinary moments in Canadian politics have come from the rejection of elite-driven, accommodation-as-usual style politics.

The effect is evident in the once-unthinkable defeat of the Meech Lake Accord, brought about by the objection of a sole Indigenous representative. Efforts were made to reassert the constitutional continuum in the form of the Charlottetown Accord, but something had already shifted: Indigenous concerns were now recognized as essential to any new political order, but a new agreement was *not*. In other words, Meech's defeat showed that Canadians could say no to the imperative of history, that legacy of loss and accommodation handed down to them as an inheritance to be tended. They did so at the risk of Quebec's exit from Canada, however, which very nearly became a reality.

These two defeats spoke volumes: a new agreement was not going to solve old problems. For what overcomes the legacy of loss is doing new things. Chambers is right to criticize the hunt for closure implied in megaconstitutional politics, but not because founding is politically constraining; rather, in the Canadian case, previous efforts at founding have been illusory all along, already hamstrung by the past. When history becomes something to be engaged and eliminated, it produces a form of politics that remains "locked in sterile combat, with none able or willing to try a different way" (Cameron 1998, 50). "We Canadians," David Cameron writes, "true children of the age of reason," believe that "every 'problem' has a 'solution,'" and so we "cried out for finality, for an end to the crisis" (50). Instead our "earnest efforts to address the national question" was "paradoxically, part of what … kept the problem in existence" (51).

So it seems we have several elements of Arendt's formula for founding in the collapse of megaconstitutionalism: people making themselves apparent in the public space, actions that are unsettling in their arbitrariness, and an "unthinkable" refusal of the temporal imperative that breaks down business as usual. We also have a powerful story of loss, first in the experiences of Indigenous peoples, and then in the desire of French and English Canada for a political union that will restore lost prestige.

It even seems that the collapse of constitutional politics has produced its own hiatus – in the form of abeyance, the agreement to shelve indefinitely the Canadian mission to right the various wrongs we bring into union. Is this enough to clear the way for founding? While not yet fully realized, Peter Russell thinks these events have made it possible to begin something new – a new kind of politics. He explains: "if Canadians are fortunate enough to kick their constitutional habit for a decent interval," the defeat of the Charlottetown agreement "will have had more positive long-term results than its majority 'No' might portend" (1993, 37). And David Cameron writes there are "grounds for believing that the present historical moment is laden with the potential for radical change" (1998, 49). He suggests it heralds "the commencement of a new and discernibly different era in our evolving political experience" (49). So the time after megaconstitutional collapse is an interlude of sorts, but it is also an opportunity for transformation in keeping with Arendt's expectations.

What, then, would be the role of absolutes in the Canadian case? Arendt maintains that absolutes such as Rights, History, God, or a sacralized concept of "the people" provide the usual suspects of modern founding, yet they do not seem prominent here. This is where the Canadian story might be at its most interesting. Arendt seems to prefer the *Aeneid*'s approach to founding over the ideological extremism of the French Revolution or even the occasionally self-deluded, occasionally brilliant American founding. The latter two cases required an absolute to stabilize the arbitrary qualities of beginning. The Romans, in contrast, merely needed a good story. The absence of consensus around any particular absolute in the Canadian case makes us less like these other modern foundings. Our shared participation in the wrenching constitutional saga, with all its high drama and driven by genuine loss, makes a better story than it does a political ideal. Moreover, the story, as Peter Russell (2004) has pointed out, forms a kind of "Odyssey." James Tully likens it to *nastawgan*, an Anishnabi word for a network of routes through a forest that defines a people, a pattern "too complex and ragged to fit any one theory" (1994, 151).

With such a legacy we will never make it into Armitage's list of modern declaratory foundings. Nor do we belong there. As Tully observes, in Canada "[n]o great founding revolution or constituent assembly" marked "an original act of state-building" (1994, 162). That Canada is an outlier is obvious enough. But an applied political theory approach also illustrates that Canada could be a rare instance of ancient founding in a modern context – a conclusion that becomes apparent only by teasing through the evidence of history in light of Arendtian theory. At the same time the deeper dimensions of Arendt's own work, its proximity to themes of loss and resilience, are brought to the surface when her theory is applied to concrete experience in the Canadian case. The great moment of founding that she celebrates, we discover, is at its most potent when we live within it, rather than look back upon it.

Which means that the exercise of applying Arendtian theory to the Canadian case delivers more than just an explanation for Canadian exceptionalism or a new perspective on Arendtian founding. It also points at a new direction for Canadian constitutionalism. Because if Canadians can release the concept of Confederation as a weak answer to the problem of founding, and resist the urge to perpetuate a politics aimed at the negation of loss, we might find we are well placed to rehabilitate an older form of founding, one that can liberate without violence by meeting the unthinkable end of things with confidence in our capacity to work together. Doing so would provide the world with an alternative model for the modern age. What this might look like in practice is still anyone's guess, but one can hope it would find a way to combine the arbitrary and demanding conditions of human freedom into a shared and evolving story. Canada's odyssey can then encompass all the stages and developments that led us here, starting from before Confederation and extending past the unthinkable megaconstitutional endings, and on to something new.

REFERENCES

Ajzenstat, Janet. 1994. "Constitution Making and the Myth of the People." In *Constitutional Predicament: Canada after the Referendum of 1992*, ed. Curtis Cook, 112–25. Montreal; Kingston, ON: McGill-Queen's University Press.

Ajzenstat, Janet. 2007. *The Canadian Founding*. Montreal; Kingston, ON: McGill-Queen's University Press.

Arendt, Hannah. 1963. *On Revolution*. New York: Penguin Books.

Arendt, Hannah. 1971. *Willing*. Vol. 2, *The Life of the Mind*. New York: Harvest Books.

Armitage, David. 2007. *The Declaration of Independence: A Global History*. Cambridge, MA: Harvard University Press.

Cairns, Alan C. 1994. "The Charlottetown Accord: Multinational Canada v. Federalism." In *Constitutional Predicament: Canada after the Referendum of 1992*, ed. Curtis Cook, 25–63. Montreal; Kingston, ON: McGill-Queen's University Press.

Cameron, David. 1998. "National Unity: Are We on the Threshold of a New Era?" *Policy Options* (September): 49–51.

Chambers, Simone. 1998. "Contract or Conversation? Theoretical Lessons from the Canadian Constitutional Crisis." *Politics & Society* 26 (1): 143–72. https://doi.org/10.1177/0032329298026001006

Cooper, Barry. 1996. "Theoretical Perspectives on Constitutional Reform in Canada." In *Rethinking the Constitution: Perspectives on Canadian Constitutional Reform, Interpretation, and Theory*, ed. Anthony A. Peacock, 217–32. Don Mills, ON: Oxford University Press.

Habermas, Jurgen. 1985. *Reason and the Rationalization of Society*. Vol. 1, *Theory of Communicative Action*. Trans. Thomas McMarthy. Boston: Beacon Press.

Hail, Michael, and Stephen Lange. 2010. "Federalism and Representation in the Theory of the Founding Fathers: A Comparative Study of U.S. and Canadian Constitutional Thought." *Journal of Federalism* 40 (3): 366–88. https://doi.org/10.1093/publius/pjq001

Hobbes, Thomas. [1651] 1968. *Leviathan*. New York: Penguin Books.

Honig, Bonnie. 1991. "Declarations of Independence: Arendt and Derrida on the Problem of Founding a Republic." *American Political Science Review* 85 (1): 97–113. https://doi.org/10.2307/1962880

Ivison, Duncan, Paul Patton, and Will Sanders. 2000. "Introduction." In *Political Theory and the Rights of Indigenous Peoples*, ed. Duncan Ivison, Paul Patton, and Will Sanders, 1–22. Cambridge: Cambridge University Press.

Jedwab, Jack. 2013. "The Founding Peoples and the Founding Events: Somewhat Different Visions East and West." Montreal: Association for Canadian Studies. Available online at http://www.acs-aec.ca/pdf/polls/Founding%20People%20of%20Canada%20Who%20and%20When.pdf

Kuo, Ming-Sung. 2009. "Cutting the Gordian Knot of Legitimacy Theory? An Anatomy of Frank Michelman's Presentist Critique of Constitutional Authorship." *International Journal of Constitutional Law* 7 (4): 683–714. https://doi.org/10.1093/icon/mop024

Levitz, Stephanie. 2015. "Advertising costs for Canada's 150th birthday rising but no party plans in sight." *CBC News*, 4 January. Available online at http://www.cbc.ca/news/politics/canada-150-ad-costs-rising-but-no-plans-in-sight-1.2889551

Lowrie, Michèle. 2005. "Vergil and Founding Violence." *Cardozo Law Review* 27 (2): 945–76.

Machiavelli, Niccolò. [1531] 1970. *The Discourses*. New York: Penguin Books.

McRoberts, Kenneth. 1997. *Misconcieving Canada: The Struggle for National Unity*. Toronto: Oxford University Press.

Noël, Alain. 1994. "Deliberating a Constitution: The Meaning of the Canadian Referendum of 1992." In *Constitutional Predicament: Canada after the Referendum of 1992*, ed. Curtis Cook, 64–80. Montreal; Kingston, ON: McGill-Queen's University Press.

Rawls, John. 1971. *A Theory of Justice*. Cambridge: Belknap Press.

Rousseau, Jean-Jacques. [1762] 1968. *The Social Contract*. Trans. Maurice Cranston. New York: Penguin Books.

Russell, Peter H. 1993. "The End of Mega Constitutional Politics in Canada." *PS, Political Science & Politics* 26 (1): 33–7. https://doi.org/10.1017/S1049096500037276

Russell, Peter H. 2004. *Constitutional Odyssey*. Toronto: University of Toronto Press.

Trudeau, Pierre. 1968. "Federalism, Nationalism and Reason." In *Pierre Trudeau, Federalism and the French Canadians*, 182–203. New York: St Martin's Press.

Tully, James. 1994. "Diversity's Gambit Declined." In *Constitutional Predicament: Canada after the Referendum of 1992*, ed. Curtis Cook, 149–98. Montreal; Kingston, ON: McGill-Queen's University Press.

Vaughan, Frederick. 2003. *Canadian Federalist Experiment: From Defiant Monarchy to Reluctant Republic*. Montreal; Kingston, ON: McGill-Queen's University Press.

Vipond, Robert. 1989. "1787 and 1867: The Federal Principle and Canadian Confederation Reconsidered." *Canadian Journal of Political Science* 22 (1): 3–25. https://doi.org/10.1017/S0008423900000810

Waite, P.B. 2001. *The Life and Times of Confederation 1864–1867*. Toronto: Robin Brass Studio.

PART IV

Ethnic Diversity and Minority Rights

12 Self-Determination Theory: Political and Psychological

MICHAEL MURPHY

Indigenous peoples in Canada face many disadvantages, but perhaps none more dire than in the area of health outcomes. Despite some recent, and encouraging, signs of improvement, to be an Indigenous person in Canada today is still to face a significantly higher risk of illness and premature mortality than a member of the non-Indigenous population. Mental health outcomes tell a similar story, with many Indigenous communities exhibiting troubling levels of anxiety, depression, post-traumatic stress disorder, alcoholism and substance abuse, and death or injury from self-inflicted violence or suicide (see, for example, Boyer 2014; Kirmayer, Simpson, and Cargo 2003; Reading and Wien 2009; Salée 2006).[1] What explains these health disparities?

Research in the broader field of health determinants suggests that the answer is complex and multifactorial (see, for example, Hertzman and Siddiqi 2009, 33; Waldram, Herring, and Young 2006, 273). Yet one particular set of factors has been identified as having an especially powerful influence on population health outcomes more generally. These are the so-called psycho-social determinants of health, which measure the psychological impact of the social environment and its deleterious effects on physical and mental well-being. Among the most commonly cited social-environmental factors are material deprivation and socio-economic inequality; a lack of social networks and a toxic social environment (including a breakdown in family relationships); substandard

1 My focus here is on Canada, but similar outcomes are experienced by Indigenous people worldwide; see, for example, Anderson et al. (2006); Cook et al. (2007); Ohenjo et al. (2006).

educational experiences; and unhealthy workplace environments. Conspicuously absent from this list is the psychological impact of the surrounding political environment. Politics is sometimes considered indirectly in relation to the kinds of public policies that are taken to be either supportive or corrosive of a healthy social environment, but precious little attention has been devoted to the direct health effects arising from an experience with what might be called an unhealthy political environment.

An applied political theory approach could help to rectify this inattention to politics, which is especially glaring in the context of the present discussion. Although there is a widely shared assumption that political self-determination is in some essential way connected to the health of Indigenous individuals and communities and, correspondingly, that colonization and the denial of self-determination have been fundamentally destructive of Indigenous physical and mental well-being, this assumption has yet to be subjected to rigorous theoretical or empirical analysis. My aim in this chapter is to take a small, and tentative, step towards filling this gap through a synthesis of insights drawn from two very different kinds of self-determination theory: one from the domain of social psychology, the other from the domain of political theory. One of the remarkable things about these two literatures is that, despite their very different theoretical and methodological orientations, they offer strikingly complementary accounts of the value of self-determination and the role it plays in human well-being. Equally remarkable is that neither of these literatures seems to have taken any notice of the other. By bridging this communication gap, and starting a conversation between self-determination theory in its political and psychological variants, I argue that there are both good theoretical reasons and some compelling empirical evidence to support the conclusion that meaningful self-determination is a factor that contributes positively to Indigenous mental health and well-being, and that the absence (or denial) of self-determination can have a decidedly negative impact on Indigenous mental health outcomes.

The chapter opens with an account of psychological self-determination theory and the three basic needs it identifies as essential to mental health. I then examine how these basic needs have been articulated in a very different, but complementary, manner within the literature on the political theory of self-determination. My ultimate aim here is to explain how communal self-determination can be viewed as in important prerequisite for individual self-determination and mental well-being. In the final section I establish the connection between political theory and practice by examining some of the available evidence linking self-determination and mental health outcomes among Indigenous peoples in Canada and elsewhere around the globe.

Self-Determination Theory: The Psychological Variant

Self-determination theory (SDT) is an empirically derived theory of human flourishing and well-being developed jointly by Edward Deci and Richard Ryan at the University of Rochester.[2] SDT is founded in a self-consciously eudaimonic conception of well-being, which conveys the idea of living a life that reflects our own values and potential. As the authors themselves put it, "the eudaimonist conception of well-being or flourishing rests on the proposition that what is most subjectively satisfying over the course of a life is activity that develops and expresses one's most reflectively valued and well-integrated human potentialities" (Ryan, Curren, and Deci 2013, 58; cf. Ryan and Deci 2002, 22–3). This conception of the good life resonates powerfully with Amartya Sen's conclusion that the path to well-being lies in ensuring that people have the freedom (or capability) to achieve the lives they themselves have reason to value (1992, 1999).

At the core of SDT lie two fundamental, and interconnected, assumptions. The first is that human beings are possessed of a natural and innate developmental drive, which is to say that people are intrinsically motivated to develop and expand their talents and capacities and to explore and understand the environments they encounter. It is through this process of self-motivated development that we realize our true potential and create, and progressively build upon, a coherent and integrated sense of ourselves as individuals. Part and parcel of this inherent developmental drive is a natural tendency to explore what Ryan and Deci refer to as our fundamentally relational nature. By this they mean that we are creatures whose sense of identity and well-being, and capacity for personal growth, are fostered partly through our relationships with other people and with the broader social groupings or communities of which we are a part (Deci and Ryan 2012b, 417; Ryan and Deci 2002, 5–6; Ryan and Sapp 2007, 73). Here we find a clue

2 This section expands upon a previous account of self-determination theory in Murphy (2015a).

as to SDT's second foundational observation, for although this inborn developmental tendency is a core feature of the human psychological architecture, healthy human development does not occur in a vacuum or in the absence of external sources of influence and support. Rather, SDT emphasizes that our success in realizing our potential and achieving a state of psychological well-being is profoundly influenced by the nature and quality of our surrounding sociocultural environments and the capacity of those environments to provide us with what Deci and Ryan refer to as our basic psychological needs (Deci and Ryan 2012b, 417; Ryan and Deci 2008, 659).

SDT identifies three basic psychological needs that are cross-developmentally and cross-culturally – in other words, universally – essential to individual mental health and well-being (Ryan and Sapp 2007, 75).[3] First and foremost is the need for autonomy. To live autonomously is to lead a life that is self-chosen, a life that accords with our own considered values, preferences, interests, and our sense of who we are as individuals (Ryan and Deci 2008, 667; Ryan and Deci 2004, 450). As Ryan and Deci put it, "[t]o the extent an action is autonomous it is characterized by feeling volitional or self-endorsed. When people are acting autonomously they are fully behind their own actions" (2011, 50).

Ryan and Deci's conception of autonomy as people self-consciously choosing and leading their own lives has much in common with the work of social and political theorists who also emphasize the relationship between autonomy and well-being. Amartya Sen, for example, endorses precisely such a conception of autonomy, and he argues that it is both intrinsically and instrumentally connected to human development and well-being: instrumentally, in that the exercise of individual autonomy is a powerful engine of economic growth and development; intrinsically, in the sense that to be autonomous is partly constitutive of what it means to live a rich and fulfilling human life (Sen 1992, 49–52; 1997, 542; 1999, 36–7; 2001, 506–12). Len Doyal and Ian Gough locate a very similar idea of autonomy at the core of their theory of human need, arguing that physical health and autonomy are the two basic needs any human being must satisfy "in order to avoid the serious harm of fundamentally impaired participation in their form of life" (Doyal and Gough 1991, 73). In parallel fashion, a number of contemporary liberal political

3 This claim to universalism has attracted charges of cultural imperialism. For their response to this charge, see Ryan and Deci (2002, 26); Deci and Ryan (2012a, 97).

philosophers have defended the view that the good life is the life lived autonomously, and that individuals who either are unable to, or are prevented from, leading a life that accords with their own freely and self-consciously determined values, goals, or ends will suffer a diminishment of their well-being (see, for example, Dworkin 1988, 20, 26, 112; Kymlicka 1995, 80–1; Raz 1986, 368–95, 408).

Ryan and Deci themselves have elaborated upon their conception of autonomy in relation to the work of philosophers such as Immanuel Kant and Gerald Dworkin. From Kant they take the idea that autonomous individuals are self-governing individuals. To be self-governing implies the experience of being the regulator or controller of one's own life, an idea that also resonates strongly with Jennifer Nedelsky's conception of the practice (and experience) of autonomy as "giving laws to ourselves," or living in accordance with laws that are self-imposed (Nedelsky 1989, 10; see also Ryan and Deci 2004, 451). At the same time, Ryan and Deci insist that autonomy, as conceived of within SDT, is not to be equated with the notion of total independence, limitless freedom, or the absence of any form of influence, regulation, or constraint on our choices or actions. On the contrary, autonomy is entirely compatible with actions taken out of a sense of duty or loyalty, actions taken in accordance with certain rules, laws, or conventions, or actions taken in response to various pressures or inducements. It is even compatible with choosing not to make choices or with granting others the authority to make decisions on our behalf. What matters in all of these cases is that we freely endorse the decisions, and the reasons behind them, and recognize them as consistent with our most basic values and commitments. Here Ryan and Deci note their agreement with Gerald Dworkin: "As Dworkin described it, autonomy entails endorsement of one's actions at the highest order of reflection … Dworkin further underscored that autonomy does not definitionally entail 'being subject to no external influences'… Rather, the issue of autonomy is whether the following of influences or inputs reflects mere obedience or coercion or, alternatively, a self-endorsed and reflective valuing of the direction or guidance that these inputs provide" (2004, 453; cf. Dworkin 1988, 21).

The opposite of autonomy, according to SDT, is "heteronomy": the experience of being restricted, controlled, or manipulated by forces (or influences) that one does not freely or genuinely endorse. Autonomy is perhaps most obviously restricted by physical coercion and restraint or a lack of rights and opportunities, but it is also compromised when we act out of necessity rather than conviction; when we are pressured or induced to act in contravention of our considered values; when we act on a desire we regard as base or unworthy; or when we passively swallow a set of rules we regard as alien or illegitimate (Ryan and Deci 2004, 450–3; 2008, 667; Ryan and Sapp 2007, 75–6, 83; cf. Nedelsky 1989, 10).[4]

Despite the similarities between the social psychology and the political theory of autonomy, one of the key distinctive features of SDT is that it places maximum emphasis on the value of autonomy as a lived experience, and it is this psychological experience of autonomy (or a lack of autonomy) that has such important implications for health and well-being. Political theorists, in contrast, almost universally view autonomy as a capacity, and it is the lack of (or frustration of) this capacity that is seen to affect well-being. Perhaps the lone exception in this regard is Nedelsky, who also defines autonomy as a capacity, but argues that "the feeling of autonomy is an inseparable component of the capacity" such that neither the feeling nor the capacity, can survive the destruction of the other (1989, 24–5). Like Ryan and Deci, therefore, her view is that, in assessing whether (or how) institutions or environments foster autonomy, our ultimate concern should be the effect of those institutions and environments on the lived experience of freedom (or unfreedom) of the people whose lives are being affected (25).[5]

The second basic need identified by SDT is competence. This "refers to feeling effective in one's ongoing interactions with the social environment and experiencing opportunities to exercise and express one's capacities … The need for competence leads people to seek challenges that are optimal for their capacities and to persistently attempt to maintain and enhance those skills and capacities through activity" (Ryan and Deci 2002, 7). Competence is properly understood not in terms of the factual attainment of any given skill or technique (such as *being* a competent political theorist or plumber). It is obviously linked to these sorts of factual achievements or successes, but again what is crucial for psychological well-being is the *experience* or *feeling* of efficacy or mastery as we engage in activities in our social environments

4 On the matter of passively following the rules that have been handed down or dictated to us compare Nedelsky (1989, 24): "many people learn to 'play the game' effectively, to do what is wanted of them, and to confidently reap the rewards handed out for compliance … [but] [i]t is not autonomy. Playing someone else's game well is not defining the path of one's own life."

5 Nedelsky does not, on the other hand, link the feeling of autonomy with well-being.

and pursue our desired ends and interests in life (7). The idea of competence has not figured prominently in the work of contemporary political theorists, at least not in the experiential sense of the term. For example, Sen emphasizes the importance to well-being of people developing the *capability* to *actively* choose and live lives they have reason to value (1992, xi). In similar fashion Raz suggests that well-being has an essentially active character, such that individuals who lack the capacity actively to pursue and successfully achieve their goals in life will necessarily suffer a diminishment of their well-being (1986, 292–7). For neither of these thinkers, however, does the feeling of efficacy that comes with the capacity to actively pursue our life goals figure in the determination of well-being. Again, the lone exception seems to be Nedelsky, who comes very close to the thinking of Ryan and Deci in suggesting that a feeling of competence is a crucial component of the feeling of autonomy, in that people who lack a sense of competence undoubtedly will feel less autonomous, less free (1989, 25; see also Deci and Ryan 2012b, 417).

Relatedness, the third basic need, speaks to the value of social connectedness, our need to feel a sense of belonging and a sense of importance to other individuals and to the larger social groupings or communities of which we are a part (Deci and Ryan 2012b, 421). The basic need for relatedness is important in its own right, but it also exists in a relationship of interdependence with the basic needs for autonomy and competence. For example, a feeling of relatedness offers us a sense of confidence and security as we explore our surrounding social environments and satisfy our basic need for autonomy. In addition, the need for relatedness itself is fulfilled through a process whereby we internalize the sociocultural values and regulations of the social groups with whom we are connected, and in this way find meaning and purpose within their bounds; crucially, however, this process of social integration will be conducive to our well-being only if it occurs autonomously, which is to say that the values and practices in question must be freely endorsed by us, for only in this way can they truly become our own (Ryan, Curren, and Deci 2013, 62–3; Ryan and Deci 2011, 51–2, 53–4; Ryan and Sapp 2007, 73, 76, 79). Moreover, in a striking parallel with some of the literature on the political theory of self-determination, SDT emphasizes that the different communities or cultures we connect with provide much of the raw material upon which autonomous choice is based. In SDT's terms, "cultures influence and provide the content for the life goals and projects people internalize," and different cultures offer raw materials that vary in terms of their propensity to "yield experiences of autonomy, competence, and relatedness" (Ryan, Curren, and Deci 2013, 63).[6]

The value of belonging has also been the subject of intensive interest among contemporary political theorists (see, for example, Guibernau 2013; Yuval-Davis 2012), many of whom describe the communal (or relational) preconditions for the development, nurture, and exercise of individual autonomy in terms that closely parallel those identified by SDT (see Doyal and Gough 1991, 76–9; Kymlicka 1995, 80–4; Nedelsky 1989, 7–13; Taylor 1985, 187–210). I take up some of these accounts in the next section of the chapter, and discuss how they have been linked both to a defence of communal self-determination and to the well-being of the individual members of self-determining communities.

To summarize the discussion so far, SDT identifies three basic psychological needs that are essential to healthy psychological development and well-being. This applies universally to all human beings, both cross-developmentally, and cross-culturally (Ryan and Sapp 2007, 71). Although the basic need for autonomy seems to be the most crucial to human flourishing, the three basic needs are mutually interconnected and interdependent, such that "the neglect or thwarting of any is expected to lead to impoverished functioning and ill-being" (Ryan and Deci 2011, 48). SDT is an empirically derived (that is, evidence-based) theory of human development and well-being, and in subsequent empirical testing across a broad spectrum of social environments its hypotheses have been borne out consistently. Whether in the domain of education, employment, health and elder care settings or intra-familial relations, in contexts where their basic needs for autonomy, competence, and relatedness are satisfied, people tend to lead healthier and more fulfilling lives, whereas in contexts where their basic needs are frustrated or undermined, poorer mental health outcomes are the result. This includes a greater tendency towards depression, anxiety, reduced self-esteem, feelings of hopelessness and passivity, alienation, and suicide ideation (Bureau et al. 2012; Deci et al. 2001; Helwig and McNeil 2011; Kasser and Ryan 1999; Ryan and Deci 2011, 48–9).

Somewhat surprisingly, self-determination theory has not had much to say about the relationship between autonomy and well-being in a specifically political context, nor has it had much to say about the

6 Compare this to the discussion below of societal cultures as "contexts of choice."

potential interdependence between individual and collective forms of autonomy and how this interdependence might influence mental health outcomes. Deci and Ryan do suggest the possibility of these linkages. For example, they argue that "the cultural, economic and political contexts within which people live have overarching and pervasive, yet often hidden, roles in supporting or thwarting the fulfillment of their basic needs" (2012a, 96; cf. Ryan and Deci 2011, 59). Or again more explicitly, "[p]olitical freedoms, economic opportunities and security (which affords freedoms), and institutional dynamics all impact a person's autonomy, and his or her capacity to fulfill basic needs" (59). They argue further that autonomy, the most important basic need, "is not just an individual affair. Across history, groups of people have struggled to protect or gain autonomy, and to be free of coercive forces from their own dictatorial governments or from invasion by other collectives" (Deci and Ryan 2012a, 85). These brief statements, however, raise at least as many questions as they answer. For example, in what specific ways does the attendant political context support or thwart the fulfilment of people's basic needs? What is the precise nature of the relationship between individual and collective political autonomy? And what role does collective autonomy play in the satisfaction of people's individual needs for autonomy, competence, and relatedness? To answer these questions, we need some help from the contemporary literature on the political theory of self-determination.

Self-Determination Theory: The Political Variant

This is a very large body of literature that encompasses many different perspectives and approaches, and I will not attempt to summarize it here. It will suffice to identify a couple of key insights that are fairly widely shared across different approaches (at least in their broad strokes), and to link them to the three basic needs identified by SDT. Some of the insights have been foreshadowed already in the discussion above.[7] The first is that there is an important relationship between collective self-determination and the individual autonomy of the members of freely self-determining communities. This relationship plays itself out in at least three different, but interconnected, ways. The first speaks to the role of collective self-determination in supporting the social

7 I have also discussed some of these insights in Murphy (2015b).

preconditions essential to developing and nurturing our very *capacity* for individual autonomy. This thesis has been explored by communitarians such as Charles Taylor, working from self-consciously Aristotelian assumptions, but very similar versions have been developed by prominent liberal thinkers such as Will Kymlicka and Joseph Raz.

Generally speaking, the argument's departure point is the observation that the realization of all of our distinctively human capacities, including the capacity for autonomy, is vitally dependent on our membership in a particular kind of cultural community – namely, a nation.[8] National membership, and national self-determination, affords us access not only to life's more practical requirements (such as safety and security), but also to a common language and a broad array of social, cultural, economic, legal, and political institutions that support a distinctive form of life. This rich sociocultural environment – what Kymlicka refers to as a cultural context of choice – nourishes and sustains individual autonomy in at least three different ways: first, by granting individuals the freedoms and opportunities they need to make choices about how to live their lives; second, by equipping individuals with the capacity to make free and informed choices and to evaluate them in relation to alternative options; and third, by providing a range of options and alternatives that have value and significance to us, options that we can explore and experiment with in the process of directing our lives in accordance with our own values and preferences (Kymlicka 1995, 75–93; Raz 1994, 133–4; Taylor 1985, 204–10). To deny people the right to self-determination is thus to deny them the ability to foster the autonomy of their own members in culturally meaningful and culturally relevant ways.[9]

---

8 This account draws partly on Murphy (2012, 50–1, 62–4).

9 It goes without saying that not all self-determining communities will choose to respect or facilitate the autonomy of their own members. Cases such as these constitute a straightforward transgression of the principle of self-determination – a principle that is *necessarily* directed towards securing the freedom of a community's constituent members. A more challenging issue stems from Ryan and Deci's observation that the means by which autonomy is satisfied, and therefore what it looks like, in practice tend to differ across cultures in relation to specific cultural beliefs, values, and priorities (2002, 26). This raises an obvious question: do some cultures do better than others in supporting the basic needs of their members, including the need for autonomy? For discussion on this point, see Deci and Ryan (2012a, 97); Doyal and Gough (1991, 69–75; 180–90); Nedelsky (1989, 25–6); Raz (1986, 391–5, 423–4); and Ryan and Deci (2008, 659).

A second way of linking self-determination and individual autonomy derives from the work of Raz, who argues that the exercise of self-government in itself is intrinsically valuable, as it affords individuals an opportunity to exercise or express their autonomy specifically in the *public and political* life of the community. Participation in self-government is both an important (and valued) expression of political autonomy, but also for many an essential aspect of their identity as community members, and as such it should command our respect and support (Raz 1994, 136). Here I would like to add another dimension to Raz's argument that is of particular relevance when speaking of Indigenous communities. It stems from the observation that self-determination also encompasses the freedom to shape and exercise self-governing powers in a manner that reflects a community's distinctive identity, traditions, and culture (see Tully 1995, 1–6, 32). This includes everything from determining the language of government, the structure and authority of the governing institutions, the nature of political participation, the character of the decision-making process, and the means by which decision makers are to be held accountable. Although this has obvious value from the point of view of respecting the freedom of people to rule themselves in their own terms, culturally appropriate governing institutions and processes are also more likely to command the legitimacy of community members. This in turn increases the chances that the institutions and processes themselves, and the decisions issuing from them, will gain the willing adherence of those who are governed by their terms (see Cornell and Kalt 1998, 2007). By comparison, when self-determination is denied, when governing institutions and processes are imposed, precisely the opposite outcome should be expected: the erosion of legitimacy and a lived experience of government that is alien to, and inconsistent with, the community members' own considered values and preferences (Tully 2002, 158; cf. Ryan and Deci 2008, 658).

Self-determination contributes to individual autonomy in a third, and closely related, way by placing people in control of jurisdictions or policy areas that are vital to their interests, well-being, and possibly even their survival as a community. In the case of Indigenous peoples, for example, jurisdictions such as education, language and culture, lands and waters, and natural resources and the environment are frequently high on the priority list. By controlling these jurisdictions, Indigenous peoples have more freedom to make decisions that reflect their needs, values, and priorities, rather than those of outsiders, which again enhances the legitimacy of those decisions and the likelihood they will be freely, and genuinely endorsed by the individuals and communities whose interests they are intended to serve.[10]

Political theorists have also had some interesting things to say about how self-determination connects up with the basic need for relatedness. One of the most frequently articulated arguments is that many individuals have a powerful sense of attachment or belonging to the nation or people of which they are a part. This sense of belonging to a distinct people with its own history, territory, language, and culture in turn contributes to people's sense of identity as individuals and to their sense of self-respect and self-esteem (Kymlicka 1995, 85–90; Raz 1994, 133–4; Taylor 1994; Tully 1995, 187–91). Echoing some of the conclusions of Ryan and Deci, theorists such as Raz and Tully further emphasize that this particular sense of belonging gives individuals an experience of safety, security, and assurance that bolsters their individual agency – their capacity to live and act autonomously in both their public and private lives (Raz 1994, 25–6, 133–4; Tully 2002, 161). Self-determination supports a sense of belonging both in a direct-material sense and in an indirect-symbolic sense. In a material sense, Indigenous communities might gain the capacity to design policies that strengthen their language and culture (and thus their sense of common identity); they might gain the authority to represent, and actively to defend, their rights and interests in the face of external pressures and threats (thus building a sense of communal solidarity); and perhaps most important, they might acquire jurisdiction over matters such as land title, economic development, resource extraction, in-migration, harvesting activities, environmental regulation, and so on, that are essential not only to their future as a cohesive and thriving community, but possibly to their very survival *as* a community.

In symbolic terms, the granting of self-determination constitutes a form of recognition of a person's distinctive cultural and political identity. It is an affirmation of one's status and dignity as a member of a people on an equal footing with other self-determining peoples. In contrast, the denial of recognition, or the granting of recognition in a diminished

10 Control over things such as education, language, and culture also has obvious implications for facilitating the capacity for autonomy among community members and, as I discuss below, control over things such as land, the environment, and natural resource development also has important implications in terms of the basic need for competence.

form, is widely recognized in the literature as a form of harm that undermines people's identity and sense of self-worth. Following Taylor, "[n]onrecognition or misrecognition … can be a form of oppression, imprisoning someone in a false, distorted, and reduced mode of being" (1994, 25). It is particularly damaging – both to a sense of belonging and to the capacity for agency it underpins – when people are subjected to ridicule or hatred or when their identities and practices are regarded as backward and inferior and in need of correction or erasure. Harms such as these can easily turn a valued source of belonging into a source of shame, humiliation, self-hatred, and paralysing self-doubt (Raz 1994, 25–6, 134). As Tully concludes, "[a] demeaning or degrading form of misrecognition tends to undermine the basic self-respect and self-esteem that are necessary to empower a person to develop the degree of autonomy and sense of self-worth that is required to participate equally in the public and private life of her society, often leading to well-known psychological and sociological pathologies" (2000, 470). Deci and Ryan undoubtedly would agree.

The link between self-determination and the basic need for competence is perhaps less obvious, but in fact it flows naturally from some of the foregoing observations. The basic insight here is that self-determination enables a community to support and sustain a range of culturally distinctive activities and practices that are highly valued by its members. For example, an Indigenous community that has jurisdiction over its land and resource base can work to ensure that continued access to traditional harvesting activities is not sacrificed to large-scale, environmentally destructive resource development and extraction activities. In so doing, the community affords its members the opportunity to satisfy their basic need for competence by exercising their skills and capacities in relation to these activities. Indeed the significance of these (and many other) activities extends well beyond the satisfaction of the basic need for competence, for they are also partly constitutive of what it means to be and feel autonomous in one's particular cultural setting. Moreover, for many individuals, such activities are very much a part and parcel of what it means to identify with and belong to their community, and to be a valued and contributing member of that community. In the absence of self-determination, and the sort of jurisdictional authority it provides, Indigenous communities have a diminished capacity both to preserve and promote these and other highly valued activities in the face of pressure from external interests, and to support their members in relation to all three basic psychological needs.

Self-Determination in Theory and Practice: Putting the Pieces Together

Two questions present themselves at this juncture: first, what do we get when we combine the insights from these two very different literatures on self-determination? and second, what can they teach us about the potential link between self-determination and Indigenous mental health? Using an applied political theory approach, I would like to offer the following tentative conclusion. If it is true that the mental health of individuals suffers when their basic needs for autonomy, competence, and a sense of social belonging are undermined by their surrounding social, cultural, or political environments; and if it is also true that these three fundamental needs are linked in crucial ways to our membership in a self-determining community, then this could help explain how a deficit of self-determination might contribute both to the poor absolute state of mental health experienced by so many Indigenous people in Canada (and elsewhere) and to the significant mental health disparities that exist between Indigenous people and the relatively more empowered non-Indigenous people with whom they share a state.[11] To embrace this conclusion is also to embrace the idea that collective self-determination is not only a fundamental human right to which Indigenous peoples, like all other peoples, are entitled as a matter of justice, but also a fundamental human need that supports and sustains the health and well-being of Indigenous communities and the individual members of those communities. As I have argued elsewhere, there is every reason to be cautious in drawing such a conclusion, the most important being that it is a product of research synthesis, rather than of direct empirical observation or testing.[12] So, to be clear, I do not claim to have proven that self-determination is the only, or even a major, determinant of Indigenous mental health; indeed, I remain open to the possibility that self-determination plays no significant role at all in Indigenous mental health outcomes. That being said, the entire thrust of the foregoing theoretical analysis leads me to believe otherwise. Moreover, even though the relationship between collective self-determination and mental health (Indigenous or otherwise) has never, to my knowledge, been the subject of direct and systematic

11 Compare Murphy (2015a, 2015b), where I suggest a similar conclusion in relation to both mental and physical health outcomes.

12 See Murphy (2014a, 37–8; 2015a).

empirical investigation, there is some indirect evidence that speaks in favour of the conclusion I am suggesting here.

Not all of this evidence deals directly with Indigenous peoples, or with the subject of self-determination for that matter. For example, recent empirical research – including a study that set out explicitly to test the conclusions of SDT with specific reference to individual political autonomy (Downie, Koestner, and Chua 2007) – indicates that respect for civil and political rights has a significant positive effect on mental well-being. Equally significant is the finding that this salutary effect remains even after controlling for the effect of civil and political rights on the level of socio-economic well-being (Diener, Diener, and Diener 1995; Downie, Koestner, and Chua 2007; Owen, Videras, and Willemsen 2008). In other words, a mental health benefit derives from what one might call the *lived experience of freedom* and empowerment or, more simply, the individual's experience of self-determination. To link this back to the issue at hand: if it is true that a deficit of communal self-determination also produces an individual experience of unfreedom (for all of the reasons cited above), then these studies provide at least indirect confirmation that an experience of communal disempowerment will have a negative effect on the mental health of individual community members.

In terms of more direct evidence, elsewhere I have summarized the results of two separate studies, one conducted in British Columbia, the other in Manitoba, that lend support to the conclusion that self-determination influences Indigenous mental health outcomes (see Murphy 2014a, 2014b, 2015a, 2015b). Again, it should be clearly stated that neither study was designed to test the relationship between health and self-determination, but in my view their findings have obvious implications in this regard. In the first of these studies, Michael Chandler and Christopher Lalonde set out to test the relationship between youth suicide and measures of what they refer to as cultural continuity among Indigenous communities in British Columbia. They measure cultural continuity using six different variables (or factors): "a) evidence that particular bands had taken steps to secure aboriginal title to their traditional lands; b) evidence of having taken back from government agencies certain rights of self-government; evidence of having secured some degree of community control over c) educational services; d) police and fire protection services; e) and health delivery services; and finally, f) evidence of having established within their communities certain officially recognized cultural facilities to help preserve and enrich their cultural lives" (Chandler and Lalonde 1998, 209).

The results of this remarkable study indicate that communities in which few or none of these factors were present had dramatically elevated levels of youth suicide, and that communities in which all of these factors were present had low to non-existent levels of youth suicide, with self-government proving to be the single most important contributing factor (Chandler and Lalonde 1998, 211–15). Chandler and Lalonde's own interpretation of these results is that communities that have made substantial progress in protecting and revitalizing their culture thereby provide an environment in which their youth feel a greater sense of identity continuity (or security), which acts as a powerful protective factor against suicide (214–16).

Interestingly, other analysts have placed far less stock in the idea that cultural revitalization and cultural identity and continuity are the primary explanatory factors, arguing instead that what the study's results really demonstrate is the positive mental health effects of increased community control or self-determination, and the sense of individual liberation, empowerment, and vitality that comes with it (Hertzman 2000, 149; Kirmayer, Simpson, and Cargo 2003, S18; Tiessen, Taylor, and Kirmayer 2009, 244; Waldram, Herring, and Young 2006, 280). Equally likely, however, is that both of these explanations hold some truth.[13] Indeed, if we examine the Chandler and Lalonde study in terms of the satisfaction of the basic needs identified by SDT, an even richer interpretation of the results becomes possible. By way of illustration, communities that have achieved all of these things would seem, on their face, to be highly conducive to the autonomy of their members – for example, by facilitating their desire to live and learn in the their own linguistic and cultural terms; to participate in shaping their political institutions and public policies; and to engage in traditional activities on their communal land base. Picking up on the latter point, communities of this kind also seem able to offer their members greater opportunities to satisfy their basic need for competence in relation to a range of activities or practices (such as harvesting and artistic pursuits) that are

---

13 Chandler and Lalonde's own indicators of cultural continuity clearly contain both measures of cultural preservation/revitalization and community control. In fact, many of these indicators seem to measure both things simultaneously – for example, securing Aboriginal title gives a community greater control over its territory, while the land itself and the activities and practices it supports undoubtedly have enormous cultural significance to individual community members.

culturally familiar, valuable to them as individuals, and valued by their fellow community members. Similarly, such communities also seem to be highly supportive of a sense of belonging: first, by helping to ensure the ongoing integrity and survival of their culture, institutions, and land base; second, by contributing to a sense of solidarity and pride among their members stemming from the vigorous, and successful, defence of core community interests; and third, by supporting the preservation and promotion of their common language, culture, and identity. For all these reasons, SDT would fully expect communities such as these – which is to say, communities that support their members' basic needs for autonomy, competence, and belonging – to exhibit good mental health and communities that lack the capacity to support these basic needs to have poor mental health, possibly including elevated levels of suicide.

The second study, by Tiessen, Taylor, and Kirmayer (2009), also focuses on the mental health of Indigenous youth, but not specifically on the plague of youth suicide. The study took place in two Indigenous communities in Manitoba. Its aim was to investigate whether the perception of community control, defined as the sense that one's community has the opportunity to control valued outcomes, has any relationship to levels of mental health and well-being among community members. Here too the results are very much in line with what one would have expected from a SDT perspective. Two points in particular stand out for attention. First, when individual youth feel that their community has greater control over valued outcomes, they themselves experience a greater sense of personal control and a sense of liberation from outside domination, and this in turn is associated with increased levels of psychological well-being (263–4). Second, the authors suggest that the experience of personal control (a measure of *autonomy*) could be connected to a positive experience of community *belonging* – positive in the sense that youth are able to "see themselves as part of an effective, valued group, instead of a powerless, dependent group that is marginalized, ignored, exploited, or otherwise devalued," an experience which increases their sense of individual (and communal) self-esteem (264).

One final bit of evidence I wish to discuss comes from the large and growing body of research into protective factors that enhance the psychological resilience of Indigenous youth and that help to shield them against the onset of severe mental health problems, including suicide. This research provides direct and compelling empirical confirmation that both a strong sense of communal *belonging* and the opportunity to gain *competence* in traditional cultural practices are key contributing factors to resilience and good mental health among Indigenous youth. It demonstrates further that a sense of competence in the performance of valued cultural activities and practices contributes positively both to an enhanced sense of belonging – in that individuals can see themselves, and are seen by others, as valuable contributing members of the community – and to an increased sense of personal autonomy and self-esteem (MacDonald et al. 2013; Wexler et al. 2013, 4; 2014, 14–16). Lastly, this research provides indirect evidence of the overarching importance of communal self-determination in supporting the basic needs of individual community members for autonomy, competence, and relatedness. I covered the reasons for this connection above, but to briefly recap: Indigenous communities that lack self-determination struggle to preserve the integrity of their lands, resources, and natural environments, and to revitalize and protect their distinctive languages and cultures and transmit them to future generations. Indeed, without self-determination, they struggle to ensure their very survival as cohesive and viable communities over time. For all these reasons, Indigenous communities that lack self-determination struggle to ensure that their members can satisfy the basic needs that SDT, and a growing body of empirical research, suggests are essential to their mental health and well-being.

Conclusion

For several decades now Canadian political theorists have been at the forefront of debates over the accommodation of religious, ethnocultural, and ethno-national diversity. One of the distinctive features of this body of work – a feature this volume seeks to highlight – is its applied nature: its commitment to speaking directly, and concretely, to the most pressing challenges of diversity accommodation both in Canada and internationally (Beiner and Norman 2001, 1–2).[14] The value of this applied political theory approach lies partly in its determination to devise strategies of diversity accommodation that combine theoretical rigour with a firm eye to what is practically feasible, and for that reason more politically relevant; but also in part, and perhaps more important, in its dedication to arriving at solutions that are not only fair and balanced, but

14 For different accounts of this way of doing political theory see Carens (2000) and Tully (2004), and the introduction to this volume.

stand to make a real, positive difference to the life circumstances of the individuals and groups to whom they are addressed. Using an applied political approach, and with the aim of extending its reach, in this chapter I have taken up the question of how the accommodation (or non-accommodation) of claims to self-determination might be affecting the mental health of Indigenous people in Canada and elsewhere. To help answer this question, I began with self-determination theory in its psychological variant. SDT provides both a theoretical account of how the erosion of our basic needs for autonomy, belonging, and competence leads to poor mental health outcomes, and extensive evidence of how these outcomes manifest themselves in different domains of human life. SDT suggests further that these basic needs are influenced by forces of a specifically political nature and by the overarching political contexts within which individuals live their daily lives. In this context the theory specifically acknowledges that the autonomy of individuals, the single most important factor contributing to good psychological health, is intimately connected to the freedom of groups or collectives, but it stops short of explaining either the nature of this particular connection or the potential relationship between collective freedom and the (other) basic needs for competence and relatedness.

Finding no further explanation of these relationships within the bounds of SDT, I turned my attention next to the political theory of self-determination. This body of work offers compelling insights into how collective self-determination nourishes and supports not only a sense of individual autonomy, but also a sense of individual identity and belonging and (to a somewhat lesser extent) a sense of competence. It also offers insights into how these three fundamental goods are connected to individual well-being. Nevertheless, the concept of well-being in this literature is generally underdeveloped,[15] and virtually no

15 For most theorists, it seems to means something like the successful achievement of our desired ends in life (for example, Dworkin 1989, 484; Kymlicka 1995, 80–1; Raz 1986, 295, 297, 370), but little attempt is made to explore how this links up with more conventional measures of well-being such as happiness, life satisfaction, positive and negative affect, or other indicators of physical or mental health. One exception is Gerald Dworkin, who further associates autonomy with a sense of personal satisfaction (1988, 112). Another exception, this one from the history of ideas, is John Stuart Mill, who associates autonomy with happiness – although he is not entirely consistent on this point, and in places argues that autonomy, or individuality, is to be valued even though it might not lead to greater happiness.

attempt has been made to link self-determination with either physical or mental health outcomes.[16] Once one combines these insights with what we have learned from SDT, however, it is possible to see how self-determination and mental health might be connected, and why the absence of self-determination might be at least part of the explanation for the crisis in mental health and well-being experienced by so many Indigenous individuals and communities. Here again it is essential to flag the tentative nature of this observation and to emphasize that, in the search for more definitive conclusions about the relationship between self-determination and Indigenous health, there is no substitute for theoretically informed, longitudinal, community-based research. This should include an examination of the health impacts of different forms and degrees of self-determination, studies of self-determination as both a psycho-social and an instrumental determinant of health outcomes, research into how self-determination interacts with other key determinants of Indigenous health, investigations of both land-based and urban Indigenous populations, and comparative research both within Canada and internationally.

At the same time, however, there is a pressing need for more theoretical research that bridges the divide between the political theory of diversity accommodation and the scientific study of population health outcomes. For example, there is a significant amount of work to be done to make sense of the (more than one hundred) different measures of freedom and control in the health sciences literature and to determine how (or whether) they map onto related constructs in the political theory literature.[17] It would also be revealing to discover why political theorists have focused almost exclusively on autonomy as a capacity, and have not devoted much time or attention to what might be called the lived experience of freedom and its impact on physical and mental well-being. Have they simply overlooked this issue, or have they perhaps avoided it for good reason? More to the case at hand, how flexible is the idea of individual autonomy, and can it be applied to Indigenous communities that do not embrace standard liberal

16 Tully is perhaps the lone exception in that he links the denial of recognition with the "well-known pathologies of oppression, marginalization, and assimilation" such as "alienation, transgenerational poverty, substance abuse, unemployment, the destruction of communities, high levels of suicide, and the like" (2000, 470; 2008, 243).

17 For a review of these terms, see Skinner (1996).

conceptions of the term? Are there other culturally specific notions of freedom and control that speak to the lived experience of Indigenous peoples, but that are not yet accounted for in either the health sciences or political theory literatures? And if self-determination does prove to be a determinant of Indigenous health, how might this change the way we seek to defend self-determination from a moral-normative point of view?

A generation of Canadian political theorists has led the field in articulating how the self-determination of peoples is intimately connected to the freedom and equality of individuals. Perhaps another generation of scholars, inspired by the potential of applied political theory, can take the lead in investigating the idea that collective self-determination might also be intimately connected to individual mental health and well-being.

REFERENCES

Anderson, Ian, Sue Crengle, Martina Leialoha Kamaka, Tai-Ho Chen, Neal Palafox, and Lisa Jackson-Pulver. 2006. "Indigenous Health in Australia, New Zealand, and the Pacific." *Lancet* 367 (9524): 1775–85. https://doi.org/10.1016/S0140-6736(06)68773-4

Beiner, Ronald, and Wayne Norman. 2001. "Introduction." In *Canadian Political Philosophy*, ed. Ronald Beiner and Wayne Norman, 1–14. New York: Oxford University Press.

Boyer, Yvonne. 2014. *Moving Aboriginal Health Forward: Discarding Canada's Legal Barriers*. Saskatoon: Purich.

Bureau, Julien S., Genevieve A. Mageau, Robert J. Vallerand, Francois L. Rousseau, and Joanne Otis. 2012. "Self-Determination: A Buffer Against Suicide Ideation." *Suicide & Life-Threatening Behavior* 42 (4): 377–93. https://doi.org/10.1111/j.1943-278X.2012.00097.x

Carens, Joseph H. 2000. *Culture, Citizenship, and Community: A Contextual Exploration of Justice as Evenhandedness*. New York: Oxford University Press. https://doi.org/10.1093/0198297688.001.0001

Chandler, Michael J., and Christopher E. Lalonde. 1998. "Cultural Continuity as a Hedge against Suicide in Canada's First Nations." *Transcultural Psychiatry* 35 (2): 191–219. https://doi.org/10.1177/136346159803500202

Cooke, Martin, Francis Mitrou, David Lawrence, Eric Guimond, and Dan Beavon. 2007. "Indigenous Well-Being in Four Countries: An Application of the UNDP'S Human Development Index to Indigenous Peoples in

Australia, Canada, New Zealand, and the United States." *BMC International Health and Human Rights* 7 (9). https://doi.org/10.1186/1472-698X-7-9

Cornell, Stephen, and Joseph. P. Kalt. 1998. "Sovereignty and Nation Building: The Development Challenge in Indian Country Today." *American Indian Culture and Research Journal* 22 (3): 187–214. https://doi.org/10.17953/aicr.22.3.lv45536553vn7j78

Cornell, Stephen, and Joseph. P. Kalt. 2007. "Two Approaches to the Development of Native Nations: One Works, the Other Doesn't." In *Rebuilding Native Nations: Strategies for Governance and Development*, ed. Miriam Jorgensen, 3–33. Tucson: University of Arizona Press.

Deci, Edward L., Richard M. Ryan, Marylène Gagné, Dean R. Leone, Julian Usunov, and Boyanka P. Kornazheva. 2001. "Need Satisfaction, Motivation, and Well-Being in the Work Organizations of a Former Eastern Bloc Country: A Cross-Cultural Study of Self- Determination." *Personality and Social Psychology Bulletin* 27 (8): 930–42. https://doi.org/10.1177/0146167201278002

Deci, Edward L., and Richard M. Ryan. 2012a. "Motivation, Personality, and Development within Embedded Social Contexts: An Overview of Self-Determination Theory." In *Oxford Handbook Of Human Motivation*, ed. Richard M. Ryan, 85–108. Oxford: Oxford University Press. https://doi.org/10.1093/oxfordhb/9780195399820.013.0006

Deci, Edward L., and Richard M. Ryan. 2012b. "Self-Determination Theory." In *Handbook of Theories of Social Psychology*, vol. 1. ed. Paul A.M. Van Lange, Arie W. Kruglanski, and E. Tory Higgins, 416–37. Thousand Oaks, CA: Sage.

Diener, Ed, Marissa Diener, and Carol Diener. 1995. "Factors Predicting the Subjective Well-Being of Nations." *Journal of Personality and Social Psychology* 69 (5): 851–64. https://doi.org/10.1037/0022-3514.69.5.851

Downie, Michelle, Richard Koestner, and Sook Ning Chua. 2007. "Political Support for Self- Determination, Wealth, and National Subjective Well-Being." *Motivation and Emotion* 31 (3): 174–81. https://doi.org/10.1007/s11031-007-9070-0

Doyal, Len, and Ian Gough. 1991. *A Theory of Human Need*. Basingstoke, UK: Palgrave Macmillan. https://doi.org/10.1007/978-1-349-21500-3

Dworkin, Gerald. 1988. *The Theory and Practice of Autonomy*. Cambridge: Cambridge University Press. https://doi.org/10.1017/CBO9780511625206

Dworkin, Ronald. 1989. "Liberal Community." *California Law Review* 77 (3): 479–504. https://doi.org/10.2307/3480555

Guibernau, Montserrat. 2013. *Belonging: Solidarity and Division in Modern Societies*. Cambridge: Polity Press.

Helwig, Charles C., and Justin McNeil. 2011. "The Development of Conceptions of Autonomy, Rights, and Democracy, and Their Relation to

Psychological Well- Being." In *Human Autonomy in Cross-Cultural Context: Perspectives on the Psychology of Agency, Freedom, and Well-Being*, ed. Valery I. Chirkov, Richard M. Ryan, and Ken M. Sheldon, 241–56. Dordrecht: Springer. https://doi.org/10.1007/978-90-481-9667-8_11

Hertzman, Clyde. 2000. "The Life-Course Contribution to Ethnic Disparities in Health." In *Critical Perspectives on Racial and Ethnic Differences in Health in Late Life*, ed. Norman B. Anderson, Rodolfo A. Bulatao, and Barney Cohen, 145–70. Washington, DC: National Academies Press.

Hertzman, Clyde, and Arjumand Siddiqi. 2009. "Population Health and the Dynamics of Collective Development." In *Successful Societies: How Institutions and Culture Affect Health*, ed. Peter A. Hall and Michèle Lamont, 23–52. New York: Cambridge University Press. https://doi.org/10.1017/CBO9780511816192.003

Kasser, Virginia G., and Richard M. Ryan. 1999. "The Relation of Psychological Needs for Autonomy and Relatedness to Vitality, Well-Being, and Mortality in a Nursing Home." *Journal of Applied Social Psychology* 29 (5): 935–54. https://doi.org/10.1111/j.1559-1816.1999.tb00133.x

Kirmayer, Laurence, Cori Simpson, and Margaret Cargo. 2003. "Healing Traditions: Culture, Community and Mental Health Promotion with Canadian Aboriginal Peoples." *Australasian Psychiatry* 11 (1 suppl.): S15–23. https://doi.org/10.1046/j.1038-5282.2003.02010.x

Kymlicka, Will. 1995. *Multicultural Citizenship: A Liberal Theory of Minority Rights*. Oxford: Clarendon Press.

MacDonald, Joanna Petrasek, James D. Ford, Ashlee Cunsolo Willox, and Nancy A. Ross. 2013. "A Review of Protective Factors and Causal Mechanisms that Enhance the Mental Health of Indigenous Circumpolar Youth." *International Journal of Circumpolar Health* 72 (1): 21775. https://doi.org/10.3402/ijch.v72i0.21775

Murphy, Michael. 2012. *Multiculturalism: A Critical Introduction*. New York: Routledge.

Murphy, Michael. 2014a. "Self-Determination and Indigenous Health: Is There a Connection?" In *Restoring Indigenous Self-Determination*, ed. Marc Woons. *E-International Relations*. Available online at https://www.e-ir.info/2014/05/26/self-determination-and-indigenous-health-is-there-a-connection/

Murphy, Michael. 2014b. "Self-Determination as a Collective Capability: The Case of Indigenous Peoples." *Journal of Human Development and Capabilities* 15 (4): 320–34. https://doi.org/10.1080/19452829.2013.878320

Murphy, Michael. 2015a. "Freedom, Self-Determination and Indigenous Well-Being." Revised version of "Self-Determination: A Basic Human Right and a Basic Human Need," presented at the conference on "Civic Freedom in an Age of Diversity: James Tully's Public Philosophy," Montreal, 24–26 April 2014. Forthcoming in *Civic Freedom in an Age of Diversity: James Tully's Public Philosophy*, ed. Dimitrios Karmis and Jocelyn Maclure.

Murphy, Michael. 2015b. "Symbolic vs Practical Reconciliation. Why Choose?" Paper presented at the European Consortium for Political Research, General Conference, Montreal, 26–29 August 2015.

Nedelsky, Jennifer. 1989. "Reconceiving Autonomy: Sources, Thoughts, and Possibilities." *Yale Journal of Law and Feminism* 1 (1): 7–36.

Ohenjo, Nyang'ori, Ruth Willis, Dorothy Jackson, Clive Nettleton, Kenneth Good, and Benon Mugarura. 2006. "Health of Indigenous People in Africa." *Lancet* 367 (9526): 1937–46. https://doi.org/10.1016/S0140-6736(06)68849-1

Owen, Ann L., Julio Videras, and Christina Willemsen. 2008. "Democracy, Participation, and Life Satisfaction." *Social Science Quarterly* 89 (4): 987–1005. https://doi.org/10.1111/j.1540-6237.2008.00595.x

Raz, Joseph. 1986. *The Morality of Freedom*. Oxford: Clarendon Press.

Raz, Joseph. 1994. *Ethics in the Public Domain: Essays in the Morality of Law and Politics*. 2nd ed. New York: Oxford University Press.

Reading, Charlotte Loppie, and Fred Wien. 2009. "Health Inequalities and Social Determinants of Aboriginal People's Health." Prince George, BC: National Collaborating Centre for Aboriginal Health. Available online at https://www.ccnsa-nccah.ca/495/Health_inequalities_and_the_social_determinants_of_Aboriginal_peoples__health_.nccah?id=46

Ryan, Richard M., Randall R. Curren, and Edward L. Deci. 2013. "What Humans Need: Flourishing in Aristotelian Philosophy and Self-Determination Theory." In *The Best Within Us: Positive Psychology Perspective on Eudaimonia*, ed. Alan S. Waterman, 57–75. Washington, DC: American Psychological Association. https://doi.org/10.1037/14092-004

Ryan, Richard M., and Edward L. Deci. 2002. "Overview of Self-Determination Theory: An Organismic-Dialectical Perspective." In *Handbook of Self-Determination Research*, ed. Richard M. Ryan and Edward L. Deci, 3–33. Rochester, NY: University of Rochester Press.

Ryan, Richard M., and Edward L. Deci. 2004. "Autonomy Is No Illusion: Self-Determination Theory and the Empirical Study of Authenticity, Awareness, and Will." In *Handbook of Experimental Existential Psychology*, ed. Jeff Greenberg, Sander L. Koole, and Tom Pyszczynski, 449–79. New York: Guilford Press.

Ryan, Richard M., and Edward L. Deci. 2008. "Self-Determination Theory and the Role of Basic Psychological Needs in Personality and the Organization of Behavior." In *Handbook of Personality: Theory and Research*, ed. Oliver

P. John, Richard W. Robins, and Lawrence A. Pervin, 654–78. New York: Guilford Press.

Ryan, Richard M., and Edward L. Deci. 2011. "A Self-Determination Theory Perspective on Social, Institutional, Cultural, and Economic Supports for Autonomy and Their Importance for Well-Being." In *Human Autonomy in Cross-Cultural Context: Perspectives on the Psychology of Agency, Freedom, and Well-Being*, eds. Valery I. Chirkov, Richard M. Ryan, and Ken M. Sheldon, 45–64. Dordrecht: Springer.

Ryan, Richard M., and Aislin R. Sapp. 2007. "Basic Psychological Needs: A Self-Determination Theory Perspective on the Promotion of Wellness across Development and Cultures." In *Wellbeing in Developing Countries: From Theory to Research*, ed. Ian Gough and J. Allister McGregor, 71–92. New York: Cambridge University Press.

Salée, Daniel. 2006. "Quality-of-life of Aboriginal People in Canada: An Analysis of Current Research." *IRPP Choices* 12 (6): 4–38.

Sen, Amartya. 1992. *Inequality Reexamined*. Cambridge, MA: Harvard University Press.

Sen, Amartya. 1997. "Development Thinking at the Beginning of the XXI Century." In *Economic and Social Development into the XXI Century*, ed. Louis Emmerij, 531–51. New York: Inter-American Development Bank.

Sen, Amartya. 1999. *Development as Freedom*. New York: Knopf.

Sen, Amartya. 2001. "What Is Development About?" In *Frontiers of Development Economics: The Future in Perspective*, eds. by Gerald. M. Meier and Joseph. E. Stiglitz, 506–13. New York: Oxford University Press.

Skinner, Ellen A. 1996. "A Guide to Constructs of Control." *Journal of Personality and Social Psychology* 71 (3): 549–70. https://doi.org/10.1037/0022-3514.71.3.549

Taylor, Charles. 1985. *Philosophy and the Human Sciences. Philosophical Papers*. Cambridge: Cambridge University Press. https://doi.org/10.1017/CBO9781139173490

Taylor, Charles. 1994. *Multiculturalism: Examining the Politics of Recognition*. Princeton, NJ: Princeton University Press.

Tiessen, Melissa, Donald M. Taylor, and Laurence Kirmayer. 2009. "A Key Individual-to-Community Link: The Impact of Perceived Collective Control on Aboriginal Youth Well-being." *Pimatziwin* 7 (2): 241–67.

Tully, James. 1995. *Strange Multiplicity: Constitutionalism in an Age of Diversity*. Cambridge: Cambridge University Press. https://doi.org/10.1017/CBO9781139170888

Tully, James. 2000. "Struggles over Recognition and Distribution." *Constellations* 7 (4): 469–82. https://doi.org/10.1111/1467-8675.00203

Tully, James. 2002. "Reimagining Belonging in Circumstances of Cultural Diversity: A Citizen Approach." In *The Postnational Self: Belonging and Identity*, ed. Ulf Hedetoft and Mette Hjort, 152–77. Minneapolis: University of Minnesota Press.

Tully, James. 2004. "Recognition and Dialogue: The Emergence of a New Field." *Critical Review of International Social and Political Philosophy* 7 (3): 84–106. https://doi.org/10.1080/1369823042000269401

Tully, James. 2008. *Democracy and Civic Freedom*. Vol. 1, *Public Philosophy in a New Key*. New York: Cambridge University Press.

Waldram, James B., D. Ann Herring, and T. Kue Young. 2006. *Aboriginal Health in Canada*. 2nd ed. Toronto: University of Toronto Press.

Wexler, Lisa, Linda Joule, Joe Garoutte, Janet Mazziotti, and Kim Hopper. 2013. "'Being Responsible, Respectful, Trying to Keep the Tradition Alive': Cultural Resilience and Growing Up in an Alaska Native Community." *Transcultural Psychiatry* 51 (5): 693–712. https://doi.org/10.1177/1363461513495085

Wexler, Lisa, Kasey Jernigan, Janet Mazzotti, Elizabeth Baldwin, Megan Griffin, Linda Joule, and Joe Garoutte. 2014. "Lived Challenges and Getting Through Them: Alaska Native Youth Narratives as a Way to Understand Resilience." *Health Promotion Practice* 15 (1): 10–17. https://doi.org/10.1177/1524839913475801

Yuval-Davis, Nira. 2012. *The Politics of Belonging: Intersectional Contestations*. London: Sage.

13 Beyond Multiculturalism: Indigenous Normativity and the Search for a Legitimate Constitution

MARC WOONS

In 2012 "Idle No More" gained force as outrage, sparked by federal legislation reducing environmental protections, grew to reflect "the historical and contemporary legacies emerging from colonization and violence throughout North America and the world. These involve land theft, treaty violations, and many misunderstandings" (Kino-nda-niimi Collective 2014, 22). Although some felt "Idle" implied inactivity, Indigenous peoples have persevered, enduring burdensome legal processes, government negotiations, and debates with Canadians, not to mention the everyday challenges that come with living under colonialism's long shadow. Ongoing Indigenous frustration stems from a belief that contemporary approaches misunderstand or dismiss their long-standing normative claims related to restitution for colonial injustices, treaties, prior occupancy, unceded sovereignty, and nationhood – herein collectively called Indigenous normativity. When the associated constitutional changes needed to secure meaningful self-determining authority over their territories are not denied for overtly moral reasons, they are deemed unreasonable, impractical, or irrelevant in the present day.[1] Even Williams, noted for critiquing those who defend liberalism on *moral* grounds, suggests that, *practically speaking*, "now and around here the [basic legitimacy demand][2] together with the historical

1 By constitutional, I am interested in the changing and living, even unwritten and understood, "basic principles and rules by which members of a community cooperate, make decisions, engage with each other and the world around them, distribute and exercise authority, and set about trying to get things done" (Cornell 2015, 2).

2 The *basic legitimacy demand* is Williams's twofold account for determining a constitutional order's legitimacy – that is, an acceptable answer to the "first political question": (1) the establishment of a cooperative political order that can handle profound disagreement and conflict with (2) "a legitimation offered which goes beyond the assertion of power" (Williams 2005, 11).

conditions permit only a liberal solution: other forms of answer are unacceptable. In part, this is for the Enlightenment reason that other supposed legitimations are now seen to be false" (Williams 2005, 8). Questioning liberal modernity and the legitimacy of western forms of government is considered futile (Fukuyama 1992; Wolfe 2009).

Some specifically sacrifice Indigenous normativity at the altar of modernity. Kymlicka (2001, 128–9), for instance, initially appears sympathetic to Indigenous arguments, writing that "Indigenous peoples do not just constitute distinct cultures, but they form entirely distinct forms of culture, distinct 'civilizations,' rooted in a premodern way of life that needs protecting from the forces of modernization, secularization, urbanization, 'Westernization,' etc" (see also Cairns 2000). Civilizational differences give them *prima facie* claims to self-determination and political authority greater than those of national minorities such as the *Québécois*. However, Indigenous peoples end up with less because the ultimate basis for the "international protection of indigenous peoples is not so much the scale of mistreatment in the past, but rather the scale of cultural difference" (Kymlicka 2001, 129). Rather than reinforcing Indigenous normativity, (ongoing) colonialism devalues central Indigenous claims to such an extent that they are no longer seen as requiring or even capable of exercising self-determination, at least in some modern Westphalian way. The dominant modern grammar cannot or will not accommodate numerically reduced, territorially dispersed, and/or culturally assimilated communities. The possibility of imagining, structuring, and exercising political authority differently loses out because they no longer matter, no longer exist, or have been irreparably damaged. In what can only be construed as a hegemonic vicious circle, Indigenous "protection" *against* liberal modernity has become irrelevant *because of* liberal modernity. Anyone who denies modern "truths that destroy those fantasies that once provided the fabric of pre-modern legitimation stories" are justifiably treated as "anarchists, or utterly unreasonable or bandits or merely enemies" (Williams 2005, 96, 136). The state lets itself off the hook. Colonialism becomes its own reward.

This chapter refutes this view, specifically using as empirical evidence the federal government's multiculturalism and land claims policy and the actions of social movements such as Idle No More. I show how an applied political theory approach can help unravel how these discourses of Indigenous self-determination relate to different strands of western political theory – in particular, liberal multiculturalism, agonism, and realism. As such, I argue that Indigenous normativity cannot be dismissed for several reasons. First, liberal modernity cannot ground uncontestable claims of ultimate authority because it is itself contestable (Larmore 2013). Indeed, Indigenous normativity historicizes modernity and corresponding notions of statehood, sovereignty, legitimacy, and so on, provincializing them for having Eurocentric and unreflective biases (Picq 2015). Some even argue that liberal modernity depends upon colonialism and the illegitimate imposition of modern forms of authority over Indigenous people (Mignolo 2011). Second, Indigenous constitutional orders, though pushed to the brink, persist as a matter of fact. The answer to who has legitimate constitutional authority "now and around here" often remains uncertain. When you travel to Waglisla (Bella Bella), are you visiting Heiltsuk lands or Canadian lands? If you hunt grizzly bears, do you honour the moratorium enacted according to Gvi'ilass[3] or hunt using a permit that derives its authority from Canadian law? Although most Canadians affirm the latter, you might get a different answer should you ask locals which laws they recognize or support. Lastly, modernity is neither fixed nor is its continued ascendance inevitable or universally desirable. This is not to say that it is rotten to the core, but that it is neither totalizing nor irrefutable. Rather, it represents but one set of ideas, susceptible to change and in competition with other conceptualizations (see Geuss 2008).

Applied political theory allows for the evaluation of different approaches to establishing constitutional legitimacy from Indigenous perspectives, given non-ideal conditions of state hegemony. I begin by suggesting that the multicultural status quo imposes an illegitimate political framework on Indigenous peoples. Despite a noticeable shift from overt exclusion and assimilation to recognition and constitutional accommodation, Canadian governments continue to load the dice, subverting fundamental questions concerning their legitimacy and locking Indigenous peoples into unjust constitutional conditions. Next I contrast multiculturalism with Tully's agonistic account, arguing that the latter better captures the fundamental nature of political conflict based on reasonable and unavoidable contestation concerning Canada's constitutional legitimacy. Establishing legitimacy demands pursuing a different political project and normative line of reasoning than multiculturalism's proposal to find a counterfactual justification for imposing an ideal-theoretic framework as legitimate on all "reasonable" citizens.

3 The Declaration of Heiltsuk Title and Rights defines this as "our governing authority over all matters related to our lands and people."

Part of our collective quest, therefore, might require cultivating civic virtues that help guide fundamental disagreements towards more consensual constitutional ends, rather than forcing "agreement" once and for all. I do nevertheless suggest that Tully's agonism could be strengthened by showing greater consideration for realist concerns. Although civic virtues undeniably help counteract state hegemony, Tully's robust constitutional vision nevertheless should be taken as one among many that inevitably – and with difficulty – must compete within the game of power politics, as opposed to displacing it. Although Tully understands such challenges, I suggest (counterintuitively, perhaps) that explicitly adopting a more realist form of agonism could do more to realize Indigenous self-determination in Canada and elsewhere.

Official Multiculturalism and Its Limits

When Prime Minister Pierre Trudeau constitutionally solidified multiculturalism in 1982, domestic and international pressure had grown to such an extent that "existing Aboriginal and treaty rights" were included despite federal and provincial resistance. The proclaimed intent has since been to give constitutional force to Indigenous normativity by creating spaces for Indigenous identities, constitutional visions, and self-determining authorities, diminishing the assimilative and exclusionary character of public institutions. This is perceived as being vital to securing Canada's constitutional legitimacy, giving it an acquired, voluntary, and consensual character. The process has been arduous. Indigenous peoples and the state struggle to define the Constitution's specific meaning through government policies, negotiations, and the courts.

I suggest that Canada's multicultural framework has failed to establish a fully inclusive and therefore legitimate constitutional order. Despite its appearance of having an acquired character, supporters of Indigenous constitutions should approach multiculturalism cautiously, with an instrumental intent, if at all, given two serious types of risk. First, multiculturalism consistently betrays its own paradoxical nature when giving Indigenous normativity its due; despite adamant claims to the contrary, it fails to break with the state's assimilationist past of arbitrarily imposing foreign institutions on Indigenous peoples. Particularly when Indigenous peoples question state control over land and resources, debate is curtailed as power relations take over, leaving important issues off the agenda and thus unresolved. This is compounded by the second type of risk: multicultural approaches put meaningful self-determination further out of reach to the extent that the state successfully entrenches a social imaginary of "permanent" solutions, effectively depoliticizing ongoing constitutional struggles. This one-two punch – of arbitrariness and the claim of permanency – advances solutions to fundamental conflicts that Indigenous peoples need not accept with any finality even when they are difficult to avoid given existing power asymmetries. These risks are highlighted across three prominent multicultural approaches: modern "treaty" negotiations, redress, and the courts.

Modern "treaty" negotiations

Every "final agreement" ratified under the British Columbia Treaty Commission (BCTC) process describes "a treaty and a land claims agreement within the meaning of sections 25 and 35 of the *Constitution Act, 1982.*" Representatives of Canada, British Columbia, and some Indigenous communities feel that the process is exemplary. Speaking to the Nisga'a Final Agreement, Chief Joseph Gosnell stated: "this treaty proves beyond all doubt that negotiations – not lawsuits, not road blockades, not violence – is the most effective, the most honorable way to resolve aboriginal issues" (*CBC News* 1998). But do such agreements give the relationship between Indigenous peoples and the Constitution a voluntary and final character? Or do they more or less mirror existing relations of domination and represent the best possible terms of surrender, if you will, given the circumstances?

Interpreting Indigenous support as entirely voluntary overlooks the unfair dilemma that they alone face when asked to ratify, under duress, agreements that threaten their way of life. More than two decades of negotiations – and a century of being ignored before that – left the Nisga'a with just two options: support the agreement and surrender over 90 per cent of their traditional lands and tax-exempt status in exchange for $200 million in compensation and control over 1,992 square kilometres, with limited self-government rights; or reject the agreement and hope to secure better terms through renegotiating, the courts, direct confrontation, or community revitalization. It is not difficult to imagine that many of the 61 per cent who supported the agreement did so *not* because they disagreed with dissenters who believed that it fell short of securing Indigenous self-determination, but because it would provide some immediate relief from their immeasurable suffering under the colonial status quo. Multiculturalists might believe that ratification equates to consent, rather than to harm reduction, or that it escapes colonialism, rather than reflecting the need to cope with its ongoing effect. The BCTC's outcomes suggest, on the contrary, that modern treaties struggle to rise above power asymmetries, reflecting instead the pressure to compromise as a result of them.

Not only do both "options" have an imposed character, but the state makes a difficult situation worse by also attempting, and largely succeeding, to inject a sense of finality. Echoing its colonial past, Canadian governments insist on extinguishing any Indigenous rights not covered under such agreements through "release" clauses that protect the state from any "known or unknown" outstanding claims and a statement that the agreement exhausts their section 35 rights. Even those who doubt that such extinguishment clauses stand up to emerging international legal norms such as the UN Declaration on the Rights of Indigenous Peoples (2007) cannot deny that the Canadian state will enforce the agreements in the meantime and defend their interpretation to the end. Should the state eventually succumb to international pressure, more damage will certainly have been done.

Some nevertheless will insist that modern treaties have a voluntary and final character. Although the debate will persist, the point is that the matter is not so cut and dried, recognizing the real possibility that, even for many who supported ratification (and most who did not), such agreements seem imposed and ultimately rooted in the state's efforts to alienate Indigenous peoples from the lands and resources they once had and still require if they are ever to secure meaningful self-determination (Corntassel 2008). Perhaps the most obvious evidence of the unacceptable risks that come with modern negotiations is the small number of final agreements ratified since the BCTC's doors opened in 1992. Only half of British Columbia's Indigenous communities have engaged in the process, and less than 8 per cent have reached final agreement (British Columbia Treaty Commission 2017, 36).

Redress

Redress also falls short of its expressed intent of setting things right with the victims of wrongful and wilful state actions. In 2008 Prime Minister Stephen Harper officially apologized for atrocities committed within residential schools, and launched the Truth and Reconciliation Commission of Canada. Yet serious problems stem from what James calls "neoliberal heritage redress," whereby "singular past government acts are abstracted from any deeper consideration of the long-term structural and attitudinal racism that tends to give rise to historical wrongs in the first place" (2013, 37). Exposing yet another link between domination and arbitrariness, the state resists redress unless claims are reduced to something amenable with liberalism, capitalism, and ongoing resource extractivism.

The general conclusion among Indigenous communities and academia is that the apology fell short of atoning for how residential schools irreversibly disrupted and harmed individuals, families, and communities by forcibly separating children from their parents and subjecting them to inhumane conditions. According to Henderson and Wakeham (2013, 12–13), the apology "occluded broader consideration of the long history of colonial genocide and its other constitutive components such as the establishment of reservations, the expropriation of land and resources, the deliberate suppression and distortion of Indigenous languages, beliefs, and cultural practices, and the disruption of kinship networks. Not to mention the present conditions of poverty, incarceration, and compromised health lived by many Aboriginal people." Mackey (2013, 54) also expresses doubt: "instead of the apology accounting for Canada's calculated expropriation of resources and the use of cultural genocide practices as a means to hold on to those resources, the apology is framed as regret for a well-meaning set of acts that caused damage to culture and families." How else could Harper proclaim, only months later at the 2009 G20 meeting, that Canada has "no history of colonialism" (Wherry 2009)? All signs suggest that the act of apology promoted not meaningful and lasting redress, but duplicity: remembering *and forgetting*, action *and inaction*.

Seemingly driven more by guilt and self-interest than by justice and restitution, the state pursues redress so that it – rather than its victims – can move forward unencumbered. Yet apologies perceived as deficient by victims provide little closure no matter how much victimizers wish otherwise. It should come as no surprise that Indigenous peoples generally did not give the apology *moral* weight, even if they acknowledged the attempt as a matter of *fact*. Responding in the House of Commons, Chief Phil Fontaine was guarded yet hopeful, saying, "the significance of this day is not just about what has been but, equally important, what is to come ... We still have to struggle, but now we are in this together. I reach out to all Canadians today in this spirit of reconciliation" (2008). Meaningful redress requires greater work through enduring struggle and continual positive engagement. Canadians have yet to meet Indigenous peoples who "reach out" hoping to find an equal and willing partner. For many the apology did not close the wound, as "it will take much more than an apology to help our communities move beyond the dark times that many of us are facing as a direct result of the residential-school experience" (Gray 2008). By refusing to accept apologies that deny aspects of historical and ongoing suffering, Indigenous peoples keep the possibility for meaningful redress alive against a state that wants to believe it has finally settled the matter. Existing redress practices leave them wondering whether things have changed and how they fit in a "new" Canada that looks much like the old on important issues related to treaties, lands, resources, and the environment, again protecting rather than challenging and transforming state hegemony.

The courts

The Supreme Court of Canada also plays a crucial role, with prominent rulings suggesting that the burden of proving sovereignty should shift to the Crown.[4] Some believe costly, lengthy, and emotional Supreme Court battles have tremendous emancipatory potential, exposing deep cracks in powerful colonial assumptions underlying the state's unilateral sovereignty claims. Echoing a common sentiment, one Indigenous leader hailed a recent ruling as a "game-changer … a strong message to all provincial leaders and Stephen Harper to deal with us in an honourable and respectful way" (APTN 2014). Although progress is undeniable, it seems more likely that the Supreme Court and the Constitution will continue to limit Indigenous self-determination, leaving the state's colonial foundations largely untouched.

Currently the Constitution neither formally recognizes the right of Indigenous peoples to self-determination nor provides them any formal way of initiating constitutional change, pinning almost all their hopes on section 35. Some believe this legal avenue eventually will grant meaningful self-determination as the Supreme Court's admission of powerful arguments rooted in Indigenous normativity will wake Canadian governments from their colonial slumber (Henderson 2013;

4 See *Haida Nation v. British Columbia* (2004); *Taku River Tlingit First Nation v. British Columbia* (2004); *Tsilhqot'in Nation v. British Columbia* (2007); and *Tsilhqot'in Nation v. British Columbia* (2014).

Hoehn 2012). Others are more cautious, seeing both the opportunities and the risks associated with the limited window section 35 provides. Ladner (2009) and Borrows (2010), for instance, affirm section 35's *potential* for promoting positive Indigenous-state relations, though they also express concerns about its ineffectiveness and ambiguousness. Borrows (2010, 199) notes that it is "increasingly used to justify government infringements of Aboriginal rights." Their focus on section 35 is perhaps best understood as pragmatic, working with the best available tools even if they are not entirely up to the job.

The legal-constitutional avenue comes with numerous risks that, even if harder to delineate, should not be overlooked. To begin with, past progress is no guarantee of eventual success, and might even put ultimate success farther out of reach. In the most optimistic of accounts, Hoehn (2012) draws on Kuhn's theory of paradigmatic scientific change to suggest that recent rulings introduce stubborn anomalies – related to Indigenous normativity – that inevitably will force Canada to abandon the "discovery" paradigm undergirding the state's unilateral assertion of exclusive sovereignty. Facing mounting pressure, the state will be forced to reconcile its de facto Crown sovereignty with de jure Indigenous sovereignty through fairer negotiations that recognize overlapping jurisdictional authority, the need for respectful dialogue, and Indigenous territorial claims. But will the Supreme Court successfully pressure reluctant Canadian governments to make institutional and legal changes that recognize the full implications of these anomalies? Or will progress always fall short as state intransigence rooted in power asymmetries and colonial creativity successfully block anything approaching extensive Indigenous self-determination?

Hoehn hastily dismisses two additional possibilities found in Kuhn's theory that deny the inevitability of stubborn anomalies leading to paradigmatic change. First, by using new arguments and/or asserting its power, the state might prove "able to handle the crisis-provoking problem despite the despair of those who have seen it as the end of an existing paradigm" (Kuhn 1996, 84). Even as legal rulings dismantle Eurocentric colonial arguments rooted in *terra nullius*, discovery, or conquest, the state raises new arguments, such as "the act of state doctrine" or the need for external recognition by great powers, to put its ultimate authority beyond dispute. Second, anomalies might linger as Indigenous concerns are downplayed, set aside, or ignored by governments that would much rather pursue other priorities. Clashing Indigenous and state perspectives have coexisted, struggled, and adapted for centuries with no clear winner in sight. This tension even exists within and across recent legal rulings,[5] none of which has clearly and explicitly given Indigenous peoples the *sine qua non* of self-determination: free, prior, and informed consent (FPIC) over all matters affecting them and their territories.

Canadian courts also have limited means of enforcement when recalcitrant governments refuse to cross their own arbitrary line in the sand – a line that leaves destructive state-building extractive industries operating without securing FPIC. Even when courts validate Indigenous normativity, they balance this against the need for stability and/or calls for renewed negotiations (Harty and Murphy 2005). Both put Indigenous peoples back into the painful, messy, and challenging world of power and politics. Calling for stability effectively defends the status quo, allowing the state to protect its position. Demanding governments pursue negotiations in good faith similarly maintains hegemonic relations as they drag their feet or agree only to terms that secure their authority over most, if not all, of the land and resources in dispute.

Finally, I would be remiss if I did not mention risks associated with mounting legal challenges using institutions and laws that are not the product of consensual agreement, but instead gain their authority from colonial assertions of the settler state's inviolable and exclusive territorial sovereignty. Not only do Indigenous peoples strengthen state claims when they recognize and thereby lend validation to the Constitution and the Supreme Court's ultimate authority; their demands for constitutional recognition and self-determination become judged according to dominant norms. Rollo writes that "the state's assertion of inviolable sovereignty over the land … pre-determines the range of acceptable conclusions we can hope to achieve through dialogue." Consequently, "for the vast majority of judges, lawyers, politicians, negotiators, and bureaucrats, [state] sovereignty is not simply a reason or consideration that can be disputed; it is the context of relationships against which these disputes are judged and resolved … Indigenous claims are either reconciled with sovereignty or they are dismissed" (Rollo 2014, 231–2).

5 Even the widely hailed 2014 Tsilhqot'in ruling applies a test for land title based on "sufficient," "continuous," and "exclusive" occupation, arguably reinventing the notion of *terra nullius* and imposing Westphalian norms in terms of territorial exclusivity. This says nothing of the fact that, by default, state sovereignty is assumed, and it is Indigenous peoples who need to appeal to the state's courts.

On this challenge, Turner (2006) surprisingly accepts that there is currently no way around the adjudication of Indigenous claims by non-Indigenous people, forcing Indigenous peoples to express themselves and their worldviews within dominant discourses in ways that people in positions of authority might understand and find acceptable. He pins his hopes on the possibility that judges and bureaucrats will become better listeners, granting greater space for Indigenous peoples to express themselves in their own ways. Turner's reasons for pragmatism are not entirely unfounded, even if his hope is likely misplaced.

Taken together, the three policy areas show just how pervasive the state is in curtailing Indigenous claims to meaningful self-determination, restitution, access to lands, and the need for shared sovereignty, imposing multicultural solutions as a supposedly fair compromise. It can accomplish this not because multiculturalism represents some pre-political, universally accepted or acceptable answer, but because the vicious circle of domination and injustice makes it possible for the state to impose its preferred solutions on those challenging its legitimacy. It is an uneven constitutional dialogue that permissively assumes – rather than permits challenges to – the state's legitimacy. Multiculturalism therefore appears to be little more than another attempt in Canada's history of containing and suppressing Indigenous peoples' legitimate constitutional struggles.

Tully's Agonistic Alternative

Here I want to make a distinction between two political ontologies with differing views of legitimacy. The first aligns closely with multicultural theory and practice, striving to *overcome* political struggle through a counterfactual universal consensus imposed as legitimate. Although multiculturalism provides some room for dissent, significant aspects of Indigenous normativity are pre-politically discredited based on a morality that comes before politics (see Williams 2005). The use of power – institutional or otherwise – is thus perceived as warranted when displacing and suppressing "unreasonable" Indigenous disagreement based on abstract understandings of justice rooted in supposed moral truths. Constitutional legitimacy therefore depends less on what actual people endorse and more on what "reasonable" people should endorse (and forms of coercion they accordingly should accept). The agonistic alternative claims it a contradiction to speak of "imposed consensus," arguing that overcoming or depoliticizing political struggle through the real or counterfactual establishment of universal agreement is fantasy. Politics is better understood as a discipline autonomous from morality "that takes place in conditions of ubiquitous, perennial, and ineradicable political disagreements and conflicts, including about the very fundamental terms of the political association itself" (Sleat 2013, 72). Although equally concerned with normative questions of constitutional legitimacy and the authoritative rules that should gain legal force, agonists reject the idea that we should start from *a priori* truths or moral arguments that authoritatively outline the goods politics should realize. The validity of laws and institutions instead are judged *a posteriori* in terms of how well they establish political order and promote cooperation in the face of irreducible conflict, with justice being – as much as we can agree – that those laws and institutions are experienced as legitimate by those actually living under them.

Supporters of Indigenous normativity can and do resist imposed solutions rooted in the first ontological understanding by pursuing political strategies honed to the second. When multicultural governments define and control the terms of engagement, pre-politically leaving certain fundamental matters aside, they circumvent the ever-dialogical and unavoidably disputed nature of constitutional politics, imposing and institutionalizing their version of the good while excluding those – the "unreasonable," the "enemies," the "unmodern" – who challenge the existing order's legitimacy. This is unfortunate because, as Mouffe warns, "the belief in the possibility of a universal rational consensus has put democratic thinking on the wrong track. Instead of trying to design the institutions which, through supposedly 'impartial' procedures, would reconcile all conflicting interests and values, the task for democratic theorists and politicians should be to envisage the creation of a vibrant 'agonistic' public sphere of contestation where different hegemonic political projects can be confronted" (Mouffe 2005, 3). Canada has been on this track for some time, earlier suppressing and now explaining away Indigenous dissent (backed by force) when it tells us that the answer is *not* a multiculturalism that denies the most significant effects of colonialism and refuses to question ultimate state sovereignty.

Lacking space to explain fully why agonists believe consensus is ultimately a chimera, even under ideal circumstances, those who understand Canada's situation well might feel almost intuitively that the second ontological understanding better captures a relationship of overt and covert – but never absent – political struggle. Indeed, if multiculturalism delivered on its promises, we would not have seen Idle No More or state-sponsored violence against Elsipogtog First Nation in 2013. Upholding the second account, Tully provides a guiding example of agonistic theory applied to Indigenous-state relations and the establishment of constitutional legitimacy. I first examine his belief that legitimacy in deeply pluralistic societies depends on following *civic virtues* capable of guiding fundamental disagreement towards more legitimate constitutional ends. Given multiculturalism's limits, I then examine how Tully sees such conflict playing out, particularly in terms of how those feeling excluded can come to see the shared constitution as legitimate using what he calls the *practices of freedom*.

Civic virtue and ancient constitutionalism

Tully believes "modern constitutionalism" – rooted in liberalism, communitarianism, and/or nationalism – unjustly imposes "an empire of uniformity" based on some historically imagined and comprehensive constitutional narrative of "all the people" that excludes or assimilates other ways of thinking, being, and acting (1995, 62–70). He contrasts this with organic "ancient constitutionalism" found within common law and Indigenous legal traditions. Despite the best efforts of "moderns" to eradicate ancient constitutionalism through theoretical reasoning, working alongside political practice, "pre-modern" traditions persist in evolving form. The challenge therefore remains of how to manage fundamental and unavoidable political diversity within a shared constitutional arrangement. An ideal and legitimate society is, for Tully (1995, 204–5), one where "the diversity of our fellow citizens evokes a sense of belonging to a constitutional association in which one's own culture (or cultures) is recognised as a constituent and interrelated part of the justice of the whole association ... One's own identity as a citizen is inseparable from a shared history with other citizens who are irreducibly different; whose cultures have interacted with and enriched one's own and made their mark on the basic institutions of society. The loss or assimilation of any of the other cultures is experienced as an impoverishment of one's own identity." Ancient constitutionalism necessarily leaves the evolving constitutional order underdetermined, filled in as diverse peoples politically engage one another in respectful ways by honouring important *dialogical civic virtues*.

When taken up by citizens, dialogical civic virtues help establish constitutional legitimacy. Tully places particular emphasis on three "conventions": mutual recognition, continuity, and consent.[6] Early Indigenous-Crown relations exemplified their usage through a form of ancient constitutionalism called "treaty constitutionalism." Tully praises early colonialists who considered Indigenous peoples co-equal nations, resisting the urge to "redescribe the Aboriginal peoples in the forms of recognition constructed by the armchair European theorists. Instead, they simply listened to how the Aboriginal negotiators presented themselves" (1995, 119). Such recognition was extended by both sides despite their different forms of government, legal traditions, and political customs. The convention of consent – what touches all should be agreed to by all – was also initially honoured in many Indigenous-state agreements as a form of *mutual* consent whereby all parties came to agree, through dialogue, to the shared rules and principles that should gain the force of law. This lent itself to the convention of continuity, highlighted in relation to the first two: "the treaty system is expressly designed not only to recognise and treat the Aboriginal people as equal, self-governing nations, but also to continue, rather than extinguish, this form of recognition through all treaty arrangements over time. Indeed, the legitimacy of non-Aboriginal governments in America depends on this continuity, for it is the condition of Aboriginal consent to recognise them" (124). In emphasizing these virtues, Tully suggests that the now-prevailing modern constitutional drive to assimilate or expel Indigenous ways of being in the world can be seen only as imperialistic and unenlightened (see Tully 2003).

The strength of the virtues comes through dialogue, not simply by lending a given (predetermined or historically contingent) constitution credibility, but by dynamically creating one that can become widely perceived as legitimate in deeply pluralistic societies. It is through dialogue that societal norms "come into being and come to be accepted as authoritative in the course of constitutional practice, including criticism and contestation of that practice" (Tully 1995, 116). Even the virtues themselves are up for discussion, rather than imposable rules that must be strictly followed. Legitimacy thus stems from defining and honouring a shared constitution through dialogical processes that progressively elaborate (and thereby strengthen) norms that can be taken

6 In more recent work, Tully talks of five principles of mutual recognition, intercultural negotiation, mutual respect, sharing, and mutual responsibility (2008a, chap. 7); although some of the names differ, the general spirit remains the same.

as authoritative to identify and resolve justice and legitimacy claims, albeit always subject to challenges and reinterpretation. This is important, because "reasonable disagreement and thus dissent are inevitable and go all the way down in theory and practice" (Tully 2008b, 96).

The differences with multiculturalism – particularly its arbitrary and final character – help explain why Tully is often unenthusiastic about present-day Canada's constitutional treatment of Indigenous peoples. Canadian history is nothing short of a fall from grace, as colonialists abandoned the civic virtues once power shifted in the nineteenth century, leaving "ancient constitutionalism" behind as self-interested settler colonial governments gained enough strength to supplant recognition and consent using coercion, force, and fraud (Tully 1995, chap. 4; 2008a, 225–8). Despite – or because of – multiculturalism, Indigenous peoples remain "unfree," dominated by hegemonic states and living under imposed institutions and laws. The primary implication is that latent forms of ancient constitutionalism need strengthening, with the question being: how can Indigenous peoples and supporters of ancient or treaty constitutionalism overcome multiculturalism's constraints?

Practices of freedom

What can be done about modern constitutions that insufficiently honour such civic virtues? Tully's later work explains how Indigenous peoples can pursue the freedom promised by ancient constitutionalism under less-than-ideal conditions of domination. Through dialogical struggle, understood broadly as comprising various forms of participation, negotiation, and contestation, we can (re)discover and (re)build constitutional legitimacy by bringing "oppressive and unjust governance relationships under the on-going shared authority of the citizenry subject to them; namely, to civicise and democratise them from below" (Tully 2008a, 4). Non-ideal dialogical struggle occurs within a threefold typology of *practices of freedom* designed to overcome obstacles blocking ancient constitutionalism's realization: negotiation, direct confrontation, and acting otherwise.

Negotiation, as Tully describes it, works best using the civic virtues – that is, without being corrupted by power – as respectful dialogue provides everyone the ability to challenge and modify existing rules, institutions, or societal norms, in the hope of provoking changes that give them an acquired character. Direct confrontation is a last resort in the face of state intransigence: "If the Crown pretends that the treaty negotiations take place within its overriding jurisdiction ... then it fails to recognise the status of Indigenous peoples, incorporates and subordinates them without justification, thus rendering the negotiation illegitimate" (Tully 2008a, 279). Acting otherwise is less intuitive, though complementary. It involves thinking and acting differently when cooperating *within* existing rules and institutions in an effort to reinterpret or challenge an existing rule or norm, all the while resisting co-optation's nefarious pull. Tully himself gives few concrete examples of such "infrapolitical resistance." Findlay, however, writes about Indigenous legal scholars who apply an "Aboriginal hermeneutic [that] works by a double gesture of compliance and circumvention ... Aboriginal resistance habitually entails cultural as well as legal performance while refusing entrapment in either law or culture (or the relations between them) as Eurocentrically understood" (2013, 219). Legal wins come from successfully performing this dance with co-optation. Tully believes acting otherwise is often underestimated and holds the most promise.

This is perhaps because, above all, Tully is optimistic that Canadians are gradually rediscovering their ancient constitutional roots not just with Indigenous peoples, but also with women, the *Québécois*, and immigrants, providing an increasingly favourable canvass for Indigenous practices of freedom to work upon. He cites Canada's separation from the British Empire through the adoption of a new flag, the 1982 repatriation of the Constitution, and citizenship rights that embrace immigrants and foreigners (Tully 2008a, 230–1, 252). Taken together, Indigenous "acting otherwise" and greater Canadian openness provide windows for critical intercultural engagement where "members of the dominant society can ... take a critical stance. These intercultural dialogues are the best and most effective way, for they enable Westerners to see their conventional horizon as a limit and the dialogues are themselves the intimations of and indispensable groundwork for a future non-colonial relationship" (277). In this regard, Tully is among other recognized non-Indigenous scholars, alongside Kymlicka and Taylor, who believe the people, if not yet the state, are warming up to the need for change.

Realist Considerations in the Search for Greater Legitimacy

Tully offers sympathetic readers much to draw upon in their desire for a constitutional order where Indigenous peoples feel at home. The practices of freedom provide tools that instil a sense of agency, revealing approaches that some might otherwise overlook. Moreover, he gives a convincing normative account of how dialogical civic virtues can peacefully guide fundamental and inescapable conflict towards legitimate constitutional ends. Although the road ahead is fraught with challenges, it is indeed a strength that Tully resists the urge simply to graft his proposals onto existing institutions of power that generally fail to respect Indigenous normativity and therefore struggle to tackle the roots of constitutional conflict. In this sense, Tully's earlier normative work on ancient civic virtues provides us a goal, while his later political work provides us important tools to help us get there, given contemporary constitutional challenges. In this section I reflect on the situation Indigenous peoples face, the suitability of the practices of freedom, and the attainability of ancient constitutionalism generally. I hope it will become clear why I fear that overemphasizing lofty civic ideals might prove distracting, even counterproductive, causing us to undervalue supporting "political" virtues more attuned to the rough ground of politics. Broader consideration should be given to how such civic virtues, or even some imperfect, next-best approximation or substitute, can be obtained in the face of hegemonic relations.

Ancient versus modern constitutionalism

The roots of my concern relate to ancient constitutionalism's morally demanding nature and its inability to escape the same fundamental contestation that is endemic of politics. Simply put, it is crucial to explore the space between the ontological claim that political disagreement and struggle are unavoidable and the normative claim that ancient constitutionalism should prevail. Recall that ancient constitutionalism rests on a shared sense of belonging such that every citizen considers it offensive when those with fundamentally different perspectives are not accorded equal respect within the greater whole. So, although Tully clearly subscribes to the idea that fundamental conflict cannot be avoided, he also makes "the normative claim that agonism *should be* valued because of its ability to uphold the pluralistic nature of society" (Rummens 2009, 385, emphasis in original). Implicit in Tully's work is the idea that supporters of modern constitutional visions who place less value on diversity are themselves "unreasonable." Prominent agonists from Connolly to Mouffe, and even Tully himself, argue that no doctrine or vision can claim legitimately (and unquestionably) to occupy the constitutional centre. This belief is so strong that these scholars extend it to the idea that dialogue, *even under ideal conditions*, cannot secure a shared constitutional vision with any finality (see Connolly 2000; Mouffe 2005). Honig (2011) calls Tully on this point, claiming that he slips into seeing his solution as the only reasonable option, thereby making the same "modern" mistake of putting it above the important role political contestation plays in establishing widespread legitimacy. Tully might bite the bullet on this point, although the implications nevertheless make it difficult to retain an optimistic perspective of ancient constitutionalism going forward, in terms of both seeing citizens adopt the civic virtues and translating the practices of freedom into actual freedom for Indigenous peoples. As will become clearer, many practical challenges arise from the unavoidable and uneven political struggle that is taking place between ancient and modern constitutionalists.

So although we might prefer Tully's constitutional vision, we cannot hold it up as anything more than one of many without first engaging in politics *within* non-ideal circumstances, where constructive dialogical political struggle is not necessarily peaceful and the outcomes are far from certain. Political disagreement goes all the way down, *even on the merits of ancient constitutionalism itself*. There will be no closing of the gap and no eradication of modern social imaginaries, only ongoing struggle between and beyond competing visions. Should consensus arise, it must come through politics, not prior to politics. The fact that political agreement can be achieved only through politics puts even greater emphasis on the "how" of instilling civic virtues and realizing greater forms of constitutional legitimacy. I therefore explore a more realist disposition that might seem more pessimistic and that, counter-intuitively perhaps, puts us on a more hopeful track, as it draws greater attention to the challenges – and one hopes, the solutions – such conflict poses.

Negotiating and acting otherwise, given hegemony and distrust

Since ancient constitutionalism could be restored from the "bottom up" using the practices of freedom, such practices need to be examined. Tully rarely describes how they might play out in any specific circumstances, but he seems to rely on a certain willingness to cooperate and level of trust that does not always exist. This seems linked to a view that colonialism is waning and circumstances are becoming more favourable. That the dominant majority is willing to surrender its position of privilege does seem overstated, however, limiting the potential for negotiations and acting otherwise in fostering intercultural respect and understanding.

To begin, Tully overlooks just how divided we are and what this might mean for balancing the practices of freedom, particularly given the sense of urgency Indigenous peoples feel and their limited capacity to pursue all avenues at once. As Honig (2011, 140) writes: "Tully keeps the focus not on the trail of tears but on the history of treaty making, as if they could be prized apart ... His reasonableness is compelling but it displaces from the realm of politics forces of fantasy, inequality, exploitation, rage, resentment, and violence that might bedevil but might also help promote and further his quest for 'justice in a post colonial age.' Progressive politics often depends on pacificism *and* protest, reasonable argument *and* extremism, realism *and* fantasy."

In fairness, there are reasons to focus on the positives, including the critical importance of drawing in those who sympathize with ancient constitutionalism. Moreover, protest, extremism, and fantasy could be understood as forms of direct confrontation. What we should take away from this, however, is that Tully's optimism leads him to emphasize – perhaps overemphasize – the emancipatory potential of negotiation and acting otherwise at some expense to practices of direct confrontation. The concern this raises is that hegemonic states can corrupt the potential of the first two, necessitating the prioritization of direct confrontation, particularly given the limited capacity of Indigenous communities, the often profoundly incompatible interests of the non-Indigenous majority, and ubiquitous feelings of distrust.

Indigenous peoples have every reason to be weary of negotiations and acting otherwise against a backdrop of state hegemony. Negotiations are useful to the extent that they establish and follow the three conventions. But in practical terms such principles have little chance of being achieved unless we first weaken or put a serious check on state hegemony. Negotiations in good faith depend on an abundance of respect and trust that is generally absent. Notwithstanding the fact that the state pursues negotiations only when it wins, largely at the expense of Indigenous peoples and their claims, even if both sides perceive cooperation as beneficial the lack of trust poses an additional challenge (Chahboun 2015). It seems that, in situations of hegemony and distrust, fruitful and fair negotiations require greater forms of security, which in turn require a greater power balance *or* other assurances that negotiations will be conducted in "good faith" (Harty and Murphy

2005; Schaap 2006).[7] Tully's idealism about negotiations comes through most when he suggests that Indigenous peoples have a responsibility to cooperate with existing colonial laws so long as faithful negotiations are ongoing (2008a, 235). What are the chances that Indigenous peoples will now see this as a productive avenue after so many broken treaties and promises, or that settler Canadians will negotiate in good faith or consider compromising on their "modern" morals or economic interests? Moreover, why should Indigenous peoples in the meantime follow the very imposed laws they bring into question, rather than continuing to follow their own? Starting off with negotiation emphasizes a process that, arguably, even if not in every case, secured benefits for settlers and sowed the seeds of mistrust at a cost to Indigenous peoples.

This is not to ignore the fact that some Canadians react positively to Tully's suggestions, curious to (re)consider ancient constitutionalism. If a larger number adopted this view, there would be a real chance of success, though I suspect most Canadians will continue to protect their constitutional privilege. Consequently, Indigenous peoples and their supporters will have to follow Tully's advice to use direct confrontation, even civil disobedience, not only to "bring the powerful to the table" (2008a, 310), but, more importantly, to transform hegemonic conditions so that sitting at the same table can be productive. For such reasons, are good-faith negotiations even possible, as the Supreme Court repeatedly demands, without prioritizing such transformation? Until then, negotiation seems more likely to exacerbate mistrust, putting meaningful self-determination and ancient constitutionalism even further out of reach.

Regarding acting otherwise, the test is whether individuals and groups can resist co-optation, a challenging endeavour particularly given overwhelming colonial power. It takes great skill and determination to resist co-optation actively and successfully (see Alfred 1999). As with negotiation, greater balance would make this easier. Tully does not mention the implications that stem from acting otherwise being a political strategy equally available to the hegemonic majority. As seen above, legal rulings uphold new principles, such as the "act of state" doctrine that undergirds ultimate state sovereignty, still advancing legal tests that separate Indigenous peoples from their lands.

7 Although challenging in itself, Pitty (2015) considers the possibility of transnational mediation by someone such as the United Nations Special Rapporteur on the Rights of Indigenous Peoples.

Indeed, what I find so paradoxical about multiculturalism is that it acts otherwise, appearing to address what it deems to be the "reasonable" heart of Indigenous normativity while selectively resisting its deeper implications. This is not to say, however, that the only way to transform power relations is through direct confrontation, though I would argue that it, and not acting otherwise, is the more fruitful approach given current circumstances. Practices of direct confrontation seem most capable of awakening members of the majority from their apathy and comfort, forcefully stressing the dialogical relationships that persist across the landscape, and exposing state hegemony and how it is used to discount and dismiss Indigenous ways of being.

We should not be surprised that a new generation of Indigenous scholars believes that any interaction with the state is a trap (Simpson 2011). As Coulthard sees it, Indigenous peoples should "collectively redirect our struggles *away* from a politics that seeks to attain a conciliatory form of settler-state recognition for Indigenous nations toward a *resurgent politics of recognition* premised on self-actualization, direct action, and the resurgence of cultural practices that are attentive to subjective and structural composition of settler-colonial power" (2014, 24, emphasis in original). This resurgent turn away from the state aims not only to prefigure Indigenous futures, but also to develop catalytic *strategies* for revitalizing Indigenous communities, giving force to Indigenous constitutions in ways that they can come to see as legitimate. This is oftentimes preferable to tacitly accepting power imbalances and naively seeking state support, because the political divide is greater than Tully describes between the majority, which prefers exclusive forms of modern constitutionalism, and Indigenous peoples who refuse to concede on important aspects of Indigenous normativity. If the two were in greater balance, incentives might exist on both sides to abandon exclusive constitutional ideas in favour of cooperation using the civic virtues. Unfortunately for ancient constitutional supporters, privilege and survival, respectively, keep non-Indigenous and Indigenous peoples apart. As a result, the political challenges ahead are much rougher as civic virtues are less available to us.

Balancing Civic and Political Virtues

Using an applied political theory approach, this chapter has evaluated current federal government multiculturalism and land claim policy in light of Tully's ancient constitutionalism. Given that ancient constitutionalism cannot pre-politically claim the constitutional centre, the civic virtues are themselves subject to political contestation. This is not to say that dialogical constitutional struggle is also up for debate; on the contrary, dialogue of a sort goes beyond peaceful debate when civic virtues fall short and certain actors who want change seek other means of challenging institutions or laws that they perceive as illegitimate. Solely promoting ancient constitutionalism is, however, susceptible to the charge that it represents utopian thinking. I do not mean this in the sense that it is universally impossible; I believe Tully and others convincingly argue that treaties *under certain circumstances* served Indigenous peoples and settlers well (see Asch 2014; Henderson 1994; Ladner 2003). It therefore meets the first criterion of, to use one prominent example, Rawls's "realistic utopia," given that it provides a constitutional order that is appealing even if it differs from the status quo. It remains to be seen, however, if ancient constitutionalism is even feasible (see Rawls 2001, 4–5). In this sense ancient constitutionalism seems utopian to the extent that it assumes that full or near-full compliance with its civic virtues is possible. Put differently, ancient constitutionalism lacks a full account of how it will be established *and* maintained.

In seeking an answer to what can be established and maintained, realists tend to believe that just as much, if not more, can be learned from studying why ancient constitutionalism worked in the first place and why it eventually lost favour. Many factors determine the rise and decline of different political orders over time, among them the availability of resources, institutions, societal norms, security, desire, ambition, and demographic changes. Ancient constitutional "moments," when they occur, are complex and contextual, borne of political necessity and reinforced by civic virtue. Tully speaks of the latter, but skims over the former. He recognizes that settlers honoured treaties when they needed help – when their survival and happiness depended on them. But the other story offers a telling account of where we are today and what might be possible moving forward. Once fed, secure, and robust in number, non-Indigenous settlers turned their backs on treaties. Narrowly emphasizing peace and sharing ignores the fact that some see war, conflict, or simply inherited power as furthering their aims, even if it comes at another's expense. It is to this story that realists are more drawn. Realists, in short, draw our attention as much to political virtues as to civic virtues. They might take their cue from studying Machiavellian *virtù* or, more likely, Weberian trade-offs that require political judgment – refining political virtues of rhetoric, leadership, interests, alliances, and so on – as a means of establishing their conception of a well-ordered society. These lessons consider our individual and collective values and goals (and the tensions that arise between them), while working with and against those of constitutional others with whom we – willingly or not – find ourselves living. Although we might appeal to principles of peaceful cooperation, we must prepare for conflict. This need not necessarily entail violence; Idle No More and the Tibetan independence movement show us that, although there are those who see an unwillingness to engage in more radical forms of confrontation as explaining the limited success of such approaches.[8]

Most of all, I worry that ancient constitutionalism is idealistic in the sense that it might not be easily (re)established or that it could misguide us as we engage in political struggle. We should consider seriously whether we can replicate conditions that (fleetingly) served us in the past, because the conditions of today differ. We cannot return to a time before broken treaties, residential schools, or environmental degradation – the modern social imaginary has emerged with force, and cannot be put back into its box. To be sure, some of this can be addressed, but no two conditions are alike. We must face the real possibility that non-agreement will endure and that, although many disagreements will be resolved through respectful dialogue, many will not be. Our actions might be better guided by recognizing this fact. In what might seem like an extreme example, Indigenous peoples and their supporters might be better served by pursuing political *virtù*, even (if only temporarily) rejecting some of the civic virtues and their own peaceful ways if it means saving Indigenous peoples from being dominated or their territories from experiencing further environmental destruction. Although violence should be avoided, such possibilities highlight how imperative it is that we creatively consider alternative constitutional approaches and arrangements more in tune with our present realities and the reluctance of "modern" citizens to surrender their exclusionary ideas and their imposition on reluctant others.

Such realism is not a form of pessimism devoid of hope; indeed, greater hope might be found from giving present political concerns their due. There is something else positive about taking a more realistic disposition: attuning our normative arguments to present realities provides more fruitful answers to the question of "what should we do?"

8 Dickinson (2015) suggests that violence helped Kosovo and Bangladesh secure self-determination while Tibet's pacifism at least partially explains its limited success.

than "elaborating our favoured utopian ideals, values or virtues and imagining an empowered agent who can enact whatever we please" (Hall 2017, 286). Turner and others have suggested this should be done from *within* Canada's legal system, but I challenge readers to imagine what this might look like using strategies more attuned to tackling such hegemonic structures. Although I leave much of the detail for another time, Indigenous activists might apply their limited resources not only to pursuing community resurgence, but also to considering whether and when it is worth using resurgence to break down barriers with settler Canadians on a more personal level, from the "bottom up," Moreover, any such strategy should not require Indigenous peoples to compromise their values, as they typically do when engaging the state through negotiation and acting otherwise. Indigenous peoples and their supporters typically argue that Canadians should educate and thereby awaken themselves, with the only "reasonable" conclusion being an ancient constitutional one. This strategy seems unlikely to work on any large scale, and indeed has not worked as multiculturalism further entrenches itself. Broader approaches appealing to settler self-interests as well as dispelling myths about Indigenous worldviews being illiberal or unmodern seem like good places to start.

Finally, I would say that the same ubiquitous world of political conflict and change that saw treaty constitutionalism decline could lead to the decline of modern constitutionalism. The better view a hopeful agonist can have of this possibility, as far as I can tell, is a realist one. A more legitimate future depends not only on political struggle using the practices of freedom, but also on Indigenous peoples and their supporters having a keen understanding of present circumstances, moral psychology, and the uncertainties of politics, recognizing that it is also through broader and more fundamental political struggle and opportunism that we will get somewhere more legitimate, as well as discover what that might look like. Indigenous peoples have few options but to persuade more of their own people as well as settler Canadians both within and outside existing state institutions that try to do the same against them. As Sleat (2013, 173) states, those who disagree "are effectively struggling against the state, a struggle that is clearly in no way equal. This inequality can undoubtedly lead to despair, resentment, anger, bitterness, and even hatred." The challenge that Indigenous peoples face every day involves channelling those emotions in the right direction, and recruiting more people to the cause by being attuned to the varied reasons that might make people willing to join.

REFERENCES

Alfred, Taiaiake. 1999. *Peace, Power, Righteousness: An Indigenous Manifesto*. Oxford: Oxford University Press.

APTN. 2014. "'Tears and cheers' greet historic Supreme Court ruling handing Tsilhqot'in major victory." *Aboriginal Peoples Television Network*. Available online at http://aptnnews.ca/2014/06/26/supreme-court-hands-tsilhqotin-major-victory-historic-ruling/, accessed 26 February 2015.

Asch, Michael. 2014. *On Being Here to Stay: Treaties and Aboriginal Rights in Canada*. Toronto: University of Toronto Press.

Borrows, John. 2010. *Canada's Indigenous Constitution*. Toronto: University of Toronto Press.

British Columbia Treaty Commission. 2017. *Reconciling Prosperity: The Role of Local and Regional Governments in Treaty Negotiations*. Vancouver. Available online at http://www.bctreaty.ca/sites/default/files/BCTreatyCommission-AR2017.pdf

Cairns, Alan C. 2000. *Citizens Plus: Aboriginal Peoples and the Canadian State*. Vancouver: UBC Press.

CBC News. 1998. "Nisga'a members sign historical treaty." Available online at http://www.cbc.ca/news/canada/nisga-a-members-sign-historic-treaty-1.167049, accessed 15 December 2015.

Chahboun, Naima. 2015. "Nonideal Theory and Compliance – A Clarification." *European Journal of Political Theory* 14 (2): 229–45. https://doi.org/10.1177/1474885114559040

Connolly, William E. 2000. "The Liberal Image of the Nation." In *Political Theory and the Rights of Indigenous Peoples*, ed. Duncan Ivison, Paul Patton, and Will Sanders, 183–98. Cambridge: Cambridge University Press.

Cornell, Stephen. 2015. "'Wolves Have a Constitution': Continuities in Indigenous Self-Government." *International Indigenous Policy Journal* 6 (1): 1–20. https://doi.org/10.18584/iipj.2015.6.1.8

Corntassel, Jeff. 2008. "Toward Sustainable Self-Determination: Rethinking the Contemporary Indigenous-Rights Discourse." *Alternatives* 33 (1): 105–32. https://doi.org/10.1177/030437540803300106

Coulthard, Glen. 2014. *Red Skin, White Masks: Rejecting the Colonial Politics of Recognition*. Minneapolis: University of Minnesota Press. https://doi.org/10.5749/minnesota/9780816679645.001.0001

Dickinson, Rob. 2015. "Tibetan Self-Determination: A Stark Choice for an Abandoned People." In *Restoring Indigenous Self-Determination: Theoretical and Practical Approaches*, ed. Marc Woons, 106–12. Bristol, UK: E-IR Publishing.

Findlay, Len. 2013. "Redress Rehearsals: Legal Warrior, COSMOSQUAW, and the National Aboriginal Achievement Awards." In *Reconciling Canada: Critical Perspectives on the Culture of Redress*, ed. Jennifer Henderson and Pauline Wakeham, 217–35. Toronto: University of Toronto Press.

Fontaine, Phil. 2008. Remarks to the House of Commons, 39th Parliament, 2nd Session, 11 June. Available online at http://www.ourcommons.ca/DocumentViewer/en/39-2/house/sitting-110/hansard, accessed 15 December 2015.

Fukuyama, Francis. 1992. *The End of History and the Last Man*. New York: Free Press.

Geuss, Raymond. 2008. *Philosophy and Real Politics*. Princeton, NJ: Princeton University Press. https://doi.org/10.1515/9781400835515

Gray, Lynda. 2008. "Why silence greeted Stephen Harper's residential-school apology." *Georgia Straight*, 12 June. Available online at https://www.straight.com/article-150021/unyas-lynda-gray-responds-prime-ministers-apology, accessed 15 December 2015.

Hall, Ed. 2017. "How to Do Realistic Political theory (and Why You Might Want to)." *European Journal of Political Theory* 16 (3): 283–303. https://doi.org/10.1177/1474885115577820

Harty, Siobhan, and Michael Murphy. 2005. *In Defence of Multinational Citizenship*. Cardiff: University of Wales Press.

Henderson, James [sakej] Youngblood. 1994. "Empowering Treaty Federalism." *Saskatchewan Law Review* 58: 241–329.

Henderson, James [sakej] Youngblood. 2013. "Incomprehensible Canada." In *Reconciling Canada: Critical Perspectives on the Culture of Redress*, ed. Jennifer Henderson and Pauline Wakeham, 115–26. Toronto: University of Toronto Press.

Henderson, Jennifer, and Pauline Wakeham. 2013. "Introduction." In *Reconciling Canada: Critical Perspectives on the Culture of Redress*, ed. Jennifer Henderson and Pauline Wakeham, 3–27. Toronto: University of Toronto Press.

Hoehn, Felix. 2012. *Reconciling Sovereignties: Aboriginal Nations and Canada*. Saskatoon: Native Law Centre, University of Saskatchewan.

Honig, Bonnie. 2011. "'[Un]Dazzled by the Ideal?': Tully's Politics and Humanism in Tragic Perspective." *Political Theory* 39 (1): 138–44. https://doi.org/10.1177/0090591710386436

James, Matt. 2013. "Neoliberal Heritage Redress." In *Reconciling Canada: Critical Perspectives on the Culture of Redress*, ed. Jennifer Henderson and Pauline Wakeham, 31–46. Toronto: University of Toronto Press.

Kino-nda-niimi Collective. 2014. "Idle No More: The Winter We Danced." In *The Winter We Danced: Voices from the Past, the Future, and the Idle No More Movement*, ed. Kino-nda-niimi Collective, 21–8. Winnipeg: ARP.

Kuhn, Thomas. 1996. *The Structure of Scientific Revolutions*. 3rd ed. Chicago: University of Chicago Press. https://doi.org/10.7208/chicago/9780226458106.001.0001

Kymlicka, Will. 2001. *Politics in the Vernacular: Nationalism, Multiculturalism, and Citizenship*. Oxford: Oxford University Press. https://doi.org/10.1093/0199240981.001.0001

Ladner, Kiera. 2003. "Treaty Federalism: An Indigenous Vision of Canadian Federalism." In *New Trends in Canadian Federalism*, ed. François Boucher and Miriam Smith, 167–94. Peterborough, ON: Broadview Press.

Ladner, Kiera. 2009. "Take 35: Reconciling Constitutional Orders." In *First Nations, First Thoughts: The Impact of Indigenous Thought in Canada*, ed. Annis May Timpson, 279–300. Vancouver: UBC Press.

Larmore, Charles. 2013. "What Is Political Philosophy?" *Journal of Moral Philosophy* 10 (3): 276–306. https://doi.org/10.1163/174552412X628896

Mackey, Eva. 2013. "The Apologizers' Apology." In *Reconciling Canada: Critical Perspectives on the Culture of Redress*, ed. Jennifer Henderson and Pauline Wakeham, 47–62. Toronto: University of Toronto Press.

Mignolo, Walter D. 2011. *The Darker Side of Western Modernity: Global Futures, Decolonial Options*. Durham, NC: Duke University Press. https://doi.org/10.1215/9780822394501

Mouffe, Chantal. 2005. *On the Political*. London: Routledge.

Picq, Manuela L. 2015. "Self-Determination as Anti-Extractivism: How Indigenous Politics Challenges International Relations." In *Restoring Indigenous Self-Determination: Theoretical and Practical Approaches*, ed. Marc Woons, 26–33. Bristol, UK: E-IR Publishing.

Pitty, Roderic. 2015. "Restoring Indigenous Self-Determination through Relational Autonomy and Transnational Mediation." In *Restoring Indigenous Self-Determination: Theoretical and Practical Approaches*, ed. Marc Woons, 72–9. Bristol, UK: E-IR Publishing.

Rawls, John. 2001. *Justice as Fairness: A Restatement*. Ed. Erin Kelly. Cambridge, MA: Harvard University Press.

Rollo, Toby. 2014. "Mandates of the State: Canadian Sovereignty, Democracy, and Indigenous Claims." *Canadian Journal of Law and Jurisprudence* 27 (1): 225–38. https://doi.org/10.1017/S0841820900006317

Rummens, Stefan. 2009. "Democracy as a Non-Hegemonic Struggle? Disambiguating Chantal Mouffe's Agonistic Model of Politics." *Constellations* 16 (3): 377–91.

Schaap, Andrew. 2006. "Agonism in Divided Societies." *Philosophy and Social Criticism* 32 (2): 255–77. https://doi.org/10.1177/0191453706061095

Simpson, Leanne. 2011. *Dancing on Our Turtle's Back: Stories of Nishnaabeg Re-Creation, Resurgence, and a New Emergence.* Winnipeg: ARP.

Sleat, Matt. 2013. *Liberal Realism: A Realist Theory of Liberal Politics.* Manchester: Manchester University Press. https://doi.org/10.7228/manchester/9780719088902.001.0001

Tully, James. 1995. *Strange Multiplicity: Constitutionalism in an Age of Diversity.* Cambridge: Cambridge University Press. https://doi.org/10.1017/CBO9781139170888

Tully, James. 2003. "Diverse Enlightenments." *Economy and Society* 32 (3): 485–505. https://doi.org/10.1080/03085140303133

Tully, James. 2008a. *Public Philosophy in a New Key.* Vol. 1, *Democracy and Civic Freedom.* Cambridge: Cambridge University Press.

Tully, James. 2008b. *Public Philosophy in a New Key.* Vol. 2, *Imperialism and Civic Freedom.* Cambridge: Cambridge University Press.

Turner, Dale. 2006. *This Is Not a Peace Pipe: Towards a Critical Indigenous Philosophy.* Toronto: University of Toronto Press.

Wherry, Aaron. 2009. "What he was talking about when he talked about colonialism." *Maclean's*, 1 October. Available online at https://www.macleans.ca/uncategorized/what-he-was-talking-about-when-he-talked-about-colonialism/, accessed 14 February 2016.

Williams, Bernard. 2005. *The Beginning Was the Deed.* Ed. Geoffrey Hawthorn. Princeton, NJ: Princeton University Press.

Wolfe, Alan. 2009. *The Future of Liberalism.* New York: Knopf.

14 Equality Rights, Multiculturalism, and Public Reason in Canada

MARK BLYTHE AND JAY MAKARENKO

Multicultural rights continue to be an ongoing debate in Canadian politics, encompassing a wide range of issues, such as the accommodation of new immigrants, federalism and Quebec nationalism, and Aboriginal self-determination.[1] Political and popular attention often focuses on the outputs of these debates and the sorts of rights and entitlements that ought to be extended to cultural, ethnic, and religious minorities. In this chapter we focus on a different question: how ought we to debate multicultural rights in a liberal democracy? The issue is the not the content of a multicultural rights regime per se, but the procedures and processes by which Canadians should debate this rights regime in public political forums. We suggest that an applied political theory might provide a useful starting point.

This chapter explores the idea of public reason as a basis for public debate, drawing from the work of American liberal political philosopher John Rawls. In Rawls's account, deliberations about constitutional essentials and matters of basic justice should be based on appeals to values that are justifiable to all in society, and should not be based on comprehensive religious, moral, or philosophical doctrines. We build upon

1 Multicultural rights in Canada can be understood as a subset of accommodation rights. To explain: the main Canadian liberal, multicultural theorist, Will Kymlicka, began in *Multicultural Citizenship* (1995) by distinguishing between "polyethnic, self-governing and special representation rights." In *Citizenship, Communities, and Identity* (2004) he changed "polyethnic" to "accommodation." His examples in both, however, are ethnic, immigrant, and religious groups. Accommodation rights should be considered more broadly to include all minority identities – ethnic, religious, gender, disability, and so on. We recast Kymlicka's narrower sense of accommodation rights as "multicultural rights."

Rawls's idea by examining how public reason might occur in the Canadian debate on multicultural rights, focusing specifically on the issue of universal versus group-differentiated approaches to the constitutional right to equality. We apply the theoretical framework of public reason to an analysis of notable instances of the political and legal dimensions of multiculturalism in Canadian politics, and we examine two case studies in this context: Supreme Court Justice William Rogers McIntyre's 1989 decision in *Andrews v. Law Society of British Columbia* [[1989] 1 SCR 143] and the federal Conservative Party's framing of the *niqab* debate in the 2015 election. The conclusion we draw here is that McIntyre's decision in *Andrews* is a valuable example of public reasoning in regards to multicultural rights, as arguments were grounded on values justifiable to all in society – specifically, principles found within the Canadian Constitution. The Conservatives' framing of the *niqab* debate, by contrast, often demonstrated a lack of public reason, with the Conservative Party regularly appealing to values that were not reasonably acceptable to Muslim Canadians, let alone most Canadians. This is not to suggest that the outcome of McIntyre's decision in *Andrews* is uncontroversial or that the Conservative Party should not have rejected special accommodation for Muslim groups, but simply that the former provides a clearer example of how a fair debate on equality and multicultural rights might proceed.

We begin by examining Rawls's account of public reason, its implication for debate in public political forums, and how it relates to his broader theory of liberal justice. The second section highlights an important issue in Canadian multicultural politics: the constitutional right to equality, and the debate between universal and group-differentiated rights. In the final sections we examine the two case studies, drawing out implications about how public reason on the issue of the right to equality should proceed in the Canadian multicultural context.

The Concept of Public Reason

In keeping with an applied political theory approach, we begin by examining an important idea in liberal political theory that will be helpful in analysing both the *Andrews* decision and the *niqab* debate. The idea of *public reason* can be found in the work of several political philosophers, including Hobbes, Kant, Rousseau, and, more recently, Jürgen Habermas, Gerald Gaus, and John Rawls. In Rawls's account, public reason addresses the question of how moral and political rules might be rightly imposed, recognizing that persons have deep disagreements about what constitutes the good life. Our applied political theory approach seeks to use Rawls's concept of public reasoning to map out a fair way to discuss political issues and events (and differences of opinion about these) in Canada.

In a multicultural society such as Canada, there is a diverse set of religious, ethnic, and cultural groups, each with its own values, moralities, and religious views. The idea of public reason holds that moral and political rules are rightly imposed only if they are justifiable, or reasonably acceptable, to all persons over whom the rules have authority. One main theme we hope to draw out is that application of public reason provides a common denominator, or shared language, from which different persons can argue for their views in a fair way or in reference to terms and principles all can reasonably accept. Public reason, therefore, differs from the concept of consent, which holds that political legitimacy requires the actual or implied consent of persons. Instead, public reason requires only that moral or political rules be justifiable to all persons, independent of whether consent is secured. Moreover, public reason does not aim at truth. As Rawls states, public reason "is not simply valid reasoning, but argument addressed to others: it precedes correctly from premises we accept and think others could reasonably accept to conclusions we think they could also reasonably accept" (1999b, 155). Public reason thus excludes argumentation based upon values or doctrines that are specific to a particular individual or group in society – for example, one cannot argue for a law or public policy because it accords with the tenets of a particular religious text. Although some in society might view them as the "truth," such doctrines nevertheless involve premises that not all in society would reasonably accept. Instead, public reason aims

> at free agreement reached on the basis of shared political values … especially when they [political and moral issues] become divisive … Abortion is a good example … of deep conflict. If we accept the idea of public reason we should try to identify political values that may indicate how this question can be settled, or a settlement approached. I have in mind the following: that public law show appropriate respect for human life, that it properly regulate the institutions through which society reproduces itself over time, that it secure the full equality of women, and finally, that it conform to the requirements of public reason itself, which, for example, bar theological and other comprehensive doctrines from deciding the case. (Rawls 2001, 117)

According to Rawls, public reason is not unchangeable in its content. As he states, it "is important that this be so; otherwise the claims of groups or interests arising from social change might be repressed and fail to gain their appropriate political voice" (1999b, 142–3). Its premises and conclusions might change over time as new evidence becomes available or as social and political values become widely challenged in society. The inclusion of these new premises, in turn, might alter the kinds of political principles that are justifiable to all in society. It is important to note, however, that, although Rawls's account of public reason requires attention to what might be reasonably acceptable to persons, he does not go so far as to require the sort of "authentic" "non-coercive," or "inclusive" forms of discourse found in much of the literature on deliberative democracy (see, for example, Bohman 1996; Dryzek 1990, 2000). This is not to suggest that Rawls's approach to public reason necessarily rejects or prohibits stronger forms of deliberative democracy, but simply that it does not require them for fair political discourse.

According to Rawls, public reason is to be relied upon when debating constitutional essentials and matters of basic justice in a liberal democratic society. The presence of value diversity motivates Rawls to articulate a political idea of justice that focuses on fair terms of social cooperation to govern the basic social institutions in society, such as the system of laws, political institutions, economic markets, public associations, and the family. Central to Rawls's liberal theory are the two principles of justice that emphasize individual liberty and equality in the distribution of social, economic, and political rights and opportunities. Although the two principles set out the basic approach to justice, specific issues of law and public policy must still be settled at the constitutional and legislative levels, and public reason should be relied upon in settling these debates. More specifically, Rawls suggests that public reason apply to the public political forum, which includes the discourses of judges, government officials, and candidates for public office (1999a, 575). In the Canadian context, this includes a broad range of institutions, such as Parliament, the provincial and territorial legislatures, the courts, the electoral process, and government programs, agencies, and tribunals.

When debating law and public policy in these public political forums, then, officials should refrain from appealing to religious or cultural doctrines, and instead appeal to premises justifiable to all. It is important to note, however, that Rawls considers public reason a duty of civility, not a legal obligation (1999b, 151). Although government officials should adhere to the idea of public reason, and be held accountable when they do not, Rawls does not advocate the coercive use of the law to do so. When a judge relies on personal beliefs in deciding a case, his or her decision should be reviewed and overturned upon appeal. Similarly, political parties that justify policies by appealing to a particular religious doctrine might be criticized in the media and defeated in the electoral process. Rawls, however, does not suggest using the law to prohibit and sanction the use of comprehensive doctrines in public political forums.

Why ought we to use public reason? Rawls grounds the idea of public reason in the value of justice itself and in the ideal of society as a fair system of social cooperation between free and equal citizens. This ideal "[p]rovides a publicly recognized point of view from which all citizens can examine before one another whether their political and social institutions are just. It enables them to do this by citing what are publicly recognized among them as valid and sufficient reasons singled out by that conception itself ... the aim of justice as fairness, then, is practical: it presents itself as a conception of justice that may be shared by citizens as a basis of a reasoned, informed, and willing political agreement. It expresses their shared and public political reason" (1996, 9). If our political principles are derived from and justified by contested moral, philosophical, or religious doctrines, the resulting terms of social cooperation and public life are unfair. In the Canadian context, for example, if political principles are justified by Christian, anglophone, or European colonial moral and religious doctrines, then the resulting terms of social cooperation might favour those cultural and ethnic groups in their life while disadvantaging groups who hold and practise alternative, and inconsistent, views of the good life. To ensure terms of social cooperation that are fair, political principles must be grounded on premises that are reasonably acceptable to all groups, whether Christian, Muslim, anglophone, francophone, European, or Aboriginal.

This does not mean, however, that comprehensive doctrines are completely inappropriate in public political debate and deliberation.[2] Public

---

2 The cases of *Rodriguez v. British Columbia (Attorney General)* [[1993] 3 S.C.R. 519] and *Carter v. Canada (Attorney General)* [[2015] 1 S.C.R. 331] on doctor-assisted death also serve to illustrate important points about public and private reasoning. In *Rodriguez*, the Supreme Court of Canada ruled against doctor-assisted death, but reversed itself in *Carter* as new evidence became available. This illustrates that public reasoning does not determine the outcome of a debate; rather, it sets the terms of reference. The other point that these two examples illustrate is a justifiable use of private reasons. If one considers the number of religious and disabled groups granted intervenor status in the cases, one sees that an appropriate use of private reason is to show a point of view – to help articulate where one is coming from, so to speak.

reason applies only to the constitutional essentials and to matters of basic justice in a liberal democratic society, which include the principles that structure the government and political process, the basic rights and liberties of citizens, and the distribution of important resources not covered by the list of basic rights and liberties (such as income and wealth). As Rawls states, "citizens and legislators may properly vote their more comprehensive views when constitutional essentials and matters of basic justice are not at stake" (2001, 91). Persons are also free to use comprehensive views when debating outside public political forums, such as private associations, the family, and religious institutions. Even within political forums, persons' religious and cultural belief systems have an important place. The introduction of comprehensive doctrines can serve to illuminate and explain the diversity of values present in contemporary democracies. Such uses of these doctrines help to explain differing points of view and experiences among diverse citizens, and have the advantage of showing "where one is coming from." Indeed, as Rawls points out, "[c]onsider, for example, a highly contested political issue – the issue of public support for church schools. Those on different sides are likely to come to doubt one another's allegiance to basic constitutional and political values. It is wise, then, for all sides to introduce their comprehensive doctrines, whether religious or secular, so as to open the way for them to explain to one another how their views do indeed support those basic political values" (1999b, 154).

Equality, Rights, and Multiculturalism

Multicultural politics in Canada encompass a wide range of debates, including the accommodation of new immigrants and demands for self-government by Aboriginal groups and Quebec. These debates have both a constitutional and legislative context. At the constitutional level, issues include Aboriginal title, multiculturalism, Quebec and federalism, and individual constitutional rights, such as freedom of religion and the right to equality. At the legislative level, multicultural politics commonly deal with the practice of key constitutional principles and the distribution of economic and social goods between different cultural and ethnic groups.

An important aspect of an applied political theory approach is to relate theory to actual political events. Here we consider how section 15 (equality rights) of the Charter of Rights and Freedoms is interpreted in the light of multiculturalism; later, we argue that this provides an excellent example of public reasoning. Section 15 provides that "[e]very individual is equal before and under the law and has the right to the equal protection and equal benefit of the law without discrimination and, in particular, without discrimination based on race, national or ethnic origin, colour, religion, sex, age or mental or physical disability." Further, subsection (1) of section 15 does not preclude any law, program, or activity that has as its object the amelioration of conditions of disadvantaged individuals or groups, including those that are disadvantaged because of race, national or ethnic origin, colour, religion, sex, age, or mental or physical disability. This Charter provision encompasses a number of constitutional entitlements that are critical to multicultural politics. Section 15, for example, prohibits the state from discriminating based on race, national or ethnic origin, colour, or religion. This entitlement is important to ensuring the state does not enact laws that give political, social, or economic advantage to some ethnic or cultural groups over others. It also promotes ethnic and cultural minority participation in Canadian society by protecting the state's ability to pursue affirmative action programs. As a result, section 15 often is an area of conflict in the politics of multiculturalism, with ethnic and cultural groups using this legal entitlement to challenge government laws and policies.

The legal notions of "equality" and "discrimination," however, are highly contestable terms in American and Canadian jurisprudence. In his influential work, "Groups and the Equal Protection Clause," the American legal scholar Owen Fiss (1976) identified three constitutional approaches to equality: the similarly situated, anti-discrimination, and group-disadvantaged principles. Comparative legal scholars, such as Gabrielle Friedman and James Whitman, have suggested the existence of competing paradigms of constitutional entitlements to equality in American and continental Europe jurisprudence, with an anti-discrimination doctrine having influence in American legal thought and practice, and a dignity approach to equality gaining acceptance in continental Europe (Friedman and Whitman 2003). A number of Canadian legal scholars have examined the Supreme Court of Canada's approach to the constitutional principle of equality. In the context of equal political participation rights, it has been argued that the Court has rejected an American libertarian model in favour of an egalitarian doctrine – see, for example, Feasby (1999); Hiebert (1998); MacIvor (2004); and Makarenko (2009). Other scholars have applied variations of Fiss's basic typology to the Canadian context. Beverley Baines (2005), for example, argues that the Court has been influenced by both American and continental European ideas about equality, and at different times in its history has endorsed the discrimination, dignity, and substantive equality constitutional principles.

The literature demonstrates an important distinction regarding the nature of the right to equality. Some advance a universal model, which is blind to socio-economic differences and attempts to achieve equality by treating everyone the same. The similarly situated principle of equality, for example, is typically understood to be a universal view, in which a person's individual characteristics and contexts are irrelevant. This universal equality principle also underpins libertarian approaches, which hold that political equality simply requires that all citizens enjoy the same basic political rights and freedoms. The fact that some enjoy more wealth or social status in the exercise of their equal political rights does not undercut equality in political participation.

Other legal doctrines tend to advocate a more group-differentiated conception of equality, which recognizes differences in persons' socio-economic contexts, and distributes rights and obligations according to those differences, including the provision of special rights to disadvantaged groups. Under the egalitarian model of political participation, for example, equal treatment in the distribution of basic political rights does not necessarily guarantee political equality: social and economic elites can use their advantages to exercise disproportionate influence on political institutions and processes, while the disadvantaged might require "special" constitutional protections or privileges in order to promote equality. The state might provide subsidies, for example, to ensure that marginalized groups have a voice, or place limits on spending to prevent the wealthy from dominating. Under this constitutional principle, the recognition of difference, in terms of both characteristics and context, as well as constitutional entitlements, is necessary.

The legal debate on group-differentiated versus universal conceptions of rights is important in the context of Canadian multiculturalism, with direct implications for the basic liberties and rights of citizens, and for the distribution of important resources to different ethnic and cultural groups. A universal approach is generally hostile to claims for "special" cultural or ethnic equality rights, such as the accommodation of particular cultural practices, targeted economic assistance for minority groups, and claims to self-determination and government. Under the universal view, equality is achieved by treating everyone the same, and special cultural and ethnic rights deviate from this perspective by granting different rights to different groups. A group-differentiated approach, by contrast, supports these "special" rights for cultural and ethnic groups, as it recognizes difference and permits different sets of entitlements for different groups based on their particular cultural, social, or economic context.

Public Reason and the Supreme Court's Decision in *Andrews*

An applied political theory approach provides a profitable way to discuss a wide range of political and judicial issues. For example, does the right to equality entail a universal approach or a group-differentiated one? Should all persons be treated the same regardless of their socioeconomic circumstances? Or should certain ethnic and cultural groups be permitted special rights and accommodations? The aim here is not to answer these fundamental constitutional questions, but to begin to identify the manner in which they ought to be publicly debated. Rawls's conception of justice provides a useful starting point: the debate should proceed fairly, based on public reason and appeals to values that are justifiable to all Canadians. But what sorts of appeals might be considered fair? What might be considered unfair? In this section we examine the Supreme Court of Canada's decision in *Andrews,* arguing that it provides an example of the application of public reason in the context of equality rights and multiculturalism.

Andrews focused squarely on the debate between universal and group-differentiated approaches to equality. More specifically, the case dealt with the citizenship requirements for entrance to the provincial bar in British Columbia. Andrews, a British subject, met all of the requirements except citizenship, and challenged the requirement on the grounds that it discriminated against non-citizens and thus violated the Charter's right to equality. At trial the Supreme Court of British Columbia concluded that the citizenship requirement was constitutional. The British Columbia Court of Appeal, however, ruled in favour of Andrews, and the Supreme Court of Canada agreed. Justice Wilson, writing for the majority, concluded that the requirement violated section 15 of the Charter, and that the violation could not be justified under section 1. Justices McIntyre and Lamer dissented on the point of the section 1 justification. The Court agreed, however, on a general approach to equality rights, with McIntyre's reasoning becoming highly influential within Charter jurisprudence.

In his interpretation of section 15, Justice McIntyre rejected the similarly situated test or doctrine that had been advanced by several lower courts at the time. According to McIntyre, this doctrine was a formalistic and mechanical notion of equality that "focuses on the equal application of the law to those whom it has application," with no requirement to consider the reasons why a law may apply to one group and not another (*Andrews* [1989], 167). Instead, McIntyre advocated an approach consistent with group-differentiated equality: consideration "must be given to the content of the law, to its purpose, and its impact upon those to whom it applies, and also upon those whom it excludes from its application" (168). Moreover, the purpose of section 15 is not to ensure identical treatment by the law, but to ensure "equality in the formulation and application of the law" (171). According to McIntyre, section 15 entails the "promotion of a society in which all are secure in the knowledge that they are recognized at law as human beings equally deserving of concern, respect and consideration" (171). Importantly, this requires the identification and accommodation of difference, taking into consideration individual characteristics and contexts. As McIntyre stated, equality "is a comparative concept, the condition of which may only be attained or discerned by comparison with the condition of others in the social and political setting in which the question arises. It must be recognized at once, however, that every difference in treatment between individuals under the law will not necessarily result in inequality and, as well, that identical treatment may frequently produce serious inequality" (164). He further stated:

> It is not every distinction or differentiation in treatment at law which will transgress the equality guarantees of Section 15 of the Charter. It is, of course, obvious that legislatures may – and to govern effectively – must treat different individuals and groups in different ways. Indeed, such distinctions are one of the main preoccupations of legislatures. The classifying of individuals and groups, the making of different provisions respecting such groups, the application of different rules, regulations, requirements and qualifications to different persons is necessary for the governance of modern society. As noted above, for the accommodation of differences, which is the essence of true equality, it will frequently be necessary to make distinctions. (168–9)

Importantly, McIntyre relied on public reason in his decision by appealing to an important shared value: the Constitution itself. Quoting Chief Justice Dickson, McIntyre outlined his basic approach to analysing the purpose of a Charter right:

> In my view this analysis is to be undertaken, and the purpose of the right or freedom in question is to be sought by reference to the character and the larger objects of the *Charter* itself, to the language chosen to articulate the specific right or freedom, to the historical origins of the concepts enshrined, and where applicable, to the meaning and purpose of the other specific rights and freedoms with which it is associated within the text of the *Charter*... If the *Charter* was intended to eliminate all distinctions, then there would be no place for sections such as 27 (multicultural heritage); 2(*a*) (freedom of conscience and religion); 25 (aboriginal rights and freedoms); and other such provisions designed to safeguard certain distinctions. Moreover, the fact that identical treatment may frequently produce serious inequality is recognized in s. 15(2), which states that the equality rights in s. 15 (1) do "not preclude any law, program or activity that has as its object the amelioration of conditions of disadvantaged individuals or groups." (169, 171)

According to McIntyre, a group-differentiated interpretation of equality is consistent with the language, values, and history of a public institution specifically, the Charter, and the Constitution. The constitutional concepts of multiculturalism and Aboriginal title, for example, provide disadvantaged minority groups special treatment in Canadian social, economic, and political life. Similarly, section 15(2) enables governments to provide special affirmative action programs for women or visible minorities to promote equality. In each case, there is a rejection of the universal ideal of identical treatment in favour of recognizing difference in individual characteristics, contexts, and treatment under the law.

McIntyre's reasoning in *Andrews* continues to be influential in Canadian jurisprudence on equality and multiculturalism. In the more recent 2008 decision in *R. v. Kapp* [[2008] 2 SCR 483], the Supreme Court returned to the question of the meaning of equality and, in doing so, highlighted McIntyre's interpretation. *Kapp* centred on the federal government's management of fisheries on the Fraser River in British Columbia. The federal government had granted local Aboriginal groups special fishing rights that it had not extended to non-Aboriginal groups. The latter challenged the government's actions, arguing that it was discriminatory to non-Aboriginals and unconstitutionally violated the right to equality under section 15(1). Chief Justice McLachlin and Justice Abella, writing for the majority, concluded, however, that the differential treatment of Aboriginals and non-Aboriginals did not constitute a violation of section 15. Drawing from McIntyre's decision in *Andrews*, they rejected a formal approach to equality, concluding instead that sections 15(1) and 15(2) work together to promote a vision of equality that recognizes difference.

Importantly, McIntyre's reasoning in *Andrews* provides an example of public reason. For McIntyre, a group-differentiated interpretation of equality was preferable because it is consistent with the Constitution and its concepts of multiculturalism and Aboriginal right and title. Under Rawls's theory, these justifications are reasonable for Canadians to accept because they are the result of legitimate liberal democratic and legal processes. They were enacted by elected officials via the processes of parliamentary government and Canadian federalism, and subsequently have been adjudicated by an independent and impartial judiciary. Further justification might stem from the enhancement of freedom of conscience and religion, as all have an interest in ensuring that the state does not limit their liberty to practise a particular faith or morality. In each case, we are appealing to basic values that it is reasonable for all Canadians in a liberal democracy to accept.

This is not to suggest, however, that McIntyre's decision is uncontroversial or that it cannot be challenged in important ways through the application of public reason. For example, McIntyre made an appeal to freedom of conscience and religion, but did not fully develop the connection in his decision. How precisely are these freedoms better served by a group-differentiated approach to equality over a universal one? One might also challenge the legitimacy of the process by which the principles of multiculturalism and Aboriginal title were enshrined in the Constitution, which was the result of a highly elitist and closed-door democratic process, as opposed to one in which Canadians were widely engaged in a substantive manner. The point here, however, is not to determine whether McIntyre was ultimately correct in his decision to endorse a group-differentiated approach to equality, but rather to illustrate an example of applied political theory or, more precisely, the application of public reason to equality rights in a multicultural context.

Public Reason and the 2015 *Niqab* Debate

Our applied political theory approach to public reason does not restrict itself to judicial discourses. It can also be used to illustrate how to deal with controversial political issues and debates. The debate regarding the *niqab* during the 2015 federal election campaign offers another useful example for developing the notion of public reason in the Canadian multicultural context.

Before considering that debate, it might be helpful to briefly recall the contours of public reason. Public reason excludes argumentation based upon values or doctrines that are specific to a particular individual or group in society. The duty of civility requires that, when debating issues in public political forums, officials are to refrain from appealing to religious or cultural doctrines, and should instead make appeals to premises justifiable to all (Rawls 1999b, 151). Public reason "[p]rovides a publicly recognized point of view from which all citizens can examine ... whether their political and social institutions are just" (Rawls 1996, 9).

The *niqab* first became an issue in 2007 in Quebec, following a public backlash against electoral procedures that permitted Muslim women to vote with their faces covered. In 2011 the issue became a federal one when the Conservative federal government announced that Muslim women must remove their *niqab* during the citizenship ceremony, when they declare their Oath of Allegiance. Zunera Ishaq, a Sunni Muslim, challenged the ban before the courts on a number of grounds, including that it violated the right to equality under section 15 of the Charter. The ban became an important electoral issue, as the Canadian courts rendered a decision against the federal government prior to and during the 2015 campaign. What is important from our perspective is how this debate ought to be framed.

We wish to draw out two general points from the Conservative Party's characterization of the *niqab* debate. First, the underlying approach to equality expressed by the party was universal, in the sense that the same rules should apply to all. On the universal approach, all persons should be treated the same, and certain ethnic or cultural groups should not be permitted special exceptions that are denied other groups, such as the right to leave their faces covered during a citizenship ceremony. A group-differentiated approach to equality, by contrast, is open to this sort of special accommodation for Muslims. The wearing of the *niqab* is an important religious and cultural practice, and requiring Muslim women to remove it might be a barrier to their completing the citizenship ceremony. As such, a special exception might be necessary to ensure equality for this particular group. Treating citizens identically, in this case, paradoxically might end up treating people unfairly by imposing additional burdens on some that others do not face.

The second point, and more important to our thesis here, is that the Conservatives' view on this issue was problematic from a public reason viewpoint. Specifically, the Conservatives' characterization of some

Islamic practices as barbaric and misogynistic strayed from fair public reasoning because it referenced beliefs that could not reasonably be shared by all Canadians – particularly Muslims. The problem is that these characterizations are grounded in personal beliefs and conclusions, not in public reason. It ended up offending many in both the Muslim and non-Muslim communities.

Even more problematic, the *niqab* debate coexisted with a broader discussion about minority cultural practices, with the Conservative government's introduction of the Zero Tolerance for Barbaric Cultural Practices Act. This legislation sought to prohibit certain minority cultural practices, such as forced marriage, and the Conservatives often framed the debate as between the traditional values of Canadians and the "barbaric" values of some minority groups. In doing so, the Conservatives appealed to premises that were not justifiable to all, and thus violated public reason. Arguing against the special accommodation of minority religious practices because they are "barbaric" or because they are not the way things are done in Canada, are not premises reasonably acceptable to Muslim Canadians, let alone many non-Muslim Canadians.

Does this mean that arguing against the wearing of *niqab* is necessarily unreasonable? No, it does not. It means public officials, and those running for office, should discuss controversial moral issues such as this in reference to public reason. For example, it is legitimate to question whether a given religious practice violates the individual rights of Canadians – in this case, Muslim women. In such a discourse we could reasonably expect to hear from Muslim women who felt their rights as Canadians were being violated, or to reference a court decision outlining such violations. Even the oft-cited "Canadian values test" could have been reasonably debated. Here the Conservatives might have outlined what are Canadian values – presumably in reference to the Charter – and showed that there are limits to the cultural practices Canadian multiculturalism can accommodate. For example, honour killings clearly cannot be tolerated in Canada in any circumstance.

What about the Liberal campaign? Did it employ public reason in this debate? Consider the following statement by Liberal leader Justin Trudeau: "You can dislike the Niqab. You can hold it up as a symbol of oppression. You can try to convince your fellow citizens that it is a choice they ought not to make. This is a free country. Those are your rights, he said. But those who would use the state's power to restrict women's religious freedom and freedom of expression indulge the very same repressive impulse that they profess to condemn. It is a cruel joke to claim you are liberating people from oppression by dictating in law what they can and cannot wear" (quoted in Patriquin 2015). Here Trudeau frames the debate quite differently. It was about one's views and one's rights. He acknowledges that it is perfectly legitimate to view the *niqab* as oppressive and try to convince others of this view, but this should be done in reference to broader public values such as the rights and freedoms Canadians enjoy. In terms of public reasoning, one might further say it is not legitimate to suppress the rights – in this case the religious freedom – of others.

What about the courts? How did they approach the issue? They decided the case not on the constitutional issues, but concluded instead that the ban violated the federal government's own Citizenship Act. The issue nevertheless has important implications for basic constitutional rights in the context of Canadian multiculturalism, with clear linkages to the debate between universal and group-differentiated equality rights. Again, the aim here is to explore the nature of the justifications the Conservative Party used in its rejection of special accommodation for Muslims. The conclusion is that the party acted in an unfair manner by often rejecting public reason and by making appeals to premises that were not justifiable to all.

Conclusion

Using an applied political theory approach, we argue that public reasoning has several important functions in diverse liberal democracies. It provides a "common language" for diverse citizens to support differing policy outcomes. It provides a fair way for courts to settle disputes. It provides a fair way for courts to consider issues raised by the fact of cultural pluralism. It shows how courts can interpret a range of rights to support differing conclusions in differing contexts and across time and place. It provides a contrast to non-public reasoning. Public reasoning is not exclusive to courts – citizens, elected officials, scholars, and so on can access it. Public reasoning provides a fair way to discuss the controversial issues that can arise in a multicultural setting such as Canada.

The oft-discussed understanding of equality coming out of the *Andrews* case – accommodation of difference is the essence of true equality – is presented here as an outcome of public reason. In the multicultural context of Canada, it further appears to be the case that the accommodation of difference often involves the public recognition of identity. One such "recognition" is the extension of multicultural, group-differentiated rights of citizenship. Yet it must be noted that other conclusions are possible. Public reasoning does not decide controversial issues; rather, it provides a fair way to discuss them. Future judicial decisions could move towards the universal conception of equality. We would expect such decisions to be grounded in public reasoning, referencing and interpreting Charter rights in ways that Canadians could be expected reasonably to accept. But this has not been the direction of Canadian judicial rulings, which have generally moved away from the universal towards the differentiated conception of equality rights.

Public reasoning is best exemplified in judicial rulings, but it can be applied by other officers of the state and citizens alike. Consider, for example, the case of Baltej Singh Dhillon. He had gone through the process of becoming member of the RCMP. The problem he faced, however, was the RCMP's strict uniform code, which would not allow Dhillon, a devout Sikh, to wear a turban while on duty. In 1989 the commissioner of the RCMP recommended lifting this ban; less than a year later, Canada's solicitor general, who oversaw the RCMP, ruled in favour of that recommendation. This is one of many examples in Canada where considering equal treatment has led to a multicultural right. Multicultural rights are a form of protection, not only of minority identities, but from discrimination as well.

As stated, however, multicultural rights are not the only kind of accommodation right. Applying public reason to the concept of equal citizenship in the context of Canada opens up a series of minority identity issues, some of which are addressed already, others are not. Some minority identities have been recognized and accommodated in Canada for decades: Aboriginal right and title were affirmed in the Constitution Act, 1982. Although beyond the scope of this chapter, gender and disability rights also can be profitably discussed through the application of the concept of public reason.

It is our main contention that, both in courts of law and in the court of public opinion, the liberal idea of public reason remains the best way to consider these kinds of disagreements in a plural democracy. Public reason allows politicians, scholars, justices, students of politics and law, and citizens to discuss peacefully and settle, if only temporarily, issues raised by the fact of diversity. The application of public reasoning is best understood as a fair process for debating the pressing questions of the day in a diverse liberal democracy. It leaves open the possibility of reversing policy and law previously thought to be fair and just, to accommodate itself to new evidence and contexts. In this sense, public reasoning is a never-ending process ever seeking to determine just what free and equal citizenship might entail in a given context.

Multicultural rights continue to be an ongoing debate in Canadian politics, encompassing a wide range of issues, such as the accommodation of new immigrants, federalism and Quebec nationalism, and Aboriginal self-determination. According to our applied political theory approach, and under Rawls's account of public reason, these debates should be based on appeals to premises that are justifiable to all in society. Structuring the debate in this manner would help to ensure adherence to just political principles and terms of social cooperation that are to the advantage of all in society, not just of dominant ethnic, cultural, or religious groups.

We have applied Rawls's theory of public reason to two case studies: Justice McIntyre's decision in *Andrews* and the Conservative Party's framing of the *niqab* debate in the 2015 federal election. McIntyre's decision is a valuable example of public reason on multicultural equality, as he appealed to premises that are reasonably acceptable to all – specifically, constitutional principles enacted by legislators via a relatively fair democratic process and interpreted through an independent and impartial judiciary. The Conservative Party's framing of the *niqab* debate, by contrast, often demonstrated a lack of public reasoning, with appeals to premises that are not reasonably acceptable to all. Again, this is not to suggest the outcome of McIntyre's decision in *Andrews* is uncontroversial or that the Conservative Party should not have rejected special accommodation for Muslim groups. It is simply that, when public officials debate multicultural rights in public political forums, they should look to the idea of public reason.

REFERENCES

Baines, Beverly. 2005. "Is Substantive Equality a Constitutional Doctrine?" In *La doctrine et le développement du droit/Developing Law with Doctrine*, ed. Ysolde Gendreau, 59–101. Montreal: Les Éditions Thémis.

Bohman, James. 1996. *Public Deliberation: Pluralism, Complexity, and Democracy*. Cambridge, MA: MIT Press.

Dryzek, John. 1990. *Discursive Democracy: Politics, Policy, and Political Science*. Cambridge: Cambridge University Press.

Dryzek, John. 2000. *Deliberative Democracy and Beyond: Liberals, Critics, Contestations*. Oxford: Oxford University Press.

Feasby, Colin. 1999. "*Libman v. Quebec (A.G.)* and the Administration of the Process of Democracy under the *Charter*: The Emerging Egalitarian Model." *McGill Law Journal* 44 (1): 5–39.

Fiss, Owen. 1976. "Groups and the Equal Protection Clause." *Philosophy & Public Affairs* 5 (2): 107–77.

Friedman, Gabrielle, and James Q. Whitman. 2003 "The European Transformation of Harassment Law: Discrimination versus Dignity." Public Law & Legal Theory Research Paper 37. New Haven, CT: Yale Law School. https://doi.org/10.2139/ssrn.383900

Hiebert, Janet. 1998. "Money and Elections: Can Citizens Participate on Fair Terms amidst Unrestricted Spending?" *Canadian Journal of Political Science* 31 (1): 91–111. https://doi.org/10.1017/S0008423900008696

Kymlicka, Will. 1995. *Multicultural Citizenship*. Oxford: Oxford University Press.

Kymlicka, Will. 2004. "Citizenship, Communities, and Identity in Canada." In *Canadian Politics*, 4th ed., ed. James Bickerton and Alain-G. Gagnon, 35–53. Peterborough, ON: Broadview Press.

MacIvor, Heather. 2004. "The Charter of Rights and Party Politics: The Impact of the Supreme Court Ruling in *Figueroa v. Canada (Attorney General)*." *Choices* (Institute for Research on Public Policy) 10 (4).

Makarenko, Jay. 2009. "Fair Opportunity to Participate: The *Charter* and the Regulation of Electoral Speech." *Canadian Political Science Review* 3 (2): 38–51.

Patriquin, Martin. 2015. "The Niqab Gambit." *Maclean's*, 9 March.

Rawls, John. 1996. *Political Liberalism*. New York: Columbia University Press.

Rawls, John. 1999a. *Collected Papers*. Ed. S. Freeman. Cambridge, MA: Harvard University Press.

Rawls, John. 1999b. *The Law of Peoples, with "The Idea of Public Reason Revisited."* Cambridge, MA: Harvard University Press.

Rawls, John. 2001. *Justice as Fairness: A Restatement*. Ed. Erin Kelly. Cambridge, MA: Harvard University Press.

PART V

Nationalism

15 Lament for a Pre-modern Nation? George Grant and Michael Byers on Canadian Identity

ANN WARD

Reflecting on the tenure of Stephen Harper, it can be argued that Canadians' sense of independence and uniqueness came under suspicion during this prime minister's time in office. Emphasizing pre-Confederation moments in our history, such as the War of 1812, and strictly subordinating Canada's actions in the world to American fossil fuel and foreign policy priorities, the Canadian nationalist could be forgiven for believing that, for the Harper government, commitment to Canadian independence was an irritating obstacle to its policy goals. Can English-Canadian nationalism, to the extent that it is a legitimate emotional and ideological perspective, be reinvigorated?

In this chapter I use an applied political theory framework to answer this question. I argue that a renewal of English-Canadian nationalism should begin by returning to an exploration of George Grant's political theorizing in *Lament for a Nation: The Defeat of Canadian Nationalism* (2000) and Michael Byers's more recent response to Grant in *Intent for a Nation: What is Canada For?* (2007). I then relate the theoretical writings of Grant and Byers to the empirical examples of the role that Canada plays in peacekeeping and combatting climate change around the world.

Three specific components of Grant's analysis in *Lament for a Nation* can contribute to a renewal of English-Canadian nationalism: the critique of capitalism, the communitarian ambiguity towards individual autonomy, and the embrace of Quebec as a distinct society. Through exploration of these three components, two key paradoxes in Grant's position emerge. First, Grant is a pro-British supporter of the Commonwealth and an English-Canadian nationalist who embraces the aspirations of Catholic Quebec. Second, Grant is a conservative who is nonetheless hostile to corporate capitalism, and endorses the economic nationalist aspirations of the New Democratic Party (NDP). He also explores the concepts of modernity and progress, as understood by him to be the deeper philosophic causes of Canada's loss of independence. Modern political theory, Grant argues, teaches freedom as the human essence, and the modern theory of progress, spearheaded by the United States, espouses the universal, homogeneous society as the key instrument for making the essence of freedom a social and political reality. For Grant, however, the progressive ideal of the global village is a threat to all local cultures, including English-Canadian and French-Canadian culture.

In his rejection of modern liberalism in the name of the supremacy of the common good over individual freedom, Grant understands himself as drawing sustenance from philosophers such as Plato and Aristotle and their conception of the *polis* and the friendship within it. I thus analyse Aristotelian political thought as providing partial grounds for Grant's concept of Canada as a community. I then move from the *polis* to English Canada as a nation, and point to nationalism as the emotive force supplementing friendship in holding citizens together. Here I investigate the relationship between the complexities of English-Canadian nationalism, as understood by Grant, and the broader international theory of nationalism articulated by Benedict Anderson in *Imagined Communities: Reflections on the Origins and Spread of Nationalism* (1983).

I conclude with a brief exploration of Byers's reflections on Canada in *Intent for a Nation*. I argue that, despite his belief that Canadians have a modern, progressive perspective that sees our natural home in the international community, Byers actually shares key points of agreement with Grant on the requirements for a renewed Canadian nationalism. In his discussion of United Nations peacekeeping, Byers clearly argues, like Grant, for Canadian independence from American foreign policy priorities; and in his discussion of climate change, Byers points directly to the dangers of American corporate capitalism and the necessary critique of the free market. I conclude that the Canadian experience, as theorized by Grant and Byers, illustrates two important elements of contemporary nationalism. First, nationalism need not be exclusive, as English-Canadian nationalism can comprehend the group rights of internal nations such as the *Québécois* or a variety of nations within a state. Second, cosmopolitanism can be a part of nationalism: in taking up the challenge of climate change, the English-Canadian nation must accept that it has an important obligation to the planet, and recognize the need to cooperate closely with other countries.

Grant and English-Canadian Nationalism

Grant explains the title of his book in the following way: "To lament is to cry out at the death or at the dying of something loved. This lament mourns the end of Canada as a sovereign state" (2000, 4). Grant is thus a nationalist or strong proponent of state sovereignty but argues that, in the 1960s, particularly with the defeat of John Diefenbaker in the 1963 federal election, Canadians experienced the culmination of nothing less than the disappearance of Canada as a sovereign nation. This disappearance, according to Grant, was quickened by the concentrated wrath of the established classes (4). The established classes or elite Grant refers to include journalists, academics, and the heads of big business centred in Toronto and Montreal. Thus, despite hailing from southern Ontario and being a professor himself, Grant has an anti-elitist bent that is directed against intellect and wealth in central Canada. Since the intellectual and business elite in this part of the country is tied to the Liberal Party, Grant's animus is also directed there.

The core of the problem with the central Canadian liberal elite, from Grant's point of view, is that they had been pursuing policies that sought to absorb Canada into, or to integrate its economy with, our more powerful neighbour to the south (Grant 2000, 5, 7). The problem with our southern neighbour for traditional English-Canadian nationalists like Grant is that America is a great liberal experiment founded on the ideology of classical liberalism. Grant emphasizes two aspects of this classically liberal ideology as particularly troubling to Canada as a sovereign nation: the protection and expansion of individual rights, and the dedication to free market capitalism. American-style capitalism, Grant argues, has given rise to huge, multinational corporations such as General Motors, IBM, and now Walmart, which Grant refers to as "private governments" that seek to control "public governments" in Washington, Ottawa, and capitals around the globe (2000, 9).

Grant's Economic Nationalism and the Critique of the Free Market

The main problem with American capitalism, according to Grant, is that it has led to the greatest empire humankind has ever known. Routinely referring to the "American Empire," Grant argues that American imperialism is not characterized by direct military or political control over other countries, such as that practised by the British, Spanish, and French in previous ages and the Soviet Union in Grant's time. Rather, the imperialism practised by America is simply "control of one state by another" (Grant 2000, 9). The main avenue through which America controls other states is the spread of free market capitalism and free trade, called the process of "globalization" today. Globalization, Grant believes, allows American multinational corporations to take control of other nations' economies and, therefore, indirectly their governments as well.

The continentalism of the liberal elite in central Canada, Grant argues, led them to pursue policies aimed at integrating the Canadian economy with the American (Grant 2000, 15). The result is that all too often Canadian business elites, working for American corporations, answer to masters whose headquarters are south of the border. According to Grant, under Liberal tutelage, "[o]ur traditional role – as an exporter of raw materials (especially to Europe) with highly protected industry in Central Canada – gradually lost its importance in relation to our role as a branch-plant of American capitalism. Our ruling class is composed of the same groups as that of the United States, with the signal difference that the Canadian ruling class looks across the border for its final authority in both politics and culture" (9). The Canadian corporate elite, whose interests and wishes are obeyed and defended by the Liberal political and intellectual elite, are, therefore, in Grant's eyes the "spearhead" of the American Empire in Canada.

Uncharacteristic of a conservative, Grant's fear of American imperialism in Canada leads him to support the economic nationalist aspirations of the federal NDP during the 1960s. According to Grant, the integration of the Canadian and American economies after 1940 meant that the nationalist aspirations of conservatives in Canada could be achieved only through some form of socialism or central economic planning to reverse this economic trend (2000, 16). Grant thus calls for unity between Canadian conservatives and Canadian socialists in the name of economic nationalism, arguing that, philosophically and ideologically, both conservatives and socialists share a necessary hostility to American liberal individualism and free market capitalism. For Grant there is a conflict between capitalism and Canadian nationalism, and both conservatives and socialists should understand this, making them natural allies (see Cooper 1978, 31; Mathie 1978, 158; Muggeridge 1978, 44). To the traditional conservative dislike of "socialism" and the attendant centralizing bureaucracy in the name of small business, Grant responds that it simply allows "private governments" – in other words, the large multinational corporations located in central Canada – to become more powerful, not less so. As Grant makes clear, only big government can combat big business. As such the Canadian nationalist, unable to combat both big government and big business simultaneously, must choose between the two, with the knowledge that there is no return to the yeoman farmer or small-town capitalist of old.

Grant's Communitarianism

Grant's nationalism, however, can seem not simply pro-Canadian, but very pro-British. Often in Grant's writing a sovereign Canada does not stand alone, but almost always in connection with the "mother country" across the Atlantic. For instance, Grant claims, "Growing up in Ontario, the generation of the 1920s took it for granted that they belonged to a nation ... To say it was British was not to deny it was North American. Such alternatives as F.H. Underhill's – 'Stop being British if you want to be a nationalist' – seemed obviously ridiculous. We were grounded in the wisdom of Sir John A. Macdonald, who saw ... that the only threat to nationalism was from the South" (Grant 2000, 5). Speaking of Diefenbaker and Howard Green, Diefenbaker's minister of external affairs, Grant says: "The character of Canada as British North America was in their flesh and bones. Yet it was their fate to be in charge of the Canadian government at the time that the English ruling class had come to think of its Commonwealth relations as a tiresome burden, when the wealthy of Canada had ceased to be connected with their British past" (33). Grant's pro-Britishness, however, is actually a symbol of his rejection of the republicanism and classical liberalism of the United States. According to Grant, "the Britishness of Canada ... was a tradition that stood in firm opposition to the Jeffersonian liberalism so dominant in the United States" (34). Thus, for Grant, Canada, as an independent and sovereign country in North America, is an inherently conservative one (see Cooper 1978, 25; Muggeridge 1978, 44–5). By "conservative" Grant means a society grounded in an older communitarian ethos that eyes the autonomy of the "individual" with suspicion.

Grant's scepticism towards the individual brings us to his reflections in *Lament for a Nation* on the deeper, underlying philosophic causes of Canada's collapse as a sovereign state. Grant focuses in on the fact that his age is an age of modernity and progress, with America as the symbol and driving force behind this modern, progressive ideal. By modernity Grant refers to the core belief of modern political theory that the human essence is freedom. Any conception of the good that seeks to place limits on human freedom is unnatural and oppressive (Grant 2000, 55). Human beings, therefore, in modern eyes, should have absolute freedom to create or recreate the world as they want it, and they want most of all the economic and sexual freedom of the individual. Thus, Grant claims, "all kinds of taste are allowed. Nobody minds very much if we prefer women or dogs or boys, as long as we cause no public inconvenience" (56). Grant sees a strong connection between the unlimited pursuit of wealth in the economic sphere and the unlimited pursuit of pleasure in the social sphere, arguing, "in the age of high technology, the new capitalism can allow all passions to flourish along with greed. *Playboy* illustrates the fact that the young executive is not expected to be Horatio Alger. The titillation of the jaded tastes of the masses serves the purpose of the corporation elites, so long as a sufficient quota of the young is siphoned off as scientists and executives ... Liberal ideology reconciles the political power of the elites with the private satisfaction of the masses" (58; see also Greenspan 1996, 203).

The modern theory of progress, Grant argues, stipulates that human beings can achieve their ideal of absolute freedom only in the universal, homogeneous society or "global village"; this is what politics should aim at or progress towards (Greenspan 1996, 204). The Canadian embrace of freedom as the political end and human good, therefore, means the disappearance of Canada (see Cooper 1978, 31; Forbes 2007, 22–3, 25–6). The problem for Canada, according to Grant, posed by the modern, progressive ideal of the universal, homogeneous society is that it makes all "local cultures," of which Canada is one, at best redundant, at worst repressive (Grant 2000, 53). As a "local culture," Canada was founded, Grant argues, on the older, pre-liberal and hence conservative principles of the Loyalists. Antithetical to the modern spirit of freedom, the conservative principles of the Loyalists allowed for the right of the community to restrain the freedom of the individual for the common good; social order and group rights took priority over individual rights. Going forward, Grant appeals to Canadian socialists on this conservative basis of limiting individual freedom for the common good (see Reimer 1978, 52). Socialists and conservatives can unite against liberals to restore Canada's independence, according to Grant, because "what is socialism, if it is not the use of government to restrain greed in the name of social good? ... In doing so, was it not appealing to the conservative idea of social order against the liberal idea of freedom? Even if socialists maintain that their policies would lead in the long run to a society of unrestrained freedom, in the short run they have always been advocates of greater control over freedom" (Grant 2000, 57).

Grant's Views on Quebec

This unique brand of Canadian conservatism is a natural fit for English-Canadian nationalism because, for Grant, the English-Canadian nation must recognize the rights of groups, not simply those of individuals (but see Bradshaw 1996, 231). Such conservative communitarianism is necessary, Grant argues, if Quebec is to be assured that its nationalist aspirations can be satisfied within Canada rather than outside it. Grant claims the "keystone of the Canadian nation is the French fact ... English-speaking Canadians who desire the survival of their nation have to co-operate with those who seek the continuance of Franco-American civilization" (Grant 2000, 21). Canadian *nation-ness* and sovereignty, Grant implies, rest on a pact between English- and French-speaking peoples who desire not to be American. American-style individualism, Grant indicates, is inconsistent with the integrity of Quebec as a historic French community – or, shall we say, "distinct society" or "nation," within Canada. According to Grant, "failure to recognize the rights of French Canadians, *qua* community, is inconsistent with the roots of Canadian nationalism. One distinction between Canada and the United States has been the belief that Canada was predicated on the rights of nations as well on the rights of individuals" (22). Grant's pro-Britishness is thus complex. It actually represents a conservative recognition of group rights that is pro-French and pro-Quebec as part of the broader Canadian community.

Grant thus suggests that the real threat to Canadian *nation-ness* and sovereignty is not a *Québécois* nationalism that could lead to separation, but rather the economic integration of English-Canadian society into a continental economy with the United States. Economic domination by the United States is such a threat to Canada because, for Grant, this leads to American domination of Canadian defence policy as well (Grant 2000, 41–2): Canadians cannot be economically dependent yet still have an independent foreign and defence policy. There is a necessary link between economics and politics, emphasizing again that, for Grant, there is a conflict between capitalism and Canadian nationalism. Grant argues that "the capitalist system makes national boundaries only matters of political formality. In small capitalist nations ... Economic control is not finally in the hands of the government, and foreign capital is able to determine possible governments by incarnating itself as an indigenous ruling class" (43). The "indigenous ruling class" that Grant refers to is the Canadian business elite working for American interests that, although determining and controlling Canadian governments, are loyal to their corporate masters south of the border. Yet why could not one earn one's pay, as it were, from an American corporation, but still have political passions for Canada? Grant responds:

> It has been said ... that Canadians have to recognize the limitations on sovereignty in a nation that lives beside the most powerful country on earth. This argument sees our case as similar to that of Poland. But ... there are clearly two chief differences between ourselves and that nation. First, the Poles have an ancient culture which has shown strength in resisting the new change. The new came to Poland not only as something Russian (that is, nationally alien) but also as something Marxist (that is, profoundly alien to a Roman Catholic people). In Canada outside of Quebec, there is no deeply rooted culture, and the new changes come in the form of an ideology (capitalist and liberal) which seems to many a splendid vision of human existence. (42)

Grant implies that, unlike Poles, *Québécois*, and many other nations and peoples, English Canadians have not developed a strong cultural identity or sense of themselves. Absent any sentiment of communal cohesion and distinctiveness north of the border, there is precious little to prevent Americanization and maintain loyalty to Canada.

Aristotle and the *polis*

In his rejection of modern liberalism in the name of the common good over individual freedom, many scholars, such as Samuel LaSelva, argue that Grant adheres to an older Christian order represented by the "Elizabethan cosmological assumptions of the Anglican Loyalists" (LaSelva 2007, 8; Muggeridge 1978, 44, 47). Yet, prior to the theology of the Reformation, not to mention Roman Catholic Christianity, Grants suggests there is an older political and philosophic tradition from which he draws. At the close of *Lament for a Nation*, he maintains: "Ancient philosophy gives alternative answers to modern man concerning the questions of human nature and destiny ... The classical philosophers asserted that a universal and homogeneous state would be a tyranny" (2000, 93). Thus Grant understands himself as drawing inspiration, if not direction, from philosophers such as Plato and Aristotle and their conception of the *polis* and the friendship within it (see also Havers 2006, 124; Reimer 1978, 55–6). Accordingly I now turn to a brief analysis of the Aristotelian conception of the human as a social and political being.

In *Politics*, Aristotle argues that the *polis*, or city, "while coming into being for the sake of living ... exists for the sake of living well," and that the human being "is by nature a political animal" (1984, 1251b29–30, 1253a2–3). Thus, although the necessities of life bring the city into being, it continues to exist for purposes beyond the strictly necessary – for the good life. Human beings are understood as social creatures whose natural home is the city and whose end is participation in the good life that only the city can provide. If the good life, however, was the accumulation of wealth and the end of the city was economic prosperity, Aristotle contends that parties to trade agreements would constitute a single city. They do not, as Aristotle argues that the city "does not exist ... for the purposes of exchange and use of one another – for otherwise the Tyrrhenians and Carthaginians, and all who have agreements with one another, would be citizens of one city" (1280a33–6; see also Cooper 1999, 365–8). I note that Grant shares with Aristotle the same ambiguity towards the pursuit of material wealth.

Aristotle asserts that, although agreements among citizens to facilitate exchange and transact business with one another are necessary for the city to exist, they are not sufficient (1984, 1280b20–3). Therefore, to aspire to the good life and for the city actually to constitute itself as a single city in the strict sense, citizens must be more than just artisans who specialize and engage in mutual exchange for material advantage. For Aristotle, such citizens resemble members of trade agreements and commercial alliances, rather than citizens in the true sense of the word. To achieve the latter, citizens must engage in communal institutions that foster the mutual affection necessary for a friendship that transcends mere utility (see also Cooper 1999, 368–71). Aristotle points to the institutions of intermarriage, religious festivals, and the pastimes of living together as "the work of affection; for affection is the intentional choice of living together. Living well, then, is the end of the city, and these things are for the sake of this end" (1984, 1280b36–40). Experience of this more elevated feeling of friendship, however, is not itself the good life and thus the end of the city. Rather, according to Aristotle, the "political partnership must be regarded ... as being for the sake of noble actions, not for the sake of living together" (1281a2–3). Aristotle, therefore, suggests that friendship among citizens can allow for and be the basis of morally virtuous actions done for the sake of the noble. Citizens, it seems, initially coming together for the sake of the useful, can continue their partnership for the sake of the noble.

Friendship, for Aristotle, is essential to politics (see also Cooper, 1999, 368–72; Tessitore 1996, 74; and Ward 2016, 103–6). In *Nicomachean Ethics* Aristotle argues that friendship among fellow citizens, or that which he calls "like-mindedness," holds cities and political communities together (2011,1155a22, 1167b2). Justice among citizens is less important than friendship as friendship, not justice, "drives out discord" and hence prevents the slide into civil strife or even war (1155a26). Aristotle attributes friendship to cities when "people are of the same judgment concerning what is advantageous, choose the same things, and do what has been resolved in common" (1167a26–8). In other words, political friendship is unity of mind among citizens in deliberation and action with regard to important matters affecting the public interest.

Friendship, built on, yet going beyond, its foundation in justice allows persons to constitute themselves most fully as citizens of one city collectively pursuing the good life for human beings. In *Nicomachean Ethics* Aristotle suggests that it is a city under a timocratic regime – the just form of majority rule – that is most conducive to creating friendship among citizens. In this discussion Aristotle makes use of relationships within the family to explain political friendship within timocracy. The friendship among citizens in a timocratic regime is analogous to the friendship between brothers. As timocratic citizens share in ruling and being ruled in turn as all "wish to be equals and equitable" and "on an equal basis," so brothers, according to Aristotle, are "equals and similar in age, and such people for the most part have the same feelings and habits" (1161a26–9). Aristotle goes further, arguing that, because brothers are born of the same parents and have a common upbringing, they are "in some way the same thing, … even though this same thing resides in separate persons" (1161b30–5). Brothers, therefore, are to each other like other selves. By implication the friendship among timocrats, like the friendship between brothers, is based on a strict equality in which each, as the same as the others, gives and receives affection in the same amount. Moreover, Aristotle suggests that timocratic citizens can share in ruling, whereby each rules and is ruled by each, because, like brothers, they regard each other as other selves (see Bradshaw 1991, 558; Homiak 2002, 93–3; Pakaluk 1998, 110; Saxonhouse 1991, 47; Sokolon 2006, 57, 66, 73, 82).

The friendship among timocratic citizens, therefore, is felt between persons, like brothers, who are closely alike and equal. Moreover, it appears that timocratic citizens who share in ruling and being ruled in turn can, like brothers, see one another as other selves. Thus, in addition to resembling most closely the friendship or unity of mind among fellow citizens that holds political communities together, the friendship among timocrats comes closest to resembling Aristotle's understanding of what he believes is true or perfect friendship (Schollmeier 1994, 75, 79, 81–8; Stern-Gillet 1995, 158–67; Tessitore 1996, 80–1; Ward 2016, 117). Timocratic friendship meets three of the requirements of true friendship: it is a like-to-like relationship, it is based on a strict equality of sameness, and timocratic citizens can view one another as other selves. Aristotle also defines friendship broadly as the condition in which two persons will the good for one another, and are aware of each other's goodwill (2011, 1156a305). In its true form, friendship is based on goodness in which the friends will the good for each other because, in themselves, "they are good" (1156b10–12). Thus, in true friendship, we feel affection for friends due to their goodness, not for the utility or pleasure we get out of the relationship. True friendship involves, therefore, a recognition of and affection for the goodness of the other. Moreover, true friendship is long-lasting, as goodness, or virtue, which friends value in each other, is a thing that lasts. Such friendship is rare, however, since good or virtuous persons are few, and it requires a long time for friends to get to know each other, as they must have confidence in each other's good character. In other words, friends must actually *be* good, not just seem good (1156b6–33, 1157a16–19; see also Sokolon 2006; Ward 2016, 74, 107; but see Burger 2008, 188–9). Friends must also enjoy spending time together: as Aristotle claims, "nothing so much belongs to friends as living together" (2011, 1157b18). Although people can have an abstract feeling of goodwill towards those among whom they do not live, or at least not wish them any ill, they "are still not quite friends, because they do not pass their days together or delight in one another, the very things that especially seem to be marks of friendship" (1158a5–10).

From *polis* to Nation

Grant, although clearly drawing inspiration from them, goes beyond the ancients in important ways. The citizens of Canada, it seems, are not "friends" in the strict sense as are the citizens of Aristotle's *polis*. Canada boasts the second-largest land mass of the world's states and hosts a population of approximately 37 million. Canada, in other words, is a nation, not a *polis*. Thus it is impossible for each of its citizens to live together and spend a long time getting to know one another personally, let alone for each and every one to be good and strictly equal – all requirements for true friendship in the Aristotelian sense to emerge. Yet it is possible that Canadians live in an "imagined political community," rather than an objective one, and are held together through the bond of nationalism as a supplement to friendship in the Aristotelian sense. Thus we can turn to Benedict Anderson's *Imagined Communities* (1983) and his theory of the "imagined political community" as the locus of modern nationalism as an additional tool to help us understand Grant's thinking on Canada.

Anderson argues that a nation is *imagined* because most of its members, unlike the citizen friends of Aristotle's *polis*, will never even hear of or come into contact with one another, let alone get to know one another personally (Anderson 1983, 6). Yet despite this anonymity between members of a nation, Anderson asserts that "in the minds of each lives the image of their communion" (6). The nation is imagined as a *community*, according to Anderson, because regardless of the socio-political inequality and economic exploitation it might contain, its members nonetheless, like the citizen friends of Aristotle's *polis*, conceive among themselves a "deep, horizontal comradeship" (7). Moreover, it is this feeling of "fraternity" among members of a nation, Anderson argues, "that makes it possible, over the past two centuries, for so many millions of people, not so much to kill, as willingly to die for such ... imaginings" (7). Nationalism is identified with this attachment to, and willingness to sacrifice for, such an imagined political entity. In Anderson's thought, therefore, the emotive force of nationalism replaces the friendship of Aristotle's *polis*.

The nation, according to Anderson, is imagined as "inherently limited and sovereign" (6). By *limited* Anderson means that a nation is always conceived of by its members as finite, with borders beyond which lie other nations. Thus, Anderson claims, "the most messianic nationalists do not dream of a day when all the members of the human race will join their nation in the way that it was possible for Christians to dream of a wholly Christian planet" (7). That nations, for nationalists, are inherently particular or exclusive to some degree reminds us of Grant's hostility to the universal and homogeneous society that he believes is the modern, progressive ideal pursued by liberals. For those dedicated to the universal, homogeneous society, there is no place, according to

Grant, for "local cultures" such as Canada to which one can be loyal (2000, 53).

Another area in which Anderson's theory of nations and nationalism and Grant's thinking on Canada merge is the role of popular media. Anderson focuses on a concept he calls "print-capitalism" to explain the rise of imagined political communities known as nations in the age of enlightenment and revolution in sixteenth-, seventeenth-, and eighteenth-century Europe and America. Print-capitalism refers to the phenomenon of publishing houses in this era that sought to maximize their circulation and profit by printing their books and newspapers in the local vernacular. In addition to being a major contributor to the decline of Latin as a privileged, pan-European language, print-capitalism, Anderson argues, "quickly created large new reading publics – not least among merchants and women, who typically knew little or no Latin – and simultaneously mobilized them for politico-religious purposes" (1983, 40). Nations quickly grew up around these "monoglot mass reading publics" as access to literature and media in a common vernacular was the means through which anonymous members of these new linguistic communities imagined their communion with each other (41).

Grant, like Anderson, focuses on media, albeit publicly controlled media, as crucial to maintaining attachment to the nation. Yet despite their convergence with respect to the importance of national particularity and the role of the media, Grant's understanding of the Canadian nation and what love of it requires does differ slightly from Anderson's theory of nationalism. For instance, as we have seen, Anderson argues that the nation is imagined as "inherently limited and sovereign" (1983, 7). By *sovereign* Anderson means that members of nations believe they, the people of the nation, are the highest political authority, and cannot be legitimately constrained by a "divinely ordained, hierarchical dynastic realm" (7). Pushing throne and altar aside, nations, according to Anderson, "dream of being free, and, if under God, directly so" (7). To the Canadian nationalist such as Grant, however, "the British Crown was a symbol of a continuing loyalty to the state- less equivocal than was expected from republicans" (2000, 69). In response to analysts who would interpret such loyalty to the British Crown and to the Crown's country of origin as *anti-national* in the Canadian context or as an indication that Canada has never developed into a nation, Grant counters that he and other Canadians do not see it this way. Rather, loyalty to the British Crown is understood as "a relation to the font of constitutional government" and "a means of preserving at every level of our life – religious, educational, political, social – certain forms of existence that distinguish us from the United States" (70).

Byers: George Grant of the Twenty-first Century?

Michael Byers, as noted, wrote *Intent for a Nation* as a response to Grant's *Lament* (see Byers 2007, 11–16). Byers shares Grant's communitarian hostility to our American neighbours, and makes a case for a unique Canadian identity on the northern part of the continent. Yet Byers argues that America is not, as Grant maintains, a modern progressive republic, but a conservative, reactionary society whose nationalist tendencies cause it to reject a cosmopolitan outlook. Canadians, on the other hand, have adopted a modern, progressive perspective that sees their natural home in the international community.

In the following analysis, I turn to the examples of the roles Canada plays in peacekeeping and combatting climate change around the world as constituting the empirical part of my applied political theory approach. The centrality of Canada's involvement in the development of international humanitarian law and the practice of peacekeeping in the years after the Second World War, Byers argues, reveals its "civic," cosmopolitan character. For instance, Byers points to the fact that, in 1948, McGill University law professor John Humphrey helped to draft the Universal Declaration of Human Rights; in 1956 future prime minister Lester B. Pearson pioneered the concept of UN peacekeeping and won the Nobel Peace Prize for it in 1957; in 1994 Roméo Dallaire, commander of UN peacekeeping forces in Rwanda during the genocide, tried to persuade the UN Security Council to enforce the prohibition against genocide; in the 1990s Foreign Minister Lloyd Axworthy promoted and supported a multilateral treaty banning anti-personnel landmines and the creation of a new International Criminal Court; and in 2005 Louise Arbour, as the UN high commissioner for human rights, spoke publicly against what she believed was American disregard for the international ban on torture in the name of the "war on terror" (Byers 2007, 25–6).

Yet Canada's leadership of the international community in these crucial areas, Byers argues, has been seriously challenged by our partnership with America in its security-driven, militaristic response to the attacks of 11 September 2001. A key symptom of this threat to the cosmopolitan character of Canada's foreign policy is the developing distaste among the Canadian armed forces for peacekeeping missions in favour of "counterinsurgency," most recently exemplified in the war in Afghanistan that, for Canada, came to a close in 2011. Byers argues that within Canada's security policy and military communities, there is a strong feeling that despite Canada's tradition of participation in UN-led peacekeeping missions, Canadian forces no longer wish to be "peacekeepers" (2007, 49). Three reasons are commonly given for such growing distaste. First, in the new reality, "terrorism" is the main threat to international security, making "peacekeeping" outmoded as opposed to "counterinsurgency" missions. Second, US-led counterinsurgency missions promote "interoperability" with US forces on the military level and alignment with US, rather than UN, foreign policy priorities on the political level. The Canadian Forces, according to Byers, view missile defence as the height of interoperability with US forces. Interoperability at this level would be very expensive, requiring that the armed forces command more of the federal government's budget, thus making Canadian generals more powerful in politics in the process (75). Third, returning to the issue of peacekeeping, there is a feeling that it is "unmanly," or unsuitable for the Canadian Forces, which have a proud and noble fighting tradition in two world wars. According to Byers, "[t]he myth that 'peacekeeping is for wimps' originates in the United States, and it found ultimate expression in US secretary of state Condoleezza Rice's October 2000 comment, 'We don't need to have the 82nd Airborne escorting kids to kindergarten'" (49).

Like Grant, who yearns for Canadian independence from American foreign policy priorities, Byers argues that Canada should reverse this trend towards "counterinsurgency" and return to its traditional "peacekeeping" role, despite the supposed preferences of the current Canadian security policy and military communities. The practical manifestation of such a change, of course, would be the Canadian Forces' withdrawal from or non-entry into missions in Afghanistan, Iraq, or now Syria that seek to kill "terrorist" fighters, and their redeployment across the globe to prevent humanitarian crises such as genocide (see Robinson 2008, 486). Byers gives five important reasons for this return to Canada's traditional peacekeeping role in humanitarian missions. First, Canada's influence on the international stage is not enhanced and might even be diminished by the Canadian Forces' participation in US-led counterinsurgency missions. Canadian contingents, numbering a few thousand at most, are very small, and make little difference compared with the hundreds of thousands of US soldiers typically deployed in such missions. In contrast, leading UN peacekeeping missions in places and situations where the US military is unable or unwilling to go would allow Canada to "punch above our weight," as it were, making Canada a more indispensable country in the eyes of the international community (Byers 2007, 50).

Second, Canadian independence in foreign policy is made possible through peacekeeping, whereas counterinsurgency promotes interoperability of the Canadian military with that of the United States, with the result that Canadian foreign policy becomes subservient to Washington. According to Byers: "The mission in Afghanistan could … lead to the development of a Canadian Forces that is focused almost entirely – in its training, ethos and equipment – on aggressive missions conducted in concert with the United States. The long-term consequences of this would be significant, especially for Canadian foreign policy, since it would diminish our ability to conduct other kinds of missions, especially those not involving the United States" (2007, 51).

The third significant reason to reassess Canada's role in counterinsurgency is the security costs. According to Byers, participation in US-led operations in Afghanistan and the Middle East makes Canadian cities targets for "terrorists" (51). Moreover, such participation has led and will lead to further Canadian violations of international humanitarian law, weakening its strong commitment since the Second World War to this important field of endeavour. Finally and perhaps most significantly, Canadian self-identity is at stake. Byers argues that Canadians think of themselves as "global citizens" uniquely placed to promote global peace and respect for international law. Seek-and-destroy missions violate and perhaps alienate Canadians from this self-perception (52).

The move towards counterinsurgency and interoperability with US forces seems to vindicate Grant's claim that nations not in control of their economy lose control of their military and foreign policies as well. Ottawa, it seems, has become a satellite or branch plant of Washington. Byers argues that Canadians, whose love of country "is rooted in the non-economic compartments of our national psyche," should reverse this trend and regain independence from American foreign policy not simply by returning to peacekeeping, but more important by confronting the challenge of climate change (Byers 2007, 16; Robinson 2008, 486). Canadian nationalism can be revived by taking up this challenge, Byers implies, when he asks: "What better manifestation of an 'intent for a nation' could one imagine than joining the charge against the greatest global threat of our time?" (Byers 2007, 151).

The problem of climate change is of particular importance for Canada because Canada is an Arctic country. The effect of climate change on the

Arctic region, one-third of which is located in Canada, is greater than in other parts of the globe (Byers 2007, 136). For instance, Byers points out that the average annual temperature in the Arctic has increased twice as much as it has globally, and that the Arctic winter of 2005–6 was the warmest on record up to that time, with temperatures averaging 4–6 degrees Celsius higher than normal (132). Due to this rise in temperature, the 2004 Arctic Climate Impact Assessment found that the average extent of sea ice cover in the Arctic in the summer had declined by 10–15 per cent over the past thirty years, and that by the end of the twenty-first century there would be no sea ice in summer at all (Byers 2007, 129). The US National Snow and Ice Data Center had a more alarming report in 2006, warning that sea ice could disappear from the Arctic as soon as the summer of 2030 (129–30).

Confronting and reducing the potential dangers of climate change cannot be done by one country alone; rather, according to Byers, it is "a collective-action problem" that requires the cooperation of "hundreds of governments, thousands of stateless transnational corporations and billions of consumers relentlessly pursuing growth inside fossil-fuel based economies" (140). Yet given Canada's role as an Arctic nation in contributing to greenhouses gas emissions into the atmosphere, Byers argues that Canadians in particular have a strong ethical obligation to our fellow human beings, especially citizens in developing countries, and to future generations to act quickly and forcefully to reduce our "carbon footprint" (139). Such measures could include steeply graduated federal and provincial transportation taxes, including higher taxes on air travel, government-supported development of "green technologies" and a shift to a "green economy," raising taxes and royalty rates on "tar sands" projects in Alberta, the introduction of stringent federal caps on industrial carbon emissions, and the development of a carbon credit trading, or "cap-and-trade," system (143–4).

Despite Canadians' unique obligation to the planet, Byers claims that both Liberal and Conservative federal governments have a dismal record on confronting climate change or reducing Canada's emissions of carbon dioxide (144–8). The reason for this failure is Canadian governments' desire to export more of our non-renewable fossil fuels to the United States. Since 1990 Canada typically has exported approximately $30 billion worth of energy to the United States annually, and the economic and political concerns surrounding such exportation has thus far trumped climate change concerns (145). Byers thus suggests that Canadians need to rethink the economic, social, and political status of the oil and gas industry. Like Grant, who believes that American multinational corporations with branch plants in central Canada are the cause of the disappearance of Canadian national independence, Byers focuses on American oil and gas industries located in western Canada as the main obstacle to the revival of a Canadian nationalism that otherwise would assume global leadership in confronting climate change.

An applied political theory approach that includes reflection on the work of both Grant and Byers shows that Canadian political theory has important insights for the world about nationalism. The Canadian experience, as theorized by Grant and Byers, illustrates that nationalism might require a critique of free trade and the world market – that there is a potential conflict between global capitalism and national independence. Also, Canadian nationalism, as articulated by Grant and Byers, can teach the world that nationalism need not be exclusive and insular. Grant's reflections on English-Canadian nationalism show that a communitarianism that recognizes internal nations, such as English Canada's recognition of the group rights of *Québécois*, can be a part of nationalism. Canadian nationalism in this sense is open and flexible. Byers's application of political theory in his discussion of peacekeeping and especially Canada's unique role in the problem and resolution of climate change shows that nationalism can also comprehend a cosmopolitanism that looks to the good of the planet. Canada, as an Arctic country, affects all other nations, and must take the lead in a global effort to reduce the effects of climate change. In taking care of itself, Canada can take care of the world.

REFERENCES

Anderson, Benedict. 1983. *Imagined Communities: Reflections on the Origins and Spread of Nationalism*. London: Verso.

Aristotle. 1984. *Politics*. Trans. Carnes Lord. Chicago: University of Chicago Press.

Aristotle. 2011. *Nicomachean Ethics*. Trans. Robert C. Bartlett and Susan D. Collins. Chicago: University of Chicago Press.

Bradshaw, Leah. 1991. "Political Rule, Prudence and the 'Woman Question' in Aristotle." *Canadian Journal of Political Science* 24 (3): 557–73. https://doi.org/10.1017/S0008423900022691

Bradshaw, Leah. 1996. "Love and Will in the Miracle of Birth: An Arendtian Critique of George Grant on Abortion." In *George Grant and the Subversion of Modernity: Art, Philosophy, Politics, Religion, and Education*, ed. Arthur Davis, 220–42. Toronto: University of Toronto Press. https://doi.org/10.3138/9781442675261-013

Burger, Ronna. 2008. *Aristotle's Dialogue with Socrates: On the Nicomachean Ethics*. Chicago: University of Chicago Press. https://doi.org/10.7208/chicago/9780226080543.001.0001

Byers, Michael. 2007. *Intent for a Nation: What is Canada For? A Relentlessly Optimistic Manifesto for Canada's Role in the World*. Vancouver: Douglas & McIntyre.

Cooper, Barry. 1978. "*A imperio usque ad imperium*: The Political Thought of George Grant." In *George Grant in Process: Essays and Conversations*, ed. Larry Schmidt, 23–39. Toronto: Anansi.

Cooper, John M. 1999. *Reason and Emotion: Essays on Ancient Moral Psychology and Ethical Theory*. Princeton, NJ: Princeton University Press.

Forbes, Hugh Donald. 2007. *George Grant: A Guide to His Thought*. Toronto: University of Toronto Press. https://doi.org/10.3138/9781442684379

Grant, George. 2000. *Lament for a Nation. The Defeat of Canadian Nationalism*. Montreal; Kingston, ON: McGill-Queen's University Press.

Greenspan, Louis. 1996. "The Unravelling of Liberalism." In *George Grant and the Subversion of Modernity: Art, Philosophy, Politics, Religion, and Education*, ed. Arthur Davis, 201–19. Toronto: University of Toronto Press. https://doi.org/10.3138/9781442675261-012

Havers, Grant. 2006. "Leo Strauss's Influence on George Grant." In *Athens and Jerusalem: George Grant's Theology, Philosophy, and Politics*, ed. Ian Angus, Ron Dart, and Randy Peg Peters, 124–35. Toronto: University of Toronto Press.

Homiak, M.L. 2002. "Feminism and Aristotle's Rational Ideal." In *Feminism & History of Philosophy*, ed. Genevieve Lloyd, 3–20. Oxford: Oxford University Press.

LaSelva, Samuel V. 2007. "To Begin the World Anew: Pierre Trudeau's Dream and George Grant's Canada." In *A Living Tree: The Legacy of 1982 in Canada's Political Evolution*, ed. Graeme Mitchell, Ian Peach, David E. Smith, and John Donaldson Whyte, 1–30. Regina: Saskatchewan Institute of Public Policy.

Mathie, William. 1978. "The Technological Regime: George Grant's Analysis of Modernity." In *George Grant in Process: Essays and Conversations*, ed. Larry Schmidt, 157–66. Toronto: Anansi.

Muggeridge, John. 1978. "George Grant's Anguished Conservatism." In *George Grant in Process: Essays and Conversations*, ed. Larry Schmidt, 40–8. Toronto: Anansi.

Pakaluk, Michael. 1998. *Aristotle: Nicomachean Ethics Books VIII and IX*. Oxford: Clarendon Press.

Reimer, James A. 1978. "George Grant: Liberal, Socialist, or Conservative?" In *George Grant in Process: Essays and Conversations*, ed. Larry Schmidt, 49–60. Toronto: Anansi.

Robinson, Paul. 2008. "Review of *Intent for a Nation: What is Canada For? A Relentlessly Optimistic Manifesto for Canada's Role in the World*." *International Journal* (Toronto) 63 (2): 485–7. https://doi.org/10.1177/002070200806300217

Saxonhouse, Arlene. 1991. "Aristotle: Defective Males, Hierarchy, and the Limits of Politics." In *Feminist Interpretations and Political Theory*, ed. Mary Lyndon Shanley and Carole Patemen, 31–52. University Park: Pennsylvania State University Press.

Schollmeier, Paul. 1994. *Other Selves: Aristotle on Personal and Political Friendship*. Albany: State University of New York Press.

Sokolon, Marlene K. 2006. *Political Emotions: Aristotle and the Symphony of Reason and Emotion*. DeKalb: Northern Illinois University Press.

Stern-Gillet, Suzanne. 1995. *Aristotle's Philosophy of Friendship*. Albany: State University of New York Press.

Tessitore, Aristide. 1996. *Reading Aristotle's Ethics: Virtue, Rhetoric, and Political Philosophy*. Albany: State University of New York Press.

Ward, Ann. 2016. *Contemplating Friendship in Aristotle's Ethics*. Albany: State University of New York Press.

16 Culture and National Identity in Quebec

RAFFAELE IACOVINO

It is challenging to squeeze an overview of the impact of Quebec on political thought in Canada into a single chapter. It is even more difficult to conceive of a project devoted to examining Canadian political philosophy without acknowledging the sheer volume and depth of normative theorizing stimulated by the movement for national affirmation in Quebec. Indeed the salience of Quebec as a particularly puzzling case lies precisely in its inclination to force observers of social and political life in Canada to account for conceptual anomalies. I employ the term "anomalies" consciously, because I want to imply that the significance of Quebec stems from an unrelenting narrative of fundamental constitutive contestation *despite* the restrictive framework of both formal institutions and prevailing moral doctrines. To state it bluntly, understanding social and political phenomena around the terms of belonging in Quebec means following the normative debates.

From a methodological perspective, applied political theory is an attractive approach in studying national and sociocultural pluralism in Quebec, and in the context of its place in Canada. The relative comfort of empirical and/or comparative analysis on the one hand, and detached abstract and universal theorizing on the other, find a meeting point of sorts in Quebec precisely because what Sujit Choudhry has dubbed "constitutive constitutional politics" (2005, 938) entails accounting for contingencies and contextual nuances related to the negotiation of existential contentions that tend to shatter the notion of a settled and consensual political community. It is within this ambiguous space – through a constant (re)examination of the sources of legitimacy around the individual and collective terms of belonging to both Quebec and the larger associative community as bounded and competing communities of reference – that Quebec as a "hard case" invites a combination of empirical and theoretical investigation on subjects as varied as the nature of sovereignty, democratic boundaries, normative reflections on federalism and constitutionalism, the place of national identity and national pluralism in liberal thought, cultural pluralism and secularism, and so on.

Using an applied political theory framework, this chapter looks at one part of the puzzle: the ongoing tensions in Quebec around the question of the limits of cultural pluralism and, by extension, the implications of this introspection on Quebec's self-conception as a nation. I begin by examining the writings of contemporary Canadian theorists of liberal pluralism such as Michel Seymour, Will Kymlicka, and Charles Taylor. I then analyse the empirical case studies of the Bouchard-Taylor Commission and the Charter of Quebec Values by applying the theoretical reflections outlined above. The argument I want to make is that Canadian political thought in relation to Quebec is grappling with a particular impasse between acknowledging the moral primacy of universal or civic conceptions of liberal justice, coupled with a commitment to pluralism, *and* Quebec's need to affirm itself as a distinct "political subject" – as a legitimating exercise in the pursuit of recognition as a self-determining collective agent. This fundamental dialectic is sustained by a particular context where the terms of belonging must account for the fact that Quebec is a minority nation whose deliberations are constrained by an associative community that controls the formal levers of citizenship. As such, if one asks the question that lies at the heart of the matter – what does it mean to belong in Quebec? – the answer will always be tinged with political considerations. It can never be grounded in a sort of abstract moral reasoning that provides for normative boundaries, because those boundaries themselves are ambiguous, contested, and subject to historical contingencies.

A little more on this point is in order. In Quebec, a society that is not formally constituted, these debates always include qualifications, sometimes implicit, that justify or explain why Quebec is having these debates in the first place. This necessarily involves considerations pertaining to Quebec's internal political sociology *as well as* the terms of its incorporation into the larger national referential space. As such, Quebec is constantly engaged in exercises around the formulation of *balises* – markers of collective identity that give meaning to a political project for national affirmation – and normative considerations inevitably will be measured against a ready-made alternative. Most nation-states do not require explicit justification for affirming their status as a host society or as a referential political space within which the markers of citizenship are considered.

Who gets to determine the terms of belonging for citizens in Quebec, and how has Quebec addressed the "who" part and the "terms of belonging" part simultaneously? This rudimentary characterization of enduring normative debates associated with Quebec's aspiration for national recognition, along with its actual initiatives for national affirmation, has resulted in the flourishing of a distinct body of political thought that seeks to frame justificatory schemes around concrete cases, rather than free-standing, abstract theory based on hypothetical choice scenarios, where collective conceptions of the "good" are clearly demarcated from the sorts of "rights" that underpin liberal justice (Dworkin 1978; Rawls 1971).[1] The explicit crafting or forging of the terms of belonging has positioned Quebec as a catalyst of sorts for the flourishing of an approach to theorizing that attributes normative force to observable contingencies associated with political sociology (Choudhry 2002, 56).[2] Above all, minority nations seek to be invested with a constituent power of their own, and the way they embody this claim in contention and negotiation with the state will vary depending on the character of this social and political mobilization as well as particular institutional possibilities and constraints. As Veit Bader

1 Although I cite Dworkin and Rawls as authoritative figures here, I want to avoid getting into a drawn-out overview of the literature on liberal conceptions of justice and its challengers. I only want to emphasize that grasping the tenor of Quebec's deliberations around national identity and citizenship involves a basic questioning of abstract reasoning that is unrooted in time and space and universal in its normative prescriptions. Indeed the notion that Quebec's particular existential quandary cannot be settled by recourse to universal principles applies to a wide range of political doctrines, including certain forms of republican thought, cosmopolitanism, and, to cite a frequent target of Quebec intellectuals, Habermasian "constitutional patriotism."

2 For a thorough formulation of this contextual turn in political theory, see Carens (2004, 118): "A contextual approach to political theory has five interrelated elements. First, it involves the use of examples to illustrate theoretical formulations. Second, it entails the normative exploration of actual cases where the fundamental concerns addressed by the theory are in play. Third, it leads theorists to pay attention to the question of whether their theoretical formulations are actually compatible with the normative positions that they themselves take on particular issues. Fourth, it includes a search for cases that are especially challenging to the theorists own theoretical position. Fifth, it promotes consideration of a wide range of cases, and especially a search for cases that are unfamiliar and illuminating because of their unfamiliarity."

contends, a satisfactory evaluative framework in such a complex setting must balance moral, ethico-political, prudential, and realist criteria, and this broader approach necessitates a contextual approach to political theory (Bader and Engelen 2003; Bader and Saharso 2004).

To begin with, it is worth reiterating that debates about the liberal-pluralist "credentials" of the affirmation and recognition of the Quebec nation must be situated appropriately within the framework of a distinct and clearly delineated national integration project in Canada. This provides the larger context. As Guy Laforest notes in regards to Quebec's recent internal deliberations around cultural pluralism, it is difficult to conceive of an authentic dialogue between the francophone majority and cultural minorities in Quebec in a formal setting that fails to recognize Quebec's status as a majoritarian political space – a host society confident in its capacity to engage in setting the parameters of this internal dialogue (2010, 137).[3] Michel Seymour makes a similar argument, adding that tensions around the perceived affront to equality engendered by the recognition of "accommodation practices" for cultural and religious minorities can only be inflamed in a larger setting where claims of national affirmation and recognition in Quebec are denied. For Seymour, Quebec's path to pluralism must confront its constitutional status: "Si le peuple québécois pouvait être reconnu et être en mesure de s'affirmer comme peuple, il pourrait être plus conciliant et ouvert à l'égard du pluralisme" [If the people of Quebec were recognized as such and affirmed as a people, they would be more open and conciliatory towards pluralism] (2010, my translation). For these Quebec theorists, Canada's brand of liberal citizenship thus subsumes the regulation of cultural relations altogether and cannot be set aside in examining developments that are internal to Quebec.

Canada not only serves as an institutional "constraint" on Quebec; it also represents somewhat of an ideational standard-bearer of the sorts of modern, liberal-universalist, and pluralist prescriptions for the forging of thin, or even "post-national" communal attachments that reject the rootedness provided by majority cultures – or indeed dismiss the integrative public salience of culture altogether as morally excessive.

3 Laforest clearly qualifies this observation, however, by explicitly noting that this contextual setting does not license the francophone majority in Quebec to forgo a commitment to ethical obligations in its deliberations around majority-minority relations.

The primary architect of this forging of a collective identity meant to bind citizens in Canada by way of universal markers and a shared conception of justice was Pierre Trudeau, who entered the prime minister's office having already formulated clear ideas about the potential value of a shared conception of justice (Norman 2001, 150) to combat forces of fragmentation.[4] Indeed, as Yves Couture contends (2014, 21), this injection of liberal neutrality as the lynchpin of an emergent Canadian identity from the late 1960s onwards constituted a laboratory for the formulation of a new kind of nation that would represent a clean break from the grip of established sociological forces – in particular, Quebec nationalism. In short, Trudeau sought to lift Canadian citizens up from the shackles of particular collective identities, which he believed were grounded in reactionary politics and emotionalism, and to inject a transcendent framework for belonging based on reason and rationality, which could be thin and conducive to a consensus wide enough to be shared across the country and form the foundations for a new marker of Canadian identity. This was Trudeau's appeal for a "Just Society." Without delving too deeply into the particulars of Trudeau's thought, it would become clear in his political prescriptions and subsequent victories that the only legitimate sources of communal attachments for Canadians would be grounded in universal conceptions of individual equality, meant to transcend particular allegiances and in effect circumscribe Canada as the community of reference. In light of the salience of context described above, Quebec's orientations thus not only must confront the moral weight of universal conceptions of liberal justice and cultural pluralism, but an actual, real-world ready-made alternative that has always called for an applied political theory approach, as developed in this volume. These competing national integration projects are inherently normative exercises.

Indeed, Trudeau's major constitutive contributions – the constitutional entrenchment of a Charter of Rights and Freedoms, multiculturalism within a bilingual framework, and a strict adherence to an equality-of-provinces doctrine – all reflect a strong commitment to rejecting perceived threats to the unity of Canada by collective identities that sought recognition as majoritarian communities. Even the

4 For a concise and cogent overview of Trudeau's political thought, see Brooks, Bickerton, and Gagnon (2003). For an authoritative examination of Trudeau's impact on the Canadian constitutional order, see Laforest (1995).

form of cultural pluralism adopted by Canadian multiculturalism was grounded in the undifferentiated recognition of constituent ethnocultural groups (Gagnon and Iacovino 2007). Culture was dissociated from language and the notion of distinct historical cultural majorities as recognized parties to a consensual pact came to be supplanted by the ideal of a single, bilingual nation (McRoberts 2004) buttressed by a rights-bearing citizenry.

~

Trudeau's victory in establishing a vision for Canada meant that options in Quebec henceforth would be evaluated against an existing blueprint that institutionalized universal conceptions of a liberal-pluralist consensus. On the surface, Quebec's rejection of this "Trudeau template" looked very much like it was rejecting a perfectly legitimate and justifiable framework for citizenship. How could one argue against the equality and freedom provided by the Charter of Rights and Freedoms? How could one reject an attempt to inject Canada with more French through official bilingualism? And how could one dismiss the benefits of a model of cultural pluralism that had history on its side and was well suited to an immigrant-receiving society that was trying to find its way? The Trudeau template, in other words, represented a project for political modernization that sought to validate and respond to the underlying liberal, democratic and progressive ambitions of the architects of the Quiet Revolution. It was a social and political emancipatory project meant to incorporate the emerging sociopolitical orientations of Quebec itself.

What Quebec's resistance to the Trudeau template came to reveal, however, was that communal attachments grounded in universal principles cannot take hold in a vacuum – they are rooted in the particular histories, institutions, identities, and cultures of constituted communities of reference. Neo-nationalists in Quebec had their own ideas for carrying out a project for political modernization, and would not simply cede this terrain to Canada. Indeed liberalism could not account for the boundaries of national identity and curtail the mobilization for collective recognition and self-determination under way in Quebec. As Norman (2001, 108–9) observes:

> It is noteworthy that when Rawls himself is claiming that justice is the first virtue of social institutions, such that it cannot be sacrificed for other goods, he is explicitly talking about a conception of justice based on

> individual rights. He is not claiming that whatever you end up calling a matter of justice, it is ipso facto the first virtue of social institutions! It is quite likely that many of the institutional changes that are debated in the constitutional politics of multination states are more or less neutral in terms of their impact on the basic civil and political rights of individual citizens ... It matters not just that one's state is just, but also that it is one's state, the state one can identify with.

Some collective identities simply want to have the right to establish the terms of social cooperation without interference. Quebec thus rejected Canadian multiculturalism, yet it clearly had moved its discourse in the direction of cultural pluralism. It rejected Canadian bilingualism based on individual choice – or the "personality principle" (Cardinal 2010) – yet recognized that the English-speaking community in Quebec ought to enjoy historical collective rights. Quebec rejected the Charter of Rights and Freedoms, yet had enacted its own charter seven years earlier. The story came to be characterized by the coexistence of liberal-pluralist frameworks as the basis for national integration projects.

This growing critique of the Trudeau template prompted a body of thought among Canadians that sought to reconcile liberalism with the challenges posed by minority nationalism. To select a couple of the more prominent normative contributions, Will Kymlicka and Charles Taylor thus began to question whether liberal neutrality is suitable to meet the challenges posed by minority nations. Kymlicka, for example, elaborates a very influential theoretical proposition that begins with the premise that, since liberal states can never be culturally neutral, universal conceptions of liberal justice as the basis for communal attachments will always privilege the culture of the majority in public life. States always privilege certain languages, interpretations of history, cultural symbols, public holidays, and so on. As such the capacity for individuals to exercise autonomy in formulating and revising their own conceptions of the good are always undertaken within particular "contexts of choice" provided by cultural identity. Although this has resulted in an attempt to justify access to one's culture as a primary right – to approach cultural pluralism through a liberal emphasis on the value of individual autonomy – Kymlicka goes further to argue that minority nations as a distinct conceptual category constitute "societal cultures," defined as a "culture which provides its members with meaningful ways of life across the full range of human activities" (Kymlicka 1995, 76), and thus ought to be granted self-government rights as a safeguard against the power of the majority culture to define and impose the terms of belonging.

For his part, Taylor introduces the notion of "deep diversity,"[5] a more robust position that shows less concern with rights and more with the salience of cultural identity in providing meaning and a sense of belonging for individuals. It is within a cultural or national community that individuals engage in a journey of self-interpretation and identity-formation. One's sense of self is thus intricately embedded in a collective dialogue that takes place within a particular community. For Taylor, minority nations can legitimately promote certain substantive goods associated with the protection and flourishing of their collective identity that trump a strict procedural adherence to universal individual rights as long as fundamental freedoms are not compromised. Indeed the liberal state can justifiably "weigh the importance of certain forms of universal treatment against the importance of cultural survival, and opt sometimes in favour of the latter" (1992, 61). Without getting bogged down in a protracted discussion of Taylor's attempt to bridge the liberal-communitarian divide, for our purposes he simply makes the claim that certain variations of liberalism that institutionalize collective conceptions of the good are not only legitimate but desirable, particularly if the alternative is to impose a set of difference-blind procedural safeguards for individuals as the basis for communal attachments. Again, what gives shape to individual self-realization are the sorts of meanings that are embedded in one's cultural membership. Quebec's project for national affirmation, to the extent that it draws on a more robust reference to culture and language, should not be taken as a force that undermines liberal citizenship in Canada; rather, its challenge is to force Canadians to see beyond the Trudeau template and accept that liberalism can take a variety of particular forms that might be more appropriate in meeting the historical and sociological challenges confronting a minority nation.

---

5 First-level diversity refers to differences in cultural membership and background, yet a shared conception of belonging – something like the undifferentiated cultural pluralism of Canadian multiculturalism. "Deep" diversity, in contrast, accepts that individuals might belong to Canada through some constituent community on different terms. Taylor seeks to show that Canada requires the adoption of deep diversity, because first-order diversity does not meet the demands of Quebecers and Indigenous peoples to belong to the associative community through the assertion of a different set of moral considerations.

Both of these important and very influential prescriptive accounts of the Canada-Quebec imbroglio reflect an approach to reconciling liberalism with robust conceptions of national identity that rests on what Michel Seymour calls the "structure of culture," which he contrasts with the actual "character of culture" (Seymour 2008). Liberalism can take hold among a wide variety of majority cultural settings through distinct institutional guideposts that should not be confused with particular cultural mores in a particular time and place. How do we determine, however, which rights are fundamental and which are linked to the well-being of the collective, and how do we reconcile this with a commitment to first-order diversity and, hypothetically, the infringement of certain individual rights? Moreover, Kymlicka offers an account of societal cultures as institutionally complete contexts for the flourishing of individual autonomy, yet does not account for a basic shortcoming: if liberal autonomy rests with membership in a societal culture, then why should the context provided by the minority nation be privileged as the site of self-government rights? Alternative and, in the case of Canada, existing societal cultures might make equally legitimate claims to delineating the boundaries of citizenship. Individuals can navigate through a variety of available contexts of choice – including those provided by the larger Canadian national integration project or even within their own ancestral cultures as a sort of denunciation of the referential claims of the minority nation. Indeed Taylor simply assumes that Quebec exists as the community of reference for its citizens, yet through the concept of deep diversity he does not explore adequately how Quebec ought to address the question of recognition of the place of minority ethnocultural groups within its own conception of the nation. These contributions go a long way to providing justifications for recognizing a plurality of collective contexts for the flourishing of liberal polities, yet they do not explicitly explore the relationship between coexisting cultural contexts.

As such, critics of multiculturalism in Quebec point to Kymlicka's use of a "silo" analogy to demarcate clearly a set of collective rights for national minorities from those afforded to ethnocultural communities as a false dichotomy. Collective identity claims cannot simply be categorized as qualitatively distinct, with a neat separation of bundles of rights, since attempts to regulate the place of culture by the larger associative community inevitably will undermine the capacity of the minority nation to forge its own collective markers. In other words, the debate in Quebec is always conditioned by the fact that Canadian citizenship is tied to Canadian multiculturalism. The main thrust of this view from Quebec thus rests on the basic idea that the imposition of Canadian multiculturalism, even if accompanied by some moderate political concessions through traditional federative instruments, will always undermine Quebec's capacity to act as a host society, prompting repeated calls for a recognition of the primacy of the Quebec nation as a constitutive pillar that supersedes multiculturalism as a uniform doctrine: recognizing a multinational polity, premised on the coexistence of societal cultures as a "structural" fact, must come prior to multiculturalism as a constitutive pillar.

This emphasis on the structure of culture as a particular subject for recognition does not reveal much about how Quebec has debated these questions internally. Indeed figuring out a particular status for an internal nation and digging deep to see how that nation is dealing with some of these tensions is another area where Quebec has contributed much to the Canadian conversation. These debates – in particular, about how Quebec has struggled to address the status of the majority culture – recently have been the source of a widespread societal discussion in Quebec.

~

Following an applied political theory approach, in this section I empirically examine the recent tensions in Quebec around the "reasonable accommodations" debate that culminated in the Commission de consultation sur les pratiques d'accommodement reliées aux différences culturelles (Bouchard and Taylor 2008) and the short-lived introduction of a Charter of Quebec Values. It is here that the formulation of Quebec's own model of cultural pluralism – interculturalism – represents an alternative path to reconciling the nation with broader moral principles. At the heart of these tensions lies the question of the status of the majority culture as a structuring agent. To reiterate, the tensions associated with navigating through this question involve not only considerations associated with prevailing norms, but also the fact that there is a ready-made civic alternative alongside Quebec's own collective project. Indeed one of the defining traits of multinational states is precisely that "what is at stake is how one defines the subject of democratic citizenship" (Resnick 2001, 284). Ongoing normative deliberations in Quebec thus emphasize the meaning and structuring capacity of the relevant political subject, and it is to these debates that I now turn.

Prior to examining Quebec's model of interculturalism, I want to emphasize that one point of consensus in Quebec's national integration project has been the primacy of French as the common public language and respect for Quebec's liberal-democratic institutions – or its civic legal infrastructure. Although the discussion that follows will highlight some persistent areas of contestation in formulating a response to cultural pluralism, these two features have been less controversial. Quebec's adherence to the provisions outlined in the Charter of the French Language, enacted in 1977, remain remarkably consistent. The Charter provides that French is the official language of Quebec: "the language of Government and the Law, as well as the normal and everyday language of work, instruction, communication, commerce and business."[6] The Charter has become a powerful symbol of social and political integration and the consolidation of national identity. English-language public schooling was made available only to children whose parents or siblings already had received English-language instruction in Canada, effectively ensuring that newcomers would be integrated through the French-language stream. It also established a series of francization initiatives, and tightened regulations of commercial activities to ensure the prominence of French in the private sector, including restrictions on the use of public signs in languages other than French.

With regards to the elaboration and scope of Quebec's model of interculturalism, it must be emphasized that it has never been the subject of actual legislative enactment – there is no "interculturalism act" – nor, in contrast to multiculturalism, does the model enjoy constitutional entrenchment. Interculturalism's actual relevance and singularity are the source of continuing debate in Quebec (Rocher et al. 2007). It has for the most part constituted a blueprint of sorts, articulated through a variety of policy statements that have changed over time and through interpretations by intellectuals and policy practitioners. As such, some have construed the intercultural model as either qualitatively distinct from multiculturalism or a simple replication with certain semantic nuances. Most of the more substantive normative debates, however, centre on defining the place of the majority culture in circumscribing public life, and it is this particular feature of the model that most clearly distinguishes it from Canadian multiculturalism. In affirming itself as a host society – as an autonomous subject of cultural policy – Quebec in effect has asserted that the terms of belonging cannot be left to the

6 See "Charter of the French Language," available online at http://www.legisquebec.gouv.qc.ca/en/showdoc/cs/C-11.

larger associative community because of its failure to recognize the collective agency of a majority culture. For Taylor, an implicit characteristic of interculturalism is that it is meant for a distinct national "story,"[7] in contrast to multiculturalism, which effectively fills an identity void following the retreat of its British connection due to demographic changes. This "dethroning of an anglo-normative understanding" (Taylor 2012, 417) effectively strips citizenship of particular cultural moorings. Interculturalism, in contrast, applies to a society still constituted by a large majority of francophones that do not seek a wholesale reformulation of their collective status. Moreover, its subject is a community whose language and culture are under constant threat as a small minority in an overwhelmingly English-speaking environment, and the struggle to overcome assimilation in this setting has for long been a source of pride and attachment. In Taylor's words:

> the story can't simply be a carbon-copy of the Canadian one. What does it look like? Something like this. Quebec society has been engaged in a long-term project not only to survive as a francophone society but to flourish; and, indeed, to flourish as a democratic society based on equality and human rights. We invite those who come here from outside to join us (those already there) in this project as full members, which means, of course, learning the language and becoming integrated into the society. But we invite them to become full members of this society, with a say like all the others, whose views and contributions count as much as those of native born. We are indeed eager to benefit from the skills and insights that they bring to us from outside. So the contrast is clear: the "multi" story decentres the traditional ethno-historical identity and refuses to put any other in its place. All such identities coexist in the society, but none is officialized. The "inter" story starts from the reigning historical identity but sees it evolving in a process in which all citizens, of whatever identity, have a voice, and no-one's input has a privileged status. (2012, 418)

Again, Taylor proceeds to defend Quebec's approach by assuming the existence of a constituted political community, in an attempt to

7 Taylor dismisses the notion that this is merely a semantic difference that represents a cynical attempt by successive Quebec governments to reject the symbolic salience of multiculturalism.

pre-empt critics who view his preferred model of cultural pluralism as a form of multiculturalism simply to be superimposed on Quebec. He categorically concedes that Quebec requires its own model, yet disregards the very real normative and sociological forces that prevent Quebec from elaborating its own approach without hindrance. The notion of simply assuming that Quebec's particular attributes are sufficient in demarcating a community of reference around a "reigning historical identity" has not in itself quelled the very real tensions inherent in simultaneously affirming a constitutive status for the majority culture while embracing cultural pluralism. Since its early formulations, the place of culture within the model has vacillated between two broad normative paradigms (Iacovino and Sévigny 2011). First, in its early formulations, the model emphasized a "culture of convergence" (Quebec 1981) – an attempt to reach out to cultural communities in a period of strained relations following Quebec's referendum on secession in 1980 – which explicitly recognized the primacy of the nation of Quebec as a *foyer de convergence* in delimiting the public sphere, with the majority culture serving as its "principal motor" (Labelle 2008, 24). Critics of the model's tendency to create a hierarchy of cultures, however, could later turn to a counterweight in a conception of the model based on the forging of a "common public culture" (Quebec 1990). This initiative, often taken as the most authoritative treatment of interculturalism to this day, represents a more pluralist and culturally neutral turn whereby the majority would engage in a "moral contract" with newcomers to ensure integration through a reciprocal engagement that eventually leads to a more consensual "fusion" of cultures. The narrative of a contract was explicit – members of minority cultures were expected to participate without shedding their cultural identities, through a commitment to the French language and a recognition of the majority culture, while the host society was tasked with ensuring that support and resources were made available for such ends. The model thus dropped the notion of a pre-existing and permanent pole of convergence, and accepted that a public culture would be the result of a hybridization of cultural influences.

These two broad outlines continue to frame the debate to this day, reflecting the basic tension between a turn to pluralism while anchoring the community of reference through the recognition of a historical majority culture. The final report of the Bouchard-Taylor Commission, in reiterating the main principles of interculturalism and recommending that the model be strengthened through legislation, opted for the adoption of its more pluralist variant, the defining features of which are as follows:

1) Québec as a nation, as recognized by all Québec political parties and the federal government, is the operational framework for interculturalism.
2) In a spirit of reciprocity, interculturalism strongly emphasizes interaction, in particular intercommunity action, with a view to overcoming stereotypes and defusing fear or rejection of the Other, taking advantage of the enrichment that stems from diversity, and benefiting from social cohesion.
3) Members of the majority ethnocultural group, i.e., Quebecers of French-Canadian origin, like the members of ethnocultural minorities, accept that their culture will be transformed sooner or later through interaction.
4) Cultural, and, in particular, religious differences need not be confined to the private domain. The following logic underpins this choice: it is healthier to display our differences and get to know those of the Other than to deny or marginalize them.
5) The principle of multiple identities is recognized, as is the right to maintain an affiliation with one's ethnic group.
6) For those citizens who so wish, it is desirable for initial affiliations to survive, since ethnic groups of origin often act as mediators between their members and society as a whole. A general phenomenon arises in this regard: almost without exception, each citizen integrates into society through a milieu or an institution that serves as a link, e.g. the family, a profession, a community group, a church, an association.
7) Multilingualism is encouraged at the same time as French as the common public language. The debate that opposes the language of identity and the common language (as a simple communication tool) is hardly promising. What is important, first and foremost, is the broadest possible dissemination of French.
8) To facilitate the integration of immigrants and their children, it is useful to provide them with the means to preserve their mother tongue, at least at the outset. This helps them to mitigate the shock of immigration by affording them a cultural anchor. It is also a means of preserving the enrichment that stems from cultural diversity.
9) Constant interaction between citizens of different origins leads to the development of a new identity and a new culture. This is what has been happening in Québec in recent decades without altering the cultural position of the majority group or infringing on the culture of minority groups.

10) Under a recent, highly promising orientation from the standpoint of pluralism, the groups present in Québec define themselves with reference to common, often universal, values stemming from their history rather than their ethnic traits. Québec is thus part of an international trend whereby societies choose to integrate diversity in light of shared values.
11) The civic and legal dimensions (and everything that concerns, in particular, non-discrimination) must be regarded as fundamental in interculturalism. (Bouchard and Taylor 2008, 40–2)

Rather than result in an anticipated closure, the commission's description of interculturalism instead prompted a public debate that looked a lot like it did before – with each intervenor interpreting interculturalism differently due to ambiguities inherent in the model – as well as virtual silence from political actors (Rocher and Labelle 2008). As Rocher and Labelle remind us, an appeal to universal values and cultural pluralism was always going to fail to address the very real political sources of these social tensions around collective identity. Even when the commissioners paid heed to Quebec's status as a minority nation and assumed it was the appropriate site for these measures, they framed it as a sort of "psycho-social" collective anxiety or malaise that could be "overcome" simply by adopting an effective framework to regulate social relations. For Rocher and Labelle, any initiatives that seek to assert the primacy of interculturalism begin to look a lot like multiculturalism unless they situate interculturalism within a formal-legal conception of citizenship, in order to clearly differentiate the project from the structuring effects of Canadian citizenship. In another piece, Labelle explicitly promotes Quebec citizenship: "ce pacte civique n'est ni neutre ni abstrait comme on tend à le lui reprocher. Bien que plusieurs de ses éléments caractérisent les démocraties libérales, il porte la marque de combats particuliers dans le contexte du Québec: la langue française, la reconnaissance politique et culturelle, etc. Son universalité s'incarne donc au sein d'une nation particulière qui doit défendre et redéfinir les marqueurs historiques de sa spécificité" [this civil pact is neither as neutral or abstract as some criticize. While several of its elements are characteristic of liberal democracies, it is marked by the particular battles of Quebec: the French language, political and cultural recognition, etc. Its universality is created within particular nation that has to defend and redefine the historical markers of its specificity] (Labelle 2008, 42, my translation). Unless the model performs this dual task, the regulation of social relations will never transcend a culturalist script, because it will always be framed as a struggle between majority and minority cultures within a larger civic referential space.

The ramifications of a turn to pluralism in Quebec on the future of the collective political project is not a new debate. Quebec intellectuals have long made explicit the link between Quebec's foray into sociocultural integration and a wider political project for national affirmation. Even wide-ranging prescriptive accounts that either wholeheartedly embrace identity pluralism or reject it altogether as an affront to the political ambitions of a cultural majority must account for the ambiguities relating to Quebec's present status. Jocelyn Maclure contends that minority nations contesting the uniformity and homogenization of majority national integration projects can do so without recourse to a substantive cultural identity meant to supersede others. As such, the political subject in Quebec has been, and ought to continue to be, defined as pluralist in its normative orientations. For Maclure, this is a permanent feature of our era, and a retreat from the public recognition of constituted identities would signal a step back for Quebec. This is because minority nations are also constituted by internal negotiations over identity by a variety of collective social actors. Yet Maclure concedes that it is precisely this internal struggle for recognition within a bounded space – this internal heterogeneity – that offers the driving force of the new nationalist discourse in Quebec. What holds the project in place, accounting for this elusive referential element, is precisely the will to self-determination, or the shared belief that this is the appropriate site for these negotiations: "This attachment to popular sovereignty or collective self-determination, rather than definitive agreement on a set of rights or on a shared identity, is the main facet of this new imaginary of belonging. In some of its variants, minority nationalism would thus be less a static quest for cultural survival than a struggle for the capacity to decide collectively which aspects of culture should be reproduced" (Maclure 2003, 48). From this perspective, in line with the approach adopted by the Bouchard-Taylor Commission, a space for deliberations about cultural identity can be delimited without recourse to some overarching institutional "refoundation" or an appeal to more conservative retrievals of the dominant structuring capacity of the majority culture. The debate around the public recognition of identity is already taking place, and comes organically to circumscribe the community of reference.

At the other end of the spectrum are those who view the promotion of a liberal-pluralist ethic as a betrayal of the neo-nationalist project for political emancipation. Inspired by the renowned sociologist Fernand Dumont, who believed that the substantive historical and cultural roots of a nation based on a collective memory could not simply be reformulated to suit a political project bent on establishing "civic" markers (Dumont 1997), some observers attribute Quebec's existential dilemma to the normative force of identity pluralism itself. Among the foremost critics of a pluralist turn in Quebec is surely Jacques Beauchemin, for whom any political project requires a clearly defined political subject:[8] "Democracy has no grounds if it cannot relate its plans for communal life to the will of a political subject that transcends divisions" (2001, 155). Asserting the liberal and civic credentials of the project for national affirmation in Quebec thus has produced a sort of "guilty conscience" among francophone Quebecers, which has "rendered intellectuals incapable of making the most obvious observation: that Quebec's project for political recognition has been brought about by one group and one group alone, namely those whose history has led them to want their nation to be called a country" (156). In part due to the introduction of the Charter of Rights and Freedoms and the dominant place of the Trudeau template more broadly, the advent of competing identity claims operating within the same normative terrain as the claims brought forth in the name of the nation has in effect torn apart the unity of the francophone majority as the political subject in Quebec and as the vehicle for political sovereignty. The only shared definition of the common good in this setting is the primacy of rights as a framework for social regulation. Yet there is no political project without the mobilizing force of a unitary political subject, and in the present moral and institutional configuration a unitary political subject comes to be equated with anti-democratic and ethnocentric values prone to exclusion. Beauchemin adds that even universal values of justice, equality, and liberty can be assumed only collectively, and it is a shared culture that prompts individuals to set aside "individual appetites" for the attainment of a common good.

Along similar lines, Joseph-Yvon Thériault contends that, although a broad consensus around a "civic and liberal conception of [Quebec] identity" (2012, 69) has been the dominant paradigm in Quebec, recent

8 Beauchemin defines a political subject as "the symbolic and institutional form through which a community arranges its diverse and potentially conflicting narratives and experiences of identity" (2001, 157); see also Beauchemin (2004).

events have begun to challenge the primacy of this path to national affirmation and political recognition. He contends that the shortcomings of the Bouchard-Taylor Commission's recommendations were precisely that they simply echoed the prevalent hegemonic discourse on the moral primacy of unrooted conceptions of cosmopolitan markers of identity: procedural liberalism for the distillation of "common values" such as democracy and gender equality, French as the common public language, and "open secularism" that links public expressions of religious faith to fundamental rights to free expression and conscience. For Thériault, however, the path to moral universalism is socio-historical – it is the product of a particular cultural mobilization, through democracy, and the vehicle of this journey is the nation. The nation cannot be defined by strictly universal principles – it is within a substantive cultural setting that the drive towards moral universalism takes shape, as a somewhat unfinished journey towards the modern ideal. Most societies seeking political recognition therefore cannot construct their national narrative around universal principles, but must emphasize the role the majority culture plays, rather than mask it. Minority nations in particular thus face accusations of illegitimacy – of "ethnic chauvinism" – against standards that cannot be met. Today, minority nations are more likely to be threatened by a "dilution in universalism" than by a move towards enclosure and cultural oppression:

> The values of modern nations are the values of modernity. The societal culture reflects rather a tradition, a national conversation, fraught with both battle and consensus, where modern ideals and values have found a way. Although tradition feeds on and manufactures identity, it is not an identity but a historical group of institutions – from school, to a situated public space, to Parliament – that formed a human plurality into a political community, so the narrative of that voyage forms the narrative of a rooted cosmopolitanism. And there is the impasse of today's Quebec nationalism ... both its detractors and its proponents are vainly seeking the values that would particularize it, when they should be seeking the political community- the historical institutions -that conveys them. (Thériault 2012, 83)

The Quebec nation, rooted in a particular culture, is the expression of a democratic project that seeks to mediate between "human culture" and a universal standard of justice as the modern ideal – the same as any other nation.

For these intellectuals, the answer to the thorny question of how to articulate a model of cultural pluralism appropriate for Quebec while acknowledging its status as a self-determining host society could be found only in rejecting cultural pluralism altogether, culminating in a sort of absolutist secularism that is explicitly tied to the historical trajectory of the majority culture. As such, the way forward was to disregard the recommendations of the Bouchard-Taylor Commission altogether, including its finding that "culture wars" did not exist to a significant degree, and to chart a new course that would rupture virtually forty years of commitment to interculturalism as the primary vehicle for integration in Quebec. Indeed, as Marissal has shown, many such voices came to form the backbone of the decision by the Parti Québécois (PQ) to seek to bring closure to the question of cultural accommodation by simultaneously affirming secularism and an elevated status for the majority culture.[9]

~

This pendulum over the cultural rootedness of the national integration project came to reveal itself forcefully with the introduction of the controversial Charter of Quebec Values (Bill 60[10]) by the minority PQ government in September 2013, only to die on the order table with the party's defeat in the 2014 provincial election. Although the Charter represented an attempt to provide a comprehensive blueprint for the adjudication of minority cultural and religious practices through the introduction of more secular republican conceptions of cultural neutrality, it nevertheless made explicit exceptions in order to recognize the privileged status of the majority culture:

> The purpose of this bill is to establish a Charter affirming the values of State secularism and religious neutrality and of equality between women and men, and providing a framework for accommodation requests. A

9 See Marissal (2014) for an overview of the influence within the PQ of Beauchemin, Thériault, and also Mathieu Bock-Côté and Éric Bédard, who have written extensively on Quebec's need to move away from a model of cultural pluralism that undermines the primacy of the majority culture.

10 The official title of Bill 60 was "Charter affirming the values of State secularism and religious neutrality and of equality between women and men, and providing a framework for accommodation requests." The text of the bill is available online at http://www.assnat.qc.ca/en/travaux-parlementaires/projets-loi/projet-loi-60-40-1.html.

> further purpose of the bill is to specify, in the Charter of human rights and freedoms, that the fundamental rights and freedoms guaranteed by that Charter are to be exercised in a manner consistent with the values of equality between women and men and the primacy of the French language as well as the separation of religions and State and the religious neutrality and secular nature of the State, while making allowance for the emblematic and toponymic elements of Québec's cultural heritage that testify to its history.

Although the main line of criticism pertaining to the Charter rested on its restrictions on conspicuous religious symbols and expression among "personnel members of public bodies," it also paradoxically alienated some advocates of more absolutist secularism by allowing for exemptions in matters pertaining to Quebec's cultural heritage. This imposition of the dictates of the majority culture clearly emerges if one looks specifically at the Charter's attempt to provide guidance regarding accommodation requests. The bill listed a series of markers meant to serve as a set of interpretive criteria to determine the legitimacy of such claims. Most were predictable: human rights, gender equality, prohibitive costs, performance, health and safety considerations, and so on. Yet authorities were also granted substantial discretion to deny accommodation requests: "When an accommodation request on religious grounds is submitted to a public body, the public body must make sure that … the accommodation requested does not compromise the separation of religions and State or the religious neutrality and secular nature of the State." Thus the notion of an environment of open exchange between cultural groups and a fusion of identities as the referential basis of a common public space was denied altogether from the outset. The provision was so broad that any request for exemptions from uniform treatment based on cultural or religious conviction likely would be denied without due consideration. In the end the Charter's intentions were rather transparent: to reconceptualize the Quebec model in a manner that undermined public recognition of cultural and religious pluralism while simultaneously introducing formal-legal opportunities to elevate the status of the majority culture in Quebec.

Perhaps the final word is best left to a novel contribution by Gérard Bouchard. In clarifying and further examining the idea of interculturalism, Bouchard reminds us that this is an old debate in Quebec, and acknowledges the difficulty of proceeding with such emotional questions in light of the collective insecurities of the majority culture.

Without reviewing his entire argument, for our purposes it is noteworthy that Bouchard identifies the distinct nature of interculturalism by noting that its main normative thrust is integrational, because it takes the foundational context and future of the majority culture into account:

> Accommodation is not unique to interculturalism and can be enacted in accordance with a variety of philosophies, sensitivities, and policies. Consequently again, we must prevent ourselves from associating accommodation exclusively with multiculturalism. Certain adjustments can seem perfectly admissible in one society and cause problems in another, even if both adhere to pluralism. In light of this discussion, we see that in the particular case of Quebec it is necessary to develop a form of pluralism that acknowledges that the francophone majority is itself a precarious minority that needs protection in order to ensure its survival and development in the North American environment and in the context of globalization. (Bouchard 2010, 441).

Moreover, a model for ethnocultural relations specific to Quebec need not privilege either defenders of the majority culture or the rights of minorities in mutually exclusive terms. The majority's preoccupations with identity could be combined with what Bouchard calls a "pluralist mindset" – a spirit of reciprocity and a commitment to interaction, and a legal framework for the protection of minorities (ibid.). Indeed Bouchard somewhat anticipates the Quebec Charter in stating that secular republicanism is inappropriate for these circumstances precisely because of the mistrust it generates, fuelling further fragmentation. The idea is to foster alliances with such groups, not marginalize them. Any way forward for Quebec therefore must involve a recognition of the existence of the majority culture. Yet Bouchard adds a qualification: any precedence attributed to the majority culture should proceed on an "ad hoc" or "contextual" basis, rather than a formal one. Indeed this concession to the majority culture stems from the Quebec case as an instance of what Bouchard calls a "duality paradigm" consisting of a clear acknowledgment of the tensions associated with a majority/minority dynamic, in contrast to the Canadian model, to which he assigns a "diversity paradigm" (ibid.).

It is this idea of "ad hoc" precedence that merits further attention as a distinctive attempt to marry the universal with Quebec's specificity. Again, since enshrining the precedence of the majority culture in a formal legal framework would create two classes of citizens, Bouchard dismisses it as illegitimate and open to potential abuses. As such, any concession to the majority culture must be carefully justified. First, he contends that any argument for precedence requires mediation through open democratic debate and compatibility with the Quebec Charter of Human Rights and Freedoms. Second, he acknowledges that this proposal is simply an extension of established political thought around the impossibility of liberal neutrality and the inevitable advancement of the values and customs of the majority culture in any society, and he claims that it is preferable to clarify their scope and impact, rather than to deny they exist. Third, drawing on inteculturalism, such concessions to the majority would constitute a kind of accommodation that minorities grant to majorities in a spirit of exchange and reciprocity, particularly in the case of Quebec, which constitutes a minority of a different kind. Fourth, as majority groups constitute the "main staples of national cultures," they have a role in protecting cultural diversity on a global scale, particularly in the context of globalization (ibid.). Fifth, and reminiscent of Thériault, Bouchard acknowledges that all societies require some symbolic anchor, rooted in identity and memory in a way that cannot be replicated by a civic legal architecture alone, that provides for "the solidarity that forms the basis for any kind of collective mobilization towards the pursuit of a common good" (455). Only the majority culture can provide this historical continuity as the lynchpin for social cohesion. Finally, on a more realistic front, Bouchard warns of the historical injustices committed on behalf of majorities that feel threatened or slighted in some way. Ad hoc precedence as a principle can serve to dampen anxieties that might result in abuses of power. He reminds us that there is no need to apologize for Quebec's national affirmation project, precisely because of its credentials in promoting liberal and democratic values.

Taken together, Bouchard believes that the ad hoc precedence of the majority culture is an inevitable component of any Quebec model:

> [T]he above argument may in a certain light run counter to the principle of formal equality between individuals, groups, and cultures. In its defence, one can say that it does nothing more than reflect and conform to a state of universal reality, namely the impossibility of cultural neutrality of nation-states. Likewise, it somewhat detracts from the ideal and abstract vision of a society formed of a group of perfectly autonomous, rational, and self-made citizens. However, it brings us closer to the complex, shifting, unpredictable, and omnipresent reality of identity dynamics and the vagaries of political life. The argument for elements of contextual precedence thus proceeds from a more sociological and realist vision of liberalism. (456)

In securing a place for contextual precedence in Quebec interculturalism, Bouchard's objective is to ensure that the debate is not dominated by a polarized climate between outright defenders of the concerns of the majority and those who seek to deny its existence as a structuring agent. Interculturalism purports to be grounded in exchange, compromise, harmonization, and reciprocity, and this requires the recognition of a majority culture, whose desire to flourish is perfectly legitimate. Bouchard does concede, however, that negotiations between minorities and majorities require an acknowledgment by the majority group that it is in a more pronounced position of power and therefore must bear the responsibility of respecting basic rights, proceed with moderation, and be willing to change in its exchanges and interactions with minorities.

In conclusion, among the world's national models of integration that "don't really exist," Quebec interculturalism is surely the most sophisticated, elaborate, and hotly contested. Quebec has grappled with the place of cultural identity in its self-conception and political project for many years, and will continue to do so. The novelty of Bouchard's approach lies precisely in his concession that abstract theorizing can get us only so far. The case of Quebec requires delving into real sociological considerations, real policy prescriptions, and the actual application of theoretical propositions in a distinct sociopolitical environment. In this sense, an applied political theory approach is a useful tool when studying the "hard case" of *Québécois* nationalism. Sometimes the particular political sociology of a given society requires us to find an equilibrium between rigid normative standards and more nuanced political considerations. Quebec is clearly an anomalous case, and I argue that Bouchard is simply stating explicitly what defenders of interculturalism in Quebec, including Taylor, have been saying for years: that formulating a place for culture in Quebec's public life must always proceed from a pluralist mindset and in the spirit of reciprocity, but must include a place for the majority culture as well. This is what has always differentiated interculturalism from multiculturalism.

REFERENCES

Bader, Veit, and E.R. Engelen. 2003. "Taking Pluralism Seriously: Arguing for an Institutional Turn in Political Philosophy." *Philosophy and Social Criticism* 29 (4): 375–406. https://doi.org/10.1177/0191453703294002

Bader, Veit, and S. Saharso. 2004. "Introduction: Contextualized Morality and Ethno-religious Diversity." *Ethical Theory and Moral Practice* 7 (2): 107–15. https://doi.org/10.1023/B:ETTA.0000032758.77152.0a

Beauchemin, Jacques. 2001. "Defence and Illustration of a Nation Torn." In *Vive Quebec: New Thinking and New Approaches to the Quebec Nation*, ed. Michel Venne, 155–68. Toronto: James Lorimer.

Beauchemin, Jacques. 2004. *La société des identités*. Montreal: Athena.

Bouchard, Gérard. 2010. "What Is Interculturalism?" *McGill Law Journal* 56 (2): 435–68.

Bouchard, G. and Taylor, C. 2008. *Building the Future: A Time for Reconciliation*. Report of the Commission de consultation sur les pratiques d'accommodement reliées aux différences culturelles. Quebec City.

Brooks, Stephen, James Bickerton, and Alain-G. Gagnon. 2003. *Six penseurs en quête de liberté, d'égalité et de communauté: Grant, Innis, Laurendeau, Rioux, Taylor et Trudeau*. Quebec City: Presses de l'Université Laval.

Cardinal, Linda. 2010. "Language Planning and Policy Making in Quebec and in Canada." In *Quebec Questions: Quebec Studies for the Twenty-first Century*, ed. Stéphan Gervais, Christopher Kirkey, and Jarrett Rudy, 184–201. Don Mills, ON: Oxford University Press.

Carens, Joseph H. January 2004. "A Contextual Approach to Political Theory." *Ethical and Moral Practice* 7 (2): 117–32. https://doi.org/10.1023/B:ETTA.0000032761.25298.23

Choudhry, Sujit. 2002. "National Minorities and Ethnic Immigrants: Liberalism's Political Sociology." *Journal of Political Philosophy* 10 (1): 54–78. https://doi.org/10.1111/1467-9760.00142

Choudhry, Sujit. 2005. "Old Imperial Dilemmas and the New Nation-Building: Constitutive Constitutional Politics in Multinational Polities." *Connecticut Law Review* 37: 933–45.

Couture, Yves. 2014. "Empire, pluralisme et démocratie: la pensée politique au Québec et au Canada anglais." In *La politique québécoises et canadienne: une approche pluraliste*, ed. Alain-G. Gagnon, 29–60. Quebec City: Presses de l'Université du Quebec.

Dumont, Fernand. 1997. *Raisons communes*. Montreal: Boréale.

Dworkin, Ronald. 1978. "Liberalism." In *Public and Private Morality*, ed. Stuart Hampshire, 113–43. Cambridge: Cambridge University Press. https://doi.org/10.1017/CBO9780511625329.007

Gagnon, Alain-G., and Raffaele Iacovino. 2007. *Federalism, Citizenship and Quebec: Debating Multinationalism*. Toronto: University of Toronto Press.

Quebec. 1981. *Autant de façons d'être Québécois: plan d'action à l'intention des communautés culturelles*. Quebec City: Ministère des communications, Direction générale des publications gouvernementales.

Iacovino, Raffaele, and Charles-Antoine Sévigny. 2011. "Between Unity and Diversity: Examining the 'Quebec Model' of Integration." In *Quebec Questions: Quebec Studies for the Twenty-first Century*, ed. Stéphan Gervais, Christopher Kirkey, and Jarrett Rudy, 249–66. Don Mills, ON: Oxford University Press.

Kymlicka, Will. 1995. *Multicultural Citizenship: A Liberal Theory of Minority Rights*. Oxford: Oxford University Press.

Labelle, Micheline. 2008. "De la culture publique commune à la citoyenneté: Ancrages historiques et enjeux actuels." In *Du tricoté serré au métissé serré: La culture poublique commune au Québec en débats*, ed. Stéphan Gervais, Dimitrios Karmis, and Diane Lamoureux, 19–43. Quebec City: Presses de l'Université Laval.

Laforest, Guy. 2010. "La Commission Bouchard-Taylor et la place du Québec dans la trajectoire de l'État-nation moderne." In *La Diversité québécoise en débat: Bouchard, Taylor et les autres*, ed. Bernard Gagnon, 125–42. Montreal: Québec-Amérique.

Laforest, Guy. 1995. *Trudeau and the End of a Canadian Dream*. Montreal; Kingston, ON: McGill-Queen's University Press.

Maclure, Jocelyn. 2003. "Between Nation and Dissemination: Revisiting the Tension between National Identity and Diversity." In *The Conditions of Diversity in Multinational Democracies*, ed. Alain-G. Gagnon, Montserrat Guibernau, and François Rocher, 41–57. Montreal: Institute for Research on Public Policy.

Marissal, Vincent. 2014. "Le choc, la charge, la charte." *La Presse* , 31 March. Available online at http://www.lapresse.ca/actualites/201403/31/01-4752879-le-choc-la-charge-la-charte.php

McRoberts, Kenneth. 2004. "Struggling Against Territory: Language Policy in Canada." In *Language, Nation, and State: Identity Politics in a Multilingual Age*, ed. Tony Judt and Denis Lacorne, 133–60. New York: Palgrave Macmillan. https://doi.org/10.1057/9781403982452_6

Norman, Wayne. 2001. "Justice and Stability in Multinational Societies." In *Multinational Democracies*, ed. Alain-G. Gagnon and James Tully, 90–109. Cambridge: Cambridge University Press. https://doi.org/10.1017/CBO9780511521577.007

Quebec. 1990. "Au Québec pour bâtir ensemble: énoncé de politique en matière d'immigration et d'intégration." Quebec City: Ministère des communautés culturelles et de l'immigration du Québec, Direction des communications. Available online at http://www.midi.gouv.qc.ca/publications/fr/ministere/Enonce-politique-immigration-integration-Quebec1991.pdf

Rawls, John. 1971. *A Theory of Justice*. Cambridge, MA: Harvard University Press.

Resnick, Philip. 2001. "Civic and Ethnic Nationalism: Lessons from the Canadian Case." In *Canadian Political Philosophy*, ed. Ronald Beiner and Wayne Norman, 282–97. Don Mills, ON: Oxford University Press.

Rocher, François, and Micheline Labelle. 2008. "L'interculturalisme comme modèle d'aménagement de la diversité: compréhension et incompréhension dans l'espace public Québécois." In *La diversité québécoise en débat: Bouchard, Taylor et les autres*, ed. Bernard Gagnon, 179–203. Montreal: Québec-Amérique.

Rocher, François, Micheline Labelle, Ann-Marie Field, and Jean-Claude Icart. 2007. "Le concept d'interculturalisme en contexte Québécois: généalogie d'un néologisme." Rapport présenté à la Commission de consultation sur les pratiques d'accommodement reliées aux différences culturelles. Quebec City. Available online at https://www.mce.gouv.qc.ca/publications/CCPARDC/rapport-3-rocher-francois.pdf, accessed 2 May 2015.

Seymour, Michel. 2008. "La nation et l'identité publique commune." In *Du tricoté serré au métissé serré? la culture publique commune au Québec en débats*, ed. Stéphan Gervais, Dimitrios Karmis, and Diane Lamoureux, 61–86. Quebec City: Presses de l'Université Laval.

Seymour, Michel. 2010. "Nationalistes ou pluralistes? Faut-il vraiment choisir?" *Le Devoir*, 9 February. Available online at https://www.ledevoir.com/opinion/idees/282682/nationalistes-ou-pluralistes-faut-il-vraiment-choisir

Taylor, Charles. 1992. "The Politics of Recognition." In *Multiculturalism and "The Politics of Recognition."* Princeton, NJ: Princeton University Press.

Taylor, Charles. 2012. "Interculturalism or Multiculturalism?" *Philosophy and Social Criticism* 38 (4–5): 413–23. https://doi.org/10.1177/0191453711435656

Thériault, Joseph-Yvon. 2012. "Universality and Particularity in the National Question in Quebec." In *Rooted Cosmopolitanism: Canada and the World*, ed. Will Kymlicka and Kathryn Walker, 69–86. Vancouver: UBC Press.

17 The Conqueror's Mask: Canada as an Empire-State

MARC CHEVRIER

In the introduction to his excellent book *The Masks of Proteus,* Philip Resnick writes, "no single, overarching theory can capture ... in all its dimensions" the nature of the modern state (1990, xi). In describing the genesis and functioning of states, Resnick likens states to the god Proteus of Greek mythology – in ancient Greek, Πρωτεύς – who was gifted with the ability to metamorphose into different creatures. The state has the same ability to wear different masks: "coercive and consensual, centralized and decentralized, democratic and anti-democratic, economic and social, sovereign and dependent" (5). Of all the masks worn by the Canadian state, I will limit myself in this chapter to examining one in particular: the mask of conqueror. I argue that military conquest founded and legitimizes the Canadian state, not only in an episodic manner but in an enduring and systematic manner. In short, Canada can be conceived of as an empire-state: it is founded upon and continues to be legitimatized by conquest.

As I will show, applied political theory is useful for understanding the history of the Canadian state. As an approach to the study of Canadian politics and history, it allows the researcher to interpret the empirical facts of history using the lens of political theory. It is also useful for understanding the legal and official discourses whose concepts are often drawn from the works of major and minor thinkers. As we shall see, conquest is not merely a historical fact; it is also a subtle intellectual construction clothed with a philosophical dress. If we look to Canada, it appears that the conquest founded and continues to legitimatize the Canadian state, on the grounds of military victories bookended by the Treaty of Utrecht in 1713 and the Treaty of Paris in 1763. Even though the conquest of 1713–63 has given rise to several differing interpretations, particularly among historians, it is rarely seen as a topic relevant to political thought. However, modern political thought, at least among liberal thinkers such as Hobbes, Hume, Locke, and Montesquieu, treats conquest as one of the possible ways to create a state and as a competitor to the idea that a state is founded by the consent of the governed. Although these thinkers see the founding of a state by consent of the governed as desirable, if not more just, they do not exclude the possibility that a founding can ignore consent and validly rely on force.

To construct my argument, I follow an applied political theory approach. I first examine empirical evidence relating to the British conquest of Canada using the primary sources of legal and historical documents. The exploration of these documents forms a solid foundation for subsequent engagement in a theoretical reflection concerning the formation of the Canadian state and its modes of legitimation. In particular, I illustrate how canonical liberal and conservative thinkers framed the concept of conquest and how those theories can be used to elucidate the meaning of the British conquest of Canada and its role in the formation of the Canadian state. We also see that the fallout from the conquest sparked a debate, little studied, among the *Patriotes* of Lower Canada and John Stuart Mill about the rights of the conquerors and those of the conquered. Interestingly, both the *Patriotes* and Mill used concepts from the seventeenth-century school of natural law to understand how conquest must include certain fundamental rights for the conquered. Finally, I argue that, even if the Canadian state has been undeniably democratized and has perfected its liberalism over time, it has maintained several characteristics of an empire-state, whereby conquest continues to be a basis of its legitimacy and defines the bonds between rulers and the ruled. As opposed to the work of Janet Ajzenstat (2003), who sees the founding of Canada as based fundamentally on the Lockean principle of consent, I argue that consent and coercion are not mutually exclusive, but are often combined in the building and legitimizing of modern states that have kept an imperial structure.

The Concept of the State in Canadian Literature

Political scientists in Canada rarely study the state – particularly the Canadian state – even though, as Resnick notes, political discourse and the social sciences have made frequent use of the concept since 1945 in both Quebec and the rest of Canada (Resnick 1990, 54–70). For example, renowned constitutional scholars such as Beaudoin (2000), Tremblay

(2000), and Morin and Woehrling (1992) barely touch on the idea of state in their analyses. There are exceptions, however, to this tradition of ignoring the state within the legal community. In one particular essay, published in 1963, Bernard Bissonnette, former judge of the Quebec Court of Appeal, offers considerations on the state that mix principles of natural law, French legal doctrine, French *personnaliste* philosophy, and papal encyclicals (1963, 165–6). In the chapter "Québec, un État?" the judge enters into a legal discussion of the state. However, this kind of theoretical discussion of the concept of state, applicable to Canada as a whole or to Quebec, is relatively uncommon, although this question did give rise to a few journal articles (Caron 1938; St-Aubin 1963). In another example, lawyers Henri Brun and Guy Tremblay attempt to make the state the central focus of Canadian constitutional law, importing concepts from Franco-German republican positivism, such as the ideas of Raymond Carré de Malberg, a legal scholar during the Third French Republic, who wrote the famous *Contribution à la théorie générale de l'État* ([1922] 2004). Similarly, among anglophone legal scholars in Canada, the concept of the state has little presence in journal articles and textbooks (Hogg 2011; Laskin 1975; Magnet 1983), although the notion of the "Crown" often takes the place of the concept of the state. This relative lack of theoretical discussion of the state in Canadian legal literature, in both languages, is similar to what has taken place in British legal literature. If one believes Kenneth Dyson, a theorist of the state in Europe, the idea of the state would be alien to the British legal tradition, which makes Britain an aberrant case within the European experience (1980, 36–43).

Moreover, if we consider the social sciences in Canada, it is mostly works of political economy, often influenced by Marxist analysis, that have studied the Canadian state, especially in analyses written in English (Panitch 1977). Aside from political economists, most social scientists appear to maintain an ambivalent relationship to the concept of the state: either they accept it in its Weberian form as a means of monopolizing legitimate violence and performing certain functions that regulate the market (Braud 1997, 50–74), or they see the state as a concept to deconstruct and to denounce as a "réalité illusoire, mais collectivement validée par le consensus" [illusionary reality that is collectively validated by consensus] (Bourdieu 2012, 25, my translation) that masks the forms of domination that various theories, ranging from Marxism to post-colonialism, have sought to reveal. Furthermore, if the concept of the sovereign state is meaningful for legal studies, it holds little interest for Canadian political scientists who are more interested in the actors operating within the state (Bélanger and Lemieux 1996, 148). Similarly, due to its adherence to liberalism largely inspired by the work of John Rawls, Canadian political philosophy has not seemed to make the state its priority (see, for example, Beiner and Norman 2001; Madison, Fairfield, and Harris 2000). Nevertheless two prominent figures in contemporary Quebec political science, Gérard Bergeron (1990) and Léon Dion (1986), have worked on the state. More recently, the collective work, *La politique québécoise et canadienne*, also devotes a chapter to the Canadian state (Graefe 2017), the political scientist Anne Legaré sums up her work in a collection of essays on the Canadian state and the Quebec nation (Legaré 2017), and a historical genesis of the Canadian state was published in Heaman (2015).

As we can see, despite some notable exceptions, there has been an overarching lack of theorization of the Canadian state in social sciences and law. The consequence of this lack of scholarly attention has been a narrow view of the origins of the Canadian state and little reflection on how those origins have important effects on contemporary politics. The use of applied political theory to introduce the concept of conquest into understandings of how the Canadian state was constructed helps nourish this much-needed reflection.

The Historical and Legal Dimensions of the British Conquest of Canada

Conquest as a concept and human activity stretches back to antiquity and is certainly an important part of the history of western civilization. One only has to think of Homer's *Iliad*, which opens with the conquest of Troy by Agamemnon's army. Although Aristotle condemned conquest and Plato disproved of the imperial expansion of the city, the Greeks practised conquest as an effective method of founding new cities and expanding territory based on the merciless principle that "la victoire fonde le droit" [victors make the law] (Bertrand 1992, 92, my translation). But the law itself observes certain prudence with regard to conquest. The Treaty of Paris of 1763, which ended the Seven Years' War and closed the chapter that American historians have called the French and Indian War, is a good example of this cautiousness. As opposed to using flowery and provocative language to describe the resolution of the armed conflict, the Treaty of 1763 "cedes and guarantees" to His British Majesty sovereignty and ownership of the part of New France that had not been assigned to him by the Treaty of Utrecht. The Royal Proclamation of 7 October 1763 was faithful to the tame and diplomatic language of the treaties of Utrecht and Paris by referring to the North American lands ceded by the French king to the British Crown as "acquisitions."

But contrary to this tactful language, the Quebec Act of 1774 invokes the language of "conquest." The Quebec Act is most famous for granting the inhabitants of the "Province of Quebec" the right to use the French laws and customs that predated the Seven Years' War. A careful reading of the text, however, shows that its often-cited section 8, which deals with the application of French law in relation to property and civil rights, is not the only important section of the act. Section 4 is equally fundamental to understanding the future of the Canadian state. In this section, the conqueror (that is, the British Crown) uses the word "conquest" to establish the legitimacy of its power, while deeming "inapplicable" the orders made by British governors in Quebec since 1764. The inapplicability of these orders is based upon the admission that, at the time of the conquest, the population of Quebec was already "enjoying an established Form of Constitution and System of Laws, by which their Persons and Property had been protected, governed, and ordered, for a long Series of Years, from the first Establishment of the said Province of Canada." It is implicitly recognized that the constitution that pre-existed the conquest of Canada continued to exercise its control over Quebec's population after the conquest because its customs were so strongly engrained and still effective. In turn, the customary force of this constitution hindered the implementation of the orders of British governors to the point where those orders became inapplicable.

It is crucial to note that section 4 recognizes that New France had a "constitution" by which persons and properties were "protected, governed, and ordered, for a long Series of Years." In Canadian constitutional history, it is rare that British imperial laws use the word "constitution." The word "constitution" did appear once, in section 1 of the Act of Union passed by Westminster on 10 February 1838 to suspend the constitution of Lower Canada. After that, it appears only once in the preamble to the Constitution Act, 1867; and the Statute of Westminster, 1931 uses the word with regard to Australia and New Zealand, but refers instead to the British North America Act when talking about Canada (sections 7 and 8). Finally, the word is used again in the Constitution Act, 1982, where the concept appears many times.

Blackstone, whose *Commentaries* were published between 1765 and 1769, a few years before the Quebec Act, helps to shed light on the scope of section 4 and its use of the term "constitution." Discussing the origins of the common law, which dates back to the period of the Anglo-Saxon kings, Blackstone observes that the "ancient collection of unwritten maxims and customs, which is called the common law, however compounded of from whatever fountains derived, had subsisted immemorially in this kingdom; and, though somewhat altered and impaired by the violence of the times, had in great measure weathered the rude shock of the Norman conquest" ([1765–69] 1979, 17). In other words, the English common law, finding its origins in old sayings and habits from before the Norman conquest of 1066, survived that conquest and even helped to soften the effects of this conquest on the conquered people of England. Section 4 of the Quebec Act replays the Norman conquest in reverse. This time, it is the turn of a fragment of France to experience conquest, and these new subjects of His Majesty retain the laws and customs of the constitution that pre-existed the conquest to lighten the yoke of their newfound status as a conquered people. In his chapter on "Countries Subject to English Law," Blackstone discusses the status of the Channel Islands of Jersey, Guernsey, Sark, and Alderney, former territories of the Duchy of Normandy that had become parts of the British Empire. Blackstone observes that these islands "are governed by their own laws, which are for the most part the ducal customs of Normandy, being collected in an ancient book of very great authority, entitled, *le grand coustumier*" ([1765–69] 1979, 104). Section 4 of the Quebec Act, therefore, confirms that New France is a British territory with a status equivalent to that of the Channel Islands: as subject to the requirements of English law, both French populations living on the two sides of the Atlantic are allowed to govern themselves according to their own customs. This apparent generosity of the conqueror is not particular to the British Empire. Indeed the art of conquest was perfected by the Romans, who, after conquering Gaul, left the vanquished with enjoyment of their customs so long as those custom did not interfere with "le commandement et l'empire" [order and empire] (Loysel [1607] 1971, iv). In sum, sections 4 and 8 of the 1774 Quebec Act dressed up the British conquest of Canada from 1714 to 1763 in Roman clothes: the conquered retained their customs, their conquerors gained their orders.

These two sections of the Quebec Act, combined with the treaties of Utrecht and Paris, establish two basic principles: a) a military victory establishes the new colonial state under the imperial sovereignty of the British Crown; and b) conquest itself is a source of rights for the conquered population. This principle is reiterated in the section 22 of the Constitutional Act of 1791, which granted the right to vote in elections for the representative legislatures of Lower and Upper Canada to people who had become subjects of Her Majesty "by the Conquest and Assignment of the Province of Canada." Conquest is implicit in the imperial law of February 1838, which suspended the constitution of Lower Canada and entrusted its administration to a special council chaired by the colonial governor, who subsequently exercised the equivalent power of a Roman dictator. However, if the Act of Union of 1840 repealed the Constitutional Act of 1791, and therefore its reference to the conquest as the basis for the granting of self-government, the Quebec Act of 1774 was not repealed, but continued to apply to Lower Canada in the period after 1840. After 1867 the Supreme Court of Canada relied on this act to interpret some provisions of the Constitutional Act of 1867.

So far I have been concerned with how the laws making up the Constitution of Canada apply to the French population living generally in Quebec. Do these legal considerations concerning the conquest of Canada apply to Indigenous peoples? For some the concept of conquest is inapplicable in this case because the French and British crowns always dealt with Indigenous people from a nation-to-nation perspective – that is, according to diplomatic protocol, and using the instruments of international law such as treaties (Lepage 2009, 3–5). At first glance British law avoids speaking about the conquest of Indigenous peoples in North America. By the Treaty of Utrecht in 1713, according to section 15, "Indians" in Canada, although "subject to the Dominion of Great Britain," are given the status of nations or "cantons," a section that British authorities interpreted as an indication that international law would continue to protect the Indigenous nations of Acadia (Henderson, Benson, and Findlay 2000, 115). Subsequently the British Crown solidified its hold on further North American territories by signing treaties with Indigenous nations outlining their rights and guaranteeing their allegiance. The Treaty of Paris and the Royal Proclamation of 1763 generalized this unique treatment of Indigenous nations compared to other conquered peoples. Section 23 of the Treaty of Paris states that the countries and territories that were conquered by the warring parties and which are not mentioned in the treaty are restored, which aims at the particular treaties in Acadia that the British had signed with Indigenous nations (Henderson, Benson, and Findlay 2000, 147).

Similarly the Royal Proclamation of 1763 reserves to the "Indians," under the sovereignty, authority and "dominion" of His Majesty, the enjoyment of their land outside the boundaries of Quebec, whose management is actually placed under the surveillance of the Crown. Some have seen this system of reserve lands as an Aboriginal protectorate – a term borrowed from James Harrington – under which "the British sovereign was not an independent or absolute authority (imperium); he had shared jurisdiction under Aboriginal compact and Treaties" (Henderson, Benson, and Findlay 2000, 151). The treaties the Crown concluded thereafter, however, especially during the Victorian period, were more acts of surrender, by which Indigenous nations ceded their lands to the Crown for little compensation, which led to the extinguishment of Aboriginal land title. Indeed Aboriginal treaties with the British Crown form a strange mixture of pacification, subjection, recognition, and empowerment, which resemble *foedera* – unequal bilateral treaties – Rome concluded with the conquered cities of the Italian peninsula, which retained a residual autonomy. If Aboriginal peoples have not been conquered formally, in a way solemnized by a capitulation and a treaty of cession, it seems that, in the long run, they have been subjugated by the British and the Canadian Crown, with effects similar to that of a conquest.

One might think that these considerations of how conquest was conceived in the legal language of the British Empire are of little interest to contemporary Canada. Yet lawyers repeatedly return to the idea of a conquest of Canada to determine the scope of a law or standard applicable to a dispute. Peter W. Hogg (2011) discusses the evolution of English-Canadian common law after the British conquest of Canada. We learn that English-Canadian lawyers did not address the conquest of Acadia as they conceived of the conquest of Lower Canada; rather, they treated Acadia like a settled colony, emptied of its inhabitants following the 1755 deportation, to which British law, both private and public, applied. Lower Canada, in contrast, is treated as a conquered colony in which the private law of the conquered people remained effective after the conquest, unless the British Parliament decided otherwise. As such the question of applicable law after the conquest nourished a long controversy before British and Canadian courts (Decroix 2011).

The legal significance of the conquest is not limited, however, to this single controversy concerning the conquered populations of Quebec and Acadia. Take again the example of Indigenous peoples, whose existing ancestral and treaty rights are enshrined in the Constitution

Act, 1982. This recognition, the scope of which is left to the discretion of the courts and governments, forces authorities in Canada to question the foundations of sovereignty. As Patrick Macklem remarks, the sovereignty of the Canadian state over Aboriginal nations is based on a legal fiction, according to which "the Crown was the original occupant of all the lands of the realm" (2001, 91). The Aboriginal occupation of Canadian land prior to contact does not invalidate this fiction because, under the legal doctrine in vogue at the time of the colonization of North America, land that was already occupied was nevertheless deemed vacant "if its inhabitants were insufficiently Christian or civilized" (92). Although various self-government agreements and land claims agreements between governments in Canada and Aboriginal nations use language that belongs to international law, these agreements still accept the consequences of the European occupation of ancestral Indigenous territories and the marginalization of Indigenous nations within Canadian political society. Indeed these agreements are similar, at least in their effects, to a settlement issued from a conquest: the conquered people retain certain rights, while Aboriginal sovereignty and title to Aboriginal lands are extinguished.

In short the Indigenous people of Canada and the descendants of the inhabitants of New France are in the same boat: both are subjects of the Canadian *empire-state*. In defining the scope of the collective rights of peoples deriving from the establishment of the federal union in 1867, governments must return constantly to the events of the British conquest of Canada and refer to founding fictions to confirm their authority. The conquest, which was the process of making extinct the sovereignty of those who inhabited Canadian territories prior to the Seven Years' War, whether they be Aboriginal or French, came to serve as the basis for Canada's entire constitutional and legal system.

Apart from the legal discourse, the conquest has also been a matter of discussion for historians. Many studies, particularly in Quebec, have been devoted to understanding the conquest, but since the 1980s historians in Quebec have gradually abandoned the theme of conquest. Historian Charles-Philippe Courtois attributes this lack of interest to the influence of multiculturalism, which is inclined "à occulter les conflits entre peuples et entre cultures" [to conceal the conflict between peoples and between cultures] (2009, 11, my translation). He also argues, "du côté du Canada anglais, la Confédération a graduellement éclipsé la conquête comme événement fondateur, conséquence du développement d'une identité nationale canadienne plutôt que britannique" [in

English Canada, Confederation gradually eclipsed the Conquest as a founding event as consequence of the development of a Canadian national identity rather than British] (11, my translation). For his part, Arthur R.M. Lower agreed that "Confederation obliterated the English Conquest" (1946, 333), yet Dale Miquelon observed that "Conquest ideologies have always informed Canadian political thought and behaviour" (1977, 9). Indeed, in recent years as well, many English-Canadian historians have treated the conquest in diverse ways (Plank 2001; Reid et al. 2004).

Moreover, the conquest appears in several works and essays, including works of political thought. In *A Fair Country,* the famous essayist John Ralston Saul states that the Royal Proclamation and the Quebec Act were "the founding of the Canadian civilization" (2008, 19). David Chennells (2001) argues that how various nationalisms are expressed within Canada is primarily explained as a consequence of the British conquest. With a more polemical tone, Brian Lee Crowley describes the concessions that the federal government has made to accommodate Quebec since the Quiet Revolution as a reversal of the conquest, which led the country to abandon its founding values inherited from Whiggism and British conservatism. Crowley writes that, "while we stooped, we did not conquer. At least not if conquering meant winning the hearts and minds of French-speaking in Quebec" (2009, 94). Philip Resnick (2005) has also examined the British roots – notably the imperial roots – of the Canadian political narrative. James Tully, when interpreting the Quebec Act in *Strange Multiplicity* (1995), relies on the writings of Whigs loyalists from the eighteenth century, touching on the old constitution of Britain derived from the Norman conquest of 1066 and on Locke's writing on this constitution in his chapter in *Two Treatises* on conquest. According to Tully, Britain's constitution guarantees the continuation of French Canada's civil and legal institutions as well as the right to approve or disallow any changes to those institutions (1995, 149–52). Like Tully, Guy Laforest (1995) was inspired by the writings of Locke to consider the imposition on Quebec of the constitutional reform of 1982 as a form of "dissolution of the government" in Locke's sense, and thus as a conquest. The conceptualization of the British conquest of Canada is essential, he believes, as a starting pointing for discussions on Canadian identity and the relationship between English Canada and Quebec (1995, 172). In short, regardless of the effects and the role attributed to the conquest of 1713–63, it is difficult to discuss the foundations of state authority, sources of law, and relations between communities and nations in Canada without presupposing the existence of a British conquest that predates and shapes the formal establishment of Canada as a country in 1867.

Conquest: A Major Theme of Modern Political Thought?

As an applied political theory approach prescribes, it is important to relate the historical events and writings described above with how conquest is treated in western political philosophy. At first glance, conquest is not a main question; rather, political theory is preoccupied by the legitimate foundation of sovereign power – notably the use of a fictional state of nature that marks the passage from an undifferentiated and divided group of people to a sovereign political body. Nevertheless several political thinkers do give the concept of conquest considerable importance, to the point that one wonders if conquest is not actually a cornerstone of their thought. Machiavelli, Rousseau, Constant, and Spencer all have treated the concept of conquest in their own way, but to understand the Canadian state, let us examine the concept of conquest in the thought of Hobbes, Locke, Hume, and Montesquieu.

Conquest has an important place in the conceptual system of Hobbes ([1651] 1968, chap. 20). For Hobbes, there are two ways of creating a state: by institution or by acquisition. Through emphasizing the first, as Foucault (1997, 80) notes, Hobbes is trying to outsmart the opponents of his time, who repeatedly stated that English power was built on the Norman conquest of England. For Hobbes the acquisition of a state, including its violent conquest, is equivalent to the institution of a state as a result of a contract between individual members of the multitude for the establishment of the Leviathan. The equivalence between creating a state through institution or through acquisition has two elements. The first element is the actual effect of institution and acquisition, which is the same: the creation of a state and often its geographical expansion. Second, conquest reproduces the state of nature on the battlefield, where the fate of the conquered is submission to the winner. Submission to the conqueror is similar to consenting to the social contract in that it is also driven by the fear of death, and the conquered give up their sovereignty in exchange for life and civil liberty. In summary, conquest can be used to supplement the territories of a state founded on a social contract because conquest replicates the state of nature. As such, conquest is likely to be used quite often and quite legitimately by a state, whether a monarchy or a democracy, to expand itself.

At first it appears that, according to Locke, the institution of a state cannot be based on conquest, but must be preceded by consent, to the extent that the leader of a just war can introduce a new government only with the consent of the subjugated population ([1689] 1986, chap. 16). This argument was meant to counterbalance the theories of conquest popular in England at the time, and Locke's criticism of those theories seems to have been motivated by fear of a French invasion during the Nine Years' War (1686–97), which saw the Augsburg League countries face off against Louis XIV after the revocation of the Edict of Nantes in 1685 (Tully 1993, 34). Moreover, for Locke, the power of the conqueror extends only to combatants, not to their families or possessions. A conquered people have the right not only to refuse to subject themselves to a despotic conqueror, but also to participate in the incorporation of the political society that issues from the conquest (Locke [1689] 1986, para. 89). This discussion should not be construed to mean that Locke prohibits the expansion of a state by conquest. Rather, he puts conditions in place so a state could grow through conquest, with the conquered people engaging in the creation of a new political contract. Furthermore, for Locke, territories left deserted or uncultivated could be legitimately appropriated by invaders seeking to make those territories productive, even if there were people already occupying those lands who were opposed to the colonization (Seliger 1968, 114). The fact that people on the lands were not using them productively justified invasion by a conqueror seeking to use the lands in a productive fashion.

For his part, David Hume develops his theory of conquest through criticism of contractualism within modern liberal thinking, which imagines that the foundation of a state is derived from a social contract among outgoing members of the state of nature. If it is desirable for political authority to be established by consent, objects Hume, we cannot find any trace in history of such an "original contract" that was present at the founding of a state and that obliges adherence by descendants of the founders. He writes: "Almost all the governments which exist at present, or of which there remains any record in story, have been founded originally either on usurpation or conquest or both, without any pretence of a fair consent or voluntary subjection of the people" (Hume [1741] 1953, 47). He adds that "conquest or usurpation – that is, in plain terms, force – by dissolving the ancient governments, is the origin of almost all the new ones which were ever established in the world" (49). As we can see, Hume tries to establish that the foundation and legitimation of the state cannot rest solely on the search for the hypothetical and impossible-to-find consent of the governed. He is adamant that "[s]ome other foundation of government must also be admitted" (50). Hume develops a prescriptive theory of the legitimation of power: it is the prescription of time that gradually confers on a monarch the authority to control the obedience of subjects. This obedience, according to Hume, stems from the innate moral sense allotted to all men, which, apart from innate natural obligations they acknowledge with regard to their families and the most unfortunate, inclines them to fulfil certain duties such as faithfulness, justice, and allegiance to the established power. Without adherence to such duties, social life would be impossible, and it is not possible to subject the foundations of men's observance to the "captious rule of logic" inherent in social contract theory. The consequence of Hume's thinking on conquest is twofold. First, for him, it is pointless to criticize the legitimacy of a state established by conquest. Second, it is also useless to try to build the legitimacy of a state through the creation of a new and rational social contract – a constitution, in the French and American sense – since a state essentially derives its legitimacy and authority from its ability to elicit obedience from its citizens. As long as a state offers citizens the opportunity to fulfil their natural duties – notably, those duties arising from justice and respect for property – it has sufficient legitimacy to govern.

In his work, Montesquieu deals with conquest in a sparse, subtle, and contradictory manner. Many of his writings testify to his condemnation of conquest: his *Lettres persanes* deny any legitimacy to conquest within the law; his *Considérations sur les causes de la grandeur des Romains et de leur décadence* paint a bittersweet and unflattering portrait of the expansive Roman republic; and his *Réflexions sur la monarchie universelle* discredit conquest as unfit for seventeenth-century European civilization. In Book X of *L'esprit des lois*, however, which precedes his famous reflections on the constitution of England in Book XI, Montesquieu develops a surprising doctrine concerning the right of conquest, which legitimizes it by recognizing that there are several advantages for the conquered people. To him, conquest appears inevitable, one of the "sortes de lois" that govern men but also preserve the residual humanity of the conquered people, which might be maintained legitimately by the conqueror, especially if it is trying to reduce tyranny. Unlike the Romans, who reserved the conqueror's unlimited right to kill and keep in bondage a conquered people, the Moderns practise a better type of conquest that is established on maxims drawn from natural law, so that the conqueror is entitled to destroy the state, but not its people. Montesquieu summarizes his thinking by this striking formula: "La société est l'union des hommes, et non pas les hommes; le citoyen peut périr, et l'homme rester" [Society is the union of men and not of men. The citizen may perish, but the man remains] (1964, 580, my translation), which emphasizes both the artificiality of the state, which can die by the effect of conquest, and the natural need for self-preservation that nonetheless must govern relations between nations, according to the laws of modern peoples. The subsequent servitude of the conquered is a transient state for Montesquieu, and conquerors have the responsibility to bring the conquered out of servitude by all means. For a monarchy that conquers, he recommends leaving the conquered people the enjoyment of their laws and customs – and it is even more necessary to leave a conquered people their social mores. As such, Montesquieu defines the ethics of modern conquest in a manner conforming to the civilizing paternalism of European colonialism. This is seen in the unpublished fragments of *De l'esprit de lois*, where Montesquieu develops a doctrine of colonies and confederations that classifies them according to the degree of domination among member states (797–9).

The School of Natural Law and the Concept of Conquest

In his conceptualization of the right to conquest, Montesquieu obviously gives primacy to the teachings of the school of natural law associated with seventeenth- and eighteenth-century lawyers Pufendorf, Grotius, Barbeyrac, and Burlamaqui (Terrel 2005–6). It is noteworthy, however, that, at the end of the eighteenth century, one of the first political essays published under the British regime in Canada invoked this same school to establish the political freedom of French Canada. The essay, by Pierre du Calvet, entitled *Appel de la justice de l'État* and published in London in 1784, contains some fascinating insights on the right of conquest. As a French Huguenot immigrant in New France at the end of the French regime, du Calvet served in the British colonial administration between 1776 and 1781 before being accused of high treason and imprisoned arbitrarily. His essay is an indictment against the "l'inquisition d'État" by the British regime and a plea for the establishment of democratic governance in Canada through a process involving the full participation of Canadians themselves. To justify the right of Canadians to participate in the foundation of their own government, du Calvet turns to the theory of natural law, under which Canadians are political actors capable of governing themselves and concluding a political agreement with their British conquerors (du Calvet [1784] 2002).

According to Christian Lazzeri, "la théorie moderne du droit naturel se caractérise par l'idée selon laquelle la puissance publique revêtant les attributs du pouvoir souverain doit son origine et sa légitimité à un accord de type contractuel entre des individus disposant de droits naturels qu'ils sont disposés ou obligés, en vertu d'une loi naturelle, à transférer, pour leur avantage, à des individus institués en détenteurs de la puissance publique" [the modern theory of natural law is characterized by the idea that public power possessing the attributes of a sovereign power has its origin and legitimacy within a contractual agreement between individuals who have natural rights that they are willing, by virtue of a natural law, to transfer to holders of public power for their own personal advantage] (2001, 465, my translation). For Grotius, a right is a capacity attached to the human person: "le droit est une qualité morale attachée à l'individu pour posséder ou faire justement quelque chose. Ce droit est attaché à la personne" [a right is a moral quality attached to the individual to possess something or do something. It is attached to the person] (1995, 35, my translation). It is this capacity that is natural to the person – it is "universelle et donc indépendante de toute appartenance à un ordre civil quelconque" [universal and therefore independent of any affiliation with any civil order] (my translation). The result is that we cannot ignore the rights of people when constituting a political body. Public power is established only through a contract between individuals assumed to be independent. In fact Pufendorf distinguishes two types of political pacts: the pact of association, which unites a people to their sovereign, and the pact of government, which decides what kind of political regime is adopted (Derathe 1995, 209–17).

Natural law theorists do not deny the right of conquest, but seek to regulate it according to standards derived from a universal natural law. The conquest destroys the conquered state, but does not remove the natural rights of a conquered people. No state can assign a government to a people without first consulting the people concerned – the conquered people retain their civil rights and the right to participate in the founding of new state institutions. For Grotius, the foundation of a state is "une réunion parfaite d'homme libres associés pour jouir de la protection des lois et pour leur utilité commune" [a perfect union of free men who join together to enjoy the protection of the laws and for their common utility] (1999, 43, my translation). Of the numerous "docteurs en droit" [doctors of law] du Calvet cites to support his argument, Pufendorf, Grotius, Locke, and Machiavelli set out very clearly the rights of a conquered people and the obligations of the conqueror. According to Pufendorf, as cited by du Calvet, conquered peoples have two destinies, chosen by the conqueror: either they are left to govern themselves within "l'économie du premier gouvernement" that was legitimized under the previous ruler; or they create a new constitution inclusive of "aux propres sujets du conquérant, mais par une association complète de privilèges, prérogatives et droits quelconques des anciens sujets, parce que sans ce complément, les peuples conquis ne pourraient être censés légitimer par leur consentement une affiliation défavorable" [the conqueror's own subjects but with a complete combination of privileges, prerogatives and rights of the old subjects, because without this addition, the conquered peoples could not be expected to legitimately consent to an unfavorable association] (du Calvet 1784, my translation). Moreover, once it has involved the conquered people in creating a new constitution, the conqueror cannot unilaterally renege on it.

References to natural law are also present in the discourse of the *Patriotes*, especially their leader, Louis-Joseph Papineau (Lamonde and Larin 1998, 469–70). According to Papineau, whose thinking was very close to that of Pufendorf, French Canada, through conquest, attained the status of a contracting party in the foundation of the colonial regime, and should enjoy all the privileges and prerogatives accorded to British subjects. As inheritors of British institutions, French Canadians have the undeniable right to a representative government, because they were granted the title of British subjects following the conquest (Lamonde and Larin 1998, 488–94). Papineau also relies on the law of nations: "Le Roi d'Angleterre ne peut avoir d'autre droit de la guerre et des gens que le droit public de l'Europe. Il est soumis aux lois du Royaume comme le simple sujet lorsqu'en temps de paix il n'est appelé qu'à veiller à leur exécution dans ses états" [The King of England can have no other law than that of war and the public law of Europe. He is subject to the laws of the Kingdom when in time of peace he is called to ensure the enforcement of laws in his states]. He adds: "Nous devons le droit d'être représenté[s] aux conditions stipulées avec nos pères dans la tranchée" [We should have the right to be represented under the conditions stipulated to our fathers in the trenches] (quoted in Lamonde and Larin 1998, 215, my translation). This is a phrase all the more remarkable as it seems to combine two approaches, that of Hobbes, for which the state can be born directly from the battlefield ("in the trenches"), and that of natural law theorists, for whom conquest does not deprive a conquered people of their right to participate in the formation of their new government. In his last public speech to the l'Institut canadien in December 1867, Papineau invoked the terms of the capitulation of 1759, which turned the habitants of French Canada into British subjects and also paid homage to du Calvet's notion that the conquered retain certain rights.

Reference to natural law continued in Lower Canada after the Act of Union. For example, Benjamin Viger deplored that the Crown distributed land to wealthy British settlers and the Anglican clergy, who often left these lands unused in order to engage in speculation, when the French-Canadian population was being forced to move to the United States because their lands had become overcrowded. In his *Aurore des Canadas*, published in October 1840, Viger outlines the limits of sovereign authority vis-à-vis the lands of a conquered people. He cites Grotius to establish that the surrender of New France to Britain did not transfer ownership of the land occupied by the people of Canada to the British sovereign. The British victory in the Seven Years' War changed the administration of the territory, but not ownership of land, which remained a protected civil right of the conquered people. By virtue of their natural right to be considered as men to be governed and not to be possessed, the French-Canadian people retained full ownership of their occupied lands, and must be consulted on any redistribution of these lands.

The reference to natural law in French Canada reappeared in a more scientific form in *Histoire du droit canadien*, by Edmond Lareau (1889), the first French-language public law treatise in Canada published after 1867. In the second part of his book, entitled "*La Domination anglaise*," Lareau does a systematic study of the legality of the British conquest of 1759–63. The study was the first of its kind, and remains unequalled. He cites several theorists of international law and natural law, such as Grotius, Vattel, Pufendorf, and Burlamaqui, to describe the change of regime and the legal effects of the conquest on civil and political rights of the people of Canada. His main conclusion is that, although the Paris Treaty of 1763 mentions only the "cession" of Canada, it was indeed a conquest, which took place under conditions specified in the terms of the capitulation. Inspired by the principles of international law, Lareau attempts to mitigate the effects of the conquest. War, which temporarily turns nations into enemies, is only a transitional state, and the general principles of international law based on equality among nations are reinstated as soon as the war is finished. Therefore, Lareau interprets the capitulation of 1759, the highest legal act of the British conquest of Canada, as follows: "C'est ainsi que l'Angleterre l'a compris, en faisant jouir les vaincus des mêmes droits que ceux de ses propres sujets; ce n'est pas une imposition de droits, mais bien une participation à un corps commun à l'empire" [Thus, England has understood by giving the defeated the same rights as those of its own subjects; that this is not an imposition of duties, but participation in a common body of the empire] (1889, 29, my translation). This participation of the conquered French Canadians in the British Empire was implicitly recognized by section 5 of the Quebec Act, which awarded the French-Canadian subjects of His Majesty the right to practise their Catholic faith throughout his empire.

References to natural law theory to determine the rights of a conquered people also appeared on the other side of the Atlantic in the writings of John Stuart Mill, in a text published in January 1838 in which the philosopher deals with the imminent nomination of Lord Durham as governor general following the Mackenzie and Papineau rebellions of 1837–38. The text is surprising in that Mill considers the rebellions a real war, governed by the law of nations, not as seditions falling under criminal law, writing: "the insurgents who fall into our hands are not criminals, who can be tried by a court of justice, but prisoners of war" (Mill [1838] 1982), 415). According to Mill, the people of Canada had a legitimate cause to take up arms, following the proclamation of Colonial Secretary Lord Russell's ten resolutions in 1837: "The people of Canada had against the people of England legitimate cause of war. They had the provocation which, on every received principle of public law, is a breach of the conditions of allegiance. Their provocation was the open violation of their constitution, in the most fundamental of its provisions, by the passing of Resolutions through Parliament, for taking their money from their exchequer without their consent." He goes on to argue that "taking away from them the right which constitutes them as members of a free state, and the violation of which, by the sense of all ages and nations, forms the casus belli between a people and their government" (417). Mill's analysis assumes, therefore, that French Canada was linked to the British Crown by the terms of allegiance in the capitulation of 1759 to which the *Patriotes* themselves often referred in their speeches. Mill also holds the 1791 constitution to be a pact between Canadians and the British authorities, whose violation gave Canadians the legitimate right to defend themselves with arms in order to restore their rights. Although insisting on the international dimension of the conflict, which would apply the law of war in the cases of the Mackenzie and Papineau rebellions, Mill actually suggests that the "war" of 1837–38 was similar to a second conquest of Canada.

Conclusion: Canada as a Conquering Empire-State

As we have seen, conquest played a pivotal role in Canada's history, in the forming of constitutional law, and in highly significant political debates, on which applied political theory can shed some light. Indeed conquest and its philosophical interpretations, illuminated by applied political theory, can help us understand the evolution of the Canadian state and its mode of legitimization. One of the prominent players in the constitutional reform of 1982, Barry L. Strayer (2013), suggests that the creation of the Dominion of Canada in 1867 was the product of neither the popular will expressed by the Canadian people nor the will of legislatures existing in Canada at the time. The Parliament of United Canada certainly approved the Quebec Resolutions in February 1865, though by a thin majority of French-Canadian deputies, but the colonial authorities subsequently amended the approved text without submitting the amended version back to legislatures in Canada. Subsequently Nova Scotia tried unsuccessfully to withdraw from the arrangements once they had been decreed by Queen Victoria. Nonetheless, says Strayer, relying on the work of the legal theorist Hans Kelsen, the legitimacy of the 1867 Constitution was hardly challenged. Summarizing the thought of Kelsen, Strayer writes: "a constitution is legitimate if it works, and it can be said to work only if it accepted by those governed by it" (2013, 31–2).

Yet Strayer does not envisage the possibility that the legitimacy of the 1867 Constitution was also founded on conquest itself, which conferred on Westminster the legal and moral authority to change the status of the colonies using the rights of the conqueror exercised by the British sovereign and its representatives since the Treaty of Utrecht of 1713. As we have seen, conquest is not merely a military exercise of interest only to historians; it is way to form a state and to legitimize its authority, as well as a source of rights that define the meaning of the obligations of the conqueror state to a conquered population. Reinterpreted by the theory of natural law that inspired many modern political thinkers and even some Canadian politicians of the nineteenth century, the rights of a conquered people might acquire considerable scope, which diminishes the dominance of the conqueror. In addition, the Canadian federal government, which favoured the gradual Canadianization of the original British North American dominion, also inherited legitimacy acquired by the imperial conquest. In many ways, the Canadian state as such was and remains an empire-state, where conquest provides, like a an inexhaustible fountain, a continuous flow of legitimacy. It should be noted that, although Canada has a history of attempts by movements, political parties, and intellectual figures to rebuild Canada on contractual bases through adopting a constitution prepared either by an assembly of representatives of all parts of the country or ratified by the entire population, all such attempts have failed. Indeed Canada was nevertheless able fundamentally to reform its Constitution in 1982 without the consent of one its founding partners, Quebec. Further, with the exception of Quebec, it was the executives of provincial governments that consented to the 1982 Constitution without even feeling the need to seek the consent of their respective legislatures (Kelly and Laforest 2004, xviii). Remarkably, some, such as Pierre Trudeau, have argued that federal deputies from Quebec could express this consent adequately without gaining the approval of Quebec's provincial representatives, as if Canada were an unitary state with an unified demos. This reminds us of de Tocqueville's famous portrayal of American federalism, which he depicts as a liberal empire where the federal government tends to act as an almost complete national government ([1835] 1981). But unlike the United States, Canada has been prone to borrow from the conservative language of David Hume and Edmund Burke, at least in constitutional matters. The Canadian government since 1867 actually has legitimized itself by means that are mostly prescriptive, such as the effect of the passage of time and the gradual acceptance of the state by citizens who have become accustomed to the political freedoms and protections it affords. However, the language of natural law, so pervasive in the nineteenth century, that defended the right to govern and the constitutional capacity of the conquered peoples has not vanished, but remains in the form of Quebec and Aboriginal nationalisms.

The work of Janet Ajzenstat (2003) certainly provides a counterpoint to these conclusions in that she argues that, despite the role the conquest played in the construction of the Canadian state, its legitimacy remains fundamentally based on the Lockean principle of consent. Conquest and consent, however, far from being contradictory, instead go together to legitimize and build a state, especially an empire-state. The eventual granting of some consent by the conquered people to the conqueror does not erase the fact that the foundation of the state was coercive and that the constitutional regime is derived from this very foundation. Noted historian Eric Hobsbawm points out that conquest cannot be maintained without seeking the cooperation of the conquered or subjected populations (2008, 53–4). In an ambitious book on UK political law, the French lawyer Denis Baranger maintains that the United Kingdom, as a political body, retains all the features of an empire in the relations between its centre (England) and its peripheral nations (Scotland, Wales, and North Ireland), notably because of the role of conquest in British legal discourse (2008, 268–302). By pushing away the homogeneity of the nation-state, through the contemporary devolution of powers to Scottish, Welsh, and Irish subnational governments, the United Kingdom today continues to perpetuate all kinds of demarcations between the English centre and the minorities on its peripheries. And if "la contrainte est un aspect de la formation d'un empire" [coercion is an aspect of the formation of an empire], adds Baranger, it is not necessarily a dominant feature of its functioning, because an empire might wish to facilitate the consent of its peripheral entities (269).

The philosopher Vincent di Norcia, evoking both the European subjugation of Indigenous nations and the conquest of New France, has argued that since its foundation Canada has presented all the structural features of an empire (di Norcia 1979). Ian Angus, for his part, believes that the progressive Hegelianism that dominates political thought in English Canada has overshadowed any discussion of empire as a structuring principle of Canada (2013, 12). In short, Canada and the United Kingdom still have much in common in the sense that both were and remain empire-states. Therefore it is not surprising that the opening phrase of the Constitution Act, 1867 clearly states the newly formed Canadian Dominion will have "a Constitution similar in Principle to That of the United Kingdom."

REFERENCES

Janet, Ajzenstat. 2003. *The Once and Future Canadian Democracy*. Montreal; Kingston, ON: McGill-Queen's University Press.

Angus, Ian. 2013. *The Undiscovered Country: Essays in Canadian Intellectual Cultivation*. Edmonton: Athabasca University Press.

Baranger, Denis. 2008. *Write the Unwritten Constitution*. Paris: Presses Universitaires de France.

Beaudoin, Gerald A. 2000. *Federalism in Canada*. Montreal: Wilson & Lafleur.

Beiner, Ronald, and Wayne Norman. 2001. *Canadian Political Philosophy*. Don Mills, ON: Oxford University Press.

Bélanger, André-J., and Vincent Lemieux. 1996. *Introduction to Policy Analysis*. Montreal: Les Presses de l'Université de Montréal.

Bergeron, Gérard. 1990. *Small State Treaty*. Paris: Presses Universitaires de France.

Bertrand, Jean-Marie. 1992. *Cities and Kingdoms of the Greek World and Political Space*. Paris: Hachette.

Bissonnette, Bernard. 1963. *Essay on the Constitution of Canada*. Montreal: Éditions du Jour.

Blackstone, William. [1765–69] 1979. *Commentaries on the Laws of England*, vol. 1. Chicago: University of Chicago Press.

Bourdieu, Pierre. 2012. *On the State*. Paris: Seuil.

Braud, Philippe. 1997. *The State*, vol. 2. Political Science. Paris: Seuil.

Caron, Maximilian. 1938. "Is Quebec a state?" *Economic News* 14: 121.

Carré de Malberg, Raymond. [1922] 2004. *Contribution à la théorie générale de l'État*. Paris: Dalloz.

Chennells, David. 2001. *The Politics of Nationalism in Canada: Cultural Conflict since 1760*. Toronto: University of Toronto Press.

Courtois, Charles-Philippe, ed. 2009. *The Conquest: An Anthology*. Montreal: Éditions Typo.

Crowley, Brian Lee. 2009. *Fearful Symmetry: The Fall and Rise of Canada's Founding Values*. Toronto: Key Porter Books.

Decroix, Arnaud. 2011. "La controverse sur la nature du droit applicable après la conquête." *Revue de Droit de McGill* 56 (3): 489–542. https://doi.org/10.7202/1005131ar

Derathe, Robert. 1995. *Jean-Jacques Rousseau and Political Science of His Time*. Paris: Vrin.

de Tocqueville, Alexis. [1835] 1981. *De la démocratie en Amérique*, vol. 1. Paris: Garnier-Flammarion.

di Norcia, Vincent. 1979. "The Empire Structures of the Canadian State." In *Philosophers Look at Canadian Confederation*, ed. Stanley G. French. Montreal: Canadian Philosophical Association.

Dion, Leon. 1986. "L'État libéral et l'expansion de l'espace public étatique." *International Political Science Review* 7 (2): 190–208. https://doi.org/10.1177/019251218600700206

du Calvet, Pierre. [1784] 2002. *Call for Justice of the State or Letter Collection King, the Prince of Wales and Ministers*. London. Reproduced in Jean-Pierre Boyer, *Appeal to the State Justice*. Quebec North.

Dyson, Kenneth. 1980. *The State Tradition in Western Europe*. Colchester, UK: ECPR Press.

Foucault, Michel. 1997. *We Must Defend Society: College in France in 1976*. Paris: Gallimard et Seuil.

Graefe, Peter. 2017. "L'État canadien." In *La politique québécoise et canadienne*, 2nd ed., ed. Alain-G. Gagnon, 133–52. Quebec City: Presses de l'Université du Québec.

Grotius, Hugo. 1999. *The Law of War and Peace*. Paris: Presses Universitaires de France.

Heaman, E.A.. 2015. *A Short History of the State in Canada*. Toronto: University of Toronto Press.

Henderson, James (Sákéj) Youngblood, Marj Benson, and Isobel Findlay. 2000. *Aboriginal Tenure in the Constitution of Canada*. Toronto: Carswell.

Hobbes, Thomas. [1651] 1968. *Leviathan*. Toronto: Collier-Macmillan.

Hobsbawm, Eric. 2008. *On Empire*. New York : Pantheon Books.

Hogg, Peter W. 2011. *Constitutional Law of Canada*. 5th ed. Toronto: Carswell.

Hume, David. [1741] 1953. *Political Essays*. New York: Liberal Arts Press.

Kelly, Stéphane, and Guy Laforest. 2004. "Introduction de l'édition en langue française." In *Débats sur la foundation du Canada*, ed. Janet Ajzenstat, Paul Romney, and William D. Gairdner, xiii–xviii. Quebec City: Presses de l'University Laval.

Laforest, Guy. 1995. *Trudeau and the End of a Canadian Dream*. Montreal; Kingston, ON: McGill-Queen's University Press.

Lamonde, Yvan, and Claude Larin, eds. 1998. *Louis-Joseph Papineau: un démi-siècle de combats, interventions publiques*. Montreal: Fides.

Lareau, Edmond. 1889. *Histoire du droit canadien*. Montreal: Librairie générale de droit and jurisprudence.

Laskin, Bora. 1975. *Laskin's Canadian Constitutional Law*. 4th ed. Toronto: Carswell.

Lazzeri, Christian. 1995. "The Theory of Natural Law in the 17th Century: The Utility as an Issue of Law and the Contract." In *A History and Explanation of the Moral and Political Philosophy*, Vol. 1, ed. Alain Caillé, Christian Lazzeri, and Michel Senellart. Paris: Flammarion.

Legaré, Anne. 2017. *Le Québec, une nation imaginaire*. Montreal: Presses de l'Université de Montréal.

Lepage, Pierre. 2009. *Myths and Realities about Aboriginal Peoples*. 2nd ed. Quebec City: Quebec Commission on Human Rights and Youth Rights.

Locke, John. [1689] 1986. *The Second Treatise on Civil Government*. Buffalo, NY: Prometheus Books.

Lower, Arthur R.M. 1946. *Colony to Nation: A History of Canada*. Toronto: Longmans, Green.

Loysel, Antoine. [1607] 1971. *Institutes coutumières*, vol. 1. Geneva: Slatkine Reprints.

Macklem, Patrick. 2001. *Indigenous Difference and the Constitution of Canada*. Toronto: University of Toronto Press.

Madison, G.B., Paul Fairfield, and Ingrid Harris. 2000. *Is There a Canadian Philosophy? Reflections on the Canadian Identity*. Ottawa: University of Ottawa Press.

Magnet, Joseph Eliot. 1983. *Constitutional Law of Canada*. Toronto: Carswell.

Mill, John Stuart. [1838] 1982. "Radical Party and Canada: Lord Durham and the Canadians." In *The Collected Works of John Stuart Mill*. Vol. 7, *Essays on England, Ireland, and the Empire*, ed. John Robson, 405–37. Toronto: University of Toronto Press. https://doi.org/10.3138/9781442654136-016

Miquelon, Dale. 1977. *Society and Conquest: The Debate on the Bourgeoisie and Social Change in French Canada, 1700–1850*. Toronto: Copp Clarke.

Montesquieu. 1964. *Complete Works*. Paris: Seuil.

Morin, Jacques-Yvan, and José Woerhling. 1992. *The Constitutions of Canada and Quebec from the French Regime to the Present Day*. Montreal: Éditions Themis.

Panitch, Leo, ed. 1977. *The Canadian State: Political Economy and Political Power*. Toronto: University of Toronto Press.

Plank, Geoffrey. 2001. *An Unsettled Conquest: The British Campaign against the Peoples of Acadia*. Philadelphia: University of Pennsylvania Press.

Reid, John G., Maurice Basque, Elizabeth Manke, Barry Moody, Geoffrey Plank, and William Wicken. 2004. *The "Conquest" of Acadia, 1710: Imperial, Colonial, and Aboriginal Constructions*. Toronto: University of Toronto Press.

Resnick, Philip. 1990. *The Masks of Proteus: Canadian Reflections on the State*. Montreal; Kingston, ON: McGill-Queen's University Press.

Resnick, Philip. 2005. *The European Roots of Canadian Identity*. Peterborough, ON: Broadview Press.

St-Aubin, Michel. 1963. "Is Quebec a State?" *Themis* 13: 51.

Saul, John Ralston. 2008. *A Fair Country: Telling Truths about Canada*. Toronto: Viking Canada.

Seliger, Martin. 1968. *The Politics of Liberal John Locke*. London: George Allen & Unwin.

Strayer, Barry L. 2013. *Canada's Revolution Constitution: 201*. Edmonton: University of Alberta Press.

Terrel, Jean. 2005–6. "About Conquest: Law and Politics in Montesquieu." *Revue Montesquieu* 8: 137–50.

Tremblay, André. 2000. *Constitutional Law: Principles*. Montreal: Éditions Themis.

Tully, James. 1993. *An Approach to Political Philosophy: Locke in Contexts*. Cambridge: Cambridge University Press. https://doi.org/10.1017/CBO9780511607882

Tully, James. 1995. *Strange Multiplicity*. Cambridge: Cambridge University Press. https://doi.org/10.1017/CBO9781139170888

PART VI

Canada in the World

18 The Legitimacy of Judicial Review: The Strength of the Weak

STEPHEN WINTER

This chapter concerns "weak-form" judicial review.[1] In a weak-form system, courts can use a bill of rights to interpret and alter legislation, but parliament[2] can gainsay the courts using ordinary legislative means. With the 1982 Charter of Rights and Freedoms, Canada was the first Commonwealth polity to develop robust weak-form review.[3] Its emulators include New Zealand's 1990 Bill of Rights (NZBORA), the United Kingdom's 1998 Human Rights Act, the Australian Capital Territory's (ACT's) 2004 Human Rights Act, and the Australian state of Victoria's 2006 Charter of Human Rights and Responsibilities Act. Despite these developments, however, weak-form review rarely appears in contemporary debates regarding the legitimacy of judicial review, in which disputants continue to presuppose that the constitutional options are limited to systems of either judicial or parliamentary supremacy (Gardbaum 2013a, 2231; Mac Amhlaigh 2016, 176). Attending to the real world of constitutional practice, this chapter demonstrates weak-form review's distinct, and potentially valuable, legitimating advantage.

Applied political theory is a useful approach for analysing an emergent constitutional model. I begin by outlining a conceptual apparatus for assessing legislative legitimacy. I use that apparatus to critique

1 The contrast between strong- and weak-form review is Mark Tushnet's. Related dicussions refer to the "dialogue model," "the new commonwealth model," or "parliamentary bills of rights." For discussion, see Gardbaum (2013b); Tushnet (2008).

2 I use "parliament" to describe an elected branch of government with the power of primary legislation.

3 This claim ignores statutory bills of rights in Saskatchewan, Quebec, and Alberta, and the 1960 Canadian Bill of Rights (see Webber 2006).

systems of both judicial and parliamentary constitutional supremacy before describing the mechanisms that constitute weak-form review in practice. The final sections address two prominent criticisms of weak-form review: the first, that weak-form systems are practically unstable; the second, that they are illegitimate. In response I argue that weak-form review is a stable constitutional model that has at least one considerable legitimating strength.

Key Concepts

Applied political theory combines the conceptual with the empirical. I start with the conceptual. The necessary concepts "rule of law," "authority," "legitimacy," and "accountability" draw from the mainstream of common law jurisprudence, supplemented by work in deliberative democracy. A primary goal of a legislative system is the *rule of law*. For law to rule, "we must be able, not merely to conform our action to what the law demands, but to act upon the law as a reason itself" (Hart 1961, 56). If laws offer reasons acceptable to the citizen, then the citizenry can rule itself according to the law. Modern polities are characterized by a complex system of law-making authorities. Political institutions exercise *authority* when they provide citizens with reasons to act and judge: legislative authority characterizes those institutions that produce reason-giving law. If legislative authority is the power to create reasonable law, then legislative *legitimacy* concerns the reasons that citizens have to endorse legislative institutions as authoritative. In complex modern polities, legitimacy is a property of a legislative system.

Legitimacy can be substantive or procedural. An institution has substantive legitimacy if conformity to its directives enables the citizenry to accomplish goods or prevent ills that are instrumental to the work of the institution itself. For example, respect for fundamental rights is a substantive basis for legal authority. It is common to perceive such rights as external limits to legislation: legislation is reasonable if and only if it does not infringe the citizen's fundamental rights (Hamburger 1993). For those of an externalist persuasion, a constitutional bill of rights specifies legal limits to law making: constitutional law "rules" the polity because it constrains the legislative process. For example, Pierre Elliott Trudeau argued that the Canadian Charter specifies "basic rights that cannot be taken away by any government" (Trudeau 1993, 322). In terms of legitimacy, constraining legislative authorities through legally enforceable rights helps citizens avoid being subject to reasonably unacceptable laws.

Although familiar, the externalist understanding of rights as constraints is inaccurate. The power to define the legal ambit of constitutional rights is the power to make law, not merely to constrain or interpret it – it is a legislative power (Waldron 2006, 1346). In both courts and parliament, law makers regularly confront hard questions about how to respect rights in domains where the values that rights protect are in conflict with other values and other rights. Examples are easy to find: hate speech, Internet privacy, and the limits to parental discipline are just a few substantive, and reasonable, areas of significant debate. In such political controversies, a bill of rights does not stand as an external limit to legislation; instead it specifies substantive public values, internal to the law, that legitimate legislative authority.

Because the substance of the law is contestable, legislative authority reposes, in part, upon procedural legitimacy. This form of legitimacy inheres in the legislative process; this chapter focuses, in particular, upon the legitimating role of *accountability*.[4] Mark Philp defines accountability as follows: "A is accountable with respect to M when some individual, body or institution, Y, can require A to inform and explain/justify his or her conduct with respect to M" (2009, 32). Using Philp's description, a legislative system of authorities (A) is accountable with respect to the law (M) when the citizen (Y) can require legislative authorities to inform, explain, and/or justify his or her conduct as regards to the law.

There are many different ways to produce legislative accountability, but regardless of the means, legitimacy improves to the extent that the legislative system realizes five criteria.[5] First, a legitimating accountability mechanism should be *public*, in the sense of being both concerned with public matters and constituted by public processes. Second, accountability mechanisms should be *open*, in terms of both access to the mechanism and its substantive content – exclusions of ideas and persons must be justifiable. Third, they should be *equal*: no citizen has a privileged ability to effect accountability. Fourth, the mechanism should be *iterative*. Fifth, the mechanism should be *effective*, enabling citizens to make the legislative authority inform, explain, and/or justify its conduct regarding the law.

4 Accountability is only one component of "input" legitimacy. An obvious addition is adherence to established "procedural rules"; see Peter (2008).

5 These criteria draw from the deliberative democracy literature, including Dryzek (2002); Gutmann and Thompson (2004); Rawls (1995).

Different accountability mechanisms realize these five characteristics to different degrees. An important example that combines all five is the parliamentary election. An election is public because it enables each citizen to exercise an equal vote, its processes and agendas are open, the election is iterated at regular intervals, and the election is effective, as citizens can use their votes to encourage politicians to justify past legislative acts and future commitments. Because elections provide accountability, they are an important means of legitimating parliament's legislative authority.

Critiquing Judicial and Parliamentary Supremacy

In this section I evaluate the legitimacy of two leading constitutional systems: those of judicial and parliamentary supremacy. If rights law requires legislative authority, then it must be legitimate, otherwise enactments pertaining to rights will not be compatible with the rule of law. And both judicial and parliamentary supremacist systems suffer from significant illegitimating defects.

Systems of judicial supremacy empower courts to use bills of rights to interpret and alter legislation, and parliaments must use extraordinary powers, such as a constitutional amendment, to gainsay judicial decisions. The United States and Germany are paradigmatic systems of judicial supremacy. Critics of judicial supremacy argue, however, that courts cannot satisfy the necessary systemic legitimacy demands (Bellamy 2007; Knopff 1998; Manfredi 1993; Morton and Knopff 2000, 149; Petter and Hutchinson 2010; Waldron 2006). Recall that legislative legitimacy concerns the reasons citizens have to endorse an institution as authoritative. There are good reasons to doubt judicial review's legitimacy on both substantive and procedural grounds. In substantive terms, people reasonably disagree over which rights polities should respect and, even more, over how the law should respect rights, and those disagreements can emerge without anyone making clear errors of reasoning (Rawls 1996, 56–7). Why should a citizen who agrees with the parliamentary enactment of a rights law treat the contrary judgment of a court as reason-giving? Judicial decisions mix conjecture with passion, incomplete knowledge, and fragmentary experience. Citizens should expect frequent judicial error. And because rights law is reasonably contestable, they will reasonably disagree over what is and what is not erroneous.

If the substantive content of the law is contestable, the hope that good judicial practice will provide procedural warrant is equally problematic.

Recall that procedural legitimacy stems, in part, from institutional accountability that is equal, public, open, iterative, and effective. Judicial review is very effective – for some citizens. Yet access to the courts is far from equal because the expense of litigation disadvantages many citizens. In terms of process, courts are highly inegalitarian, and preserve, to a degree unsurpassed by other political institutions, medieval customs of privilege, dress, and form. Nor are courts open: legal doctrines of standing prevent broad participation, and appellate courts can focus on legal technicalities, ignoring reasons germane to the rightness or wrongness of the particular case. In terms of iteration, judicial supremacy makes the opinions of a few appellate judges into permanent law for the many – that is, until such time as those same judges decide to contradict themselves. These points are widely recognized – see the results of a survey reported in Bowcott (2015). How can people "act upon the law as a reason itself" if they have good reason to think the law could be wrong in substantive content and derive from a flawed procedure? From an accountability perspective, judicial supremacy suffers from an acute legitimacy deficit.

For that reason, one might prefer a system of parliamentary supremacy. In such a system, politicians have the final authority over rights law. Courts may offer suggestions, but must defer to parliament's authority. The reason that systems of parliamentary supremacy might be more legitimate is not that politicians are better at avoiding substantive error; rather, to some, it appears that parliament has superior procedural legitimacy (Bellamy 2007, 27; Waldron 2006, 1375). As noted above, parliamentary practice clearly embodies the five accountability criteria. Through rallies, petitions, select committee presentations, and, pre-eminently, elections, parliaments are held to account by the citizenry through mechanisms that are equal, open, public, iterative, and effective. The parliamentary supremacist need not exclude the courts from the legislative process, but when parliament and courts disagree, parliament's superior accountability provides a "tie-breaking" reason to be the final authority.

The accountability argument for parliamentary supremacy over rights law sounds fine in theory, but when applied in real politics, parliaments are liable to significant accountability failings. Modern polities count their voters by the millions, making the accountability of parliament to most citizens ineffective regarding any particular law (Kumm 2007, 26–7). And parliament is not accountable to all citizens equally. Control of parliament depends, inevitably, upon minority support. Not only do governments garner minorities of the popular vote (and even smaller minorities of the electorate); in an age of targeted campaigning, political office depends upon the swing votes of fractional minorities. Those all-important popular elections are not open contests, but instead are heavily moderated by the circumstances of what Jeffrey Winters calls "civic oligarchy" (2011, 208–9ff). The private workings of money, technical expertise, and party hierarchy obstruct modern politics, while wider social and economic structures erect systemic obstacles to both the political ideas of and participation by those disadvantaged by race, gender, wealth, and class. Parliamentary activity is not wholly public: government dominates parliament, the cabinet dominates government, the Prime Minister's Office dominates the cabinet, and, in terms of effectiveness, all levels of government are increasingly constrained by supranational organizations and institutions such as the World Trade Organization and the global bond market.

In terms of the accountability criteria, real-world parliaments are unequal because some citizens exercise more influence than others, closed to marginalized citizens and systemically excluded issues, non-public because private interests can make the law pander to their preferences, and ineffective because most individuals are politically powerless. The iterations of elections are independent of the citizenry, and might occur at times that are not conducive to reflection on particular rights law. As Annabelle Lever remarks, "[e]lections are too blunt, too infrequent, and typically raise too many issues for electoral consideration for them to provide a good means of holding legislators accountable for violations of rights – or, indeed, for much else" (2009, 811).

The defender of parliamentary supremacy might think that the flaws of existing parliaments are reasons to improve them. And so they are. There is reason, however, to doubt the perfectibility of legislative systems: legislative authorities must be built using the "crossgrained crooked wood" of humanity (Kant 1799, 421); therefore even the best legislative systems will be marred by structural imperfection and injustice. If human infirmity means both judicial and parliamentary institutions are perpetually and irreparably flawed, citizens will be subject regularly to procedural and substantive legislative deficiencies.

Weak-Form Review

In the face of these illegitimating defects, weak-form review offers some legitimating advantages. Weak-form constitutional systems are constituted by mechanisms that enable both judicial and parliamentary authority regarding rights. Weak-form systems realize this authoritative plurality by combining four mechanisms: an interpretation article, the judicial power of annulment or provision for non-justiciable "declarations of inconsistency," a notwithstanding power, and a "reasonable limits" clause.[6] Because these countervailing mechanisms constitute both parliaments and courts as authorities over rights, constitutional pluralism provides avenues of accountability for the citizen.

The first mechanism is the practice of judicial interpretation. A weak-form system enables judges to use a bill of rights to interpret the law. Given two or more possible interpretations of a law, a bill of rights enables a court to legislate a meaning it believes is more rights-congruent. In Canada the interpretative powers of the judiciary are particularly strong: it can use the Charter to "read down" laws – confining the extension of a law – and to add provisions to a law by "reading in." An example of the latter power is *Haig v. Canada* ([1992] CanLII 2787 (ON CA)), in which the Ontario Court of Appeal used the Charter to make sexual orientation a prohibited ground of discrimination under the Canadian Human Rights Act.

The second power accorded to weak-form courts concerns what happens when the law cannot be interpreted as consistent with the bill of rights. Canadian courts can annul inconsistent legislation; other weak-form courts can issue declarations of inconsistency.[7] Parliaments are not required to legislate in response to these declarations – they can ignore them, but also, importantly, they can choose how they will amend legislation in response. The declaration often enables special procedures to facilitate a parliamentary response; in the United Kingdom, a declaration allows parliament to "fast-track" legislation to bring the law into conformity. In Victoria and the ACT, a declaration obliges a cabinet minister to table a response in parliament.

Turning to the powers of the weak-form parliament, both the Canadian and the Victorian Charters enable parliament to override judge-made law with a "notwithstanding" (*non obstante*) clause. Because that

6 Weak-form systems often have other provisions, such as parliamentary oversight committees and the provision for parliamentary reports on compliance. My thesis focuses on the legislative powers of the court and parliament.

7 In the United Kingdom, these are called "declarations of incompatibility"; in the Australian state of Victoria, they are declarations of "inconsistent interpretation." These are merely terminological differences.

clause enables parliament to legislate, notwithstanding judicial decisions on rights law, for a renewable five-year period,[8] a court's power to alter and annul legislation is conditional on parliamentary restraint. If parliament decides that the court did, or will, act unreasonably, it can make law through ordinary mechanisms.

Lastly, weak-form systems include a "reasonable limits" clause.[9] For example, section 7 (2) of the Victorian Charter reads: "A human right may be subject under law only to such reasonable limits as can be demonstrably justified in a free and democratic society." Not only does a reasonable limits clause recognize the contestable character of rights-law, it also offers both courts and parliament influence over its development. The use of the reasonable limits clause by courts is important and often remarked (see, for example, Choudhry 2006), but its use by parliament is observed less frequently. A good example is the 1994 Canadian case, *Daviault v. The Queen* ([1994] 3 S.C.R. 63). In 1989 Henri Daviault committed a sexual assault after he had drunk a large amount of brandy. In his defence Daviault argued that he was so inebriated that he could not form the intent to commit a criminal offence. After the Quebec courts ruled against Daviault – contemporary case law held that drunkenness is no defence against assault – the Supreme Court of Canada used the Charter to allow intoxication as a defence. In response, Parliament amended the Criminal Code to give effect to the original prohibition, arguing that a legislative provision disallowing a defence of intoxication is a reasonable limit in the context of vulnerable women and children (Kelly 2005, 248). At the time of writing, that provision of the Criminal Code remains effective: intoxication is not an effective defence in cases of assault.[10]

The countervailing powers that weak-form review vests in courts and parliament provide multiple means by which the law can be made accountable to the citizenry. Within the judiciary, the powers of interpretation, annulment, and declaration also offer the citizen accountability tools. Citizens seeking a particular interpretation of the law can

8 Canada's notwithstanding clause applies only to sections 2 and 7–15, and thereby excludes rights of voting and citizenship. The Victorian Charter is not limited in this way.

9 The United Kingdom's Human Rights Act lacks a general limits clause in part because specific limitations to particular rights are set out by the European Convention on Human Rights, to which the act gives effect.

10 This was confirmed by the Supreme Court of Canada in *R. v. Tatton*, [2015] 2 S.C.R. 574.

simply ask the courts to make the law as citizens would understand it. Similarly both the powers of nullification and declaration provide means by which citizens can use judicial institutions either to change the law or to issue weighty opinions on how the law should change. Turning to parliament, the notwithstanding power subjects any judicial determination to a potential parliamentary override for which the citizenry, in turn, will have an opportunity to hold parliament accountable. Because the five-year period for renewal exceeds the maximum parliamentary term, renewal can occur only after an election. Similarly the reasonable limits clause provides a mechanism for parliament to offer reasoned and weighty determinations of rights law within an institutional framework that enables citizens to engage in the legislative process through select committee submissions, protest, lobbying, and elections.

Varying arrangements of these powers create weak-form systems that differ from one another in terms of the relative strength of parliament and the courts. For heuristic purposes, one can depict these systems on a continuum (depicted in Figure 18.1), with powers of judicial review ranging in relative strength.[11] New Zealand sits closest to the parliamentary supremacy pole because, while courts in that country can use NZBORA to interpret statutes, "read down" regulations, and issue declarations of inconsistency, they are denied powers of annulment, and parliament does not have a standard means of response to declarations of inconsistency (Winter 2017). A little further to the right are the ACT, Victoria, and the United Kingdom, where courts are expressly empowered to issue declarations that require parliamentary attention and complex committee-based systems for intra-institutional dialogue. Furthest to the right sits Canada, where judges use an entrenched bill of rights to read down, read in, and annul legislation. Canada remains a weak-form constitutional system because those judicial powers are balanced by the ability of Canadian legislatures to use the Charter's "reasonable limits" and "notwithstanding" clauses to make rights law in the face of contrary court decisions through the ordinary course of legislation.

My thesis is that weak-form constitutional systems possess a legitimating advantage when compared to the traditional rival systems of parliamentary and judicial supremacy. Because weak-form systems

---

11 The depiction is heuristic; for a critique of this representation of a single-axis continuum, see Kavanagh (2009, 416–19).

Figure 18.1. The Relative Strength of Weak-Form Review

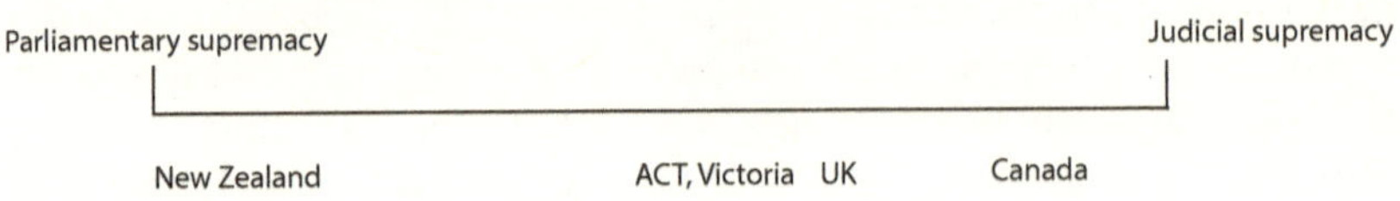

enable both the judiciary and parliament to exercise countervailing authority over rights law, the system as a whole is more accountable to the citizen. That claim, however, is subject to two major points of criticism, one empirical and one theoretical.

The Instability Hypothesis

I first address an empirical concern. A number of influential scholars endorse what I call the "instability hypothesis" (Allan 2006a; Campbell 2009; Geddis 2009; Hiebert 2011; Kelly 2011; Tushnet 2003, 2008). The hypothesis claims that weak-form review is unstable and will tend to evolve rapidly into a system of judicial supremacy or to revert to a system of parliamentary supremacy. Using the continuum depicted in Figure 18.1, the hypothesis suggests that systems positioned towards the left will revert to parliamentary supremacy, while systems on the right will evolve into systems of judicial supremacy. Those who favour the hypothesis often focus on developments in the most "mature" weak-form systems, New Zealand and Canada, and argue these polities demonstrate opposing tendencies. On one hand, New Zealand's impuissant review practice provides evidence of a "rever[sion] to parliamentary sovereignty *simplicita*" (Geddis 2009, 469). On the other hand, it is said that Canada's system is weak-form in appearance only, and in practice differs little from the paradigmatic system of judicial supremacy: the United States of America (Huscroft 2008, 76; Waldron 2006, 1356–7). Either way, practical instability means that weak-form review fails (Tushnet 2003, 838).

Evidence for the instability hypothesis takes at least two different forms, which one can call the "hard" and "soft" arguments. The "hard" argument concerns effective power, and the threat to weak-form stability is desuetude. Unused powers diminish in legitimacy and, ultimately, in effectiveness. A good example is the governor general's legislative veto. Once significant, its disuse, accompanied by a failure to develop legitimating arguments, has meant the loss of that power. Legislative authority develops in an existential game of use it or lose it (Vermeule 2012, 422). If actors do not use the powers a legislative system accords them, other agents will occupy the unused political space.

Hard-power evidence for the right-hand slide into judicial supremacy includes the fact that Canada's federal parliament has never used the Charter's notwithstanding clause. Similarly the UK parliament tends to treat declarations of incompatibility as commands to change the law. The key causal factor is parliamentary reticence. Once a court begins to use a bill of rights to alter legislation, parliaments are reluctant to contradict it (Allan 2006b, 913–14). Similarly, judicial reserve enables the leftward slide into parliamentary supremacy. The usual example is New Zealand.[12] After NZBORA was passed in 1990, New Zealand courts shrank from employing robust powers of interpretation and the declaration of inconsistency. A culture of judicial deference led to claims that the courts were using NZBORA merely to supplement the common law's "principle of legality" review, and therefore failed to realize NZBORA's potential (Geiringer 2008, 62–3). Denied both substantive power and support by professional opinion, New Zealand courts have failed to use NZBORA to occupy legislative space.

Upon closer scrutiny, the "hard" evidence turns out quite weak, for it is clear that parliamentary systems that lie to the right side of the continuum retain significant legislative power vis-à-vis conflicting judicial decisions. At the time of writing, the UK parliament has been resisting for nearly ten years a series of domestic and European rulings, including a declaration of inconsistency, that prisoners have a right to vote. In Canada, the "strongest of the weak," parliament is influential in determining which values warrant Charter protection and the extent of that protection, often in contrast to judicial determinations. Whereas those who favour the instability hypothesis focus on the federal failure to use the notwithstanding clause, Canadian parliaments have, less spectacularly, used the Charter's "reasonable limits" clause (section 1) to exercise significant influence over rights jurisprudence (Roach 2006, 349f). Examples of Canadian "push back" against judicial decisions include laws pertaining to rape-shield provisions (*Seaboyer v. The Queen*, [1991] 2 S.C.R. 577), restrictions on tobacco advertising (*RJR-MacDonald Inc. v. Canada (Attorney General)* [1995] 2 S.C.R. 112), and the aforementioned

12 Further evidence is provided by the record of judicial deference regarding Canada's 1960 Bill of Rights.

defence of intoxication (*Daviault*) (Kelly 2005, 248). In *Attorney General v. Bedford* ([2013] 3 S.C.R. 1101), the Supreme Court of Canada used the Charter to strike down the criminal prohibition of prostitution. In response, in Bill C-36, parliament criminalized the purchase of sexual services, with a preamble arguing that prohibition is a reasonable limit that responds to pressing demands of dignity and safety.[13] Those cases of parliamentary "push back" demonstrate the continued authority of parliament to make rights law despite judicial opposition.

Moreover, the Canadian federal government's disuse of the notwithstanding power is not clear evidence of its desuetude. Constitutional history contains a number of disused mechanisms that return to life; the best example is the US Supreme Court's power of annulment. Established in *Marbury v. Madison* ([1803] 5 U.S. 137), it was not used to annul federal legislation until *Dred Scott v. Sandford* ([1857] 60 U.S. 393). During the intervening period, however, the Supreme Court often annulled state legislation. Canada's notwithstanding power is similarly operative at the provincial level (Hogg, Thornton, and Wright 2007; Kahana 2001). Far from atrophying into desuetude, the notwithstanding clause remains political salient. This was apparent in recent discussions concerning religious dress, including the 2014 debate over Quebec's Charter of Quebec Values and the 2015 federal election campaign (*CBC News* 2014, 2015). The notwithstanding clause is a further reason that judicial review is an important but not supreme part of Canada's complex legislative system.

Turning to the left side of the continuum, the case for reversion in New Zealand requires the judiciary to have lost powers that NZBORA envisions. It is hard to see, however, what powers the judiciary "lost," and easy to discover powers it "gained." NZBORA did not grant the courts the power to issue declarations of inconsistency. That power was made salient by the judiciary through repeated contemplation *obiter dicta*. Twenty-five years after NZBORA was originally promulgated, the High Court issued New Zealand's first declaration of inconsistency in a case pertaining to the voting rights of prisoners (*Taylor v. Attorney-General* [2015] NZHC 1706). The declaratory power was confirmed by the Court of Appeal (*The Attorney-General v. Taylor* [2017] NZCA 215). As for the point that rights-preferring interpretation is merely the "principle of

13 The details of this interaction are more complicated than I have space for in this chapter; for more information, see Canada (2015).

legality's" old wine in a new bottle, this is not evidence of "reversion," but rather the unsurprising point that jurisprudence is a developmental process: the new builds upon the foundations of the old. It is clear that the courts are using NZBORA to exercise review powers beyond that of "legality." This includes real legislative change. For example, in a case concerning a flag-burning protest (*Morse v. The Police* [2011] NZSC 45), the Supreme Court used NZBORA to make its interpretation of "offensive behaviour" more rights-consistent.

The practical experience of robust and sustained pluralist authority over rights law exercised by both courts and parliaments in mature weak-form systems is evidence against the hard-power version of the instability hypothesis. There is, however, an alternative soft-power version of the instability thesis. This soft-power argument suggests that weak-form review affects the legislative process in a manner conducive to judicial supremacy. The dynamic operates within the parliamentary legislative process. Parliamentarians know that the courts will review legislation. Seeking both to protect themselves from public criticism and to preserve their legislative aims, parliaments vet legislation with regard to its rights-compliance. That intra-parliamentary vetting for rights-compliance becomes, in practice, anticipating the court's judgment (Hiebert 2011, 42; Morton 1992, 639). Legal analysis displaces traditional parliamentary considerations, such as constituent opinion and common morality, as compliance testing depicts the development of rights law as a technical problem best addressed by legal experts. Hence, through anticipatory restraint and a perversion of the legislative process, weak-form review encourages parliaments to defer to the courts by adopting judicial language and judgments.

As evidence in favour of the instability hypothesis, soft-power claims for judicial supremacy are weak. The suggestion that legal reasoning *displaces* moral and political engagement seems implausible. The legal cases that drive rights jurisprudence often draw specific attention to pertinent moral values; therefore studying case law can help both politicians and other citizens understand the relevant principles and arguments (Kumm 2007, 5–12). Perhaps some might worry about parliamentarians thinking about rights in a legalistic manner (Campbell 2011, 461), but it is hard to see how the sharing of concepts between parliaments and courts constitutes judicial supremacy. As for the concern with anticipatory restraint, parliaments regularly proceed with legislation that they are advised is likely to face difficulties with review (Hiebert 2011, 54); Canada's Bill C-36 criminalizing prostitution is a recent and clear example.

The soft-power argument concerns how judicial review changes parliamentary behaviour. Therefore it is not evidence of reversion to parliamentary supremacy. As for the right-hand slope towards judicial supremacy, soft power is the wrong kind of evidence to support the hypothesis. The instability hypothesis claims that any significant power of judicial review will quickly engender judicial supremacy. Yet the evidence for the soft-power argument positions parliament as an independent agent seeking to influence court judgments. In fact it is evidence that weak-form review is a distinctive model.

To conclude, support for the instability hypothesis is weak. First, empirical evidence from the most mature weak-form systems, Canada and New Zealand, indicates that weak-form review produces distinctive and stable pluralistic arrangements of "hard" legislative power. Second, the soft-power argument presupposes that both parliaments and courts remain effective legislative authorities. Therefore it is the wrong kind of evidence for the instability hypothesis. It is, instead, behavioural evidence of a substantially distinct constitutional model.

The Legitimacy of Weak-Form Review

I now turn to theoretical questions of legislative legitimacy and the rule of law. Critics condemn weak-form judicial review for enabling judicial encroachment into domains in which parliamentary authority should be pre-eminent (Allan 2006a; Hiebert 2011; Huscroft 2008). Some scholars ascribe superior legitimacy to the elected parliament on accountability grounds because judicial review involves unelected judges' supplanting laws made by popularly accountable parliaments (Bellamy 2007; Waldron 2006). The fact that review is "weak" is irrelevant, for the vital issue is the legislative authority of the courts. The courts' "privileged position" in defining rights law raises "fundamental questions about the legitimacy of judicial review" (Petter 2010, 143).

In response, I develop the argument that weak-form systems have a legitimacy advantage over both systems of parliamentary and judicial supremacy because they facilitate institutional accountability that is more effective, open, public, equal, and iterative. The argument stands upon two conceptual points: the citizen focus of legitimacy, and a systemic conception of the legislative process.

The citizen focus of the argument distinguishes it from cognate approaches. Previous discussions of mutual accountability between court and parliament presuppose a dialogue in which each institution is accountable to the other.[14] Those discussions draw from theoretical traditions in which civil freedom is served through institutional "checks and balances." The theory of checks and balances is classical in its origins,[15] but is now often associated with James Madison ([1788] 2003). For Madison, dividing political authority among differently constituted branches of government helps a polity avoid tyranny because one faction cannot dominate government by seizing control of a single institution.

The framework of applied political theory helps us see how weak-form review develops the classical theory of the mixed constitution in a novel direction. The point is not to leverage the antagonism of distinct institutions. Recall that I defined legislative legitimacy as the reasons citizens have to endorse legislative institutions as authoritative. The question one must ask, given a citizen focus, is not what weak-form review does for parliament or courts, but what it does for the citizenry. The goal of a legislative system is the rule of law, and the hunch is that reasonable law will be more likely if the citizenry can make the system more accountable as a whole. The aspiration is to enable citizens to use both parliament and courts to obtain accountability regarding the law.

The second conceptual point is that legitimacy is a property of a legislative system. The respective critics of judicial and parliament supremacy tend to focus on the deficiencies of particular institutions. That scrutiny is misplaced. Legislative legitimacy is systemic property. In a large and complex constitutional system, not all authoritative nodes need be procedurally identical or held to common standards of accountability. One should judge the components of an imperfect political system by how they contribute to the quality of the system as a whole. Here, the thought is that the accountability of the legislative system to the citizen might be improved by designing a network in which no single element is supreme, and differently constituted institutions exercise overlapping authority.

The accountability argument for weak-form review understands legitimacy in terms of a complex and pluralistic legislative system.

14 This tendency is apparent among authors discussing the Canadian practice (and theory) of "Charter dialogue"; see Hogg, Thornton, and Wright (2007).

15 Discussing the Spartan constitution, Polybius argues that the division of power among different institutions produced stability: "The force of each being neutralized by that of the others, neither of them should prevail and outbalance another, but that the constitution should remain for long thanks to the principle of reciprocity" (2011, 317).

It follows the recent "deliberative turn" in political theory in which mechanisms for legislative accountability extend beyond parliamentary elections (Dryzek 2002, 1–7; Mansbridge et al. 2012). That broad framework includes a large number of local, national, and even international accountability mechanisms, leaving voting as the legitimating device *primes inter pares*. Recognizing that each authoritative "node" in a non-ideal legislative system is subject to substantive contestation, error, and procedural inequity, a constitutional structure of "distributed accountability" involves multiple political forums whose mechanisms for accountability operate differently.[16] Weak-form review's legitimacy advantage is that, by multiplying mechanisms for accountability, it can make political systems more effective, open, equal, public, and iterative.

It will help develop the argument if one distinguishes (roughly) between two forms of accountability: the broad and the narrow. The distinction concerns both to "whom" the institution is accountable and "what" it is accountable for – recall that these were the variables Philp terms Y and M. Parliamentary elections provide broad accountability because candidates for office are accountable to a large number of voters, at least potentially, for all their past acts and future commitments. Electoral accountability is also broad in the sense that there are no enforceable strictures on why people vote for different candidates (or abstain). Different voters will select candidates based on differing assessments of differing sets of legislation. This is good. Mechanisms of broad accountability enable new issues to be put on the public agenda and old ones removed from it, encourage coherent policy packages, and allow citizens to vote according to both prospective and retrospective considerations. The ability of citizens to effect accountability through elections is a tool for, and of, legislative legitimacy.

In the real world, however, the broad form of electoral accountability is inequitable, coarse grained, and unpredictable, and leaves the individual citizen at the mercy of millions of other voters. Therefore, in addition to broad accountability mechanisms, a polity can improve systemic legitimacy by incorporating institutions of narrow accountability. Judicial review offers two forms of narrow accountability. In the first instance, judicial review narrows the scope of what the legislative system is being held accountable for, and focuses upon particular elements

16 The point builds on Goodin's description of "distributed deliberation" (2008, 192–203).

of legislation in isolation. In the course of particularized scrutiny, courts provide an institution in which interested parties can present complex and extended arguments, benefit from previous examples of similar cases, and address impartial judges. This makes the system more open, as citizens can raise previously overlooked or discounted reasons.

As a narrow form of accountability, judicial review makes the legislative system more public in terms of its reasonableness. Review cases require judges, politicians, and citizens to use a bill of rights to justify particular decisions on contested normative issues. There are clear benefits to articulating and assessing the reasonableness of the law's operation away from the hurly-burly of parliamentary deal making. Review makes public officials engage in a public process of deliberation, involving them in "publicly articulating, explaining, and most importantly, justifying public policy" (Chambers 2003, 308). The above-mentioned legislative response to the *Bedford* decision is a good example of the Canadian parliament using the justifying language of the Charter. In such a process, a bill of rights provides a public political standard for assessing legislation.

The second way judicial review provides for "narrow" accountability is its responsiveness to individuals. This makes the system more effective, iterative, and equal. In terms of iteration, weak-form review provides a stable constitutional framework for citizens to have the law re-examined. Individual citizens can subject legislation to an authoritative "second look," but that "second look" is itself conditional upon further iterations. The *Bedford* decision demonstrates that citizens who "lose" a bill of rights case in court can return to parliament. No legislative provision is final, in the sense of being incontestable, as weak-form review institutionalizes the practice of re-examining the reasonable basis for particular laws.

Further, weak-form review improves the legislative system's effective accountability because it gives "individuals the standing to call the government to account" (Walen 2009, 341). In court the citizen's success does not depend, as in an electoral contest, upon first getting a political party to endorse a requested change or convincing the gatekeeping media to promote the case in a manner that will convince thousands of others to change their vote. Instead the citizen is afforded an opportunity to argue that legislation affects her in a way contrary to public standards in a forum in which counterargument will be aired and those invested with authority can assess the relevant arguments (Kumm 2007, 16).

The fact that the citizen has the capacity to force an authoritative assessment of the law serves the values not only of publicity and openness, but also of equality. In the first instance, a rights case enables the citizen to pursue substantive claims for equal treatment, if the case concerns the nature of equality under law. But even in cases that do not concern substantial questions of equality, the citizen's power to procure a hearing constitutes a means in which citizens are equal. A legitimate polity aims to realize the equality of citizens in terms of their capability for effective political action. Courts provide a forum wherein citizens can enact a particularly valuable form of equality: the act of political reasoning. Courts are argumentative spaces in which the citizen can act politically, using reason in an effort to make law.

The legitimating virtue of weak-form review is not that it produces better law, but that it incorporates mechanisms through which citizens can make the legislative system accountable. The discussion represents the accountability of the legislative system as a pluralistic relation between the citizenry and multiple legislative institutions. Weak-form review has a legitimating advantage over systems of either parliament or judicial supremacy insofar as it offers the citizen countervailing mechanisms for broad and narrow accountability. In a non-ideal system, where some institutions will serve some citizens better than others, multiplying the number of authoritative institutions can promote a more open, public, equal, iterative, and effective legislative system. Some citizens who are disadvantaged by the electoral system will be better served by the courts. Others will prefer electoral forums and other parliamentary mechanisms. Still others might be better served by human rights commissions, administrative tribunals, ombudsmen, public inquiries, and royal commissions. If plurality facilitates legitimacy, the argument provides broad support for a complex interlocking system of rights authorities.

Conclusion

Contemporary discussions of judicial review tend to focus on a binary option set, asking us to choose between judicial and parliamentary supremacy. Critics are rightly suspicious of both systems. Informed by an applied political theory framework, I argue that weak-form review offers a distinctive "third" constitutional model with a legitimacy advantage. Drawing upon both political theory and constitutional practice, I have shown how weak-form review augments the citizenry's ability to engender accountability by multiplying institutions with authority over rights law. Differently composed, with different remits and different procedures, the multiple scrutiny provided by weak-form pluralism would make the legislative system more accountable by making it more open, more equal, more public, more iterative, and more effective.

Legislative accountability is important to legitimacy. If both parliaments and courts will make decisions on rights law that are substantially contestable and procedurally deficient, one might prefer, on legitimacy grounds, a pluralist system that facilitates the law's accountability to the citizen. No authority is ultimate and no law as final. Contestation is the stuff of politics.

REFERENCES

Allan, J. 2006a. "Portia, Bassanio or Dick the Butcher? Constraining Judges in the Twenty-First Century." *King's College Law Journal* 17 (1): 1–26. https://doi.org/10.1080/09615768.2006.11427627

Allan, J. 2006b. "The Victorian Charter of Human Rights and Responsibilities: Exegesis and Criticism." *Melbourne University Law Review* 30: 906–22.

Bellamy, R. 2007. *Political Constitutionalism: A Republican Defence of the Constitutionality of Democracy*. Cambridge: Cambridge University Press. https://doi.org/10.1017/CBO9780511490187

Bowcott, O. 2015. "Only one-quarter of Britons believe legal system is fair." *Guardian*, 2 December. Available online at https://www.theguardian.com/law/2015/dec/02/only-one-quarter-of-britons-believe-legal-system-is-fair-survey-shows, accessed 7 December 2015.

Campbell, T. 2009. "Slaying the Hydra: Living Tree Constitutionalism and the Case for Judicial Review of Legislation." *Problema Anuario de Filosofía y Teoría del Derecho* 3: 17–36.

Campbell, T. 2011. "Parliamentary Review with a Democratic Charter of Rights." In *The Legal Protection of Human Rights: Sceptical Essays*, ed. T. Campbell, K.D. Ewing, and A. Tomkins, 453–71. Oxford: Oxford University Press.

Canada. 2015. Department of Justice. "Technical Paper: Bill C-36, *Protection of Communities and Exploited Persons Act*." Ottawa. Available online at http://www.justice.gc.ca/eng/rp-pr/other-autre/protect/p1.html

CBC News. 2014. "Notwithstanding clause would be used to pass secular charter." 31 March. Available online at http://www.cbc.ca/amp/1.2592700

CBC News. 2015. "Gilles Duceppe favours notwithstanding clause to ban niqab at citizenship ceremonies." 22 September. Available online at https://

www.cbc.ca/news/politics/canada-election-2015-notwithstanding-clause-bloc-1.3239021

Chambers, S. 2003. "Deliberative Democratic Theory." *American Political Science Review* 6 (1): 307–26. https://doi.org/10.1146/annurev.polisci.6.121901.085538

Choudhry, S. 2006. "So What Is the Real Legacy of *Oakes*? Two Decades of Proportionality Analysis under the Canadian Charter's Section 1." *Supreme Court Review* 34: 501–35.

Dryzek, J. 2002. *Deliberative Democracy and Beyond: Liberals, Critics, Contestations.* Oxford: Oxford University Press. https://doi.org/10.1093/019925043X.001.0001

Gardbaum, S. 2013a. "The New Commonwealth Model of Constitutionalism." *German Law Journal* 14 (12): 2229–48.

Gardbaum, S. 2013b. *The New Commonwealth Model of Constitutionalism.* Cambridge: Cambridge University Press.

Geddis, A. 2009. "The Comparative Irrelevance of the NZBORA to Legislative Practice." *New Zealand Universities Law Review* 23: 465–88.

Geiringer, C. 2008. "The Principle of Legality and the *Bill of Rights Act*: A Critical Examination of *R v Hansen*." *New Zealand Journal Public and International Law* 6: 59–94.

Goodin, R. 2008. *Innovating Democracy: Democratic Theory and Practice After the Democratic Turn.* Oxford: Oxford University Press. https://doi.org/10.1093/acprof:oso/9780199547944.001.0001

Gutmann, A., and D. Thompson. 2004. *Why Deliberative Democracy?* Princeton, NJ: Princeton University Press. https://doi.org/10.1515/9781400826339

Hamburger, P. 1993. "Natural Rights, Natural Law, and American Constitutions." *Yale Law Journal* 102 (4): 907–60. https://doi.org/10.2307/796836

Hart, H.L.A. 1961. *The Concept of Law.* Oxford: Oxford University Press.

Hiebert, J.L. 2011. "Governing Like Judges?" In *The Legal Protection of Human Rights: Sceptical Essays*, ed. T. Campbell, K.D. Ewing, and A. Tomkins, 40–65. Oxford: Oxford University Press. https://doi.org/10.1093/acprof:oso/9780199606078.003.0003

Hogg, P.W., A.A.B. Thornton, and W.K. Wright. 2007. "Charter Dialogue Revisited – or 'Much ado about metaphors.'" *Osgoode Hall Law Journal* 45 (1): 1–65.

Huscroft, G. 2008. "Rationalizing Judicial Power: The Mischief of Dialogue Theory." In *Contested Constitutionalism: Reflections on the Charter of Rights and Freedoms*, ed. J.B. Kelly and C. Manfredi. Vancouver: UBC Press.

Kahana, T. 2001. "The Notwithstanding Mechanism and Public Discussion: Lessons from the Ignored Practice of Section 33 of the Charter." *Canadian Public Administration* 44 (3): 255–91. https://doi.org/10.1111/j.1754-7121.2001.tb00891.x

Kant, I. 1799. "The Idea of a Universal History in a Cosmopolitan Point of View." In *Essays and Treatises on Moral, Political and Various Philosophical Subjects*.Volume 1. Trans. W. Richardson. London: Royal Exchange. Available online at https://archive.org/details/essaysandtreati01kantgoog

Kavanagh, A. 2009. *Constitutional Review under the UK Human Rights Act*. Cambridge: Cambridge University Press.

Kelly, J.B. 2005. *Governing with the Charter: Legislative and Judicial Activism and Framers' Intent*. Vancouver: UBC Press.

Kelly, J.B. 2011. "A Difficult Dialogue: Statements of Compatibility and the Victorian Charter of Human Rights and Responsibilities Act." *Australian Journal of Political Science* 46 (2): 257–79. https://doi.org/10.1080/10361146.2010.517181

Knopff, R. 1998. "Populism and the Politics of Rights: The Dual Attack on Representative Democracy." *Canadian Journal of Political Science* 31 (4): 683–705. https://doi.org/10.1017/S0008423900009604

Kumm, M. 2007. "Institutionalising Socratic Contestation: The Rationalist Human Rights Paradigm, Legitimate Authority and the Point of Judicial Review." *European Journal of Legal Studies* 1 (2): 1–32.

Lever, A. 2009. "Democracy and Judicial Review: Are They Really Incompatible?" *Perspectives on Politics* 7 (4): 805–22. https://doi.org/10.1017/S1537592709991812

Mac Amhlaigh, C. 2016. "Putting Political Constitutionalism in Its Place." *International Journal of Constitutional Law* 14 (1): 175–97. https://doi.org/10.1093/icon/mow010

Madison, J. [1788] 2003. "No. 51 The Structure of the Government must Furnish the Proper Checks and Balances Between the Different Departments." In *The Federalist Papers*, ed. C. Rossiter. New York: Signet Classics.

Manfredi, C.P. 1993. *Judicial Power and the Charter*. Norman: University of Oklahoma Press.

Mansbridge, J., et al. 2012. "A Systemic Approach to Deliberative Democracy." In *Deliberative Systems*, ed. J. Parkinson and J. Mansbridge, 1–26. Cambridge: Cambridge University Press. https://doi.org/10.1017/CBO9781139178914.002

Morton, F.L. 1992. "The Charter Revolution and the Court Party." *Osgoode Hall Law Journal* 30 (3): 627–52.

Morton, F.L., and R. Knopff. 2000. *The Charter Revolution and the Court Party*. Toronto: University of Toronto Press.

Peter, F. 2008. *Democratic Legitimacy*. New York: Routledge.

Petter, A. 2010. "Rip Van Winkle in Charterland." In *The Politics of the Charter: The Illusive Promise of Constitutional Rights*, ed. A. Petter. Toronto: University of Toronto Press.

Petter, A., and A. Hutchinson. 2010. "Rights in Conflict: The Dilemma of Charter Legitimacy." In *The Politics of the Charter: The Illusive Promise of Constitutional Rights*, ed. A. Petter, 117–34. Toronto: University of Toronto Press. https://doi.org/10.3138/9781442698864-007

Philp, M. 2009. "Delimiting Democratic Accountability." *Political Studies* 57 (1): 28–53. https://doi.org/10.1111/j.1467-9248.2008.00720.x

Polybius. 2011. *"The Histories: Books 5–8 (W. R. Paton, Trans.),"* ed. F. Walbank, and C. Habicht. Cambridge, MA: Harvard University Press.

Rawls, J. 1995. "Political Liberalism: Reply to Habermas." *Journal of Philosophy* 92 (3): 132–80.

Rawls, J. 1996. *Political Liberalism: With a New Introduction and the "Reply to Habermas."* New York: Columbia University Press.

Roach, K. 2006. "Dialogue or Defiance: Legislative Reversals of Supreme Court Decisions in Canada and the United States." *International Journal of Constitutional Law* 4 (2): 347–70. https://doi.org/10.1093/icon/mol008

Trudeau, P.E. 1993. *Memoirs*. Toronto: McClelland & Stewart.

Tushnet, M. 2003. "New Forms of Judicial Review and the Persistence of Rights- and Democracy-Based Worries." *Wake Forest Law Review* 38 (2): 813–38.

Tushnet, M. 2008. *Weak Courts, Strong Rights: Judicial Review and Social Welfare Rights in Comparative Constitutional Law*. Princeton, NJ: Princeton University Press.

Vermeule, A. 2012. "The Atrophy of Constitutional Powers." *Oxford Journal of Legal Studies* 32 (3): 421–44. https://doi.org/10.1093/ojls/gqs010

Waldron, J. 2006. "The Core of the Case Against Judicial Review." *Yale Law Journal* 115 (6): 1346–406. https://doi.org/10.2307/20455656

Walen, A. 2009. "Judicial Review in Review: A Four-Part Defense of Legal Constitutionalism, A Review Essay on *Political Constitutionalism*." *International Journal of Constitutional Law* 7 (2): 329–54. https://doi.org/10.1093/icon/mop007

Webber, J. 2006. "A Modest (but Robust) Defence of Statutory Bills of Rights." In *Protecting Rights without a Bill of Rights: Institutional Performance and Reform in Australia*, ed. T. Campbell, J. Goldsworthy, and A. Stone, 263–88. Aldershot, UK: Ashgate.

Winter, S. 2017. "Magna Carta's Promise: Strengthening the Declaration of Rights-Inconsistency." In *Magna Carta and New Zealand: History, Politics and Law in Aotearoa*, ed. S. Winter and C. Jones, 207–27. London: Palgrave Macmillan. https://doi.org/10.1007/978-3-319-58439-3_11

Winters, J. 2011. *Oligarchy*. Cambridge: Cambridge University Press. https://doi.org/10.1017/CBO9780511793806

19 Canada and the International Responsibilities to Protect and Prosecute in Cases of Mass Atrocity

KIRSTEN J. FISHER AND CRISTINA G. STEFAN

Originating from a common foundation of liberal cosmopolitanism, the Responsibility to Protect (R2P) and the Rome Statute, the founding treaty of the International Criminal Court (ICC), were conceived with the common objective of protecting individuals from crimes considered to be of concern for the international community based on their unique character (Badescu 2011; Drumbl 2007; Fisher 2009; Luban 2004; Vernon 2002). R2P is activated by genocide, crimes against humanity, war crimes, and ethnic cleansing; the ICC's current jurisdiction covers genocide, crimes against humanity, and war crimes.[1] With a common purpose, parallel emergence at the turn of the twenty-first century, and contemporary introduction into the fore of United Nations Security Council resolutions, R2P and the international responsibility to prosecute atrocity crimes are norms whose time has come. Individually and together, they play important roles in the protection of individuals globally.

Canada was instrumental in the emergence of both the R2P norm and the ICC. Canadians identify with both as representing a duty of international cooperation and protection of human rights. The R2P norm is the product of the 2001 report of a Canadian-sponsored commission, the International Commission on Intervention and State Sovereignty (ICISS). Canada played a central role in the establishment of the ICC by contributing to the development of the Rome Statute and by being

1 The fourth crime in the Rome Statute is the crime of aggression. The consensus decision reached at the States Parties' 16th session in December 2017 allowed the activation of the Rome Statute dealing with the crime of aggression to begin on 17 July 2018.

the first country to ratify and complete the necessary implementing legislation for it in 2000, thereby pushing forward the emergence of the Court. Although Canadians generally identify with a history and ideology encapsulated in both the R2P norm and international criminal law, in recent years Canada's reputation and self-identity as a middle power promoting liberal institutionalism has begun to wane, if not abate, especially in its relationship with R2P and the ICC. And, in their short existences, the emerging norms of the responsibilities to protect and prosecute have met real-world challenges in the stumbling blocks of international politics.

Applied political theory can be used to formulate prescriptions to correct the deficiencies in the currents practices of the UN Security Council and its implementation of R2P. The pressing conceptual and political task of this chapter, then, is to consider in what form and from whom this attention ought to originate. Despite some variation, all cosmopolitan views emerging from liberal political theory regard all human beings, regardless of their political affiliation, as citizens in a single global community. Although no state can embrace this sentiment fully by denying the existence of special obligations between the state and its citizens, Canada has a history, and embraces an identity, of pursuing its foreign policy according to a liberal cosmopolitan stance. It is against this history that we examine the moral obligations for promoting legitimate human rights–protecting institutions – that is, institutions that are both themselves morally justified and politically stable. Arguably those with greater ability have greater levels of obligation to promote and support these global institutions. Given its history, we argue that Canada has a significant opportunity, and also a moral duty, to right its course in terms of renewing the commitment to liberal cosmopolitanism that has waned in recent years, and again offer guidance and support for international cooperation and human rights protection. Part of this moral duty can be met by helping these two institutions shed their inherent political biases, which hinder their ability effectively to protect and promote human rights globally as intended.

We apply the theoretical principles that flow from this liberal cosmopolitan theoretical framework to an empirical presentation of the history, development, and current functioning of the institutions associated with the ICC and R2P. We begin by providing the context of the Canadian involvement with both R2P and the ICC. We show that Canada was the "norm entrepreneur," working to increase the legitimacy of these institutions by promoting global acceptance of basic human rights and protecting norms underpinning R2P and the ICC. We then argue that the condition currently inherent in both – namely, the UN Security Council's powerful influence over each – leaves them at risk of partiality and injustice. The Security Council's power allows decisions to be made based on the morally problematic self-interests of its permanent members. The legitimacy of global institutions, however, is strengthened or weakened by basic levels of international support and representation; political acceptability must underwrite the institutions charged with bringing otherwise accepted norms into being. For this reason, we argue in the second section that the current conditions of the international response to grave and systematic human rights abuses are morally insufficient. In the final section we discuss Canada's potential role and moral duty in promoting a restructuring of the Security Council's influence that would bring R2P and ICC activities more in line with the moral international responsibilities to protect and prosecute.

Canada's Historical Involvement with R2P and the ICC

Canada has a history of foreign policy grounded in liberal cosmopolitan principles, such as the belief that the "ultimate units of moral concern are individual human beings," as recognized and supported by the United Nations charter and the human rights regime (Held 2010, 230), belief in collective decision making, and "avoidance of harm and the amelioration of urgent need" (232). Canada has long held itself to be a global leader in peacekeeping, the promotion and protection of human rights, and the development of international justice (Dorn 2006; Stoett and Kersten 2014, 229). Support for this role has existed for so long that it has become part of the national identity, and "is a celebrated part of what Canada is as a nation, and even who Canadians are as a people" (Dorn 2006, 7). Canada was among the first UN members to participate in a UN peacekeeping operation, when it sent a contingent to Korea as part of the United Nations Temporary Commission on Korea in 1948. In 1948 Canada contributed a contingent to the first peacekeeping-type mission operated by UN observer groups in Palestine. It was a Canadian, Foreign Minister Lester B. Pearson, who invented modern peacekeeping with his proposal for a UN peacekeeping force in the 1956 Suez Crisis. After Suez an ideational framework increasingly shaped the views of foreign policy makers and Canadian responses to international events, with Canadians participating in every UN peacekeeping mission from the Suez Crisis until the end of the 1980s (Badescu

2010). This changed during the first half of the 1990s, although Canada remained among the top ten contributors to the UN peacekeeping list until 1997 (Dorn 2006, 16).

Building on this early Pearsonian commitment to peacekeeping, in the latter half of the 1990s, under the political leadership of then-foreign minister Lloyd Axworthy, Canada pushed the human security agenda to the forefront (Donaghy 2003). Axworthy's views placed the security of individuals at the centre of international relations, and used a human security framework to replace the more traditional preoccupation with the security of states. It was in the late 1990s that human security became regarded as an important theme in Canadian foreign policy, albeit this did not last long enough. It echoed the long-standing views of the Canadian public on the importance of helping others to keep global order. During the years when Canada was most recently a non-permanent member of the Security Council (1999 and 2000), Ottawa manifested its willingness to use military force in response to "humanitarian emergencies" (Hynek and Bosold 2009, 740–1). Post-Axworthy, the focus was less on the grand design of human security and more on finding practical ways to implement the agenda.

It was in this context that Canada played a key role in the emergence of both the R2P and the ICC. First, in regard to the R2P norm, in September 2000 the Canadian government established the ICISS to address the quest for solving the humanitarian intervention conundrum, a challenge posed by then-UN secretary-general Kofi Annan. The commission was chaired by former Australian foreign minister Gareth Evans and UN secretary-general special adviser Mohamed Sahnoun. Two Canadian scholars, Gisèle Côté-Harper and Michael Ignatieff, served as commissioners. Although established by the Canadian government, ICISS was an independent commission, whose report reflected its balance in composition, its comprehensiveness, outreach, and innovativeness.[2] The concept of R2P was then endorsed in the 2004 report of the UN High-Level Panel, entitled *A More Secure World: Our Shared Responsibility* (United Nations 2004) and in the 2005 report of former UN secretary-general Annan, *In Larger Freedom* (Annan 2005). Its most significant normative advance came in September 2005, when heads of state and

2 The balance in its composition was reflected by the two co-chairs and by its inclusion of commissioners, academics, and politicians from both the North and South, with opposing positions on the intervention-sovereignty debate.

government supported R2P in paragraphs 138 and 139 of the World Summit Outcome Document. This moment marked the first time the concept was endorsed in an universal forum, which was also the largest gathering of heads of state and government to date. The UN Security Council has made specific references to R2P on several occasions since then, and the UN secretary-general has issued yearly reports on R2P, starting in 2009, to be discussed by the General Assembly.

R2P has been described as "the most dramatic normative development of our time" (Thakur and Weiss 2009, 22). Two particular elements are worth mentioning in this context – namely, the demand-driven nature of the ICISS and the significant role Canada played, as norm entrepreneur, in the emergence of R2P. The former is important, since the ICISS was created after a recognition of the failures to protect civilians in the 1990s from the scourge of war and genocide. The 1994 Rwandan genocide epitomized such failures and the need for new policy responses designed specifically to address similar crises. The need to find a consensus on the contested concept of humanitarian intervention increased demands for an answer when the ICISS was launched (Badescu 2011, 121). Indeed the Canadian government appointed the commission "to wrestle with the whole range of questions- legal, moral, operational, and political – rolled up in this [humanitarian intervention] debate, to consult with the widest possible range of opinion around the world, and to bring back a report that would help the Secretary-General and everyone else find some new common ground" (ICISS 2001, vii). The R2P report shifted the debate from the right of external actors to intervene in the internal affairs of states where gross violations of human rights take place to the responsibility of sovereign states to protect their populations in the first place, which proved to be a very clever and efficient formulation.

The role ICISS played in R2P's normative development was the result of a combination of fine research work and good ideas,[3] on the one hand, and of building political momentum and having the necessary political weight to advance such ideas, on the other (Badescu 2011, 120). If a commission produces work that is restricted to the former, it risks being irrelevant. If it seizes the opportunities to advance its central thesis and receives enough political weight – as R2P did after the release of the ICISS report through the Canadian diplomatic machine – it might

3 For more details on the power of ideas, see Thakur, Cooper, and English (2005).

become another success, such as the anti–land mine or ICC campaigns. The literature on international norms describes "persuasion by norm entrepreneurs" as a key mechanism in the first stage of a norm's "life cycle" (Finnemore and Sikkink 1998, 895). Canada's efforts to advance R2P up to its September 2005 endorsement in the UN Summit Outcome Document best illustrates this. The Canadian government was rightfully dubbed "R2P's state champion" (Thakur and Weiss 2009, 34) for being the main advocate of R2P in the first four years after the release of the ICISS report.

Canada's role as norm entrepreneur began with its decision in September 2000 to answer Kofi Annan's call to UN member states in the fall of 1999 to find a compromise on humanitarian intervention by establishing the ICISS. This decision was a perfect example of entrepreneurial leadership (Riddell-Dixon 2005, 1074). In sponsoring the ICISS and later on in promoting R2P, Canada built on its ongoing commitment to multilateralism and human security, and especially on its focus, in recent years, on promoting civilian protection. In 1999 and 2000, during its non-permanent membership in the Security Council, Canada lobbied for the adoption of two UN resolutions on civilian protection – Security Council Resolutions 1265 and 1296 – that marked the council's recognition for the first time of the need to protect civilians in general, not just humanitarian workers. Canada thus was already influential in introducing concerns about the safety of civilian populations and about human rights law and international humanitarian law into discussions at the UN.

Canada started its advocacy campaign for R2P as soon as the ICISS report was released in December 2001 by promoting it both at home and abroad, among UN officials, other states, and non-governmental organizations (NGOs). The Canadian government invested significant resources of time, money, and reputation in the R2P campaign. An office inside the Global Issues Bureau within the Department of Foreign Affairs and International Trade (DFAIT) was specifically mandated to promote the R2P framework, advocate the adoption of the recommendations in the ICISS report, and build a constituency of support among "like-minded" friends. In line with the country's active promoter reputation, many Canadian embassies abroad conducted briefings on R2P. Apart from raising the issue of R2P bilaterally, Canada also raised it in multilateral forums such as La Francophonie. Canadian officials used powerful rhetoric to make sure R2P language was included in declarations, official documents, and political statements, and placed on the agendas of various conferences and workshops on security.[4] By calling attention to R2P and the recommendations in the ICISS report in its own statements, Canada helped "build" the language of R2P.

Attracting civil society to promote R2P was part of the Canadian government's strategy. From 2001 to 2005 Canada funded civil society roundtable discussions all over the world using money from a $10 million human security program fund that DFAIT was using for policy development on various human security issues, including R2P. DFAIT also sponsored several NGOs – including the World Federalist Movement–Institute for Global Policy, the primary organizer of NGO support for R2P, and a Canadian NGO, Project Ploughshares, whose work included developing a series of consultations in Africa on R2P – to seek feedback on the potential role of civil society in promoting R2P.[5]

Through persuasion, Canadian initiatives were directed towards convincing a critical mass of actors to embrace R2P. These efforts culminated with the Canadian officials' work behind the scenes for months in preparation for the 2005 World Summit to ensure that R2P would be included in the Outcome Document. In the final forty-eight hours before reaching an agreement in the negotiations, then-prime minister Paul Martin made personal phone calls to five heads of the most opposing governments in the General Assembly, including Pakistan. As a result of this last-minute personal diplomacy, in at least three of the five cases the permanent representatives in New York indicated the following day that they were under instructions from their capitals to change their position on R2P (Badescu 2011, 127).

Similarly Canada played a pivotal role both in promoting the norm of international prosecution for atrocity crimes and in establishing the ICC by providing human and material resources to guide its development and early work. As was the case in regards to R2P, the ICC was conceived as a response to a significant moral demand for a better way for the international community to deal with mass atrocities. After the UN Security Council created two ad hoc tribunals to investigate atrocity crimes committed in the former Yugoslavia (the International Criminal

4 Confidential interviews conducted with senior DFAIT officials by Cristina Stefan, Ottawa, 2–3 May, 1–2 August 2006.

5 The specific examples of Canadian efforts to promote R2P were gathered from interviews conducted with officials from various DFAIT divisions by Cristina Stefan, Ottawa, 2–3 May, 1–2 August 2006.

Tribunal for the former Yugoslavia) and Rwanda (the International Criminal Tribunal for Rwanda), there was a push for a permanent and independent institution that could react more quickly to crimes committed, while also, it was hoped, having a deterrent effect.

The Canadian delegation to the Rome Conference played a brokering role in the negotiations regarding significant elements concerning how the ICC would look. These included the Court's jurisdiction, definitions of the crimes within its jurisdiction, and the Court's procedures and general principles. The Canadian government's website demonstrates a continuing pride in the country's guiding role in the establishment of the Court: "After five weeks of negotiations, delegates at the Conference had made tremendous headway on hundreds of technical issues related to the creation of the ICC. However, substantial divisions still existed on difficult issues … Accordingly, it fell to the Chair of the Committee of the Whole, Philippe Kirsch, with the assistance of a Bureau of coordinators, to draft a final, global proposal for the ICC … On the final day of the Conference, the final proposal that was drafted under Canada's leadership received broad approval" (Canada 2018). Indeed the Canadian lawyer and senior diplomat Philippe Kirsch was a central figure in the drafting of the Rome Statute, the establishment of the Court, and the steering of its initial work once it was established. Kirsch first chaired the Committee of the Whole at the Diplomatic Conference of Plenipotentiaries on the Establishment of an International Criminal Court in Rome, held in 1998, then chaired the Preparatory Commission for the International Criminal Court from 1999 to 2002, and then became the first president of the Court from 2003 to 2009.

The foundational treaty for the ICC, formally known as the Rome Statute of the International Criminal Court, was first open for signature on 17 July 1998, and was signed by Canada on 18 December, indicating an intention to ratify. On 29 June 2000, Canada became the first country to adopt legislation to implement the Rome Statute domestically, and ratified the statute on 7 July. The significance of Canada's "leadership and ratification" were noted by William Pace, convenor of the NGO Coalition for an International Criminal Court: "Canada is a major peacekeeping nation, a member of the Security Council and NATO, and is the first to simultaneously complete ratification of the Rome Statute while enacting comprehensive national cooperation legislation. The Canadian example and legislation will greatly assist other nations in their efforts toward ratification" (Coalition for an International Criminal Court 2000). As was the case with its relationship with R2P, however,

Canada's relationship with the ICC became strained under the Harper government, which was vocal and conservative about the Court's budget, in a way that could be seen as detrimental to the Court's growth and effectiveness.

The Responsibilities to Protect and Prosecute

To be morally sufficient, an institution or doctrine must, minimally, not interfere with the satisfaction of basic human rights. In the case of an institution that imposes international order, it must be shaped so that all persons subjected to it are, if not equally able to benefit from it, not harmed by its arrangement. When an institutional order that coercively limits actions alternative to its own and itself avoidably fails to protect human rights, it is violating a duty of justice (Pogge 2005). Although the conceptions of global responsibilities to protect and to prosecute in cases of atrocity stem from a morally sound cosmopolitan foundation, the current global order that is entrusted to meet these responsibilities is far from adequately arranged to do so. An applied political theory approach, then, demands that the divide between theory and reality be minimized, while recognizing that the dictates of ideal theory might not be possible and that our theorizing and recommendations must remain within the confines of practical reality.

In the conceptions of the responsibilities to protect and to prosecute, however, there is promise. Both global responsibilities are young, and their respective layers are at different stages of diffusion as far as international norms are concerned. There is continuing criticism about both, which is to be expected, but they are spreading worldwide in line with their universal agendas. Both responsibilities originate from a liberal cosmopolitan foundation (Fisher 2012, 8–29) and both resemble novel ways to establish the global rule of law based on the universal promotion and protection of human rights (Kersten forthcoming). As suggested in the 2001 ICISS report, R2P is first and foremost a moral imperative, stemming from our "common humanity" (ICISS 2001, 2). The responsibility to prosecute, as embodied in the ICC, makes this institution an innovative form of cosmopolitanism, developed from, and enhancing, Kant's conception of cosmopolitan law (Kant [1785] 1993), which aims to hold accountable individuals most responsible for atrocity crimes (Fisher 2012, 8). Both R2P and the ICC reflect challenges to the convention of international realism, extending the rule of law and concern for the individual from inside national borders to the international sphere.

To various extents, both the responsibilities to protect and to prosecute have been institutionalized at the international level, embedded in various treaties and conventions, supported by the United Nations, recommended by leading NGOs, and endorsed by some key states. Out of the two, the responsibility to prosecute is the one most embedded within international law (Leonard and Roach 2009, 60–3), which has implications for its practice, thus making it "the safest legally – and morally – to invoke" (Mills 2013, 341).

Historically, criticisms of international criminal law typically are based on two sets of questions, both alluding to the legitimacy of the system of law. The first concerns authority, and deals with the legal and moral basis for the judicial institution's existence and with the prosecution of those it deems in violation of promulgated criminal law. The second comprises questions regarding the objectivity and justness of the legal structure as a legitimate system of law. The norm entrepreneurship in which Canada engaged helped to establish the first, but the second form of legitimacy is compromised by current international politics. International criminal justice, as embodied in the ICC and other institutions, captures the essence of the responsibility to prosecute. We focus on the ICC in the remainder of this chapter to discuss the latter, and particularly on the influence of the UN Security Council, which seems to introduce problems of overstepped authority, political biases, and partiality. In a similar vein, the selectivity of the Security Council's invoking of R2P opens it up to criticism that focuses mainly on legitimacy concerns.

Legitimacy, in the context of international judicial institutions, is based not only on the legal system's accordance with particular just foundations and principles, but also on the perception of legitimacy by both international and local populations. Perceived legitimacy is not "whether or not a particular criminal justice approach can be justified as legitimate on a theoretical level … whether or not various local and international communities are likely, as a practical matter, to 'buy in' to the approach and treat the activities of the institutions involved as legitimate" (Dickinson 2003, 301). Rather, the approach must be seen to exist as a legitimate authority over those it has jurisdiction, and to administer the law objectively, fairly applying the law to all subjects within its jurisdiction. Over its short existence, international criminal law has faced numerous challenges to its legitimacy and its ability to pursue "justice" in a just and objective manner. Challenges that were once touted as a result of growing pains could shortly hamper the enterprise of international criminal law in being regarded as anything more than a political tool.

The ICC, a unique institution of international criminal law, faces the criticism of being a political instrument in an unjust global system. In this way, its authority as an arbiter of justice and right behaviour is undermined. In and of itself, the Court has faced criticisms for lacking democracy, inspiring debates as to whether this lack negatively affects the Court's legitimacy (Fichtelberg 2006; Morris 2002). It is its relationship with the UN Security Council that is most problematic in terms of the Court's real and perceived lack of authority as a just global legal order. An important question is whether the Court acquired legitimate political authority through international sources or tenets of international criminal law. Questions of authority deal with the legal basis for the judicial institution's existence. As a treaty-based institution, the ICC is on firm ground to investigate and prosecute situations connected to member states that have submitted to its jurisdiction – the only ones, in fact, over which it has jurisdiction, with the exception of cases referred by the Security Council. This arrangement between the ICC and its member states lends the Court straightforward legal authority over cases that arise from the member states, but limits its ability to be a genuine global institution until all states have ratified the Rome Statute. The influence of the Security Council, written into the Rome Statute, allows the Court more global reach, but arguably negatively affects its legitimate authority. The ICC can establish jurisdiction in one of three ways: a member state can refer a situation, the Security Council acting under Chapter VII of the UN Charter can refer a situation, or the ICC prosecutor can initiate an investigation in accordance with Article 15 of the Rome Statute. The first and the third options can set in motion only investigations concerning member states.

The UN Charter, which outlines the powers and functions of the Security Council, positions it as primarily responsible "for the maintenance of international peace and security" (Article 24). The Security Council is not the only UN organ to possess this responsibility, but while it shares this responsibility with the General Assembly and the International Court of Justice, the Security Council has grown to be understood as the paramount organ for this task. It is not only the Charter that determines the Council's role; as with any living constitution, practise also shapes it. Since the end of the Cold War, the Security Council has become active in many conflicts, and although some interpret this as the Council's fulfilling its mandate, others feel it has overstepped its reach. In regards to international criminal law, the Security Council established the first two international criminal tribunals (on the former Yugoslavia and Rwanda). Before this occurred, there was no expectation that international trials would be established and, in fact, some argue that the Security Council overstepped its Chapter VII authority by ordering the creation of the tribunals. Arguably the Council "came to demonstrate an extraordinarily broad interpretation of its responsibility to maintain international peace and security" by establishing these courts (Chesterman 2001, 121).

Although it is a court independent of the UN, the ICC's special relationship with the Security Council is being used to initiate investigations that could not otherwise be opened. If the Council refers a situation to the ICC for investigation, the membership status of the state is extraneous. Cases referred by the Council are open to concerns regarding not only authority, but also objectivity. Because of the unique condition written into the foundation of this treaty-based institution, the Security Council is in a position to affect the work and reputation of the Court by generating a condition in which its caseload is shaped by the concerns and self-interests of permanent members of the Council, while not all of the members are themselves member states of the Court and therefore not under its jurisdiction. More specifically, because of this unique referral system, the cases that make it before the ICC reflect not necessarily the worst or most deserving of all situations globally in which international crimes occurred; rather, the Court's caseload reflects its members and their judgment expressed through Security Council votes. Therefore, there exist in this arrangement remarkable conflicting challenges, such as the need for the Council to refer some cases not otherwise under its jurisdiction, while recognizing that Security Council votes themselves can reflect bias.

We can explore what these questions mean practically, since the Security Council has evoked both the R2P doctrine and referral to the ICC in recent years. The institutionalization of R2P and ICC referral options is a significant step forward as a means to protect and promote basic human rights globally. Nevertheless, without some alteration to the way the Security Council can employ them, the legitimacy of both as effective and just instruments is questionable. The recent and ongoing political changes and transitions in the Middle East and North Africa underscore this issue, with the recent situations of Libya and Syria demonstrating some of the problems. In the wake of the political uprisings known as the Arab Spring, there were calls for the involvement of the ICC and

R2P in both Libya and Syria to deal with widespread and systemic violence (Blomfield 2011; Human Rights Watch 2013). The international community's involvement in Libya and lack of involvement in Syria demonstrates the political challenges related to both implementing R2P and ICC referrals. The Security Council, "despite having an obligation to authorize international action when civilians are being slaughtered, has failed repeatedly to do so" in Syria, with Russian and China vetoing four resolutions (Matthews and Paikin 2015).

The ICC's involvement or lack of it in these countries positioned the Court to face particularly damning criticisms regarding its legitimacy (Fisher 2014). Because none of the Arab Spring countries but Tunisia was a member state of the ICC, the only way to initiate ICC investigation into these cases was by means of referral to the Security Council.[6] With the exception of Libya, which received the Council's unanimous vote to be referred to the ICC for investigation of its government led by Muammar el-Gaddafi (Security Council Resolution 1970), no other Arab Spring country received attention from the Court. The last draft resolution, proposed by France, for the Security Council to refer Syrian crimes to the ICC, was vetoed by both Russia and China in May 2014. In this particular instance, all the other thirteen members of the Security Council backed the measure. There have been six so-called double-vetoes (Russia and China) in regards to Syria. Russia, however, has used its veto power in the Security Council more than China. Russia's use of the veto in April 2018 against a US-drafted resolution to investigate chemical weapons use in Syria aimed at identifying the perpetrators was the twelfth time it had managed to block action directed at its Syrian ally.[7] The lack of Security Council attention to Syria is arguably partly because of the ties between the Arab Spring countries and permanent members of the Council that possess veto power and can protect their allies from investigation by blocking any attempts to refer a case to the ICC. Bahrain and Yemen have close ties with the United States, and Syria has ties with both China and Russia. To some critics, this state of affairs reeks of politics in the absence of objective justice (Chulov 2011).

6 Bahrain, Egypt, Syria, and Yemen are all signatory states, each having signed the Rome Statute in 2000, but none has ratified the statute and none is therefore a full member or is under the jurisdiction of the ICC.

7 Numerous draft resolutions on Syria were vetoed by both Russia and China, starting with S/2011/612.

Despite the great strides forward in its pursuit of accountability for international crimes, the ICC's relationship with the Security Council is so problematic as to affect its legitimacy, both perceived and real. At the same time, this relationship allows the Court more universal reach (thus bolstering its legitimacy), and creates a more politicized foundation for its caseload (thus diminishing its legitimacy). As Hehir and Lang argue, the current international order needs to be reformed to ensure a better integration of R2P and the ICC into international law and practice by "altering the Security Council's powers and developing new judicial structures to enable the more consistent application of international law" (2015, 153). The authors make a compelling case for the unjustness, and therefore illegitimacy, of the current system, using R2P and the ICC "as evidence of the framework being consolidated that enables the selective and arbitrary use both of military force and punitive censure rather than strengthening the formal procedures of a normative legal order" (155). The effectiveness and legitimacy of both human rights–protecting institutions are compromised by the exceptional powers held by the permanent members of the Security Council. Simply put, "we cannot expect R2P or the ICC to operate in a manner consistent with normatively sound principles of legal theory" if the international legal order remains unchanged (155). Hehir and Lang make some reasonable suggestions for reform, which they argue are both necessary and possible to create a more just political and legal order, if political will exists to pursue them. They advocate for a more explicit constitutional order, in which the powers and practices of law making are separated from law enforcement. Included in this reform would be a more purposeful law-making, or legislative, function in which norms such as R2P can be translated into rules or laws.

Applied political theory implies that we move beyond exclusively focusing on abstract moral arguments and consider how they can be actualized in contemporary political contexts – in this case, in the global governance structure. Rather than evaluate particular recommendations, we want to show that reform is needed and that Canada has a significant role to play as state champion of this reform. The UN Security Council wields a great deal of power, especially in regards to military intervention (under Chapter VII) for the protection of individuals and the prosecution of atrocity crimes. Interestingly, Hehir and Lang argue that the current condition of Security Council power and the fact that the international political and legal order is shaped by practice as much as by written law allows the five permanent members of the Council to continue to increase their power, and as they become "increasingly more powerful, the efficacy of moral advocacy will arguably diminish" (2015, 163). If we accept Hehir and Lang's conclusion, not only is Security Council reform necessary, but not reforming it has increasingly negative consequences. The status quo is bad, but the need for reform is more pressing than ever.

Canada's Role

With its history Canada is well positioned to promote policies that could contribute to the more objective application of R2P and ICC referrals. In recent years, however, Canada has taken an approach more detrimental to international justice and global human rights protection. For example, Canada chose not to support a Swiss-led initiative calling on the UN Security Council to refer the situation in Syria to the ICC: "Canada's silence on this symbolic gesture marks a subtle but notable shift in attitude away from endorsing the role of international criminal justice in international affairs" (Stoett and Kersten 2014, 230). As noted, Canada has also focused on budget concerns and advocated a more conservative approach to the operations of the ICC, a sign of Canada's weakening commitment to international justice (Ochieng and Jennings 2014). In what can be interpreted as an attempt to subvert the use of international criminal law, then-foreign minister John Baird threatened that Palestine would lose access to Canadian aid if it referred its situation to the Court (Heinbecker 2015; *National Post* 2012).

Nevertheless, Canada can reverse this course. And it should. Even if the Harper Conservative government failed to invest the diplomatic energy to advance both R2P and the work of the ICC, addressing serious human rights violations remains an issue of interest to Canadians. And with the election of a new Liberal government in the fall of 2015, Canadians are optimistic about change, which could take the form of Canada's meeting its moral obligations to support and legitimate human rights–protecting institutions by helping to ensure that these institutions are both morally justified and politically stable. Since the UN Security Council has such inherent influence over the situations in which the international community intervenes either militarily under R2P or judiciously with the ICC, and reform of the Security Council is necessary to ensure objective assessment in line with the interests of justice, a moral duty to support and promote reform exists for all actors who are contributing to the structural injustice (Pogge 2005; Young 2006). All states, as members of the UN system, have this responsibility to work towards change, but Canada, we argue, might possess a stronger responsibility than others.

One area where improvement could be achieved and the impact could be high relates to specific organs within international organizations such as the UN, with significant decision-making power and influence in regard to the responsibilities to protect and to prosecute. The idea that reform of the Security Council is needed is not new: calls for reform have a long history stretching back almost to the creation of the UN itself. More recent attempts at reform include the Accountability, Coherency and Transparency initiative, which built on the work of the Small-Five (Costa Rica, Singapore, Switzerland, Jordan, and Liechtenstein). This group wanted to revive efforts to reform Security Council working methods, and sponsored a draft resolution in the General Assembly on 3 May 2012 for "Enhancing the accountability, transparency and effectiveness of the Security Council," which included an appeal to permanent members of the Council to "[refrain] from using a veto to block Council action aimed at preventing or ending genocide, war crimes and crimes against humanity."[8] The twelve vetoes by Russia and six vetoes by China over the past seven years of Syria's civil war explain the need for Security Council members to adhere to the ACT Code of Conduct in mass atrocity situations. To date 113 UN member states and 2 observers have signed the ACT Code of Conduct. The UN General Assembly's 2016 initiative is a great alternative to the Security Council's deadline regarding referring the situation in Syria to the ICC.

The General Assembly established the International, Impartial and Independent Mechanism (IIIM) for Syria in 2016 to investigate atrocities and to ensure an alternative route to accountability could be provided. It goes without saying that the IIIM needs member states to provide technical assistance and voluntary contributions, and that it also cannot stop the fighting, the crimes, and the suffering of Syrian civilians. In the absence of a Security Council referral to the ICC, however, it could work towards ensuring that those responsible for committing war crimes in Syria eventually will be held accountable and face justice. France has been at the forefront of this initiative,[9] with a conference in Paris held

8 See Costa Rica, Jordan, Liechtenstein, Singapore and Switzerland, "Revised Draft Resolution: Enhancing the accountability, transparency and effectiveness of the Security Council," UN Doc A/66/L.42/Rev.1 (3 May 2012), paragraph 20.

9 In an address to the 68th Session of the UN General Assembly in September 2013, French president François Hollande asked the five permanent members to "collectively renounce their veto powers" in cases of mass atrocity crimes.

by the French foreign ministry on 21 January 2015 as one example of a diplomatic effort towards limiting the use of the veto in the Security Council in cases of mass atrocities and to raise the political cost for their doing so. The initiative called for a "statement of principles" to be signed by the five permanent members that would affirm their commitment to refraining from using the veto. Support for such an initiative "would represent a major leap forward in the fight to protect populations from some of the world's gravest crimes" (Matthews and Paikin 2015), but it is not enough. The French proposal is obviously just one part of the broader reform needed to adapt the Security Council to the multipolar reality of the twenty-first century, and especially to make the Council more effective in addressing mass atrocities. More serious reform is necessary, and this is where Canada can, and should, step in and resume its position as an honest broker of research and ideas.

As Iris Marion Young argues, it is not only that agents "bear responsibility for structural injustice because they contribute by their actions to the processes that produce unjust outcomes" (2006, 119), but that "differences of kind and degree [of responsibility] correlate with an agent's position within the structural processes" (127). Peter Singer similarly argues that, if one is in a better position to provide assistance, then the moral argument follows that one should act (1972, 232). Young suggests that an agent's power and ability, among other characteristics, influence its responsibility. Furthermore, in line with a cosmopolitan ethic of protection, which is more "salient" in liberal states than in non-liberal states (Wendt 1999, 234, 238; see also Bukovansky et al. 2012), Canada indeed has a "special" responsibility to do more to advance the two responsibilities it initially supported, in this case through assisting with Security Council reform.

Arguably, then, Canada, with its history and reputation as an honest broker of international justice, possesses a stronger responsibility to promote the necessary reform of the UN Security Council to bring the international community's work in line with normatively sound principles of justice. Canada was instrumental in bringing about and championing R2P as a strong solution to a recognized problem, and this experience, along with its reputation as a peaceful and liberal middle power and its relative wealth, positions Canada as uniquely powerful and able to succeed in this very challenging political battle. Building on its early Pearsonian commitment to peacekeeping and its experience championing R2P, Canada again could help to overcome the impotence of the Security Council in the face of responsibilities to protect and prosecute. It is in this context that we suggest a Canadian initiative that would go beyond the French proposal, which, while apparently pragmatic in that it did not seek to abolish the veto but only to persuade the five permanent members not to cast one, was perhaps only a band-aid to cover more serious issues of systemic injustice.

By building on its previous work with R2P, Canada could initiate and support an independent commission that would offer recommendations regarding Security Council reform to further strengthen R2P and free the ICC from barriers to its administering objective international criminal law. This dedicated commission would be tasked with researching and evaluating options and likely outcomes, just as was the ICISS at a time when a resolution was needed on the "humanitarian intervention" debate. The commission could incorporate many of the ideas already articulated in disparate fashions, such as those put forward by Hehir and Lang and others. In championing such an initiative, Canada could again help to build language and advocate for change, but minimally it should help the international community produce a platform of ideas from which to start, and it should aim to regain its historical position as an honest broker of ideas to promote international cooperation and the protection of human rights. Indeed we would argue that Canada has the moral duty to do so. It is through the lens of applied political theory that Canada needs to find a significant middle ground between practical realities and political compromises, on the one hand, and ideal liberal cosmopolitan theory, on the other.

REFERENCES

Annan, Kofi. 2005. *In Larger Freedom: Towards Development, Security and Human Rights for All*. Report of the Secretary General. New York: United Nations.

Badescu, Cristina G. 2010. "Canada's Continuing Engagement with United Nations Peace Operations." *Canadian Foreign Policy* 16 (2): 45–60. https://doi.org/10.1080/11926422.2010.9687307

Badescu, Cristina G. 2011. *Humanitarian Intervention and the Responsibility to Protect: Security and Human Rights*. London: Routledge.

Blomfield, Adrian. 2011. "Syria: President Bashar al-Assad faces indictment by the International Criminal Court." *Telegraph*, 24 April.

Bukovansky, Mlada, Ian Clark, Robyn Eckersley, Richard Price, Christian Reus-Smit, and Nicholas J. Wheeler. 2012. *Special Responsibilities. Global Problems and American Power*. Cambridge: Cambridge University Press. https://doi.org/10.1017/CBO9781139108812

Canada. 2018. "About Canada and the International Criminal Court." Available online at http://www.international.gc.ca/world-monde/international_relations-relations_internationales/icc-cpi/about-a_propos.aspx?lang=eng

Chesterman, Simon. 2001. *Just War or Just Peace?* Oxford: Oxford University Press.

Chulov, Martin. 2011. "Libyan government asks why ICC isn't also seeking to prosecute Syria." *Guardian*, 16 May.

Coalition for an International Criminal Court. 2000. "Canada Ratifies Treaty to Establish a Permanent International Criminal Court." New York.

Dickinson, Laura. 2003. "The Promise of Hybrid Courts." *American Journal of International Law* 97 (2): 295–310. https://doi.org/10.2307/3100105

Donaghy, Greg. 2003. "All God's Children: Lloyd Axworthy, Human Security, and Canadian Foreign Policy, 1996–2000." *Canadian Foreign Policy* 10 (2): 39–58. https://doi.org/10.1080/11926422.2003.9673326

Dorn, Walter. 2006. "Canada: The Once and Future Peacekeeper?" *Peace Magazine*, October–December.

Drumbl, Mark. 2007. *Atrocity, Punishment, and International Law*. Cambridge: Cambridge University Press. https://doi.org/10.1017/CBO9780511611100

Fichtelberg, Aaron. 2006. "Democratic Legitimacy and the International Criminal Court: A Liberal Defence." *Journal of International Criminal Justice* 4 (4): 765–85. https://doi.org/10.1093/jicj/mqk002

Finnemore, Martha, and Kathryn Sikkink. 1998. "International Norm Dynamics and Political Change." *International Organization* 52 (4): 887–917. https://doi.org/10.1162/002081898550789

Fisher, Kirsten J. 2009. "The Distinct Character of International Crime: Theorizing the Domain." *Contemporary Political Theory* 8 (1): 44–67. https://doi.org/10.1057/cpt.2008.21

Fisher, Kirsten J. 2012. *Moral Accountability and International Criminal Law*. London: Routledge.

Fisher, Kirsten J. 2014. "Selectivity, Legitimacy and the Pursuit of Post-Arab Spring International Criminal Justice." In *Transitional Justice and the Arab Spring*, ed. Kirsten J. Fisher and Robert Stewart. London: Routledge.

Hehir, Aidan, and Anthony Lang. 2015. "The Impact of the Security Council on the Efficacy of the International Criminal Court and the Responsibility to Protect." *Criminal Law Forum* 26 (1): 153–79. https://doi.org/10.1007/s10609-015-9245-4

Heinbecker, Paul. 2015. "Canada's bluster over Palestine's ICC bid betrays its principles." *Globe and Mail*, 28 January.

Held, David. 2010. "Principles of Cosmopolitan Order." In *The Cosmopolitan Reader*, ed. Garrett W. Brown and David Held, 229–47. London: Polity.

Human Rights Watch. 2013. "UN Security Council: Heed Call for Justice in Syria." 14 January. Available online at https://www.hrw.org/news/2013/01/14/un-security-council-heed-call-justice-syria

Hynek, Nik, and David Bosold. 2009. "A History and Genealogy of the Freedom-from-Fear Doctrine." *International Journal* (Toronto) 64 (3): 735–50. https://doi.org/10.1177/002070200906400309

ICISS (International Commission on Intervention and State Sovereignty). 2001. *The Responsibility to Protect: Report of the International Commission on Intervention and State Sovereignty*. Ottawa: International Development Research Centre.

Kant, Immanuel. [1785] 1993. *Grounding for the Metaphysics of Morals*. 3rd ed., trans. James W. Ellington. Indianapolis, IL: Hackett.

Kersten, Mark. Forthcoming. "A Fatal Attraction? The UN Security Council and the Relationship between R2P and the International Criminal Court." In *Mobilising International Law for "Global Justice,"* ed. Jeff Handmaker and Karin Arts. Cambridge: Cambridge University Press.

Leonard, Eric, and Steven Roach. 2009. "From Realism to Legalization: A Rationalist Assessment of the International Criminal Court in the Democratic Republic of Congo." In *Governance, Order and the International Criminal Court: Between Realpolitik and a Cosmopolitan Court*, ed. Steven Roach, 55–70. Oxford: Oxford University Press. https://doi.org/10.1093/acprof:oso/9780199546732.003.0003

Luban, David. 2004. "A Theory of Crimes against Humanity." *Yale Journal of International Law* 29: 85–167.

Matthews, Kyle, and Zach Paikin. 2015. "Opinion: Canadian leadership is needed to end Syria's suffering." *Gazette* (Montreal), 27 March. Available online at http://montrealgazette.com/news/world/opinion-canadian-leadership-is-needed-to-end-syrias-suffering

Mills, Kurt. 2013. "R2P^3: Protecting, Prosecuting, and Palliating in Mass Atrocity Situations?" *Journal of Human Rights* 12 (3): 333–56. https://doi.org/10.1080/14754835.2013.812421

Morris, Madeline. 2002. "The Democratic Dilemma of the International Criminal Court." *Buffalo Criminal Law Review* 5 (2): 591–600. https://doi.org/10.1525/nclr.2002.5.2.591

National Post. 2012. "Canada's $300-million humanitarian aid to Palestinians under review." 4 December.

Ochieng, Lilian, and Simon Jennings. 2014. "ICC Secures Budget Increase." London: Institute for War & Peace Reporting, 20 January.

Pogge, Thomas. 2005. "Human Rights and Human Responsibilities." In *Global Responsibilities: Who Must Deliver on Human Rights?* ed. Andrew Kuper, 3–36. New York: Routledge.

Riddell-Dixon, Elizabeth. 2005. "Canada's Human Security Agenda: Walking the Talk?" *International Journal* (Toronto) 60 (4): 1067–92.

Singer, Peter. 1972. "Famine, Affluence, and Morality." *Philosophy & Public Affairs* 1 (3): 229–43.

Stoett, Peter, and Mark Kersten. 2014. "Beyond Ideological Fixation: Ecology, Justice, and Canadian Foreign Policy under Harper." *Canadian Foreign Policy* 20 (2): 229–32. https://doi.org/10.1080/11926422.2014.934857

Thakur, Ramesh, Andrew Cooper, and John English. 2005. *International Commissions and the Power of Ideas*. New York: United Nations University Press.

Thakur, R., and T.G. Weiss. 2009. "R2P: From Idea to Norm – and Action?" *Global Responsibility to Protect* 1 (1): 22–53. https://doi.org/10.1163/187598409X405460

United Nations. 2004. High-Level Panel on Threats, Challenges and Change. "A More Secure World: Our Shared Responsibility." A/59/565. New York, 2 December. Available online at http://www.un.org/en/ga/search/view_doc.asp?symbol=A/59/565

Vernon, Richard. 2002. "What Is Crime against Humanity." *Journal of Political Philosophy* 10 (3): 231–49. https://doi.org/10.1111/1467-9760.00151

Wendt, Alexander. 1999. *Social Theory of International Politics*. New York: Cambridge University Press. https://doi.org/10.1017/CBO9780511612183

Young, Iris Marion. 2006. "Responsibility and Global Justice: A Social Connection Model." *Social Philosophy and Policy* 23 (1): 102–30. https://doi.org/10.1017/S0265052506060043

20 Immigration and Borders in Canada: Looking Outward, Looking Inward, and Breaking Away from Legacies

MIREILLE PAQUET

Canadian political theorists have been at the forefront of contemporary theoretical developments when it comes to citizenship, multiculturalism, and belonging. This innovative body of applied political theory scholarship has been partially contingent on the constitutive "conditions" of Canada: national and linguistic diversity as well as regional and economic disparities. These create excellent opportunities for the use of an applied political theory approach. In particular, immigration is a subject that lends itself to applied political theory, especially as the diversification of source countries of Canadian immigrants increasingly opens up questions of justice, equity, and conceptions of the nation. This chapter tackles debates around immigration through applying the work of liberal theorist Joseph H. Carens to a qualitative case study of Canada's Express Entry program, using primary documents from the federal government. In doing so, I illustrate how an applied political theory approach is an effective way to study Canadian immigration policies and politics.

Since the 1980s international immigration levels to Canada have remained high and keep increasing – in 2013 Canada welcomed 258,953 newcomers (Canada 2014b). Always a large component of the country's population growth, international immigration has been the largest contributor to Canada's demographic development since the early 2000s (Canada 2014a). Despite its importance, the process and management of immigration has not been a top item on Canadian political theorists' agenda. In the background of Canada's contribution to theorizing multiculturalism and diversity, issues related to immigration and borders have been tackled by only a handful of Canadian scholars. Indeed, with some rare exceptions – in particular, the work of Carens –

Canadian political theory has not dealt head on but only indirectly with these issues. Instead, theorists have focused either upon the outward effect of Canada's policies or inward upon the effect of borders and immigration on the nation and on newcomers. Carens's work combines these two directions, and is recognized internationally as one of the most comprehensive contemporary political theories to engage with these questions. By reviewing his work, I hope to demonstrate the importance of Carens's contribution to the study of these issues, and to show, in dialogue with empirical material, the importance for Canadian political theory of engaging with issues of immigration and borders.

Using Carens's perspective, I consider Canada's Express Entry system, in place since January 2015. This system established new methods for the selection of economic immigrants and gave Canadian employers a renewed role in the management of immigration. I show that this new procedure represented a break from the largely imperfect legacy of equal membership for immigrants in Canada. As such it marked a return to a classical version of liberalism – focused on limited state intervention, individual economic independence, and a reverence for market forces – after years of immigration policy that attempted to aligned with contemporary principles stemming from egalitarian liberalism. I conclude that Express Entry has limited even further Canada's contribution to the fight against global inequalities through international immigration.

Immigration and Borders as a Domain of Enquiry

The study of immigration and borders, from a political theory standpoint, should refer to the means – as well as the associated policies and discourses – by which states select potential migrants and shield themselves from those seen as unwanted newcomers. These means include elements such as selection grids and point systems; different models of immigrant attraction; relationships between states in the management of human movements; spaces and methods of immigrant detention and expulsion; and how borders are patrolled and secured. As such, immigration and borders as a domain of enquiry is distinct in its focus on the formal and physical inclusion or exclusion of immigrants. It leaves aside states' responses associated with immigrants' naturalization and integration, as well as the social and political dynamics of ethnocultural recognition and diversity management.

In formal terms, I posit an analytical distinction between "immigration and borders" and the fields of human rights and diversity policy. In doing so, it is useful to build on the work of the Canadian political scientist Miriam Smith, who proposes we "think about human rights and diversity policies as a specific policy sector," as a way to consider "how various policies and state practices recognize peoples' rights and provide redress when they are violated, how public policies allocate or redistribute economic advantage to specific groups, and how policies and institutions create barriers or openings for political mobilization and participation for different groups in the political process" (2009, 835). Smith's proposition for such a domain of enquiry is rooted in a desire to see Canadian political scientists analyse these questions outside assumptions about Canada's political culture – for example, using statements such as "Canadians are inherently more open to diversity than are Americans or Europeans." Avoiding such an approach, according to Smith, would make it easier to highlight the fact that the policies and the politics of multiculturalism are part of larger political processes that generate differences in power and resources in Canada, as elsewhere (Smith 2009).

Using the same logic, a focus on immigration and borders, as opposed to ethnocultural recognition and diversity management could highlight dynamics and power relations still less often considered in mainstream Canadian political science. Indeed Canada's scholarly productivity regarding integration and multiculturalism generally has left dynamics specific to immigration and borders less explored by applied political theory. As a result, the work of political scientists has contributed to a certain depoliticization of immigration and borders. More important, as a result, this work has not challenged the elements that structure immigration policy in Canada nor the role the Canadian state plays in the construction and production of the "diversity" it seeks to understand and, more broadly, to integrate.

Although the distinction between immigration/borders and ethnocultural recognition/diversity management is artificial, three specific justifications support the need to distinguish them nonetheless. First, there are differences between the two subjects when it comes to the role of a clearly defined political community. More broadly, issues of immigration and borders present unique challenges for political theory. For example, discussions about the legitimacy of borders present major challenges to several of liberalism's central assumptions. Since these assumptions are central to mainstream Canadian political theory on immigrant integration – for example, in Will Kymlicka's (1995) seminal work – clumping the two domains of enquiry together makes it harder to identify and explore these challenges.

Second, and building on Smith's argument, the analytical distinction between "immigration and borders" and policies regarding human rights and diversity is a potent tool to question societal beliefs. Indeed it destabilizes the assumption that diversity issues in Canada – and to a lesser extent, human rights – are solely the result of immigration-related dynamics. In addition to ethnicity, "race," and "culture," they also concern socio-economic status, gender, sexuality, and national or linguistic minorities. By the same token, the distinction demonstrates the normative problems associated with the reflex to discuss the need for accommodation and the dynamics of integration as solely spurred by the presence of "newcomers" in a society.

Third, by making the separation, I argue that it will be easier to have mainstream discussions of issues such as the racialized and neocolonial character of Canadian immigration policy, both in applied political theory and in public policy analysis. To be sure, these topics are already being discussed extensively (see, as examples, Abu-Laban 1998; Bhuyan et al. 2017; Thobani 1999; Tungohan 2017). Yet, a lot more could be done to acknowledge them in research on immigration-related issues in Canada.

Focusing on immigration and borders as a domain of enquiry is, ultimately, only an analytical distinction, and should serve only as such. Many political actors involved in struggles about immigration and borders resist this distinction. They challenge current Canadian policy by highlighting troubling connections between the state's immigration strategies and the conditions newcomers experience. Yet in order to correct the current bias in Canada's political theory, this distinction nonetheless could be productive and generative as long as it is used mindfully.

Immigration and Borders in Canadian Political Theory

The epistemological and ontological consequences of the dynamics described above are clear: a lot of the theoretical and normative work on immigration and borders in Canada has dealt with these issues indirectly or in combination with broader sets of concerns usually attached to diversity management. This is in stark contrast to the growing body of empirical studies dealing with immigration and borders stemming

Table 20.1. Directions of Canadian Scholars Concerned with Immigration

	Outward	Inward
Example of concerns and themes	Global inequalities, the brain drain, neocolonialism, open borders	Racialization, intersectionality, political and socio-economic equality, citizenship
Examples of authors	Karmis and Koji (2009); Shachar (2009); Sharma (2006)	Abu-Laban and Gabriel (2002); Vukov (2000)

Note: This table is only indicative, not exhaustive; exclusion is related solely to space constraints.

from Canadian scholars and the intellectual production of activists and community organizations.[1]

A clear structure nonetheless emerges from the Canadian theoretical literature concerned with immigration and borders. First, the contributions that do not engage directly with these issues can be divided into two groups: the outward-looking scholars and the inward-looking scholars. Second, evident in this literature is the dominance of the work on immigration and open borders produced by Joseph Carens. Interestingly, all of the work surveyed in this section meets the criteria of the applied political theory approach described in the introduction to this volume: it involves empirical analysis, and links political theory with political events or practices.

As indicated by the name, inward and outward scholars produce work that focuses on the internal or external dynamics related to immigration. These inductive categories are not mutually exclusive, and scholars might produce work in both categories and alternate over time. Table 20.1 presents some examples of themes and concerns illustrative of both categories.

The outward direction is concerned with Canada as a receiving state and its effect on the welfare of others, beyond the nation. Scholars working with this perspective engage with themes such as global inequalities, the brain drain, neocolonialism, open borders, and (global) norms. The inward-looking contributions tackle the effect of immigration and

1 For example, the Canadian chapters of the collective No One Is Illegal are active in the production of knowledge regarding immigration and borders that engages both with normative and empirical issues. For more information, see the website at http://www.nooneisillegal.org/.

borders on lives inside Canada – not so much the effect on the "Canadian" population as the ways immigration policy affects the existence of individuals and groups who are (or were) targeted by state action. These scholars engage with themes such as racialization, intersectionality, political and socio-economic inequalities, and varied concepts of citizenship.

Not all of these authors are political theorists, but they all produce work with a normative engagement that is in dialogue with political theory. It is also important to note that several Canadian authors are now empirically concerned with the translation and evolution of political theories and norms in politics and public policies. Triadafilos Triadafilopoulos's work, for example, has demonstrated the variegated influence of international norms – especially human rights – on naturalization and immigrant selection policies in Canada and elsewhere after the Second World War (Triadafilopoulos 2010, 2012). In the same line, focusing on Canada between 1867 and 1967, Christopher G. Andersen (2012) has traced the influence of two different versions of political liberalism – liberal internationalism and liberal nationalism – on the management and control of the country's borders.

Inward and Outward: Carens's Case for Open Borders

In relation to the two directions taken by Canadian scholars, Joseph H. Carens – not only Canada's pre-eminent theorist when it comes to immigration and borders, but also one of the precursors of the larger debate about open borders in contemporary political theory – has produced a body of work that encompasses both the inward and the outward perspectives. Indeed his political theory "from the ground up" (Carens 2013, 9–13) has produced considerable insights on topics such as how to deal with the need for inclusion created by immigration, the acceptable immigrant selection criteria for democratic societies, and, more broadly, the ways immigration policies could support the fight against global inequalities.[2] His work exemplifies Canada's tradition of applied political theory. Since Carens considers that the state has to play an active role in achieving equality, his approach is rooted in liberal

2 This section is based on Carens's most recent book, *The Ethics of Immigration* (2013). I concentrate on this book since it offers a rich synthesis of Carens's contributions to the liberal theory of immigration over the past twenty years.

egalitarianism – a leading contemporary political philosophical current in Canada (as exemplified by the work of Will Kymlicka) and in the world (for example, John Rawls).

Carens's approach is twofold. First, he considers issues related to inclusion, belonging, and immigrant selection in relation to what he considers to be broadly shared "democratic principles." Second, moving beyond what he sees as the frustrating conclusions produced by this analysis, Carens proposes a reframing of the issues surrounding immigration away from the realm of control and towards the principle of open borders and their contribution to furthering social justice. In dealing with current policies and political debates, Carens uses "democratic principles" as his benchmark. Using a purposely broad term to represent a consensus that encompasses actors of several political orientations, he argues that these principles

> refer to the broad moral commitments that underlie and justify contemporary political institutions and policy throughout North America and Europe – things like the ideas that all human beings are of equal moral worth, that disagreements should normally be resolved through the principle of majority rule, that we have a duty to respect the rights and freedom of individuals, that legitimate government depends upon the consent of the governed, that all citizens should be equal under the law, that coercion should only be exercised in accordance with the rule of law, that people should not be subject to discrimination on the basis of characteristics like race, religion, or gender, that we should respect norms like fairness or reciprocity in our policies and so on. (Carens 2013, 2)

Aside from the question of the content of integration and diversity management policies,[3] Carens also apply these principles to the selection of permanent and temporary migrants. With regard to temporary workers, selected on the basis of a state's economic needs, he argues that democratic principles require either that the duration of their stay be limited or that a time threshold be established after which these individuals would acquire the right to stay (2013, 113–14). That is to say, democratic principles should limit a state's capacity to maintain

3 According to Carens, these should be only sparingly different from the rights granted to and policies affecting nationals and only for a short time after arrival. He also makes a strong case against differentiating rights based on citizenship status in favour of recognizing the belonging and participation of permanent residents (2013, 119–24).

indefinitely a group of migrants in categories such as guest workers and temporary foreign workers. These principles should also guide states in recognizing the effect of time – the duration of stay, which carries the implicit recognition of one's contribution to the host society – as a factor giving weight to equality and inclusion claims for temporary migrants. This time principle could, on the other hand, justify some short-term exclusion from social benefits, but Carens insists on the importance of providing equal working conditions for both nationals and foreign workers (2013, 116). In this context, the centrality of equal rights for democratic justice should trump any economic interests of the state.

In line with the same democratic principles, Carens is also concerned with the criteria states use to select permanent migrants. Recognizing that states consider this decision to be their sovereign prerogative (2013, 173 and 191), he defends the idea that this freedom should at least be limited by a prohibition again discrimination based on "race," ethnicity, or "culture." He also argues for the moral obligation of states to allow family reunification via migration (2013, 190), while also proposing that family ties, as a criterion for inclusion, should be considered more broadly to include "secondary family ties" as a way to go beyond ethnocentric conceptions of the family (2013, 180). Reviewing commonly used criteria, Carens identifies concerns about national security and social order as acceptable justifications for exclusions (2013, 187), but advocates for a clear acknowledgment of the slippery slope such exclusions might represent. On the other hand, working within the context of sovereignty and democratic principles, Carens recognizes that economic inclusion and exclusion criteria are acceptable, even if they might be "ungenerous" or "unjust" from a global justice standpoint (183).

Having explored the implications of "democratic principles" for permanent and temporary immigrant selection, Carens moves his focus to a reframing of the questions in a way that allows for a consideration of global justice and the pursuit of substantive human rights. Indeed, his conclusions regarding exclusion and inclusion by democratic states remain limited in their capacity to consider the global effect of "just" state decisions in the face of considerable inequalities among states. Accordingly Carens argues for a critique of exclusion rooted in the principle of open borders and with the reiteration of mobility as an individual human right. This argument is not about negating the current international order; Carens attempts his demonstration with sovereign states as the starting point of reflection.

Based on premises of equality, Carens offers three central justifications for a world without borders. First, control of migration by states is a clear infringement of freedom of movement. Second, especially in the context of inequalities among states, limiting freedom of movement is in effect limiting equality of opportunity. Third, freedom of movement via open borders is a potent tool for social justice. Thus, "a commitment to equal moral worth entails some commitment to economic, social, and political equality, partly as a means of realizing equal freedom and equal opportunity and partly as a desirable end in itself. Freedom of movement would contribute to a reduction of existing political, social, and economic inequalities" (2013, 228). These three reasons support a strong criticism of the role of affluent states in the creation and perpetuation of global inequalities (2013, 234). Acknowledging critics who consider that this proposal would lead to a flight of human resources – including a "brain drain" – from poor to rich states and limit consideration of the conditions that provoked the decision to immigrate, Carens suggests his proposal could complement other attempts at global structural changes. Yet the embodiment of freedom of movement, via open borders, as a human right remains central for Carens as an extension of states' commitment to democratic principles (2013, 236–7).

This argument encounters resistance, however, with respect to its effect on political communities' and nations' capacity to self-govern and to manage their own criteria for justice and inclusion. Central critics of Carens consider that his proposal might endanger the sense of belonging and solidarity among members of a political community – sentiments that render redistribution, justice, and cohesion possible (Walzer 1983). Further, critics argue that open borders would make it impossible to differentiate and – to a large extent – reward explicit commitment to a political community by rights and privileges associated with belonging.[4] In response Carens proposes that, despite open borders, "political communities [would continue to matter] morally" (2013, 287), and he rejects the idea that exclusion is the only way to constitute them. Instead, time of residence – implying participation and contribution – and the decision to commit to a specific place would remain good principles for inclusion in a political community, in a world characterized by open borders.

Carens's perspective is the best through which to reflect on recent changes to Canada's immigrant selection system. As the most comprehensive

4 Carens (1987, 1999) reviews these objections in detail, while Meilaender (1999) provides a good summary of the criticisms.

theory on the topic, it allows for a consideration of the internal and external dynamics involved in the management of migration. In addition, Carens's perspective allows for a balanced and simultaneous attention to the issues associated with both temporary and permanent migration. As Canada increasingly blurs the line between these two categories – especially with the implementation of the Expression of Interest system – this represents an important analytical asset. More broadly, Carens's egalitarian argument for open borders forces us to denaturalize and denormalize, at the outset of our analysis, the procedures and policies the Canadian state deploys to manage international immigration.

Breaking Away from Legacies: The Express Entry System

Having discussed Carens's work, the next step in an applied political theory approach is to look at empirical evidence. To do so I turn to the case of the Express Entry system. In 2013 the Canadian federal government announced the development of a new immigrant processing procedure, to be implemented at the beginning of 2015. This procedure – called "Expression Entry" and inspired by processing systems implemented in New Zealand and Australia – was part of a broader agenda of reform of Canada's immigration regime initiated by the Conservative government of Stephen Harper in 2008, during its second mandate. The Express Entry system has considerable implications for Canadian immigration and borders. Using Carens's egalitarian perspective as a starting point, it is clear that several elements of the Express Entry program represent a break from Canada's legacy of equal membership for immigrants. More broadly, the program further shrinks Canada's contribution, via international immigration, to the fight against global inequalities. It conflicts with Carens's objectives of open borders and inclusion/exclusion criteria that align with "democratic principles," as well as with the overall goal of advancing global equality.

The Express Entry system is applied to the category of economic migrants and targets – specifically, individuals aiming to enter Canada under the following programs: the Federal Skilled Worker Program, the Federal Skilled Trades Program, and the Canadian Experience Class (Canada 2015a). Provinces may also select individuals who apply via this system and invite them to become Provincial Nominees. As of January 2015, it is the only mechanism by which these individuals in these categories may apply to become permanent residents of Canada. Figure 20.1 presents Citizenship and Immigration Canada's general representation of the Express Entry procedure.

Figure 20.1. The Express Entry System

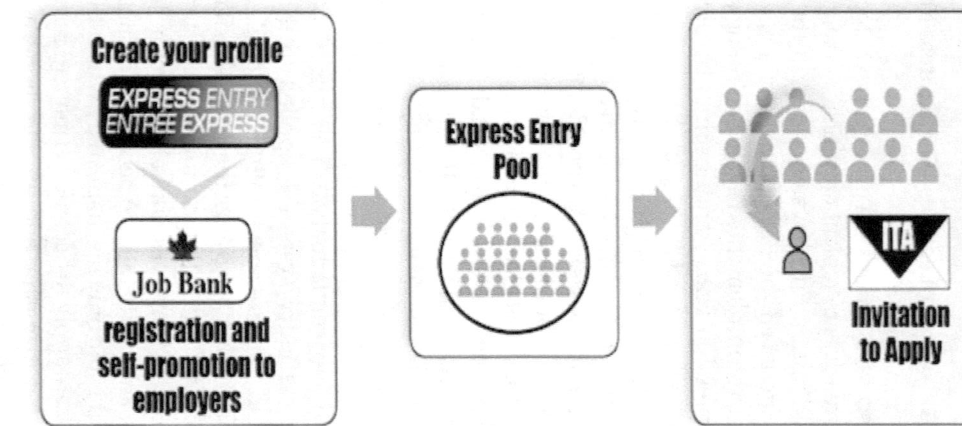

Source: Canada 2015c.

Under the Express Entry system, immigrant selection is a formal two-step process, rather than the single application in use before 2015. In the first step, applicants are required to present an expression of interest to immigrate, via an electronic profile with Citizenship and Immigration Canada (CIC). This expression of interest must include information relative to applicants' education, experience, and skills. It must also include information about their level of proficiency in either English or French, as tested and assessed prior to the application.[5] In addition, applicants must provide information either about a job offer they might have received in Canada or a provincial nomination they might have been awarded. For applicants who do not have an offer or a nomination, the expression of interest must be accompanied by the creation of a job seekers' account with a government management job bank. Using this individual data, CIC establishes applicants' eligibility to join a pool of immigration candidates using criteria based on ministerial instructions and on Canada's Immigration and Refugee Protection Act (2001). Currently, to be eligible to enter the pool, Express Entry candidates must have work experience in a National Occupational Code (NOC) 0, A, or B occupation.

In the second step of the Express Entry procedure, pooled candidates are evaluated by governments (federal, provincial, and territorial) and by employers. The federal government uses a formula called the "Comprehensive Ranking System" that measures skills and experience, characteristics of the applicant's partner (such as language skills and education), skills transferability, and actual job offers or provincial nominations (Canada 2015b). From this evaluation, candidates are ranked inside the pool in relation to the other candidates accepted in the first step of the Express Entry procedure. Based on the alignment of needs and skills/experience, candidates could then be invited to apply for permanent residence in Canada. The minimum Comprehensive Ranking System score applicants need to receive an invitation to apply for permanent residency is not static, nor is the number of invitations extended for each round. These are determined in relation to government planning of immigration levels, but ultimately are decided via ministerial instructions stemming from the minister of citizenship and immigration. Table 20.2 sums the

5 Testing and assessment is not managed by Citizenship and Immigration Canada; instead, candidates must pay private organizations that provide such evaluations (Canada 2015d).

Table 20.2. Ministerial Instructions on Invitations to Apply for Permanent Residency, Canada, 2016

Date of Ministerial Instruction	Minimum Comprehensive Ranking System Score Required	Number of Invitations to Apply Issued
6 January	461	1,463
13 January	453	1,518
27 January	457	1,468
10 February	459	1,505
25 February	453	1484
9 March	473	1,013
23 March	470	1,014
6 April	470	954
20 April	468	1,018
7 May	534	799
18 May	484	763
1 June	483	762
15 June	488	752
29 June	482	773
13 July	482	747
27 July	488	755
20 August	490	754
24 August	538	750
7 September	491	1,000
21 September	438	1,288
12 October	484	1,518
19 October	475	1,804
2 November	472	2,080
16 November	470	2,427
30 November	786	559
16 December	497	1,936
22 December	475	2,878

Source: Canada 2017.

2016 set of ministerial instructions regarding the Express Entry program. Note that the number of invitations to apply does not correspond to the number of permanent residents who entered Canada.

Table 20.2 illustrates the tap-on, tap-off approach associated with Express Entry and the very active nature of ministerial involvement in the management of the selection system. In the near future, employers will be able to select candidates from the pool as a way to fill job vacancies, provided they have been approved by CIC and have demonstrated efforts in the past to find a Canadian to employ. This will be facilitated by a job bank, managed by the government, which matches applicants with prospective employers.

Finally, the pool of candidates ranked according to the Comprehensive Ranking System is only in place for a short time. After a year, the government empties the pool, and the applications of candidates who have not been invited to apply or who have not received a job offer or provincial nomination will expire. Candidates who wish to try again must resubmit an expression of interest to immigrate to Canada and update all of the relevant information. The process of creating the pool and ranking applicants then starts anew for another year.

The Express Entry system breaks from the pre-2015 processing system, at least conceptually, in several ways. The most crucial way is that it limits the capacity of individuals to submit freely a complete application to immigrate to Canada. Although the presentation of an expression of interest to immigrate to Canada remains available, only a certain number of applicants receive the authorization to apply formally for permanent residence in Canada. Second, the system explicitly rejects any obligation on the part of the federal government to consider applicants on the basis of the order of the applications or the time spent in an applicant pool; furthermore, the government retains the right to empty the pool of candidates for any reason and at any moment. Third, Express Entry explicitly recognizes a direct role for private actors – employers and business operators – in the selection of permanent immigrants to Canada (Canada 2013b). Although economic interests have always been at the heart of Canada's immigration regime, post–Second World War policies and institutions that were developed to manage immigration gave precedence to the state. Instead of letting private actors do the lion's share of the recruitment and settlement work, the regime forced them to interact with the state to pursue their immigration interests. The centrality given to the state's role allowed for the realization of broader nation-building objectives with regard to immigration, as well as a relative – yet considerable – egalitarian liberalization of Canada's immigration policies after the 1960s.

The decision to move to a two-step process followed the general ambition put forward by the Harper government in its 2008 Economic Action Plan to "strengthen Canada's immigration system, bringing the people this country needs to help to foster economic growth and making sure all Canadians will prosper in the long-term" (Canada 2013a). Other justifications then followed. The need to modernize and streamline the immigration processing and evaluation system – a long-standing concern of the Harper government, especially following its "tackling" of the Federal Skilled Workers backlog – was cited as a reason to put the new system in place, while the built-in mechanisms permitting the government to limit or purge extra candidates were a response to this justification.

Skills shortages and the need to respond to a variety of region- or industry-specific labour market requirements was also presented as a justification for the implementation of the Express Entry system. Following criticisms of the human capital–inspired selection model in place since the late 1980s, several innovations were put in place to better align the demands of Canadian labour markets with the immigrants the federal government selects. These include the creation of the Provincial Nominee Program, the expansion of the Temporary Foreign Worker Program, the establishment of a list of preferred occupations for Federal Skilled Workers, and the creation of the Canadian Experience Class (Paquet and Larios 2018).

Finally, Express Entry has been presented as a way to address issues related to the poor economic integration outcomes of federal skilled workers, especially when it comes to the acquisition of work experience in Canada and the recognition of foreign training, skills, and experience in the Canadian labour market. By controlling for applicants' qualifications at the onset of the migration process, while they are still abroad, and by theoretically ensuring access to a job at the level of applicants' qualification at their moment of arrival in Canada, the Express Entry system, in the eyes of policy makers, is intended to promote better economic integration.

Express Entry, Democratic Principles, and Global Inequalities

The implementation of the Express Entry system mirrors Canada's early migrant attraction and settlement programs (Hawkins 1988; Vineberg 2012). Rooted in different iterations of classical liberalism (Andersen

2012), these aimed at recruiting suitable farmers, then workers, to benefit the country's economic and demographic development. As part of these early efforts, the state played only a limited role (border control, quarantine management, visa issuance). Economic interests – capital or landholders – had a direct influence in the making of immigration policies, and *laissez-faire* remained the guiding principle. Building on the qualitative policy evidence presented above, Carens's perspective helps highlight three central tensions with this breakaway from egalitarian liberalism in both discourse and policy.

First, via its two-step system, the Express Entry system effectively makes it even harder to enter the country, thereby limiting any semblance of freedom of movement in relation to Canada. As such, the system reiterates Canada's non-commitment to mobility as a transnational human right. The consequence is indeed a limitation of equality of opportunity for potential migrants and, in the short, medium, and long term, a limitation of new forces that might counter global inequalities. Indeed these added barriers to movement limit circular mobility, a now-recognized dynamic that counterbalances the "brain drain" (De Haas 2005). By allowing people to move back and forth between sending and receiving countries, migrants are able to spread the resources gained by immigration across different contexts. Therefore free movement can represent a potent tool against the continual accumulation of financial and human capital in rich countries, based on the extraction and exploitation of resources in other regions of the world.

In addition it is important to recognize that the system as it is set up – and especially its demands for pre-arrival evaluation, its reliance on a job offer, and its ranking of candidates inside a pool – is stacked against particular types of migrants and benefits only specific individuals. Specifically, as indeed was the case in Canada's previous selection regimes (Abu-Laban and Gabriel 2002; Karmis and Koji 2009), it emphasizes skills and access to capital and social/professional networks that tend to be more accessible to men and to individuals belonging to upper classes in several societies (including Canada). As a result the system limits even further the freedom of movement for some groups – namely, women, poor and less educated people, and minorities.

Second, the Express Entry system formalizes the legitimacy of economic actors (employers and firms) in the management of immigration and borders. Although economic actors have always played a role in Canada's immigration regime, the Express Entry system allows them able to interact directly with potential permanent residents. This creates several tensions with the "democratic principles" Carens hopes to see states abide by when it comes to their immigrant selection schemes. Economic actors might be less prone to avoid discriminating on the basis of "race," "culture," or religion when selecting potential employees abroad. Further, they might be in a better position to justify discriminatory practices using arguments rooted in the logic of the market, such as the effectiveness of employees, better integration into the existing employee pool, and cultural similarities with clients. Since states now align only in small part with these "democratic principles," it is crucial to emphasize that economic actors face an even more limited set of normative pressures to act according to these principles.

Third, when it comes to membership, the Express Entry system also formalizes expectations regarding participation and what states owe to newcomers. Carens's perspective presents participation and length of stay as elements that reinforce the general principle according to which states ought to grant rights and facilitate the integration of immigrants living on their territory (Carens 2013, 4). By making direct access to a job a central feature of membership, the Express Entry system also reinforces expectations about immigrants' participation in the economy and self-reliance as conditions for inclusion. The policy implication of such a paradigm, over time, might well be a dismantling of the public infrastructure supporting immigration settlement and integration, with a job considered the primary mechanism of settlement and integration. Generally the formalization of these expectations and the ratification of a formal role for economic actors in immigrant selection could also have the consequence of limiting views regarding the roles and responsibilities of the Canadian state in regard to immigrants living on its territory.

To be sure, these issues were already present in Canada before the inception of the Express Entry selection procedure. The break this system represents, however, reinforces the dynamics of exclusion already in process in Canada, and limits the potential of the country's immigration system to combat global inequalities. On a broader scale, by making economic participation the only factor of belonging, the system could increase the differentiation of practical and lived citizenship between newcomers and Canadian citizens. The effects of this differentiation on substantial equality and on the already limited spaces for newcomers and new citizens to exist politically in Canada could be considerable.

Conclusion

Despite the election of a Liberal government in Ottawa in October 2015, no announcements have been made about dismantling the Express Entry system. The move away from Canada's imperfect contemporary legacy of egalitarian liberal immigration policy quite probably will continue, despite some sporadic punctuation – for example, Canada's response to the Syrian refugee crisis. Carens's perspective – a comprehensive theoretical account that looks simultaneously inward and outward – provides an excellent analytical base to show that the Express Entry system furthers several problematic tendencies inherent in Canada's contemporary management of immigration and borders. Indeed applied political theory makes it possible to link immigration policy reform and important questions regarding democracy, freedom, and citizenship. In addition to limiting freedom of movement, the Express Entry system further dismantles the proactive role of the state in supporting equality for migrants. Instead it instils new forms of legitimacy for economic actors, who, in addition to continuing to influence the direction of immigration policy, are now able to act directly as decision makers. It also formalizes even more injunctions about the independence of newcomers towards the state, reinforcing economic autonomy and contribution as necessary conditions for inclusion. In a way, the policy innovation the Express Entry system represents – aimed at addressing some issues attributed to previous selection mechanisms – is thus a return to the classical liberalism that animated Canada's early migration policies and settler recruitment programs (Andersen, 2012).

The enhancement of already existing characteristics of Canada's immigration system is also paired with some breaks from existing legacies: the Express Entry procedure limits individuals' capacity to apply freely to move to Canada, rejects any obligation on the part of Canada to consider candidates in their order of application, and gives a new role to economic actors in the selection of immigrants. All of these disruptions must be considered in the context of broader changes to Canada's immigration system promoted by the Harper Conservatives while in office (Paquet and Larios, 2018). These include, for example, a revamping of naturalization procedures in favour of a more stringent set of conditions for citizenship (Paquet 2012; Winter 2014) and an unprecedented increase in the number of temporary foreign workers accepted in the country. Also central in this change was a slow but steady slip in the already limited immigration policy-making capacity of Parliament into the hands of the immigration minister, as demonstrated by his role in making day-to-day decisions regarding the Express Entry administration via ministerial instructions.[6] These changes demonstrate that political ideas are potent factors influencing immigration and border policies in Canada, and that considerable room remains to develop the insight of Canadian political theory on these topics.

This is where the challenge lies: using the Canadian experience to imagine alternatives to current policies. From the standpoint of applied political theory, Carens's argument for open borders remains a powerful starting point to think about this. By disrupting the legitimacy of national borders and arguing instead for freedom of movement as a central driver of equality, his perspective highlights central tensions in the "Canadian model" when it comes to migration. Indeed Canada's self-representations as a country welcoming of immigration and championing multiculturalism remain rooted in discourses and logic revolving around the contribution and utility of migrants for the Canadian economy and society. Absent from these positive representations, however – which are used to justify state action and to market Canada abroad (Kymlicka 2008) – are the consequences of Canada's immigration policies on source countries. The economic effect of the brain drain and the social and emotional consequences of programs that support gendered migration, to name but two, are never considered in conjunction with newcomers' contributions to Canada. Also absent is genuine consideration of the effects of Canada's foreign, military, and economic policies on the production of international migrants and on freedom of movement across the globe. Although the Canadian state likely will not move towards open borders in a near future, a genuine egalitarian immigration policy for the twenty-first century should at least attend to the causes and effects of international migration and national border policies.

REFERENCES

Abu-Laban, Yasmeen. 1988. "Keeping 'em Out: Gender, Race and Class Biases in Canadian Immigration Policy." In *Painting the Maple: Essays on Race, Gender, and the Construction of Canada*, ed. V. Strong-Boag, S. Grace, J.M. Anderson, and A. Eisenberg, 69–82. Vancouver: UBC Press.

Abu-Laban, Yasmeen, and Christina Gabriel. 2002. *Selling Diversity: Immigration, Multiculturalism, Employment Equity, and Globalization*. Peterborough, ON: Broadview Press.

Andersen, Christopher G. 2012. *Canadian Liberalism and the Politics of Border Control, 1867–1967*. Vancouver: UBC Press.

Bhuyan, Rupaleem Daphne Jeyapal, Jane Ku, Izumi Sakamoto, and Elena Chou. 2017. "Branding 'Canadian Experience' in Immigration Policy: Nation Building in a Neoliberal Era." *Journal of International Migration and Integration* 18 (1): 47–62.

Canada. 2013a. "Backgrounder – 2014 Immigration Levels Planning: Public and Stakeholder Consultations." Ottawa: Citizenship and Canada. Available online at https://www.canada.ca/en/immigration-refugees-citizenship/news/archives/backgrounders-2013/2014-immigration-levels-planning-public-stakeholder-consultations.html, accessed 19 March 2015.

Canada. 2013b. "The Role of Employers in an Expression of Interest System." Ottawa: Citizenship and Canada. Available online at https://www.canada.ca/en/immigration-refugees-citizenship/corporate/transparency/consultations/expression-interest-system/role-employers.html, accessed 19 March 2015.

Canada. 2014a. "Canadian Demographics at a Glance." Cat. no. 91–003-X. Ottawa: Statistics Canada.

Canada. 2014b. "Facts and Figures 2013: Immigration Overview – Permanent and Temporary Residents." Ottawa: Citizenship and Immigration Canada.

Canada. 2015a. "Entry Criteria and the Comprehensive Ranking System." Ottawa: Citizenship and Canada. Available online at http://www.cic.gc.ca/english/express-entry/criteria-crs.asp, accessed 19 March 2015.

Canada. 2015b. "Express Entry – Comprehensive Ranking System (CRS) Criteria." Ottawa: Citizenship and Canada. Available online at https://www.canada.ca/en/immigration-refugees-citizenship/services/immigrate-canada/express-entry/become-candidate/criteria-comprehensive-ranking-system/grid.html, accessed 19 March 2015.

Canada. 2015c. "Express Entry System: Employer Outreach Information Session." Ottawa: Citizenship and Canada. http://www.cic.gc.ca/english/resources/publications/employers/express-entry-presentation-fall2014.asp, accessed 20 March 2015.

Canada. 2015d. "Fill Out Your Profile – Skilled Immigrants (Express Entry)." Ottawa: Citizenship and Canada. Available online at https://www.canada.ca/en/immigration-refugees-citizenship/services/immigrate-canada/express-entry/become-candidate/fill-profile.html, accessed 19 March 2015.

Canada. 2017. "Ministerial Instructions respecting Invitations to Apply for Permanent Residence under the Express Entry System." Ottawa: Citizenship and Immigration Canada. Available online at https://www.canada.ca/en/immigration-refugees-citizenship/corporate/mandate/

policies-operational-instructions-agreements/ministerial-instructions/previous-express-entry-ministerial-instructions.html, accessed 20 September 2017.

Carens, Joseph H. 1987. "Aliens and Citizens: The Case for Open Borders." *Review of Politics* 49 (2): 251–73. https://doi.org/10.1017/S0034670500033817

Carens, Joseph H. 1999. "A Reply to Meilaender: Reconsidering Open Borders." *International Migration Review* 33 (4): 1082–97. https://doi.org/10.2307/2547364

Carens, Joseph H. 2013. *The Ethics of Immigration*. Oxford: Oxford University Press.

De Haas, Hein. 2005. "International Migration, Remittances and Development: Myths and Facts." *Third World Quarterly* 26 (8): 1269–84. https://doi.org/10.1080/01436590500336757

Hawkins, Freda. 1988. *Canada and Immigration: Public Policy and Public Concern*. 2nd ed. Montreal; Kingston, ON: McGill-Queen's University Press.

Karmis, Dimitrios, and Junichiro Koji. 2009. "L'instrumentalisme néolibéral et l'hospitalité coloniale: une critique de la politique canadienne de sélection des immigrants." In *Les politiques publiques au Canada: Pouvoir, conflits et idéologies*, ed. D. Karmis and L. Cardinal, 103–31. Quebec City: Presses de l'Université Laval.

Kelley, Ninette, and Michael Trebilcock. 2010. *The Making of the Mosaic: A History of Canadian Immigration Policy*. 2nd ed. Toronto: University of Toronto Press.

Kymlicka, Will. 1995. *Multicultural Citizenship: A Liberal Theory of Minority Rights*. Oxford: Oxford University Press.

Kymlicka, Will. 2008. "Marketing Canadian Multiculturalism in the International Arena." In *The Comparative Turn in Canadian Political Science*, ed. L.A. White, R. Simeon, R. Vipond, and J. Wallner, 99–120. Vancouver: UBC Press.

Meilaender, Peter C. 1999. "Liberalism and Open Borders: The Argument of Joseph Carens." *International Migration Review* 33 (4): 1062–81. https://doi.org/10.2307/2547363

Paquet, Mireille. 2012. "Beyond Appearances: Citizenship Tests in Canada and the UK." *Journal of International Migration and Integration* 13 (2): 243–60. https://doi.org/10.1007/s12134-011-0233-1

Paquet, Mireille, and Lindsay Larios. 2018. "Venue Shopping and Legitimacy: Making Sense of Harper's Immigration Record." *Canadian Journal of Political Science* 51 (4): 817–36. https://doi.org/10.1017/S0008423918000331

Shachar, Ayelet. 2009. *The Birthright Lottery: Citizenship and Global Inequality*. Cambridge, MA: Harvard University Press.

Sharma, Nandita. 2006. *Home Economics: Nationalism and the Making of "Migrant Workers" in Canada*. Toronto: University of Toronto Press.

Smith, Miriam. 2009. "Diversity and Canadian Political Development." *Canadian Journal of Political Science* 42 (4): 831–54. https://doi.org/10.1017/S0008423909990692

Thobani, Sunera. 1999. "Sponsoring Immigrant Women's Inequalities." *Canadian Woman Studies* 19 (3): 11–16.

Triadafilopoulos, Triadafilos. 2010. "Global Norms, Domestic Institutions and the Transformation of Immigration Policy in Canada and the U.S." *Review of International Studies* 36 (1): 169–93. https://doi.org/10.1017/S0260210509990556

Triadafilopoulos, Triadafilos. 2012. *Becoming Multicultural: Immigration and the Politics of Membership in Canada and Germany*. Vancouver: UBC Press.

Tungohan, Ethel. 2017. "From Encountering Confederate Flags to Finding Refuge in Spaces of Solidarity: Filipino Temporary Foreign Workers' Experiences of the Public in Alberta." *Space and Polity* 21 (1): 11–26.

Vineberg, Robert. 2012. *Responding to Immigrants' Settlement Needs: The Canadian Experience*. New York: Springer. https://doi.org/10.1007/978-94-007-2688-8

Vukov, Tamara. 2000. "Penser l'immigration comme spectacle: les bases coloniales de la nation canadienne." *Recherches Feministes* 13 (2): 121–30. https://doi.org/10.7202/058100ar

Walzer, Michael. 1983. *Spheres of Justice: A Defense of Pluralism and Equality*. New York: Basic Books.

Winter, Elke. 2014. *Becoming Canadian: Making Sense of Recent Changes to Citizenship Rules*. Montreal: Institute for Research on Public Policy.

Contributors

Mark Blythe writes and teaches in the topic areas of political philosophy and Canadian politics at the University of Alberta and Concordia University of Edmonton. His research is centred on contemporary liberal political philosophy. Mark received his doctorate from the University of Alberta. His dissertation was a series of emendations to John Rawls's theory, "Justice as Fairness." Mark has published several papers in the field of political philosophy focusing on capability theory, Rawlsian liberalism, and pluralism in Canada.

Marc Chevrier is a jurist and professor of political science at the Université du Québec à Montréal. He specializes in political systems (Quebec, Canada, western Europe) and in political philosophy; law and politics; and literature and politics. His books include: *Le Temps de l'homme fini* (2005); *La république québécoise* (2012); and *Par-delà l'école-machine* (editor, 2010). He has also co-edited many other books on the theory of democracy, French politics, and sex and gender.

James Farney is Associate Professor and Department Head of Politics and International Studies at the University of Regina. His primary research interests are Canadian party politics, political institutions, and religion and politics. He is the author of *Social Conservatism and Party Politics in Canada and the United States*, and editor (with David Rayside) of *Conservatism in Canada*. He is currently working with Clark Banack (Alberta) on a book examining the different ways that Canadian provinces fund and regulate religious schools and with Julie Simmons (Guelph) on an edited volume on Canadian federalism in the Harper era.

Kirsten J. Fisher is Assistant Professor of Global Governance in the Department of Political Studies at the University of Saskatchewan. She is the author of *Moral Accountability and International Criminal Law* (Routledge, 2012), *Transitional Justice for Child Soldiers* (Palgrave Macmillan, 2013), co-author/co-editor of *Transitional Justice and the Arab Spring* (Routledge, 2014), and author or co-author of multiple articles on the ethics and politics of international criminal law.

Catherine Frost is Associate Professor of Political Science at McMaster University. She has been a visiting fellow at the Hebrew University of Jerusalem and at McGill University, a policy adviser in government, and a communications adviser in the private sector. Her work appears in the *Journal of Political Philosophy, Constellations, Review of Politics, Canadian Journal of Communication, Mortality, Irish Political Studies, Information Society*, and in edited collections. She is the author of *Morality and Nationalism* (Routledge, 2006).

Neil Hibbert is Associate Professor of Political Studies at the University of Saskatchewan, where he specializes in contemporary political theory. His primary research interests include theories of social justice and the sources of motivation and solidarity in the context of diverse societies and welfare states. He is currently working on challenges of political legitimacy and obligation within and beyond the state.

Raffaele Iacovino is Associate Professor and Supervisor of Undergraduate Studies in the Department of Political Science at Carleton University. His interests include Canadian and Quebec politics, federalism, citizenship and immigration, and citizenship education. He has also held the positions of Invited Professor of Quebec Studies at McGill University; Postdoctoral Fellow at the Canada Research Chair on Democracy and Sovereignty at l'Université du Québec à Chicoutimi; and Skelton-Clark Postdoctoral Fellow of Canadian Affairs in the Department of Political Studies at Queen's University. He is the co-author, with Alain-G. Gagnon, of *Federalism, Citizenship, and Quebec: Debating Multinationalism* (University of Toronto Press, 2007), which won the 2011 Canada Publishing Award for Japan (International Council for Canadian Studies).

Brooke Jeffrey is Professor of Political Science at Concordia University, where she teaches Canadian politics and public administration. A former federal public servant, she left the bureaucracy in 1984 to serve as

Director of the Liberal Research Bureau, and was a Liberal candidate in the 1993 federal election. She is the author of *Divided Loyalties: The Liberal Party of Canada, 1984–2006*, and is currently completing work on a planned second volume, *Road to Redemption: The Liberal Party of Canada, 2006–17*.

Steven Lecce is Associate Professor of Political Theory at the University of Manitoba. He is the author of *Against Perfectionism: Defending Liberal Neutrality* (University of Toronto Press, 2008) and numerous articles about political theory. He is also co-editor of *Fragile Freedoms: The Global Struggle for Human Rights* (Oxford University Press, 2017). He is currently working on a manuscript entitled *Equality's Domain*.

Jay Makarenko writes on political theory and Canadian politics. His interests include contemporary liberal thought, liberty and egalitarianism, the Canadian Charter of Rights and Freedoms, and political participation. Jay has a PhD from the University of Alberta in political philosophy. His thesis explored John Rawls's idea of the fair value of equal political liberties and its practical application to Canadian and American jurisprudence. He has published and presented several papers on fair political participation.

David McGrane is Associate Professor of Political Studies at St Thomas More College and the University of Saskatchewan. His latest book is entitled *The New NDP: Moderation, Modernization, and Political Marketing* (UBC Press). He is active in his community as a member of the City of Saskatoon's Environmental Advisory Committee, Chair of the Political Action Committee of the Saskatoon & District Labour Council, and President of the Saskatchewan NDP.

Michael Murphy is a professor in the Political Science Program at the University of Northern British Columbia, where he held the Canada Research Chair in Comparative Indigenous-State Relations (2006–15). His recent publications include *Multiculturalism: A Critical Introduction* (Routledge, 2012); "Self-Determination as a Collective Capability: The Case of Indigenous Peoples," *Journal of Human Development and Capabilities* (2014); "Self-Determination and Indigenous Health: Is There a Connection?" *E-International Relations* (2014); and "Multiculturalism," *Oxford Bibliographies in Philosophy* (2018).

Darin Nesbitt teaches political science, with a focus on political philosophy, ethics, and the politics of literary utopias and dystopias, at Douglas College, New Westminster, British Columbia. His past scholarly publications have explored rights and recognition, property rights, British Idealist ethics, and democracy and education. Dr Nesbitt's current research interest revolves around the normative issues raised by assisted death and the subsequent policy challenges resulting from the Canadian federal government's medical aid-in-dying legislation.

Mireille Paquet is Associate Professor of Political Science at Concordia University and co-directs the Centre for Immigration Policy Evaluation. Her research focuses on immigration and public policy, Canadian politics, and public administration.

Paul Saurette is a professor at the School of Political Studies, University of Ottawa. His current research and teaching focus is on contemporary theories of ideology and discourse analysis, political communication, and the conservative and progressive movements in Canada and the United States (including a particular focus on the anti-abortion movement). His books include *The Kantian Imperative* (2005); and *The Changing Voice of the Anti-Abortion Movement in Canada and the US* (2015, with Kelly Gordon).

Marlene K. Sokolon is Associate Professor of Political Science at Concordia University. She specializes in Ancient Greek political thought, but has broad research interests in political emotions, politics and literature, deliberative democracy, justice and ethics, and questions arising from the intersection of biology and culture. She is the author of *Political Emotions: Aristotle and the Symphony of Reason and Emotion* (Northern Illinois University Press, 2006), and is working on a book on conceptualizations of justice in Euripides.

Cristina G. Stefan (formerly Badescu) left Canada in 2014 to join the University of Leeds in the United Kingdom, where she is also the Co-Director of the European Centre for the Responsibility to Protect. Her research on human protection, responsibility to protect, and norm studies has appeared in monographs such as *Humanitarian Intervention and the Responsibility to Protect: Security and Human Rights*, and in journals, including *Global Governance, International Studies Perspectives, European Journal of International Security, Canadian Journal of Political Science, Canadian Foreign Policy Journal*, and *Security Dialogue*.

Kathryn Trevenen is an Associate Professor at the Institute for Feminist and Gender Studies as well as the School of Political Studies, University of Ottawa. Her current research and teaching focus is on social/political theory – in particular, gender, queer, disability, and culture studies – as well as questions related to the politics of the classroom and the importance of critical pedagogy in the contemporary university context.

Jill Vickers is Distinguished Research Professor and Emeritus Chancellor's Professor in Political Science at Carleton University. A Fellow of the Royal Society, she has been active in civil society as President of the Canadian Political Science Association, the Canadian Association of University Professors, and the Canadian Research Institute for the Advancement of Women. She was also parliamentarian of the National Action Committee on the Status of Women, which mobilized women's advocacy groups to incorporate gender rights in the Charter of Rights and Freedoms. Author of many books and articles on the political dynamics of gender, race, and nation, she is currently editing an international handbook on gender, diversity, and federalism, and working on her theoretical text about gender's interaction with nationalism and nation building.

Ann Ward is Professor of Political Science at Baylor University. Before coming to Baylor in 2017, she was a member of the Philosophy and Political Science Departments at Campion College, University of Regina. Her most recent book is *Contemplating Friendship in Aristotle's Ethics* (SUNY Press, 2016). She is also the author of *Herodotus and the Philosophy of Empire* (Baylor, 2008). Her most recent edited collection is *Classical Rationalism and the Politics of Europe* (Cambridge Scholars Publishing, 2017), and has co-edited with Lee Ward, among other collections, *Natural Right and Political Philosophy: Essays in Honor of Catherine Zuckert and Michael Zuckert* (University of Notre Dame Press, 2013). She has published widely in scholarly journals, including *POLIS: The Journal of the Society for Greek Political Thought, Perspectives on Political Science, European Journal of Political Theory,* and *The European Legacy: Toward New Paradigms*.

Lee Ward is Professor of Political Science at Baylor University, where he teaches political and constitutional theory. He previously taught at Campion College at the University of Regina and at Kenyon College, and was a Postdoctoral Fellow in the Program in Constitutional Government at

Harvard University. He is the author of *The Politics of Liberty in England and Revolutionary America* (Cambridge University Press, 2004); *John Locke and Modern Life* (Cambridge University Press, 2010); *Modern Democracy and the Theological-Political Problem in Spinoza, Rousseau and Jefferson* (Palgrave Macmillan, 2014); the editor of John Locke's *Two Treatises of Government* (Hackett, 2016); and co-editor, with Ann Ward, of *The Ashgate Research Companion to Federalism* (Ashgate, 2009).

Stephen Winter is a Senior Lecturer in Political Theory at the University of Auckland. He has a long-standing interest in the theory and practice of rights and constitutions. His most recent publication in this area is *Magna Carta and New Zealand: History, Politics and Law in Aotearoa*, co-edited with Chris Jones (Palgrave Macmillan, 2017).

Marc Woons is a Doctoral Fellow with the Research Foundation – Flanders, and Researcher at the University of Leuven's Research in Political Philosophy, Leuven Institute. His interest is the intersection of power and justice in multinational contexts, with a particular focus on European politics and Indigenous nationalism. His work has been featured in *Settler Colonial Studies*, *AlterNative*, and *St Antony's International Review (Oxford)*. He is also the editor of *Restoring Indigenous Self-Determination* (E-IR Publications, 2015); and *Critical Epistemologies of Global Politics*, with Sebastian Weier (E-IR Publications, 2017).

www.ingramcontent.com/pod-product-compliance
Lightning Source LLC
LaVergne TN
LVHW090757070826
844660LV00022B/1009

* 9 7 8 1 4 4 2 6 2 8 4 3 4 *